Marriage Notices

From the

Southern Christian Advocate

1867–1878

By

Brent Howard Holcomb
Certified Genealogist

HERITAGE BOOKS
2024

HERITAGE BOOKS

AN IMPRINT OF HERITAGE BOOKS, INC.

Books, CDs, and more—Worldwide

For our listing of thousands of titles see our website
at
www.HeritageBooks.com

Published 2024 by
HERITAGE BOOKS, INC.
Publishing Division
5810 Ruatan Street
Berwyn Heights, MD 20740

International Standard Book Number
Paperbound: 978-0-7884-2769-5

INTRODUCTION

The *Southern Christian Advocate* was the publication for the Methodist Conferences of South Carolina, Georgia, and Florida, for the period covered in this volume. It was published in Macon, Georgia, through the issue of May 28, 1878. After a brief hiatus the *Southern Christian Advocate* was re-established in Columbia, South Carolina, as the publication for the South Carolina Conference. Publication continued in Macon for the Georgia and Florida conferences, but the title of the newspaper was changed to the Wesleyan Christian Advocate with the issue of June 4, 1878. I have included in this volume the marriage notices which appeared in the four June, 1878, issues of the *Wesleyan Christian Advocate*, since the South Carolina ministers appear to have been still sending in marriage notices to be published and because these issues are available on the some roll of microfilm.

This volume includes only the marriage notices, but in this twelve year period over 5,000 such notices appeared in this newspaper. The death and obituary notices were published in a separate volume by the author in 1993.

The marriage notices which were published in the Southern Christian Advocate are largely from South Carolina, Georgia, and Florida, but there are a significant number of marriage notices from North Carolina and Alabama with a few notices from other states as well. All of the marriage notices are of interest, as a marriage notice might name a parent or another relative of the bride which would not appear on a marriage license. Additionally, there have been relatively few marriage records published for the period covered in this volume. It is not unusual to find notices of couples for which the bride and groom were residence of different counties, especially in Georgia. Since South Carolina did not require marriage licenses until 1911, the notices of South Carolina marriages are very valuable. North Carolina's marriage license law did not take effect until 1868. Therefore, the North Carolina marriage notices are of value as well.

Brent H. Holcomb
April 13, 1994

MARRIAGE NOTICES FROM THE SOUTHERN CHRISTIAN ADVOCATE 1867-1878

Issue of January 25, 1867

On 18th December, by Rev. A. J. Cauthen, W. A. Ruff and Miss Sue Lever, of Richland, S. C.

By the same, Jan. 3, 1867, Wm. Hinnant, of Fulton, Arkansas, and Miss Lucy Powel, of Fairfield, S. C.

At Warrenton, Ga., on the morning of November 1st, by the Rev. J. M. Dickey, Mr. E. D. L. Mobley, of Atlanta, and Miss Rowena J. Hale, of the former place.

In the Methodist E. Church, at Culloden, Ga., January 15th, by Rev. Wesley F. Smith, Mr. James F. Ross, of Sumter co., Ga., and Miss E. B. Rutherford, of Culloden, Ga.

On the 15th inst., by Rev. P. M. Ryburn, Mr. T. N. Kirkpatrick, of Georgiana, Ala., and Miss M. L. Hames, of Troup Co., Ga.

On 19th December, 1866, by Rev. Geo. L. W. Anthony, Rev. J. M. Lowrey, of the North Georgia Conference, to Miss Sophia A. G. Davis, of Gwinnett co., Ga.

By Rev. W. J. Cotter on the 7th inst., Mr. M. L. Tidwell to Miss M. Swint.

By the same, on the 10th inst., Mr. Robt. Stripling to Miss Mary C. Emory, all of Harris county, Ga.

In Cokesbury, S. C., December 12, 1866, by Rev. S. H. Browne, Mr. W. G. McGee to Miss Sophronia, daughter of Capt. S. A. Hodges, all of Cokesbury, S. C.

In Newberry, S. C., December 13, 1866, by the same, Rev. Thomas A. Edwards of the South Carolina Conference, to Miss Caroline Mc. P. daughter of the late Rev. Dr. Kilgore.

In Marion co., Ga., January 15th, by Rev. J. T. Ainsworth, James Stevens, to Miss Margaret James.

In Whitefield co., Ga., January 16th 1867, by Rev. J. M. Richardson, Mr. William H. Martin, of Tilton, to Miss Julia E. Davis.

By the same, on the 3d January, Mr. Tilmon Leatherwood to Mrs. Martha Hampton, all of Whitefield co.

On the 27th November 1866, by Rev. A. R. Lovejoy, Mr. W. T. Sibley to Mrs. Mary J. Mathews, all of Meriwether co., Ga.

On 13th December, 1866, by the same, Maj. John F. Jones, of Early co., to Miss Mollie F. Mitchell, of Meriwether co., Ga.

On the 16th December, 1866, by the same, Mr. Lyman H. Blalock to Miss Alice G. Floyd, all of Meriwether co., Ga.

On the 18th December, 1866, by the same, Mr. R. R. G. Williams to Miss E. V. Wilkinson, all of Meriwether co., Ga.

On the 8th inst., by Rev. P. M. Ryburn, Mr. John W. Miller, of West Point, and Miss Mary Elizabeth Phillips, of Troup co., Ga.

On 8th January 1867, by Rev. C. P. Murdock, Mr. John T. Haskew to Miss Carrie E. Sanford, all of Madison co., Florida.

Issue of February 1, 1867

On the 27th December, 1866, by Rev. Thomas B. Lanier, in Burke co., Ga., Mr. John C. Templeton, to Mrs. Mary E. McColough.

By the same, January 3, 1867, Homer V. Borrow to Miss Emma E. Stone, all of Burke co., Ga.

By the same, January 17, 1867, Mr. Edwin N. Palmer to Miss Ella E. Bullard, daughter of N. Bullard, Esq., Burke co., Ga.

By the Rev. George C. Clarke, January 25th 1867, Mr. F. M. Griffith of Macon Co., Ga., and Miss Henrietta J. Shines of Houston co., Ga.

On 20th January, by Rev. J. Rush, Mr. John S. Fuller and Mrs. Manda A. Freeman, both of Meriwether co., Ga.

On 15th inst., by Rev. J. M. Kenney, Mr. John A. Nichols to Miss Louisa E. Jackson, daughter of John S. Jackson, all of Clarke co.

On 17th January, by Rev. John R. Parker, Capt. Howard W. Newman of Winchester, Tenn., to Miss Maggie A. Donaldson, of Canton, Ga.

By the Rev. J. M. Goss, M. D., on Dec. 20th 1866, Mr. Nemon L. Nance, of Clarke co., Ga., to Miss Mary M. Camp, of Jackson co., Ga., daughter of Berryman S. Camp.

In Jacksonville, Florida, December 29th, 1866, by Rev. W. A. McLean, Mr. W. S. Skinner and Mrs. Elizabeth Dobson.

In Gainesville, Ga., on the 10th January, by Rev. W. T. Caldwell, Mr. Thomas G. Campbell to Miss Elgivia E. Redwine, both of Gainesville.

On the 15th inst., by Rev. J. M. Boyd, Rev. J. B. Traywick, of the South Carolina Conference, and Miss Carrie E. Buzhardt, of Newberry District, S. C.

By the Rev. H. D. Moore, 8th January 1867, Mr. Peter McLaren to Mrs. Julia A. Pace, all of Albany.

On the 27th Jan. by Rev. W. T. Robinson, Mr. Alfred Scarborough, of Sandersville, Ga., and Miss Mary Brinn, of Macon, Ga.

Recently, by Rev. F. W. Baggarly, Rufus Shell to Harriet Head, Wm. W. Reeves to L. E. Head, T. J. Wells to S. B. Haston, W. T. Stallings to M. S. Freeman, R. W. Andrews to Lilly H. Williams, Dudley Parks to Emma Bridges, James A. C. Tidwell to L. B. Coppage, eldest daughter of W. N. Coppage of Spalding co., Ga.

On the 22d of January 1867, by Rev. S. D. Clements, A. H. Freeman, attorney at law, Greenville, Ga., and Miss Medora McClendon.

SOUTHERN CHRISTIAN ADVOCATE MARRIAGE NOTICES 1867-1878

In Gilmer co., Ga., January 10th 1867, by Rev. B. B. Quillian, Mr. M. K. Chadwick and Miss Salina Harris.

Issue of February 8, 1867

On January 1st, 1867, by Rev. J. E. Evans, in Columbus, Ga., Mr. J. W. Williams to Miss Susie Robinson, daughter of the late Rev. W. W. Robinson, of the Georgia Conference.

On 15th Jan., by Rev. J. M. Kenney, J. A. Nichols to Miss Louisa E. Jackson, daughter of John S. Jackson, all of Clark county.

On the 30th January, by the Rev. D. R. McWilliams, Mr. E. A. Keebler to Mrs. L. C. Bird, both of Effingham county.

On the 20th January, by Rev. C. A. Fulwood, Mr. Newton Williams to Miss Susie Ellison, all of Talbot county, Ga.

In Scriven co., Ga., on the 24th of January, by Rev. T. A. Pharr, Mr. Samuel S. Lines to Miss Nannie B. Brown, formerly of Richland, Va.

By the Rev. J. M. Dickey on 17th Jan. 1867, in Warren co., Ga., Captain S. T. Flynt to Mrs. Hattie Lester.

By the same, in Warren co., Jan. 24th, 1867, Lieut. N. E. A. Lewis to Miss S. W. Rogers.

By the same, January 31st, 1867, Mr. H. G. Davis to Miss Martha F. Hayes, all of Warren co,. Ga.

December 20, 1866, by Rev. W. B. Jarrell, Mr. W. W. Colding of Scriven, to Miss Annie D. Morrell, of Effingham co., Ga.

January 17, 1867, by Rev. J. M. Stokes, Mr. William Waters to Miss Sallie A. Thompson, all of Scriven co., Ga.

Issue of February 15, 1867

In Macon, Ga., on the 12th inst., by Rev. J. W. Burke, Mr. John A. Burgess of North Carolina to Miss Mollie C. Askew, of Macon, Ga.

In Macon, Ga., on the 12th Feb, by Rev. J. W. Burke, John Goodman to Sarah P. Williams, all of Macon, Ga.

On Feb. 3, 1867, in Eufaula, Ala., by Rev. W. Shepard, Major Wilson M. Bates to Mrs. Sarah E. Hughes.

By Rev. T. B. Lanier, January 31, in Habersham, Ga., Mr. J. D. Salmon to Miss Emlia M. Davant.

In Americus, Ga., on the 6th inst., by Rev. Chas. R. Jewett, Mr. Wm. C. Mathews, of Washington co., Ga., to Miss M. Valeria, daughter of Mrs. Harriet R. Clayton, of Americus.

SOUTHERN CHRISTIAN ADVOCATE MARRIAGE NOTICES 1867-1878

Issue of February 22, 1867

By Rev. W. F. Robinson on 17th Feb., Mr. Edward Wimberly and Miss Mary Harvey, both of Macon, Ga.

By Rev. L. M. Kenney, in Athens, Georgia, on the 10th inst., Mr. John Lilly, to Miss Charity E. Hughes.

In Stewart co., Geo., on the 31st of January, by Rev. L. J. Davies, Mr. Marquis L. Everett to Miss Eliza J. S., daughter of Judge Loverd Bryan, all of Stewart co.

In Barnesville, Ga., Feb. 7th 1867, by Rev. Morgan Bellah, Mr. John D. Thomas of Alabama, to Miss Flora, daughter of Rev. Daniel Kelsey of the Georgia Conference.

By Rev. W. W. Oslin, on the 29th Jan., Mr. John M. Fulkenberry, of Russell co., Ala., to Miss Clarissa A. West of Harris co., Ga.

Also by the same, on the 13th Feb., Mr. Henry A. Kimbrough to Miss Laura Walker, daughter of James S. Walker, of Harris co., Ga.

At Fort Browder, Jan. 22, by Rev. M. C. Turrentine, Dr. A. C. Crymes to Miss Mattie Wilson, all of Fort Browder, Ala.

By Rev. E. S. Tyner, on 2nd Jan. Mr. Franklin Holly to Miss Ann Casey, all of Marion co., Fla.

By the same, Jan. 12, Mr. Bryant Weaver to Miss Elizabeth Colson.

On 22nd Jan., by Rev. W. T. Hamilton, Mr. Z. D. Gamlin, of Catoosa co., Ga., to Miss V. C. Renfro, of Walker co., Ga.

In Shelby co., Ga., on the 9th of Jan., Mr. G. W. Williams, to Macon Co., Ga., to Miss Sallie L. Little of Schley co., Ga.

Also, on the 15th of Jan., in Americus, Ga., Mr. Wm. W. Wimbush of Schley co., Ga., to Miss R. C. Danels, of the former place.

Also, on the 29th Jan., Mr. Jessie Cox, of Macon co., Ga., to Miss Martha E. Vivins, of Schley co., Ga.

By Rev. G. H. Wells, on 6th Feb., 1867, Mr. Keneth Floyd to Miss Missouri Kirton, daughter of Stephen Kirton, all of Horry District, S. C.

On the 6th Feb 1867 by the Rev. John E. Sentell, Mr. Thomas E. Ivey of Scriven co., Ga., to Miss M. T. Martin of Liberty co,. Ga.

On 12th Feb 1867, by the Rev. John Sentell, Mr. J. L. Bird to Miss S. Louisa Johnson, both of Liberty co., Ga.

Issue of March 1, 1867

By Rev. P. C. Harris, Feb'y 20th 1867, Mr. Robert A. Alexander, of Thomas co. and Miss Betsey Thomas, youngest daughter of Rev. Hamilton W. and Jane Sharpe, of Lowndes Co., Ga.

By Rev. Thos. B. Lanier, 7th of Feb. 1867, Mr. W. H. Saxon to Miss Clara C. Goodwin. By the same Feb. 21, P. Duncan Cox to Miss T. Allana Fulcher, all of Burke co., Ga.

On the 14th inst., by the Rev. C. A. Fulwood, Mr. Moses M. White to Miss Mary Williams, all of Talbot co., Ga.

On the 13th of Feb., 1867, at Attapulgus, Ga., by Rev. John W. Mills, Mr. Daniel Griffis to Miss Lula Howren, daughter of Rev. Robt. H. Howren, of South Georgia Conference.

Near Madison, Ga., Feb. 12th, by Rev. W. R. Foote, Mr. John B. Nebhut, of LaGrange, Tenn., to Miss Emma L. Jones, daughter of Rev. Jas Jones, of the Georgia Conference. (Memphis Advocate please copy.)

On 3d of Feb. 1867 by Rev. B. Ousley, Mr. T. F. Gibson, of Athens, Tenn., to Miss Maggie C. Vaughn, of Thomasville, Ga., daughter of Gen. Vaughn, formerly of Tennessee.

By Rev. T. B. Harben, on 30th Jan., Mr. Samuel Pendry to Mrs. S. A. Peterson, all of Baker co., Ga.

On 12th of Feb., at the residence of Judge J. H. Hines, Hon. Thos. O. Wicker to Miss Almira Bird, all of Washington co., Ga.

On the 31st of Jan., by Rev. George E. Smith, Mr. J. Albert Perkins to Miss Mattie E. Lundie, all of Coweta co., Ga.

By Rev. John Calvin Johnson, Jan. 10th 1867, Mr. Samuel H. Smith to Miss Mary A. Simonton, all of Clarke co., Ga.

By the same, Jan. 17th 1867, Mr. Andrew J. Elder to Miss Sarah Susan Elder, all of Clarke co,. Ga.

By the same, February 12th 1867, Mr. Arthur M. Jackson, of Walton co., Ga., to Miss Sarah E. Hester of Green co., Ga.

Issue of March 8, 1867

In Taylor county, Georgia, on the 28th February, 1867, by Rev. G. L. W. Anthony, Mr. Charley Guttenberger to Miss Emma Peacock.

On the 14th February 1867 by Rev. J. O. A. Cook, Mr. Benjamin Seay, of Alabama, and Miss Kitty George, of Cuthbert, Randolph county, Ga.

On the 27th February, by Rev. H. H Parks, Dr. Marcus A. Daniel of Elbert county, Ga., and Miss Martha T. Wilkerson, of Athens, Ga.

By the Rev. W., A. Dodge, on the 31st January 1867, Mr. Josiah Johnson and Miss Sophia, youngest daughter of Zachariah R. and Mary Jones, all of DeKalb county, Ga.

By the same on the 12th of February, Mr. James Jackson and Miss Mary C., daughter of Robert F. E. and Lucy, Jones, all of DeKalb county, Ga.

By the same on the 3d January, Mr. Elijah Braswell and Miss Sallie Chupp, all of DeKalb county, Ga.

By the same on the 20th December 1866, Mr. Louis Baily amd Miss Correna Marbutt, all of DeKalb county, Ga.

On the 25th of February 1867, by Rev. D. J. Myrick, Mr. Hinton C. Zuber to Miss Eleanor E. Hall, both of Oglethorpe county, Ga.

On the 21st of February at Laurens C. H., S. C., by Rev. Jas. T. Kilgore, Capt. William H. Franks to Miss Nannie M., daughter of the late Rev. D. L. Ballew, formerly of Georgia.

On the 21st of February by Rev. F. A. Kimbel, Mr. Frederick, B. Yarborough, of Arkansas, to Miss Rebecca A. Crowder, of Merriwether county, Ga.

On the 21st of February by Rev. R. A. Conner, Mr. L. D. Walton to Miss Jane McLean, daughter of Dr. McLean, all of Columbia county, Ga.

On the 18th February by the Rev. W. H. Wicker, Virgil A. White to Miss Sallic A. Griffith, all of Floyd county, Ga.

In Butts county, on 20th February, by Rev. Wesley F. Smith, Mr. D. R. Walker, of Upson county, and Miss Mollie E. Ward, daughter of Maj. B. F. Ward,of the former place.

On the 14th February, at the residence of Dr. Johnson, in Lenoir, N. C., by Rev. J. C. Hartsell, Capt. P. J. Johnson, of Burk county, to Miss Jane Corpening, of Caldwell, N.C.

In Midway, Ga., on 20th February, by Rev. R. W. Bigham, Capt. J. Hardeman, of Jones county, and Miss Dollie Whitaker of Midway.

On 21st Feb., in Macon co., Ga., Mr. Crawford Winbush, of Schley co., Ga., to Miss Roselle C. Waters, of the same county.

On 21st Feb., by Rev. J. F. Norman, Leut. Y. T. Bobo to Miss Mattie A. Dillard, all of Union District, S. C.

On Feb. 6th, by Rev. A. J. Cauthen, Dr. John Lever, of Biehland, to Miss Nannie Ruff, of Fairfield, S. C.

By the same, Feb. 21st, Capt. John Hinnant to Miss Maggie Willingham, all of Fairfield, S. C.

Issue of March 15, 1867

On the 21st Feb., at the residence of Capt. W. B. Johnson, West Point, Ga., By Rev. P. M. Ryburn, Mr. Lawrence Higgins of Albany, Ga., to Miss Nannie S. Gartin, all of Lebanon, Ky.

By the same, on the 5th of March, Mr. S. C. Truett to Mrs. E. W. Bass, both of West Point, Ga.

By Rev. W. M. D. Bond, Feb. 17th 1867, Mr. J. H. McNeal to Miss M. E. Livingston, all of Sumter co., Ga.

By the same, on 21st of Feb., Mr. H. J. Randit, of Pulaski county, to Miss S. J. Williams of Harris county, Ga.

On the 28th Feb., by Rev. J. R. Gaines, Mr. R. J. Bates of Cherokee co., Ga., to Miss Bettie J. Brown, of Milton county, Ga.

By Rev. W. T. Robison, on 7th March, Mr. T. A. Judge to Miss Elizabeth E. Harvey, of Macon, Ga.

By Rev. J. R. Little, on 29th of Jan., 1867, Mr. W. H. Fitzgerald to Mrs. Ellen E. Armfield, all of Monroe, N. C.

By the same, on 7th of January 1867, Mr. J. E. Hinson to Miss Pocahontas Tapscott, all of Monroe, N. C.

Issue of March 22, 1867

In Henry co., by the Rev. G. T. Embry, Mr. Emory M. Owen and Miss Sarah J. Granade, March 7, 1867.

On the 14th Feb., by Rev. B. J. Baldwin, M. D., Mr. Joseph T. Perry, of Stewart co., Ga., to Miss Georgia A. Tucker, at the residence of A. M. Moreland, Esq., Randolph co., Ga.

By the same on the 21st of Feb., Mr. W. S. Bell, of Stewart co., Ga. to Miss M. Emma Jarrel of Richland, Ga.

In Lumpkin, Geo., March 10th, by Rev. L. J. Davies, Mr. John F. Craft, of Hart co., Ga. to Miss S. Ellen Goss, daughter of the Rev. Mr. Goss, of the former place. N. B. Christian Index please copy.

On the 27th of Feb. 1867, in Mobile, Ala., by the Rev. J. J. Gace, Mr. Michael Sefers of Greenvlile, Ala., to Miss Josephine Finche of Mobile, Ala.

By the Rev. Ewing Johnston, on the 14th March 1867, Mr. Jacob D. Johnson and Miss Sarah Bell, all of Richmond co., Ga.

By the Rev. J. H. D. McRae, Mr. Thomas Stanford to Mrs. Susan W. Farnell, all of Columbia co., Fla.

In Rutherford co., N. C., by Rev. W. Bowman, Feb. 14, 1867, Thos. Alison of Transylvania co., N. C., to Ellen E., daughter of M. H. Kilpatrick, Esq., of Rutherford co., N.C.

Issue of March 29, 1867

On the 14th of March, by the Rev. A. W. Harris, Mr. N. J. Harris to Mrs. M. J. Groover, all of Nashville, Berrien co., Georgia.

On the 14th of March, 1867, by Rev. Isaac Marden, Mr. John J. Sapp to Miss Martha Blackwell, all of Suwannee co., Fla.

On the 9th of March, 1867, by Rev. Wm. S. Foster, Mr. D. M. Sanders to Miss J. A. DuPree all of Cherokee co., Ga.

By Rev. J. Finger, Mr. T. F. Wilkinson, of Savannah, Ga., to Miss Mattie M. Hill, of Catawba co., N. C.

On the 21st of January, by the Rev. Henry D. Moore, John W. Orr, to Miss Annie E. Wright, all of Albany, Ga.

By the same, on the 20th of March, George C. Bell, of Terrel co., Ga., to Miss Mattie P., daughter of Mr. Perry Duncan, of Dougherty co., Ga., formerly of Greenville District, S. C.

On March 17th, 1867, at Sylvania, Ga., by Rev. J. M. Stokes, Mr. Jas. P. Stewart to Miss Temperance E. Scott, all of Sylvania, Ga.

On January 31st, by Rev. W. B. Jarrell, Mr. L. Dow Shepherd to Roxy A. Boykin, all of Scriven co., Ga.

On February 12th, by the same, Mr. Joseph B. Jarrell to Miss Bettie S. Morrell, of Effingham, co., Ga.

On February 21st, by the same, Mr. Paul G. Boykin to Miss Henrietta Anderson, all of Scriven co., Ga.

On the 20th of February, 1867, at Clay Springs, Orange co., Fla., Mr. T. B. Burleson, of Marion co., Fla., to Miss Henrietta Waterman, of the former place.

In Augusta, Ga., on the 18th inst., by Rev. A. Wright, Mr. Carbett L. Lawrence to Miss Savannah A. Barton.

On the 10th of March, 1867, by Rev. C. A. Mitchell, Mr. Benjamin B. Davis to Miss Elizabeth Nichols, all of Clarke co., Ga.

In Houston, Ga., February 13th, by the Rev. E. H. McGehee, Mr. Jno. Prater, of Crawford co., Ga., to Miss Ida McKay.

In Marshallville, Ga., March 21st, by the same, Mr. Jno. Martin to Miss Cordelia Johnson.

Issue of April 5, 1867

By Rev. A. C. Mixon, on the 26th of March, 1867, Mr. J. A. McMullan of McDonough, GA., to Miss M. E. Harris, daughter of Henderson H. Harris, Esq., of Newton county, Ga.

By the same, on the 22d of January 1867, Mr. Flournoy Ivy to Miss Mattie Knowles, daughter of Morris Knowles, Esq., all of Jasper county, Ga.

On the 7th of March by Rev. M. F. Malsby, Dr. Wm. A. Watson to Miss Lizzie McAlpin, all of Jackson county, Ga.

On the 20th of March, at the residence of Col. Phil. Dell, Newnansville, East Florida, by Rev. J. J. Seely, Mr. F. P. Olmsted to Miss S. A. Dell.

In Thomasville, March 19th 1867, By Rev. N. B. Ousley, O. G. Bartley, Co. C. 16th Regt. U. S. Infantry, to Mrs. Anna Cole of Thomasville, Ga.

In Thomasville, March 19th 1867, by Rev. N. B. Ousley, Mr. Eaton Douglas to Miss Emma Allen, all of Thomasville, Ga.

On the 27th ult., by Rev. H. H. Parks, Mr. Jas. O'Ferrell to Miss Martha F. Mason, both of Athens, Ga.

Issue of April 12, 1867

By Rev. W. F. Robinson on the 7th April, Mr. Frank Jones and Miss Agnes Byas, of Macon, Ga.

By Rev. J. M. Austin, April 4, Mr. B. Haesler to Mrs. Francis M. Lawes, all of Burke co., Ga.

On the 27th March, by Rev. C. A. Evans, Captain H. L. Rockwell of Lumpkin, Ga., to Miss Cornelia Skinner of Atlanta.

By the Rev. A. G. Dempsey in Cobb co., Ga., March 15, 1867, Mr. Sidney Burdan of Hart Co., Ga., to Miss Emily F. White.

On the 19th of March by the Rev. W. M. D. Bond, Mr. James Roach and Mrs. Mary J. Hargrove, all of Sumter co., Ga.

By the same, March 21, Mr. Hiram E. Sloan and Miss Mary C. Ray, all of Sumter co., Ga.

Issue of April 19, 1867

March 20th in Marion S. C., by the Rev. S. H. Browne, at the residence of the bride's father, Rev. W. C. Powers, of the South Carolina Conference, Mrs. M. Louisa McEachin, daughter of Gen. Wm. Evans.

On the 12th March by Rev. J. E. Watson, Mr. M. M. Tat to Miss Sarah J. Webster, both of Union District, S. C.

By the same on the 26th March, Mr. E. Coyl to Miss Louisa Scott, both of Union District, S. C.

March 26th by Rev. Henry D. Moore, Mr. David L. Fudge to Miss Clara C. Bostick, all of Dougherty co., Ga.

By Rev. Thos G. Herbert, on the evening of the 26th of March 1867, Rev. Geo. F. Round, of the South Carolina Conference, to Miss Julia Hammond, daughter of the late Col. Herbert Hammond and Mrs. Elizabeth Hammond, all of Anderson C. H., S. C.

By the Rev. D. R. McWilliams, Mr. Benj. A. Porter to Miss Susan A. Berry, both of Effingham co., Ga., April 10th 1867.

On the 10th April 1867, by the Rev. John E. Sentell, Mr. J. T. Grive* to Miss N. E. Darsey, all of Liberty co., Ga.

On the 28th March, at the residence of John B. Crump, Leon co., Fla., by Rev. Sam'l Woodberry, Dr. William Thomas Snipes to Miss MaryAnn Willis.

Issue of April 26, 1867

Married by Rev. S. A. Clarke, Feb. 237, Mr. J. C. Sanderford to Miss Mattie J. Quaige, Jonesville, Ga.

By the same, March 28th, on Doboy Island, Mr. W. H. Patterson to Miss M. C. Hebert.

By the same on 16th April, Mr. James Maulden to Miss Rhoda C. Williams, all of Clarke county, Ga.

On 4th April by Rev. Jas. H. Tart, at the residence of Mr. John Cox, Mr. C. W. Cox of All Saints Parish, S. C., to Miss M. E. Wall, of Marion District, S. C.

Issue of May 3, 1867

The 14th day of March by Rev. F. M. Hunt, Mr. Jno. F. Ogletree of Monroe co., and Miss Fannie P. daughter of the late Judge Gilbert J. Green.

On the 18th inst., by Rev. A. M. Wynn, Mr. Geo. P. Walker and Miss Annie G. Sausey, both of Savannah.

In Culloden, April 17th, 1867, by Rev. Wesley F. Smith, Mr. Thomas D. Smith and Miss Anna P. Trippe, all of Culloden.

April 23d, 1867, by Rev. J. M. Stokes, Mr. Wm. H. Beard to Miss Laura Best, all of Scriven co., Ga.

By Rev. W. F. Robison, April 25th, Mr. Robert Walker to Miss Julia Arnold of Macon, Ga.

Issue of May 10, 1867

By Rev. W. M. Kennedy, May 2nd, Mr. Edwin T. Davis to Miss Mattie T. Jones.

By Rev. J. B. Wardlaw, on the 25th of April, in Miller co., Ga., Mr. Taylor Scott, to Mrs. Sophia Batts.

Near Georgetown, S. C., April 25th, by Rev. P. F. Kistler, Dr. H. D. Green, of Bishopville, to Miss Eliza P. Coachman, daughter of Elijah P. Coachman, Esq.

By Rev. J. C. Hartsell, at the residence of H. J. Moor, on 10th April, Mr. John C. Sherrill to Miss Bell V. Moon, of Catawba co., N. C.

By the same, at the residence of Henry Link, on the 12th April, Mr. John Fry to Miss Emma Lane, of Hickory Station, N. C. (Episcopal Methodist at Raleigh, please copy).

April 7th, by M. F. Malsby, Mr. J. H. Kirkpatrick to Mrs. L. J. Wills, all of Jackson co., Ga.

April 30th, by Rev. T. S. L. Harwell, Mr. John W. Jones to Miss M. E. Scroggins, all of Troup co., Ga.

In Macon, April 30th, by Rev. Joe S. Key, Mr. Franklin L. Groce, of Griffin, to Miss Florida H. Hollingsworth, of Macon, Ga.

On May 2nd, by Rev. Wm. W. Mood, Mr. Alonzo W. Flagler to Miss Ella, daughter of Samuel M. Matthews, all of Williamsburg District, S. C.

Issue of May 17, 1867

In Columbia, S. C., on the 24th April 1867, by the Rev. Wm. Martin, John H. Bremer of Charleston, S. C. to Miss Lavinia C. Loomis of Columbia, S. C.

On the 5th inst., by Rev. A. Gray, Mr. W. H. Lloyd to Miss M. Z. Parker, both of Newton County, Ga.

By the Rev. W. M. D. Bond, on 1st of May, Mr. Wm. L. Parker to Miss Sarah F. Robinson, all of Sumter county, Ga.

On the 27th April by Rev. N. B. Ousley, at the residence of C. G. Bartley, Mr. Wm. E. Fletcher, 16 U. S. Infantry, to Miss G. A. Moss, of Thomasville, Ga.

By Rev. J. M. Austin, May 1st, Rev. Charles J. Oliver, of the South Georgia Conference, to Miss Nancy A. Reeves, of Burke county, Ga.

Issue of May 24, 1867

On the 9th inst., at the residence of Judge Brooke, by Rev. Wm. M. Overton, Mr. Thos. Jeff. Overton and Miss Sarah Rice Brooke, of Taliaferro co., Ga.

In Henry co., Ga., by the Rev. G. T. Embry on the 12th inst., Mr. Wm. F. Moseley and Miss Mary A. Bowen, both of Henry co., Ga.

At the Chalybeate Springs, Meriwether co., Ga., April 30, 1867, by Rev. R. W. Dixon, Mr. Eugene E. Love and Miss Francis G. Cheney, all of Meriwether co., Ga.

By Rev. W. F. Robison on the 16th May, Mr. John J. Nelson and Miss Amanda Carter of Macon, Ga.

On the 7th May by the Rev. James Dunwody, at the residence of Col. W. Laidler, Mr. J. N. Smith to Miss A. M. Laidler, all of Houston co., Ga.

By the Rev. J. R. Danforth, at the bride's residence, on the 21st inst., Mr. Wm. A. Havis of East Baton Rouge, La., and Mrs. Mary A. Townsend of this city.

Issue of May 31, 1867

At Cedar Keys, Fla., by the Rev. Jas. P. DePass, Mr. Thos E. Chairs to Miss Clara McQueen, April 24, 1867.

On April 28th, by the Rev. James Griffith, Mr. N. B. Newsom and Miss Emma Leroy, second daughter of H. H. Leroy, Esq., of Reynolds, Ga.

At the residence of the bride's father, by Rev. A. Nelson Hollifield, May 16th, 1867, Mr. W. Bugg, of Oglethorpe co., to Miss Mary C. Wheeler, daughter of Lawrence F. Wheeler, Esq., of Green co., Ga.

In Henry co., Ga., on the 21st of May, by the Rev. G. T. Embry, Mr. Wm. J. Livingston and Mrs. Sarah E. Martin.

On the 5th of May, at the residence of the bride's sister (Mrs. A. M. Simms), Mr. Samuel J. Arnold, of Coweta co., Ga., to Miss Monterey Houston, of Fayetteville, Ga., by Rev. J. T. Lowe.

At Cave Spring, Ga., May 16th, 1867, by Rev. B. B. Quillian, Mr. M. T. Sewell to Mrs. M. A. Herren, all of Floyd co., Ga.

At Alexandria Church, Oswitchie, in Russell co., Ala., on Thursday evening, the 23d of May 1867, by Rev. Jos. B. Cottrell, Mr. Albert E. Patterson, formerly of Spartanburg, S. C., and Miss Lizzie S. Dalden of Russell co.

Issue of June 7, 1867

On the 25th May, at the residence of Mr. A. Wimberly, by Rev. W. J. Wardlaw, Mr. W. T. Lane to Miss A. L. Alsobrook, all of Fulton county, Ga.

On the 23d of May 1867, by Rev. J. A. Wood, of the South Carolina Conference, Mr. S. W. Hamilton to Miss Sallie L. Green, of Polk co., N. C.

In Lumpkin, Ga., on the 28th of May, by Rev. L. J. Davies, Mr. John W. Simmons, son of Rev. J. C. Simons, to Miss Mary C., daughter of Mr. J. G. Singer, all of Lumpkin, Ga.

Issue of June 14, 1867

On May 28th in Georgetown, S. C., by Rev. J. A. Porter, Mr. W. C. McMillan, of Marion, S. C., to Miss Mattie L. Porter, of Georgetown, S. C., daughter of the officiating minister.

On May the 22nd, by Rev. Josephus Anderson, Mr. John Cromartie to Miss Annie Blake, all of Leon co., Fla.

On June 4th, 1867, by the Rev. J. E. Sentell, Mr. Thomas F. Lanier to Miss Mary F. Floyd, all of Liberty co., Ga.

In Barbour co., Ala., May 18th, by Rev. D. S. T. Douglas, Mr. M. C. Merritt to Miss M. E. Owens.

Issue of June 21, 1867

By the Rev. G. F. Hughes, at the residence of Edwin P. Williams on the 4th of June, Mr. George G. Bristol, of Clay county, N. C., to Miss Sallie J. Williams, of Nacoochee Valley, Ga.

On 28th May, by the Rev. T. J. Rutledge, Mr. T. J. Johnson of Rome,m Ga., to Miss Fannie Griffith of Glennville, Ala.

Also, by the same, on 8th June, Mr. W. Eugene Besson of Eufaula, Ala., to Miss Sallie Graves, of Glennville, Ala.

Issue of June 28, 1867

At Jacob Hinely's, June 13, 1867, by Rev. D. R. McWilliams, Mr. T. S. Flood of Savannah, and Miss Amanda E. Hinely, of Effingham co., Ga.

By Rev. J. W. Jackson on 9th of June, at the residence of Dr. J. W. Price, Mr. Amon McManus to Miss Charity Higgins, all of Columbia co., Florida.

On 6th ult., by Rev. J. T. Ainsworth, Dr. H. Spinks to Miss M. c. Wats, all of Marion co., Ga.

By the Rev. J. R. Teat, on the 29th May, Mr. Rob't Pollok Ballar, of Cobb co., to Mrs. Nancy Burke, of Stewart county, Ga.

Issue of July 5, 1867

On the 19th June by Rev. Wm. W. Mood, Capt. Geo. P. Anderson of Greenville District, S. C., and Miss Mag. G., daughter of Col. D. D. Wilson, of Williamsburg Dist., S. C.

On 18th June 1867, in Hernanda co., Fla., by Rev. W. H. Thomas, Rev. E. H. Giles of the Florida Conference, to Miss Mary J. Tranham, formerly of Ocala, Fla.

On May 14th, 1867, by Rev. J. J. Workman, Mr. P. A. McDavid and Miss Fannie M., daughter of Dr. J. M. Sullivan, all of Greenville Dist., S. C.,

By the Rev. E. H. McGehee, on 25th June, at the residence of Mr. O. H. Walkton in Crawford co., Ga., Mr. Jehu G. Postell to Miss Lizzie J. Walton.

On June 27, 1867, in Conwayboro, S. C., by Rev. J. H. C. McKinney, Mr. Samuel S. Beaty to Miss Mary E. Burroughs, both of Horry District, S. C.

On 15th June 1867 at the residence of Mrs. M. C. Beaty in Conwayboro, S. C., by Rev. J. H. C. McKinney, Mr. B. Lewis Beaty to Miss Fannie C. Grissette, both of Horry District, S. C.,

Issue of July 19, 1867

June 12, 1867, by Rev. W. Bowman, at the bride's father's, Dr. J. L. Rucker of Rutherford co,. N. C., to Miss Bettie, daughter of Rev. T. M. Fanning of Henderson co., N. C.

By Rev. W. Bowman, June 27, 1867, at the residence of Dr. Jas Bivings, Dr. A. J. Nesbitt of Spartanburg, S. C., to Miss E. A. Patton, of Ashville, N. C.

On the 11th July, by the Rev. S. H. J. Sistrunk, Mr. David H. Riley to Mrs. Susan Calhoun, all of Houston co., Ga.

By Rev. J. H. D. McRae, on the 4th July, at the bride's father's, Mr. John Coon to Miss Sarah Burns, all of Columbia co., Fla.

Issue of July 26, 1867

On the evening of the 11th in Newnan, by Rev. F. M. Daniel, Mr. John H. Cooke and Mrs. Savannah A. Morris, all of Newnan.

On 16th inst., at the residence of Alfred Windsor, Esq., by Rev. W. C. Bass, Isaac Bledsoe, Esq., of this city and Miss Sallie Rice of Bibb co.

In Henderson, Houston co., Ga., on the 7th inst., by Rev. E. H. McGehee, Mr. F. W. Pool to Miss S. D. McGehee.

On 11th July, Dr. R. R. Mitchell of Rome Ga., to Miss H. Addie Stokes, of Montgomery, Ala.

On 16th July, Rev. Wm. T. Pattillo, of Lee co., To Miss Sallie V. Cole, of Macon Co., Ala.

By Rev. James Dunwody at the residence of Mrs. S. C. Killen, Mr. M. P. Sherron, to Miss S. D. Killen, all of Houston co., Ga.

On 22d July, by Rev. W. F. Robison, Mr. Marion G. Rainwater, and Mrs. Jessie F. Saunders, both of Macon, Ga.

In Macon, Ga., July 10,. By Rev. Jos. S. Key, Mr. J. W. Fears and Miss Mary E. Roberts.

In Vineville July 17, by Rev. Jos. S. Key, Mr. H. B. Hays of Cherokee, Ala., and Miss Loretta Virgin, of the former place.

Issue of August 9, 1867

On the 28th of July by Rev. W. F. Robinson, Mr. William Dewberry and Miss Elizabeth Cannon, both of Macon, Ga.

In Jonesboro, on the 25th July, by the Rev. G. R. Embry, Mr. W. E. Carnes and Miss Minerva C. Morrow, all of Jonesboro.

On Thursday morning, Aug. 1, 1867, at St. John's Church, in Savannah, by Rev. C. F. McRae, Mr. Charles A. Hall of Macon and Mrs. Julia B. Shoer, of that city.

At Mulberry St. Church, by Rev. Jos. S. Key, on the 25th June, Mr. Robert J. Lightfoot and Miss Ellen T. Ross, all of Macon.

At the bride's residence, on the 4th of August, by Rev. W. F. Robison, Mr. John R. Booker, of Prince Edward co., Ga., and Miss Martha E. Schofield, of Macon, Ga.

By Rev J. E. Watson, at the residence of Dr. Thos Littlejohn, Mr. M. Smith to Miss Talula Cooper,. all of Union District, S. C.

Issue of August 16, 1867

At the residence of Major Ward, of Henry co., Homer V. Hardwich to Miss Mildred P. Ward.

On the 1st of August 1867, by Rev. J. R. Gaines, Mr. Hugh T. Winn to Miss Frankie E. Latimer, all of Cobb co., Ga.

July 5th 1867, at the residence of Col. Thos Pierce in Summerville, Emanuel co., by Dr. L. B. Bouchelle, Mr. L. G. Reid of Lexington, Ky., and Miss Martha A. Pierce, of Burke co., Ga.

By the Rev. J. H. C. McKinney, Aug. 1, 1867, Mr. Lewis S. Cooper to Miss Mary A. Lewis, both of Horry District, South Carolina.

Issue of August 23, 1867

In Atlanta, August 14th, by Rev. Atticus G. Haygood, Mr. Charles E. Boynto, and Miss Myra A., youngest daughter of the late Green B. Haygood, Esq.

In Putnam county, Ga., on Tuesday the 30th of July 1867, By Rev. Mr. Hitchcock, Mr. William R. White to Miss Sallie A. Knight, daughter of Rev. J. W. Knight of Putnam county, Ga.

On the 14th inst., by Rev. W. M. Brumly, Mr. John D. Ray of Newnan, Ga., to Miss Mary P. Rawson, daughter of Mr. E. E. Rawson, of Atlanta, GA.

SOUTHERN CHRISTIAN ADVOCATE MARRIAGE NOTICES 1867-1878

Issue of August 30, 1867

In Lake City, Fla., August 8th, by the Rev. Jas. P. DePass, Mr. J. S. Beckman to Miss Dora A. Hancock.

By Rev. James Dunwody, July 18th 1867, at the residence of Mr. D. W. Buff, Mr. Thomas Marchman to Miss Fannie J. Buff, all of Houston county, Ga.

By Rev. James Dunwody, Aug. 15, 1867, at the residence of Mr. J. C. Benson, Mr. J. Hamilton Laidler to Miss Sallie Benson, all of Houston county, Ga.

By Rev. G. T. Embry on the 12th inst., Mr. Elbert Beavers to Mrs. Mary N. Simes, in Henry county, Ga.

By Rev. J. R. Little, August 24, 1867, at the residence of A. N. Lawson, Esq., Mr. M. W. Cuthbertson, of Monroe, to Miss Nettie F. Wadsworth, formerly of Rowan county, N. C.

On July 24th 1867, by Rev. J. H. Lockhart, Mr. Alex. Lamb of Russel county, Ala., to Miss O. J. Whitten, of Lee county, Ala.

In Athens, Ga., by Rev. H. H. Parks, 9th of July, Jas. G. McCurdy to Miss Sarah R. Kinney, both of Athens, Ga.

By the same, 16th of July, J. A. Patat to Miss Anne E. Royal, both of Athens, Ga.

By the same, 3d of August, F. Patat to E. J. Kirby, both of Athens, Ga.

By the same, 20th Aug., Benj. F. Culp to Miss Selina A. Moon, Athens, Ga.

By the same, 22d Aug., Hugh R. Bernard, of Tenn., to Miss Bettie Weatherly, of Athens, Ga.

At Bland Wallace's Sr., near Buena Vista, by Rev. J. T. Ainsworth on 18th ult., Mr. John Wallace, of Stewart county, Ga., to Miss Martha Lasier, of Randolph county.

August 20, 1867, by Rev. J. H. C. McKinney at the residence of Mr. Wm. P. Melson, in Conwayboro, S. C., Mr. Malcom C. Brewer, of Moore county, N. C., to Miss Carrie L. Bruton, of Horry District.

Issue of September 13, 1867

Aug. 22d, by Rev. L. M. Wilson, Rev. Frank Brandon of the Montgomery Conference, to Miss Carrie Woodward of Jacksonville, Ala.

By Rev. J. B. Wardlaw, Aug. 20th, near Colquit, Miller co., Ga., Dr. William P. Chapman, and Miss Dora C. Swearingen.

August 22d 1867, by Rev. J. M. Stokes of Scriven co., Ga., Mr. Alex. E. Morgan, of Nashville, Tenn., to Miss Georgia Lawton.

Aug 1, 1867, by Rev. J. H. C. McKinney, Mr. Lewis S. Cooper to Miss Mary A. Lewis, both of Horry Dist. S. C.

On the 13th Aug., By Rev. E. S. Tyner, Mr. James V. Avry and Miss Ann Byrun, all of Ocala, Fla.

By the Rev. J. W. Jackson, Mr. John Junius Sheperd, of Washington co., Ga., to Miss Martha Jane Howel, of Columbia co., East Fla.

Issue of September 20, 1867

In Catawba co., N. C., by Rev. J. C. Hartsell, on the 5th instant, Mr. Monroe L. Williams to Mrs. Harriet M. Hull. Episcopal Methodist at Raleigh please copy.

At South Butler, Ala., on Sept. 1st, by the Rev. H. J. Hunter, Mr. Thomas Sneed to Mrs. Mary O. Cottenham.

Issue of September 27, 1867

By Rev. John E. Sentell, Sept. 11th, 1867, Mr. T. A. Floyd to Miss Laura Freeman, both of Liberty co., Ga.

In Henry co., Ga., Sept. 19, by the Rev. G. T. Embry, Mr. J. T. Lewis and Miss Nancy M. Carroll.

By Rev. W. Lane, Dr. Robt. T. Barton to Miss Mary S. Rivers, both of Jefferson co., Ga.

In Greenville, Ga., August 17 at 8½ o'clock, A. M., by the Rev. S. D. Clements, Mr. C. D. Williams and Miss Fannie Gresham.

Issue of October 4, 1867

On September 19, 1867, In Clayton county, Ga., by the Rev. James Jones, Mr. Wm. B. Ragan, of Newton county, to Miss Sallie L. Jones, daughter of E. L. Jones, all of Ga.

By the same, Sept 22nd 1867, Mr. H. H. Barfield, To Miss W. P. Carrol, all of Campbell county, Ga.

At Enon, Ala., on 17th September, by Rev. W. H. Ellison, Mr. Wm. L. Anthony to Miss Arcadia Davis.

At Bronson, Fla., on 17th Sept 1867, By Rev. E. J. Knight, Mr. H. P. Jackson, to Miss M. F. Shands, the youngest daughter of the Rev. A. Shands.

In Fort Valley, Ga., by Rev. E. H. McGehee, on the 25th of Sept., Mr. J. D. Houser to Mrs. I. N. Rumph.

Issue of October 11, 1867

By Rev. W. J. Cotter at Whitesville, Harris co., Ga., July 30th, Mr. Thos. J. Hunt to Miss Sallie Hogan.

By the same in Harris co., Ga., Sept. 18th, Mr. H. C. Watson to Miss L. L. Langford.

By the same at Whitesville, Oct. 18, Mr. J. J. Hadley to Miss Kate Bishop.

In Baptist Church, Macon., Ga., on the 2nd inst., by Rev. J. W. Burke, Robert J. Anderson and Miss Julia F. Coley.

In Lumpkin, Ga., on 3d Oct., by Rev. L. J. Davies, Mr. M. J. Lunquest, of Cuthbert, Ga., to Miss Cornelia Cravey, of the former place.

On the 22d Aug. in the Methodist Church, Cheraw, S. C., by Rev. W. L. Pegues, Rev. Robt Lee Harper of Hamilton, Canada West, to Miss Mary Sanders, of Cheraw, S. C.

On 18th Sept. by Rev. Wm. W. Mood, Mr. Wm. C. Hemingway of Conwayboro, S. C., and Miss Ellen, daughter of the late J. A. Hemingway of Williamsburg Dist., S. C.

On 29th Sept. by the same, Mr. James E. Davis and Miss Anna M., daughter of Capt. Wm. R. Cookroy, all of Clarendon Dist.. S. C.

On Sept. 8th 1867, by Rev. J. J. Workman, Mr. John F. Clardy to Miss Maggie A. Orr, all of Anderson Dist., S. C.

By the same, Sept. 17, Mr. E. S. Griffin to Miss Sallie M. Smith, both of Pickens Dist. S. C.

By the same, Sept. 29, Mr. Sion J. King to Miss E. Ann Sitton, both of Anderson Dist., S. C.

Issue of October 18, 1867

By Rev. W. F. Robison, October 3d, Mr. Geo. S. Westcott to Miss Lucy Cleghorn, all of Macon, Ga.

In Butler, Ga., by Rev. James Griffith, Rev. James D. Anthony, of South Georgia Conference to Miss E. J. Alexander.

Also, by the same, October 1st, at the residence of Dr. Edwards, Mr. J. A. McCants to Miss M. A. Edwards, all of Butler, Ga.

On 3d October, in Twiggs co., Ga., by the Rev. R. B. G. Walters, Mr. R. H. O. McLendon of Lawrence co., Ga., to Miss Camilla V. Ward, of Twiggs co., Ga.

On 8th Oct. by the same, Mr. James Howell to Miss Emma Underwood, all of Johnson Co., Ga.

By Rev. T. B. Russell in Houston co., Ga., Oct. 6th 1867, Mr. J. W. Melvin to Mrs. Sarah Amerson.

By the same, in Fort Valley, Ga., Oct. 8th 1867, Mr. Charles G. Grey to Miss C. E. Wiggins.

Issue of October 25, 1867

In Montezuma on 17th Oct., by Rev. Chas. R. Jewett, Mr. J. E. DeVaughn to Miss S. Virginia, daughter of Mr. W. W. McClendon, all of Montezuma, Ga.

On 13th of Oct., by Rev. Samuel Bellah, Jesse Brown to Mrs. Elizabeth Morris, both of Milton co., Ga.

Issue of November 1, 1867

On Oct. 17th in Quitman, Ga., by Rev. O. L. Smith, D. D., Mr. James L. Beaty of Quincy, Fla., to Miss Mary B. Cobb.

In Pickens District ,S. C., by Rev. C. H. Ellis, on the 21st Aug., Mr. M. Vann Estes, to Miss Lou Sharp. Athens Watchman pleas copy.

By Rev. H. J. Hunter, Rev. Wm. W. Graham of the Montgomery Conf. to Miss Julia A., daughter of James and Harriet Watson, on the evening of Oct. 16, 1867, at Wesley Chapel, South Butler ct., Montgomery Conf.

At the Methodist Church in Bennettsville, on the evening of the 3d inst., by Rev. Tracy R. Walsh, Mr. John H. McCollum to Miss Josephine T. Walsh.

On 17th Oct. 1867, by Rev. J. R. Gaines, Mr. Aaron M. Puckett of Alpharetta, Ga., to Miss Olivia C. Daniel, of Canton, Ga.

In Walker co., Ga., Oct. 2, by Rev. Wiley T. Hamilton, J. G. Putman and Miss Margaret Thurman.

Issue of November 8, 1867

On Oct. 22d, by Rev. J. J. Workman, Mr. William A. Davis of Newberry to Miss Sade Q. Payne of Greenville Dist. S. C.

By Rev. W. J. Cotter, Oct. 3d, Mr. F. M. Smith to Miss N. J. Hall.

By the same, Oct. 24, Mr. J. T. Burton, To Miss L. B. Blackmon, all of Harris co., Ga.

At Rome, Ga., on 30th October, by the Rev. C. A. Stillwell, the Rev. William F. Robison of the So. Ga. Conference and the Miss Savannah E. Stillwell, daughter of the officiating minister.

On 10th October, near Auburn, Lee co., Ala., by Rev. L. F. Dowdell, Mr. Cornelius Slaughter, to Miss Mary S. P., daughter of Elisha Hightower, Esq., all of Lee county, Ala.

In Augusta, Ga., October 20th by Rev. G. H. Pattillo, Mr. H. Rawls and Miss Jane E. Carter.

In Augusta, Ga., October 30th by Rev. G. H. Pattillo, Mr. M. E. Hill and Miss Mary P. McCann.

On 17th October, by Rev. John R. Parker, Amos M Evans and Laura M. Barnes, all of Cherokee county, Ga.

On Thursday, October 24th, by Rev. J. W. McRoy, Mr. Stobo R. Perry and Miss Georgia C. Willis, both of Colleton dist. S. C.,

By the same, October 27th, Mr. Augustus Verdier and Miss Mary E. A. Dandridge.

Issue of November 15, 1867

October 22, 1867 by Rev. E. G. Gage, Mr. Thos. A. White of Tenn., to Miss F. J. Dale of Marion, N. C.

October 29th, by the same, Mr. W. B. Mitchell, of Rutherfordton, N. C., to Miss Sallie J. Neal, of Marion, N. C.

November 5th, by the same, Mr. D. J. A. Greenlee of McDowell county, N. C., to Miss Mary R. Burgin, of Marion, N. C.

On November 6th, by Rev. Arminius Wright, Mr. Pulaski F. Campbell to Miss Sallie W. Eve, daughter of Dr. Jos. A. Eve, all of Augusta, Ga.

On the 17th Oct., at the residence of the bride's father, Col. Hammond, By the Rev. W. L. Curry, Mr. H. D. Watts to Miss Mollie J. Hammond, all of Baker co,. Ga.

By the Rev. J. H. D. McRae, on the 5th of Nov., 1867, Mr. Charles M. Henry to Miss Susan H. Hunter, all of Columbia county, Fla.

On the 22nd Oct., 1867, in Sumter co., Ga., by Rev. B. F. Breedlove, Mr. G. W. Sinius, of Americus to Miss Odie Rylander, daughter of M. E. Rylander.

By the same on Oct. 22nd, Mr. R. R. Arrington to Miss E. Williams, both of Sumter co., Ga.

By the same, Oct. 24th 1867, Mr. John Ed. Thomas to Miss Marietta M. West, of Sumter co., Ga.

In Wadesboro, N. C., on the 29th of October by Rev. F. Milton Kennedy, Mr. John W. Richardson to Miss Lottie C. Leak, all of Anson co., N. C.

On the 31st of July by Rev. F. Auld, Mr. Washington Sharp, of Abbeville, to Miss Mary J. Eppes, of Laurens, S. C.

In Fulton county, Ga., on the 17th October, by Rev. W. L. Wardlaw, Mr. A. C. Sewell to Miss N. M. Baker, daughter of Mr. Julius Baker, all of Fulton co., Ga.

In Fort Valley, Ga., on the 29th of Oct., by Rev. E. H. McGehee, Mr. Jas. R. Turrentine to Miss Nannie Bazemore.

In the M. E. Church at Americus, Ga., on the 23d of Oct., by Rev. S. Anthony, Mr. A. D. Gatewood to Miss H. W. Furlow, second daughter of Hon. T. M. and Mrs. M. Furlow, all of Americus.

On 6th November, by Rev. R. W. Milner, Mr. Jose T. Quillian of Cobb co, Ga., to Miss Margaret E. Smith, of Cherokee co., Ga.

Issue of November 22, 1867

On the 7th inst., Athens, Ga., by Rev. H. H. Parks, Mr. S. M. Herrington, of Scriven co,. Ga., and Miss Mattie F., daughter of Col. Jno. I. Huggins of Athens Ga.

By the same, 7th inst., Mr. J. W. Eberhart and Miss M. E. Dottrey, both of Athens, GA.,

By Rev. W. M. D. Bond, on 10th Oct., J. L. Murray of Houston co., Ga., to Miss M. A. E. Slone, of Sumter co,. Ga.

On 21st Oct., by the same, Mr. Wm. F. Marsh to Mrs. Mary A. Cobb, all of Sumter co,. Ga.

In Walker co., Ga., Oct. 23, by Rev. W. T. Hamilton, Rev. John McDonald and Miss Margaret A. Alexander.

In Walker co., Ga., Nov. 13, by the same, Rev. T. P. Harris and Mrs. Jane Lenar.d

Near Lafayette, Ga., Nov. 14, by the same, W. A. Farris and Julia A. Gober.

On 10th November 1867, by Rev. J. A. Wood of the S. C. Conference, Mr. James Tinsley to Miss Elizabeth West, all of Spartanburg District, S. C.

In Athens, Ga., on the 12th inst., by Rev. Jos. S. Key, Dr. H. E. Carlton and Miss Helen C. Newton.

Issue of November 29, 1867

On the 10th Nov., by Rev. Wm. W. Mood, Mr. W. H. Kennedy, of Manning, So. Ca., and Miss Julia, daughter of Capt. John E. Scott, of Williamsburg district, S. C.

On the 19th Nov., by Rev. Wm. W. Mood, Dr. Robert Y. McLeod of Kershaw district, So. Ca., and Miss Almira W., daughter of Wm. Rogers, Esq., of Bishopville, So. Ca.

Nov. 12th by Rev. A. J. Dean, Mr. W. P. Bridges of Harris co., Ga., to Miss Lucy E. Fort of Talbot co., Ga.

On 17th Nov., by Rev. Jno. R. Parker, Mr. E. J. McConnell and Miss Sallie J. Houston of Hickory Flat, Ga.

On the 15th October by the Rev. W. A. Gamewell, at the residence of Col. J. L. McDowell in Rutherford co., No. Ca., Dr. J. Harvey Gilkey of Marion, No. Ca. and Mrs. Adella J. McJunkin of Union, So. Ca.

By Rev. W. S. Baker, October 24, 1867, Capt. A. A. Beall to Miss Mattie J. Hughes, all of Irwinton, Ga.

By the same, October 31st at the residence of Mr. James Pierce, Esq., Mr. Jethro D. Vanlandingham to Miss Cyntha Pierce, all of Wilkinson county.

By Rev. W. Knox, at the residence of the bride, Nov. 29th 1867, Mr. Lemuel Sheppard of Scriven co., and Mrs. Amanda A. Tyson of Effingham county.

In Sumter co., Ga., Nov. 29, 1867, by Rev. B. F. Breedlove, John S. Lee, Jr., of Houston co., and Miss Henrietta P. Gass.

On 20th Nov., by Rev. W. J. Wardlaw, Mr. D. W. Connally to Miss M. A. Witcher.

By the same, Nov. 29th, Mr. J. W. Christian to Miss A. P. Connally.

Also at the same time, Mr. J. B. Wardlaw to Miss Susan J. Connally, all of Fulton co., Ga.

Issue of December 6, 1867

By the Rev. J. H. D. McRae, on the 24th Nov., Mr. Henry C. Marcum to Miss Rebecca F. Hutchinson, all of Columbia co., Fla.

By the same on the 29th Nov., Mr. Wesley Gainey to Miss Sarah Taylor, all of Columbia co., Fla.

In All Saints Parish, S. C., by the Rev. J. H. Tart, Mr. B. B. Cox to Miss Catharine Branton.

On the evening of the 21st Nov. 1867, at the residence of the bride's father, by Rev. W. T. Caldwell, D. Albert Meaders of Hall co., to Mattie W. Pitchford, of White co., Ga.

Issue of December 13, 1867

Nov. 11th, by Rev. J. M. Stokes, Benj. F. Scott, jun., of Sylvania, and Miss Laura V. Nunnaly, of Bascom, Ga.

Nov. 20th by the same, Mr. Wm. M. Bryan and Miss Anna E. Jarrell, all of Scriven co., Ga.

In Talbotton, Ga., Nov. 28, 1867, by Rev. R. W. Dixon, Dr. Seaborn K. Oneal of Talbotton, Ga., and Miss Eleanor T. Worrell, daughter of Hon. E. H. Worrell of Talbotton, Ga.

By the Rev. Thos. B. Lanier, at the Bride's sister, Mr. J. A. Lamberts to Miss Francis Skinner, Oct. 24, 1867

By the same, Oct. 24, Mt. Littleton Joiner to Miss Jane Barefield.

By the same, Nov. 15, at the bride's mother in Habersham, Mr. John T. Reeves to Miss Florence M. Chance.

By the same, Nov. 28, at the bride's grandfather, Mr. J. Bell's, Mr. R. C. Wimberly to Miss Georgia Bell, all of Burke co., Ga.

In Whitfield co,. Ga., near Dalton, Nov. 21, by Rev. J. M. Richardson, Mr. William C. Quillian and Miss Sarah J. Tye.

In Monroe co., by Rev. Wesley F. Smith, Nov. 14, Mr. Francis Grove and Miss Mary Stroud.

By the same in Barnesville, Nov. 28, Mr. J. A. Stafford and Miss Ellen Reeves.

By the same, in Upson co., Dec. 3d, Mr. James Marchman of Troup co., Ga., and Miss Civility Stephens, of the former place.

Issue of December 20, 1867

In Henry co., Ga., by the Rev. G. W. Embry, on the 4th of Dec., Mr. G. W. Parks of DeKalb co., to Miss M. F. Albert.

In Jonesboro, Ga., by the same on 20th Dec., Mr. William A. Wilson and Miss Mollie J. Key

In Clayton co., by the same on the 23th Dec., Mr. B. Deen and Miss Lucy J. Christian

In Clayton co., by the same, Dec. 12th, by the Rev. D. Nolan, Mr. Wm. M. Campbell and Miss Janie T. Dixon.

Nov. 11th, by the Rev. W. R. Branham, at the residence of the bride's father, Judge John Berry of Hancock co., Ga., to Indiana V., eldest daughter of J. J. Griffin, Esq.

On the 21st Nov., in Cuthbert, Ga., by Rev. J. O. A. Cook, Robert D. Chapman and Miss Eugenia A. McNeil.

On 12th Dec., by Rev. J. V. M. Morris, Mr. W. H. H. Barnes of Baldwin co., to Miss Norie Denham of Putnam co., Ga.

By Rev. A. J. Dean, Dec. 3rd, Mr. R. E. Fort of Talbot co., Ga., to Miss M. E. Bridges of Harris co., Ga.

Issue of January 3, 1868

Nov. 5th by Rev. T. S. L. Harwell, Mr. James Ould to Miss Sarah J. Hardy, all of Troup co., Ga.

By the same, Nov. 24, Mr. W. J. Malone to Miss Anna Oslin, all of Troup co., Ga.

On the 27th Nov., near Auburn, Ala., by Rev. L. F. Dowdell, Mr. Luther M. Dowdell to Miss Maggie Hugueley, all of Lee co., Ala.

On Nov. 21st, by Rev. J. B. McGehee, Mr. W. Capers Freeman of Merriwether co., and Mrs. Mary E. Potts, of Troup co., Ga.

By Rev. J. R. Little, Nov. 28th 1867, Mr. S. M. Nabers of Laurens, S. C., to Miss Annie C., daughter of the late Rev. W. A. McSwain of the S. C. Conference.

Issue of January 10, 1868

By Rev. T. S. L. Harwell, Dec. 15, Mr. Crawford Moon to Miss Emily Reynolds, all of Troup co., Ga.

By Rev. J. H. Grogan, Nov. 26, Isaac R. Hall to Miss Mary E. Dillard, all of Oglethorpe co., Ga.

By the same, Dec. 19, John T. Hurt to Miss Hallie L. Smith, all of Oglethorpe co., Ga.

By the same, Dec. 27th, L. M. Dadisman to Miss Susan Snellings, all of Elbert co., Ga.

On the morning of the 26th Dec. at the residence of the bride's father, by the Rev. Dr. R. W. Lovett, Mr. Wm. R. Lovett and Miss Mary E. Oliver, all of Scriven co., Ga.

Nov. 20, by Rev. D. J. Myrick, Robt T. Johnson and Miss S. Virginia Hutcheson, all of Oglethorpe co., Ga.

By the same Dec. 12., Benj. O. Bigby and Miss Alemeta A. Stevens, both of Lexington, Ga.

By the same, Dec. 25, Edward L. West of Hancock co., to Miss Utensa A. Winter of Clarke co., Ga.

On Tuesday evening, Dec. 17, by Rev. J. Lee Dixon, Mr. Cantey Richbourg of Clarendon to Miss Isadora, daughter of G. Wesley Smith, Esq., of Richland District, S. C.

At Thomasville, Ala., Dec. 12, by Rev. J. W. Shores, Mr. Jas. R. Harden to Miss Mollie S. Braddy.

In Talbotton, Ga., Dec. 18, by the Rev. G. H. Pattillo, Mr. Daniel Jenkins of Charleston, S. C., and Miss Annie E. Rush, daughter of Rev. L. Rush of No. Ga. Conference. Charleston papers please copy.

Dec. 23, at Mrs. Yates, by Rev. E. G. Gage, Mr. D. L. Stuart of Lincolnton, N. C., to Miss Eliza L. Gibson of Columbia, S. C.

In Methodist Church, Enon, Ala., on Dec. 19, by Rev. Dr. Ellison, Mr. Wesley A. Oliver to Miss Minnie E. Jefferson, both of Enon.

On 20th Nov. in Columbia co., Ga., by Rev. R. A. Conner, Dr. J. A. Dozier to Miss Lizzie Dozier.

By the Rev. Geo. C. Clarke, at his own house, near Fort Valley on the 23d of Dec., Mr. Isaac Vinson and Mrs. Sarah A. McDonald, all of Houston co., Ga.

In Irwinton, Ga., by Rev. W. F. Robison, on 18th Dec., Mr. M. J. Guyton of Laurens co. and Miss Cornelia Fisher, of the former place.

In Dahlonega, Ga., Dec. 22, by Rev. G. Hughes, Capt. Amzi Rudolph of Dahlonega, Ga., and Miss Fannie, daughter of Col. Wier Boyd of Dahlonega, Ga.

On the 18th Dec., at the residence of A. T. Barco, Leon co., Fla., by Rev. T. K. Leonard, M. D., Mr. Daniel T. Forrest to Miss Susan F. Hutto

On the 16th inst., by Rev. H. H. Parks, James I. McRee and Miss S. A. Hinton, both of Athens, Ga.

By the same 17th inst., Mr. C. D. Camp of Campbell co., Ga., and Miss Annie C. Whorton, of Athens, Ga.

In Horry District, S. C., on 22d Dec by Rev. G. H. Wells, Mr. B. H. Pinner to Miss Hannah M. Dusenbery.

By Rev. Thos. B. Lanier on 18th Dec., at Mrs. A. Herringtons, the bride's sister, Mr. Geo. W. Reeves to Miss Kittie Prescott.

By the same on 19th Dec., Mr. Crawford T. Herrington to Miss Annie A. Reeves, all of Burke co., Ga.

Dec 10th by Rev. S. H. J. Sistrunk, Dr. C. McStewart of Jones co., Ga., and Miss Laura Bryan, of Houston co.

By the same on the 17th inst., Mr. Frank Henderson of Henderson, to Miss Hattie Bacon of Haynesville, Houston co.

On 5th Dec., by Rev. J. R. Gaines, Mr. John B. Mathis of Forsyth co., Ga., to Miss Marietta A. A. Mays, of Cobb co., Ga.

By the same on 26th Dec., Mr. S. C. Brown of Forsyth co., Ga., to Miss Sallie E. Teasley of Alpharetta, Ga.

By Rev. J. H. D. McRae, Mr. Geo. Brunson to Miss P. A. Goodman.

By the same, James T. Chastain to Miss N. E. C. Miller, all of Columbia co., Fla.

On Dec. 17, by Rev. W. Shapard, Augustus H. Allston and Annie M. Ott, both of Eufaula, Ala.

Dec. 31, by the same, Rev. Frank E. Manson and Mattie Baker, both of Eufaula, Ala.

By Rev. John Calvin Johnson on 10th Dec., Mr. Francis P. Griffith to Miss Celestia A. Thrasher, all of Clarke co., Ga.

By same on 12th Dec., Mr. Andrew J. Royston to Miss Lucy A. Thompson, all of Clarke co., Ga.

By same on 12th Dec., Mr. Mark E. Stovall of Greene co., Ga., to Miss Eva E. Marable of Clarke co., Ga.

By same on 17th Dec., Thomas W. Davenport of Clarke co., Ga. to Miss Sallie A. Atkinson of Morgan co., Ga.

By same on Dec. 19th, John F. W. Osborn to Miss Eugenia Elder, all of Clarke co. Ga.

Issue of January 17, 1868

By Rev. R. J. Johnson the 25th of Dec., in Calhoun, Ga., Capt. W. L. Williams to Miss e. M. Martin, all of Calhoun, Ga.
By the same, on 4th January 1868, Mr. H. B. Herrington of Terrel co., Ga. To Miss C. C. Dobbins, of Gordon co., Ga., Parson's fee O. K.

On the 24th Dec., 1867, by Rev. J. Lewis, Jr., Mr. LaFayette Powell to Miss Camilla W. Simmons.

By Rev. O. L. Smith, Jan. 7th 1868, Mr. E. S. Remington of New York City, to Mrs. Jane L. Livingston, Of Quitman, Ga.

By Rev. C. A. Crowell, Dec. 31, Mr. Larken Johnson to Miss Emma Murray, daughter of Moses Murray, all of Calhoun co., Ga.

On Nov. 27th, by Rev. Paul C. Morton, near Gainesville, Capt. W. S. Erwin, of Clarksville, to Miss Ruth S. Clark, of Hall co., Ga.

By the same, on the 1st ult., Mr. W. Henderson to Miss Julia F. Biggers, both of Habersham co., Ga.

By Rev. J. W. Jackson, on 1st January, Mr. W. J. Boon, of Georgia, to Miss Sallie J. Perry, of Columbia co, East Fla.

By the same on 7th January, Mr. W. Y. Hunter to Miss Mary E. E. Roberts, all of Columbia co., East Florida.

January 5th 1868, in Bainbridge, Ga., by Rev. A. J. Dean, Mr. Frank McIntyre to Miss Mary Willis.

By Rev. John E. Sentell, on 18th Dec., 1867, Chas. G. Johnson to Mrs. S. J. Brantley, all of Liberty co., Ga.

By the same, on 2d January 1868, Mr. S. D. Bradwell of Liberty co., To Miss Lizzie L. Clifton, oldest daughter of Col. Wm. Clifton of Tatnall co., Ga.

Issue of January 24, 1868

At Enon, Ala., Dec. 17, 1867, by Rev. W. H. Ellison, Mr. B. R. Barkesdale to Miss E. C. Crawford.

At Enon, Ala., Dec. 18, 1867, by Rev. W. H. Ellison, Mr. W. A. Oliver to Miss M. E. Jefferson.

On Jan. 5th 1868, in Union Springs, Ala., by Rev. W. M. Motley, Mr. J. S. Leak to Miss H. A. McRae. Madison Examiner please copy.

On 28th of Nov. 1867, by the Rev. S. D. Clements, Mr. Wm. T. Holmes, Jr. of Talbot Valley, to Miss Jennie H. Evans, of Pleasant Hill, Ga.

In Darlington, S. C., on the evening of Jan. 8th, by Rev. A. J. Stafford, M. J. G. McCall to Miss L. J. Dargan.

By the Rev. F. Milton Kennedy in the Methodist Church at Wadesboro, N. C., Dec. 30th 1867, Mr. J. M. Little of Wadesboro, N. C., to Miss M. C. Steele of Thomas co., Ga.

On Jan. 9th 1868, by Rev. Jas. M. Wright, Capt. J. M. McNeely to Miss Eugenia Tison, both of Glennville, Ala.

Issue of January 31, 1868

On the 31st Dec. 1867, by Rev. P. M. Ryburn, Mr. Wm. A. Gilbert of Athens, Ga., to Mrs. Carrie Pearson of Troup co., Ga.

By the Rev. S. D. Clements, January 14, Mr. H. M. Bryan, of Bellvue, to Miss Alice O'Neal, of Geneva, Ga.

January 1, 1868, by Rev. J. E. Watson, Mr. D. P. Bushart to Miss Mary E. S. Meadors, all of Newberry Dist.

On 16th January by Rev. W. A. Rogers, Lieut. David W. Patterson of Griffin, Ga., to Miss Henrietta Stilwell of Spaulding co., Ga.

In Augusta, Ga., January 15, by Rev. G. H. Pattillo, Mr. Josiah Miller and Miss R. H. Hays.

By Rev. W. P. Pledger, January 3, 1868, Mr. Wm. M. Johnson to Miss Mary S. Ward, all of Forsyth, Ga.

By Rev. Thos. B. Lanier at the bride's grand fathers, I. Jinkins, Mr. John T. Roberson to Miss Emily Scott, Jan. 2, 1868.

By same, Jan. 23, Mr. Willoby Chance to Miss Dio Davis, all of Burke co., Ga.

On the 9th inst., by Rev. H. H. Parks, W. P. Loving and Miss Nancy Ann Williams, both of Athens, Ga.

By the same 17th inst., Mr. Edmund B. Adams, Walton co., Ga., and Mrs. Julia A. Walker, Athens, Ga.

On 15th Jan. 1868 in Allsaints Parish, S. C., by Rev. James H. Tart, Mr. L. D. Bryan of Horry District to Mrs. E. Blume, daughter of Capt. Thomas Randall.

Nov 7th 1867 by Rev. J. _. Penny, Mr. Andrew Byrd to Miss Sarah Westbury, both of Colleton district, S. C.

By the same, Nov. 21, 1867, Mr. Daniel Byrd to Miss Julia M. Westbury, both of Colleton district, S. C.

Nov 19, 1867, by the same, Mr. Stephen W. Ackerman to Miss Mary C. Johnston, both of Colleton district, S. C.

Nov 2-, 1867, by the same, Mr. A. W. Patrick to Miss Cinthia Proctor, both of Colleton district, S. C.

Issue of February 7, 1868

On the 23d January by Rev. J. T. Ainsworth, Rev. Charles G. Johnson to Miss Martha D. Gibbs, all of Twiggs co., Ga.

On the 18th January, at the residence of Mr. Robert Morris, Georgetown, Quitman Co., Ga., by Rev. J. O. A. Cook, Mr. Isaac T. Hill and Miss Eugenia T. Morris.

In St. James' Church, Augusta, Ga., Jan. 29, by Rev. G. H. Pattillo, Mr. William J. Freeman and Miss Mildred A. Taliaferro.

On 19th Jan. at Graham's T. O., S. C., by Rev. D. J. Simmons, Dr. Sam'l H. Tindal to Miss Sallie Redford, both of Barnwell District, S. C.

On the 24th December 1867 at the residence of the bride by the Rev. J. L. Brockman, Mr. John W. Brandon of Cherokee co., Ala., to Miss Anna C. Fullwood of Polk co., Ga.

On the 23d January by Rev. R. S. L. Harwell, Mr. Robt. A. Hardy to Miss Martha Truman, all of Troup co., Ga.

On Jan. 16th by Rev. W. J. Wardlaw, Mr. Wm. Connally and Miss Molly Silvey.

Also by the same, on 23d Jan., Mr. Wm. R. Hooper and Miss Lou S. Green, all of Fulton co., Ga.

On the 30th Jan. by Rev. W. P. Smith, Mr. J. W. Hightower of Barnesville and Miss Mattie Blalock of Upson co., Ga.

Issue of February 14, 1868

On 23d January, by the Rev. J. M. Richardson, Mr. G. W. Hair to Miss E. L. Cady, all of Whitefield Co., Ga.

By the same, on January 26th in Murray co., Ga., Mr. C. G. Hollman to Miss M. A. Loller.

By the same, Jan. 30th, Mr. S. W. Mote to Miss Sarah A. Simmons.

By W. P. Pledger, Jan. 30th 1868, Mr. C. P. Toney, to Miss Alice A. Stone, all of Forsyth, Ga.

In Hamilton, Ga., Jan. 28th 1868, by Rev. W. A. Parks, S. J. Webster to Miss M.D. Walker.

On 23d January in Edgefield District, S. C., by the Rev. D. Derrick, J. W. Lagrone to Miss A. P. Smith, daughter of Mrs. Charlotte Smith.

By Rev. G. L. W. Anthony, on 26th January 1868, at the residence of Rev. James Griffith, of Butler, Ga., Mr. W. F. Baggett to Miss Rebecca Griffith, all of Taylor co., Ga.

In Troup co., Ga., January 30th 1868, by Rev. J. W. McGehee, Mr. R. H. Jackson to Miss Bunnie E. Norwood.

By the Rev. J. R. Little, February 5th 1868, Mr. R. Fulton Howard of Providence, to Miss Amanda, eldest daughter of T. D. Winchester, Esq., Monroe, N. C.

Issue of February 21, 1868

By Rev. R. H. Howren on the 29th Dec 1867, Mr. S. J. Barineau to Miss Lizzie E. Howren, daughter of the Rev. R. H. Howren of the So. Ga. Conference, all of Decatur co., Ga.

On 20th Nov 1867, by Rev. A. N. Wells, the Rev. R. R. Dagnall of the S. C. Conference, to Miss Mary E. Hellams, of Laurens District, S. C.

On 9th Jan. 1868 by Rev. R. R. Dagnall, Mr. Harvey Curry to Miss Ann Hellams of Laurens District, S. C.

In Monroe co., Feb. 6th 1868, by Rev. Wesley F. Smith, Mr. J. W. Lester and Miss Avis M. Clements, all of Monroe co.

In Crawford co., Ga., on the 9th inst., at the residence of the bride's brother, Dr. W. L. Jones, by the Rev. I. L. Avant, Mr. A. R. Opry of Houston co., Ga., to Miss Ella Jones of the former place.

In Macon on the 5th inst., by Rev. J. S. Key, Dr. M. G. Crumley of Atlanta to Miss A. J. Tindal of Macon.

In the Methodist Church in Buena Vista, Ga., Feb. 67 by Rev. G. T. Embry, Mr. D. C. N. Burkhalter and Miss Berta Brown.

By Rev. J. R. Little, Feb. 12th 1868, Mr. R. V. Houston to Miss Celestia A., youngest daughter of Maj. D. A. Covington, all of Monroe, N. C.

By the Rev. G. W. Persons on 13th inst., at the residence of Mrs. George Lowman, Crawford co., Mr. J. W. Collier to Miss M. C. Lowman.

By the same and at the same time and place, Mr. T. B. Simpson to Miss M. A. Martin.

In Talbot co., Jan. 29th 1868 by Rev. R. B. Lester, Mr. R. J. Walton and Miss H. M. Willis.

In Putnam co., Ga., Dec. 16th by Rev. D. Kelsey, Mr. W. H. Pelote to Miss M. C. Vincent.

Dec. 12 by the same at Monticello, Mr. J. Morgan of Clinton to Miss M. A. Penn of the former place.

In Upson co., Jan. 15th by the same, Mr. J. A. Colquitt to Miss S. A. Black.

On 24th Dec., by Rev. J. H. Grogan, G. T. Snellings to Miss S. E. Kinckesw[?], all of Elbert co., Ga.

On 8th Jan. by same, B. W. Tillman of Fla., to Miss S. A. Starke of Elbert co., Ga.

Issue of February 28, 1868

On Feb. 9, by Rev. R. F. Evans, Mr. Jas Ward to Miss Amanda Massey, both of Thomas co., Ga.

By Rev. J. P. Duncan at Oglethorpe, Ga., Mr. Wm. Pelham to Miss Talulah Hansel, daughter of the late Major Hansel.

At the residence of Rufus W. Smith in Greene co., Ga., on 2nd Feb., by Rev. O. A. Mitchell, Mr. John H. Jernigan and Miss Siberia D. Mane.

At the residence of the bride's mother, Tuesday evening, Feb. 18, by Rev. A. J. Stafford, Mr. Andrew Woods to Miss Martha S. Gibson, both of Darlington, S. C.

Nov. 28th 1867 by Rev. J. H. C. McKinney, Wm. F. Hardy to Miss Joanna Oliver, both of Horry district, S. C.

Jan 9th by same, B. B. McCracken to Miss Julia E. Beaty, both of Horry district, S. C.

Jan 23d, by the same, Mr. Asa Causey to Miss Ann E. Beaty, both of Horry district, S. C.

Issue of March 6, 1868

On Feb. 25th 1868, by Rev. W. A. Parks, in Harris co., Ga., at the residence of Mr. Charles Smith, Mr. Reuben Mobley to Miss Kittie E. Simpson.

By Rev. T. S. L. Harwell, Feb. 18, 1868, Mr. S. A. Smith of Sumter co., Ga., to Miss M. J. Moore, of LaGrange, Ga.

on the 12th Feb., 1868, at the bride's father, Col. Campbell, by Rev. E. S. Tyner, Mr. J. M. Dell to Miss A. E. Campbell, all of Alachua co., East Florida.

By Rev. W. H. Stanton, on the 20th Feb., at the residence of the bride's mother, Dr. W. A. Reynolds to Miss Frances E., daughter of Mrs. Gresham, all of Warrior Stand, Ala.

On 13th of Feb. 1868 by Rev. J. A. Wood of S. C. Conference, Mr. Wm. M. Reed to Miss Mattie Splawn, all of Polk co., N. C.

On Feb. 5th 1868, by Rev. H. D. Moore, Green E. Hood to Miss Cynthia A. Barton, all of Albany, Ga.

By the same, Feb. 20th, Thos. B. Barton to Miss Agness Smith, all of Albany.

Issue of March 13, 1868

On the 27th ult., by Rev. Chas. A. Fulwood, Mr. Roderick Leonard and Miss Mattie J. Matthews, all of Talbot co., Ga.

On the 18th ult., by same, Mr. Geo. W. Edwards, and Miss Sallie Millican, all of Talbot co., Ga.

In Covington, Ga., on Feb. 25th, by Rev. H. J. Adams, Oscar Thomason, Esq., of Madison, Ga., to Miss Florence Usher.

By Rev. W. H. Potter, in Brothersville, Ga., on the 27th ult,. C. E. Clarke to Miss Martha B. Allen.

Also, by the same, Mr. Geo. W. Hughes to Miss M. Eugenia Clarke.

Issue of March 20, 1868

On Feb. 6, 1868, by Rev. R. J. Corley, Mr. John H. Flowers to Miss Josephine Arnow, both of St. Marys, Ga.

On the 10th inst., by rev. P. H. Brewster, Martin Graham, Esq., of Forsyth co., to Miss M. E. Mauldin, of Cherokee co., GA.

On Feb. 24th, by Rev. W. H. Fleming, Mr. A. Oline Watson, of Cokesbury, to Miss S. Addie, daughter of the late Rev. J. G. Humbert, of Laurens District, S. C.

In Bainbridge, Ga., Feb. 25th, 1868, by Rev. A. J. Dean, Mr. James E. Crawford to Miss Mattie A. Dickinson.

By the same, March 3d, near Bainbridge, Ga., Mr. John E. Dickinson, to Miss Eliza A. Crawford.

By the same, March 10th, Mr. L. F. Lester to M. K. Dickinson, all of Bainbridge Ga.

On the 13th ult., by Rev. J. W. Rush, Dr. Thomas B. Maddux to Miss Jennie Lela Watts, both of Perry county, Ala.

Issue of March 27, 1868

By Rev. J. P. Duncan, 11th inst., in Baker co., Mr. John Nolan, West Point, to Miss Mattie Elliott.

On Feb. 4th, 1868, in LaGrange, Ga., by the same, Mr. Robt. O. Douglass and Miss Jennie Kimbro.

By Rev. J. J. Workman, Jan. 19th 1868, at Enoree Factory, Greenville Dist., S. C., Mr. Walker Graham and Miss Rachal Spivy.

By the same, March 1st, at Batesville, S. C., Mr. Isra Brown and Miss Frances Dyer.

Issue of April 3, 1868

On Feb. 6th, 1868, by Rev. W. W. Stewart, Mr. Coley Bryan of Dooly co., to Miss Cordilia Manning of Houston co., Ga.

On Feb. 18th, by Rev. W. W. Stewart, Mr. J. W. Oglevie to Miss E. Barton, all of Houston co., Ga.

On Feb. 27th, by Rev. W. W. Stewart, Mr. J. F. Hodges to Miss Olivia Davis, all of Houston co., Ga.

On 1st March, 1868, by Rev. David L. Slaton, Mr. M. A. Sandford to Miss Carrie D. Thomas, all of Tallapoosa co., Ala.

On March 18th, 1868, by Rev. J. H. C. McKinney, Mr. Jasper Guiton to Miss F. C. Beaty, both of Horry District, S. C.

On March 19th, 1868, by Rev. J. H. C. McKinney, Mr. A. S. Anderson to Miss Melvina Cartwright, both of Horry District, S. C.

On Sunday morning, March 22, 1868, by the Rev. J. J. Morgan, Mr. J. T. Tapper and Miss Jane P. Bowen, all of Washington, Ga.

On the 24th of Feb., by Rev. A. N. Wells, Mr. W. H. Clifton to Miss Laura Eudora, daughter of Mrs. Martha Ferguson, all of Union District, S. C.

On 26th March, in the M. E. Church in Canton, Ga., by Rev. J. R. Gaines, Dr. John M. Turk of Alexandria, Ala., to Miss V. F. Shockley, of Canton, Ga.

By Rev. J. E. Irby, Feb. 20th 1868, Mr. R. Crowder of Anson, to Miss Martha E.,eldest daughter of Dr. James W. Doster, of Union, North Carolina.

On March 3d, by Rev. J. W. Shores, Mr. A. D. Fielder to Miss L. J. Wood, all of Bullock co., Ala.

Issue of April 10, 1868

On the 19th March, Mr. J. S. Crockett and Miss Sue H. Manson, daughter of Rev. F. E. Mason.

By Rev. S. Woodbery, on 12th March 1868, Mr. B. B. Woodbery, to Miss M. E. Jones, daughter of R. F. Jones, Esq., of Quincy, Fla.

Issue of April 17, 1868

In Crawford county, Ga., March 26th, 1868, by Rev. E. H. McGehee, Mr. John Royal to Miss Elizabeth Harris.

In Houston co., Ga., April 8th, 1868, by the same, Mr. J. M. Ward of Burke co., Ga., to Miss Cornelia F. Allen.

By Rev. R. A. Conner, March 11th, Mr. John Bynum to Miss Fannie Reynolds, all of Columbia co., Ga.

On the 8th of April,by Rev. W. F. Robison, L. C. Ryan, Esq., to Miss Elenora Bozeman, both of Hawkinsville. Ga.

By Rev. J. A. Wood, on the 23d of March 1868, Mr. Samuel Reed, to Miss Titha A. Splawn, all of Polk co., N. C.

On March 12th, by Rev. E. A. Lemmond, Mr. Philip Grenning, late of England, to Miss Lizzie Lefler, of Mt. Pleasant, N. C.

In Trinity Church, Savannah, Ga., April 1st, 1868, by Rev. Geo. G. N. MacDonell, Mr. W. J. Marshall to Miss Eliza Knight Godfrey, both of Savannah, Ga.

By Rev. W. Lane, on 5th April, 1868, Mr. W. A. Hall to Miss Permelia Vanlandingham, both of Wilkinson co., Ga.

Issue of April 24, 1868

By Rev. T. B. Russell, in Fort Valley, Ga., April 7, 1868, Mr. W. D. Wells to Miss E. C. McAffee.

By Rev. Shelton R. Weaver, on 19th March, Dr. P. F. M. Greer to Miss Lizzie Blocker, all of Clay co., Ga.

Feb. 18th, by the Rev. W. S. Baker, Mr. W. L. Bray of Cartersville, Ga., and Miss Georgia E. Richardson of Lumpkin, Ga.

On March 19th, by the same, Mr. Lackington C. Randle and Miss Mary E. Bryan, all of Stewart co., Ga.

On March 31st, by the same, Mr. Joseph L. Bond, of Claiborn Parish, La., and Miss Jessie L. Carter, of florence, Ga.

On 3d of March, 1868, at the residence of Mr. A. Pooser, East Fla., by Rev. J. J. Sealy, Mr. R. M. Davis, to Miss S. E. M. Beckwith of Columbia, S. C.

At Chunnenuggee Ridge, Ala., by Rev. Joseph B. Cottrell, Col. M. B. Locke of Union Springs, and Miss Johnnie Beatrice Blackmon, daughter of Homer Blackmon, Esq.

On the following morning at the same place, by the same, Dr. A. H. Herring, of La., and Miss L. L. Randle, of Chunnenuggee.

On 14th April, in Union Springs, Ala., by the same, Rev. Wm. M. Motley, of the Montgomery Conference, and Miss Mary E. Threadgill, daughter of Wm. Threadgill, Esq.

Issue of May 8, 1868

In Palmetto, Ga., on 13th of April, by Rev. T. J. Davies, Rev. James T. Lowe, of the North Georgia Conference, to Miss Emma T. Scarborough, of Palmetto.

On the 22d April, by Rev. Jos. P. Prickett, Rev. Oscar A. Allen of Campbell county, to Mrs. G. V. Howell, of Cobb co., Ga.

By Rev. W. A. Florence, April 23, Mr. Wm. M. Bonds and Miss Nancy B. Harris, both of Gwinnett co., Ga.

On the 23d April, in the Methodist Church at Cuthbert, Ga., by Rev. James O. A. Cook, Mr. L. A. Smith and Miss Mary Lou Russell, all of Cuthbert, Ga.

By Rev. John W. Reynolds, Sunday morning, April 12, Mr. C. J. Bains to Miss S. E. Stripling, of Crawford co., Ga.

By Rev. Lewis Lawshe, Mr. J. P. Hellings, to Miss Nancy E. Bankston, daughter of henry Bankston, Esq., Fulton co., Ga.

At Waynesboro, Ga., April 15th, by Rev. I. S. Hopkins, Mr. H. H. Perry and Miss Charlotte E. Carter.

In Columbus, Ga., April 28th, by Rev. Lovick Pierce, D. D., Dr. Wm. A. Mitchell of Glennville, Ala., to Annie T., daughter of Dr. Thos. H. Dawson, of Russell co., Georgia.

Issue of May 15, 1868

By Rev. J. C. Crisp, Wm. O. Thompson and Miss Miria E. Peninger, both of Union co., N. C.

On the same day by the same, Rev. Wm. C. Owen of the Baptist Church, Lancaster District, S. C., and Miss Lucinda Mullis, of Union co., N. C., being the fifth marriage of the said Rev. Mr. Owen.

At Fort Gaines, Ga., April 28th, R. H. Moomaugh of Louisville, Ky., to Miss E. F. Farrior of Fort Gaines.

By Rev. W. S. Black, April 23, Mr. R. Wicker to Miss Mattie Pope, both of Newberry, S. C.

On 2d May by Rev. J. W. McRoy, Mr. F. A. Bruce and Miss M. W. Coburn, daughter of Rev. J. R. Coburn, of the S. C. Conf.

By Rev. J. A. Wood, on the 22d of April 1868, Mr. J. A. Duncan to Miss M. M. Green, all of Polk co., N. C.

On April 16, by Rev. R. A. Conner, Mr. A. Lazenby to Miss M. Fuller, daughter of Mr. F. Fuller, all of Columbia co., Ga.

In Columbus, Ga., April 26th, by Rev. Lovick Pierce, D. D., Dr. Wm. A. Mitchell of Glennville, Ala., to Annie T., daughter of Dr. Thomas H. Dawson, of Russell co., Ala.

On the morning of the 2d inst., by Rev. J. T. Lowe, Mr. J. R. Smith of Palmetto, to Miss L. Arnold of Coweta co.

Issue of May 22, 1868

On the 26th April, by Rev. J. W. Shores, Mr. John A. Stewart to Miss Annie E. Johnson, both of Pike co,. Ala.

On the 10th May, in the Methodist Church, Marion N. C., by Rev. J. R. Griffith, Mr. R. W. Brown, of McDowell co., and Miss Adelia Bobbitt, of Warren co., N. C.

On the 10th May, in the Methodist Church, Marion N. C., by Rev. J. R. Griffith, Mr. Alfred Raoul, of Ala., to Miss Ella J. Neal, of Marion, N. C.

In Ocala, Marion co., Fla., on 19th March, by the Rev. J. Rast, Miss Josephene Clonts, daughter of the Rev. M. A. Clonts, of the Florida Conference, to Mr. Milledge V. Bouknight, of Alachua co.

March 17, 1868, by Rev. W. A. Gamewell, Mr. Donald Fleming, formerly of Columbia, S. C., and Miss Anna E. Bobo, second daughter of Simpson Bobo, Esq., of Spartanburg, S. C.

Issue of May 29, 1868

By Rev. W. S. Baker, May 13, Mr. H. H. Mansfield of Miss E. E. Beall, all of Lumpkin co., Ga.

In Macon, on the 26th inst., by Rev. J. W. Burke, Mr. Robert L. Henly to Miss Mary R. Elfe, all of this city.

By Rev. W. W. Oslin, May 20th, Mr. P. H. Ferguson of Winchester, Tenn., and Miss Mary E. Weems of Monticello, Ga.

On May 20th, near Columbus, Ga., by Rev. A. M. Wynn, Louis F. Garrard to Miss Anna F. Leonard, daughter of the late Van Leonard.

On May 6th by Rev. J. H. Traywick, Mr. F. P. Wells of Edgefield District, S. C., to Miss Fannie Marvin of Lincoln co., Ga.

On May 10th, by Rev. J. B. Traywick, Mr. Albert Blum, late of Switzerland, to Mrs. Sarah Weeks of Abbeville Dist., S. C.

Issue of June 5, 1868

By Rev. D. L. Branning, May 13, Mr. S. J. Vance of Putnam co., Ga., to Miss Harriet C. Hall of Marion co., Fla.

On May 18, by Rev. W. P. Jones, Rev. G. W. Stephens of Madison co., Fla., to Mrs. Sarah Horrid of Jefferson co., Fla.

By Rev. R. B. Crawford, on 29th April 1868, near Glennville, Ala., Mr. J. H. Mitchell of Russell co., to Miss Anna E. Humber of Fort Valley, Ga.

By Rev. H. T. Bussy, April 21, Mr. Wm. O. McRae of Irwin co., Ga. to Miss Sarah J. McKinnon, daughter of Laughlin and Mary McKinnon of Telfair co., Ga.

Issue of June 12, 1868

By Rev. D. J. Branning, on 23d May, Mr. M. L. Bartley to Miss S. J. Barrington, both of Putnam co, Fla.

Issue of June 19, 1868

On June 3, by Rev. W. S. Bowman, Rev. A. R. Danner to Miss Mary H. Green

On June 9, by Rev. H. H. Parks, Athens, Ga., Mr. T. J. Fain and Miss Martha A. Hemphill.

By the same, June 10, Mr. H. P. England of Union co., Ga., and Mrs. E. Henrietta Patrick, Athens, Ga.

In Abbeville Dist., S. C., May 7, 1868, by Rev. W. P. Mouzon, T. O. Hill to Mrs. Dicey Trible.

On the 2nd inst., by Rev. S. H. J. Sistrunk, Mr. T. J. Peddy of Houston co., to Mrs. Elizabeth Barnes, of Dooly co., Ga.

Issue of June 26, 1868

On the 11th June, in M. E. Church at Cave Spring, Ga., by Rev. A. M. Thigpen, Mr. Wesley Connor and Miss Eddie Simmons, daughter of Mrs. Shelton Simmons.

On June 3, by Rev. John W. McRoy, Mr. P. J. Malone and Miss Olivia Ann Stokes, daughter of Capt. Benjamin Stokes of Colleton Dist., S. C.

By Rev. L. T. Mizell on 16th inst., Mr. D. F. McClatchey of Marietta, Ga., to Miss Adie Reynolds, eldest daughter of Dr. A. Reynolds, of Powder Springs, Ga.

At the house of the bride's brother, on 2d April 1868, by Rev. A. B. Stephens, Mr. Hosea Robinson to Miss L. M. B. Cox, daughter of the late Col. R. Cox, all of Greenville, S. C.

In the Methodist Church in Greenville, S. C., on June 11th 1868, by rev. A. B. Stephens, Mr. Peter Ingraham, of S. W. Ga., to Miss Evadna DeCamps of Greenville, S. C.

In Houston co., Ga., on the 17th inst., by Rev. Chas. R. Jewett, Mr. Wm. T. Pearson to Miss Mary E., daughter of Mr. Henry H. Briscoe, all of the above county.

Issue of July 3, 1868

On 9th June, at the house of D. A. Rutledge, by Rev. H. J. Hunter, Mr. Jas. Flowers of Butler co., to Miss emma J. Rutledge, of Crenshaw co., Ala.

On June 18, in Schley co., Ga., at the residence of R. W. Wilkinson, By Rev. R. F. Williamson, Mr. C. C. Muse of Atlanta, to Miss Ella Hill of West Point.

By Rev. W. Knox, on 18th June, at the residence of the bride, in Houston co,. Ga., Mr. J. A. Hafer and Mrs. Elizabeth Riley.

In Barbour co., Ala., June 9, by Rev. Dr. W. H. Ellison, Dr. J. J. Winn to Miss Mary V. Crews.

By the same at Clayton, Ala., June 11, Mr. J. C. McEachern, to Miss Victoria Williams.

On June 18, near Clarksville, Ga., by Rev. F. G. Hughes, J. A. Griggs, to Miss Jane Haddock.

By Rev. R. H. Howren, June 21, in Savannah, Mr. Stephen Boineau to Miss Mary L., Smith, only daughter of the late J. J. Smith.

Issue of July 10, 1868

On 3d of March 1868, By Rev. W. C. Lovejoy, Mr. T. H. Phillips of Macon, Co., Ala., to Miss Fannie Jeter, of Meriwether co., Ga.

By Rev. W. H. Fleming, June 9th, Mr. Jared D. Sullivan of Laurens, S. C., to Miss Rosalie A. Moore, daughter of Mrs. R. A. Moore of Abbeville Dist., S. C.

By the Rev. W. H. Fleming, June 10th, Mr. John S. Brooks, of Abbeville, to Miss Anna A. Gadsden, youngest daughter of F. Gadsden, Esq., of Charleston, S. C.

SOUTHERN CHRISTIAN ADVOCATE MARRIAGE NOTICES 1867-1878

Issue of July 17, 1868

In Anson co., N. C., on 20th ult., by Rev. E. W. Thompson, Maj. J. M. Wall to Miss Helon Billingsley.

By Rev. J. M. Austin on 9th July, Mr. J. E. Weddon to Miss Martha L. Renfroe, all of Sandersville, Ga.

In Culloden, Monroe co., Ga., by Rev. W. F. Smith, June 25th 1868, Mr. Jas. L. Winfield and Miss Joanna L. Woodward, daughter of Col. O. S. Woodward of the former place.

On 2nd inst., near Augusta, Ga., by Rev. R. A. Conner, Mr. Wm. B. Ferrell to Miss Frances A. Lawrence.

Issue of July 24, 1868

By Rev. John E. Sentell on 10th June, 1868, Mr. J. S. Warnell to Miss Mary S. Bradley, both of Liberty co., Ga.

On 12th July at the residence of the bride's father, By Rev. J. C. Crisp, Mr. Eli Conder to Miss Amanda V. Wentz, both of Union co., N. C.

On the 24th June, by Rev. Wm. M. Brearley, Mr. H. K. DuBose of Darlington C. H., to Miss Hennie J., eldest daughter of the late Gen. J. M. Blakeney, of Chesterfield District, S. C.

On 2d of July 1868, by Rev. J. M. Lowrey, Mr. E. R. Thornton of Campbelton, Ga., to Mrs. Nancy J. Baxley of Gwinnett co., Ga.

By Rev. J. M. Lowrey, July 9th 1868, Mr. Elisha W. Strickland, of Forsyth co., Ga., to Miss Mattie A. Bragdon, of Gwinnett co., Ga.

In Houston co., Ga., July 12, 1868, by Rev. J. L. Avant, Mr. William B. Hurdle, to Miss Ceana J., daughter of Isaiah Walton, all of Houston co., Ga.

On the 8th July 1868 by Rev. Wm. C. Power, Mr. Silamon McLean of Robison co., N. C., to Miss M. A. Manning, of Marion District, S. C.

On the 1st of July 1868 by Rev. C. D. Smith, at Mt. Zion Church in Macon co., Ga., Mr. A. J. Dula of Lenoir N. C., and Miss Mary S., daughter of the late Eli McKee, of Macon co., N. C.

On the 12th July, by Rev. W. F. Cook, Mr. D. M. Young, of Marietta, to Miss Harriet Burt, of Cobb co.

Issue of July 31, 1868

At Alexander, Burke co., Ga., July 1st 1868 by Rev. I. S. Hopkins, Mr. J. J. Gresham and Miss Ella U. Lassater.

In Fort Valley, Ga., June 28, by Rev. E. H. McGehee, Mr. B. F. Avera to Miss Missouri Lewis.

In the Methodist church, July 8th, by Rev. W. S. Black, Mr. W. E. Higgins to Miss Malinda Langford, all of Newberry, S. C.

Issue of August 7, 1868

On 23d July 1868 by Rev. G. Hughes, Mr. W. H. Price to Miss Susan O. Merk, both of Dahlonega, Ga.

On the 7th July at Bottsford, Sumter co., Ga., by Rev. B. F. Breedlove, Capt. H. R. Dean, formerly of S. C., to Miss Georgia E. McTyeire of the above place.

In Cuthbert, Ga., July 1, 1868, by Rev. J. M. Bonnell, D. D., J. A. Edwards of houston co., Ga., to Miss Emma J. Miller, of Tampa, Fla.

By Rev. W. Lane, July 19, 1868, Mr. Luther A. Hall to Miss Anna G. Boatright, both of Irwinton, Ga.

July 14, 1868, by Rev. Jno. W. Reynolds, Mr. G. H. Bossill of Crawford co., to Miss Mary E. Horns, of Culloden, Ga.

July 21, 1868 by the same, Mr. A. C. Perkins of Monroe co., to Miss Mary C. Leseuer of Culloden, Ga.

Issue of August 14, 1868

In Hamilton, Ga., August 4, 1868, by Rev. W. A. Parks, Mr. J. H. Cowart to Miss Salatha A. Kimbrough.

By Rev. F. A. Branch, at the Methodist Church in Jacksonville, Fla,. on the 5th of Aug., Dr. Wm. M. Bostwick to Miss Eliza S. Jones, all of Jacksonville.

On 23d July, at the residence of J. H. Freeman, by Rev. W., F. Roberts, Mr. I. L. Davis to Miss Meriam Freeman, all of Wilkinson co., Ga.

At Richmond Factory, Richmond co,. Ga., on July 20, by Rev. W. Ewing Johnston, Mr. Geo. Saunders to Miss Mary Burch.

Issue of August 21, 1868

July 17, 1868, by Rev. W. A. Dodge, Mr. J. J. Akers of Miss, to Miss M. A. McDaniel of Gwinnett co., Ga.

July 30, 1868, by Rev. John R. Parker, Mr. Thomas Goudelock of Hall Co., to Miss Kate Garvin, of Lumpkin co., Ga.

Issue of September 4, 1868

At Greenville, on 18th inst., in the Methodist Church, by Rev. A. B. Stephens, Mr. I. Mims Sullivan to Miss Jennie Stokes, daughter of I. M. Stokes, Esq., all of Greenville, S. C.

Issue of September 11, 1868

Aug 23 by Rev. J. W. Shores, Mr. Evan Lee to Miss Lizzie Kendrick, both of Pike co., Ala.

Issue of September 18, 1868

In Marietta, Ga., Sept, 2, 1868, by Rev. W. F. Cook, Mr. W. E. Gramblin of Atlanta, Ga., to Miss Sarah W. Reed, of the former place.

Sept. 9 by Rev. John R. Parker, J. W. Davis, of Gainesville, Ga., to Mrs. Ann E. Harris, of Atlanta, Ga.

Issue of September 25, 1868

On Sep. 6, 1868, by Rev. C. J. Oliver, Miss Martha Fleming to Mr. Geo. M. Wheeler, all of Atlanta.

By Rev. J. J. Workman, Sept. 10th 1868, Mr. J. N. Bramlett to Miss Maria L. King, all of Greenville District, S. C.

On 25th Aug., by Rev. J. C. Crisp, Mr. H. J. Helms to Miss Nancy J. Byrum, all of Union co., N. C.

On 13th Sept. by the same, Mr. R. P. Kaziah to Miss Emoline Stilwell, all of Union co., N. C.

Issue of October 2, 1868

In Atlanta, on the 15th inst., by Rev. W. M. Crumley, Wm. A. Hemphill and Miss Mary A., youngest daughter of Jas. H. Anderson, all of Atlanta.

In Athens, Ga., Sept. 18, 1868, by the Rev. Dr. Lipscomb, Thomas F. Green, Jr., Esq., of Milledgeville to Miss Ella B. Lipscomb.

By the Rev. Geo. C. Clarke, Sept. 17th 1868, Mr. Geo. E. Waddy, of Griffin, and Miss L. J. Carnes, of Jonesboro.

On Sept. 9th 1868, by Rev. W. F. Easterling, Mr. J. J. Willie to Mrs. Laura C. Fowdren, all of Jefferson co., Fla.

By Rev. J. R. Little, September 9th 1868, Mr. James M. Pistole to Miss Alice, daughter of M. and R. Osborne, all of Monroe, N. C.

Issue of October 9, 1868

By Rev. R. W. Bigham, Oct. 1, in LaGrange, Ga., Rev. D. D. Cox, of the S. Ga. Conference, to Miss Annie Adelia, a daughter of the late Judge O. A. Bull.

On Sept 8, by Rev. W. S. Black, Mr. F. Pearson of Newberry to Miss Sallie Blease, of Edgefield, S. C.

On Sept. 20, by Rev. T. Alonzo Harris, Mr. James A. Andrew to Mrs. Susan A. Glenn, both of Oglethorpe co., Ga.

By Rev. I. M. Richardson, Aug. 18, 1868, at the residence of Dr. L. A. Folsom, near Dalton, Mr. William T. Cowles, of Thomaston, to Miss Nellie D. Wyche, of Whitfield.

By the same, Sept. 22, 1868, Mr. I. A. Carden to Mrs. Francis A. Gentry, all of Dalton, Ga.

By the same, Sept. 24, 1868, Mr. I. D. King to Miss Mary E. Fraker, both of Whitfield, Ga.

SOUTHERN CHRISTIAN ADVOCATE MARRIAGE NOTICES 1867-1878

Issue of October 16, 1868

By the Rev. F. P. Browne, Sept. 29th 1868, Dr. Ormond Pinkerton, of Cartersville, to Miss Mary R. Starr, of Gordon county, Ga.

Sept. 20, by Rev. W. T. Hamilton, Mr. P. E. Hudgins to Miss Caroline Malony, all of Chattooga co., Ga.

By the same, Sept. 23, Mr. S. W. McWhorter, of Walker co., Ga., to Miss M. L. Powell, of Chattooga, Ga.

Issue of October 23, 1868

Sept 18 by Rev. F. G. Hughes, Mr. Thomas W. Leonard of white co., Ga., to Miss Victoria Barr, of Habersham co, Ga.

Oct 13, by the same, Mr. Francis L. McKinney to Miss Mary J. Williams, all of Nacoochee Valley, Ga.

Oct. 6, in Henry co., Ga., by Rev. W. T. Read, Mr. Levi A. Turner to Miss Tommie L. Glass.

Oct, 15, by Rev. E. A. Seed, Mr. Robert B. Kean to Miss Sallie F. Dozier, all of Columbia co.

Oct. 8, at Trinity Church, by Rev .Geo. G. N. MacDonell, Mr. Wm. B. Mell to Miss Annie E. a. George, both of Savannah, Ga.

Oct. 11, by Rev. S. D. Clements, Mr. Edward P. Powers, of Alabama, to Miss Florence E. Douglass, of Muscogee co., Ga.

Oct. 1, in Bainbridge, Ga., by Rev. A. J. Dean, Mr. W. T. Smith to Miss Rebecca Waters, all of Bainbridge, Ga.

Oct. 8, by the same, Mr. J. S. Hopson to Miss Mary Strickland, all of Bainbridge, Ga.

Oct. 13, in Talbot co., Ga., by Rev. G. L. W. Anthony, Mr. Wm. R. Johnson, of Taylor co., to Miss Mary A. H. Freeman, of Talbot co., Ga.

Oct. 1, by Rev. J. W. Shores, Mr. D. A. McCaskill to Miss Fannie Davis, all of Pike co., Ga.

Issue of October 30, 1868

On the 22nd inst., at the residence of the bride's father by Rev. P. M. Ryburn, Mr. Lewis S. Schnessler of West Point, Ga., to Miss Sallie S. Trammell of Chambers co., Ala.

In La Grange, Ga., Oct. 15th, by Rev. R. W. Bigham, Mr. N. Tumlin, of Bartow county to Miss Frances Ophelia Wilkes, of La Grange.

In La Grange, Ga., Oct. 20th by Rev. R. W. Bigham, Mr. E. W. Marsha, of Atlanta, to Miss Achsah Turner of La Grange.

By the Rev. W. C. Dunlap, Oct. 15th, Mr. Jacob Sherman to Miss Catherine Ward, both of Bartow county, Georgia.

Married, at Abbeville C. H., South Carolina, on Oct. 18th, by the Rev. Alex. J. Smith, Dr. Henry J. Mouzon and Miss Sarah V. Mouzon, eldest daughter of the Rev. W. P. Mouzon, and formerly of Charleston, South Carolina.

By Rev. W. P. Pledger, in the Methodist Church, Forsyth, Ga., Oct. 22nd, Mr. F. O. Mays to Miss Emma B. Bean.

By the same, Oct. 15, Mr. J. R. Fryer of Burke co., Ga., to Miss Catharine G. Turner of Monroe co., Ga.

Oct. 11th, by Rev. G. Hughes at the residence of A. G. Wimpy, Mr. L. Q. Meadows to Miss Sarah J. O'Conner, all of Dahlonega, Ga.

By Rev. W. W. Stewart, Mr. Z. Y. Edmondson of Putnam co., Mrs. L. D. Coombs of Houston co., Ga., Oct. 8th 1868.

By the same, Mr. Jas. D. McDonald to Mrs. D. A. Roquemore, all of Houston co., Ga. Oct. 15, 1868.

Issue of November 6, 1868

Octo. 27, in Marshallville, Ga., by Rev. E. H. McGehee, Capt. Thos. J. Massey to Miss Mary S. Massey.

Oct. 13, by Rev. W. A. Dodge, Mr. Jabez Loyd to Mrs. Juda C. M. Pool, all of DeKalb co., Ga.

Oct. 20, by Rev. J. N. Myears, Mr. W. C. Ramsey to Miss F. J. Ranson, all of Fulton co., Ga.

Oct. 27, at the residence of Judge W. J. Weekes, in Talbotton, Ga., by Rev. R. W. Dixon, Mr. W. T. Dennis, to Miss Virginia A. Stallings, all of Talbotton.

Sept. 10, in Henry co., Ala., by Deacon Williams of the Baptist Church, Robt. Pitman, Esq., to Mrs. Dicey Odom.

Oct 15 by Rev. J. W. McRoy, Mr. Benj. King to Miss Josaphine Coger.

Oct. 22, by Rev. J. F. Mixon, Mr. Edmond L. Newton to Miss Martha Julia Bailey, all of Newborn, Ga.

Oct. 8, by Rev. C. A. Mitchell, Mr. Alpheus Broome to Miss Josephine Andrews, both of Green co., Ga.

Oct. 1, by Rev. J. C. Crisp, Mr. J. M. Slagle of Lancaster, to Miss Nancy E. Collins, of York dist., S. C.

Oct 11 by the same, Mr. Thos Polk to Miss Sarah A. Rice, both of Union co., N. C.

Oct 22 by the same, Mr. R. S. Billue to Miss Martha Walker, both of Union co., N. C.

Oct 29, by Rev. W. T. McMichael, Mr. E. M. Crowley, of Ware co., Ga., to Miss Martha McDonald, eldest daughter of Rev. Wm. McDonald, of Ware.

At the same time and place, by the same, Mr. H. H. Smith to Miss Estelle Cuyler, daughter of Mrs. D. M. Hood.

Sept. 23, by Rev. J. H. D. McRae, at the residence of the bride's father, Mr. J. J. Brunch to Miss E. F. Ellis.

Oct. 8 by the same, Mr. J. D. Adams t Miss J. E. Jackson, daughter of Rev. J. w. Jackson, Fla. Conf.

Oct 8, by the same, Mr. H. Hared, to Miss O. L. Cooper.

Oct. 28, by the same, mr. W. T. Henry to Miss M. T. Hunter, all of Columbia co., Fla.

Oct. 13, by Rev. T. S. L. Harwell, Mr. N. H. Sledge of Troup co., to Miss Ella L., daughter of Dr. E. d. Pitman, of La Grange, Ga.

Oct. 15 by the same, Mr. J. J. Adams to Miss A. E. Davis, all of Troup co., Ga.

Oct. 27 by the same, Mr. J. F. Wright to Miss Matilda Traylor, all of Troup co., Ga.

Issue of November 13, 1868

On the 26th October 1868, by Rev. G. Hughes, Col. Robert H. Moore to Miss Lucinda Morrison, daughter of Mr. A. F. Morrison, all of Dahlonega, Ga.

On the evening of the 29th October, at the residence of Maj. Beck, by the Rev. J. M. Richardson, Mr. Samuel B. McCamy to Miss Kate L. Carter, all of Murray co., Ga.

On 6th October, by Rev. Thos. B. Lanier, Mr. John A. Lester to Miss Sallie Rogers.

By the same, Nov. 1st at Bethany Church, Captain Samuel J. Heath, to Miss Leonora N. Buxton, all of Burke co., Ga.

By the Rev. D. Derrick, 22d October 1868, Mr. T. G. Smith of Edgefield District, S. C., to Miss Mary A. Leaphart of Lexington Dist., S. C.

By the Rev. W. T. Caldwell, on 27th October 1868, at the residence of Milton Bass, Hancock co., Ga., Judge W. L. Coleman, of Glascock co., to Miss Ann E. Bass, and Mr. John W. Moate, of Dooly co., to Miss Carrie Grabilla Bass.

By the same, October 28th, 1868, Mr. B. J. Clarke to Miss Sallie E. Dickson, both of Hancock co., Ga.

At Conyers, Nov. 4, by the Rev. J. L. Stewart, Dr. A. A. Stewart to Miss E. H. Davis.

In Sumter county, Ga., Oct. 13th 1868, by Rev. B. G. Breedlove, Mr. A. H. Harvey to Louisa Picket.

Oct. 28th by Rev. S. D. Clements, Mr. C. B. O'Neal and Miss Mary J. Passmore, all of Harris co., Ga.

Issue of November 20, 1868

Oct. 19, in Taylor co., Ga., by Rev. Jas. Griffith, Mr. Jas. Kimbrel and Miss A. C. Smith.

On Oct. 29, by the same, Mr. J. Pope and Miss Leona, eldest daughter of David Ballard, all of Taylor co.

On Nov. 3, by the same at E. B. Waters, Esq., Mr. T. W. Sistrunk and Miss Sarah W. Chapman, all of Butler.

On Nov 10, 1868, by Rev. M. H. Fielding, J. J. Wilkins of Lowndes co,. Ga., eldest son of the Rev. J. H. Wilkins, formerly of Terril co., Ga., to Miss Emily C. Wheatley, of Stockton Ga., formerly of Thomas co,. Ga.

On Nov. 4, by Rev. W. E. Johnston, Mr. J. J. Tinley of Bibb co., to Miss M. Jennie Winter of Richmond co., Ga.

In Jackson co., Fla., on Sunday 1st inst., at 3 o'clock, P. M., by Rev. W. R. Talley, A. McNealy, Esq., to Mrs. Lavinia Byrd, consort of the late John Byrd, Esq.

On 14th ult., by Rev. T. A. Harris, Mr. H. O. Parish to Miss Rebecca G. Dorough, both of Oglethorpe co., Ga.

By Rev. J. J. Workman, Oct. 1, Mr. T. A. Burdett and Miss M. A. Smith, all of Greenville Dist., S. C.

By the same, Oct. 29, in Camden, S. C., Mr. W. E. DeLoach of Barnwell to Miss Beckie R., daughter of the late W. C. Workman, Esq.

By the same, Nov. 5, Mr. W. Holland and Miss Hattie E., daughter of Dr. J. M. Sullivan, all of Greenville, S. C.

In Richmond co., Ga., on 3d inst., by Rev. I. s. Hopkins, Mr. C. N. Churchill and Miss A. E. Catlin.

Issue of November 27, 1868

Nov. 21, by Rev. A. W. Roland, Mr. John W. Almond to Miss Mary M. Waldrop, all of Newton co., Ga.

Nov 12, by Rev. A. J. Cauthen, Oscar Cappel to Miss Mattie Howell of Richland District. S. C.

Nov. 2, in Buena Vista, Ga., by Rev. G. T. Embry, Mr. Wm. D. Stallings to Miss Zeula Brooks.

Nov. 9, by the same, Mr. A. C. Adkins to Miss Evaline Brooks, all of Buena Vista. Ga.

Nov 18, at St. Peter's Church, Beaufort Dist., S. C., by Rev. A. J. Stokes, Clarence A. Graeser of Columbia, S. C,. To Miss Margaret A. Dibble of Charleston, S. C.

Nov 17, in Camden, S. C., by Rev. C. H. Pritchard, Rev. C. Thomason of the S. C. Conference to Miss Mary Wragg, second daughter of the late Rev. Saml Wragg Capers.

Oct. 28, by Rev. J. H. Grogan, Geo. W. Alexander of Lexington, Ga., to Miss Vedona T. Vail of Elberton, Ga.

Oct. 29 by the same, Jos. N. Olds to Miss Sallie E. DuBose, all of Elbert co., Ga.

Nov. 12, by the same, Rev. John R. Parker of the No. Ga. conference to Miss Sallie A. low, of Hall co., Ga.

Nov 5, by Rev. E. G. Gage, Dr. W. D. Cornwell to Miss R. M. Allen, all of Newberry, S. C.

Oct. 26, at Montgomery, near Savannah, by Rev. Geo. G. N. MacDonell, Mr. Alexander Armstrong of Savannah, to Miss Ella I. Willett of Chatham co.

Nov. 5, at Savannah by the same, Mr. Jas. G. Dent to Miss Ellen Meashin, both of Savannah, Ga.

Nov. 12, by the same, Mr. Robt. H. Vorus[?] of Stewart co., Ga., to Miss Ida Zittrouer, of Savannah, Ga.

Issue of December 4, 1868

Nov. 17, by Rev. H. H. Wild, Mr. H. V. Napier of Macon, Ga., to Miss Anastatia Blackwar of Chunneuggee, Ala.

By the same on the same evening, Mr. D. H. Elder to Miss Nancy C. Graham, all of Bullock co., Ala.

On 19th Nov., at Canton, Ga., by Rev. P. H. Brewster, Mr. C. A. Dowds, to Miss Seletie F., eldest daughter of Rev. J. R. Gaines of the N. Ga. Conference.

In Twiggs co., Ga., Nov. 24, 1868, by Rev. J. Blakely Smith, Mr. S. T. C. Murray to Mrs. M. F. Jarvis, all of Twiggs co.

Nov 25, by Rev. A. J. Cauthen, Mr. M. Kirkland to Miss Emmie Cook, all of Fairfield, S. C.

By the same, Nov. 26, Mr. B. F. Davidson of Charlotte, N. C., and Miss J. A. Duvall of Winnsboro, S. C.

In Harris co., Ga., Nov. 15, by Rev. W. A. Parks, W. B. McGehee to Miss Ida McGehee.

Issue of December 11, 1868

Nov, 25, 1868, by Rev. W. H. Hunt, W. W. O'Caine to Miss Callie P. P. Hutchinson, all of Columbia co., Fla.

At. Mt. Airy, Hancock co,. Ga., by Rev. W. H. Potter, Judge J. E. Berry, Sr., to Mrs. Ann Elizabeth Devereaux.

By R. H. Howren, Mr. I. Morgan to Miss Lizzie Heidt, all of Effingham co., Ga., Nov. 1868.

Nov. 26, by Rev. S. D. Clements, Mr. Jesse B. Butts, of Upson co., and Miss Mildred O. Burt, of Talbot co.

On the 1st inst., by Rev. C. A. Fulwood, Mr. W. A. Sealey and Miss Susan E. Adams, eldest daughter of Augustus Adams, Esq., all of Talbot co., Ga.

At the residence of the bride's brother, Mr. W. H. Lancaster, in Houston co., Ga., Nov. 2d, 1868, by Rev. I. L. Avant, Mr. Thos. W. Vinson to Miss Harriet A. J. Lancaster, all of Houston co., Ga.

Dec. 3d, by Rev. Josiah M. Gable, Mr. S. N. Green to Miss N. Lou Mankins, of Cobb co., Ga.

By Rev. M. M. Crumley, on Nov. 17, W. B. Bass to Miss Rosa M. Anderson, of Atlanta, Ga.

Issue of December 18, 1868

On the 10th day of December 1868, by the Rev. J. J. Morgan Mr. N. J. Newsome to Miss Lou J. Riddle, all of Washington co., Ga.

By Rev. V. A. Sharp in the Methodist Church, Nov. 10th, Mr. W. S. Guthrie, late of Tennessee, to Miss Carrie E., eldest daughter of Dr. John M. and Mrs. Margaret Craton, of Rutherfordton, N. C.

By the same, Nov. 12th, Mr. Wm. R. Tanner, of Spartanburg, S. C., to Miss M. Lizzie, daughter of Col. W. A. Tanner, of Rutherfordton, N. C.

By Rev. R. W. Dixon, December 3d, 1868, Prof. Jno M. Proctor of Collinsworth Institute, to Miss Anna H. Forbes, all of Talbotton, Ga.

By the same, December 8th 1868, William E. Ragland to Mis sAugusta B. Kimbrough, all of Talbotton, Ga.

In Thomaston, Upson co., Ga., December 10th, by Rev. D. Kelsey, Mr. James w. Hightower to Mrs. Catharine A. Snead.

By the same, December 10th, in Upson co., Mr. Russell F. Cariker to Miss Eliza F. Reeves.

On Nov. 25th by the Rev. T. E. Wannamaker, Mr. Geo. Boyleston, of Barnwell, to Miss Carrie Riley, of Orangeburg, S. C.

By the same on December 3d, Mr. J. M. Keller to Miss Sallie Boyd, first daughter of the officiating clergyman, all of Orangeburg, S. C.

On December 6 by the Rev. M. Langford, M. A. S. Ray to Miss Harriet L. Armstrong, all of Warren co., Ga.

In Houston County, Georgia, December 10th, by Rev. E. H. McGehee, Mr. J. E. Hay ito Miss Louzana Hampton.

In Houston County, Georgia, December 10th, by Rev. E. H. McGehee, Col. Lewis A. Rumph to Miss E. Emma McGehee.

SOUTHERN CHRISTIAN ADVOCATE MARRIAGE NOTICES 1867-1878

Issue of January 1, 1869

Dec. 1st, by Rev. F. Milton Kennedy, Rev. A. J. Stafford of the South Carolina Conference to Miss Parthenia A., daughter of the late Nathan Beverly, of Wadesboro, N. C.

Dec. 14 in Macon, by the Rev. J. Blakely Smith, Edward D. Ballard to Miss Maggie Johnston

By the same, Dec. 23, Arthur D. Thompson of Savannah, to Miss Mary Anna Hays, of Macon, Ga.

Dec. 22 by the Rev. J. H. Nall, Mr. Thos. J. Anderson of Macon, Ga., to Miss Annie E. Sullivan, of Americus, Georgia.

Nov. 25, by the Rev. John E. Sentell, Mr. John E. McCall to Miss mary A. Wells, all of Liberty county, Ga.

Nov. 10 by the Rev. J. W. Cook, Mr. Wm. J. Fischer, of Newton co., to Miss Caroline E. Horton, of Jasper co., Georgia.

Issue of January 8, 1869

At the residence of Peter C. Sawyer, near Macon, on the night of the 30th Dec., by the Rev. J. W. Burke, Orren E. Massey to Fannie E. Holstern, all of Bibb co.

On the 11th Oct., 1868, by Rev. Wm. S. Foster, Mr. Elijah R. Howell to Mrs. Sarah A. Hames.

By the same, on 9th Nov., Mr. James Spears to Miss Frances C. Dupree.

By the same, on 9th Dec., 1868, Mr. Eli Cornwell to Miss Martha Ilchers, all of Cherokee co., Ga.

In Quitman, Georgia, Dec. 23rd, by Rev. O. L. Smith, Mr. John Tillman to Miss M. Lawson Wyche.

In Pike co., Ala., on 23rd Dec., by Rev. J. Wilson Shores, P. F., B. H. Meredith Gillis to Miss Mollie Lewis, daughter of Elisha Lewis, Esq.

In Dalton, Ga., Dec. 13th 1868, by Rev. J. T. Norris, Lieut. Wm. R. Gocto, of Arkansas, to Miss Anna M. Sims of Dalton, Ga.

On Dec. 17th 1868, by Rev. J. R. Gaines, Mr. William M. Chambers, of Cherokee co., Ga., to Miss Martha B. Dunn, of Pontotoc co., Miss.

In Perry, Ga., on 10th Dec., by Rev. W. C. Bass, George C. White, Esq., to Miss Emma C., daughter of Dr. P. B. D. Cutter, all of Perry, Ga.

On the 9th Dec., in McDonough, by Rev. Wm. d. Hardy, Mr. James W. Alexander to Miss Mary Brown, all of Henry co., Ga.

By Rev. E. S. Tyner, in Ocala, Fla., on the 15th Dec., 1868, Mr. W. E. McGahagin to Miss Emma C. Gartrell, daughter of the late Rev. W. J. Gartrell.

By the same, on the 10th Dec. 1868, at the bride's father's, Mr. J. B. Thomas, Mr. J. M. Shaw to Miss M. F. Thomas, all of Alachua co., Fla.

On 22nd Dec. 1868, by Elder W. J. Collins, Mr. L. B. C. Evans to Miss I. L. Logan, all of Houston co., Ga.

By the Rev. Geo. C. Clarke, Dec. 24th 1868, Mr. Lamar Collier, eldest son of Hon. John Collier, to Miss Luta Zachry, all of Atlanta, Ga.

SOUTHERN CHRISTIAN ADVOCATE MARRIAGE NOTICES 1867-1878

In Cartersville, Taylor co., Ga., Dec. 1st 1868, by Rev. G. L. W. Anthony, Mr. Henry Searcy to Miss M. V. Perkins.

By the same, Dec. 27th 1868, Mr. John F. Parker to Miss Sarah Ruffin.

In Greensborough, Ga., on the 15th Dec., by Rev. Dr. L. M. Smith, Mr. James P. McCall to Miss Claude Weaver.

In Hamilton, Harris co., Ga., Dec. 2nd, 1868, by Rev. W. A. Parks, Mr. Jas. M. Kimbrough to Miss Sallie Mobley, daughter of Col. James M. Mobley. Texas Advocate please copy.

Nov. 15th, by Rev. A. R. Lovejoy, Capt. Milton P. Tucker to Miss G. C. Beckwith,all of Greenville, Ga.

In Greenville, Ga., by the same, Dec. 10th, Mr. Wiley T. Thornton to Miss Novilla Adams, all of Merriwether co., Ga.

In Griffin on 10th Dec., by Rev. H. A. Adams, Mr. Thos. H. Harris of Macon to Miss Mary M. Merk.

By the same in Fayette co., on 15th Dec., Chas. W. Hobnett of Macon Co., Ala., to Miss Ella Gray.

By Rev. T. B. Russell, in Houston co., Ga., on 17th Dec., 1868, Mr. W. Cooper Clarke to Miss Fannie Draper.

By Rev. W. W. Oslin, Dec. 22nd, Mr. H. w. Walker to Miss Indian E. Robinson, all of Jasper co., Ga.

By same, Dec. 16th, Mr. Wm. King to Miss Ellen Maddux, all of Jasper co., Ga.

By same, Dec. 26th, Mr. James E. Niblett to Miss Martha J. Morgan, all of Jasper co., Ga.

On the 17th Dec. at Henry O. Williams', Thomson, Ga., by Rev. A. B. Thrasher, Mr. W. B> jones of Morgan co., to Mrs. Joseph M. Harrell, of the former place.

By Rev. Dr. Manson, Mr. T. A. Ward to Miss Missouri Glass, daughter of J. F. Glass, of Henry co.

In Talbotton, Ga., Dec. 22nd 1868, by Rev. T. A. Brown, Dr. J. W. Lee of Milford, Ga., to Miss Jennie L. Strickland of Talbotton.

Also, in Talbot co., Ga., Dec. 22nd, by the same, Mr. William H. Culpepper to Miss Ellen N. Biggs, both of Talbotton.

By Rev. John W. Reynolds, at the residence of W. Rickerson, Esq., Nov. 19th, Mr. James Wilson to Miss Mary C. Rickerson, all of Crawford co., Ga.

By the same, Dec. 12, Mr. Samuel S. A. Moon to Miss Mary E. Smith, all of Culloden, Ga.

By the same, Dec. 12th, Mr. John T. Hilton, to Miss Amanda C. Watson, all of Upson co., Ga.

By the same, same time and place, Mr. Henry C. Michael to Miss Mary A. Watson.

In Union Church, on Sunday, Dec. 29th, by the Rev. S. Y. Sims, Mr. Holloway S. Crook to Miss Lidia T. Hester, all of Chambers co., Ala.

At the residence of Judge W. W. Anderson, Warren co., Ga., Dec. 22nd, 1868, by Rev. W. T. Caldwell, Mr. Wm. D. Brantley of Hancock co., Ga., to Miss Mittie M., daughter of Rev. L E. Culver, of Troy, Ala.

By the same Dec. 22nd, 1868, Mr. John G. Collins, to Miss Sarah E. Waller, both of Hancock co., Ga.

Issue of January 22, 1869

At Cotton Valley, Ala., Nov. 26, 1868, by Rev. B. B. Ross, Mr. C. E. Dill to Miss Maggie McBryde.

On Nov. 29, by the same, Mr. S. W. Menefee to Miss Lou M. Campbell, all of the above Cotton Valley, Macon co., Ala.

By the same, on 23d December 1868, Mr. W. H. Harris of Cotton Valley, Ala., to Miss Mary Oswalt, of Hunnicutt, Ala.

In Talbot co., Ga., Jan., 14, 1869, by Rev. T. A. Brown, Wm. J. J. Smith of Macon, Ga., to Miss Nancy E. McCrary of Talbot co., Ga.

On 25th Dec. at the house of the bride's father, by Rev. James N. Myears, Mr. Newton Cunard of Jasper co., Ga., to Miss Nancy E. T. Myears, of Walton co., Ga.

At the residence of Mr. George Bell, 7th Jan 1869, by Rev. R. H. Eakes, Mr. Joseph Black and Miss Catharine Bell, all of Forsyth co., Ga.

On 10th Oct. 1868 by Rev. R. F. Williamson, Mr. Jas. Dixon to Miss Ellen Acock, all of Macon co., Ga.

Jan 7th in the Methodist Church in Albany, Ga., by Rev. Henry D. Moore, Mr. J. J. White of Albany, Ga., and Miss Dora C. Hutchings, of Louisville, Ky.

Dec. 16, 1868, by Rev. J. W. Shores, Rev. Hugh M. Gillis of the Montgomery Conf., to Miss Mary N. V. lewis, of Pike co., Ala.

On Dec. 22nd 1868 in Lee co., Ala., by Rev. M. S. Andrews, Rev. Tho. F. McGehee of Meriwether co., Ga., and Mrs. M. A. Ogletree.

By Rev. S. D. Clements, Dec. 22, Mr. F. F. Holmes of Talbot to Miss Kate Mahone of Bellevue, Ga.

On 3d Jan, by Rev. D. J. Myrick, Wm. H. Jones of Madison co., Ga., to Miss Lou Dawson of Oglethorpe co.

By the same on 4th Jan., Dr. Wm. H. Jarrell of Oglethorpe co. to Miss Nettie S. Vincent of Athens, Ga.

By Rev. J. A. Wood of the S. C. Conf., Dec. 24, 1868, Mr. W. L. Morris to Miss Carrie Williams, all of Polk co., N. C.

In Taylor co., Ga., by Rev. Jas. Griffith, Dec. 17th, Mr. Lavendor of Wilkerson co., Ga., to Miss P. Bynum of the former place.

By the same on same date, Mr. J. D. Stralnaker and Miss S. Ogburn, all of Macon co., Ga.

By the same Dec. 23, Mr. E. D. Hicks and Miss Julia Arington, in Reynolds, Ga.

By the same, Dec. 24, Mr. J. F. Humphries and Miss A. Carter, all of Taylor co.

By the same, Dec. 31, H. J. Ruffin and Miss W. V. Jinks, all of Taylor co.

By the same, Jan. 31, 1869, Mr. Thos. Johnson and Miss Streetman, all of Taylor co., Ga.

Near Broxton's Bridge, S. C., Dec. 31st, 1868 by Revs. L. B. Barn and L. Wood, Dr. Malcom V. Wood of Beaufort to Miss R. Anna, second daughter of Capt. J. G. Varn of Colleton.

On Dec. 17, 1868, by Rev. I. L. Avant, Mr. E. E. Shine to Miss Millie E., eldest daughter of Mr. Elijah Vinson of Houston co., Ga.

By Rev. J. H. McRae, Dec. 13, Mr. L. G. Stringfellow of Columbia co., to Miss Rebecca Turner, of Bradford co., both of Fla.

By the same on Dec. 17, Mr. B. C. Prevatt of Columbia co., and Miss Celia Sasser of Bradford co., both of Fla.

By the same Dec. 24, Mr. B. F. Bouchillon and Miss Delia A. Smith, both of Bradford co., Fla.

By the same, Dec. 30, Mr. J. J. Vinzant and Miss Elsie Prevatt, both of Columbia co., Fla.

By the same on same evening, Mr. C. A. Markum and Miss Susan Newmons, both of Columbia co., Fla.

By the same on 31st Dec., Mr. John Odom and Miss Martha M. Williams, both of Columbia co., Fla.

Issue of January 29, 1869

In the Methodist Episcopal Church, at Talbotton, Ga., on the 14th inst., by Rev. Thos. T. Christian, Mr. William H. Martin and Miss Mattie C. Callier, all of Talbotton, Ga.

By the Rev. J. M. D. McRae, on the 6th Jan. 1869, Mr. Elijah Mattox and Miss E. A. A. Bryant, both of Columbia co., Fla.

By the same on the 3rd Jan., Mr. J. W. Lord and Miss Mary A. Trueluck, both of Columbia co., Fla.

On 20th Jan., by the Rev. J. H. Grogan, at the residence of S. C. Starke, Esq., Elbert co., Ga., Mr. Thomas W. Hill of Wilkes co., Ga., to Miss Mary J. Starke.

In the Methodist Church, Cheraw, So. Ca., Dec. 27th 1868 by Rev. F. Milton Kennedy, Mr. Samuel Reid to Miss Cornelia Walsh, daughter of the late Rev. Tracy R. Walsh.

On Dec. 31st, 1868 by Rev. Wm. A. Sampey, Mr. Wm. E. Maulden, Esq., to Mrs. Nancy J. Kelly, daughter of Judge D. Carmichael, all of Newton, Ala.

On Jan. 19th 1869, by Rev. J. R. Gaines, Mr. Henry H. Rogers to miss Martha J. Perry, all of Milton co., Ga.

On Oct 25th, 1868, by J. W. Turner, Mr. Wm. St. John to Miss Elizabeth McKibben, of Henry co., Ga.

On Dec. 25th, by the same, Mr. J. M. Bradley to Miss Mary Shuptrine, of Liberty co., Ga.

On Jan. 7th, at the residence of Mrs. Gay, LaGrange, Ga., by Rev. R. W. Bigham, Mr. John Ragland and Mrs. Fannie Wales.

In Jackson co., Fla., during the holidays of December, by Rev. W. R. Talley, Mr. Jas. A. Cain to Miss Lee America, daughter of Marshal Warren, Esq.

On 14th Jan., by Rev. J. J. Little, Mr. Isaac H. Askin, of Monroe co., and Miss Lou Williams, of Harrison co., Ga.

On the 19th Jan., by S. R. Weaver, Mr. Angus M. Score, of Alabama, to Miss Sue A. Stovall, of Stewart co.

On the 21st Jan., by W. P. Pledger, Mr. William E. H. Searcy, of Monroe co., Ga., to Miss Eugenia Pauline Rogers, of Forsyth, Ga.

[issue of February 5, 1869 missing]

Issue of February 12, 1869

In Russel co., Ala., Dec. 3rd, 1868, by Rev. W. B. Neal, Mr. W. M. Boswell[?], to Miss A. E. Scott.

By the same, Jan. 28th 1869, in Lee co., Ala., Mr. Martin Guthrie, of Bullock co., Ala., to Miss Mary F. Pattillo.

On the 14th Jan., 1869 by Rev. H. J. Mashburn, Mr. E. M. Thompson of Jefferson, Jackson co., Ga., to Miss S. J. Johnson, of Oglethorpe co., Ga.

By the same, on 26th Jan. 1869, Mr. William J. McDonald, of Homer, Banks co., Ga., to Miss Ellas C. Butler, of Gainesville, Hall co., Ga.

On the 21st inst., by Rev. E. A. Steed, Mr. Jas. T. Flanigan to Miss Mattie A. Avary, all of Columbia co., Ga.

On 19th Jan 1869, in Lexington, Ga., by Rev. T. Alonzo Harris, Mr. J. W. Manley, of Franklin co., to Miss Sarah C. England, of Lexington.

On the 26th ult,. by Rev. S. S. Sweet, Mr. Wm. A. Brown, of Jefferson co., and Miss Amelia Glisson, of Burke co, Ga.

On Feb. 4th, in Berrien co., by Rev. J. W. Simmons, Mr. John S. Lovejoy to Miss Annie V. Carroll, daughter of Judge Carroll.

In Perry, Ga., Feb. 2nd, 1869, by Rev. W. Knox, Mr. J. N. West of Bainbridge, Ga., and Miss M. T. Cox, of Perry, Ga.

Issue of February 19, 1869

On Feb. 2nd, at Pleasant Hill, by Rev. R. J. Corley, Dr. E. Manes, of Florida, to Miss Ann Bedell, of Talbot co., Ga.

In the Methodist Church at Spartanburg, S. C., on Sunday, Jan 31, by Rev. M. A. Gamewell, Mr. Wm. C. Kirkland, third son of the late Rev. W. C. Kirkland, of the S. C. Conference, and Miss Alice F. Burnett, only daughter of Rev. J. S. Burnett, formerly of the Holston Conference.

By Rev. W. P. Pledger, Feb. 4th 1869, Col. A. D. Hammond of Forsyth, GA., to Miss Mary Holland, of Monroe co., Ga.

On Dec. 23, 1868 by Rev. W. F. Roberts, Mr. H. H. Bailey to Miss Sallie Robertson.

By the same Dec. 27th 1868, Mr. J. L. Wynn to Miss Amanda Howel, all of Wilkinson co., Ga.

By the same, Feb. 2, 1869, Mr. Lewis Metts of Laurens co., Ga., to Miss Rachel A. Fordham, of Wilkinson co., Ga.

At Ansonville, N. C., Feb. 3, 1869, by Rev. F. Milton Kennedy, Mr. Julius Heilbron to Miss Wilmer Myers.

Also by the same, Feb. 4, Mr. John Treadaway to Mrs. Phoebe Griggs, all of Anson co., N. C.

On Feb. 2, by Rev. E. A. Steed, Dr. Wensley Hobby of Louisiana, to Miss Mamie P. Lamar, of Columbia county, Ga.

In Upson co., Jan. 13, 1869, by Rev. W. F. Smith, Mr R. T. Jackson and Miss Fannie M. Holloway.

By the same, Feb. 2, in Upson co., Mr. Wm. F. Chancellor and Miss L. A. E. Allen.

By Rev. R. J. Johnson on Jan. 26, J. F. Eapy of Jackson co., Ga., to Miss Mary Allen of Gwinnett co., Ga.

On Jan. 4, 1869, by Rev. W. F. Quillian, Mr. W. Y. Cochran to Mrs. Sarah M. Garrison, both of Banks co., Ga.

In Baker co., Ga., Jan. 12, 1869, by Rev. A. J. Dean, Mr. W. R. Clifton to Miss Sabra Matthis.

By same, in Bainbridge, Ga., Jan. 12, 1869, Mr. D. J. G. McNair to Miss N. A. Patterson, all of Bainbridge, Ga.

By same, in Decatur co., Ga., Jan. 26th 1869, Mr. M. P. Hoyl of Bainbridge, Ga., to Miss Lou Bates, of Decatur.

In Albany, Ga., Feb. 9, by Rev. H. D. Moore, Mr. Saml R. Cade of Abbeville, S. C., to Miss Sallie C. Slaughter of Albany.

At Warrenton, Ga., Jan. 26, 1869 by Rev. J. Lewis, Jr., M. O. Wilkie and Miss H. Virginia Hubert.

Issue of February 26, 1869

In McDowell co., N. C., on 1st Jan 1869 by Rev. J. R. Griffith, Mr. Alfred Rutherford of Tennessee, to Miss Sallie Goode, of McDowell, N. C.

In McDowell co., N. C., on the 9th of Jan. 1869 by Rev. J. R. Griffith, Mr. Richard Camp to Miss Caroline Kayler.

In McDowell co., N. C., on the 10th of Jan. 1869 by the same, Mr. M. Poteet to Miss Mary Smith.

In McDowell co., N. C., on the 17th of Jan. 1869 by the same, Mr. Jno R. Simmons to Miss Jane Flemming.

In McDowell co., N. C., on the 27th of Jan. 1869 by the same, Mr. M. M. Craig of Colorado to Miss Rebecca Brown of McDowell co.

In Burk co., N. C., on the 10th of Feb. 1869 by the same, Mr. Samuel Dunvant of Virginia to Miss Virginia Corpening of Burk, N. C.

On Jan. 14th 1869, by Rev. J. B. Traywick, Mr. Harrel Tolbot to Miss Gable, the former of Abbeville, and the latter of Edgefield Dist., S. C.

On Jan. 21st 1869 by the same, Mr. James McCain of Abbeville to Miss Mary Stone, of Edgefield Dis., S. C.

On Feb. 19th, 1869, by the same, Mr. James Mayson of Edgefield, to Miss Mattie Tibert, of Abbeville Dist., S. C.

By Rev. W. D. Heath, Jan. 7th 1869, Mr. A. H. Foster and Mrs. A. M. Chambers of Catoosa co,. Ga.

By the same, Feb. 7th 1869, Mr. Benjamin F. Blackburn and Miss Emma J. Sloan, of Catoosa co., Ga.

By same, Feb. 11th 1869, Mr. John H. Keener and Miss Mary J. Derrick, of Greysville, Ga.

In Russell co., Ga., Feb. 11th 1869, by Rev. B. B. Crawford, Mr. Thos. S. Paschal to Miss Mattie Upshaw.

On the same day by same, in Barbour co., Ala., Mr. Joseph Blackstock to Miss Sallie Davis.

By Rev. J. R. Little, Feb. 10th 1869, Mr. P. A. Brock of Cheraw, S. C., to Miss Mattie E., second daughter of Wm. E. and Sarah Horne, of Anson co., N. C.

On Feb 16th, by Rev. D. O'Driscoll, Mr. John Stephens and Miss S. M. R. Patterson, both of Cusseta, Ga.

By Rev. J. J. Workman, Jan. 31st, 1869, Mr. Henry A. Smith and Miss Wylie C. Simpson.

By same, Feb. 7th, Mr. Simmons Taylor and Miss Elisabeth Rogers.

On Feb. 17th 1869, by Rev. P. L. Herman, Capt. S. W. Carter of Yancy co. to Miss Laura J., youngest daughter of James and Elizabeth Avery, of Burke co., N. C.

On Tuesday evening, 16th inst., by the Rev. William Martin, Mr. J. J. Roach and Miss Ella Irine, daughter of Capt. Rufus D. Senn, all of Columbia, S. C.

At the residence of Mrs. Myrick, by Rev. John W. Reynolds, Jan 27th, Mr. Ira F. Jordan of Alabama and Miss Missouri M. Flagan, of Crawford co., Ga.

By Rev. A. B. Stephens, Feb. 4th, in Anderson co., S. C., Mr. James Paine and Miss Fannie Gambell.

By same on 10th Feb., Mr. J. K. Bates and Miss Annie Redfearn, all of Greenville, S. C.

Feb. 9th, by Rev. P. M. Ryburn, Mr. Grant J. Anderson of Union Parish, La., and Miss Annie A. Fletcher, of Merriwether co, Ga. Nashville and N. O. Advocates please copy.

On the 28th inst., at Pool's Furnace, Bartow co., Ga., by The Rev. P. H. Brewster, Mr. Zachary T. Moss to Miss Emma L., eldest daughter of Capt. Benj. G. Poole.

In Atlanta, at the residence of L. B. Davis, Esq., by the R. F. Williamson, Dr. C. H. Smith of Schley co., to Mrs. Susie M. Berry.

Near Union Point, on 9th inst., by Rev. Philip B. Robinson, Judge D. A. Newsom and Miss Maggie W. Carlton, both of Green co.

On Wednesday evening, Feb. 17th 1869, at the Second Presbyterian Church, Charleston, S. C., by the Rev. Lovick Pierce, D. D., Mr. Ellison A. Smyth, son of the Rev. Dr. Smyth, and Miss Julia, daughter of L. Gambell, of Charleston, and granddaughter of the officiating minister.

On 17th Feb., by the Rev. J. M. Bonnell, Mr. Simeon D. Rogers of Hancock co., to Miss Emma Clancey, second daughter of Michael J. Clancey, Esq., of Macon.

Issue of March 5, 1869

Feb. 11, 1869, by Rev. R. B. Lester, Mr. H. D. Leitner of Columbia co., Ga., to Miss Anna E. Jackson of Talbotton, Ga.

On Feb. 23, 1869, by Rev. R. R. Johnson, Mr. W. S. Gramling of Atlanta, to Miss Fannie C. Chambers of Carroll co., Ga.

SOUTHERN CHRISTIAN ADVOCATE MARRIAGE NOTICES 1867-1878

On Feb. 14, by Rev. R. A. Conner, Mr. J. Reynolds to Miss Lucy E. Hardy, all of Columbia co., Ga.

On Jan. 16, by Rev. L. T. Mizell, Mr. R. Stricklin of Campbell co., Ga., to Miss Cornelia M. A. Quillian, daughter of Rev. J. B. C. Quillian, of Cobb co., Ga.

By Rev. J. M. Dickey in Green co., Mr. Wm. T. Jackson to Miss Mary A. E. Brooks.

In Decatur co., Ga., Feb. 17, 1869, by Rev. A. J. Dean, Mr. H. Satterfield of Bainbridge, Ga., to Miss M. E. Farish of Decatur.

On 14th inst., by Rev. J. H. Zimmerman, Mr. M. J. Boyd of Newberry, S. C., to Miss Maggie Stone of Edgefield, S. C.

In Beaufort Dist., S. C., Jan. 21, by Rev. L. C. Loyal, Mr H. M. Parnells to Mrs. Hattie C. Johnson, daughter of Mr. Henry E. Solomons, all of said District.

On Feb. 18, 1860 by Rev. J. R. Gaines, Mr. Augustus A. Downs of Canto, Ga., to Miss Sarah R. Smith of Cobb co., Ga.

At Col. Thos Jones, near Thomasville, Ga., Feb. 2, 1869 by Rev. W. M. Kennedy, Mr. T. P. Jones of Thomas Co., Ga., to Miss Livinia J. Chairs, of Tallahassee, Fla.

In Atlanta, at the residence of L. B. Davis, Esq., by the Rev. R. F. Williamson, Dr. C. H. Smith of Schley County, to Mrs. Susie M. Berry.

Issue of March 12, 1869

By Rev. Jas. P. DePass in Lake City, Fla., Dec. 22, 1869, Mr. James McNiell to Miss Hannah L. Carter.

By the same Dec. 28, 1868, Lake City, Fla., Mr. John Miller to Miss Fannie Ferrand.

By the same Feb. 18, 1869, Lake City, Fla., Mr. Thomas Lloyd to Miss Mattie A. Hancock.

By the same in Lake City, Fla., March 3, 1869, Mr. James E. young to Miss Louisa D. Wright.

by Rev. H. H. Parks, Jan 6, Mr. James H. Colquitt and Miss Elizabeth D. Barnett, both of Floyd co., Ga.

By the same, Feb. 2, Mr. James R. Blount, of Macon, Ga., and Miss Ida M. Graves, of Rome, Ga.

By the same, Feb. 24, Mr. C. J. Groves and Miss Ella Graves, both of Rome, Ga.

In Augusta, Ga., Feb. 20 by Rev. G. H. Pattillo, Mr. John T. Miller and Miss Anna M. Frazier.

In Augusta, Ga., Feb. 26, by the same, Mr. Lucius M. Dyer and Miss Eliza Napier.

By the Rev. J. V. M. Morris, in Baldwin co., Ga., Feb. 9, 1869, Mr. Edy Z. Brown to Miss Mary E. Harper.

By the same in Baldwin co., Ga., Feb. 18, 1869, Mr. Eli Harrell to Miss M. A. Blunt.

By the Rev. J. Chambers on the 28th Feb. in Alpharetta, Milton co., Ga., Mr. Melvil P. Brown, of Lebanon, Tenn., to Miss Martha C. Grover, daughter of Rev. Milton Grover, of Alpharetta, Ga.

By Rev. J. C. Hartsell, on 28th Feb 1879 at the parsonage in Chesterfield, Mr. James Smith to Miss Rosa White, all of this county.

On the 25th Feb., by Rev. D. E. Starr, Mr. J. T. Starr to Miss Mary Kiblin, all of Clayton co., Ga.

On 18th Feb., by Rev. Mr. Barr of Lincolnton, Mr. A. A. Morris of Gaston co., to Miss Jane Kistler, daughter of Lawson H. and Mary E. Kistler.

Issue of March 19, 1869

By Rev. Jas. M. N. Low, Feb. 11, 1869, Mr. W. A. Ethridge of Randolph co., to Miss Mary Jane Sanders of Clay co., all of Ga.

By the same, March 4, 1869, Mr. J. F. Pate to Miss Rachel L. Cobb of Clay co., Ga.

By Rev. V. A. Sharpe, March 4th, at the residence of Dr. J. M. Craton, Mr. __. H. Mills to Miss Mary Craton, all of Rutherfordton, N. C.

By Rev. A. Gray, Feb. 25, Mr. M. Waldrop and Mrs. M. A. Christian, both of Newton co., Ga.

In McDonough, Henry co., Ga., on 2d day of March, by Rev. D. Nolan, Mr. D. B. Bivins to Miss Eugenia J. Reed, both of Henry co, Ga.

On Feb. 24, by Rev. J. A. Reynolds in Broom Town Valley, Chattooga co., Mr. W. R. Wyatt to Miss Ella Merrell, all of said county.

By Rev. R. F. Evans at Bethany, Ga., March 10, 1869, Dr. J. B. Randall to Mrs. Lucy A. Griffin.

Feb. 24th, by Rev. W. M. Watts, at his residence, Taylor's Creek, Mr. J. W. Bird[?] of Liberty co., and Miss M. R. Hogan of Meriwether co., Ga.

Issue of March 26, 1869

At St. Luke's Church, Columbus, Ga., on the 17th inst., by Rev. Jas. E. Evans, Mr. Orlando N. Dana of Macon, Ga., to Miss Fannie S. White, of the former city.

On 3rd March in Hackensack, N. J., by Rev. W. A. Gamewell, Mr. Henry L. Bruns, formerly of Charleston, S. C., and Miss Kate L. Gamewell, third daughter of John N. Gamewell, formerly of Camden, S. C.

By Rev. James M. Armstrong, in Richmond co., Ga., March 11th 1869, Mr. Howell C. Walker and Miss Corinne L. Greiner.

By Rev. J. J. Workman, Feb. 8th 1869 at the residence of the bride's mother, Mr. Benjamin P. Randall of Greenville co., to Miss Hettie Snow of Spartanburg co., S. C.

In Jackson co., Fla., on the 24th Jan., by Rev. H. P. Waugh, Mr. Wm. H. Knapp to Miss Mollie A. A., daughter of Rev. B. F. Blow, of the Montgomery Conference.

Issue of April 2, 1869

In Meriwether co., Ga., at the residence of Mr. Noah Hamby, Jan. 27, 1869, by Rev. W. C. Lovejoy, Mr. B. F. McLaughlin to Miss Eliza Hamby.

On Thursday, March 25 by Rev. T. E. Wannamaker, Mr. A. Watson of Edgefield to Miss Annie R., daughter of Dr. W. W. Wannamaker, St. Matthews, S. C.

March 23, by Rev. J. M. Austin, in Thomasville, Ga., Mr. S. R. Robinson to Miss Julia E., daughter of Robt. R. Evans, deceased, all of Thomasville.

By Rev. J. W. Reynolds, March 18, Mr. C. A. Hardin of Barnesville, Ga., to Miss Elizabeth [sic] of Crawford co., Ga.

SOUTHERN CHRISTIAN ADVOCATE MARRIAGE NOTICES 1867-1878

In Cuthbert, Ga., March 11, 1869, by Rev. J. B. Owen, Mr. E. J. Lavina to Miss Mary A. Goodwin.

In Leon co., Fla., March 17, 1869, by Rev. A. J. Woldridge, Mr. J. Felkel to Mrs. Rebecca Barnes.

By Rev. J. E. Sentell, on March 10, 1869, Mr. J. H. Eason of Tatnall co., Ga., to Miss Sarah J. McCall of Liberty co., Ga.

By the same on March 16, 1869, Mr. Wm. A. Sheppard to Miss Mary J. L. Baggs, both of Liberty co., Ga.

On March 11, by the Rev. S. D. Clements, Mr. T. J. Taylor to Miss Ophelia A. Kimbrough, all of Harris co., Ga.

In Auraria, Ga., on 4th March 1869, by Rev. G. Hughes, Dr. J. E. Cobb of Dawsonville, Ga., to Miss Lizzie M. Wood of the former place.

In LaGrange, March 17, by Rev. P. A. Heard, Dr. G. B. Ridley to Miss M. E. Beall.

On March 4, by Rev. T. J. Rutledge, Mr. H. Pope of rome, Ga., to Miss Mittie Bilbro of Tuskegee, Ala.

Feb. 21, 1869, at Irish Grove, Mo., by Rev. J. M. Stokes, Mr. J. Turner of Atchison co., Mo., to Miss Mary J. Hewlett, late of Scriven co., Ga.

Issue of April 9, 1869

By the Rev. W. F. Easterling, March 4th 1869, Mr. Geo. Dawkins of Jefferson Co., Fla., and Miss Isabella Branch, of Leon.

On March 24th 1869, by Rev. W. F. Easterling, Mr. Wm. R. Taylor and Miss Sarah S. Skinner, both of Jefferson co., Fla.

On February 16th, by Rev. J. W. Shores, Mr. Alexander McBryde to Miss Celia Ann Clenny, all of Pike co., Ala.

In Fort Valley, by Rev. E. H. McGehee, on 25th March, Mr. J. B. Willis of Bibb co., and Miss Anna, daughter of Mr. Jno. M. Walden, of Fort Valley, Ga.

Issue of April 16, 1869

On April 6, 1869, near Thomaston, Ga., by Rev. J. R. Weaver, Mr. B. F. Lee of Crawford co., and Miss Mary C. Sandwich of the former place

On April 8, 1869, in Midway, Ga., by Rev. W. H. Potter, Saml. A. Cook, Esq., of Albany Ga., and Miss Anna M., daughter of Dr. Thos. F. Green.

In Colleton co., S. C., on 21st Jan. 1869 by Rev. J. L. Sifly, Mr. J. M. Wetsel and Miss Sue E. Wethers.

By the same in same co., S. C., on Feb. 3, 1869, D. A. Rumph and Miss Sallie J. Murray.

By same, in same co., on Feb. 11, 1869, Mr. P. Shuler and Miss Virginia G. Murrer.

By same in same co., on Feb. 16, 1869, Mr. Wm. Shider and Miss Maggie R. Dukes.

Issue of April 23, 1869

At the Methodist Church, in Marietta, Ga., April 7, 1869, by Rev. G. W. Yarbrough, H. A. Dunwody, Esqr., and Miss Hattie Morris.

By Rev. M. F. Malsby, Mr. G. W. M. Whitehead to Miss h. Williams, all of Social Circle, March 31, 1869.

Also, April 1st, Mr. J. O. Sheppard to Miss Mary Whitehead, all of Social Circle.

On the 13th of April, at the residence of Mr. John A. Cromartie, Miscosukie, Florida, by Rev. Dr. Leonard, Mr. B. Fuller Hart to Miss ellen Anna Dennis.

Near Clarksville, Ga., on 30th March 1869, by Rev. F. G. hughes, Mr. James J. Taylor to Miss Marietta Nix.

On the 15th inst., by Rev. R. H. Timmons, at the residence of Mrs. Wall, Thomas E. holmes to Mrs. E. A. Mackay, all of Carroll co., Ga.

On Wednesday, 31st March 1869, in LaGrange, Ga., by Rev. Wm. M. Cunningham, D. D., William J. Speer and Miss Geraldine Z., youngest daughter of Dr. John F. Moreland.

At Ansonville, N. C., March 23d, 1869, by the Rev. F. Milton Kennedy, Mr. Lewis James Williams of Yadkin co., to Miss Sallie Alie Smith of Ansonville.

Issue of April 30, 1869

In Elberton, Ga., by Rev. A. G. Worley on April 13, Rev. Wm. A. Florence of no. Ga. Conference and Mrs. Cornelia J. Jones of Elberton, Ga.

On April 15, 1869, by Rev. Wm. M. Crymes, R. C. Kennedy of Stewart co., Ga., to Mrs. Carrie Harp of Brooksville, Randolph co., Ga.

In Monroe co., Ga., April 15, 1869, by Rev. Wesley F. Smith, Mr. Henry G. Smith to Miss Nannie J. Wooten.

On Feb. 11, by Rev. W. F. Quillian, Mr. W. A. Quillian to Miss Clarissa M. Dean, both of White co., Ga.

Issue of May 7, 1869

On 22d of April 1869 by the Rev. Jno W. Kelly, Mr. C. L. Fike to Miss Mary A. Goodwin, all of Laurens District, S. C.

In Gadsden co., Fla., on the 27th April, 1869 by Rev. Dr. Leonard, Mr. Jesse A. Johnson to Miss Georgia A. Bowen.

Issue of May 14, 1869

On May 4, 1869, by Rev. I. L. Avant, Mr. F. Glazier to Miss Carrie E. W. Seago, youngest daughter of Rev. Wm. Seago, of Houston co., Ga.

By Rev. T. T. Christian, April 27, Mr. W. W. Kearing of Texas, to Miss Mary J. Davis, of Talbot co, Ga.

On April 27, by Rev. F. Auld, Mr. R. S. Goodgion to Miss Mary H., daughter of Capt. G. W. Sullivan, all of Laurens co, S. C.

By Rev. J. E. Sentell, April 2, 1869, Rev. Wm. M. Hayes of the So. Ga. Conf., to Miss Laura E. Hemstead, formerly of St. Marys, now of Darien, Ga.

On April 13 at Farmington, Ga., by Rev. W. R. Branham, Mr. J. W. Hinton of Oxford, Ga., to Miss Lula, daughter of Dr. Price of the former place.

April 15, 1869 at the residence of E. S. Price, Esq., by Rev. R. S. Dagnall, Mr. T. N. Price Jr. of Richland and Miss Carrie A. Rice of Barnwell, S. C.

On March 4, 1869, by the same, Mr. R. Bishop of Richland to Mrs. Sarah Dawkins of Kershaw, S. C.

March 14, 1869, by same, Mr. D. Hays to Miss Lou Shirah, all of Kershaw, S. C.

March 14, 1869 by same, Mr. Henry C. Wilson to Miss Mary L. Watts, all of Fairfield, S. C.

In Bartow co., by Rev. J. L. Pierce, Thursday, April 22, J. K. Ward to Miss Fanie Ward.

In Gadsden co., Fla., May 6, 1869, by Rev. Dr. Leonard, Mr. S. W. Sadler to Miss Sabena F. Newberry.

By Rev. T. A. Seals, at the residence of the bride's father, Mr. S. D. Mayes to Miss S. F. Brinkley, on morning of the 4th inst., all of Warren co., Ga.

Issue of May 21, 1869

March 16th 1869, By Rev. James P. dePass, Mr. G. Crawford Mattox to Miss Sue V. Henry, all of Columbia co., Fla.

By the same, May 6th 1869, Mr. Alexander Dudly of Savannah, Ga., to Miss Martha J. Watkins, of Baker co., Fla.

In Savannah, Ga., April 22nd 1869, by Rev. Geo. G. N. MacDonell, Mr. Dallas M. Bennett to Miss Anna Maria Holland.

By the same, April 26th 1869, Mr. Seaborn H. Wade to Miss Mary A. Thompson, daughter of Col. W. T. and Mrs. Caroline Thompson of Savannah, Ga.

In Sumter, S. C., on the 4th inst., by the Rev. Henry M. Mood, Mr. Wm. H. Lockwood of Marion, S. C., to Miss Laura M. Hill, formerly of Waterford, Miss.

May 13th at the bride's father's, Appling co., Ga., by Rev. W. M. Kennedy, Mr. Daniel Bateman to Miss Jane Whitehead, all of Appling county.

By Rev. J. H. D. McRae, at Way Key, Fla., April 1st, Mr. W. H. McRary and Miss Anne E. Burns.

On the 6th inst., by Rev. D. D. Cox, Mr. Milton Young, formerly of Augusta, Ga., to Miss virginia Parade, of Savannah, Ga.

On the 11th May, by Rev. T. J. Rutledge, Rev. Geo. R. Lynch of Wetumpka, Ala., to Miss Mary E. Bedell, of Auburn, Ala.

Issue of May 28, 1869

On 20th inst., by Rev. Wm. Martin, Mr. M. M. Wolfe of Charlotte, N. C., to Miss Hattie A., daughter of Capt. Rufus D. Senn of Columbia, S. C.

On May 12, at the residence of the bride's father, by Rev. Jas. O. Vernon, Maj. M. Bell of Atlanta, to Miss Mary C. Cox of Banks co., Ga.

May 20, by Jno. W. Reynolds at the residence of C. W. Fouche, Esq., Mr. S. M. Duke of Griffin to Miss Mary A. Truitt of Barnesville, Ga.

In Taylor co., on the 9th inst., by Rev. R. F. Williamson, Mr. W. C. Carter to Miss Jane T. Speer, all of Taylor co.

May 4, by Rev. G. E. Smith, J. W. Turner, of No. Ga. Conf., to Miss Mary J. Hunnicutt of Coweta co., Ga.

Issue of June 4, 1869

On 16th May by Rev. R. B. G. Walters, Mr. W. G. Webb and Miss Mary Harrison, all of Washington co., Ga.

By the same, on 27th May, Mr. James F. Freeman of Wilkinson co., Ga., to Miss Mary F. Moye, of Johnson co., Ga.

May 26th, 1869, by Rev. H. H. Parks, Rev. W. P. Kramer of the No. Ga. Conference to Miss Janie F. Mobley, daughter of Hon. Saml. Mobley, of Floyd co., Ga.

May 6th by Rev. D. O'Driscoll, Mr. Emory Jefferson and Miss Caroline McLester, both of Chattahoochee co., Ga.

By Rev. J. J. Workman, May 23d, 1869, Mr. Russell C. Johnson and Miss Sallie A. P. Gambrell, all of Anderson co., S. C.

In Green co., May 30th ,by Rev. Thos. F. Pierce, Mr. Wm. Massey, of Wiltshire, England, to Miss Sarah Ann Randall.

Issue of June 11, 1869

In Crawford co., Ga., June 1st 1869, by Rev. I. L. Avant, Mr. A. H. Barnes to Miss Fannie, second daughter of Samuel Low, all of Crawford co., Ga.

In LaGrange, Ga., June 1st, 1869, by Rev. R. W. Bigham, Mr. J. M. Tomlinson and Miss Addie Bull, daughter of the late Hon. O. A. Bull.

On 26th ult., by Rev. S. S. Sweet, Mr. J. F. Bates and Miss Eugenia Herrington, of Burke co.

In Hawkinsville, on 3d inst., by Rev. Chas. R. Jewett, Mr. J. L. Bohannon and Miss Sallie E., daughter of Judge C. M. Bozeman, all of Pulaski co., Ga.

By Rev. H. H. Parks, 26th of May at Judge Mobley's near Rome, Ga., Rev. Wm. P. Kramer of the North Ga. Conference and Miss Janie E. Mobley.

Issue of June 18, 1869

Near Athens, Ga., on the 23d May last, by Rev. C. A. Evans, Rev. Amicus W. Williams of North Ga. Conference to Miss Alice C. Nance of Clarke co.

In Athens, June 3rd, by Rev. C. A. Evans, Col. J. d. Matthews of Lexington, to Miss Sarah Emma Mitchell, of the former place.

On the 6th inst., by Rev. Morgan Callaway, Mr. Alphonso T. Strother to Miss Georgia Holliday, both of Lincoln co.

On the 27th May, by Rev. R. F. Jones, Mr. J. B. Goodwyn of Coweta, and Miss Cattie Pope of Merriwether co., Ga.

By Rev. F. F. Reynolds, at his residence, June 3rd 1869, Mr. Louis Witkowski to Miss Mary G. Daniels, all of Bethany, Ga.

On 27th April 1869 by Rev. G. H. Round, Mr. G. W. Cochran to Miss Laura E. Puett, all of Caldwell county, N. C.

In Jackson co., Fla., on the 27th ult., by Rev. W. Rothchild Talley, Mr. Charlie Knowles to Miss Bettie Baxter.

On the 3rd of June, by Rev. J. T. Ainsworth, Mr. Ambrose P. Hilliard to Mrs. elizabeth K. Heath, both of Mitchell co., Ga.

In Augusta, Ga., June 2nd, 1869, at the residence of Dr. Jas. Milligan, by Rev. W. H. Clarke, Mr. Henry L. Graves, of Newton co., Ga., to Miss Henrietta D. Killigan.

Issue of June 25, 1869

In Oglethorpe co, Ga., by Rev. T. A. Harris, June 3, 1869, Mr. C. Jacks to Miss Janie Brightwell, both of said county.

By Rev. A. Nettles, June 13, 1869, Mr. C. Mickler to Mrs. Caroline Bickley, all of Lexington, S. C.

By Rev. H. Tyler, June 13, 1869, Rev. Jas. B. Scarborough to Mrs. P. W. Cheak, both of Madison co., Ga.

In Monticello, Ga., June 9, at the residence of Dr. W. D. Maddux, by Rev. M. W. Arnold, Mr. A. M. Robinson, formerly of Newborn, Ga., to Miss Jennie Maddux, both of this place.

Issue of July 2, 1869

In Charleston, S. C., June 1st, 1869, by the Rev. J. Mercer Green, Mr. William H. Cox to Miss Mary A. Robinson, both of Charleston, S. C.

Issue of July 9, 1869

By Rev. W. J. Cotter on 1st July, Mr. W. A. Post and Miss S. G. Arnold, all of Grantville, Ga.

On June 16, at the residence of Wm. Johnson, Esq., by Rev. Wm. C. Bass, Mr. J. D. Drew of Houston co., Ga., and Miss Mary F. Howard of Bibb co., Ga.

In Thomasville, Ga., June 30, by Rev. J. M. Austin, Mr. J. T. Pittman to Miss Mary A. Denson, all of Thomasville.

Issue of July 16, 1869

On 5th inst., at Smithville, Ga., by Rev. Chas. R. Jewett, Mr. J. A. R. Bennett of Macon, Ga., to Mrs. Florence Maudeville of the former place.

On the evening of the 8th inst., by Rev. W. C. Bass, Mr. J. W. Hancock to Miss Julia E. Ives, both of Bibb co., Ga.

On July 8, in Bibb co., by Rev. J. Blakely Smith, Mr. A. S. McGregor to Miss Frances D. Jones.

Issue of July 23, 1869

On July 1st, by Rev. A. L. Smith, Mr. Jno. B. Sample of Abbeville District and Miss Mary A. Boulware of Laurens District, S. C.

Issue of July 30, 1869

On July 14, 1869, near Grooversville, By Rev. J. W. Talley, Mr. C. D. Groover to Miss Alice C. Joiner, all of Brooks co., Ga.

On the 30th inst., by Rev. S. S. Sweet, Wm. R. Miller, Esq., and Miss Fannie H. Williams, all of Burke co., Ga.

SOUTHERN CHRISTIAN ADVOCATE MARRIAGE NOTICES 1867-1878

Issue of August 6, 1869

In Baldwin co., Ga., July 21, 1869, by the Rev. J. V. M. Morris, Mr. A. F. Bayne to Miss Bettie H. Singleton, of Midway.

Issue of August 20, 1869

In Campbell co., Ga., by Rev. Geo. W. Yarbrough, July 20th, 1869, Mr. J. M. Gorman and Miss Ophelia M. Austell.

In Brooks co., Ga., July 15th, by Rev. O. L. Smith, D. D., Mr. Samuel A. Graves and Miss Fannie E. Perdue.

In Columbia co., Ga., August 5th, by Rev. R. A. Cannon, Mr. George Dermond to Miss Amanda V. Jones, daughter of Mitchel Jones, all of the former place.

Issue of August 27, 1869

On 17th Aug., by Rev. W. M. Watts, F. G. Hodges, of Bullock co., to Miss Martha E. Byrd, of Taylor's Creek, Liberty co., Ga.

On 12th Aug., 1869, Mr. Malachi Key to Miss sallie E. Whitlow, all of Warrior Stand, Ala.

Issue of September 17, 1869

In Monticello, Ga., Sept. 1st, by Rev. D. Kelsey, Mr. Wm. A. Reid to Miss Agnes Broddus, daughter of Dr. C. Broddus, Monticello, Ga.

In Decatur, Ga., Sept. 21, 1869, by Rev. W. H. Clarke, Maj. W. H. Howard and Miss Sallie Avary, daughter of Dr. J. C. Avary.

On 7th Sept., by Rev. A. M. Thigpen, Mr. James s. Baker and Miss Nannie Stone, all of West Point, Ga.

On 25th August, by Rev. John R. Parker, Rev. John H. Mashburn, of the North Ga. Conference, to Mrs. Nancy M. Butler, of Gainesville, Ga.

On 2d Sept. 1869, at the residence of the bride's father, Mr. A. Hague, by the Rev. E. S. Tyner, Mr. F. P. Thomas and Miss Fanie P. Hague, daughter of Mr. A. Hague, all of Alachua co., Fla.

Issue of September 24, 1869

In the Methodist church at Talbotton, Ga., Sept. 8, by Rev. Thos. T. Christian, Capt. S. w. Thornton, of Talbot co., and Miss Julia Weeks, daughter of Judge W. J. Weeks, of Talbotton, Ga.

On Sept. 5, in Columbia co., Ga., by Rev. R. A. Conner, Rev. B. K. Benson of the N. Ga. Conference, to Mrs. Mary A. Basford of the former place.

On Aug 22d, by Rev. L. P. Neese, H. W. Leazer to Miss Lucinda F. Harman, both of Floyd co., Ga.

Issue of October 1, 1869

On the 9th Sept., in Spalding co., by the Rev. D. E. Starr, Mr. S. H. Nipper of Henry co., to Mrs. Kittie Perdue.

Issue of October 8, 1869

On Sept. 16 by Rev. A. R. Danner, Mr. E. D. Patrick to Miss Julia C. Knight, all of Charleston co.

By the same on 23d Sept. Mr. John Nettles to Miss Frances Patrick, all of Charleston co.

On Sept 23d, 1869, by Rev. W. S. Black, S. G. Major to Miss Elisa Carter, all of Abbeville District, S. C.

By Rev. F. B. Davies, on Sept. 16, at the residence of Mr. Augustus A. Davis, Dr. T. R. Kendall, of Upson co., and Mrs. Julia F. Thomas, of Monroe co,. Ga.

In Richmond co., Ga., at the residence of the bride's father, on Sept. 23d, by Rev. W. Ewing Johnston, Dr. J. T. Seago to Miss Mattie L. Brown, all of Richmond co.

On Sept. 23d, 1869 in Wilkinson co., Ga., by Rev. C. W. Smith, Mr. W. H. Fitzpatrick to Miss Lizzie Massey.

Also on 3d Oct., 1869 by the same, Mr. L. M. Harmon of Putnam co., to Mrs. E. F. Lisenby of Wilkinson co.

Issue of October 15, 1869

By Rev. A. J. Dean, Sept. 14th, 1869, Dr. Elbert Peacock of Bainbridge, Ga., to Mrs. Delia P. Crawford, of Decatur county, Ga.

By Rev. A. J. Dean, Sept. 30th, 1869, Mr. A. Brown to Miss C. A. Whitaker, both of Decatur co., Ga.

On the 5th inst., by Rev. T. J. Rutledge, Mr. Thos. H. Clower of Auburn, Ala., to Miss Georgia A. Bedell, of Columbus, Ga.

By Rev. M. S. Andrews, near Auburn, Ala., Aug. 12th, Mr. Thomas S. Phillips of Loacapeka, to Miss G. C. Lamar, daughter of Dr. W. H. Lamar.

On the 7th of Oct. 1869, by the Rev. J. J. Morgan, Dr. Harris Fisher to Miss Julia E. Guyton, all of Laurens co., Ga.

Issue of October 22, 1869

On Sept. 30, by Rev. D. O'Driscoll, Mr. Julius Shipp and Miss Mollie Hewell, both of Cusseta, Ga.

In Jefferson co., Ga., on Oct. 6, 1869, by Rev. H. d. Murphy, Mr. W. H. Fay to Mrs. Julia Rhenet, daughter of Rev. N. A. Hayles.

On the 7th inst., by P. A. Brewster, Mr. J. N. Simpson to Miss S. M. Taylor, all of Cherokee co., Georgia.

Issue of October 29, 1869

By Rev. W. A. Gamewell, Oct. 3d, 1869, Mr. A. B. Mulligan of Charleston, S. C., to Miss Florence C. Idest, daughter of Jno. B. Archer of Spartanburg, S. C.

Rev. J. J. Workman, Oct. 10th 1869 at Rocky Creek Baptist Church, Mr. Geo. W. Bramblett of Williamston, S. C., to Miss Sallie L. Walker, of Greenville, S. C.

By the same Oct. 13th 1869 at Ebenezer M. E. Church, South, Thos. R. League, M. D., to Miss Anna Crighton, all of Greenville county, S. C.

In Wilkinson co., Ga., at Jos. N. Meadors', Esq., on the 24th Oct., by Rev. C. B. Anderson, Rev. Jesse Peacock to Miss Marietta R. Anderson, of Forsyth co., N. C.

SOUTHERN CHRISTIAN ADVOCATE MARRIAGE NOTICES 1867-1878

In Columbia, S. C., October 20, 1869, the Rev. P. J. Shand, Mr. John L. Root to Miss Cornelia Loomis, all of the above named place.

Issue of November 5, 1869

By Rev. E. H. McGehee in Fort Valley, Mr. Duncan McNeill of Sumter co., Ga., and Miss Margaret A. Sloan, of the former place.

By Rev. A. J. Dean, Oct. 19, 1869, T. J. Thompson of Bainbridge, Ga., to Miss Catharine Nichalson of Decatur Co., Ga.

By same, Oct. 19, 1869, M. W. Bates of Decatur co., Ga., to Miss F. A. Crawford of Bainbridge, Ga.

In Macon, Ga., on 21st ult., by Rev. W. C. Bass, Mr. James H. Campbell and miss fannie, only daughter of Maj. D. E. Blount, all of Macon, Ga.

On the evening of the 26th ult., at the residence of the bride's father, by Rev. W. F. Robison, Mr. Richard L. Stapler and Miss Fannie Rawls, daughter of Judge Daniel Rawls, all of Hawkinsville, Ga.

Issue of November 12, 1869

On the 2d inst., at Col. Wm. J. Anderson's in Fort Valley, by Rev. Chas. R. Jewett, Dr. R. T. Persons and Miss Mary Barry.

By the same at the same time, Col. E. M. Brown and Miss Mattie Barry.

On 28 October, 1869, by Rev. Amos Johnson, Mr. George W. johnston, to Miss Sarah A. Benton, all of Warren co., Ga.

On the 14th Oct., near Greenwood, by Rev. H. P. Waugh, Mr. Jacob V. Dansby of Selma, Ala., to Mrs. Eliza E. Cravey, of Jackson co., Fla.

On the evening of the 21st Oct., by the same, and at the same place, Mr. Junius Rawls to Miss Statira A. Watts, all of Jackson co., Fla.

At the residence of and by Rev. W. C. Lovejoy, Mr. L. D. F. Rosser to Miss Leonora Freeman, all of Merriwether co., Ga.

In Alachua circuit, East. Fla., 30th Sept., by Rev. E. L. King, his second son, E. Lawrence King and Miss M. P. Moore, daughter of Dr. T. W. Moore of Chester District, S. C.

Oct. 12th, by Rev. A. M. Wynn, Mr. Wm. A. Willingham, of Forsyth, and Mrs. Mary J. Woodruff, daughter of Dr. M. Woodruff of Columbus, Ga.

By Rev. J. Chambers, Oct. 20th, Mr. G. W. C. Jones of Milton co., Ga., to Miss Fannie D. Smith of Alpharetta.

In Eatonton, Ga., on the 28th Oct., by Rev. W. P. Kramer, Mr. W. S. Reid to Miss Mary B., daughter of B. F. Adams, Esq., of Eatonton.

By the Rev. J. E. Sentell, on the 26th of Sept. 1869, Mr. B. Darsey to Mrs. L E. Harnage, all of Liberty co., Ga.

October 27th 1869 by Rev. D. R. McWilliams, Mr. Robert E. Hendry of Harris co., Ga., and Miss Anna E. Hightower, of Stewart co., Ga.

At Pacific Methodist College, Vacaville, Sunday, Oct. 10th 1869 by Bishop E. M. Marvin, Mr. L. E. Burgstiner of Sanel, to Miss Mary E. Thomas, of Vacaville, formerly of Oxford, Ga.

Issue of November 19, 1869

By Rev. J. J. Singleton on Nov. 3, 1869, Mr. M. C. Gay of Newton co., to Miss Julia L. Bryan of Oxford, Ga.

By Rev. Madison S. Hamilton on the evening of Oct. 28, at the bride's residence in Jefferson co., Ark., the Hon. James A. Hudson and Mrs. Mary E. Ingrum.

Oct. 28, 1869, by Rev. E. D. Dashiel, Mr. Bond E. Chrietzberg to Miss Belle P. Perkins, both of Chappel Hill, Texas.

On Oct. 14, 1869, by the Rev. Dr. Y. M. Farabee, Mr. A. S. Peters to Miss Sarah J. Pemberton, all of Sumter co., Fla.

Oct. 28, by W. W. Stewart, Mr. Hardy Woodall of Talbot co., to Miss Emma, daughter of Bushrod Johnson of Houston co, Ga.

At Lake City, Fla., by Rev. J. H. D. McRae, Mr. L. B. Trask of Savannah, Ga., and Miss M. E. Kennedy of Lake City, on Oct. 16, 1869.

By Rev. D. O'Driscoll, Nov. 8, 1869, Mr. James Wright of Marion co., Ga., and Miss Martha Haynes of Stewart co., Ga.

On Nov 1, by Rev. J. H. Kilpatrick, Dr. J. B. Moore and Miss Mary Eley, daughter of John H. Eley, Esqr., all of Greene co., Ga.

On the morning of Nov 11, by Rev. T. J. Rutledge, Rev. S. D. Clements of So. Ga. Conference, Albany Station, to Miss Fredonia C. Dozier of Muscogee co., Ga.

By Rev. R. J. Harwell, Mr. S. P. Kenny to Miss N. E. Jackson, Sept. 16, 1869, all of Clarke co., Ga.

By Rev. J. Chambers in Cobb co., Mr. J. A. Garrison of Milton to Miss Nancy Keplen.

By Rev. H. P. Pitchford, 9th inst., Mr. Jas. N. Mathews to Miss Ophelia, daughter of Wm. Houghton, deceased, all of Harris co., Ga.

By the same, 10th inst., Mr. Steven J. Pearson to Miss Mary, daughter of --- Mathews, deceased, all of Harris co., Ga.

Issue of November 26, 1869

In the Methodist Church in Talbotton, Ga., on the 15th inst., by Rev. Thos. T. Christian, Dr. Wesley F. Tignor of Columbus, Ga., to Miss Eliza M. Cottingham, of Talbotton, Ga.

By Rev. J. R. Little, Oct. 28th near Cross Hill, Dr. E. T. McSwain to Miss Janie, eldest daughter of Capt. J. J. McGowan, all of Laurens, S. C.

Nov. 3d, 1869, by Rev. F. Milton Kennedy, Mr. W. A. Rose of Fayetteville, N. C., to Miss Emma Barrett, of Anson co., N. C.

By the same, Nov. 9th, Dr. Joseph H. Foster to Miss Lottie Brown, all of Lancaster, S. C.

Nov. 7th, by Rev. W. T. Capers, Mr. Charles C. Smith to Miss Irene, eldest daughter of Dr. B. C. Hart, all of Cokesbury, S. C.

On Nov. 11th 1869, by Rev. B. E. L. Timmons, Mr. Oscar Lee and Miss Jennie Jenkins, of Muscogee co., Ga.

On the 11th Nov., by the Rev. A. W. Harris, Dr. Jas. W. Talley, of Mill Town, to Miss M. Holtzendorf, of Stockton, Ga.

On 9th Nov., 1869 by Rev. W. W. Tidwell, Mr. William H. Bledsoe to Miss Camilla Green, all of Macon co., Ga.

Also on the 11th, by the same, Mr. George A. Potter, of Taylor co., to Miss Sophronia Dixon, of Macon co., Ga.

Oct. 20th, by Rev. A. M. Wynn, Mr. Wm. B. Moore to Miss Susan Long, both of Columbus, Ga.

By the same, Nov. 2d, near Columbus, Ga., Mr. B. L. Kimbrough to Miss Mary Havillah Pace.

By the same, Nov. 4th, Mr. Alexander A. Pacetty to Miss Ella S. Snow.

By the same, Nov. 11th,Mr. Thomas Chapman to Mrs. Anna E. Thomas, both of Columbus, Ga.

Issue of December 3, 1869

In Talbotton, on the 16th Nov., by Rev. T. T. Christian, Dr. Wesley F. Tignor, of Columbus, Ga., to Miss Eliza M. Cottingham, daughter of Jas. D. Cottingham, of Talbotton, Ga.

At Timmonsville, by Rev. J. R. Little, Nov. 28th, 1869, Mr. F. L. Liles, formerly of Lancaster co., to Miss H. E. Hayes, of Cheraw, S. C.

On Marshallville, Ga.,2 on Nov. 23, by Rev. W. C. Bass, Marshall J. Hatcher, Esq., of Columbus, Ga., and Miss V. Hammie, only daughter of W. H. Felton, Esq., of the former place.

On Oct. 31, by Rev. R. F. Jones, Mr. T. G. Alexander of Atlanta, and Miss Sallie A. Williams, of Meriwether co., Ga.

By Rev. H. P. Pitchford, Nov. 16, Mr. Benj. A. Clark of Muscogee co., Ga., to Miss A. D., daughter of Mr. Joseph Miller, of Harris co., Ga.

On Nov. 2nd, in Burke co., Ga., by Rev. N. B. Ousley, Mr. R. M. Cook of Augusta, to Mrs. R. A. Hudson.

On Nov. 17, by Rev. N. B. Ousley, Mr. Edward A. Carter to Miss S. Augusta Lawson, all of Burke co., Ga.

By Rev. J. M. Austin, nov. 17, Mr. John M. Stephens of Thomasville, to Miss Janie F. Mitchell of Thomas co., Ga.

On Nov. 23d, by Rev. D. L. Branning, Mr. N. B. Ivey, formerly of Wilmington, N. C., to Miss Susan A., daughter of Judge Ozias Budington, of Middleburg, Fla.

On Nov. 4, 1869, by Rev. Jas. C. Stoll, Mr. Arnold Livingston, to Miss Laura, second daughter of Rev. T. J. Mellard, all of Charleston co., S. C.

By Rev. W. P. Pledger in Butts co., Ga., Nov. 21st, 1869, John D. Dumble, Esq., to Mrs. Martha E. Goddard, daughter of Mrs. Wilkinson.

By the same, at the same time and place, Mr. William M. Harben to Miss Lucia Wilkinson.

On Sept. 15, by Rev. A. J. Cauthen, Mr. T. G. Wade of Lancaster to Miss A. M. Bookter, of Richland District, S. C.

By the same, Nov. 23, Mr. G. W. Gibson to Miss Marion, eldest daughter of Dr. T. R. Center, all of Fairfield District, S. C.

Issue of December 10, 1869

On Dec. 2nd, by Rev. J. M. Bonnell, D. D., Mr. Geo. F. Wing to Miss Ocie Anna G. Heath, eldest daughter of J. F. Heath, all of Macon.

At the residence of Augustus Reid, Esq., in Troup co., Ga., Nov. 25th, by Rev. R. W. Bigham, Mr. J. T. O'Neale of Russel co., Ala., and Miss Sidney Reid, daughter of the late Hon. Sam'l Reid, of Troup.

Also by the same, Nov. 30th, in LaGrange, Ga., Mr. B. H. Whitfield and Miss Eliza H. Stone.

On the evening of the 25th Nov., by Rev. M. F. Malsby, Mr. J. w. Garrett to Miss M. E. Butler, all of Social Circle, Ga.

On the 25th Nov. 1869, at the Methodist church at Talbotton, the Rev. Thos. T. Christian, Mr. Thos. E. Fell and Miss Amanda F. Harvey, all of Talbotton.

In Burke co., on the 25th Nov., by Rev. T. B. Lanier, Mr. Godfrey DeGilsey Etta, of New Orleans, to Miss Eugenia C. Barton, of Burke co., Ga.

On 25th Nov., by Rev. W. M. Watts, Mr. J. A. Sheftell to Savannah, to Miss R. A. Wilkins, of Effingham co, Ga.

By the same, on the 1st Dec., Mr. J. R. Rahn to Miss A. E. Shearouse, all of Whitesville, Ga.

On 25th Nov. 1869 by Rev. R. R. Gadnall, Mr. F. A. Koon to Miss Ida Z., third daughter of G. W. and Jane R. Smith, all of Richland co, S. C.

In Colleton, S. C., on the 25th Nov 1869, by Rev. L. Wood, Mr. Aaron S. Varn to Miss Emma E. Wingard.

On Nov. 21st, at the residence of H. C. Merritt, Esq., of Henry co., Rev. W. P. Rivers, Dr. Jno. R. Price, to Miss Laura R. Turner.

By the Rev. Jno. H. Harris, Nov. 16th, Mr. Jno. T. Nash and Miss Eliza L. Clinton, all of Henry co,. Ga.

By the same, Nov. 18th, Mr. Silas Oglesby, of Henry co. and Miss Mittie Brown of McDonough, Henry co., Ga.

By the same, Nov. 25th at the residence of Judge Q. R. Nolan, McDonough, Ga., Capt. W. T. Evans of Ringgold, Ga., and Miss Mattie A. Nolan, of Morgan co., Ga.

On the 14th Nov., by Rev. E. H. Giles, Mr. Thomas Davis and Miss Alice Evans, all of Marion co., Fla.

By Rev. Joseph M. Gable, Nov. 7th 1869, Mr. W. G. Self to Miss A. Pitts, both of Cobb co., Ga.

By the same, Nov. 23d, Rev. E. P. Gaines of Cobb co., Ga., to Mrs. Mary A. Sharp, daughter of W. Oslin, of Coosa co., Ala.

By the same, Nov. 25th, Mr. E. W. Gillham to Miss S. E. McKee, both of Cobb co., Ga.

Issue of December 17, 1869

On Nov 26, by Rev. Wm. W. Mood, Mr. James K. Neatherry of Franklin co., Ga., to Miss Bell, daughter of Dr. T. J. Roach, of Columbia, S. C.

On Dec 9, by the same, Mr. Joseph B. Ballew of Laurens, S. C., to Miss Cattie, daughter of Mr. Joseph A. C. Gruber of Columbia, S. C.

On 23d Nov., by Rev. W. E. Jones, Mr. A. P. Jones to Miss Lena Miller, all of Harris co., Ga.

On 23d Nov, by Rev. T. E. Wannamaker, Mr. J. A. Laws to Miss Sallie Paulling, all of St. Matthews, S. C.

By the same, Nov 25, Mr. James Moss to Miss Maggie Holman, all of Orangeburg, S. C.

By the same, Dec. 3d, Mr. Wm. T. Rives to Mrs. M. A. Butler, all of St. Matthews, S. C.

In Lumpkin co., Ga., on 2d Dec. 1869, by Rev. G. Hughes, Capt. John W. Owen, of Banks co., Ga., to Miss Lucy Smith, of said county.

On Nov. 18, by Rev. Wm. G. Pritchard, Rev. Robt. F. Mountain of the Montgomery Conference, to Miss Mary A. Woods, of Tallapoosa co., Ala.

On Dec. 14, 1869, by Rev. C. W. Smith, Thomas J. Hunt, of Talbot co., Ga., to Miss Mary L. Butts, of Macon, Ga.

Issue of December 24, 1869

On the 9th December, by Rev. Isaac C. Harris, Mr. John Dobbins to Mrs. P. A. Carmichael, all of Adam's Station, Ga.

By Rev. R. W. Dixon, in Macon county, Ga., November 25th 1869, John I. Hudson, of Americus, Ga., to Miss Emma C. Hicks, of Macon county, Ga.

By the same in Sumter county, Ga., December 14th, Emmette M. Gruson, to Miss Meily M. Hooks, all of Sumter county, Ga.

On December 14th, by Rev. John M. Bowden, Mr. John J. Barfield, to Miss Martha A. L. McGehee, all of Campbell county, Ga.

In Fort Valley, on the 14th December, by Rev. S. H. J. Sistrunk, Mr. Jacob C. Slappey and Miss Stella, daughter of Maj. Sterling Neal, of Fort Valley.

By Rev. Atticus G. Haygood, at Trinity Church, on the evening of the 18th Nov., Mr. J. I. Miller and Miss Sallie A., youngest daughter of Capt. Lovick P. Thomas, all of Atlanta.

By the same, Dec. 2d, Rev. W. A. Dodge of the North Georgia Conference, and Mrs. Marietta Chandler, daughter of Zachariah Jones, Esq., of DeKalb county.

On the 15th Dec., by Rev. J. T. Ainsworth, Mr. H. B. Ainsworth, of Thomasville, Ga., to Miss Permelia Evritte, of Thomas co., Ga.

On 23d Nov., by Rev. S. D. Clements, Mr. Thos. W. Glaze, of Sumter co., and Miss Fannie Miller, of Dougherty co., Ga.

On the 14th Dec., by the same, Mr. Jno. F. E. McKay, of Florida, and Miss Mary Copeland, of Harris co., Ga.

On 23d Nov., by Rev. H. F. Jones, at the same time and place, Mr. R. P. Rosser and Miss Alice Lee. Also, Mr. H. J. Hightower and Miss Fannie Lee, all of Meriwether co., Ga.

On the 16th Dec., by Rev. Rev. L. C. Peek, Mr. Wesley A. Pue and Miss Rebecca F. Jordan,all of Thomas co., Ga.

On the 18th Nov. 1869, by the Rev. Dr. J. M. Farabee, Mr. John L. Peters to Miss Martha L. Pemberton, all of Sumter co., Fla.

At Cave Springs, Ga., Nov. 16th, 1869, by Rev. J. F. Mixon, Mr. Jas. R. Barber, Esq., of Cedartown, Ga., to Miss Lou Wood, all of the former place.

On the 6th Dec., 1869, by Rev. C. P. Murdoch, Mr. A. L. Gilbert of Atlanta, Ga., to Miss K. M. Livingston, of Putnam co., Fla.

On the 7th inst., in Hancock co., by Rev. J. Lewis, Mr. T. C. Turner to Miss A. B. Mason.

By Rev. W. J. Cotter on the 21st inst., Mr. Thos. E. Zellers to Miss Ella C. Moreland, all of Grantville, Ga.

Issue of January 7, 1870

By Rev. John Calvin Johnson, 16th December, Mr. H. T. Elder to Miss S. A. Marshall. All of Clark county, Ga.

By same, 19th December, Mr. J. G. Southerland, to Miss M. S. Whitehead. All of Clark county, Ga.

On December 26th, by Rev. W. F. Roberts, Mr. J. L. Roberts of Jefferson county, Fla., to Miss Mattie J. Tarpley, of Irwinton, Ga., daughter of the late Edward J. Tarpley.

By J. T. Payne, on the 2d inst., J. L. Willis, Esq., of Dawson, Ga., to Mrs. Hettie Dennis, of Americus, Ga.

On 28th December 1869, by Rev. Wm. A. Parks, Capt. J. A. Terell, of Dadeville, Ala., to Miss G. A. Bonner, daughter of Judge Z. bonner, of Carroll county, Ga.

On the 16th, by Rev. F. M. T. Brannon, H. C. Jones to Miss Adrian Davis. All of Troup county, Ga.

By the same on the 23d December, S. A. Johnson to Mrs. E. C. Johnson. All of Troup county, Ga.

On 30th December 1869, by Rev. W. E. Johnston, Mr. A. E. Burch, to Miss M. J. McDade. All of Richmond county.

In Charleston county, S. C., December 7, 1869, by Rev. J. C. Stoll, Mr. L. C. Mellard to Miss Mattie C. Clark.

By the same, on 26th December, Mr. John Myers, to Miss Etenona, daughter of L. C. Myers, all of Orangeburg county, S. C.

On 23d December 1869, by Rev. J. W. Simmons, Dr. B. F. Coleman, to Miss Statie, daughter of Dr. Lewe Sessions, of Union Springs, Ala.

In Upson county, Ga., November 25th, by Rev. D. Kelsey, Mr. C. A. Black to Miss E. P. Holloway.

On 23d December 1869, by Rev. Amos Johnson, Mr. J. R. Johnson to Miss S. A. Hughes. All of Warren county, Ga.

On the 22d December, by Rev. J. T. Ainsworth, Z. J. Arthur to Miss Mary Harrison. Both of Mitchell county, Ga.

By the same on 23d December, Rev. Wesley Lane, of the South Georgia Conference, to Miss M. E. McKinnon, of Thomas county.

By Rev. A. G. Worley, on December 9, 1869, Mr. L. R. Johnson to Miss F. S. Butler.

By the same on December 15th 1869, Mr. F. O. Baily, to Miss F. C. H. Brown. All of Elbert county, Ga.

By Rev. U. G. Tigner, November 23d, Mr. T. F. Johnson of Atlanta, to Miss M. E. Gilmer, of Talbot county.

On 22d December 1869 by Rev. John W. McRoy, Mr. B. A. Jeter, of Unionville, S. C., to Miss M. S. Hill of Union county, S. C.

In Perry by the Rev. W. knox, December 21st, 1869, Mr. A. H. Fry, to Miss Katie Cox.

On December 15th, 1869 in Gadsden county, Fla., by Rev. A. J. Dean, Mr. W. P. Sims of Bainbridge, Ga. to Miss E. C. Nicholson, of the former place.

At Lofton's Church, in Jefferson county, Ga., on the 26th inst., by the Rev. W. A. Hayles, Mr. Wm. Arnold to Mrs. M. E. Pugeley. All of Jefferson county.

On the 23d December, 1869 by Rev. W. M. Watts, Mr. J. J. Martin to Miss E. E. Swindle. All of Liberty county, Ga.

On the same day by the same, Mr. M. F. Stubbs of Tatnall county, to Miss F. M. Stephens, of Liberty county, Ga.

In Meriwether county, Ga., December 19th 1869 by Rev. Henry J. Ellis, Mr. Z. P. Lee to Miss W. E. Rosser.

In Louisville, Ga., on the 15th December 1869 by Rev. H. d. Murphy, Mr. W. J. Pierce to Miss F. M. Kelley. Both of Jefferson county.

Issue of January 14, 1870

Dec. 14, at the residence of the bride's father, by Rev. C. A. Crowell, Mr. Gilford E. Bell of Columbus, Ga., and Miss Louisa M. Crymes, adughter of Rev. W. M. Crymes, of Weston, Ga.

Dec. 16, by the same, at the residence of the bride's father, Mr. Wm. J. Hayes of Randolph co., Ga., and Miss Louisiana Mulkey, daughter of Rev. H. V. Mulkey, of Terrell co., Ga.

Dec 23d, by the same, at the residence of the bride's father, Mr. Edwin Scoville of Macon, Ga., and Miss Susan E. Hoyl, of Dawson, Terrell co., Ga., only daughter of Rev. Thos. I. Hoyl.

Dec. 23d, by the same, at the residence of the bride's father, Mr. N.L. Holmes and Miss Loouilla A. Fulton, daughter of Mr. John Fulton, all of Randolph co., Ga.

By Rev. R. W. Dixon in Sumter co., Ga., Dec. 20th 1869, James m. Cook and Mrs. Sallie Wliliams, all of Sumter co., Ga.

In St. Matthew's Parish, S. C., on Thursday evening, Dec 23d, 1869, by the Rev. W. P. Mouzon, Mr. Virgil C. Dibble and Miss Eliza C., daughter of Dr. R. W. Bates.

Nov. 25th 1869, by the Rev. W. B. Merritt, Rev. Malcom Hair and Miss Sue McMichael, all of Marion co., Ga.

At Cave Spring, Ga., January 3, 1870, by Rev. B. B. Quillian, Mr. John W. Mann and Miss Martha J. Cowey, all of Cave Spring.

On 26th Dec., by Rev. N. D. Morehouse, Mr. R. Spear and Miss Laura Blitch, all of Effingham co., Ga.

On the 23d Dec. 1869, at the residence of the bride's father, by Rev. F. F. Reynolds, Dr. H. Carwell of Washington Co., Ga., to Miss C. Van Murphy, of Jefferson co., Ga.

At the residence of Mr. Wesley Nance, by Rev. A. W. Williams, Mr. Jacob Peterson, late from Denmark, to Miss Olivia Lampkin, of Clarke co., Ga., Dec. 20th 1869.

In Clarkesville, Ga., on the 28th Dec., by Rev. F. G. Hughes, Capt. Garnett McMillan to Miss Julia W. Erwin.

On the same day by the same, Mr. Andrew A. Ivester to Miss Elizabeth A. Franklin, all of Habersham co., Ga.

By Rev. J. R. Mayson, in DeKalb co., Dec. 28th 1869, Mr. John G. Marshall of Savannah, Ga., and Miss Mary J. Gew, of DeKalb co., Ga.

By Rev. T. S. L. Harwell, December 27th 1869, Mr. Charles W. Shepard to Miss Mary E. Mattox, all of Liberty co., Ga.

On the 14th Dec., by the Rev. M. D. Wood, Maj. T. H. Mitchell, of Gwinnett co., Ga., to Miss M. A. Quillin, of DeKalb co., Ga.

On Nov. 25th 1869, by the Rev. R. H. Howren, Mr. R. D. Nunerly, to miss Susan Scott, at Sylvania, Scriven co., Ga.

On Dec. 31st by Rev. B. J. Johnson, Dr. John T. Clower to Miss D. Ann Brandon, all of Gwinnett county, Ga.

Issue of January 21, 1870

On Jan. 6, 1870, by Rev. Morgan Bellah, Mr. A. M. Lambdin to Miss Susan w., daughter of Rev. Jas. B. Hanson, all of Barnesville, Ga.

On the 13th inst., at the residence of Dr. Cook, by Rev. Dr. Leonard, Mr. Moses L. Sanderlin to Miss Sarah M. Graham, all of Columbia co., Fla.

On Dec. 2, 1869, by Rev. A. J. Stokes, Mr. John Rodger to Mrs. A. E. Winebrenner, all of Unionville, S. C.

On Dec. 21, 1869, by the same, Mr. Franklin Wofford of Spartanburg, to Miss Mattie Murphy of Union, S. C.

On the evening of Dec. 30, 1869, by the Rev. J. M. Richardson, Mr. G. T. McCurdy to Miss Cornelia Brinkley, all of Whitfield, Ga.

On Jan. 13, 1870, by the same, Mr. Nathan Wofford of Banks co., Ga., to Miss Ella L. Rogers, of Whitfield.

By Rev. D. R. McWilliams, in Lumpkin, Ga., Dec. 23, 1869, Mr. Olin Pitts of Newton co., Ga.,to Miss Mollie L. Porter, of Lumpkin, Ga.

SOUTHERN CHRISTIAN ADVOCATE MARRIAGE NOTICES 1867-1878

Issue of January 28, 1870

Dec. 23d, at the residence of the bride's father, By Rev. A. B. Stephens, Mr. James S. Bell of Colleton, S. C., and Miss Isabella J. Stephens, daughter of Reuben Stephens, of Colleton, S. C.

Dec. 30th 1869, by the Rev. J. J. Giles, Mr. Warren Kennon to Miss Tempy Ann Folsom, both of Lowndes co., Ga.

Jan. 4th 1870, by the Rev. S. D. Clements, Mr. T. H. Freeman and Miss Sarah R. Page, all of Harris co., Ga.

Jan. 6th 1870, by the same, Mr. Jas. S. Morgan and Miss AManda M. Holmes, all of Muscogee co., Ga.

Jan. 18th 1870, in Sparta, Ga., by the Rev. M. P. Pledger, Mr. Milton Bass to Miss Margaret M. Sterling.

Jan. 16th 1870, in Bibb co., by Rev. H. J. Harvey, Mr. Thomas Lee and Miss Mary Bullock.

Issue of February 4, 1870

By Rev. James N. Myears, in Carroll co, Ga., Jan. 27, 1870, John T. Brown and Miss Mary E. Webb, all of Carroll co., Ga.

On Jan 11, 1870, at Austin, Arkansas, by Rev. J. M. Cline, Mr. C. T. Harrell of Darlington, S. C., and Miss H. J. G., daughter of Dr. C. J. Flinn, formerly of Darlington, S. C., now of Austin, Ark.

On Jan 26, by Rev. Henry M. Mood, Oliver F. Hoyt and Mary Catharine Mood, all of Sumter, S. C.

By Rev. J. Rast, Jan. 20, 1870, A. Warren Mizell of Lake Butler, Bradford co., Fla., and Miss Oni May Heath of Gainesville, Alachua co,. Fla.

On Jan. 26, 1870, at the residence of the bride's mother, by Rev. J. T. Payne, Mr. W. H. Ludy to Miss Emily E. Gammage, all of Terrell co., Ga.

On Thursday evening, January 20, at the residence of the bride's father, by the Rev. Bishop W. M. Wightman, D. D., W. W. Pemberton, of Charleston, S. C., and Mary A., second daughter of Dr. R. W. Bates, of Orangeburg District, S. C.

On 20th inst., near Cokesbury, by Rev. W. H. Fleming, Mr. G. W. Rampy to Miss Ella H. Carter, all of Abbeville, S. C.

In Sparta, Ga., on the morning of the 20th inst., by Rev. Dr. Curtis of South Carolina, George F. Pierce, Jr., to Harrie Hayes, eldest daughter of Rev. W. J. Harley. No cards.

On Dec 14, 1869, by Rev. Wm. Hutto, Mr. Angus P. Dantzler to Miss Mary M. Dantzler, all of Orangeburg.

On the 11th inst., by the same, Mr. Jacob D. C. Pendarvis to Miss Rachel L. Weathers, of Colleton District, S. C.

On the 20th inst., by the same, Maj. P. P. Moorer to Mrs. Eliza Murray of Colleton District, S. C.

At Sharon church, Anderson co., S. C., on Nov 25, 1869, by Rev. J. L. Stoudemire, Mr. S. L. Johnston to Miss N. E. Brewer.

By the same, on Jan 20, 1870, Mr. R. M. Martin to Miss Emma Gaines, all of Pickens co., S. C.

On Jan. 20, 1870, by Rev. R. R. Johnson, Mr. W. M. England to Miss MAttie S. Nunnally, all of Oglethorpe co., Ga.

Issue of February 11, 1870

At the residence of Mr. J. r. Harris in Quincy, Fla., Jan. 5th 1870, by Rev. Dr. Woldridge, Mr. Wm. W. Wilson to Miss Mariah Harris, daughter of Mr. J. R. Harris.

By the same at the residence of the bride's uncle, Mr. J. Gregory, Ochesee, Fla., Jan. 25th 1870, Mr. Wm. Munroe to Miss Florence Gregory.

By the same in Quincy, Fla., Feb. 1st 1870, Mr. Geo. W. Dismuke to Miss Alice Munroe, daughter of Mr. William Munroe.

By Rev. W. A. Dodge, Jan. 6th 1870, Mr. Roland C. Tilly of Floyd co., Ga., and Miss Lou Jones, daughter of Col. C. M. Jones, DeKalb co., Ga.

By the same, Jan. 23d, 1870, Mr. George Rakestraw and Miss Mary E. Etheredge, of the former place.

In Charleston co., S. C., Jan. 27th 1870 by the Rev. James C. Stoll, Mr. J. W. Hamlet of Va., to Miss Susan B., youngest daughter of Mr. Louis Hart, of Charleston co., S. C.

On 23d Jan. 1870, by Rev. J. M. N. Low, Mr. Russell C. White to Msis Grazilla M. Mlils, all of Calhoun co., Ga.

On 28th Jan. 1870 by Rev. J. O. A. Cook, Mr. Joseph H. Maunds and Msis ella Cumly, all of Talbotton, Ga.

On 23d Jan. 1870 by Rev. James Harris, Mr. John Joiner to Miss Mary A. R. lester, all of Dooly co., Ga.

Dec. 24th 1869, by the Rev. W. B. Neal, Mr. F. A. Lockhart to Miss M. E. Pruitt, daughter of Rev. M. Y. Pruitt, of Salem, Lee co., Ala.

Issue of February 18, 1870

By Rev. John W. McRoy, Jan. 6, 1870, Middleton Lake and Miss Drusilla Ann Gillam of Union co., S. C.

By the same, Feb. 3, 1870, R. Chamberlain and Miss Jane Fallin, both of union co,. S. C.

By the same, Feb. 8, 1870, Joseph Kelly of Fairfieled co. and Miss Sarah C. Slattery of Newberry, Union co., S. C.

Jan. 26, at Capt. Charles Smith's, Cokesbury, S. C., by Rev. W. H. Fleming, Misses Lou C. and Sallie E. Smith, the foremr to Mr. E. M. Hix of Laurens, the latter, to Mr. John Kennerly of Edgefield.

On Jan 27, at Spartanburg Female College, by Rev. S. B. Jones, Mr. Julien H. Porcher and Miss Susan B. Jones.

On Jan 17, by Rev. R. L. Wiggins, Dr. T. F. Munroe to Miss M. H. Jones, both of Quincy, Fla.

On Jan 20, by Rev. F. Auld, Mr. L. R. Millhouse of Barnwell co. to Miss Lulie Funderburk of Orangeburg co., S. C.

On 25th Jan. by the same, Dr. A. J. Horger to Miss Agnes C. Culler, all of Orangeburg co., S. C.

On Feb 2 by the same, Mr. George A. Smack to Miss Emma J. A. Millhouse, all of Orangeburg co., S. C.

On Feb. 1, in Elberton, by Rev. A. G. Worley, Capt. James J. Burch to Miss Ida R. Jones, all of Elbert co., Ga.

On Feb. 3, by B. J. Johnson, Mr. James T. E. Craig to Miss Eugenia E. Peeple, all of Gwinnett co., Ga.

By the same on Jan. 22, Dr. Samuel J. Hinton to Miss Allie Stanley ,all of Gwinnett co., Ga.

On Feb. 3, in Tuskegee, Ala., by Rev. B. B. Ross, Mr. J. P. REad of Warriot Stand, Ala., to Msis Emma Yarborough, of Upshur co., Texas.

By same on same day at Cross Keys, Ala., Mr. Watson Walker to Miss Mollie Trimble of Macon co., Ala.

On the 30th ult., by Rev. Wm. Hutto, Mr. Lewis Rickenbacker to Miss Caroline Lowe.

On the 1st inst., by same, Mr. John Patrick to Miss Matilda Ackerman.

On the 3d inst, by the same, Mr. William Westberry to Miss Julia Connor, all of St. George's, Colleton, S. C.

On the 2nd inst., by Rev. S. S. Sweet in Jefferson co., Ga., Silo S. Smith and msis Sarah A. Perkins.

At Bear Creek, Ga., Janaury 25, 1879, by Rev. Josh H. Harris, Mr. A. Henderson and Miss Irene Adair, all of Henry co., Ga.

By Rev. H. H. Parks, on the 8th inst., at Dr. Beale's, Mr. Lambeth Hopkins and Miss C. Augusta Beale, all of Richmond co, Ga.

By the same on 9th inst., at Mrs. J. C. Harrisons, Mr. Claude N. Wynne of Augusta, Ga., and Miss Claude A. Hopkins, of Richmond co., Ga., daughter of the late Mr. Lambeth Hopkins.

On Jan 14, 1870, by Rev. W. C. Lovejoy, Dr. W. P. Ragland of Heard co., to Mis sMary J. Boozer, of Troup co., Ga.

Issue of February 25, 1870

By Rev. J. R. Tucker in Edgefield District, S. C., Dec. 23d 1869, Mr. R. S. Wright and Miss Lavinia Cogburn.

In the Methodist E. Church in Culloden, Feb. 189th,by Rev. Wesley F. Smith, Mr. H. M. Hogan of East Macon, and Miss Mattie Andrews, of the former place.

Feb. 10th in Abbeville co., S. C., by Rev. W. H. Fleming, Mr. S. T. Munday and Miss Cynthia W. Lomax, daughter of W. A. Lomax, Esq.

On the 18th of Jan., by Rev. M. J. Wellborn, Mr. George P. Massingale, of Nashville, Tenn., and Miss Julia B. H. Smith.

By Rev. John Calvin Johnson, in Watkinsville, on 15th Feb. 1870, Mr. Henry S. Anderson, of Clarke co., Ga., to Miss Sallie S. White, of the former place.

On Jan. 26th 1870, by Rev. W. F. Quillian, Mr. Aaron H. Hardy to Miss J. Ashmore, both of Lincoln co., Ga.

On the 13th of Feb. 1870, by Rev. John M. Bowden, Mr. Jno. L. Duke to Mrs. M. E. Duke, all of Campbell co., Ga.

Issue of March 4, 1870

Feb. 24, at the residence of Mr. Archibald Nicholson, by the Rev. SAmuel Woodbery, Mr. M. N. Fletcher to Miss Martha E. Gee, all of Gadsden co., Fla.

By Rev. A. J. Dean, Feb. 10, 1870, Mr. J. C. Patterson to Mrs. S. A. Hoover, all of Decatur co., Ga.

By the same, Feb.16, 1870, Mr. John howell of Gadsden co., Fla., to Miss S. E. Martin of Decatur co., Ga.

By Rev. T. R. Barnett on Jan. 13, John A. Scott to Miss Frances Tompkins, both of Sumter co., Fla.

At the Methodist Church in Greenville, S. C., by Rev. S. A. Weber, Mr. William H. Cammer to Miss Eliza Dyer, daughter of Geo. B. Dyer, Esq.

By Rev. W. T. Hamilton on Feb. 23, 1870, at Red Ctiy, Ga., Mr. William Ransome of Bedford co, Tenn., to Mary E., daugther of Capt. James H. Huff, of the former place.

By Rev. A. G. Carpenter, Feb. 3, Mr. H. L. Patterson to Miss Ruth E. Ellis, all of Cumming, Ga.

By Rev. D. J. Myrick, Feb. 10, 1870, O. S. Porter to Mrs. Julia A. Camp, both of Covington, Ga.

By Rev. G. T. Embry on Feb. 24, Rev. H. C. Fentress of the So. Ga. Conf., to Miss A. S. Sessions, daughter of Rev. J. J. Sessions.

Issue of March 11, 1870

On 14th Dec. 1869, by Rev. Lovick Pierce, D. D., Dr. E. D. Allfriend, of Sparta, to Miss Mary S. Pierce.

By the same, on 1st March 1870, James A. Harley, Esq., of Sparat, to Miss Anne T. Pierce-- both daugthers of Bishop George F. Pierce.

Feb. 16th, by Rev. L. B. Bouchelle, Mr. John T. Smith and Miss L. J. Meeks, all of Amenuel co., Ga.

By the same, Feb. 27th, Mr. Henry Bish and Miss Ophelia Dye, both of Emanuel co., Ga.

By the same, March 3d, Dr. W. W. Duffie and Miss Sally M. Moseley, both of Burke co,. Ga.

by Rev. J. M. Lowry, Feb. 15th 1870, Mr. Alexander S. lundy and Miss Matilda M. Lee, all of Green co., Ga.

By the same, Feb. 22d, 1870, Mr. Charles E. Little and Miss winnie F. Copeland, all of Green co., Ga.

Feb. 20th by Rev. T. S. L. Harwell, Rev. A. C. DeLamar to Miss Sallie E. Blanton, all of Harris co, Ga.

By the same, Feb. 24th 1870, Mr. J. W. Williams of Troup co., Ga., to Miss M. V. Tucker, of Harris co., Ga.

On 29th Dec. 1869, by Rev. Wm. C. Power, Mr. Thomas H. Bethea to Miss Bettie H. McLaurin, both of Marlboro' District, S. C.

SOUTHERN CHRISTIAN ADVOCATE MARRIAGE NOTICES 1867-1878

In Cokesbury, S. C., March 2d 1870, by Rev. A. J. Stafford, Mr. Charles L. Smith to Miss Lynn Allen.

At Graniteville, S. C., March 3d 1870, by Rev. E. G. Gage, Mr. Lucius A. Moore to Miss Anna Moore, both of Raytown, Ga.

Issue of March 18, 1870

On 3d inst., at the residence of the bride's father, by Rev. Dr. Leonard, Mr. James W. Bradley to Miss Sarah Atwell, of Suwanee co, Fla.

In Georgetown, Ga., Feb. 14, by Rev. E. H. McGehee, Mr. Thomas G. Hester of Stewart co., Ga., to Miss Susan V. Bethune.

On Jan. 4, 1870, by Rev. H. H. Porter, Mr. J. D. Temple to Miss A. Farmer.

On Feb. 24, 1870, by Rev. H. H. Porter, J. W. Patrick to Mrs. M. J. Wilkins, daughter of Dr. Anderson, all of Springplace, Ga.

In Atlanta, Jan. 6, 1870, by Rev. W. P. Harrison, D. D., Dr. Charles H. Montgomery of Whitesville, Ga., to Miss Virginia Chamberlain of Atlanta.

In Tallapoosa co., Ala., Jan. 25, 1900, by Rev. W. P. Harrison, D. D., Mr. Richard P. Glenn of Atlanta, to Miss Elizabeth Taylor, of Tallapoosa co., Ala.

In Atlanta, Jan. 27, 1870, by Rev. W. P. Harrison, D. D., Mr. Henry H. Newton to Miss Martha A. Lester.

In Atlanta, Feb. 11, 1870, by Rev. W. P. Harrison, D. D., Mr. Banks Crawford to Miss Jennie Hudgens.

In Atlanta, Feb. 24, by Rev. W. P. Harrison, D. D., Mr. Samuel Baker, of Midway, Ala., to Miss Martha M. J. Smith of Atlanta.

In Atlanta, Feb. 24, 1870, by Rev. W. P Harrison, D. D., Mr. Levi J. Smith to Miss Annie M. Cozart.

In Atlanta, Feb. 27, 1870, by Rev. W. P Harrison, D. D., Mr. W. A. Brown to Miss Jane Boyd.

Issue of March 25, 1870

On the 8th Feb. 1870, by Rev. William Hutto, Mr. Grecian Murray to Mrs. Sarah Livingston, all of Charleston District, S. C.

By the same on the 17th Feb. 1870, Mr. Henry M. Dantzler to Miss Mary Ann Shuler, all of Orangeburg Dist., S. C.

On the 27th Feb. 1870, in Richmond co., at the residence of the bride's uncle, Mr. Jesse Tinly, by Rev. W. Ewing Johnson, Mr. Howard H. Smith to Augusta, to Miss Amanda E. Arington, of Richmond co, Ga.

In the Methodist Church at Anderson, S. C., by Rev. A. B. Stephens, Mr. James B. Pegg to Mrs. A. M. Foran, both of Anderson, S. C.

On Feb. 24th 1870, by Rev. A. J. Cauthen, Mr. J. W. Boozer and Miss Alice Hughes, all of Newberry, S. C.

On March 17th 1870, by Rev. R. H. Howren, Mr. T. R. Johnson to Mrs. M. A. Robinson, all of Washington co., Ga.

At the residence of Col. T. T. Dorough, March 8th, 1870 by Rev. Thomas Crymes, Dr. A. W. Brawner to Miss Mattie Z. Dorough, all of Carnesville, Ga.

On March 17th 1870, by Rev. J. Rast, Mr. Elias H. Futch to Miss Rebecca J. Whitehead, all of Baker co., Fla.

Issue of April 1, 1870

By Rev. J. W. Simmons, March 24, Mr. Edgar P. Williams and Miss Mary L. C., daughter of James L. Lovejoy, Clinch co., Ga.

March 17, 1870, by Rev. W. Lane, Mr. Willis J. Parnel, of Thomasville, Ga.,and Mrs. Eliza H. Brown, of Leon co., Fla.

In Dahlonega, Ga., at the residence of A. G. Wimpy, Feb. 24, 1870, by Rev. J. W. Hutchins, Mr. Ben A. Martin, of Liberty Hill, Pike co., Ga., and Miss Mollie E. O'Connor, of Dahlonega, Ga.

In Gwinnett co., Ga., March 13, by Rev. R. A. Conner, Mr. Z. B. Betts of Jackson co., to Mrs. Margaret J. Kilgore, daughter of Jordan Stanton, of the former place.

By Rev. A. W. Williams, March 10, Mr. William Sefstrum, to Miss Mollie Lampkin, eldest daughter of William H. Lampkin, all of Clarke co., Ga.

Issue of April 8, 1870

At the residence of Judge E. F. Lawson, by Rev. N. B. Ousley, Dr. Thomas Gedell to Miss Emma Carter, all of Waynesboro, Ga.

By the Rev. James M. Myers, on the 24th March, 1870, Mr. John W. Brooks and Miss Cyntha E. Allen, all of Carroll co., Ga.

Issue of April 15, 1870

By Rev. W. Hutto, 29th ult., Mr. Durant Jackson to Miss Sarah L. Weathers, all of Colleton Dist.

On the 5th inst., by Rev. W. Hutto, Mr. Middleton Waters to Mrs. Bars, all of Colleton District.

On 5th inst., by Rev. W. Hutto, Mr. J. S. Martin of Charleston to Miss Eliza Dantzler, of Orangeburg Dist.

By Rev. Thos. J. Simmons, March 22, 1870, Mr. S. R. C. Adams to Miss N. C. Mitchell, all of Whitfield co., Ga.

By Rev. Thos. J. Simmons, March 29, 1870, Mr. James Buchanan to Mrs. Rachel Stone, all of Whitfield co., Ga.

By Rev. Thos. J. Simmons, March 31, 1870, Mr. J. A. Millirous to Miss Margaret Potts, all of Whitfield co., Ga.

By Rev. Thos. J. Simmons, March 31, 1870, Mr. M. R. Yeagle to Miss Charlotte V. Noblet, all of Whitfield co., Ga.

On 31st March 1870, by Rev. N. D. Morehouse, Mr. H. M. Little to Mrs. M. L. Cordry, all of Sandersville, Ga.

On the 2d March, by Rev. W. M. Watts, Mr. W. H. Bradly to Miss Susie Bird, all of Taylors Creek, Ga.

By Rev. W. M. Watts, on March 30, Mr. Eli Bradly to Miss Sarah J. Bird, of the same place.

By Rev. L. P. Neese, on March 22, Mr. J. A. Johnson to Miss A. T. Hanes, all of Jonesboro, Ga.

By Rev. A. E. Cloud, Mr. R. W. Jones, to Miss Georgia A. Turner, all of Jonesboro, Ga.

Issue of April 22, 1870

Feb. 3d, 1870, by Rev. W. Bowman, Mr. John H. Hudson to Miss Mary A., daughter of Jenkins Adams, of Pickens, S. C.

By Rev. W. Fowman, March 15th 1870, Judge Irvin H. Philpot to Miss Jane M., daughter of Isaac Alexander, all of Pickens, S. C.

By Rev. C. A. Mitchell, on the 31st March, 1870, Mr. Wm. H. Wright, of Hancock co., Ga., to miss Catharine Morton, of Jones co., Ga.

By Rev. J. K. Armstrong, March 30th, Mr. G. Harris of Muscogee, to Mrs. Caroline Parham of Stewart co., Ga.

In Columbus, Ga., April 10th 1870, by Rev. O. L. Smith, Mr. Hamilton Boland to Miss Maria C. Davis.

Issue of April 29, 1870

In Forsyth, Ga., April 12, 1870, by Rev. Thomas G. Scott, Mr. A. B. C. Davis to Miss Hattie E. Wilder.

By Rev. W. Lane, Mr. Jonas Courtney to Miss Sallie Roberts, both of Leon co., Fla.

On April 20, in Trinity Church, Charleston, by Rev. W. P. Mouzon, Dr. P. T. Pendleton, of Sparta, Ga., and Miss Mattie A. Nelson, daughter of Samuel A. Nelson, of that city.

At the residence of the Rev. C. I. Shelton, 10th inst., by Rev. L. A. Darsey, J. T. Wooten, Esq., and Miss Susannah Fletcher, all of Telfair co., Ga.

In Orangeburg co., S. C., March 24, 1870, by Rev. James C. Stoll, Mr. Thos. P. Evans to Miss Martha Shuler, all of Orangeburg co., S. C.

By Rev. James C. Stoll in Orangeburg co., S. C., April 7, 1870, Mr. Louis R. Evans to Miss Mary A. Evans, all of Orangeburg co., S. C.

By Rev. James C. Stoll in Georgetown co, S. C., April 14, 1870, Mr. Augustus J. McKay of Charleston co., S. C., to Miss S. Elizabeth Bailey of Georgetown co., S. C.

Issue of May 6, 1870

On 21st April 1870, by Rev. R. W. Flournoy, J. T. Good, Esq., and Miss Georgia A. Berry, both of Jeffersonville, Twiggs co., Ga.

By the Rev. Thos. B. Lanier, April 28th 1870, in Bryan co., Ga., at Mr. Henry E. Smith's, Mr. Robert H. Guyton of Effingham co., Ga., to Miss Julia A. Smith, of Bryan co.

On April 28th 1870, at the bride's residence by Rev. J. H. C. McKinney, Rev. R. M. Harrison, of the S. C. Conference, to Mrs. C. A. Abney, of Edgefield co., S. C.

Issue of May 13, 1870

Near Opelika, Ala., on 3d inst., by Rev. L. J. Davies, Rev. John M. Bowdon, of the North Ga. Conf. to Miss Eliza M., daughter of John Akers, Esq., lately of Troup co., Ga., now of the former place.

By Rev. R. B. G. Waters, on April 28, 1870, Mr. Henry G. Miller to Miss Mary B. Williamson, all of Johnson co., Ga.

By Rev. J. P. Duncan, 4th inst., Rev. Robt. A. Rogers, formerly of the Ga. Annual Conference, to Mrs. J. Jennie Hill, all of Spaulding co., Ga.

In Greenville, Ga., April 28, by Rev. Alex. M. Thigpen, Mr. J. E. Adams to Miss Eliza H. Gresham.

On April 3d 1870, by Rev. David Nolan, Mr. R. T. Crawley, of Newton co., to Miss Nannie J. Garlington, of Henry co., Ga.

By Rev. H. C. Fentress, at the residence of the bride's father, Pulaski co., Ga., April 18, 1870, Mr. Martin B. Smith to Miss Elephair N. J. Garrett.

May 5, 1870, by Rev. E. G. Gage, Mr. Curtis Varn to Miss Nancy A. Johnson, and Mr. James Gault to Miss Eliza J. Johnson.

Issue of May 20, 1870

On the 5th May 1870, by Rev. J. J. Morgan, Mr. Thos. M. Tarply, of Wilkinson co., to Miss Anna Linder, of Laurens co., Ga.

In Charleston co., S. C., April 28th 1870, by Rev. James C. Stoll, Mr. Peter J. Mims to Miss Olivia C. Murray, all of Charleston co., S. C.

On May 11th at the residence of Mr. F. W. Brogdon, of Effingham co., Ga., by Rev. Thomas B. Lanier, Mr. Thos. J. Cox of Bryan co., Ga., to Miss Sarah V. Griner, of Effingham co., and Mr. Allen Crawford to Miss Elizabeth C. Griner, latter of former, Effingham co., Ga.

In Cuthbert, Ga., April 26th, 1870, by Rev. E. H. McGee, Mr. Thomas A. Goodrum to Miss charlie Harris.

By the Rev. J. H. D. McRae, on the 2d May 1870, Rev. Samuel Galloway of Quincy, to Miss Nettie Munroe, of Lake City, both of Florida.

Issue of May 27, 1870

By Rev. Thos. B. Lanier, May 15, at the bride's mother's in Whitesville, Effingham co,. Ga., Mr. Asa Ernest, of Bibb co., Ga., to Laura A. Tool, of Effingham co., Ga.

At the church, by Rev. W. F. Cook, pastor, April 14, Mr. Henry J. Johnson to Miss Joe Reudy, all of Rome, Ga.

In Randolph co., Ga., May 8th, by Rev. J. K. Armstrong, Mr. Irwin Cannon to Miss M. A. Suggs.

By Rev. W. F. Cook, May 15, Rev. James Lamberth to Miss Alethia A. Langston, of Floyd co.

Issue of June 3, 1870

At the Methodist Church in Albany,Ga., May 24th 1870, by Rev. G. H. Pattillo, Rev. J. M. Marshall of So. Ga. Conference, and Mrs. Amanda M. Sims, formerly of Coweta co., Ga.

On May 5th 1870, by Rev. J. B. Traywick, Capt. Thos. L. Williams of Greenville, Tenn., and Miss Mary M. Simpson, daughter of Hon. R. F. Simpson, near Pendleton, S. C.

At Henderson, Ga, on May 24th 1870, by Rev. W. W. Stewart, Mr. C. J. holmes of Houston co., and Miss E. P. McGehee, of the former place.

On the morning of 25th May 1870, by Rev. R. B. Lester, Mr. Miller H. McAfee and Miss Maggie Love Smith, daughter of H. P. Smith, all of Macon, Ga.

In Columbus, Ga., May 25th 1870, by Rev. O. L. Smith, D. D., Mr. John T. Harrison and Miss Mary C. Jones.

Issue of June 10, 1870

In Charleston co., S. C., May 15, 1870, by Rev. Jas. C. Stoll, Mr. Watson J. Wetherford of Charleston co., to Miss Ada Shuler, of Orangeburg co., S. C.

At the residence of Mr. E. Ponder, by Rev. L. A. Darsey, May 29, 1870, Mr. Benjamin Inman of S. C., and Mrs. Mary Bass of Burke co., Ga.

May 10, by Rev. A. J. Cauthen, Dr. J. L. LaBorde and Miss Ada, eldest daughter of Capt. J. R. Kinsler, of Richland, S. C.

May 12 by Rev. A. J. Cauthen, Mr. -- Abrams and Miss Anna Lake, of Newberry, S. C.

On 1st inst., in Harris co., Ga., by Rev. S. P. Callaway, W. Frank Pattillo, of Atlanta, and Miss Mary E. Moss.

Issue of June 17, 1870

By Rev. John Calvin Johnson, in Watkinsville, Clarke co., Ga., on 26th May 1870, Mr. Aaron E. Beardin to Miss Eliza J. Langford.

By same, at same place, 9th June 1870, Daniel W. Bradford to Miss Ann E. Hall.

At Union Springs, Ala., on 1st June 1870, by Rev. P. A. Heard, Mr. Robert Beall, of LaGrange, Ga., to Miss Annie L. Hayes, of Union Springs.

On 25th May 1870,l by Rev. J. T. Turner, Mr. Wm. B. Heys to Miss Mattie A., youngest daughter of Turner Dixon, all of Sumter co., Ga.

On the 2d June 1870, in Culloden, Ga., by Rev. J. O. A. Cook, Dr. James T. Jelks to Miss Susie E. Cook.

Issue of June 24, 1870

By Rev. Thos. P. Pierce, in Washington, June 7, Mr. W. W. Simpson of Sparta, to Mrs. lucy A. DuBose, of Wilkes co., Ga.

Near Lumpkin, Ga., on May 12, by Rev. D. S. T. Douglas, Mr. William A. Rawson to Miss Florida I. Fort.

On Sunday, June 5, 1870, by W. T. Laine, Mr. G. I. A. McCrary to Miss Salina A. Casey, all of Fulton co., Ga.

Issue of July 1, 1870

In Milledgeville, on the 15th inst., by Rev. A. M. Thigpen, Mr. Henry W. Thomas to Miss Amanda J., daughter of Col. N. C. Burnett.

In Amultaliga, June 16th 1870, by Rev. Dr. J. M. Farabee, Mr. John Wynn to Miss Mary Clardy, all of Hernando co., Fla.

On June 2d, 1870, in Scriven co., Ga., by Rev. W. T. McMichael, Mr. William J. Scott to Miss Mary C. Anderson.

On June 2d, 1870, by Rev. L. P. Neese, Mr. A. A. Morris to Miss M. A. Jones, all of Jonesboro, Ga.

On 3d June 1870 by Rev. Manning Brown, Rev. J. L. Shuford of the So. Ca. Conf. to Mrs. Mary A. Bell, of Fairfield co., S. C.

On 23d inst., by Rev. Geo. T. Embry, Mr. William T. Robinson to Miss Mattie I. Glenn, daughter of James B. Glenn, of Terrel co.

Issue of July 8, 1870

On June 22, by Rev. Dr. J. M. Farabee, Mr. Wily W. Carrithers to Mrs. Jane Mein, all of hernando, Fla.

On the 12th inst., by N. D. Morehouse, Wm. N. Carey and Eugenia Moye, both of Washington co., Ga.

In Greenville, Ga., June 28, by Rev. Alex. M. Thigpen, Mr. John E. Shuttles and Miss Ella, daughter of Dr. A. G. Floyd.

Issue of July 15, 1870

By Rev. R. H. Howren, June 28th 1870, Mr. Joseph H. Hines to Mrs. H. A. McConnell, all of Washington co., Ga.

On the 29th June 1870, by Rev. Wm. W. Mood, Mr. Wm. D. Hornsby to Miss Julia V. Smith, all of Richland District, S. C.

On the 7th July 1870, by Rev. Wm. W. Mood, Mr. H. Oscar Duke of Fairfield District, S. C., to Miss Emma I. Lomas, of Richland District, S. C.

By the same and at the same time, Mr. David G. Cloud of Fairfield District, S. C,. to Miss Lizzie Bell Lomas, of Richland District, S. C.

By Rev. L. A. Darsey on the 3d inst., at Fulwood's Chapel, Mr. O. W. L. Harn of Emanuel co., Ga., to Miss Sophia Murphey, of Burke co., Ga.

In the city of Montgomery, on 5th July 1870, by Rev. O. R. Blue, Mr. Timothy I. Jones to Miss Ellen F. Blue.

In Columbia co., Fla., July 7th 1870, at the residence of the bride's father, by Rev. Dr. Leonard, Mr. Granville W. Bryant to Miss Annie E. Corley.

Issue of July 22, 1870

In Houston co., Ga., July 7, 1870. by Rev. I. L. Avant, Mr. M. B. L. McDowell, formerly of Taylor co., Ga., to Miss Georgia A. Vinson, granddaughter of Josiah Vinson, Esq., of the former place. Western Methodist please copy.

July 10th by Rev. C. J. Tool, Mr. Boze Kitchens to Miss Penellie Rayborn, all of Glasscock co., Ga.

Issue of July 29, 1870

By Rev. W. W. Oslin in the Methodist Church at Barnesville, July 7th 1870, Mr. John P. McClane to Mrs. C. E. Dozier, both of Pike co., Ga.

By the same, July 17th 1870, Mr. W. C. Alsabrook of Fulton co., to Mrs. J. E. J. Childs, of Barnesville, Ga.

By Rev. J. J. Workman, July 11th 1870, Mr. Alonzo C. Martin to Miss Zilphia C. Cann of Abbeville co., S. C.

July 17th 1870, Mr. Augustus S. Munroe to Mrs. Susan W. Black, by H. W. Long, Esq., all of Marion co., E. Florida.

In Madison, Ga., on 21st of June 1870, by Rev. W. R. Foote, Mr. J. Emory Nolan to Miss Alice H. Robertson.

Issue of August 5, 1870

In Bradford co., Fla., July 21, 1870, by Rev. Dr. Leonard, Mr. Vastine J. Valentine to Miss Mary Jane Berling.

By Rev. E. E. Duncan, July 28, 1870, Mr. W. Franklin Hughey to Miss Arie H. Rutherford, all of Madison co., Fla.

Issue of August 12, 1870

In Fort Valley, Ga., July 31st, 1870, by Rev. R. B. Russell, Mr. C. W. Beington, of Fort Valley to Miss Annie N. Richardson, of Albany, Ga.

By Rev. J. H. Grogan, Dr. Charls Webb to Miss Myra F. Benson, both of Hartwell, Ga.

Issue of August 19, 1870

On Aug. 9, 1870, by R. R. Johnson, Mr. H. H. Colquit and Miss Bettie Winfrey, all of Oglethorpe co., Ga.

July 16th, by Rev. W. S. Bird, Rev. Geo. C. Leavel of the Florida Conference, to Miss Elizabeth E. Barwick of Monticello, Florida.

July 28 by Rev. L. P. Neese, assisted by Rev. W. R. Branham, Mr. F. M. Arnold of Fayette co., Ga., to Miss Maggie Burnsides of Jonesboro, Ga.

On Aug. 11, by J. T. Cherry, J. P. Mr. Nectar McSwain to Miss Nancy A., daughter of William A. Stokes, all of Bibb co., Ga.

Issue of August 26, 1870

August 11th 1870, in Jasper co., Ga., by Rev. A. W. Rowland, Mr. Enock D. John of Galveston, Texas, to Miss Martha S. Allen.

Near Cave Spring, Ga., August 14th 1870, by Rev. B. B. Quillian, Mr. James R. Cakely to Miss Hattie L., daughter of Allen Pledger.

Issue of September 9, 1870

On the 21st of August, at the residence of Col. Telbests, by Rev. J. I. E. Bird, Mr. B. S. Sheats, to Monroe, Walton county, Ga., to Mrs. Sarah Hill, of Carroll county, Miss. Christian Index will please copy.

August 29, 1870, by Rev. G. W. Ivy, at Bridgewater, Burke county, N. C., Mr. John Rutherford to Mrs. Elizabeth C. D. Jenkins, of Little Rock, Ark., daughter of L. and P. A. E. Denison of the State of New York.

On July 28, 1870, by Rev. M. G. Jenkins, Mr. Daniel McAlpin, to Miss Mary, daughter of Rev. J. Smith, all of Grimes county, Texas, formerly of Alabama.

By Rev. Geo. W. Yarbrough, Aug. 25th, Mr. Joseph H. Kenner, of Baltimore, and Miss Mary B. Tibbs, of Dalton, Ga.

By Isaac Ingram, Esq., at the residence of Col. W. E. Teasley, Aug. 23, 1870, Capt. W. R. D. Moss, to Miss Mollie Grogain, all of Canton, Ga.

Issue of September 16, 1870

On Sabbath morning, August 28, by Rev. H. J. Ellis, Mr. Asbury H. Arnold to Miss Ellen A. Simms, all of Coweta co.

Near Shady Dale, Jasper co., Sept. 7, 1870, by Rev. F. B. Davies, Mr. V. A. Jordan to Miss M. L. Geiger, and Mr. M. W. Spearman to Miss J. L. Geiger.

Issue of September 23, 1870

By Rev. J. R. Little, Sept. 7, 1870, Mr. Wm. A. Liles to Miss Adam, daughter of Rev. D. Barentine, near Cheraw, S. C.

In Rome, Ga., Sept. 6, 1870, by Rev. W. F. cook, Mr. N. G. Bayard Jr., to Miss Grace Battey, all of Rome, Ga.

Sept. 8, 1870, near Clyattville, at the house of the bride's father, by M. M. Caswell, J. P., Mr. B. J. Newsom, to Miss G. A. Bragall, of Lowndes co., Ga.

Near Cave Spring, Ga., Sept, 5, by Rev. B. B. Quillian, Mr. Anderson Clement, to Mrs. Nancy Ann Allerd, all of Polk co., Ga.

At the residence of Thos. M. Pace, Esq., in Cedartown, Ga., on the 3d of Aug., by Rev. Jno. A. Reynolds, Mr. Elkana Pace, of Ala., to Miss Georgia A. Walker, of the former place.

By Rev. J. B. Jefcoat, Sept. 1, 1870, Mr. S. A. Stewart, to Mrs. Martha Carpenter, all of Orange co., Fla.

By Rev. J. B. Jefcoat, Sept. 7, 1870, Mr. J. A. Hux, of Sumter co., to Mrs. Mary K. Ballad, of Orange co., Fla.

By Rev. J. B. Jefcoat, Sept. 8, 1870, Mr. C. W. Mills, to Mrs. Eliza C. Stewart, all of Orange co., Fla.

In Cuthbert, Ga., Sept. 15, 1870, by Rev. E. H. Mcgehee, Mr. Wm. B. Gorton, to Miss Amanda Andrews.

Issue of September 30, 1870

Near Cave Spring, Ga., Sept. 20, by Rev. B. B. Quillian, Mr. W. F. Whitfield, to Miss Maggie, daughter of Thomas Pledger.

In Perry, Ga., on Sept. 22, by Rev. Walter Knox, Maj. John B. Cobb of Macon, and Mrs. Alice Culler Leak.

On Sep. 15, 1870, by Rev. I. L. Avant, Mr. Leander West, of North Carolina, to Miss Harriet E., daughter of Rev. Lucius G. Evans, of Crawford co., Ga.

In Kansas City, Missouri, on the 6th September, by the Rev. J. W. Lewis, Hon. James Jackson of Macon, Ga., and Mrs. Mary S. Schoolfield, of the former place.

On the 12th inst., by Rev. W. Hutto, Mr. William Way to Miss Mary Curry, all of Colleton co.

SOUTHERN CHRISTIAN ADVOCATE MARRIAGE NOTICES 1867-1878

On the 14th inst., by Rev. W. Hutto, Mr. Wesley Hutto to Miss Emma Whetsel, all of Colleton co., S. C.

On the 23d inst., by Rev. W. Hutto, Mr. Joseph Heaton to Miss Julia Appleby, all of Colleton co., S. C.

Issue of October 7, 1870

On Sept. 1, at the residence of the Rev. William Seay, Stewart co., by the Rev. S. R. Weaver, John T. Baker of Mitchell co., Ga., To Miss Frances M. Seay, of Stewart co., Ga.

Sept. 5, 1870, near Clyattville, at the house of the bride's father, by M. M. Caswell, J. P., Mr. B. J. Newsom to Miss G. A. Bray, all of Lowndes co., Ga.

In LaGrange, Ga., Sept. 28, 1870, by Rev. D. D. Cox, Maj. John W. Park of Greenvlile, Ga., and Miss Sallie C. Bull, daughter of the late Judge O. A. Bull, of LaGrange, Ga.

By Rev. John Calvin Johnson, on 25th Aug., 1870, Thomas F. Trible to Mary E. Puryear, all of Clarke co., Ga.

By the same on 23d Sept. 1870, Albert A. Edge to Sallie J. Dawson, all of Watkinsville, Clarke co., Ga.

By the same on 25th Sept. 1870, Joseph E. P. Trible to Sarah A. E. Edwards, all of Clarke co., Ga.

On Sunday morning, Sept. 25, 1870, by the Rev. Geo. C. Clarke, Mr. R. W. Smith, to Miss Sarah C. Dixon, all of Decatur co., Ga.

Issue of October 14, 1870

Sept 27th 1870, by Rev. J. L. Shuford, Mr. Thomas Woods of Chester co., to Miss C. A. Hawthorn of Fairfield co., S. C.

On Sep. 25, by Rev. J. T. Kilgo, Maj. Abram Jones of Edgefield to Mrs. Mary J. Lee, of Leesville, S. C.

On Sept. 28, 1870, by Rev. W. F. Roberts, Mr. Isaac A. Bosh of Colquitt, Ga., to Miss Calista Sheffield of the same place.

On Sept. 6, 1870, by Rev. Z. D. Cottrell, at the residence of Dr. James Hamilton, Subligna, Chattooga, Ga., Miss M. T. Hamilton, his daughter to Mr. S. H. Shy, of Madison, Ga.

Issue of October 21, 1870

At the Methodist parsonage in Darlington circuit, Oct. 6th 1870, by the Rev. P. G. Bowman, W. Capers Harrell, M. D., to Miss Mary Zelime, daughter of the officiating minister.

By Rev. N. D. Morehouse, on 6th Oct., Marabo H Boyer, to Vivianna B. Skrine, all of Sandersville, Ga.

Oct. 6th, by Rev. J. T. Ainsworth, Mr. Julius C. Day, to Miss Sarah E. Stewart, both of Mitchell co., Ga.

At same time and place by Rev. J. T. Ainsworth, George W. Ott, to Miss Sarah E. Rosey, both of Mitchell co., Ga.

On Sabbath morning, Oct. 9th, at the residence of W. G. Morgan, by the Rev. G. W. Barker, Mr. James F. Baggents, to Miss Amanda Morgan, all of Pike co, Ala.

SOUTHERN CHRISTIAN ADVOCATE MARRIAGE NOTICES 1867-1878

By Rev. L. C. Peek, Oct. 6th 1870, at the residence of the bride's father (James L. Lovejoy), Mr. Robert Holtzendorf, to Mrs. Stalina Lamb, all of Clinch co., Ga.

Issue of October 28, 1870

By Rev. T. R. Barnett, on 1st Sept., Wm. Tomkins to Miss Susan A. Knight.

By Rev. T. R. Barnett, on Sept. 30, Mr. G. W. Wiggin of Macon co., Ga., to Miss Emma Brown, of Sumter co., Fla.

By John Calvin Johnson, in Clarke co., Ga., on Oct. 19, Mr. George W. Anderson to Miss Cornelia I. Willoughby.

By John Calvin Johnson, on Oct. 20, Mr. William H. Marable to Miss Sallie P. Anderson.

By John Calvin Johnson, Mr. Matthew H. Jones to Miss Martha A. T. Butler.

On Oct. 12, near Hurtville, Russel co., Ala., by Rev. D. M. Banks, Dr. C. H. Franklin to Miss Sallie F. Banks.

On Oct. 20, by Rev. A. M. Campbell, at the residence of the bride's father, Mr. O. J. Davis, Mr. M. H. Cutter to Mrs. M. A. Cannon, daughter of Mr. J. O. Davis, all of East Macon, Ga.

On Oct 9, by Rev. P. C. Harris, Mr. John C. Crittcell to Miss Hannah E. Davis, all of Decatur co,. Ga.

On Oct. 13, 1870, by Rev. T. S. L. Harwell, Mr. James W. Williams to Miss Emma S. Ridgeway, all of Troup co., Ga.

By Rev. C. M. McClure, Oct. 5, Mr. George B. Burtz of Fulton co., Ga., to Miss Cora C. Garrison, of Cobb co., Ga.

On Oct. 13, by Rev. F. A. Kimbell, Mr. Madison Harralson and Miss Lou C. Cozart, all of the city of Atlanta.

On Oct. 4, by Rev. F. A. Kimbell, Mr. Robert Elder and Miss Mollie Foster, all of Forsyth, Ga.

On Sept. 29, by Rev. F. A. Kimbell, Mr. Kirk Britt and Miss Mary Howell, all of Monroe co., Ga.

Issue of November 4, 1870

On Oct. 18, by N. D. Morehouse, Col. J. C. Dell, to Miss F. C. Sharpe, all of Scriven co., Ga.

In Athens, Ga., Oct. 18th 1870, by Rev. E. G. Murrah, Mr. John Bird, to Miss Tallulah Norris. Athens papers please copy.

On Thursday evening the 20th Oct., by Rev. L. T. Mizell, Mr. David L. McEachern, to Miss Mary A. Baggett, all of Cobb co., Ga.

Issue of November 11, 1870

On 12th Oct., by Rev. J. O. A. Cook, in the Methodist Church, Talbotton, Ga., Jos. A. Allison and Miss Sallie S. Matthews, all of Talbot co.

Oct. 20, 1870, at the residence of Mr. Terry, Columbia co., Fla., by Rev. Dr. Leonard, Mr. John G. Dyall to Miss Permelia E. Stalnaker.

On 20th Oct. 1870, by Rev. Wm. W. Mood, Mr. Thos. D. Lomas and Miss Sue L. Coon, all of Richland Dist. S. C.

By Rev. W. T. Hamilton on Oct. 20, Mr. W. H. Willson to Miss M. R. Quillian of Whitfield co., Ga.

By Rev. E. J. Rentz, at Major Picketts, in Sumter co., Ga., Oct. 27, Mr. John R. King to Msis Emma F. Pickett.

By Rev. G. W. Ivy in McDowel co., N. C. Oct. 12, Capt. T. Parks, of Burke co., N. C., to Miss Lou D. Neal, daughter of J. Neal

By Rev. G. W. Ivy, on 27th Sept., Mr. J. Parks to Miss Lou H. Hunter, daughter of Jos. B. Hunter, all of Burke co., N. C.

In Sumter co., S. C., by Rev. L. Wood, on 27th Oct. 1870, Mr. Joseph E. Baskin to Miss Laney, daughter of Edmund Stuckey.

On Oct. 30, 1870, by Rev. W. P. Howell, Thos. M. Gur to Miss Harriet A. Davidson, daughter of E. F. Davidson, all of Cleburne co., Ala.

On Oct. 26, by Rev. W. K. Turner, Rev. Dr. V. H. Shelton to Miss Virginia M. Sexton, all of Alachua co., Fla.

In Americus, Ga., Nov. 2, by Rev. G. H. Pattillo, Col. B. F. Brown to Albany, Ga., and Miss Savannah Bell, of the former place.

Issue of November 18, 1870

In Desoto Ga., Oct. 25th, by Rev. W. F. cook, Mr. C. F. McCrary of Rome, Ga., to Miss Molie C. Mitchell, of the former place.

On the 8th Nov., by Rev. J. Blakely Smith in Bibb co., Rev. Chalres R. Jewett, of the South Georgia Conference and Miss Annie S., daughter of Mr. Ellis W. Howard.

On the 9th Nov., by Rev. John G. Motley, Mr. O. G. Motley of tuskegee, ALa., to Miss Carrie H. Lamar, of Macon, Ga.

On the 20th ult., by Rev. W. Hutto, Mr. William Shetsel to Miss Eliza Harlee, all of Colleton.

On the 3d inst., by Rev. W. Hutto, Mr. John Shuler of Orangeburg, to Miss Henrietta Kizer of Colleton.

On the 8th inst., by Rev. W. Hutto, Mr. Augustus B. Murray to Miss Susan Weathers, all of Colleton.

By the Rev. Dr. Hillyer, on Wednesday Nov. 9, at the Baptist Church, Forsyth, Ga., Mr. Wm. M. Pendleton, of Macon, to Miss Lizzie D. Talmage, of Forsyth.

On Oct. 27th, by Rev. W. A. Florence, Rev. Thos. H. Timmons, of the North Georgia Conference, and Miss Mary E. Booth, of Madison, Ga.

Also, by the Rev. W. A. Florence, on Nov. 10th, Mr. Elbert L. Campbell, of Jasper co., Ga., and Miss Eudora J Peacock, of Madison, Ga.

Issue of November 25, 1870

Thursday at 11 o'clock A. M., by Rev. Wesley J. Smith, at the residence of the bride's mother, M. D. Stroud, and Miss Ella Sanders, both of Crawford county, Ga.

On Nov 11, by Rev. W. S. Black, Mr. T. H. Parrott of Darlington, S. C., to Miss Fanny, eldest daughter of Rev. S. Jones of the S. C. Conference.

In the M. E. Church, Auburn, Ala., Nov. 1, by Rev. W. E. Lloyd, Mr. D. G. Owen, of Pleasant Hill, Ga., and Miss Sallie B. Read.

On Nov. 13, 1870, by Rev. B. E. L. Timmons, Mr. Milton Davis and Miss Emily Freeman, all of Wilkinson co., Ga.

By Rev. T. A. Brown, on Nov. 17, Simpson Fulscher of Burke co., to Miss Julia Hughes of Houston co., Ga.

By Rev. R. H. Howren, Oct. 24, 1870, Mr. Wm. Morgan to Miss Annie Hunt, all of Washington co,. Ga.

By Rev. A. Gray, at Lawrenceville, Ga., on Nov. 13, W. Scott Thomas and Miss Mary C. Garmany, both of the former place.

On the 15th inst., by Rev. R. B. Lester, Mr. John B. Lightfoot to Mrs. Harriet A. Lightfoot, all of Macon, Ga.

On Nov. 10, by Rev. John Inabinet, Mr. Malechia Inabinet to Miss Anna Walsh, all of Orangeburg co.

Issue of December 2, 1870

On 17th Nov., in the Methodist Church, Talbotton, Ga., by Rev. J. O. A. Cook, Mr. J. L. Dozier of Columbus, to Miss Anna W. Persons, of Talbotton, Ga.

On 17th Oct., at the residence of Rev. N. Athons in Stewart co., Ga., Mr. Josiah Colley to Miss Corra Atson.

On 10th Nov., by Rev. W. R. Foote, Mr. B. M. Stovall to Miss M. O. Few, all of Morgan co., Ga.

By Rev. A. W. Moore, on the 13th instant, Mr. Vandiver Robinson to Miss Mary E. Anderson, both of Laurens co.

By Rev. S. G. Chiles, Mr. W. A. Pierce to Miss S. E. Waldren, on the 20th Oct., 1870, all of Jefferson co., Ga.

On the 4th inst., by Rev. T. A. Seals, Mr. A. Walter Mershon to Miss Eugenia C. Flynt, all of Tallafero co., Ga.

By Rev. T. A. Seals, on the 17th inst., Mr. Thomas J. Burkhalter to Miss Anna Scruggs, both of Warrenton, Ga.

In Culloden, by Rev. Wesley F. Smith, oct. 20th 1870, Mr. John jones to Mrs. S. C. jones.

In Monroe co., Oct. 26, 1870, Rev. Wesley F. Smith, Mr. S. C. Boykin, of Ala., to Miss Bettie H. O'Neal.

In Crawford county, Oct. 17th 1870, by Rev. Wesley F. Smith, Mr. Mack D. Stroud to Miss M. Ella Sanders.

In St. Luke M. E. Church South, on Wednesday Nov. 23d, by Rev. O. L. Smith, D.D., Mr. Joel A. Walker of Macon ,Ga., to Miss Cornelia F. Watt, of columbus, Ga.

On Oct. 23, by Rev. W. F. Quillian, Mr. J. L. Ware, to Miss T. E. Bussey, all of Lincoln co., Ga.

Nov. 16, near Cave Spring, Ga., by Rev. W. F. Cook, Col. J. N. Glenn of Lawrenceville, Ga., to Miss Sallie Floyd Johnson of the former place.

By Rev. Thos. G. Herbert, on 10th Nov 1870, Mr. Jno Proctor and Miss Lou B., daughter of J. J. Cooper of Abbeville co., S. C.

Nov. 24, by Rev. J. T. Ainsworth, Mr. B. A. Trice, to Mrs. Donie E. Cook, both of Baker co.

Nov. 2, by Rev. W. Lane, Mr. A. F. Berry and Miss Annie E. Copeland, both of Leon co., Florida.

Nov. 16, by Rev. W. Lane, Mr. John B. Thomas and Miss Anna F. howard, both of Thomas co., Ga.

Sept. 22, by Rev. W. S. Baker, Mr. W. J. Hodges, to Miss Nannie S. Barton.

In Quincy, Fla., by Robert L. Wiggins, Mr. John R. Franklin of Brunswick, Ga., to Miss Rosalie Nathans, of the former place

Nov. 10, 1870, by Rev. Morgan Bellah, Mr. Thos. W. Story and Miss Sallie Howel, all of Pike co., Ga.

Nov. 15, 1870, by Rev. Morgan Bellah, Mr. W. T. Lipsey and Miss W. Fossett, all of Pike co., Ga.

Nov. 23, 1870, By Rev. Morgan Bellah, Mr. James L. Lasseter and Miss Mattie M. Daniel, all of Pike co., Ga.

Issue of December 9, 1870

On the 30th November AD 1870, at the residence of Mr. John Niblack, by Rev. Dr. Leonard, Mr. John C. Paxon of Walton co., Ga., to Miss Lanora Niblack, of Columbia co., Florida.

on 15th November, by Rev. Thos. H. Timmons, Mr. Camillus M. Patterson to Miss Emma D. Beall, both of Putnam co., Ga.

At the residence of the bride's mother, by Rev. W. M. Kennedy, on the evening of the 29th Nov., Gen. John C. Vaughn, of Sweet Water, E. Tenn., to Miss Florence, daughter of Thomas and Lavinia Y. Jones, of Thomas co., Ga.

By Rev. T. S. L. Harwell, Nov. 20th 1870, Mr. W. L. Mobley to Miss S. A. Mallory, all of Troup co., Ga.

On the 10th Nov., at the residence of the bride's father, by Rev. W. F. Robison, Mr. Abram Chance of Burke co., to Miss Virginia E. Oliver, of Scriven co.

By Rev. E. G. Murrah, Nov. 22d, Mr. Larkin Tomlin to Miss Susan Kinny.

By Rev. E. G. Murrah, on 24th Nov., Mr. William Briant to Miss Gussie Maxwell.

On 29th Nov., by Rev. Jno. H. Harris, Mr. Thos. Brinn to Miss Josephine Bell, all of Henry co., Ga.

By Rev. Jno. H. Harris, Dec. 1st, Mr. Jos. M. Foster to Miss Rebecca Raven, all of Henry co., Ga.

On the 23d inst., by Rev. R. H. Rogers, Mr. Geo. W. Dossette to Miss Nannie B. Leach, all of Spalding co., Ga.

On the 17th inst., by Rev. F. Auld, Mr. John O'Cain to Miss Jennie C. Richards, all of Orangeburg co., S. C.

By Rev. J. M. Bowden, on Thursday evening, Dec. 1st, Mr. Jno. I. Miller to Miss Ambrosia A. Pitman, all of Corinth, Heard co., Ga.

Issue of December 16, 1870

In Grace Church, Sacramento, Cal., on 23d Nov. by Rev. J. H. C. Bonte, Mr. John Boggs of Colusa, Cal., to Miss Lou E., daughter of F. R. Shackelford, Macon, Ga.

In Columbia co., Fla., Dec. 4, 1870, by Rev. Dr. Leonard, Mr. Matthew J. Floyd to Miss Sarah V. Ruff.

In Columbus, Ga., by Rev. O L. Smith, Dec. 1st, 1870, Mr. A. L. Harrison and Miss Gertrude A. Street.

Nov. 24th, at the house of the bride's father, by Rev. C. J. Oliver, Mr. Robert H. jones to Miss Gertrude Hall, all of Floyd co., Ga.

At Grooversville, Dec. 8th, by Rev. Capel Raiford, Mr. Emanuel Brown to Miss Lessa J. Joiner, all of Brooks co.

By Rev. Thos. B. Lanier, Mr. George M. Ganann to Miss Hannah E. Groverstine, Nov. 29.

By Rev. Thos. B. Lanier, Dec. 7th, J. G. Morgan to Miss Susan A. Dasher, all of Effingham co., Ga.

In Marshallville, 1st Dec., by Rev. B. F. Breedlove, Mr. T. M. Tarpley of Irwinton, Ga., to Miss A. F. Vanlandingham of the former place.

On Dec. 6, by Rev. B. F. Breedlove, Mr. Jesse Waite to Miss C. S. Royal, both of Fort Valley, Ga.

On Dec. 8, by Rev. B. F. Breedlove, Mr. F. A. Adams to Miss Emma Rumph, all of Houston co., Ga.

Issue of January 4, 1871

Near Monticello, on the evening of the 15th Dec., 1870, by Rev. F. B. Davies, Mr. A. C. Potter to Miss S. L. Pope.

In Glennville, Ala., on the 29th Nov., by Rev. W. A. McCarty, Mr. A. G. Hitchens to Miss Carrie V. Rivers, all of Glennville.

In Cartersville, Ga., Nov. 10th 1870, by Rev. J. L. Pierce, Rev. B. B. Quillian, of Cave Spring, Ga., to Miss Lizzie Gaines of the former place.

On 15th Dec., by Rev. T. S. L. Harwell, Mr. Jas. Piper to Miss Lizzie Borders, all of Harris co., Ga.

By Rev. Joseph M. Gable, December 11th, at Mt. Pleasant Church, Mr. Wm. W. Wells of Atlanta, Ga., to Miss Virginia E. Baxter, grand daughter of Jesse Oslin, Esq., of Cobb co., Ga.

By Rev. Joseph M. Gable, December 11th, at Mt. Pleasant Church, Mr. A. D. Hays to Miss Ida W. Baxter, grand daughter of Jesse Oslin, Esq., of Cobb co., Ga.

Dec. 8th by Rev. W. J. Wardlaw, at the residence of the bride's father, Mr. Sumner E. Butler, of Selma, Ala., to Miss Lizzie F. Perkerson, of Fulton county, Ga.

By the Rev. Wm. B. Neal, at the bride's fathers, Rev. N. Pattilla, Nov. 20th 1870, Mr. H. N. Hargrove to Miss May Pattilla, all of Lee co., Ala.

By Rev. Wm. B. Neal, Dec. 10th 1870, Mr. H. N. Traywick to Miss Sarah L. Turk, near Loachapoka, Ala.

At the residence of the bride's father, Dr. J. S. Russell, Dec. 7th, 1870, by Rev. E. S. Tyner, Mr. Charles L. Wolf to Miss Lucy A. Russell, all of Jefferson co., Fla.

On 26th Oct., by Rev. W. K. Turner, Rev. Dr. V. H. Skelton to Miss Francis M. Sexon, all of Jefferson co., Fla.

On Dec. 1st by Rev. L. B. Bell, Mr. Howell Robbins to Miss Eliza Ann Smith, daughter of Col. Thomas Smith, all of Coosa co., Ala.

On Dec. 6th, by Rev. L. R. Bell, Mr. John A. Blyen, of Talbot co., Ga., to Miss M. L. Rodgers, daughter of William and Mariah Rodgers of Coosa co., Ala.

On the 24th Nov., near Camak, Ga., by Rev. T. A. Seals, Mr. W. F. Norman, to Miss Mary E. Brinkley, all of Warren co.

In Washington, Ga., on the 13th inst., by Rev. T. A. Seals, Rev. B. F. Farris to Miss Lydia E. Norman, daughter of Rev. G. G. Norman, late of Wilkes co., Ga.

In Columbia county, Florida, December 20, 1870, by Rev. Dr. Thomas K. Leonard, Miss Mattie Y., second daughter of Hon. Joseph Price, to Mr. James M. Perry.

At the residence of J. V. T. Wright, Esq., Dec. 20, by Rev. Jas. T. Kilgo, Mr. Gamewell M. Smith to Miss Amelia C. Wright.

On the 24th Nov., by Rev. C. J. Oliver, Mr. Robert H. Jones to Miss S. Gertrude Hall, all of Floyd co., Ga.

Issue of January 11, 1871

Dec 21, by Rev. J. W. Shores, Mr. Geo. T. Jones of Bullock Co., to Miss Sarah E. Northcutt of Pike co., Ala.

At Oxford, Ga., Dec. 15, 1870, by Rev. J. Lewis, Jr., Rev. C. C. Spence of Covington, Ga., and Miss Mattie F. Harper of Oxford, Ga.

On Dec. 27, 1870, by Rev. H. d. Moore, Mr. Duncan C. Phillips to Miss Sallie A. E. Bickley, eldest daughter of Simon P. Bickley of Talbot co., Ga.

At the Methodist Church in Thomaston, Nov. 16, by Rev. D. Kelsey, Mr. R. Riviere to Miss Fannie L. Payne.

By Rev. John R. Parker, 21st Dec., Mr. C. L. Hutchins of Gwinnett co., Ga., to Miss Lula Starr of Nacoochee Valley, Ga.

In Columbia co., Fla., Dec. 15, 1870, by Rev. Dr. Leonard, Mr. George S. Legrone to Miss Sarah C. Feagle.

In Culloden, Tuesday morning, Dec. 20, by Rev. Wesley F. Smith, Mr. Andrew A. Morgan of Crawford county, and Miss Joe L. Smith of the former place.

In Culloden, Tuesday evening, Dec. 20, by the Rev. Wesley F. Smith, Mr. Joseph L. Fincher of Upson county, and Miss Martha A. Hamlin of the former place.

Issue of January 18, 1871

On Dec. 15th 1870, by Rev. D. J. Simmons, Mr. F. W. Renneker to Miss E. J. Steinmyer, daughter of J. F. Steinmyer, all of Charleston, S. C.

On Dec. 11th 1870, by Rev. B. E. L. Timmons, Mr. Isaac O. Bower to Miss Olive E. Bishop, all of Irwinton, Ga.

At the residence of the bride's father, on the 29th Dec., by the Rev. John N. Wilcox, Mr. Tillmon D. Joiner to Miss Emily S. Skinner, all of Burke county.

Dec. 20th 1870, by the Rev. I. L. Avant, Mr. E. M. Mathews, of Crawford co., Ga., to Miss Mittie Bateman, of Houston co., Ga.

On Dec. 23d 1870, by Rev. I. L. Avant, Mr. M. R. Joyner to Miss Indiana G. Walton, of Crawford co., Ga.

On Dec. 1st 1870, by Rev. I. L. Avant, Capt. B. F. Vinson, of houston co., Ga., to Miss Jane E., daughter of J. T. Cherry, Esq., of Bibb co., Ga.

On Dec. 58th [sic], 1870 by Rev. I. L. Avant, Mr. John L. Bryant, to Miss S. P. Bryant, both of Crawford co., Ga.

By Rev. Jno. M. Bowden, on the 3d of Jan 1871, Mr. James B. Bryant to Miss Ellorah Thornton, of Palmetto, Ga.

On the 3d inst., at the residence of the bride's mother, by Rev. W. D. Bussey, Wm. B. Thomas of Macon, to Miss Nannie B. Wooten, of Lumber city, Ga.

On Sunday, Jan. 1st 1871, by Rev. J. W. McRoy, Mr. A. C. Zeigler to Miss Mary J. Austin, both of Orangeburg co., S. C.

By Rev. T. S. L. Harwell, Dec. 21st 1870, Mr. Thomas S. Cotton to Miss Eliza j. Harwell, all of Troup co., Ga.

On the 22d of Dec. 1870, by Rev. F. Auld, Mr. William V. Izlar to Miss Anna A., daughter of Col. Paul S. Felder, all of Orangeburg, S. C.

On the 15th of Dec., 1870, by Rev. W. A. Hayles, Mr. Edwin A. Cook to Miss Sallie E. Joiner, all of Jefferson co., Ga.

On the 4th inst., at Bethany, Mr. Benj. A. Reynolds to Miss Jennie E. Moore, all of Jefferson co., Ga.

On the 22d Nov., 1870, at the residence of the bride's father, Col. Geo. W. Wilson, by the Rev. J. R. Harrison, Dr. E. J. Frederick of S. C., to Miss J. F. Wilson, of Bortetourt [sic] county, Virginia.

On the 6th Dec. 1870, by Rev. V. A. Sharp, Mr. H. S. Taylor to Miss Mary, only daughter of J. D. McClure, all of Rutherford, N. C.

By Rev. V. A. Sharp, Dec. 20th, George W. Nanney to Miss Louisa, second daughter of Isham Wood, all of Rutherford, N. C.

By Rev. V. A. Sharp, Dec. 22d, Preston T. Goforth to Miss Jane Poteet, formerly of Burke co., N. C.

In Dutch Bend, Autauga, co., Ala., Dec. 15th, by Rev. Wm. A. Edwards, R. P. Houser to Mrs. Mary Dejarnett.

By Rev. J. L. Sifley, on Dec. 4th 1870, Mr. Brantley Ulmer to Miss Adelia Keitt, both of Orangeburg co., S. C.

By Rev. J. L. Sifley in Orangeburg co., S. C., on 20th Dec., Mr. Ralph Layton to Miss Salena Rush.

By Rev. J. B. Traywick, Mr. Joseph W. Major to Miss Maggie Webb, both of Anderson co., S. C.

On the 22d Dec., 1870, by Rev. D. J. Myrick, at the bride's fathers, Joseph J. Daniel to Miss Rosa Lydia Andrews, all of Liberty co., Ga.

Issue of January 25, 1871

Near White Sulphur Springs, Ga., Dec. 11, 1870, by Rev. W. J. Cotter, Mr. J. W. McKee to Miss Mollie C. Robinson.

In Marshallville, Jan. 6., by Rev. B. F. Breedlove, Mr. D. B. Frederick to Mrs. E. R. Mellard.

On the 4th inst., at the residence of Capt. Wm. G. Newman, in Atlanta, Ga., by Genl. C. A. Evans, Dr. Robert N. Payne of Ga., to Mrs. Sallie E. Payne of Miss.

By Rev. H. H. Parks, Dec. 14, 1870, Geo. M. Gordon, Esq., of Scotland, and Miss Mary J. Williams, of Richmond co., Ga.

By Rev. H. H. Parks, Dec. 28, A. P. Woodward and Miss Katie F. Royal, Augusta, Ga.

By Rev. H. H. Parks, Jan. 5, 1871, Col. Garland Snead and Mrs. Hennie R. McGolrick, Augusta.

By Rev. H. H. Parks, Jan. 11, Mr. Geo. F. Lamback and Miss Mery Belle Fargo, Augusta.

On Dec. 13, 1870, by Rev. A. Bray, Mr. John C. Flowers to Miss Laura E. Brown, both of Newton co., Ga.

In Newnan, Ga., by Rev. R. W. Bigham, Jan. 8, 1871, Mr. A. Jones and Miss Lula Bridwell.

In Coweta co., by Rev. R. W. Bigham, Jan. 11, 1871, Capt. Jas. H. Wragg of Rome, Ga., and Miss Laura C. Overby.

Near Camilla, Ga., Jan. 12, by Rev. J. T. Ainsworth, Mr. James H. Palmer to Miss Mollie E. Cox.

On 12th inst., by Rev. Chas. R. Jewett, Mr. Jno. B. Chisholm and Miss Mary A. ,daughter of Mr. Robt. R. Evans, all of Thomasville, Ga.

At the residence of Rev. H. McClenaghan, Jan. 10, 1871, by Rev. W. Thomas, Mr. J. Knight Gibson and Miss E. Eliza Black, all of Marion co., S. C.

By Rev. O. L. Smith, Jan. 17, 1871, Mr. Frederick Wilhelm of Salem, Ala., and Mrs. Ann Eliza Gilmore, of Columbus, Ga.

In Harris co,. Ga., Jan. 12, 1871, by Rev. A. J. Dean, Mr. John F. Boyd of Muscogee co., Ga., to Miss Leola Miller of the former place

By Rev. Thos. B. Lanier, Jan. 18, 1871, Mr. John F. Tool of Whitesville, Effingham co., Ga., to Miss Sally J. Brown of jefferson co., Ga.

In Orangeburg co., S. C., Nov. 3, 1870, by Rev. James C. Stoll, Mr. James Way to Miss Missouri Bull, all of Orangeburg co., S. C.

By Rev. James C. Stoll in Charleston co., S. C., Nov. 24, 1870, Mr. David Thomas to Miss Carrie Thomas, of Charleston co., S. C.

By Rev. James C. Stoll in Charleston co., S. C., Dec. 20, 1870, Mr. Henry Bunch to Miss Mary Bunch, all of Charleston co., S. C.

By Rev. James C. Stoll in Charleston co., S. C., Dec. 22, 1870, Mr. Reuben Martin to Miss Mary Rush, all of Charleston co., S. C.

By Rev. James C. Stoll in Charleston co., S. C., Jan. 5, 1871, Mr. Freddie Evans to Miss Lizzie Dantzler, all of Orangeburg co., S. C.

Issue of February 1, 1871

On the 15th of Jan. 1871, By Rev. J. A. Wood, Mr. James M. Gambrell of Ninety Six, to Miss E. C. Clinkscales of Williamston, S. C.

By Rev. J. W. McGehee, Jan. 5th 1871, at the residence of Rev. Hiram Dorman, Mr. Sanford T. Harrison to Miss Antionette M. Dorman, both of Harris co., Ga.

By Rev. John Calvin Johnson, in Clarke co., Ga., on 29th Dec. 1870, Mr. James T. Bowden to Miss Malissa Faulkner.

By Rev. John Calvin Johnson, in Greene co., Ga., on 5th Jan. 1871, Mr. Wiley B. McRae to Miss Laura A. McWhorter.

By Rev. John Calvin Johnson, in Clarke co., Ga., on Jan. 5th 1871, Mr. James E. Whitehead to Miss Sarah A. S. Southerland.

On 4th Jan., by Rev. James Griffeth, George Ingham to Miss Maggie Tomlin, all of Taylor co., Ga.

Jan. 19th 1871, at the residence of Rev. Thos. F. Pierce, Union Point, Ga., by Rev. Geo. W. Yarbrough, Mr. Joel F. Thornton to Miss Annie Foster Pierce.

Jan. 19th 1871, at the residence of Rev. Thos. F. Pierce, Union Point, Ga., by Rev. Geo. W. Yarbrough, Mr. Ed G. Williams to Miss Kate Pierce.

Jan 12th 1871, by Rev. J. M. Richardson, at the residence of the bride's mother, Mr. Henry W. Williams, of Springplace, Ga., to Miss Clara M. Ransom, of Fairmount, Gordan co., Ga.

On 17th Jan., by Rev. J. M. Richardson, Mr. John C. Harris to Miss Sallie A. Brown, all of Springplace, Ga.

By Rev. T. S. L. Harwell, Jan. 10th 1871, Mr. J. G. Andrews to Miss E. A. Cotton.

By Rev. T. S. L. Harwell, Jan. 10th 1871, Mr. G. W. Poer to Miss L. A. Cotton, all of Harris co., Ga.

By Rev. F. A. Kimbell, Jan. 17th 1871, Mr. J. D. Proctor to Miss Julia I. Mays, all of Forsyth, Ga.

On the morning of the 24th inst., by Rev. F. M. Daniel, at the residence of Dr. L. McLester, Cuthbert, Ga., Mr. Enoch Brown, of Dawson, to Miss Lucinda G. McLester, of the former place.

By Rev. J. W. Simmons, at the residence of Mr. Wm. C. Matthews, in Washington co., Jan. 18th, Robert W. Hardwick to Miss Zimmie S. Matthews.

On the 26th inst., by Rev. H. H. Parks, Rev. Clement C. Cary to Miss Callie Benson, all of Augusta, Ga.

By the same, 26th inst., Jno. W. Smith to Mrs. Anna M. German, all of Augusta, Ga.

By the same, 19th inst., Jay O. Gailey, of Athens, Ga., Miss Nellie G. Adam, of Augusta, Ga.

On Dec. 15th 1870, by Rev. R. H. Jones, Mr. William L. Fain, of Atlanta, Ga., to Miss Fannie L. Gower, of Cartersville,Ga.

Issue of February 8, 1871

By Rev. W. M. Watts, Jan. 4, Mr. E. B. Daniel to Miss M. E. Laing, all of Liberty co., Ga.

By Rev. W. M. Watts, Jan. 25, Rev. A. J. Hughes to Miss M. A. Rodgers, all of Liberty co., Ga.

In Cuthbert, Ga., on Jan. 5, 1871, by Rev. R. B. Lester, Mr. Sid B. Trapp to Miss Mollie E. George.

On Jan. 24, by Rev. J. T. Ainsworth, Mr. Wm. L. Davis to Miss Bettie E. Walker, both of Mitchell co., Ga.

On Jan. 25, by Rev. J. T. Ainsworth, Mr. Wm. T. Huff to Miss Sallie V. Scurry, both of Butler co., Ga.

At the residence of the bride's father, Jan. 15, by Rev. F. F. Reynolds, Mr. A. M. Baxter to Miss Eunice Strickland, all of Gwinnett co., Ga.

By Rev. F. F. Reynolds, Jan. 26, at the residence of the bride's father, Mr. E. S. Wiley to Miss A. O. Brandan, all of Gwinnett co., Ga.

In Muscogee, Jan. 26, 1871, by Rev. S. D. Clements, Mr. Ozias Thomaston to Miss Sumantha H. White.

By Rev. J. R. Little, Jan. 11, 1871, Mr. J. B. Withers of Valdosta, Southwestern Georgia, to Miss C. M. Ivy, of Lancaster, S. C.

On Dec. 28, 1870, by Rev. W. F. Roberts, Mr. James A. Williamson to Miss Emma F. coleman, both of Early co., Ga.

By Rev. Thos. F. Pierce, Jan. 5, Mr. B. S. Irwin of Washington to Miss Sallie Hill of Wilkes co., Ga.

By Rev. Thos. F. Pierce, Jan. 18, Mr. Alexander Smith of Washington to Miss Sallie Swann, all of Green co., Ga.

At the residence of Dr. J. S. Russell's, Jan. 17, 1871, by Rev. E. S. Tyner, Mr. B. P Murphey to Miss Mattie A. Russell, all of Wahkeenah, Fla.

At the residence of Rev. W. F. S. Powell near Newnan, Ga., by Rev. R. W. Bigham, Jan. 17, Mr. A. P. Brewster to Miss Sue Powell.

Jan. 17, by Rev. J. B. Traywick, Mr. Marion Newton to Miss Ellen Martin, both of Anderson co,. S. C.

Jan. 19, 1871, by Rev. Jones, D. D., Mr. W. B. Candler, of Villa Rica, and miss Lizzie Slaughter of Atlanta.

On Jan. 26, in Rome, Ga., by Rev. W. F. Cook, Rev. C. J. Oliver, of the North Ga. Conference to Miss Fannie T. Shropshire, of Floyd co., Ga.

Issue of February 15, 1871

Dec. 29th 1870, by the Rev. W. H. Graham, in Pike co., Ga., Mr. W. H. Bowden of Meriwether, to Miss C. P. Range, of Pike co., Ga.

By the same on the 5th Jan. 1871, Mr. Henry Nelson to Miss Martha A. Rucker, all of Pike co., Ga.

On Feb. 2d, 1871, by Rev. W. Williams, W. W. Walker, Esq., to Miss Loula Moring, all of Crawfordville, Wakulla co., Fla.

By Rev. G. Hughes on 22d Jan. 1871, Mr. A. S. Welchel to Miss Julia A. Neisler, both of Lumpkin co., Ga.

By Rev. W. W. Stewart, on Jan. 26th 1871, Mr. J. S. Wall to Miss Adda Smith ,all of Marion co., Ga.

In Macon co., Jan. 31st, by Rev. J. B. McGehee, Mr. William Wooten, of Dawson, to Miss Anna Stevens.

In Pike co., Ga., on the 22d Jan. 1871, by Rev. J. B. Hanson, Mr. J. W. Peurifoy to Miss Hettie Maddux, daughter of the late Rev. P. N. Maddux.

In Fort Valley, Ga., Jan. 18th 1871, by Rev. B. F. Breedlove, Mr. M. T. Colyer to Mrs. S. L. Andrews.

On 31st Jan. 1871, by Rev. J. J. Sealy, Mr. Jos. G. Little to Miss Fannie Fagan, of Newnanville, E. Fla.

By Rev. W. Hutto, on 7th Feb., Mr. Hansford Moorer to Miss Mary Weathers, all of Colleton co.

On the 2d Feb., by Rev. C. Raiford, Mr. Anthony W. Ivey to Miss Rebecca M. Peacock, all of Thomas county.

By the same, on the 5th Feb., Mr. James M. Stansell to Miss Martha J. Harrell, all of Thomas co., Ga.

Issue of February 22, 1871

In Meriwether co., Ga., Feb. 2, by Rev. Alex. M. Thigpen, Mr. E. H. Blount and Miss Mary J. Smith.

On the 9th of Feb., by Rev. Geo. C. Leavel, Mr. John W. Hinson of Gadsden co., Fla., to miss Penny Maxwell, of Decatur co., Ga.

Jan 19, by Rev. A. W. Walker, Mr. Samuel Guilds to Miss Hannah Harrell, all of Georgetown, S. C.

Feb 2, in Georgetown, S. C., by Rev. A. W. Walker, Mr. William Thompson to Miss Agnes Sian.

Feb. 2, by Rev A. W. Walker, Mr. George R. Mercer to Miss Kate Haselden, both of Georgetown, S.. C.

By Rev. A. J. Dean, Jan. 26, 1871, Mr. G. Peddy of Ala., to Miss Sally Twilley, of Columbus, Ga.

By Rev. A. J. Dean, Jan. 26, 1871, Mr. D. McSwain to Miss M. J. Wallace, all of Columbus, Ga.

By Rev. A. J. Dean, Feb. 5, 1871, Mr. W. J. Vickery to Miss M. E. Riley, all of Columbus, Ga.

By Rev. A. J. Dean, Feb. 7, 1871, Mr. S. Thriff to Miss M. Wadsworth, all of Columbus, Ga.

By Rev. A. J. Dean, Feb. 7, 1871, Mr. J. C. Parr to Miss Ophelia Agniero, all of Columbus, Ga.

At Belinger chapel, Jan. 12, by Rev. W. A. Clarke, Mr. J. B. Bates to Miss S. E. Barker.

At same place and time, by Rev. W. A. Clarke, Mr. W. A. Riley to Miss R. P. Barker, all of Barnwell co., S. C.

In Crawford co., Jan. 12, 1871, by Rev. Wesley F. Smith, Mr. B. S. Scott of Forsyth ,Ga., and Miss Lizzie B. Moran of Crawford co.

On Jan 19, 1871, by Rev. F. Auld, Mr. Robert A. Price to Miss Leak C. Bell, all of Orangeburg co,. S. C.

On Jan 22, by Rev. F. Auld, Mr. John A. Rast to Miss Asenath R. Pooser, all of Orangeburg co., S. C.

In Troup co., Ga., Feb. 1, by Rev. W. J. Cotter, Mr. James H. Greene to Miss Fannie A. Market.

On the 5th inst., by Rev. J. H. Zimmerman, Dr. H. E. Unger of Lexington co., to Miss Ann C. Bouknight, of Edgefield co., S. C.

By Rev. Thos. B. Lanier, in Whitesville, Effingham co., Ga., Mr. Z. H. Powers to Miss Sarah E. Rahn.

On 5th Feb., at Conyers, Ga., by Rev. J. L. Stewart, Mr. S. H. Lamanda to Miss S. S. Stewart.

On same day, by Rev. J. O. Stewart, Mr. J. C. Farmer to Miss Eugenia Hudson.

In Crawfordville, Fla., Feb. 3d, by Rev. W. Williams, W. W. Walker to Miss Louisa Moring.

By Rev. J. W. McRoy, Feb. 15th 1871, W. H. Matheney to Miss Narcissa A. Hutto, both of Barnwell, S. C.

Issue of March 1, 1871

On the 31st Jan. at the residence of Mr. U. B. Harrold, Americus, Ga., by Rev. W. B. Merritt, Miss M. A. M. Fogle of Columbus, Ga., to Mr. Wm. Lewis Pfohl, of Salem, N. C.

Near Shady Dale, Jasper co., on 16th Feb., by Rev. F. B. Davis, Mr. T. H. Kennon of Newton co., to Miss M. E. Speerman of Jasper co.

By the same, Mr. James T. Goodman to Miss Emily Dawkins, all of Jasper co., Ga.

By Rev. W. A. Faries, on 5th Jan. 1871, Judge S. Stovall to Mrs. Matilda F. Magruder, all of Columbia co., Ga.

By the same, on 5th Feb., 1871, Joseph Isham to Miss Ann E. Albra, all of Columbia co., Ga.

By the same, Thomas E. Benning to Miss Pattie M. Crawford, on 7th Feb., 1871, all of Columbia co., Ga.

Feb. 2d, 1871, by Rev. F. A. Kimbell, Mr. Augusta W. Bramlett to Miss Georgia A. Hill, all of Monroe co., Ga.

On Feb. 1st, 1871, by Rev. S. D. Clements, Mr. Geo. A. Redding, to Miss Marie L. Passmore, all of Harris co., Ga.,

In Cuthbert, Ga., Feb. 15th, by Rev. J. R. Owen, Mr. John B. Lee to Mrs. Lou A. Carter.

Issue of March 15, 1871

Near Pendleton, S. C., Feb. 23, 1871, by Rev. Hugh McLees, Mr. Wm. M. Graham of Bolton, Miss., and Miss M. J. Simpon [sic] of Anderson co., S. C.

In Crawford co., Ga., Feb. 16, 1871, by Rev. I. L. Avant, P. D. McCarty, Esq., of Macon Co., Ga., to Miss Mary Ann, eldest daughter of Rev. Lucius G. Evans, of Crawford co., Ga.

On Feb. 23, 1871, by Rev. Arthur L. Kennedy, Col. S. P. Hutchinson of Columbia co., Ga., to Mrs. E. Jennie Stone of Edgefield co., S. C.

Jan 26, 1871, by Rev. J. P. Bailey, Mr. J. A. Richey to Miss Emma M. Weems, both of Bartow co., Ga.

On Feb. 22, by Rev. D. J. Myrick, in Covington, Ga., Mr. Alfred S. Mandeville of Athens, Ga., to Miss Ann Eliza Woodson of Covington, Ga.

In Eufaula., Ala., Feb. 1, by Rev. A. J. Briggs, Benj. Leroy and Emily S. Wiggins.

Feb. 14, in Eufaula, by Rev. A. J. Briggs, J. M. Flournoy and Emily P. Williams.

Feb. 23, in Eufaula, by Rev. A. J. Briggs, N. T. Christian and Mary C. Williams.

By Rev. J. H. D. McRae, on Feb. 19, Mr. George Witt and Miss Louisa Taylor, all of Columbia co., Fla.

By Rev. G. Hughes, on Feb. 23, 1871, Mr. Mayor B. Rice of Forsyth co., GA., To Miss M. L. Smith of Lumpkin co., Ga.

By Rev. H. H. Parks, Feb. 21, Mr. Geo. Maul to Miss Emeline E. Walker, both of Richmond co., Ga.

By Rev. H. H. Parks, Feb. 28, Mr. Henry N. Freeman to Miss Annie W. Taliaferro, both of Augusta, Ga.

On the 23d Feb., by Rev. John Inabinet, Mr. Joseph W. Hodges of Abbeville co., to Miss Amy C. Sistrunk, of Orange co.

On 23d Feb., by the Rev. W. C. Dunlap, Mr. Elbert S. Cassady to Miss Bettie Strange, daughter of Benj. Strange, all of Chatooga co., Ga.

In Georgetown, S. C., on 21st Feb., by Rev. A. W. Walker, Mr. Edwin D. Doar to Miss Alice Croft.

By Rev. L. P. Neese, Mr. Newton A. Glass to Miss Virginia Hightower; Mr. I. S. Bellah to Miss N. I. Askew, all of Henry co., Ga.

On the 1st of March 1871, by Rev. A. W. Harris, Mr. J. P. Rivers, of clay co., to Miss Margaret Glisson, of Putnam co., all of Fla.

Also, by Rev. A. W. Harris, on the 2d of March, 1871, Mr. E. C. Summerlin to Miss Ellen Gnan, all of Green Cove Spring.

In Orangeburg co., S. C., Feb. 2d, 1871 by Rev. James C. Stoll, Dr. C. T. Thompson to Mrs. Jewella J. Stocker, all of Orangeburg co., S. C.

By the same in Orangeburg co., S. C., Feb. 14th 1871, Mr. Mr. A. P. Avinger to Miss M. E. Shuler, all of Orangeburg co., S. C.

By the same in Orangeburg co., S. C., March 2, 1871, Mr. Lewis Dantzler to Miss Catharine Bull, all of Orangeburg co., S. C.

On 9th Feb., by Rev. R. B. Tarrant, Miss Narcissus Inabinet of Orangeburg, to Mr. A. C. Free, of Barnwell co.

On 23rd Feb. by the same, Mr. Vastine Livingston to Miss Carrie Zeiglar, all of Orangeburg co.

Feb. 28th 1871, by the Rev. S. D. Clements, Mr. Geo. P. Lynch to Miss Colistia A. Slayton, all of Harris co., Ga.

By Rev. F. B. Davies, on the 21st Feb., Mr. Eli S. Glover, to Mrs. Sarah A. Hunter, all of Monticello, Ga.

Near Hillsboro, Ga., on the 2d of March, by Rev. F. B. Davies, Mr. Francis C. Goolsby, of Jasper co., to Miss Carrie E. White of Jones co., Ga.

Issue of March 22, 1871

On March 2, in Macon, by Rev. H. J. Harvey, Mr. Robt. L. Cain and Miss Annie E. Legg.

On Jan. 25, by R. F. Jones, Mr. L. W. Bohannan and Miss Ida Barnett of Coweta co., Ga.

On Feb. 28, by R. F. Jones, Mr. Jno. W. Peavy and Miss Hattie Williams of Merriwether co., Ga.

On March 2, 1871, by Rev. J. R. Mayson, at the residence of Mr. Charlie Sentell, Mr. Lee F. Heflin of Fulton co., to Miss V. M. Reynolds of Fayette co., Ga., daughter of the late Rev. Edward W. Reynolds of the North Ga. Conference.

In White co., Ga., March 5, 1871, at the residence of Mr. C. Meadors, grandfather of the bridegroom, by Rev. B. E. L. Timmons, Mr. George Quillian of Hall co., Ga., to Miss Amanda, daughter of the Rev. A. F. Underwood of the Baptist Church of White co,. GA.

At the residence of Dr. Henry S. Wimberly of Twiggs co., Ga., on the 8th inst., by Rev. A. A. Robinson, Mr. John E. Taylor to Miss Alice L. Wimberly.

Issue of March 29, 1871

On the 2d March, by Rev. W. Hutto, Madison Smith to Miss Harriet Howell, all of Colleton co., S. C.

On the 5th March, 1871, by Rev. W. F. Norton, Mr. George Allen to Miss Ella Parks, all of Montgomery co., Ala.

In Covington, Ga., March 7th 1871, by Rev. C. A. Evans, Mr. Wm. A. Hemphill to Mrs. Emma B. Luckie.

In Georgetown, Ga., on 12th March, by Rev. E. H. McGehee, Dr. F. M. Bledsoe to Mrs. Minnie Goode.

In Eufaula, Ala., March 6, by Rev. A. J. Briggs, George Vaughn to Maliere Gibson.

On the 16th March, by Rev. A. J. Briggs, in Eufaula, J. J. Creyan to Maggie Buett.

Issue of April 5, 1871

At Jesup, Wayne co., Ga., by Rev. W. M. Kennedy, Mr. M. Carter to Miss Helen Lee, all of that place.

On 28th Feb. 1871, by Rev. J. A. Mood, Mr. Saml. F. Fant, to Miss Fannie J. Lysles [sic], all of Newberry, S. C.

By Rev. J. A. Mood, near Newberry, S. C., March 2, 1871, Mr. James Culbreath of Edgefield, S. C., to Miss Abbie Merchant, of Newberry, S. C.

By Rev. R. W. Flournoy in Jefferson co., Ga., at the residence of Mr. T. N. Polan, on the evening of the 22d of March, Dr. Isaac C. Vaughn to Miss Mattie L. Whigham.

In Decatur co., Ga., March 22, 1871, by Rev. R. W. Dixon, Hunter Satterfield, of Bainbridge, Ga., to Miss sallie Bowie, of Decatur co., Ga.

On March 15, in Summerville, by Rev. L. B. Bouchelle, Mr. J. D. Dunford, of Texas, to Miss Ann E. Dye of Emmanuel co., Ga.

By Rev. L. B. Bouchelle, March 21, Mr. G. D. Wells and miss Mary F. inman, both of Summerville, Ga.

By Rev. W. F. Robison, on 21st March, Mr. Wm. B. Dukes to Mrs. S. W. Black, both of Harris co., Ga.

By Rev. W. F. Robison, on 28th March, in Harris co., Ga., Mr. James Luttrell of Tenn., to Miss J. A., daughter of Judge Torly.

Issue of April 12, 1871

March 28th, by Rev. Thos. T. Christian, Mr. H. J. Martin to Miss Carrie Oslin, all of Pleasant Hill, Talbot co., Ga.

Near Monticello, Ga., on 21st March, by Rev. F. B. Davies, Mr. James L. Campbell to miss Martha Elder.

By Rev. L. A. Darsey, on the 26th March, Mr. James Gould to Miss Emma F. Chitty, all of Bulloch co., Ga.

In Talbot co., March 21st, by Rev. T. A. Seals, Mr. Ansel B. Phelps, of Warrenton, Ga., to Miss S. Emma Leonard, of former place.

In Augusta, Ga., on 4th inst., by Rev. T. A. Seals, Mr. E. P. Heath to Miss Lucy D. Buford, all of Warrenton.

On the 26th March, by Rev. W. P. Rivers, Mr. J. L. Erwin to Miss J. D. Coney, both of Floyd co., Ga.

Issue of April 19, 1871

In Schley co., Ga., March 19, by Rev. R. F. Williamson, Rev. W. B. Merrett of Americus, Ga., to Miss Fannie Williamson of Schley co,. Ga.

In the M. E. Church, Dec. 25, 1870 at Lewisburg, West Virginia, by Rev. P. S. E. Seixas, Rev. Geo. G. Smith, Jr., to Miss Nannie Lynn Lipps, daughter of John Lipps, Esq.

On April 5, 1871, by Rev. Alex. P. Wright, Mr. W. B. Cunningham to Miss Julia A. Boston, all of Lowndes co., Ga.

By Rev. W. D. Heath, March 21, Mr. James F. Dillard to Miss Lizzie Hutcherson, all of Oglethorpe co., Ga.

Issue of April 26, 1871

In Rome, Ga., April 8th by Rev. W. F. Cook, Mr. Albin Omberg to Miss sue M. Gregory, all of Rome, Ga.

Near Dalton, Ga., on 6th April, by Rev. W. T. Hamilton, Mr. John L. King to Mrs. Martha E. Keys.

By Rev. B. F. Breedlove, in Fort Valley, Ga., April 9th, Mr. J. M. Horn to Miss M. C. Vinson.

By the same near Fort Valley, Ga., April 20th, Mr. W. V. Culler of S. C., to Miss Anna M. Houser.

Issue of May 3, 1871

April 4th by Rev. J. W. Kelly at Brook Green on the Waccamaw, Rev. D. W. Seale of the S. C. Conf. to Miss Anna Larricott.

In Cave Spring, Ga., April 13, 1871, by Rev. B. B. Quillian, Mr. H. G. Peters of Rome, to Miss Lou Stoffragen, late of Taladega, Ala.

On the evening of the 18th April, in Jefferson co., miss., by Rev. Samuel Montgomery, Mr. Emory A. Maddux, of Georgia, to Miss M. Arlone Torrey.

On the 6th April 1871, Mr. George t. Brown, of Leon co., Florida, to Miss Margaret C. McKinnon, of Thomas co., Ga.

Near Long Cane, Troup county, Ga., April 18th, by Rev. J. S. Sappington, Hon. Hiram Dennis, to Miss Susan A. L. Brady.

In Thomson, Ga., on the 23d of April 1871, by Rev. F. P. Brown, Dr. C. O. Rush, and Miss Ella T. Bevens, both of Thomson.

In Pulaski co., Ga., on 12th April, by Rev. H. C. Fentress, Mr. W. H. Pool to Miss N. E. L. Wynn.

April 19th, by Rev. A. A. Robinson, Mr. John D. Lawson, of Americus, Ga., to Miss Mary E. Wimberly, of Twiggs county, Ga.

At the Methodist Episcopal Church, in Athens, Ga., on 29th April by the Rev. Eustace W. Spear, Miss Susie T. Hill of Athens, to Mr. Robert H. Johnston, Jr., of Griffin, Ga.

Issue of May 10, 1871

By Rev. R. H. Luckey, 30th March, Mr. Abraham Foreman to Miss Josephine Peacock, all of Thomas co., Ga.

By Rev. R. H. Luckey, on 27th April, Mr. W. Dudley Peacock to Miss Mary H. williams, all of Thomas co., Ga.

On 9th April by Rev. J. C. Crisp, Leroy Burns to Miss H. H. Tapp, both of Spartanburg co,. S. C.

On 25th April by Rev. W. Hutto, Mr. Thomas M. Sloan of Charleston, S. C., to Miss Enora M. Moorer, of Colleton, S. C.

On 27th April by Rev. W. Hutto, Mr. Abram E. Shuler to Miss Julia W. Edwards, all of Orangeburg, S. C.

In Monroe co., near Crawford's Station, on the 2d inst., by Rev. J. W. Burke, Mr. H. C. Fryer, of Blakely, Ga., to Miss Emma C. Etheridge, of the former place.

On the 23d April by Rev. J. C. Crisp, Mr. W. H. West to Miss Nancy A. West, all of Spartanburg, S. C.

On 6th April by Rev. R. B. Tarrant, Mr. C. J. Straman to Miss Rosa Odom, all of Orangeburg, S. C.

Issue of May 17, 1871

By Rev. W. T. Hamilton at the residence of James H. Huff, Red Clay, Ga., May 4th, Mr. E. W. Dagnall to Miss Lizzie C. Senter.

April 25th, in Jacksonville, Fla., in St. John's Episcopal Church, by Rev. R. H. Weller, Rev. Frederic Pasco, of the Florida Annual Conference, M. E. Church, South, to Miss Maria C., daughter of the late Judge Doggett, of Jacksonville.

On the 4th inst., by Rev. L. T. Mizell, Mr. Joseph H. Murray of Watkinsville, to Miss Eugenia P. Reynolds of Powder Springs, Ga.

On 25th April, by Rev. Jas. E. Hughes, Hon. A. W. Johnson to Miss Mary J. Mashburn, all of Forsyth co., Ga.

On May 3d, by Rev. J. T. Ainsworth, George W. Mayo to Miss Mattie McGregor, both of Baker co., Ga.

Issue of May 24, 1871

On the 10th of May, by the Rev. F. P. Brown, Dr. Wm. A. Collins of McDuffie co., to Miss Bertie Dozier, of Columbia co., Ga.

On the 11th May, by the Rev. James N. Myers, Mr. J. J. Willard, of Rome, Ga., to Miss Jessie S. Candler, of Carroll co., Ga.

Issue of May 31, 1871

In Milledgeville, Ga., May 17th, by Rev. A. J. Jarrell, Dr. C. P. Hartwell, of Albany, to Mrs. Mary W. Hodges, of Milledgeville.

On the 16th of May, 1871, by Rev. E. F. Anderson, Mr. Richard B. McRee of Clark, Ga., to Mrs. Mollie Z. Suber, widow of Prof. Thos. S. Zuber, of Fort Deposit, Ala.

By Rev. William M. Jerdone, April 1, 1871, in the M. E. Church, South, in Ocala, Mr. Joseph H. Sears, of Plymouth, Mass., and Miss Emilie C. Stowe, of New Haven, Conn.

By Rev. W. J. Cotter, on the 11 inst., in Troup co., Ga., Mr. J. W. Sledge, to Mrs. Mary E. Hill.

In Sparta, Ga., May 2d, by Rev. A. J. Jarrell, Dr. Charles S. Strother, of Barnesville, to Miss Lula Lamar, of Sparta.

On the 11th inst., at the Methodist church in Hawkinsville, by Rev. Chas. A. Fulwood, F. H. Bozeman, Esq., to Miss Celia Lester Lucas, all of Hawkinsville, Ga.

May 11th, by Rev. J. T. Ainsworth, H. c. Hays, to Miss Mary H. Tenison, both of Mitchell co., Ga.

In McDuffie co., Ga., May 4th 1871, by Rev. Amos Johnson, Mr. Joseph Dunevent, to Miss Mary S. R. Ticen.

In Tallahassee, Florida, on May 9th, by Rev. T. W. Moore, Mr. Joseph A. Edmondson, to Miss Louisa M. Damon, all of said city.

On the 17th May, by Rev. F. A. Kimbell, Dr. Wm. E. Murphey, of North Alabama, to Mrs. Sarah A. Lindsay, of Lagrange, Ga.

In Florence, Ga., May 2d, by Rev. J. D. Waddell, Mr. H. H. Hill, to Miss R. E. V. Latimer, all of Florence, Ga.

Issue of June 7, 1871

By Rev. W. H. Graham, May 14, 1871, Mr. W. P. Elliott to Mrs. W. A. Chandler, all of Pike co., Ga.

By Rev. W. H. Graham, May 21, Mr. George W. Stocks to Miss Lucy A. Hawkins, all of Pike co., Ga.

On the 16th May, at her father's residence, by Rev. Jno. J. Little, Mr. William H. Phelps to Miss Mancy F. Bowden.

By Rev. Jno. J. Little, on the 23d May, Mr. William H. Wyche to Miss Margaret A. Chunn, all of Meriwether co., Ga.

By Rev. J. B. Hanson, May 23d, in Barnesville, Ga., Mr. R. M. Murphy to Miss Dora Lee, daughter of W. A. Lee, late of Virginia.

On the 24th May, by Rev. J. Chambers, Mr. James G. Tanner to Miss Maggie E. Blalock, all of Carrollton, Carrol co., Ga.

By Rev. Jas. T. Lowe, on the 28th May, Mr. Cepkas R. Spearman to Matilda R. StJohn, all of Troup Co., Ga.

May 25th, 1871, by the Rev. Geo. C. Clarke, C. W. Duncan, son of Rev. John P. Duncan, of N. Ga. Conf., to Miss Missouri F. Kidd, of Baker co., Ga.

Issue of June 14, 1871

By Rev. W. Lane, on 6th April 1871, Mr. George T. Brown, of Leon co., Fla., to Miss Margaret C., daughter of Mr. K. and Ann McKinnon, of Thomas county, Ga.

On the 1st inst., by the Rev. J. H. Zimmerman, Henry Hill, Esq., to Miss G. E. Strother, all of Edgefield co., S. C.

May 25th 1871, in Whitesville, Harris co., Ga., by Rev. R. S. L. Harwell, Mr. W. A. Harwell, of Troup co., Ga., to Miss Ella T., daughter of T. J. Shepard, of Liberty co., Ga.

In Columbia co., Fla., June 1st 1871, by Rev. T. K. Leonard, Mr. William H. Perry to Miss Eugenia Tanner.

On the 16th of May 1871 ,by Rev. E. S. Tyner, Mr. H. C. Ferris to Miss Ada M. Britt, all of Tampa, Fla.

Issue of June 21, 1871

In Perry, Ga., June 7, 1871, by Rev. Walter Knox, Mr. Charles M. Brown to Miss Mary E. Mann, all of Perry.

June 1, 1871, at the residence of the bride's father, in Calhoun co., Ga., by Rev. T. A. Armistead, Mr. Osgood A. Barry, of Cuthbert, Ga., to Miss Eliza J. Allison, of Calhoun co., Ga.

On June 6, 1871, at Coleman's Station, Ga., by Rev. B. J. Baldwin, Mr. Benjamin G. Blanten, of Talbot co,. Ga., to Miss Lela Marshall, daughter of Daniel Marshall.

On April 27, 1871, by Rev. B. J. Baldwin, Mr. T. J. Lanier, of Water Valley ,Miss., to Miss m. J. Mounger, daughter of Judge E. Mounger, of Randolph co., Ga.

By Rev. E. G. Murrah in Reynold's Chapel Church, in Hancock co., Ga., Mr. E. A. J. Harris, of Talbot co., Ga., to Miss Willie M. Garrand.

In Zebulon, on 6th inst., by Rev. J. P. Duncan, Mr. J. M. Ware, of Barnesville, to Miss Nannie, daughter of Judge Green, of the former place.

By Rev. J. L. Sifly, April 19, 1871, Col. J. O. Brock to Miss Warington E. Oliver, both of Clarendon, S. C.

By Rev. J. L. Sifly, June 8, 1871, Mr. George W. Smith of Columbia, S. C., to Miss Miranda E. Broughton, of Clarendon, S. C.

Issue of June 28, 1871

In East Macon, on the 30th ult., by Rev. J. W. Burke, Mr. John glowers to Miss Sarah A. Givin.

On the 3d June, by Rev. W. T. Hamilton, Mr. A. E. Stockburger, of Whitfield co., to Miss C. M. Nance, of Catoosa co., Ga.

In Varnell Station, Ga., June 15th, by Rev. W. T. Hamilton, Mr. Elijah Cagle to Miss N. L. Whittimore.

On 14th June, by Rev. D. J. Myrick, Mr. John P. Harris to Miss Betty A. Groves, in Shiloh Church, both of Newton co., Ga.

At the residence of the bride's father, Judge N. Land, on the 8th June, by the Rev. Warren Aiken, Mr. F. H. Land, of Twiggs co., Ga., to Miss Mona A. Land, of Cass co., Ga.

On June 15th, by Rev. J. L. Shuford, Mr. Wm. McConnell of Fairfield, S. C., to Mrs. Mary M. Coogler, of Lexington, S. C. Christian Neighbor please copy.

Issue of July 12, 1871

On June 25th 1871, by Rev. Jas. W. Parks, Henry C. Johnson, Esq., to Mrs. Emily m. Johnson, all of Dawsonville, Ga.

On 11th June 1871, by Rev. Wm. T. Norman, the Rev. John B. Wade, of hart co., to Mrs. Kizziah Pledger, of Elbert co., Ga.

On May 16, by Rev. E. H. Giles, Mr. C. G. Waterman, of Orange co., Fla., to Miss Jettie R. Forbes, of Sumter co., Fla.

In the Methodist Church at Nacoochee Valley, 11th April 1871, by Rev. John r. Parker, Mr. A. P. Williams to Miss A. H. Allan.

On the 28th May, by Rev. W. S. Black, Mr. J. I. Coffee of Alabama, to Miss W. F. Watkins, youngest daughter of Mr. W. T. Watkins of Stanley co., N. C.

Issue of July 19, 1871

In Milledgeville, Ga., June 29th, by Rev. A. J. Jarrell, Mr. B. B. Adams to Miss Eudora Wright, all of Milledgeville.

At the circuit parsonage of Marion ct., S. C. Con., by Rev. W. W. Jones, Mr. John Jordan to Miss Maggie L. Johnson, all of Orangeburg Dist., S. C.

In Newnansville, Fla., July 5th 1871, by Rev. J. M. Stokes, Mr. Michael H. lucy to Miss Jennie E. Wilson, all of Newnansville.

Issue of July 26, 1871

By Rev. J. W. Simmons in Sandersville, June 15th, Mr. James W. McLendon of west Point, to Miss Annie E., daughter of Rev. A. C. c. Thomson, of Sandersville.

In Dawson, Ga., on the 13th inst., by Rev. E. H. McGehee, Mr. Horace G. Chase to Miss Martha L. Gardner.

Issue of August 2, 1871

By Rev. J. C. Crisp, May 21st 1871, Mr. James Wood to Miss M. A. Cobb, both of Cedar Hill, Spartanburg co., S. C.

By Rev. J. C. Crisp, June 15th in Spartanburg co., S. C., Mr. J. W. Burnet of Greenville City, S. C., To Miss L. E. Jackson

By Rev. J. C. Crisp, June 18th, Mr. Tho. Timmons to Miss Jane Robison, both of Cedar Hill, Spartanburg co., S. C.

By Rev. J. C. Crisp, July 9th, Mr. M. A. Ragan to Miss L. E. McKlewreath, both of Spartanburg co, S. C.

By Rev. J. C. Crisp, July 16th, Mr. Tho. Miller to Miss B. L. Timmons, both of Cedar Hill, Spartanburg co, S. C.

July 16, by Rev. E. J. Knight, Mr. John Dawkins to Mrs. Dorcas Kersey, all of Jefferson co., Fla.

By Rev. E. J. Knight, July 16, Mr. W. W. Gray of Thomas Co., GA., to Miss Idella L. Johnson of Jefferson co., Fla.

In Columbus, Ga., July 20, 1871, by Rev. A. J. Dean, Mr. Wm. R. Martin to Mrs. Mary Summerville.

July 24, by Rev. O. L. Smith, Mr. Frank M. Bradley of Texas, to Miss Martha E. Rainey of Columbus, Ga.

Issue of August 9, 1871

On Sunday, 13d [sic] ult., by Rev. W. J. Scott, Rev. Sanford Leake of the N. G. Conference, to Miss Nannie E. Smith, of Catoosa co., Ga.

Issue of August 16, 1871

On the evening of the 26th July 1871, by Rev. James N. Myers, Mr. Lucius P. Riggs to Miss Leah J. Kinney, all of Carroll co., Ga.

On the 3rd of August by Rev. W. H. Hunt, Mr.Adam I. Smith to Miss H. R. Bethea, all of Columbia co., Florida.

On 3rd August, by Rev. C. J. Toole, Mr. D. W. Eddding to Mrs. Laura S. Renolds, all of Emanuel county, Georgia.

Issue of August 23, 1871

By Rev. E. J. Knight, August 10, 1871, Mr. Paul J. Poppell to Miss Susan A. Houck, all of Jefferson co., Fla.

At the residence of the bride's father, in Orangeburg co., S. C. July 16, 1871, by the Rev. D. J. Simmons, Mr. Wm. Bird to Miss Frances A. Edwards.

In Newton co., Ga., August 10, 1871, by Rev. Albert Gray, Mr. J. S. Butler of Virginia, to Miss M. J. Pharr of the former place.

Issue of September 6, 1871

On the 20th inst., by Rev. W. Hutto, Mr. John Whetsel to Miss Hettie Pendarvis, all of Colleton co., S. C.

Issue of September 13, 1871

By Rev. W. G. Hanson, Sept. 3d 1871, J. R. Mann to Mary M. Wallace, all of Spalding co., Ga.

Issue of September 20, 1871

August 31st, by Rev. L. B. Bouchelle, J. C. Johnson to Miss E. Sherrod, All of Emanuel county, Ga.

24th Aug. by Rev. J. B. Campbell, R. W. Davis to Miss Jane F. McKenzie, all of Beaufort county, S. C.

At Talbotton, Ga., Sept. 20th, by Rev. F. A. Branch, Daniel V. Biggs, of Talbort county, and Miss Stella Florence, eldest daughter of Rev. S. R. Weaver of the So. Ga. Conf.

In Columbia county, Fla., Sept. 7, 1871, by Rev. Thomas K. Leonard, George W. Price, to Miss Mary E. Perry.

Issue of September 27, 1871

In Macon, on 21st inst., by Rev. J. W. Burke, W. T. Mozo, Esq., and Miss Voctoria L. Brown, all of Macon.

Bu Rev. F. M. T. Brannon, Sept. 5th 1871, Wm. L. Rector to Miss Emma A. Lovejoy, all of Hogansville, Troup county, Ga.

On the 19th inst., at the residence of the bride's father, Major T. S. Jones by Rev. Lewis Solomon, F. H. Land to Miss Minnie N. Jones, all of Twiggs co., Ga.

In Hamilton county, Tenn., Sept. 14th by Rev. W. J. Scott, Mr. S. M. Ellis to Miss Maryi E. Green, daughter of A. P. Green, Esq.

In Tampa, Fla., Sept. 1st 1871, by Rev. E. S. Tyner, Mr. T. E. Spencer of Tampa, to Miss Mary G. Spencer, of White Sulpher Springs, Fla.

Issue of October 4, 1871

Sept. 21, by Rev. P. M. Ryburn, Joseph P. Wallace to Miss Elizabeth A. Barrett, all of Marietta, Ga.

On the 5th Sept., by Rev. F. Auld, Edward B. Rush to Miss Carrie C. Barrett, all of Orangeburg, S. C.

By Rev. F. Auld, on the 21st Sept., Maj. J. J. Salley to Miss Fannie R. Barton, all of Orangeburg, S. C.

Issue of October 11, 1871

By Rev. L. P. Neese, 14th of September, W. L. Warterson to Miss F. M. Morrow. All of Jonesboro, Ga.

Issue of October 18, 1871

By Rev. W. G. Hanson, Oct. 3d, Mr. Chappell McMullen to Miss Mattie A. Grant, all of Monroe co., Ga.

By Rev. J. C. Crisp, on 6th September, at the residence of Mr. Jacob Morgan, Mr. F. S. C. Bryce, of Carroll co., Ga., to Miss S. A. Wynn, of Spartanburg, S. C.

By Rev. W. Hutto, on the 21st September, Mr. Daniel D. Smith, of Colleton, to Miss Theodosia J. Hart, of Orangeburg, S. C.

On the 5th September, by Rev. J. E. Watson, Mr. Rhett Riley to Mis sMary Zeigler, all of Orangeburg co., S. C.

On the 26th September, by the same, Mr. Lawrence D. Clarke to Miss Rosa Gaskins, all of Orangeburg co., S. C.

In Lafayette on 4th inst., by the same, Mr. John P. Smith to Miss S. E. Rogers, both of Walker co., Ga.

On 28th September, by Rev. F. M. T. Brannon, Mr. Thos. J. Jones to Miss virginia S. Johnston, all of Hogansville, Troup co., Ga.

At Cornith, Heard co., Ga., September 28th, by Rev. J. T. Lowe, Dr. William Amis to Miss Josephine Miller.

On October 2d, by the same, Mr. J. M. Hamby to Miss Abthia L.Turner, all of Meriwether co., Ga.

In Augusta, Ga., September 27th, by Rev. I. S. Hopkins, Mr. J. W. Huckabee to Mrs. Harriet B. Denby.

Issue of October 25, 1871

In Sparta, Ga., Oct. 3d, 1871 by W. P. Pledger, David Dickson, Esq., of Hancock co., Ga., to Miss Clara C. Harris, daughter of Col. Benjamin T. Harris, of the former place.

By Rev. M. Puckett, Oct. 15th, 1871, Charles B. Sewell, of Cobb co., to Miss Hassie Evans, of Cherokee co., Ga.
By Rev. W. Carson Dunlap, on the 26th of Sept., at the residence of the bride's father, Mr. G. T. Horton of Chattooga, Co., Ga., to Miss Hattie Gilbert, of Cherokee co., Ala.

On Thursday the 12th ult., by Rev. J. M. Bowden, Mr. Richard Morris of Palmetto, to Miss Mary C. Cockran, of Campbell co., Ga.

Issue of November 1, 1871

By Rev. John Calvin Johnson, 5th Oct., 1871, Mr. John E. Barnhart, of Greensboro, Ga., to Miss Anna Stephens of Watkinsville, Ga.

By the same, 19th Oct 1871, Mr. James W. Jackson to Miss Mary Louise McRee, all of Clarke co., Ga.

By Rev. W. H. Graham, Oct. 6th 1871, Mr. W. R. Howe to Miss M. V. Hunt, all of Pike co,. Ga.

By the same, Oct. 13th, Mr. R. N. Lefsy to Miss C. P. Howel, all of Pike co., Ga.

At the residence of Mr. Thomas in Elbert co., Ga., on 18th Oct., 1871 by Rev. A. G. Worley, Mr. Z. A. Tate to Miss Cora E. Thomas, daughter of Judge Thomas, deceased.

On 10th Oct., in Brunswick, Ga., by Rev. J. O. A. Cook, Capt. Eugene Albert Thomas to Miss Mary Talulah Dillon.

On 20th Sept., by Rev. J. E. Watson, Mr. L. D. Clarke to Miss Rosa V. Gaskin, all of Orangeburg co., S. C.

In Milledgeville, Ga., Oct. 19th, Capt. Wm. Thos. Conn to Miss Henrietta Miller.

By Rev. S. S. Sweet, on Oct. 19th, Mr. J. H. Shinholser to Miss Audent V. Wood.

On 19th Oct., 1871 by Rev. J. M. Bowden, Mr. Franklin H. Steed of Palmetto, to Miss A. M. Perkins of Coweta co., Ga.

By Rev. Jno. T. Norris, on 18th Oct., in Cartersville, Ga., Rev. Walker Lewis of Fort Valley, Ga., to Miss Lula Trammell, of the former place.

On Oct. 5th, by Rev. H. H. Parks, Mr. Wm. D. Villard of Burke co., Ga., to Miss Mary L. Royal of Augusta, Ga.

On the 8th inst., by the same, Mr. Edward E. Harley to Miss Martha Cane, both of Augusta, Ga.

By the same on 13th Oct., Mr. Theo. O. Brown to Miss Matilda M. Slack, both of Augusta, Ga.

By the same, Oct. 22d, Mr. John O. Heath to Miss Catharine McGrath, both of Augusta, Ga.

Issue of November 8, 1871

Oct. 22d, 1871, by the Rev. S. D. Clements, Mr. Robt. Hinton, of Talbot co., Ga., to Miss Mary E. Slaughter, of Harris co., Ga.

On the 19th of Oct. in Camden, S. C., by Rev. A. J. Stokes, Capt. Wm. Clyburn to Miss A. T. Reed, daughter of Jas. F. Reid.

On the evening of the 21st Oct., by Rev. T. A. Seals, Mr. H. b. Shiver,s of Warren co., and Miss Carrie M. Coleman of Hancock co., Ga.

By Rev. T. A. Seals on the 30th Oct., Mr. Walter Scott and Miss Augusta Wilder, all of Warrenton, Ga.

On 11th Oct., 1871, by W. W. Tidwell, Mr. T. S. Brooks of Macon co., to Miss Elizabeth Battle, of Taylor co., Ga.

By Rev. C. W. Smith, October 31st, in Wilkinson co., Ga., Mr. Jas. B. Stevens to Miss Sue Brewer.

Issue of November 15, 1871

At Aiken, S. C., on 1st Nov. 1871, by Rev. Lucius Cuthbert, Mr. John H. Loomis, of Columbia, S. C., to Miss E. Augusta Hendrix, of Aiken, S. C.

On 8th Oct., by Rev. W. J. Cotter, Mr. R. Ward to Miss L. A. Thomas, all of Troup co., Ga.

By the same on 19th Oct., Mr. R. A. Crawford to Miss L. Cunningham, all of Troup co., Ga.

On 7th Nov., in Sparta, Ga., by Bishop Pierce, Mr. R. Henry Thomas, of California, to Miss Susie W. Turner of Sparta, Ga. San Francisco *Spectator* please copy.

On 3d Oct., by Rev. Wm. C. Power, Mr. Houston Manning to Miss Mattie R., daughter of Col. E. T. Stackhouse, both of Marion Dist., S. C.

On Oct. 19th, at the Rock, Upson co., by Rev. J. P. Duncan, Mr. Thomas Black to Miss Lou Collier.

By Rev. R. R. Dagnall, Oct. 25th 1871, Mr. W. S. Tyler to Miss annie L. Foreman, all of Barnwell co., S. C.

By the same, on Nov. 1st, 1871, at the residence of Mrs. W. A. Slater, Mr. M. O. Eubanks of Barnwell co., S. C., to Miss Lizzie J. Dagnall, of Georgia.

On Nov. 1st, 1871, by Rev. I. J. M. Goss, M. D., LL. D., at the bride's residence, in Walton co., Ga., Mr. Lucius A. Hawkins to Miss Louisa Browning.

On 12th Oct. 1871, at the bride's grandfather's in Walton co., Ga., by the same, ,Mr. Charles L. Pattillo, of Jackson co., Ga., to Miss Nancy E. Aycock.

At the residence of the bride's father, Oct. 19th, 1871, by Rev. D. J. Simmons, Mr. Asbury Dukes to Miss Susan McElhany, all of Orangeburg co., S. C.

On 2d Nov 1871, in Orangeburg co., S. C., by the same, Mr. Young M. E. Davis to Miss Henrietta Nettles; also, Mr. Gideon Hutto to Miss Angeline S. Davis.
By L. P. Neese, Oct. 24th 1871, Geo. M. Hayes, of Newton co., Ga., to Miss Janes Dabney, of Henry co., Ga.

By Rev. W. Lane, on 7th Nov 1871, Mr. Phillip M. McKinnon to Miss Jane M. Williams, both of Thomas co., Ga.

On Oct. 22d, at Rome, Ga., by Rev. W. F. Cook, Rev. C. N. McLeod, of Ala. Conference, to Miss Mary Landrum.

On Nov. 2d, at Marietta, Ga., by Rev. W. F. Cook, Wm. S. Thomson, of Atlanta, Ga., to Miss Nena Danner, of the former place.

Near LaGrange, Ga., on 29th August, by Rev. Alex. M. Thigpen, Mr. James F. Ogletree to Miss Lula Ella, daughter of Mr. Frank Stinson.

By the same, on Oct. 5th, Mr. J. William Boyd to Miss Eliza Williams, all of Greenville, Ga.

In Troup co., Ga., by the same, Oct. 26th, Mr. Hal. Crowder to Miss Jennie Leslie.

In the Methodist Church at Newton, on the 8th inst., by Rev. James T. Ainsworth, Mr. James W. Nesbitt to Miss Mary E. McGregor, both of Baker co., Ga.

On Nov. 1st, in Palatka, Fla., by Rev. S. S. Moore, Mr. Geo. C. Middleton, of Palatka, to Miss Susan J. Smith, of Darien, Ga.

Issue of November 22, 1871

On 2d Nov., by Rev. J. R. Littlejohn, Mr. Jas. W. Atwater of Thomaston, to Miss Antoinett E. Respress of Taylor co., Ga.

By Rev. J. R. Littlejohn, on Nov. 7th, Mr. B. J. McCants to Miss Leonora McCants, both of Taylor co., Ga.

Nov. 8th, 1871, at the residence of the bride's father in Barnwell co., S. C., by the Rev. D. J. Simmons, Mr. Theophilus F. Barton, of Orangeburg co., S. C., to Miss Mary Raysor, daughter of Rev. Thos. Raysor, M. D., of the So. Ca. Conference.

On 19th Oct., by Rev. B. E. L. Timmons, Mr. J. S. Brownlow to M. F. McKinney, all of White co., Ga.

By Rev. B. E. L. Timmons, Oct. 21st, Mr. Hellum Hunt to Miss M. A. Sears, all of White co., Ga.

By Rev. B. E. L. Timmons, Oct. 26th, Mr. John Meaders of White co., Ga., to Miss Mattie Lambert, of Clarke co., Ga.

By Rev. B. E. L. Timmons, Mr. E. L. Dorsey to Miss S. A. Gilstrap, all of White co., Ga.

By Rev. W. F. Robison, on 1st Nov., Mr. J. P. Terry to Miss Fannie B. Freeman, of Harris co., Ga.

By Rev. W. F. Robison, on 8th Nov., Mr. Simri R. Murphy to Miss Laura P. Bedell, of Hamilton, Ga.

By Rev. W. F. Robison, on the evening of the 8th Nov., Mr. Jas. H. Carter, of Talbotton, Ga., to Miss Carrie A. Benning, of Harris co., Ga.

On 26th Oct., by Rev. L. Wood, Mr. Ira Porter Bull of Orangeburg, to Miss Mattie Caroline, youngest daughter of Gabriel Hodges, of Cokesbury, S. C.

By Rev. W. W. Oslin, Oct. 26th, Mr. G. W. Stolvey to Miss America Marchman, all of Putnam co., Ga.

By Rev. W. W. Oslin, Nov. 9th, Mr. G. E. Herbert to Miss Fannie J. Bearden, all of Putnam co., Ga.

By Rev. W. A. Fariss, on 2d Nov., Mr. George W. Olive to Miss Annie M. Hatcher, both of columbia co., Ga.

Nov. 9th, by Rev. S. R. Weaver, at the bride's mothers, in Talbot county, Mr. George T. Fouch to Miss Mary Binns.

Nov. 8th, 1871, by Rev. W. M. Watts, Mr. Edward Humphrey of Blackshear, to Miss Rebecca J. Pugh, of Thomas co., Ga.

On the 26th Oct., by Rev. Robert L. Wigins, Mr. Chas. A. Huntington, late of this county, to Miss Elizabeth V. Wyatt, of this, Gadsden co., Fla.

In Clarendon co., Oct. 10th, 1871, by Rev. J. L. Sifley, Mr. Harvey J. Eadon to Miss Clara Brogdon, all of Clarendon co.

In Clarendon co., Oct. 1st, by Rev. J. L. Sifley, Mr. Jas. M. Brown to Mrs. Mary S. Nettles, all of Clarendon.

In Elberton, Ga., Nov. 7th, 1871, by Rev. F. G. Hughes, Gerard W. Allen to Miss Addie M. Stanford, all of Elberton, Ga.

On Nov. 8th, by Rev. F. Auld, Mr. Andrew C. Dibble of Bamburg, S. C., ot Miss Mary J. Clark, of Orangeburg, S. C.

By Rev. B. C. M. Brooks, Nov. 7th, 1871, Rev. W. A. Greene of the south ga. Conference to Miss Carrie M. Gardner, of Taylor co., Ga.

At the Methodist Church, in East Macon, on the 31st ult., by Rev. John W. Burke, Mr. Amos A. Subers to Miss Wayne Massey.

Issue of November 29, 1871

Married by Rev. J. R. little, on the 16th of Nov., 1871, Mr. Judson W. Hasseltine to Miss Mary R., third daughter of Mr. and Mrs. D. W. Brown, all of Lancastersville, S. C.

Married on the 15th inst., in Thomasville, Ga., by Rev. Chas. R. Jewett, Mr. E. Burke Baldwin, of Marshallville, Ga., and Miss Clara S., daughter of Judge Robt. H. Hardaway, of the former place

On the 9th of November, near White Sulpher Springs, Ga., by the Rev. John W. McGehee, Mr. William P. Merritt, of Henry co,. Ga., and Miss Sallie J. Tucker, of Meriwether co., Ga.

In Jasper co., Ga., Sept. 7th 1871, by Rev. A. C. Mixon, Mr. John H. Moseley, of White Springs, Fla., to Miss Mary P. Spears, of the former place.

Married, by the Rev. F. M. T. Brannan, on 31st Oct., 1871, J. W. Lee of Walker county, Ga., to Miss Julia Pricket, of Meriwether co., Ga.

On Nov. 14, by the same, Philip Powledge, of Meriwether co., Ga., to Miss Lizzie Means, of Troup co.

By the same on Nov., 14, J. A. Bailey of Ala., to Miss N. A. Sewell, of Meriwether co,. Ga.

Married on the 16th of Nov., by Rev. F. B. Davies, Mr. Joseph G. Tollison to Miss S. Emma Talmadge, all of Monticello, Ga.

Married on the 19th of Nov., by the Rev. S. S. Sweet, Dr. John W. Shinholser and Miss Martha A. Heard, all of Bibb co.

Married in Georgetown, Ga., Oct. 8th, by Rev. E. H. McGehee, Mr. Alexander Balkcom to Miss Josephene E. Warren.

In Dawson, Ga., Nov. 23d, by Rev. E. H. McGehee, Mr. W. N. Thornton to Miss Nettie Hearn.

In Dawson, Ga., Nov. 23d, by Rev. E. H. McGehee, Mr. Andrew J. Baldwin to Miss Berta Crouch.

On Nov. 15th, by Rev. James R. Smith, Mr. R. A. Thornton to Miss Sarah V. Moore.

On the 16th, Mr. Wilson Smith to Miss Mary A. Watkins, all of Butts co.

On 5th November, at Mile Creek, by L. N. Robins, Esq., Frank Owens to Miss Narcissa Norris, all of Pickens County, S. C.

On 12th November, by the same, J. N. Arnold to Miss Sarah C. Moss, all of Pickens county, S. C.

In Terrell county, Ga., on the 15th November, by the Rev. G. T. Embry, Mr. R. A. Brown, of Americus, Ga., to Miss Sue Payne, of Terrell county. Ga.

By Rev. W. W. Oslin, Nov. 21st, Mr. Geo. W. Dennis, Jr., to Miss Carrie E. Pearson. All of Putnam county, Ga.

By Rev. W. W. Oslin, Nov. 23rd, Mr. Walter F. Beall, to Miss Sue J. Johnson. All of Putnam county, Ga.

In Jefferson county, Ga., on 15th November, Mr. John T. Cheatham to Miss Sarah E. Clark.

By John Calvin Johnson in Farmington, Clarke county, Ga., on 31st October, Mr. Weldon W. Price, to Miss Callie A. Overby, daughter of the late Hon. Basil H. Overby.

By the same, in Clarke county, Ga., on 14th November, Mr. John H. Freeman, of Gwinnett county, Ga., to Miss Louvinia G. Matthews, of Arkansas.

Issue of December 6, 1871

Nov. 23d, 1871, in Morgan co., Ga., by the Rev. J. L. Lupo, Mr. John H. Cox, of Madison, Ga., to Miss Mary M. Furlow, daughter of Mr. Charles Furlow.

On the 23d Oct., at the Methodist Church in Griffin, Ga.,by Rev. John W. Heidt, Dr. John W. Vinson, of Fort Valley, to Miss Fannie L. Johnson, of former place, daughter of the late Rev. Marcus D. C. Johnson.

By Rev. J. W. Heidt, on the 14th Nov., Mr.Daniel S. Muse, of Meriwether co., to Miss Leila E. Williams, daughter of Mr. John M. Williams, of Griffin.

By Rev. J. W. Heidt, on the 23d nov., Mr. Huger W. Johnston, of New York, to Miss Emma O. Johnson, daughter of Mr. Charles H. Johnson, of Griffin.

By Rev. J. W. Heidt, on the 22d Nov., Dr. William E. Sweeny, of Augusta. Ga., to Miss Anna Morgan, daughter of Rev. Thomas Morgan, of Griffin.

By Rev. J. W. Heidt, on the 23d Nov., Rev. Willard W. Wadsworth, to Miss Ada B. Stevens, daughter of Mr. Geo. W. Stevens, all of Griffin.

On the 23d Nov., by Rev. S. S. Sweet, Mr. D. M. Slocumb to Miss Sallie E. Jones, all of Houston co., Ga.

On the 23d Nov., at the residence of James Jones, Esq., in Houston county, by Rev. S. S. Sweet, Mr. L. L. Watson to Miss Mary A. Jones.

In Barnesville, Ga., 22 Nov., by Rev. John P. Duncan, Rev. William F. Lewis, son of Rev. Josiah Lewis, of No. Ga. Conference, to Miss Mary Hulit Speer.

On the 23d Nov., by Rev. A. Nettles, Mr. Thomas McCay of Charleston co., to Miss Margaret R. Bailey, of Georgetown co., S. C.

On the 1st Nov., 1871, by Rev. W. F. Quillian, Dr. A. C. Quillian to Miss Jane C. Parks, all of Lincoln co., Ga.

Oct. 23d, by Rev. J. T. Lin, Mr. Frank L. Miller to Miss Nannie S. Baker, both of Cave Spring, Ga.

In the Methodist Church, Cave Spring, Ga., Nov. 23d, by Rev. J. T. Lin, Mr. John A. Traylor, of New Orleans, to Miss Leila Murrell, of Ga.

By Rev. J. H. Baxter, Nov. 23d, 1871, Mr. H. L. Wheeless, of Meriwether co., Ga., to Miss Mary D. Lyon, of Willks co., Ga.

At the residence of Mr. Hermon Weisbroad's, on Nov. 21st, 1871, by Rev. E. S. Tyner, Mr. W. D. Archer, of Key West, Fla., to Miss Daganheart, of Tampa, Fla.

Issue of December 13, 1871

On the 19th Oct., in Cuthbert, Ga., by Rev. R. B. Lester, John T. Wade, of Macon, to Miss Fannie V. Phelps of Cuthbert.

On the 21st of Nov., by Rev. R. B.Lester, William H. Amons to Miss E. J. Yarbrough, all of Cuthbert.

On Nov. 29th, 1871, by Rev. S. D. Clements, Mr. Charles Hill to Miss Fannie Pearson, all of Harris co., Ga.

On Nov. 29th 1871, at the residence of the bride's mother, by Rev. W. D. Heath, Mr. H. J. E. England to Miss A. M. Colquitt, all of Oglethorpe co., Ga.

On the 15th Nov., by the Rev. W. C. Dunlap, at the residence of the bride's father, Mr. Thos. T. Carroll to Miss Ada Johnston, all of Chattooga co., Ga.

On 21st Nov., by Rev. W. C. Dunlap, at the residence of the bride's father, Rev. John B. McFarland of the No. Ga. Conference, to Miss Louisa A. Hamilton, all of Chattooga co., Ga.

By Rev. John Calvin Johnson, Nov. 30th 1871, in Watkinsville, Clarke co., Ga., Mr. John I. Montgomery, of Madison co., to Miss Jennie Wall, of the former place.

By Rev. J. C. Johnson, on Nov. 30th, Mr. Drury B. Jackson, to Miss Susan J. McRee, all of Clarke co., Ga..

By Rev. L. P. Neese, on 9th Nov., 1871, Manson D. Roundtree to Miss Sallie Harris, all of Henry co., Ga.

At the Methodist Church, in East Macon, on 6th inst., by Rev. John W. Burke, Mr. john W. Richards to Miss Henrietta M. Brown.

On 18th Nov., by Rev. W. M. C. Conley, Mr. J. S. Lanier, to Bulloch co., to Miss Percilla Lang, of Tattnall co.

By Rev. Alex. M. Thigpen, Dec. 7th, Mr. John H. Houser, of Perry, Ga., to Miss Fannie A., daughter of Mr. Z. Thigpen, of Clinton, Ga.

On 30th Nov., by Rev. F. M. Hunt, in Pike co., Ga., Mr. John J. Bush, of Monroe co., Ga., to Miss Fannie Leak.

On 23d Nov., in Salem, Ala., by Rev. J. H. Lockhart, Mr. J. Y. Allen, Esq., of Thomaston, Ga., to Miss R. C. Pruitt, daughter of Rev. Moses y. Pruitt, of Salem, Ala.

On Nov. 22d, by Rev. J. W. Stipe, Mr. P. W. Brown to Miss Mattie P. Webb, all of Baldwin co., Ga.

Near Talbotton, on 30th Nov., by Rev. F. A. Branch, Mr. William S. Couch, of Talbot co., to Miss Mary A., daughter of Col. Lee, of Muscogee co.

At Talbotton, on 6th ult., by Rev. F. A. Branch, Mr. John T. Waterman, of Perry, to Miss Anna E., daughter of Mr. T. A. Brown, of Talbotton.

By Rev. J. W. Knight, in Watkinsville, Ga., on the 23d Nov., Mr. John A. Swift, of Stone Mountain, to Miss Nettie Johnson.

Issue of December 20, 1871

By Rev. Manning Brown, on the 5th of Dec., at the residence of the bride's father, Rev. G. W. Gatlin, of the S. C. Conference, to Miss M. Agnes Ledingham, of Richland District, S. C.

Dec. 6, by W. H. Hunt, Mr. David B. Paxton, to Miss Florida V. Mattox, all of Columbia co., Fla.

At Troup Factory, on the 5th Dec., by Rev. W. J. Cotter, Mr. Leslie W. Dallis to Miss Low Leslie.

In Sparta, Ga., on the 14th of Dec., by Rev. W. P. Pledger, Mr. Jno. G. Daniel to Miss M. Emma Sasnett, daughter of the late Dr. Wm. J. Sasnett.

On the 12th Dec., by Rev. J. J. Tooke, at the bride's fathers, Mr. W. S. Kilby to Miss A. E. Duke, all of Taylor co., Ga.

By Rev. A. Seals, on the morning of the 23d of Nov., Mr. A. J. Mayes to Miss Mary Swain, all of Warren co., Ga.

In Greene co., Ga., Dec. 5th, by Rev. J. L. Lupo, Mr. William B. Watson to Miss Lavinia Catchings.

Nov. 16th, by Rev. I. L. Avant, Mr. Isaac M. Jordan to Miss Julie E., eldest daughter of Mr. G. W. Thames, of Crawford co., Ga.

Dec. 7th, by J. T. Cherry, Esq., Mr. D. H. Wootten, of Telfair co., Ga., to Miss Theodosia R., eldest daughter of Mr. Daniel Guerry, of Bibb co., Ga.

Issue of December 27, 1871

On 5th Dec., by Rev. R. B. Tarrant, at the residence of the bride's father, Mr. A. H. wolfe to Miss M. L. Zeigler, of Orangeburg co.

At the residence of the bride's mother, on 14th inst., by Rev. W. J. Hatfield, Mr. F. H. McEachern to Miss Sally Jane Lee, all of Sumter co., S. C>

In Columbus, Ga., on 5th inst., by Rev. Chas. R. Jewett, Rev. J. B. Hartwell from China, to Miss Julia C. Jewett, of Macon, Ga.

By Rev. H. Tyler, Nov. 21st 1871, Mr. M. A. Heler to Miss M. A. Cromer, all of Anderson co., S. C.

By Rev. H. Tyler, Dec. 7th 1871, Mr. W. D. Dobbins to Miss Mattie E. Ramply, all of Anderson co., S. C.

By Rev. H. Tyler, Dec. 14th 1871, Mr. James T. Drake to Miss E. S. Wardlaw, all of Anderson co., S. C.

By Rev. J. H. Baxter, Nov. 26th, 1871, near Wahsington, Wilkes co., Ga., MR. George c. Cosby to Miss Julia Freeman.

In Savannah, Ga., November 22d, by the bride's father, Mr. W. B. Daniel of Albany, Ga., to Miss S. J. Urquahrt Evans, daughter of Rev. J. E. Evans, South Georgia Conference.

By Rev. R. W. Bigham, in Newnan, Ga., Nov. 28th, 1871, Hon. J. S. Bigby to Miss Lizzie McClendon.

By Rev. R. W. Bigham, on Dec. 13th, 1871, Mr. J. R. Peacock of Quitman, to Miss Katie Neely, of Newnan, Ga.

By Rev. W. A. McLean, in Jacksonville, Fla., Dec. 10th 1871, Mr. James Vinzant to Miss Fannie M. Sellors, all of Duval co., Fla.

By Rev. R. M. T. Brennan, on Dec. 10th 1871, Daniel C. Gentry to Miss Rebecca D. Thompson, all of Corinth, Heard co., Ga.

Issue of January 10, 1872

In Oxford, Ga., December 14th, 1871, by Rev. J. Lewis Jr., Mr. W. A. Parham to Mis Ella J. Evans.

In Griffin, Ga., at the residence of Joseph Boyd, on the 21st of December, by Rev. Mr. Hale, Mr. H. A. DeLaPerriere, of Atlanta, son of General H. DeLaPerriere, of Jackson county, Ga., to Miss M. R. Samples, of Merriwether co., Georgia.

By the Rev. W. Ewing Johnston, on the 5th of December, at the residence of the bride's father, Mr. Geo. W. Duval to Miss Anna T. M. Burch, all of Richmond county.

By the Rev. W. Ewing Johnston, on the 14th of December, at the residence of the bride's father, Mr. Louis V. Winter to Mrs. Artemecia M. [?], all of Richmond county.

By Rev. S. R. Weaver, at the residence of the bride's father, in Talbot co., Ga., Mr. Wm. --kin and Miss Sarah Adams, on the 3rd day of Jan. 1871.

By Rev. S. R. Weaver, Dec. 20th, 1871, at the residence of the bride's father, in Talbot co., Ga., Mr. Wm. Benn and Miss Martha Lumpkin.

By Rev. S. R. Weaver, Dec. 20, 1871, at the residence of the bride's father, Thomas J. Walker and Miss Susan J. Kellum.

By Rev. F. R. C. Ellis, at Valdosta, on the 13th of December, W. Watson Twitty, of Camilla, to Miss S. M. Coachman, of Valdosta, Ga.

By Rev. Thomas K. Leonard, in Columbia co., Florida, on the 20th of December 1871, Mr. A. B. Brown to Miss Mary A. A., youngest daughter of Mr. Langley Bryant.

By Rev. Geo. C. Leavel, on the 6th of December, 1871, in Gadsden county, Fla., at the residence of Dr. Henly, Mr. Jno. Byrd to Miss Mary J. Foster, daughter of Rev. L. F. Foster.

By Rev. J. R. Mason, December 20th 1871, at the residence of the bride's father, Mr. Daniel D. Barrett, of Cobb county, Ga., to iss Sallie Smith, of Cherokee county, Ga.

By Rev. R. M. T. Brannan, on Dec. 27th, 1871, Robert Milton, to Miss Mary J. Thompson, all of Hogansville, Troup co., Ga.

In Taylor co., on 12th inst., by Rev. R. F. Williamson, Rev. J. F. Griffeth to Miss Emma Pyror, all of Taylor co.

In Schley co., on 30th ult., Rev. R. F. Williamson, CApers Stephens to Miss Laura Williamson.

On the 21st Dec., by Rev. C. A. Fulwood, Mr. N. W. Jelks to Mis sMollie Bozeman, all of Hawkinsville.

By Rev. J. H. Baxter, in Gainesville, Ga., Dec. 21st 1871, Dr. Thomas C. Gower, of Cartersville, to Miss Mary E. Simmons, of the former place

By Rev. J. H. Baxter, near Gainesville, Ga., Dec. 24th, Mr. Joseph W. Webster to Miss Mary J. Barrett.

On the 22d of Dec., by Rev. B. E. Manget, at the residence of the bride's father, Mr. Thomas J. Williams, of Ala., to Miss Sallie E. Gamage, of Talbotton, Ga.

On the 22d of Dec., by Rev. V. E. Manget, at the Methodist Church in Centreville, Ga., Mr. H. C. Trussell to Miss F. Eugenia Williams, all of Talbot co., Ga.

Dec. 20, by Rev. W. A. Clark, Rev. A. G. Gantt, of the South Carolina Conference to miss Emma C. Browning, of the Charleston District, S. C.

Dec. 21st, by the Rev. Jno. H. Harris, Mr. James A. Spears of Butts co., to Miss conie Thurman, of Henry co., Ga.

On Nov. 23d, by Rev. W. B. Neal, Mr. Thos. W. Harison to Miss Martha J. Capps, daughter of Rev. W. M. Capps, all of Lee co., Ala.

By Rev. W. B. Neal, Dec. 14th, Mr. Mike Harvey of Opelika, Ala., to Miss -- Dumas, of Russel co., Ala.

In Monticello, Nov. 22d, by Rev. F. B. Davies, Dr. J. F. Webb to Miss Annie J. Broddus.

In Jasper co., Ga., Dec. 15th, by Rev. F. B. Davies, Mr. Sam A. Flournoy to Miss Eva Roby.

In Jasper co., Ga., Dec. 31st, by Rev. F. B. Davies, Mr. James M. McMichael to Miss Ella McCarthy.

Dec. 7th, by Rev. T. B. Lanier, at Mr. J. L. Hawks', Mr. Eldridge M. Floyd, of Savannah, to Miss Valaria H. Zittroner of Efingham co,. Ga.

Dec. 12th, by Rev. T. B. Lanier, Mr. William P. Chapman, of Wilkinson co., Ga., to to Miss Louisa _ Sinquefield, of Effingham co,. Ga.

By Rev. L. Alonzo Darsey, on 13th December, 1871, Mr. John G. Blitch, of Savannah, Ga., to Mrs. Laura M. Young, of Bullock county, GA.

On the 20th of December 1871, in Eatonton, Ga., by the Rev. W. R. Fotte, Mr. J. Hudson Adams to Miss Florence A. Reid, both of Eatonton, Ga.

By the Rev. J. B. C. Quillian, Hon. C. C. Green of Fulton county, to Miss Lou J., daughter of the late Joseph H. Wilson, Esq., Campbell county, Ga.

By Rev. A. Nettles, on the 28th December, Mr. Wm. G. Richardson to Miss Mary E. Cooper, all of Williamsburg county, S. C.

On the 21st of December, 1871, at the residence of the bride's father, by Rev. Alex. P. Wright, Mr. Henry Walker, of Florida, to Miss Sallie H. Beaty, of Lowndes county, Ga.

By Rev. J. J. Singleton, on 16th November 1871, Mr. Wiley A. Clements, to Miss Mary C. Rogers.

By Rev. J. J. Singleton, on 10th December 1871, Mr. John W. Evans to Miss Dora V. Turk.

By Rev. J. J. Singleton, on 24th December 1871, Mr. A. S. Redding to Miss Vista Allen.

At the residence of the bride's father in Orangeburg county, S. C., December 21st, by Rev. D. J. Simmons ,Mr. F. Marion Green to Miss Josephine L. Izlar.

On the 20th of November 1871, in Orangeburg county, S. C., by Rev. D. J. Simmons, Mr. George Bonnette to Miss Mary Bosard.

In Greenwood, S. C., November 22, 1871, by Rev. John McLees, Mr. G. Marshall Jordan to Miss Nannie C., daughter of Mr. and Mrs. John Creswell.

By Rev. James L. Martin, at the residence of the bride's father, on December 21, 1871, Mr. Thomas S. Moorman, of Newberry C. H., to Miss Marie Witherspoon, eldest daughter of Dr. Jos. L. Wardlaw, of Abbeville C. H.

By Rev. Y. F. Tigner, of the South Georgia Conference, at the residence of the bride's father, Nov. 26, 1871, 10½ o'clock A. M., Mr. Jacob R. Cobb to Miss Susan J. Fulsom.

By Rev. Y. F. Tigner, on the morning of the 31st December 1871, at the residence of the bride's father in Cusseta, Ga., Mr. Daniel L. McGlaun, son of David G. McGlaun, to Miss Eva L. Bond, daughter of Rev. W. M. D. Bond, of the South Georgia Conference, all of Chattahoochee county, Ga.

Issue of January 17, 1872

By John Calvin Johnson, on 12th December, 1871, Mr. William B. Dicken to Miss Susan A. Cook, all of Clarke county, Georgia.

By the same, on the 21st December, 1871, Mr. Thomas P. Maynard to Miss Philo B. Hinesby, all of Clarke county, Ga.

By the same, on 3d January, 1872, at the residence of Pope Barrow, Esq., Col. David C. Marrow to Miss P. F. Sawyer, all of Oglethorpe county, Ga.

On the 27th December, in the Methodist Church at Monticello, Fla., by the Rev. F. A. Branch, Mr. John W. Garwood of Monticello, to Miss Lou Bowie, daughter of the late Rev. J. K. Glover, of the Florida Conference.

On the 4th January, in the Methodist Church at Talbotton, Ga., by the Rev. F. A. Bra ch,, Major Robert A. Mathews to Miss Laura E. Leonard, both of Talbotton.

By Rev. W. J. Cotter, on the 31st December, Mr. J. S. Perry to Miss M. A. Morris.

By the same, on the 3d Janaury 1872, Mr. C. J. Bailey to Miss Mattie Embry, all of Troup co., Ga.

By Rev. F. F. Reynolds, in Gwinnett co., Dec. 29, 1871, Mr. Joseph Oliver to Miss Mary Pate.

Issue of January 24, 1872

By Rev. J. C. Crisp, Oct. 18th, Mr. J. L. Tucker to Miss Emily Kimrell, both of Cedar Hiil, Spartanburg county, S. C.

By the same, Dec. 24th, Mr. Wm. Hammett of Greenville county, to Miss Lizzie E. Stone, of Cedar Hill, Spartanburg county, S. C.

By the same, Jan. 11th, in Spartanburg county, Mr. Ervin Holtzclaw of Greenville county, to Miss R. Addie West.

On the 28th Dec., by the Rev. J. J. Cassidy, the Rev. W. P. H. Connerly, of the Alabama Conference, to Miss Joanna Brett, of Marianna.

In Macon, Ga., on the 9th inst., by the Rev. J. W. Burke, Mr. Wm. O. Wadley of Screven county, Ga., to Annie, eldest daughter of the late Rev. Geo. H. Hancock.

By Rev. R. H. Howren, on the 28th Dec., 1871, Mr. Wm. R. Cox, of Burke county, to Miss L. E. Kittles, of Scriven county, Ga.

On the 12th Dec., at the residence of the bride's mother, in Hancock county, Ga., by Rev. E. G. Murrah, Mr. A. S. Babb[?] to Miss Ella Simmons.

By the Rev. G. S. Johnston, in Schley county, Ga., on the 21st of Dec. ,1871, Mr. Wm. D. Murray to Miss Catharine Howe.

In Orangeburg county, S. C., Jan. 4th 1872, by Rev. D. J. Simmons, Dr. H. N. FAir to Miss Cordelia W. Pooser.

By Rev. W. J. Cotter on the 14th inst., Mr. F. L. Smith, to Miss M. E. Gilbert, all of Troup county, Ga.

By Rev. W. J. Cotter on the 16th inst., Mr. O. D. Hardy, to Miss B. McGee, all of Troup county, Ga.

Jan 3d, by Rev. J. W. Mcroy, Mr. Joshua S. Coburn to Miss Eliza Buche.

On the 24th Dec., at Corinth, Heard county, Ga., by Rev. James T. Lowe, Col. W. P. Moseley, formerly of Virginia, to Miss Juvernia R. Lowe, of Chattooga county, Ga.

By Rev. J. R. Mayson, at the residence of Dr. A. Smith, in Acworth, Ga., Dec. 27th, Mr. James H. Ross to Miss Susie Smith.

By Rev. J. R. Mayson, Jan. 11th, at the residence of Mrs. MAry Winn, Mr. Benson O. Boulton to Miss Lula Winn.

By Rev. Geo. G. N. Macdonell, Jan. 3d, Mr. Louis L. Carswell to Miss Mary A. Sexton, both of Savannah, Ga.

By Rev. G. G. N. Macdonell, Jan. 9th, Mr. Owen B. H. Johnston, of Savannah, to Miss Ellie C. Peirson, of Sparta, Ga.

By Rev. G. G. N. Macdonell, Jan. 10th, Mr. James B. Harris to Miss Ruth A. Glass, both of Savannah, Ga.

By Rev. G. G. N. Macdonell, Jan. 10th, at Trinity Church, Mr. William H. Ross to Miss Ella F. Stevenson, both of Savannah, Ga.

In Camilla, Ga., Jan. 16th, by Rev. J. T. Ainsworth, Wm. O. Butler, of Decatur county, to Miss Sarah A. Cox, of Camilla.

By Rev. D. Comfort, December 28th, Mr. W. H. Scruggs of Brooks county, Ga., to Miss Susie M. Peek, of Thomas county, Ga.

Issue of February 7, 1872

In Houston county, Ga., Dec. 13th, by Rev. J. B. McGehee, Mr. W. Richardson Davis, to Miss Fannie Virginia Lane.

Dec. 20th in Green county, Ga., by Rev. Geo. W. Yarbrough, Mr. Julius Gerding, of Eatonton, Ga., to Miss Flem Curtwright, of Green county, Ga.

In the M. E. Church at Quitman, Ga., on the 21st Dec., by Rev. J. J. Giles, Mr. E. A. Morse to Miss Sallie C. Talley, youngest daughter of Rev. J. W. Talley.

At George's Station, Colleton county, S. C., Dec. 21st, by Rev. James C. Stoll, Mr. Ben. O. Evans, of Orangeburgh county, S. C., to Miss Sue Street, of Colleton county.

By Rev. J. E. Sentell, on the 28th of Jan., Mr. A. E. Choate to Miss A. C. Pennick, all of Cochran, Ga.

At the residence of the bride's father, near Madison, Florida, on Jan. 23d, by Rev. Wm. R. Johnson, Mr. S. M. Hankins to Miss A. Z. Hawkins, all of Madison county.

In Colleton county, S. C., Jan. 11th, by Rev. P. F. Kistler, Mr. Richard Cummings to Miss Jane N. Ackermon.

On the 21st Jan., by Rev. J. E. Watson, at the residence of Mr. William Cornwell, Mr. Martin Cornwell, of Chester, to Miss Agnes Cornwell, of York, S. C.

By Rev. Jesse Tomlin, Jan. 2d, near Haw Ridge, Coffee county, Ala., Mr. I. J. Stewart, of Dale county, Ala.s, to Miss Fannie E. McNair.

By Rev. J. H. Mashburn, on the 16th Jan., Mr. George W. Roberts to Miss Americus L. Spencer, both of Hall county, Ga.

In Monticello, Ga., on 18th Jan., by Rev. E. G. Murrah, Mr. E. H. Stephens, of Upson county, Ga., to Miss Susie O. Anderson, of the former place.

By Rev. E. G. Hurrah, in Eatonton, Ga., on 24th Jan., Mr. E. B. Smith, of Jasper county, to Miss E. V. Adams, of the former place.

By Rev. J. V. M. Morris, Jan. 7th, Julius H. Bugg, of Oglethorpe county, Ga., to Miss M. Edwards, of Clarke county, Ga.

At Dickson, Ala., on the 18th Jan., by Rev. Mr. Stevenson, T. H. Ward, Esq., of Ga., to Miss Loutie Dickson, of Ala.

On Jan. 14th, by Rev. J. R. Littlejohn, Mr. M. H. Riley to Miss Sallie E. Searcy, both of Taylor county, Ga.

On Jan. 18th, by Rev. J. R. Littlejohn, Mr. E. T. McCord, of Talbot county, to Miss Ellen C. Spear, of Taylor county, Ga.

On the 25th January, by the Rev. Thos. T. Christian, Dr. James W. Pitts, of Columbus, to Mrs. Sarah A. Clark, of Muscogee county.

On the morning of the 14th ult., at the residence of Mr. W. D. Terrell, in Putnam county, by Rev. A. M. Marshal, Rev. W. J. Alexander to Miss Celestra J. Sadler.

At Thomson, Ga., on the 18th January, by Rev. A. B. Thrasher, Mr. Charles W. Arnold to Mrs. Martha W. Young, all of McDuffie county.

On January 31st, 1872, by Rev. John W. McRoy, Mr. David T. Kennerley to Miss Julia C. Fogle, both of Barnwell county, S. C.

Issue of February 14, 1872

On the 30th January, at the residence of the bride's step father, in Sumter county, by Rev. S. S. Moore, Dr. A. A. Stivender, of Leesburg, Fla., to Miss Sarah Macon.

On 25th January 1872, by Rev. J. B. Elder, Mr. William N. Barfield to Miss Frances E. Ogletree of Spalding county, Ga.

By Rev. W. F. Robison, on 15th January, Dr. Thos. S. Jenkins to Miss L. L. Stubbs, both of Harris county, Ga.

By Rev. L. Wood, on 30th January 1872, Dr. James S. Riley, of Corinth, Miss., to Miss Mattie Taylor, daughter of John C. Waters, Esq., of Abbeville county, S. C.

On 1st inst., by Rev. P. G. Reynolds, Mr. Robert E. Millican, of Chattooga county, to Miss Sallie Brunson, of Floyd county, Ga.

In Bradford county, Fla., February 1st 1872, by Rev. Thomas K. Leonard, Mr. John W. Oseen to Miss Susannah Gay.

By Rev. J. A. Kennedy, at his residence near Gainesville, Fla., on 27th December, Mr. A. T. Zetrouer, to Miss Lottie K. Feasted.

Issue of February 21, 1872

By Rev. J. H. Baxter, in Gainesville, Ga., Feb. 8th, William T. B. Wilson to Miss Massina Smith.

On 17th December, by Rev. Jere Reese, at the minister's residence, Mr. R. B. Traylor of Troup county, Ga., to Miss Virginia B. McDonald, of Barbour county, Ala.

In Vineville, January 13th, by Rev. F. Milton Kennedy, Mr. Wm. H. Virgin to Miss Annie E. Holt, daughter of Gen. Wm. S. Holt.

In Camilla, Ga., Feb. 8th, by Rev. James T. Ainsworth, Mr. Thomas A. Barrow of Decatur county, to Miss Jennie Turner, of Camilla.

At the residence of the bride's father, Major B. Pye, in Forsyth, Ga., on the evening of February 1st, by the Rev. Dr. Jones, Mr. D. H. Talley, of Murfreesboro, Tenn., to Miss Mary R. Pye, of the former place.

Feb. 1st, by Dr. A. T. Mann, at St. James Church, Augusta, Ga., Mr. W. F. Holleyman to Miss Mary A. Parks, daughter of Rev. H. H. Parks.

On the 31st Dec., by Rev. Robert L. Wiggins, Mr. Arnold Hague to Miss Antonette Vardaman, all of Harris county, Ga.

On the 31st Jan., by Rev. Robert L. Wiggins, Mr. Joseph L. Biggers of Muscogee county, to Miss Minerva Cox, of Harris county.

By Rev. Robert L. Wiggins, on the 11th of Jan., Mr. Z. A. Bonner of Carrol county, to Miss Mary O. Scott, of Harris county.

In Albany, Ga., on Thursday evening, Jan. 25th, by Rev. R. J. Corley, Mr. Jas. P. Brinson to Mrs. Martha Outzs.

In Albany, Ga., on Tuesday evening, Feb. 6th, by Rev. R. J. Corley, Mr. C. W. Arnold to Miss Mattie Wiseman.

In Baker county, Ga., on Thursday evening, Feb. 8th, at the residence of Mr. B. F. Cochran, by Rev. R. J. Corley, Mr. A. S. McCollum to Miss Hattie Everingham.

Jan. 29, by the Rev. J. C. Love, the Rev. R. L. Harper, of the South Carolina Conference, to Mrs. Harriet Clapp, of Iuka, Miss.

Issue of February 28, 1872

On February 14th, 1872, by Rev. N. C. Thomas, Mr. Felix F. Darden to Miss Gabriella Dyer, of Warren county, Ga.

By Rev. A. C. Mixon, January 25th 1872, Mr. James N. Shaw to Miss Serena C. Kelly, both of Jasper county, Ga.

On February 8th, in Meriwether county, Ga., by Rev. Thomas H. Gibson, Mr. James A. Sibley to Miss Elizabeth Evans.

By Rev. Lowndes A. Darsey, on 15th inst., at Cochran, Ga., Mr. D. M. Ryle to Miss M. R. Pennick.

In Cumming, Ga., on 14th November, 1871, by Rev. W. T. Caldwell, Rev. Geo. E. Gardner of the North Georgia Conference, to Miss Mary R. Bell, daughter of Hon. H. P. Bell

On January 23d, by Rev. A. J. Cauthen, Sam. Barnes to Miss --- Grant, of Abbeville, S> C.

At the residence of the bride's father, in Bradford county, Fla., February 15th 1872, by Rev. Dr. Leonard, Mr. William F. Hunt to Miss Julia D. Dubose.

By A. A. Day, Esq., in Coffee county, Ga., February 8th 1872, Mr. Eli Dudley of Polk county, to Miss F. A. Wooten, of Telfair county, Ga.

On 17th December 1871, in Forsyth, Ga., by Bishop George F. Pierce, Mr. F. N. Wilder to Miss Laura V. Allen, both of Forsyth, Ga.

In Brooks county, on 15th February, by Rev. C. Raiford, Mr. W. F. Dean to Mrs. M. F. Dampier.

On 11th January, near Notsaulga, Ala., by Rev. L. F. Dowdell, Mr. Thomas L. Ware to Miss M. A. Cameron.

By Rev. D. D. Cox, November 9th, 1871, Mr. Harrison Smith to Mrs. M. L. Watts, all of Atlanta, Ga.

By Rev. D. D. Cox, November 12th, 1871, Mr. John L. Weaver to Mrs. Annie Patrick, all of Atlanta, Ga.

By Rev. D. D. Cox, December 21st, 1871, Mr. Lorenzo D. McDonald to Miss Carrie O. Mills, all of Atlanta, Ga.

By Rev. D. D. Cox, January 25th, 1872, Mr. James Williamson, to Miss Emma Pierce, all of Atlanta, Ga.

By Rev. D. D. Cox, January 28th, 1872, Mr. A. P. Smith to Miss N. E. Weems, all of Atlanta, Ga.

By Rev. H. P. Myers, in St. Marys, Ga., February 1st, 1872, Mr. Orlando W. Peck, of Cedar Keys, Fla., to Miss Ella M. Rackliff, of St. Marys.

In Atlanta, Ga., February 15th 1872, by Rev. C. A. Evans, Mr. W. T. Ashford to Miss Jennie Kirkpatrick.

In Macon, on 22d inst., by Rev. John W. Burke, Mr. Louis L. Harrison, of Alabama, to Miss Julia R. Munsun, of Macon, Ga.

At Dawson, Ga., on 21st January, by Rev. J. G. Parks, Mr. J. B. Jobson to Miss Sallie L. Norman.

Issue of March 6, 1872

Feb. 23d, by Rev. Wesley P. Smith, F. Reynolds Pool to Miss A. English, all of Warren co., Ga.

By Rev. A. G. Gantt, on the 20th of Feb., Mr. Jacob Carson to Miss Hattie A. Weeks, all of Charleston county, S. C.

By Rev. W. T. McMichael, at the residence of the bride's mother in Scriven county, GA., Jan. 23d, Mr. H. T. Matthews to Miss Mary Norton, daughter of the late John W. Babcock, of Macon.

In Madison, Florida, on Feb. 9th by Rev. Wm. R. Johnson, Mr. Collin Forsythe to Miss C. Durst, both of Ellaville, Florida.

By Rev. W. A. Clarke, Feb. 23d, Robert Phillips to Miss Dorcas Way, all of Colleton county, S. C.

On the evening of the 13th February, at St. John's Lutheran Church, by the Rev. Thos. William Dosh, Louis O. Dargan, of Darlington, S. C., to Miss J. Anna, daughter of F. R. Wickenberg, of Charleston.

On the 27th of Feb., by Rev. Robert L. Wiggins, Mr. W. B. Lloyd of Cotton Valley, Ala., to Miss Lucy J. Walker, of Muscogee county, Ga.

On the 22d of Feb., in Spalding county, Mr. James R. Ellis to Miss Mary L. Blanton.

By the Rev. S. D. Clements, January 30th, Mr. David L. Jones to Miss Cordelia A. Autry, all of Harris county.

By the Rev. S. D. Clements, Feb. 22d, Mr. James Gafford to Miss Mary Christian, all of Chattahoochee county, Ga..

By Rev. Dr. Leonard, Feb. 27th, at the residence of Mr. James A. Mathis, Columbia county, Fla., Mr. Samuel A. Ruff of Tustenugee, Fla., to Miss Susan F. Martin, of Edgefield, S. C.

On Feb. 11th, by Rev. C. R. H. Hays, Mr. B. F. McCrary to Miss Edna Montgomery, both of Taylor county, Ga.

On 25th Feb., at Dickey's Church, Gowensville circuit, Greenville county, S. C., by Rev. J. C. Crisp, Mr. J. H. Hightower to Miss H. A. Dickey, both of Greenville county, S. C.

By Rev. P. F. Kistler, Feb. 18th, at Boone Hill, Colleton county, S. C., Mr. Henry Bunch to Miss Julia, daughter of Middleton Sweet, Esq.

By Rev. P. F. Kistler, Feb. 28th, near Bacon Bridge, Colleton county, S. C., Mr. W. W. Bunch to Miss Sallie Bee, daughter of the late Cap. Jos. Bee.

At Double Wells, Arkansas, by Rev. Andrew Hunter, Mr. Albert B. Craig, of Bradley county, to Miss Sallie E. McGehee, daughter of Maj. S. M. McGehee, of Jefferson county.

Issue of March 13, 1872

On the 15th of February, by Rev. Wm. C. Power, Mr. M. Davis Nesmith of Williamsburg District, to Miss Esther A., daughter of Thomas R. Sessions, Esq., of Georgetown, S. C.

By Rev. W. K. Turner, at Ocala, February 27th, 1872, Mr. Thomas P. Kennedy, of Tampa, Fla., to Miss Ida J. Cathcart, of Ocala, Fla.

On January 26th, 1872, by Rev. E. J. Knight, at the residence of the bride's father, Mr. Hilliard Jones, of Bartow, Polk county, Fla., to Miss Julia Townsend, of Jefferson county, Fla.

In Macon, on the 7th inst., by Rev. J. W. Burke, Mr. William Finch, of Augusta, Ga., and Miss Mary J. Jobson, of Macon.

In Macon, at the Lanier House, on the 7th inst., by Rev. J. W. Burke, Mr. John R. Scott of Athens, Ohio, and Miss Annie Moore, of Barnesville, Ohio.

On February 29th 1872, by Rev. W. P. Kramer, Dr. W. C. Nixon to Miss Emma O. Pinson, of Floyd county, Ga.

On 21st December, at the bride's father, in Clarke county, Ga., by Rev. D. C. Oliver, Mr. Eppy F. Bond, of Franklin county, Ga., to Miss Emma C. Thompson, of the former place

By Rev. Dr. Leonard, March 3d, 1872, Mr. David E. Ruff, of Tustenuggee, Fla., to Miss Lucinda E. Harris, of Bradford county, Fla.

On February 28th 1872, at the residence of the bride's father, by Rev. Samuel Woodbery, Mr. W. G. Fletcher to Miss Mary C. Bowen.

By Rev. J. Blakely Smith, at the residence of Mrs. Bolfeullet, in Macon, Ga., on the 5th of March, William Keefer to Miss Annie E. Worswick.

By Rev. N. D. Morehouse, on 10th December, Mr. Joel W. Hadden, to Miss Fanny Worthy, both of Clay county, Ga.

By Rev. N. D. Morehouse, January 2d, in Savannah, Ga., Mr. E. Hilton, to Miss Ella Lenair, both of Scriven county, Ga.

By N. D. Morehouse, on 15th inst., in Quitman county, Mr. J. C. Leay, of Montgomery, Ala., to Miss Ella Z. Lancaster.

Issue of March 27, 1872

In East Macon, Ga., on the 14th inst., by Rev. J. w. Burke, Solomon H. Crosby to Miss Celestra R. Waltz.

On 31st January, by Rev. John Halsten, Rev. John W. Davis to Mrs. Mary Davis, all of Carroll County, Ga.

On 27th February, by Rev. W. L. Pegues, Mr. Daniel Skipper to Miss Sally Gittems, all of Marlboro, S. C.

By Rev. L. B. Bouchelle, March 7th, Mr. G. A. Cowart To Miss M. A. Redding, all of Emanuel county, Ga.

By Rev. Geo. G. N. MacDonell, in Fernandina, Fla., March 5th, 1872, Mr. Samuel B. Rawls to Mrs. Hannah N. Pelot.

On the 26th February, at the residence of the bride's father, by Rev. G. W. Gatlin, Mr. J. Andrew Mitchell, of Lexington county, to Mrs. Sallie b. Lark, of Newberry County. *Newberry Herald* please copy.

In Monticello, on 29th February, by E. G. Murrah, Mr. Henry Glover, of Macon, Ga., to Mrs. Jennette Keith, of the former place.

On 14th March, by Rev. W. C. Bass, William J. Lavar to Mrs. Jennie G. Ross, all of Bibb county, Ga.

At the bride's father, March 8th, by Rev. Thos. B. Lanier, Mr. Edwin B. Rahn to Miss Sarah J. Berry, all of Effingham county, Ga.

On January 11th, by Rev. J. A. Mood, at the residence of the bride, Dr. O. B. Mayer to Mrs. L. C. Kinard, all of Newberry, S. C.

By Rev. J. A. Mood, February 23d, Mr. Thomas Cook of Fayetteville, to Miss Colin M. Chapman, of Newberry, S. C.

On February 1st, by Rev. Wm. Hutto, Mr. John A. Tharp to Miss Nancy O. Verelle, all of Abbeville county, S. C.

On March 5th, by Rev. Wm. Hutto, Mr. M. W. Coleman, of Walhalla, to Miss Ludie C. Meriman, of Greenwood, Abbeville county, S. C.

On March 3d 1872, in Crawford county, Ga., at the residence of the bride's aunt, by Rev. I. L. Avant, Mr. Walter J. Jones to Miss A. Josephine McDonald, only daughter of the late Dr. R. McDonald, of Houston county, Ga.

By Rev. J. A. Mood, February 29th, Mr. Francis M. Shrumpert [sic] to Miss Lillie E. Merchant, all of Newberry, S. C.

At the residence of the bride's mother, in Walker county, Ga., March 6th 1872, by Rev. D. J. Weems, Mr. Wesley Lupo, son of Rev. James L. Lupo, to Miss Lula J. Trunnell.

By Rev. J. Lewis, Jr., February 23d, 1872, Mr. Wm. H. Fuller to Miss Elizabeth M. Flournoy, all of Athens, Ga.

On 25th February, by Rev. F. B. Davies, Mr. Joseph Robinson to Miss Frances K. Hardeman, all of DeKalb county.

By Rev. F. B. Davies, on the 14th March, Mr. Charles P. Lively, of Norcross, to Miss Marcilla E., daughter of Judge H. H. Walker, of DeKalb county.

Issue of April 3, 1872

By Rev. J. R. Mayson, March 14th, at the residence of the bride's father, Mr. Samuel House to Miss W. J. Grisham, all of Cobb county, Ga.

By Rev. J. R. Mayson, March 24th, Mr. J. R. Carrell to Miss Mary Wilson, all of Cobb county, Ga.

By Rev. R. R. Dagnall, on 17th of March, Mr. Isaac N. Eubanks to Miss Susan V. Green, both of Barnwell county, S. C.

March 13th, by Rev. J. M. Stokes, Mr. John C. Gramling to Miss Sarah E. Townsend, all of Madison county, Fla.

March 12th, at the residence of William Jefferies, Esq., by the Rev. J. L. Dixon, Mr. M. S. Lynn to Miss Rebecca Jefferies, all of Union county, S. C.

In Macon co., on the 25th March, by Rev. J. W. Burke, Mr. Henry C. Cameron to Miss Laura Follendore.

Issue of April 10, 1872

By Rev. E. P. Bonner, on 26th March 1872, William D. Tutt, Esq., of Lincoln county, Ga., to Miss S. Leonard Freeman, of Columbia county, Ga.

On March 7th, by Rev. A. J. Cauthen, B. B. Allen to Miss Mattie M., daughter of C. T. Latimer, all of Abbeville, S. C.

In Marion county, S. C., April 2d 1872, by Rev. James C. Stoll, Mr. W. D. Carmichael to Miss Agnes Harllee; all of Marion county, S. C.

By Rev. B. J. Johnson, on 14th March, Mr. Daniel W. Arnold to Miss Keran J. Hames, all of Henry county, Ga.

In Macon, Ga., on 4th inst., by Rev. J. W. Burke, Mr. John W. Watson to Miss Dollie A. E. Mullins.

Issue of April 17, 1872

On the 24th March, by Rev. N. Osborn, Mr. T. W. Tabor to Miss M. A. Cole, all of Gilmer county, Ga.

In Warrenton, by Rev. Wesley F. Smith, March 21st, Mr. Joseph L. Scruggs, of Jefferson county, to Miss Sarah J. Scruggs, of the former place.

On March 7th, by Rev. J. J. Giles, at the residence of the bride's father, Rev. J. T. Webb, Mr. James W. Roundtree to Miss Anna J. Webb, all of Lownds county, Ga.

On April 4th, by Rev. John M. Bowden, Mr. William Cranford, of Coweta county, to Miss Celestia C. Smith, of Fayette county, Ga.

On 24th March, at the bride's father, Henderson, Rusk county, Texas, by Rev. D. M. Stovall, Mr. Emory S. Puryear, of Henry county, Ga., to Miss Ophelia F. Cox.

On the 28th March, by Rev. B. L. Hume, Dr. T. J. Walker of Griffin, to Miss Emma L. West of Morgan county, Ga.

Issue of April 24, 1872

On April 9th, in Savannah, Ga., by Rev. E. Lathrop, D. D., of Stamford, Conn., Mr. G. Hal. Cotter, son of Rev. W. J. Cotter, to Miss A. B. Fairchild, daughter of L. J. B. Fairchild.

By Rev. W. A. McLean, in Jacksonville, Fla., April 3d, 1872, Mr. W. P. Pledger to Mrs. Mary A. Hagins, all of Duval county, Fla.

On April 11th 1872, in Meriwether county, Ga., by Rev. Thomas H. Gibson, Mr. Edward J. Wyche to Miss Mary L. Chunn.

On February 4th 1872, by the Rev. B. Sanders, Mr. Richard West to Miss Mary Winters, all of White county, Ga.

On March 31st, 1872, at the residence of the bride's father, in White county, Ga., by Rev. B. Sanders, Mr. Jhon [sic] A. Ledford to Miss E. Jane Ash.

On April 14th, by Rev. Sanford Leake, Mr. William Sims, of Tennessee, to Miss Margaret Tatum, of Whitfield county, Ga.

By Rev. T. W. Moore, Miss Marian G. Collins to Capt. William A. Shaw, all of Jacksonville, Fla.

In Randolph county, Ga., April 18th, by Rev. B. F. Breedlove, Mr. J. P. Sharp, of Dawson, Ga., to Miss M. N. Bailey.

Issue of May 1, 1872

By Rev. Thos. B. Lanier, April 11, Mr. Thos. E. Rahn to Miss Rebecca M. Morgan, all of Effingham county, Ga.

By Rev. Thos. B. Lanier, April 17, Mr. Andrew J. Simmons to Miss Agnes J. Shearouse, all of Effingham county, Ga.

On April 18th, by Rev. I. Z. T. Morris, at the residence of the bride's father, in Montgomery, Ala., Mr. Charles B. Lasser to Miss Lou A. Alred.

On April 18th, by Rev. I. Z. T. Morris, in Herron St., Church, Montgomery, Ala., Mr. John S. Bowman to Miss Ruth R. Gorden, all of Montgomery, Ala.

In Cokesbury, S. C., on the 17th of April by Rev. L. Wood, Dr. B. C. Hart to Mrs. Henrietta M. Gladney, late of Aberdeen, Miss.

In Bradford county, Florida, April 18th, by Rev. Dr. Leonard, at the residence of Mr. Josiah Ward, Mr. Samuel P. Crews to Miss Cynthia C. Ward.

In Warrenton, April 18th, by Rev. Wesley F. Smith, Rev. Allen C. Thomas of the North Ga. Conf., to Miss Nannie H. Hubert, of the former place.

On the 18th April, at the residence of the bride's father, by Rev. Clement Vaughn, Irvine Chipley, of S. C., to Bessie, daughter of Dr. J. T. Coxe, of Macon, Ga.

On the 6th March, by Rev. J. Baxter Platt, Mr. A. W. Davis to Miss M. T. Lowery, all of Chesterfield county, S. C.

Issue of May 8, 1872

In Cave Spring, Ga., 25th inst., by Rev. W. P. Rivers, Rev. P. M. Bartlett, D. D., of East Tennessee, to Miss Florence, youngest daughter of the late Col. A. Alden, and granddaughter of Ex-Governor Lumpkin. *Telegraph and Messenger* please copy.

By Rev. W. A. McLean in Jacksonville, Fla., April 11th 1872, Mr. Z. F. Hundley to Miss Margaret L. Sparkman, all of Duval county, Fla.

On April 14th, at the residence of the bride's father, Rev. W. C. Patterson, by the same, Mr. W. D. Rodgers to Miss Mollie Patterson, all of Lancaster, S. C.

In Calverton, Ga., April 23d 1872, by Rev. W. T. Caldwell, Mr. Richard H. Moore, to Miss Missouri M. Culver.

By Rev. J. E. Little, April 24th 1872, Mr. William G. Clark to Miss Mary F. Sadler, all of Lancasterville, S. C.

At Summerville, S. C., April 24th by Rev. Paul F. Kistler, Mt. Thos. J. Harlee to Miss Edith Dursene[?].

Issue of May 15, 1872

At the residence of the bride's father, near Cuthbert, Ga., on 25th May, by Rev. B. F. Breedlove, Mr. Edward Burtchell to Miss Willie Knowles.

In Barnesville, May 5th, by Rev. J. P. Duncan, Mr. Robert Greer Mathews to Miss Mary Ellen Blalock, all of Upson county, Ga.

At the Asbury Parsonage, Augusta, Ga., April 9th, by Rev. L. J. Davies, Mr. John S. Powell, of Fort Payne, Ala., to Miss Dollie, daughter of the late Rev. J. C. Simmons, No. Ga. Conf.

In Madison county, Florida, May 1st, by Rev. E. L. T. Blake, Mr. John M. Raysor, of Jefferson county, Fla., to Miss Mary Emma, only daughter of Rev. S. G. Chiles, of the So. Ga. Conference

In New Hope church, Lawrenceville ct., April 21st, by Rev. C. A. Conaway, Rev. F. F. Reynolds, of the North Georgia Conference, to Mrs. Z. B. Coffee, daughter of Dr. Griffin.

April 25th, by the Rev. Mr. Reid, Mr. William R. Talley to Miss Carrie Harry, all of Lowndes county, Ga.

On the 5th of May, by Rev. L. C. Peek, Mr. Frederick Miller to Mrs. Emma Armstrong, all of Thomas county, Ga.

In Philadelphia, Pa., on 28th April, by Rev. R. H. Allen, Mr. Wm. R. Thomson, of Philadelphia, to Miss Ann E. Leak, of Griffin, Ga.

By Rev. T. J. Simmons, on 18th of April, at the residence of A. C. Leak, Esq., Mr. S. F. Owen to Miss Jane Long, all of Whitfield county, Ga.

Issue of May 22, 1872

On May 8th, 1872, by Rev. W. D. Kirkland, Mr. John Rantin to Miss Abigail Reid, all of Columbia, S. C.

At the residence of the bride's father, in Hernando county, by Rev. S. S. Moore, on May 1st, Mr. Geo. Sumner to Miss Mary Cray, all of Hernando county, Fla.

On April 4th, at the residence of the bride, in Hernando county, Fla., by Rev. T. J. A. Brown, Rev. Dr. J. M. Farabee to Miss Julia M. Goss.

By Rev. Dr. J. M. Farabee, April 17th, 1872, Mr. Henry B. King to Miss Lucy A. Allen, daughter of Early A. and Gennet Allen, all of Hernando county, Fla.

On May 1st, 1872, by Rev. L. W. Rast, Rev. George S. Anderson, formerly of Virginia, now pastor of the Baptist Church in Madison, Florida, to Miss Isabella C. Spigener, of Orangeburg county, S. C.

May 1st, at the residence of Mr. LeConte, by Rev. Jno. A. Reynolds, Mr. J. L. Camp, of Rome, Ga., to Mrs. J. M. Stone, of Bartow county, Ga.

In Athens, Ga., May 9th 1872, by Rev. J. Lewis, Jr., Mr. Linton W. Stephens to Miss Fannie L. Huggins.

By Rev. J. V. M. Morris, in Oglethorpe county, Ga., April 30th, 1872, Mr. Rob. Eidson to Miss Elizabeth Boling.

By J. V. M. Morris, in Clarke county, Ga., May 9th 1872, Barton E. Thrasher to Miss Sallie F. Hattaway.

By Rev. J. V. M. Morris, in Clarke county, Ga., May 9th, Rev. James H. Baxter of the North Georgia Conference, to Miss Fannie P. Thrasher.

By Rev. J. V. M. Morris, in Clarke county, Ga., May 9th, Seaborn J. Fulilove to Miss Clara A. Thrasher.

Issue of May 29, 1872

On the 16th inst., by Rev. Mr. Radford, Mr. Edwin B. Calhoun to Miss Nannie McBee, both of Polk county, Ga.

On May 2d, 1872, by Rev. W. G. Booth, assisted by Rev. W. M. Watts, at the bride's father, Mr. C. C. Daniel, to Miss A. E. Lang, all of Liberty county, Ga.

On the 15th inst., near Dawson, by Rev. W. G. Parks, Mr. David C. Armstrong, of Notasulga, Ala., to Miss Susie R. Harris, daughter of Maj. E. J. Harris.

At the residence of the bride's father, on May 16th, by Rev. Wm. M. Verdery, Mr. Benj. F. Fleming to Miss Laura E. Saulter, all of Jefferson county, Ga.

On May 15th, by Rev. R. F. Evans, Mr. Henry S. Wimberly, Jr., son of Dr. H. S. Wimberly, to Miss Mary S. Coombs, daughter of Mr. James Coombs, all of Twiggs county, Ga.

May 5th, by Rev. John H. Harris, Mr. Edward H. S. Fife and Miss Sallie Hand, all of Henry county, Ga.

By Rev. John H. Harris, May 16th, in McDonough, Mr. Isham D. Crawford and Miss Lizzie Lemon, all of Henry county.

By Rev. John H. Harris, in McDonough, May 16th, Mr. G. A. McKibben and Miss Mary E. Knott, all of Henry county.

In Cusseta, Ga., May 14th, 1872, by Rev. S. D. Clements, Mr. John L. Harp and Miss Georgia V. Mitchell.

At the Methodist Church in Albany, on the morning of the 15th of May, 1872, by Rev. R. J. Corley, Mr. Enoch C. Jones and Miss Amelia F. Jones, all of Baker county, Ga.

Issue of June 5, 1872

By Rev. W. F. Quillian, May 9th 1872, Mr. George H. Langford of Watkinsville, Ga., to Miss Hattie Craig, of Banks county, Ga.

At the residence of the bride's father, in Weston, Ga., May 19th, by Rev. E. J. Rentz, Mr. J. D. Dantzler to Miss Fannie Blar.

On May 7th, 1872, by Rev. W. T. Caldwell, Mr. Benjamin C. Culver to Miss Sallie T. Davis, both of Hancock county, Ga.

On May 23d, 1872, by Rev. W. T. Caldwell, Mr. N. H. Coleman to Miss A. L. Cody, both of Hancock county, Ga.

On May 21st, 1872, by Rev. W. A. Florence, Mr. William B. Lamkin to Miss Mattie C. Freeman, all of Columbia county, Ga.

On May 23d, 1872, at the residence of the bride's father, in Washington county, Ga., by Rev. Jas. A. Roper, Mr. James M. Thigpen to Miss Annie E. Riddle.

Issue of June 12, 1872

At the residence of Judge Daniel Nolby, in McDonough, Ga., by Rev. John H. Harris, on the 29th of May, Mr. A. W. Crookshank to Miss Delia Nolby, all of McDonough, Ga.

By Rev. N. D. Morehouse, on 16th May, Dr. W. T. Rogers to Miss A. B. Credille, all of Randolph county, Ga.

By Rev. N. D. Morehouse, on 21st May, James P. Goodall to Mrs. M. A. Sams, all of Randolph county, Ga.

On the 16th May, by Rev. J. N. Myers, at the bride's father's, Mr. William A. Eady to Miss Virginia Dickson, all of Carroll county, Ga.

On the 26th May, by W. H. Hunt, Mr. Simpson Pernell to Mrs. Mary F. Smith, all of Columbia county, Fla.

At the residence of the bride's mother, Mrs. E. M. Shearer, in Okolona, Miss., on the 16th May, by Rev. A. C. Allen, Morgan C. Shell, Esq., of houston, Miss., to Mrs. Sallie M. Wilcox, of Okolona, Miss.

On June 2d, by Rev. R. F. Williamson, Mr. R. E. Wilkison to Miss Anna Taylor, all of Schley county, Ga.

On June 2d, by Rev. R. F. Williamson, Mr. James A. Harden to Mary E. Daniel, all of Schley county, Ga.

Issue of June 19, 1872

At the M. E. Church, South, at Aiken, S. C., on the 6th inst., by the Rev. George J. Griffiths, Mr. Henry T. Nicholas, of Edgefield, S. C., to Miss Laura Dagnall, late of Burke county, Ga.

On the 6th of June, at Live Oak, Fla., by Rev. Josephus Anderson, D. D., Rev. E. S. Tyner, of the Florida Conference, to Miss Etta Green, of Live Oak.

At the residence of Mr. Thomas Reaves, Esq., May 30, by Rev. Wm. Thomas, Mr. F. R. Twitty to Miss Mary E. Talbot, all of Lancaster county, S. C.

At the residence of the bride's father, J. J. Horton, Esq., June 6th, by Rev. Wm. Thomas, Mr. Nathaniel Gay to Miss S. Rebecca Horton, all of Lancaster county, S. C.

In Houston county, Ga., on the 4th inst., by Rev. E. H. McGehee, Mr. Zachary B. Gunn to Miss Virginia Woodsen.

Issue of June 26, 1872

On 21st May, in St. Luke's Church, Columbus, Ga., by Rev. Joseph S. Key, Mr. Thomas J. Watt of Muscogee county, to Miss Indiana Lloyd, of Columbus.

By the Rev. J. L. Skipper on 9th June, at the residence of the bride's mother, Mr. S. M. Dunn, to Miss Secludy Caloway, all of Conecuh county, Ala.

On the 12th June, at the residence of the bride's mother, by the Rev. J. L. Skipper, Mr. N. B. Purrnal, of Covington county, Ala., to Miss Laurah A. Binson, of Butler county, Ala.

In Atlanta, on 6th June, by Rev. Clement A. Evans, Mr. Henry S. Johnson, to Miss Emma Rawson, daughter of Mr. E. E. Rawson, all of Atlanta, Ga.

In Talbot county, Ga., June 12th, by the Rev. D. R. McWilliams, Mr. T. R. Massengale to Miss Sallie E. Rush, daughter of Rev. L. Rush, of the North Georgia Conference.

By Rev. J. J. Workman, at St. Peter's Church, June 10th, Jules A. Herard, Esq., to Miss Elizabeth A., daughter of Maj. W. G. Roberts, of Beaufort county, S. C.

On 29th May, at the residence of Thos. Bradley, in Liberty county, by Rev. W. S. Booth, Mr. James Butler to Miss Sallie Bradley, both of Liberty county, Ga.

By Rev. W. G. Booth, on 12th June, at Angus Martin, of Liberty county, Mr. Angus Lang to Miss Addie Martin, both of Liberty county, Ga.

In Allendale, May 23d, by Rev. T. E. Wannamaker, Mr. George E. Hudgins of Charleston, S. C., to Miss Rosa G., second daughter of the officiating clergyman.

Issue of July 3, 1872

On 11th June at Smithville, Ga., by Rev. D. O'Driscoll, Mr. William Paten, of Macon, to Miss Sallie Copeland, of Smithville.

In Macon, Ga., on the 27th inst., by Rev. John W. Burke, Mr. Geo. C. Boutwell, to Miss Hattie B. Lidden.

Issue of July 10, 1872

May 30, by Rev. W. A. Florence, Mr. Robert A. Lassiter, to Miss Fannie E. McDaniel, all of Columbia county, Ga.

On the 27th June, at Red Clay, Ga., by the Rev. S. Leake, Mr. George D. Stuart to Miss Mollie J. Parker.

At Athens, Ga., June 23d, 1872, by Rev. J. Lewis, Jr., Mr. Wm. E. Stanley, and Miss Mary Ann Chasteen.

In Talbotton, Ga., on the 27th inst., by Rev. Thos. T. Christian, Mr. John L. Truslow, of Chattanooga, Tenn., to Miss Julia B. Howard, of the former place.

Issue of July 17, 1872

On 4th July, at the Residence of the bride's father, in Richmond county, Ga., by Rev. E. Ewing Johnston, Mr. Joseph H. Green to Miss Sarah W. Parish, all of Richmond county.

Issue of July 24, 1872

At Cave Spring, Ga., July 7th, by Rev. B. B. Quillian, Mr. H. D. Barr to Miss Sue M. McCulley, both of Oxford, Ala.

By Rev. John Calvin Johnson, in Jackson county, Ga., on 11th day of July, Col. W. W. Lowrance, of Tishemingo county, Miss., to Miss Mary J. Bell, of former place.

Issue of July 31, 1872

By Rev. Joseph M. Gable, July 19, 1872, Mr. John M. Spinks, to Miss Samantha E. Thomas, both of Cobb county, Ga.

Issue of August 7, 1872

In Bainbridge, Ga., July 21st, by Rev. W. Knox, Walter W. Keep, editor *Live Oak* (Fla.) *Times*, to Miss Pauline C. Biles.

In Decatur county, July 23, by Rev. W. Knox, D. A. C. Funderburk to Miss S. J. Yates.

In Mikesville, Florida, July 23d, by Rev. Dr. Leonard, Mr. Thomas C. Carrol to Miss Evelina S. Townsend, of Columbia county, Florida.

July 30th, by Rev. Joseph M. Gable, Mr. George M. Bradley of Polk county ,Ga., to Miss Elizabeth Donehoo, of Cobb county, Ga.

At Brown's Hotel, on the evening of the 31st of August, by Justice Coxe, Mr. William b. Miller to Miss Willie Williams, both of Burke county, Ga.

Issue of August 14, 1872

In the Methodist Church in Talbotton, Ga., July 10th, 1872, by Rev. R. W. Dixon, Thomas B. King, of New York, to Miss Eliza M. Pou, of Talbotton, Ga.

By Rev. Jas. O. Branch, in Macon, Ga., on 7th August, 1872, Mr. Solomon Braney to Miss Sallie R. Kelsey, both of Richmond county, Ga.

At the residence of the bride's father, on July 21st, 1872, by Rev. J. H. Mashburn, Mr. D. H. Venable to Miss S. H. Carrington.

On July 11th, 1872, by Rev. M. L. Banks, Mr. Taylor Eaddy to Mrs. Emily Stone, both of Williamsburg county, S. C.

By Rev. M. L. Banks, August 1st, 1872, Mr. W. Bennet Miller to Miss Margaret M. Britton, both of Williamsburg county, S. C.

Issue of August 21, 1872

On the 8th of August, by Rev. S. S. Sweet, Mr. C. H. Fretwell to Miss S. E. Phillips, of Quitman, Brooks county, Ga.

In Saludaville, S. C., August 11th, by Rev. W. D. Kirkland, Mr. J. Hilton to Miss Mary A. Loyal, daughter of Rev. L. C. Loyal of the So. Ca. Conference.

Issue of August 28, 1872

By Rev. Henry J. Evans, Mr. A. Henry Graham to Miss Emiline N. Graham, at the residence of Burton Graham, all of Walker county, Ga.

By Rev. W. W. Oslin, at the Eatonton hotel, August 7th, Mr. W. H. Hearn, of Eatonton, to Miss Hattie C. Pelot, of Mount Meigs, Ala.

By Rev. Geo. G. N. MacDonell, August 8th, at Lawton, No. 12, A. & g. R. R., Mr. John C. Wright, of Savannah, Ga., to Miss Almira J. Hankins, of LaFayette county, Florida.

Issue of September 11, 1872

On August 11th, by Rev. W. F. Quillian, Mr. C. W. Meaders, to Miss Georgia Blackwell, all of Hall county, Ga.

By Rev. Joseph M. Gable, August 28th, 1872, Mr. Mark Reeves to Mrs. Nancy E. Haygood, all of Cobb county, Georgia.

By the Rev. S. H. J. Sistrunk, on July 19th, at Mrs. Gausey's of Houston county, Mr. William Fulwood, of Houston, to Miss Charity Mitchel, of Taylor county, Ga.

By Rev. W. Hutto, August 29th, Mr. Jas. T. Clemm to Miss Susan C. Brant, all of Abbeville, S. C.

In Columbia, S. C., August 29th, by Rev. W. D. Kirkland, Mr. J. M. Kirkpatrick of Charlotte, N. C., to Miss L. G. Burns, of Columbia, S. C.

By Robert L. Wiggins, August 6th, 1872, Mr. Thomas H. Pitchford, of Alabama, to Miss Cornelia C. A. Pitchford, of Cataula, Harris county, Ga.

Issue of September 18, 1872

At Hickory Flat, Ga., Sept. 1st, by Rev. L. F. Burtz, Mr. David R. Gaines to Miss Martha J. Johnson, all of Cherokee county, Ga.

Issue of September 25, 1872

By Rev. L. C. Peek, on the 10th September, Mr. Elijah Merritt, of Florida, to Miss Julia Ann Akins, of Thomas county, Ga.

By the Rev. L. C. Peek, on the 13th September, Mr. William S. Davis to Miss Elizabeth S. Hays, both of Thomas county, Ga.

On the 6th inst., by Rev. S. S. Sweet, Mr. Henry Arnold to Miss Zephie Evans, of Brooks county, Ga.

Issue of October 2, 1872

On August 14th, 1872, in White county, Ga., by Rev. B. Sanders, Mr. Joseph L. Lawson to Miss Mary Hamilton.

By Rev. B. Sanders, September 15th 1872, Mr. John W. Allen to Miss E. A. Helton, all of White county, Ga.

On September 1st, 1872, by Rev. W. H. Thomas, at the residence of Hon. John King, Camden county, Ga., Wm. T. Atkins, of Fernandina, Fla., to Miss Marian F. King.

On September 19th, 1872, by W. H. Hunt, Mr. William N. Buchanon to Miss Mary Jane Knight, all of Columbia county, Florida.

By Rev. J. L. Sifly, on 12th inst., in Manning, S. C., Rev. Abner Ervin, of the South Carolina Conference, to Miss Esther Carpenter, of Manning, S. C.

Issue of October 9, 1872

On 11th Sept., in Ridgeville, S. C., at the residence of brother George Baxter, by the Rev. A. R. Danner, Mr. George T. Goodwin to Miss Agnes Brown, all residents of the above place.

At the residence of the bride's father, by the Rev. W. F. Cook, Mr. Jemmie B. Hill to Miss Susie Whitely, all of Rome, Ga.

Sept. 17, at the residence of the bride's father, by Rev. Hiram Dorman, Mr. Charles H. Turner, of Carroll county, Ga., to Miss Sue C. Fletcher, of Meriwether county, Ga.

By Rev. W. C. Dunlap, in Mt. Harmony Baptist Church, on the 12th of Sept., Mr. R. R. Johnson to Miss E. M. Hendon, both of Chattooga county, Ga.

By Rev. W. C. Dunlap, at the residence of the bride's father, on the 19th of Sept., Mr. Wm. A. Simmons, of Chattooga county, to Miss M. H. McWhorter, of Walker county, Ga.

By Rev. W. C. Dunlap, on the 24th of Sept., at the residence of the bride's mother, Mr. E. A. Johnston to Miss S. E. Powell, both of Chattooga county, Ga.

In the city of Atlanta, Sept. 15th, by Rev. W. P. Harrison, Mr. G. H. Boutell to Miss S. A. Dale.

In Atlanta, at the Second Baptist Church, Oct. 1, by Rev. W. P. Harrison, Mr. B. B. Crew to Miss Tillie C. Maffit.

In Atlanta, at the Second Baptist Church, Oct. 1, by Rev. W. P. Harrison, Mr. William H. Patterson to Miss Flora Brown.

Issue of October 23, 1872

In Houston county, Ga., on the 2d inst., by Rev. E. H. McGehee, Mr. L. S. Tounsley to Miss Susie Tucker.

In Griffin, Ga., August 13th, by Rev. John W. Heidt, Capt. M. Fletcher Tutwiler, of Virginia, to Miss Nina E. Johnson, of former place.

In Griffin, Ga., August 25th, by Rev. John W. Heidt, Mr. Thomas J. Bowen, of Spalding county, to Miss Eliza Reeves, of former place.

In Griffin, Ga., October 1st, by Rev. John W. Heidt, Dr. William B. Jones, of Burke county, to Miss Emory C. Freeman, of former place.

Near Grifin, Ga., October 1st, by Rev. John W. Heidt, Mr. James K. Johnson, of Griffin, to Miss Susie M. Crawley of Spalding county.

On October 3d, 1872, 1872, by Rev. Jas. A. Rosser, Mr. Lorenzo D. Lasseter to Miss Ella V. Smith, all of Burke county.

In West End, on 8th inst., at the residence of the bride's father, Col. boynto, by Rev. Dr. W. H. Pegg, Col. A. W. Tigner to Miss Miriam Boynton.

At the residence of the bride's father, Wm. Woods, on October 3d, by G. W. McMullen, Esq., Mr. John Miller to Miss G. A. E. Woods, all of Henry county, Ga.

In Marion county, S. C., August 27th 1872, by Rev. James C. Stoll, Mr. B. F. Fenegan to Miss Maggie Platt, all of Marion county, S. C.

On October 2d, in Jonesboro, by Rev. Robert Logan, Mr. William J. Land to Miss Lula E. Melson, of the former place.

In Atlanta, Ga., October 10th 1872, by Rev. Alex. M. Thigpen, Mr. Colin M. Fraser to Miss Susie E., daughter of Mrs. Ann M. Cozart.

Issue of October 30, 1872

Oct. 15th, by Rev. P. A. Heard, Mr. Geo. H. Hammond, of Atlanta, to Miss Florida Floyd, of Covington.

On the 16th of Oct., by Rev. W. F. Quillian, Mr. Z. T. Suddath to Miss E. A. Winters, all of Banks county, Ga.

On the 24th of Oct., by Rev. Rev. W. F. Quillian, Mr. D. E. Brewer to Miss E. P. Norwood, all of Banks county, Ga.

In Bibb county, Ga., on the 23d Oct., by Rev. J. W. Burke, Capt. W. T. Reid, of Eatonton, to Miss Amanda M. Gantt, of Bibb county.

At St. Paul's Church, Columbus, Ga., Oct. 22d, by Rev. Joseph S. Key, Mr. John W. Collier, of Atlanta, Ga., to Miss Sallie E. Wright, daughter of Rev. Arminius Wright, pastor of St. Paul's Church.

SOUTHERN CHRISTIAN ADVOCATE MARRIAGE NOTICES 1867-1878

Issue of November 6, 1872

On October 10th, 1872, by Rev. W. F. Smith, Mr. James P. Johnson, of McDuffee county, to Miss Indiana E. Edwards, of Warren county, Ga.

On October 6th, by Rev. A. Gray, Mr. Nathan E. Lee to Miss Emma Glass, both of Newton county, Ga.

On October 24th, by Rev. A. Gray, Mr. J. C. Nelms, of Rockdale county, Ga., to Miss Lucy Treadwell, of Newton county, Ga.

On October 1st, by Rev. J. M. Dickey, Rev. B. J. Johnson, of the North Georgia Conference, to Miss G. Josephine Bankston, of Fulton county, Ga.

On October 24th, at the residence of the bride's father, by Rev. H. W. Sharpe, Mr. James R. Van to Miss Lizzie McKinnon, daughter of John McKinnon, Sen., all of Thomas county, Ga.

On October 17th, by Rev. James A. Rosser, Dr. J. C. Brigham to Miss Julia D. Odom, all of Burke county, Ga.

On October 3d, by Rev. J. N. Wilcox, Mr. L. D. J. Chance to Miss Frances Reeves, all of Burke county, Ga.

On October 24th, in Milton county, Ga., by Rev. S. J. Bellah, Mr. Jacob P. Neese to Miss Aurelia S. A. Hooke, daughter of Dr. J. C. P. Hook, deceased.

On October 22d, near Perry, Houston county, Ga., by Rev. A. J. Dean, Mr. Geo. F. Riley to Miss E. M. J. Calhoun.

On October 23d, in the Methodist Church at Bennettsville, S. C., by Rev. John A. Porter, assisted by Rev. Wm. Martin, Mr. G. W. Huggins to Miss Sarah Waring Porter.

On October 17th, at the residence of the bride's mother, Mrs. A. G. Caldwell, near Hazlewood, S. C., by Rev. W. McDonald, Mr. F. R. Simonton to Miss Sallie E., daughter of Rev. J. W. J. Harris, deceased, of S. C. Conference.

Issue of November 13, 1872

By Rev. J. H. D. McRae, at Mr. Mathew's on 13th August, Mr. N. Mizell to Miss Zemton Doke, all of Bradford county, Fla.

By Rev. J. H. D. McRae, at Mr. Hatchell's on September 12th, Mr. W. H. A. Roberts to Miss Sue Long, all of Columbia county, Fla.

By Rev. J. H. D. McRae, on September 26th, Mr. Welshin Marcum to Miss Martha Roberts, all of Columbia county, Fla.

By Rev. J. H. D. McRae, at Major G. U. Ellis', on October 2d, Dr. T. C. Hunter to Miss Leonora A. Townsend, all of Columbia county, Fla.

Near Bethany, Ga., on October 24th 1872, by Rev. H. D. Murphy, Mr. James H. Ponder to Miss Mary Perkins.

At the Methodist Church in Tallahassee, Fla., on October 17th, 1872, by Rev. Dr. Josephus Anderson, Judge D. W. Gwynn to Miss Emma, daughter of Dr. Miles Nash, all of Tallahassee.

Near Bethany, Ga., on 24th October 1872, by Rev. H. D. Murphy, Mr Enoch Gibson to Miss Caroline Perkins.

By Rev. W. P. Pledger,in the Methodist Church, Madison, Ga., on October 20th, Mr. M. A. Peteet to Miss Ola A. Robertson.

In Houston co., Ga., on October 24th, by Rev. E. H. McGehee, Mr. Josian Bass to Miss Mattie W. McCoy.

At the residence of the bride's mother, in Snow Hill, Wilcox county, Ala., by Rev. D. M. Hudson, on October 31st 1872, Rev. D. J. Wright, of the Alabama Conference, to Miss Sallie Hall.

By Rev. R. B. G. Walters, on November 3d, 1872, at the residence of the bride's mother, Mr. Isaac L. Moye to Miss Margaret Ann Walters, all of Johnson county, Ga.

On November 4th 1872, by Rev. James N. Myers, Rev. James Baskin to Miss Rhoda Bledsoe, all of Carroll county, Ga.

In Talbot county, Ga., November 6th, 1872, by Rev. R. W. Dixon, Algernon J. Perryman, of Talbotton, Ga., to Miss Hattie C. Smith, of Talbot county.

At Hillsboro, Ga., October 29th 1872, by Rev. J. L. K. Smith, Mr. John McCollough to Mrs. Frances E. Alexander.

Issue of November 20, 1872

In Crawford county, Ga., Nov. 7th, by the Rev. I. L. Avant, Mr. Benjamin A. Heartley to Miss Eliza J. Perkins, daughter of Furney G. Perkins, deceased.

On the 8th of Nov., by Rev. R. A. Conner, in the Methodist Church in Jefferson ,Jackson county, Ga., Mr. Wm. E. Hatcher, of Columbia county, to Miss M. Fannie Conner, of the former place, and daughter of the officiating minister.

By Rev. J. J. Singleton, Oct. 8th, Mr. D. E. Willis to Mrs. Lizzie Simmons, of Monroe county, Ga.

By Rev. J. J. Singleton, Oct. 17th, Mr. James R. Hill to Miss Fannie O. Chambless, of Monroe county, Ga.

By Rev. J. J. Singleton, Nov. 6th, Mr. S. B. Price, of Macon, Ga., to Miss Mary L. Perkins, of Monroe county, Ga.

Oct. 10th, at the residence of the bride's mother, by Rev. J. A. Kennedy, Mr. L. L. hill formerly of Lincolnton, N. C., to Miss Louisiana Zetrouer, daughter of the late John R. Zetrouer, all of Alachua county, Fla.

By Rev. W. W. Oslin, Nov. 6th, M. J. Mon. Johnson to Miss Sryphosia M. Rosser, both of Eatonton, Ga.

Issue of November 27, 1872

In Warrenton, Nov. 14th, 1872, by Rev. Wesley F. Smith, Rev. Joshua M. Parker, of the North Georgia Conference, to Miss Laura V. Neal, of the former place.

At Blackville, S. C., Nov. 14th, 1872, by Rev. J. W. McRoy, Mr. Samuel McInis of Hamilton co., Fla., to Miss Henrietta Holman, of Barnwell county, S. C.

On the 7th of Nov., by the Rev. W. Ewing Johnston, Mr. Joseph W. Parish to Miss Katie Shaw, all of Richmond county, Ga.

On the 12th of Nov., by Rev. W. Ewing Johnston, Lord George M. Gordon, of Scotland, to Miss Annie E. F. Winter, of Richmond county, Georgia.

By Rev. John W. McRoy, W. Aldrich to Miss Collins, eldest daughter of Jeremiah Collins, all of Barnwell county, S. C.

On Nov. 7th, by Rev. John L. Harris, at Bear Creek, Henry county, Ga., Mr. Wm. A. Speer to Miss Roxey Bivins.

On Nov. 11th, by Rev. John L. Harris, Mr. J. D. Nipper, of Henry county, Ga., to Miss Fannie J. Adair, of Greenville, Ga.

On 7th Nov., 1872,by Rev. J. O. A. Cook, Mr. M. J. Colson to Miss Laura R. Frazer.

On Nov. 7th, by Rev. A. G. Gantt, Covert B. Nelson, of Williamsburg, to Miss Amanda C. Orvin, of St. Johns Berkley, Charleston county, South Carolina.

On Oct. 24th, by Rev. J. E. Penney, Mr. Andrew J. Penney to Miss Haggie Penney, all of Abbeville county, S. C.

In Talbot county, Ga., on 5th Nov., by Rev. J. B. McGehee, President Andrew Female College, A. M. C. Russel, to Miss Annie E. Mounger.

In Georgetown, Ga., on Nov. 10th, by Rev. J. B. McGehee, Mr. Thos. M. Bryan to Miss M. T. Warren.

By the Rev. J. J. Singleton, Nov. 21st, 1872, Mr. C. F. Turner, of Thomaston, Ga., to Mrs. Eliza Smith, of Monroe county, Ga.

By Rev. J. J. Singleton, Nov. 21st, 1872, Dr. Samuel H. Grey, to Miss Lula Hollis, both of Monroe county, Ga.

Issue of December 4, 1872

In Columbia county, Fla., at the residence of Captain Simeon L. Sparkman, by Rev. Dr. Thomas K. Leonard, November 20th 1872, Mr. John William Niblock to Miss Frances A. Fry.

On the 27th Nov., by Rev. W. C. Bass, H. J. Winn, Esq., of Monroe county, to Miss Mary E., third daughter of Robert Bowman, deceased, of Bibb county, Ga.

At the Methodist Church in Tampa, Fla., November 6th, by Rev. E. F. Gates, Dr. Chas. J. Mitchell, of Ft. Mead, Fla., to Miss Nellie M. Spencer, of Tampa, Fla.

At the residence of the bride's father, in Meriwether county, Ga., November 19th 1874, by Rev. T. H. Gibson, Mr. Wm. D. Varner to Miss Mattie C. Underwood.

By Rev. Loundes A. Darsey, on November 7th, 1872, Robert A. Ponder, Esq., to Miss Ella A. Gordon, both of Burke county, Ga.

By Rev. L. A. Darsey, on November 21st, 1872, Green B. Robinson, Esq., of Burke county, Ga., to Miss Lizzie Ponder, of Jefferson county, Ga.

On November 14th, by Rev. E. G. Murrah, at the residence of the bride's mother, in Monticello, Ga., Mr. Samuel Minnifee of Palmetto, Ga., to Miss Lizzie Jordan, of the former place.

By Rev. E. G. Murrah, November 14th, at the residence of the bride's father, in Jasper county, Ga., Mr. Sam'l Hearn, of Eatonton, Ga., to Miss Carrie Wyatt.

By Rev. J. J. Singleton, November 26th, 1872, Mr. Thomas D. Johnson, of Jonesboro, to Miss Emma L. King, of Monroe county, Ga.

By Rev. J. J. Singleton, November 27th, 1872, Mr. H. F. Lester, of Atlanta, Ga., to Miss Julia H. Ivey, of Monroe county, Ga.

Near Cave Spring, Ga., November 21st, 1872, by Rev. B. B. Quillian, Mr. James M. B. Grisham to Miss Eliza O. Pledger, daughter of Allen Pledger.

In Polk county, Ga., November 24th, 1872, by Rev. B. B. Quillian, Mr. E. Marbut to Mrs. Lodocey Wharton.

In Quitman county, Ga., November 20th, by Rev. B. F. Breedlove, Mr. Joseph Baily to Miss Bethia Jenkins.

In Randolph county, Ga., November 26th, by Rev. B. F. Breedlove, Mr. Allen Baker, of Alabama, to Miss M. C. Pyles.

Issue of December 11, 1872

By the Rev. S. A. McCook, at the bride's house on the 22d day of September, Mr. Joseph Nail to Mrs. Elizabeth Daniel, both of Wakulla county, Fla.

By Rev. S. A. McCook, on the 31st day of October, Mr. A. M. Anderson to Miss Eliza Causseaux, all of Wakulla county, Fla.

By Rev. S. A. McCook, near Wakulla Springs, on 7th November, Mr. Wm. W. Causseaux to Miss Elizabeth Ferrell, both of Wakulla county, Fla.

By Rev. S. A. McCook, at the bride's father's A. M. Ferrell, on the 26th day of November, Mr. S. K. Causseaux to Miss Edney Ferrell, all of Wakulla county, Fla.

On the evening of Nov. 28th in the Methodist Church in Quitman, Ga., by Rev. Alex. P. Wright, Mr. George W. Averett to Miss Mattie J. Wattles, all of Quitman, Ga.

By Rev. Henry M. Mood, on the 28th Nov., Rev. Wm. M. Mood, of the South Carolina Conference, to Miss M. E. Gregory, daughter of W. S. Gregory, Esq., of Union county, S. C.

Nov. 21st, by Rev. J. R. Mayson, at the residence of Dr. E. Mattox, in DeKalb county, Ga., Emory V. M. Mahaffey, of Jackson county, Ga., to Miss Fannie K. Mattox.

On the 31st of October near Bishopville, S. C., by Rev. Allan McCorquodale, Mr. A. Clarance Durant to Miss C. C. Dixon, third daughter of Wm. K. and S. P. Dixon.

Nov. 12th, by Rev. S. J. Hill, W. B. Hill of York County, to Mrs. A. E. Houser, of Orangeburg, S. C.

Dec. 3d, by Rev. J. W. Hinton, Mr. John H. Abel of Macon, Ga., to Miss Laura E. Brooks.

By Rev. J. M. Austin, Dec. 2d, in Lumpkin, Stewart county, Ga., Mr. M. G. Robinson, of Nottaway county, Virginia, to Miss N. Virginia Richardson, of Lumpkin, Ga.

At Tustenuggee on the 28th of Nov., by Rev. Dr. Thomas K. Leonard, Mr. A. T. Smallwood to Miss Rosa R., eldest daughter of Hon. Thomas R. Collins, all of Columbia county, Fla.

By Rev. Manning Brown, on the 20th Nov., Rev. John Kelly McCain, of the South Carolina Conference, to Miss Fannie, daughter of Samuel G. Henry, Esq.

Nov. 10th by Rev. T. S. L. Harwell, Mr. L. Green of Harris county, Ga., to Miss Sallie O. Sledge, of Troup county, Ga.

By Rev. T. S. L. Harwell, Nov 17th, Dr. B. G. Poer of Harris county, Ga., to Miss F. O. Shepard, daughter of T. J. and S. Shepard, of Liberty county, Ga.

In Macon, Ga., Dec. 4th, by Rev. J. W. Hinton ,Mr. T. O. Vinson of Crawford county, Ga., to Miss Mary E. Robertson, of Bibb county, Ga.

In Franklin, Ga., Nov. 28th, by Rev. Jno. H. Bowden, Dr. William C. Baily, of Palmetto, to Miss Malodia M. Wilkinson, of the former place.

At Pinson's Hotel, Cave Spring, Ga., Nov. 28th, by Rev. B. B. Quillian, John W. Propst to Miss Sallie Littlejohn, both of Jacksonville, Ala.

In Cartersville, Ga., Nov. 20th, by Rev. John T. Norris, Mr. James W. Thomas, of Nashville, Tenn., to Miss M. Emma DeJarnette, of Cartersville, Ga.

In St. John's Berkley, November 27th, by Rev. P. F. Stevens, Rev. W. D. Kirkland, of the South Carolina Conference, to Mrs. M. Marion Porcher.

Issue of December 18, 1872

At the residence of Dr. Brown in Bulloch co., Ga., on Dec. 3d, by the Rev. W. T. McMichael, Mr. Charles Evans of Screven county, to Miss Ida Brown, of Bulloch county.

By Rev. W. W. Oslin, Nov. 29th, 1872, Mr. W. D. McDade to Miss Lou E. Caswell, all of Putnam county, Ga.

By the Rev. John Calvin Johnson, in Watkinsville, Clarke county, Ga., on 14th Nov. 1872, Mr. George W. Mason, of Athens, Ga., to Miss Beulah A. Booth, of the former place.

By the Rev. John Calvin Johnson, in Clarke county, Ga., on 28th Nov. 1872, Mr. Robert E. Kirkpatrick, of Athens, Ga., to Miss Salina J. Epps.

By the Rev. John Calvin Johnson, on 3d Dec. 1872, William R. Little, Esq., of Carnesville, Ga., to Miss Dudley Few, of Clarke county, Ga.

By the Rev. John Calvin Johnson, on 5th Dec. 1872, Mr. Pleasant Lewis to Miss Nancy E. Harrison, all of Clarke county, Ga.

On the 26th of Nov., in Covington, Ga., by Rev. F. G. Hughes, Mr. Eugene B. Heard, of Elbert county, to Miss Sallie M. Harper, of the former place

On Dec. 6th, at the residence of S. W. McMichael, by the Rev. W. W. Stewart, Mr. Wm. P. Hunt to Miss Patona E. Hatcher, all of Marion county, Ga.

On Dec. 9th, by Rev. Lowndes A. Darsey, John E. Barnett, Esq., to Miss Emma Attaway, both of Eastman, Ga.

On 5th Dec., by Rev. J. H. Zimmerman, Mr. Joseph P. Brownlee to Miss Emma C. Mellard, daughter of Rev. T. Mellard, all of Charleston county, S. C.

By Rev. J. B. Platt, Dec. 3rd, 1872, Mr. L. L. Spencer, to Miss Harriet S. Robeson, all of Chesterfield county, S. C.

Oct. 27th 1872, at the residence of the bride's father, by the Rev. W. Thomas, Mr. H. W. Mobley, to Miss Jane Robinson, all of Lancaster co., S. C.

Nov. 21st, 1872, at the residence of the bride's mother, by Rev. W. Thomas, Mr. James Blake to Miss Belle Tillman, all of Lancaster county, S. C.

Issue of December 25, 1872

At the residence of Mr. Henry R. Brown, by Rev. J. R. Little, December 5th, 1872, Capt. William F. Rutledge of Lancaster, to Miss Eugenia A. Brown of Liberty Hill, S. C.

By Rev. Joseph M. Gable, December 10th 1872, at the residence of the bride's father, Mr. Jos. T. Hamby of Marietta, Ga., to Miss T. E. Gober of Cobb county, Ga.

On the 28th November, at the residence of the bride's father, by Rev. R. B. Tarrant, Mr. Thos. Murphy, to Miss M. M. Livingston, all of Orangeburg county, S. C.

In Bartow county, Ga., on the evening of the 12th, by Rev. Jno. A. Reynolds, Mr. W. V. Dishroon, to Miss O. N. Gilreath, youngest daughter of Geo. H. Gilreath.

By the Rev. C. H. R. Hays, on the 17th December, 1872, Mr. J. G. McCantz, to Miss J. J. Murrey, all of Taylor county, Ga.

December 5th 1872, by Rev. W. H. Hunt, Mr. J. A. Langford, to Mrs. Elmira Walker, all of Columbia county, Florida.

In Warrenton, Ga., December 11th, 1872, by Rev. Wesley F. Smith, Mr. Wm. H. Latimer, to Miss Hattie E. Smith, both of the above place.

On 10th December, 1872, by Rev. J. M. Venable, Mr. Allen L. Venable, to Miss Mary E. Lyle, all of Jackson county, Ga.

At the residence of J. W. Stuckey, Esq., on Sunday, December 8, 1872, by Rev. S. A. Weber, Mr. Ladson Crosswell, to Miss Sarah Reynolds, all of Bishopville, S. C.

On November 6th, 1872, at the residence of the bride's father, by the Rev. W. B. Neal, Mr. Reuben Trotter, to Miss Fanny Fuller, all of Lee county, Ala.

By the same on the 21st November 1872, at the residence of the bride's father, Mr. Wm. M. Burt, to Miss Annie M. Van, all of Salem, Lee county, Ala.

By the same on the 4th December 1872, at tl.e residence of the bride's father, Rev. R. L. Wiggins, of the South Georgia Conference, to Mrs. A. E. Kimbrough, of Lee county, Ala.

In Fort Gaines, Ga., December 5th, 1872, by Rev. T. A. Brown, H. C. Vinson of Early county, to Miss Lucia P. Watts, of Fort Gaines, Ga.

In Fort Valley, Ga., December 19th, 1872, by Rev. T. A. Brown, Mr. G. D. Brown, to Miss Lou Jordan, both of Fort Valley, Ga.

By the Rev. Jno. T. Whitaker, at the residence of Mr. G. M. Gordys, on the 12th December, 1872, Mr. Wm. F. Gay, to Miss Josephine Johnson, both of Harris county, Ga.

On the 12th inst., by Rev. J. H. Zimmerman, Mr. Thomas Livingston, to Miss Ella H. Wessinger, all of Orangeburg county, S. C.

On the 21st November, 1872, by Rev. B. E. Ledbetter, Mr. Lewis M. Turner, to Miss Alice Hudson, daughter of J. E. Hudson, Esq., all of Canton, Ga.

On December 12th, at the residence of the bride's father, by Rev. Joshua Bradford, Rev. Robt. P. Martin of the North Georgia Conference, to Miss L. M. Thomas, daughter of Rev. B. T. Thomas of Gwinnett county, Ga.

On the 12th inst., by the Rev. D. H. Moore, at the residence of the bride's mother, Mr. J. M. Webb, to Miss Susie McNeice, all of Crawford county, Ga.

On the evening of December 5th, 1872, by Rev. W. D. Kirkland, Mr. Wiley B. Burnet of Baltimore, Md., to Miss Annie R. Jones, daughter of Abram Jones, Esq., of Edgefield county, S. C.

Issue of January 8, 1873

November 27th, 1872, by Rev. I. L. Avant, Mr. A. J. Long to Miss Laura Aultman, both of Crawford county, Ga.

In Bibb county, Ga., December 15th, 1872, by Rev. I. L. Avant, Rev. Lucius G. Evans of Crawford county, Ga., to Mrs. Hattie M. Bartlett, of Bibb county, Ga.

December 28th, 1872, Rev. I. L. Avant, Mr. Wm. F. King, of Houston county, Ga., to Miss Augusta A. Heartly, of Crawford county, Ga.

In the Methodist Church, at Graniteville, S. C., December 24th 1872, by the Rev. J. Claudius Miller[?], his daughter Anna M., to B. W. Hard, Esq., of Graniteville, S. C.

In Macon, on the 1st, inst., by Rev. J. W. Burke, Mr. J. M. Bazemore, to Mrs. Anna Parish.

In Mikesville, Florida, December 17th, 1872, by Rev. Dr. Thomas K. Leonard, Mr. James Means, of Texas, to Miss Lucretia, youngest daughter of Mr. John Lites, of Columbia county, Fla.

At 4 P. M., the 18th December, 1872, in Columbia county, Fla., by Rev. Dr. Thomas K. Leonard, Mr. Season W. Wright, of Jacksonville, Fla., to Miss Martha Frances, eldest daughter of Mr. Thomas J. Walker.

In the Methodist Church, Columbia county, Fla., December 22d 1872, by the Rev. Dr. Thomas K. Leonard, Mr. Isaac J. Brown to Miss Lillie E., daughter of Rev. Dr. Anderson Peeler.

In the city of Macon, on the 25th ult., by Rev. J. W. Burke, Mr. W. T. Nelson to Mrs. Sallie Gevers, all of Macon, Ga.

At the residence of the bride's father, in Warren county, Ga., December 19th 1872, by Rev. Jas. M. Armstrong, Mr. Jas. W. Hill to Miss J. J. Lewis.

By the Rev. D. M. Banks, on the 11th of December, 1872, at the Methodist Church, at Glennville[?] Mr. M. J. Caldwell of Bullock county, Ala., to Miss Sallie E. Glenn, of Russel county, Ala.

On the 5th December 1872, by Rev. J. F. Sleigh, Mr. John C. Seybt[?], to Miss Sarah, daughter of Peter Suber, all of Newberry county, S. C.

December 15th, 1872, by W. H. Hunt, Mr. John E. Pernell to Miss J. E. Milling, all of Columbia county, Fla.

November 20th 1872, in Richmond county, Ga., by Rev. James T. Barton, Mr. Richard H. P. Day to Miss Mary L. T. Avret.

December 22d, 1872, in Richmond county, Ga., by Rev. James T. Barton, Mr. William B. Beale to Miss Elvira L. Johnson.

December 26th, 1872, by Rev. Wm. T. Capers, Mr. Joseph J. Botts, to Miss Sallie A. Arnold, daughter of the late Lewis Arnold, all of Abbeville county, S. C.

By H. P. Jackson, November 28th 1872, at the Church in Bronson, Fla., Rev. R. M. Ellerby[?] of the Florida Conference, to Mrs. A. Williams, of Bronson, Fla.

On the 19th December 1872, near Cokesbury, S. C., by the Rev. Wm. C. Power, Mr. Warren Stribling, to Miss Anna Mundy.

In Macon, Ga., on the 1st inst., by Rev. J. W. Burke, Mr. T. G. Holt, of Houston county, Ga., to Miss Lizzie Sheffield, of Macon, Ga.

On the 19th December, 1872, at the residence of the bride's father, near Cusseta, Ga., by Elder W. J. Mitchell, Mr. E. T. Hickby, to Miss Georgia Wardlaw, all of Chattahoochee county, Ga.

On the 25th December, 1872, by Thos. W. --zard, Esq., in Forsyth county, Ga., at the residence of the bride's mother, Mr. Joseph E. Doss to Miss M. C. Wills, fourth daughter of Mason Wills, deceased.

On Thursday, December 19th 1872 by Rev. Jos. M. Bowden, Mr. Quincy M. Landrum, to Miss Nancy J. Gosden, all of Fayette county, Ga.

On the 6th December, 1872, in Quitman, Ga., by Rev. S. S. Sweet, Wm. Dart, Esq., of Brunswick, Ga., to Miss Mattie R. Edmondson, of Quitman, Ga.

On the 19th December, 1872, in Quitman, Ga., by Rev. S. S. Sweet, Mr. Clinton Brown to Miss Georgia A. Holzendorf, of Quitman, Ga.

December 5th, 1872, by Rev. George C. Leavel, Mr. J. W. Becton to Miss Martha Rodgers, all of Hillsboro county, Fla.

In Georgetown, Ga., December 17th, 1872, by Rev. J. B. McGehee, President Andrew Female College, Mr. E. B. McCrary of Americus, Ga., to Miss E. V. Dozier.

By Rev. J. B. McGehee, in Cuthbert, Ga., December 19th, 1872, Mr. Thomas J. Marr to Miss Donie W. Shine.

In Decatur, Ga., Dec. 27, 1872, by Rev. F. B. Davies, Rev. R. W. Bigham, of the North Georgia Conference, to Miss S. J. Davies.

In Atlanta, Ga., Dec. 31st, 1872, by Rev. F. B. Davies, Mr. Albert A. Clarke, of Decatur, to Miss P. N. Randall, of Atlanta.

At Thomasville, Ga., Jan. 1st, 1873, by Rev. J. F. Mixon, Joseph P. Smith, Esq., to Miss Allen D. Williams, both of Thomasville.

In Cherokee county, Ala., Dec. 31st 1872, by Rev. B. B. Quillian, Mr. A. S. Baker, of Cave Spring, Ga., to Miss Lizzie Wade.

By Rev. R. H. Howren, on the 26th of November 1872, Mr. J. W. Ramsey, of Brooks county, Ga., to Miss Ella Ramsey, of Thomas county, Ga.

By Rev. R. H. Howren, on the 26th December 1872, Mr. Wm. Grey, of Texas, to Miss Mary T. Howren, of Brooks county, Ga.

On the evening of the 27th December 1872, at the residence of the bride's father, in Cusseta, Ga., by Elder W. J. Mitchell, Mr. D. J. Fussel[?], to Mrs. M. J. Kelly.

On the evening of December 17th 1872, by the Rev. T. E. Wannamaker, Dr. W. T. C. Bates, to Miss Minnie B., daughter of Dr. W. W. Wannamaker, all of Orangeburg county, S. C.

In Wilkes county, Ga., December 19th, 1872, by Rev. S. M. Baxter, Mr. G. B. Smith to Miss Lucy J. Combs.

In Walker county, Ga., November 24th 1872, by the Rev. H. H. Porter, Mr. Nuton J. Rainey to Carrie Rea, daughter of the Rev. W. T. Rea.

On the 19th December 1872, by the Rev. H. H. Porter, Mr. W. T. Waters, to Miss W. A. Lawrence, of Chattooga county, Ga.

On the 24th December 1872, by the Rev. H. H. Porter, Mr. Daniel Stout,
of Walker county, Ga., to Mrs. Fanny J. Smith, daughter of Rev. W. T. Rea, of Chattooga county, Ga.

Issue of January 15, 1873

On the 5th Dec., 1872, by Rev. W. Hutto, Mr. George Hughes to Miss Lizzie Nichols, all of Abbeville county, S. C.

On the 31st Dec., 1872, by Rev. W. Hutto, Mr. James McRacken, of Abbeville, to Miss Nina Ross, daughter of Dr. B. A. Ross, of Edgefield county.

At the residence of Mr. J. W. Green, by the Rev. A. R. Danner, 24th Dec., 1872, Mr. Christopher Langley, of Barnwell county, to Miss Susan G. Green, of Ashepoo, S. C.

On the 2d Jan. 1873, at the residence of the bride's father, by Rev. A. R. Danner, Mr. Reuben Owens, to Miss Alice E. Cummings, all of Colleton county, S. C.

At the residence of Mr. R. H. Brunson, by Rev. A. C. Baynard, Dec. 22d 1872, Mr. J. H. Bostick to Miss Nettie R. Brunson, all of Beaufort county, S. C.

By Rev. A. C. Baynard, Dec. 31st, 1872, at the residence of the bride's father, Mr. C. H. Stuart to Miss E. E. Bostick, all of Beaufort county, S. C.

On the evening of the 17th Dec., 1872, at the residence of the bride's father, Mr. thomas Goodwin to Miss M. E. Biggs, both of Talbot county, Ga.

Jan. 5th 1873, at the residence of Mr. Sam. Lary, by Rev. A. C. Thomas, Mr. John Lary to Miss Rebecca Warren, all of Hancock county, Ga.

Jan. 21, 1873, by Rev. A. J. Cauthen, Eugene Moore, Esq., of Athens, GA., to Miss Emma Cozbey, youngest daughter of W. C. Cozbey, Esq., Lowndesville, S. C.

On the 2d Jan, 1873, at the residence of the bride's father, by the Rev. David Nolan, Mr. Columbus F. Jones to Miss Palestine Rentfrow, both of Fayette county, Ga.

Issue of January 22, 1873

On Jan. 14, near Oglethorpe, by Rev. J. B. Wardlaw, Mr. Chas. L. Royal, of Smithville, to Miss Charlotte McMurrian, of Macon county, Ga.

By S. S. Clements, on the evening of Dec. 26, Mr. W. D. Christian, of Meriwether county,k to Miss Rosa L. Onerly, of Coweta county, Ga.

In Jonesboro, Clayton county, Ga., on the 12th of January 1873, by Rev. J. T. Smith, Mr. Wm. O. Betts, to Miss Amanda D. Sims, all of Clayton county, Ga.

By Rev. J. J. Singleton, January 12, 1873, Mr. Alfred H. Bramlett to Miss Mary B. Zellner, both of Monroe county, Ga.

By Rev. W. W. Oslin, Dec. 22d, Mr. Thos. J. Branam to Miss Amanda J. Fitts, all of Putnam county, Ga.

By Rev. W. W. Oslin, Jan. 8th, Mr. J. W. Haskins to Miss A. T. Webster, all of Putnam county, Ga.

At the residence of Mr. Daniel Campbell, Jan. 12th 1873, by Rev. W. A. Greene, Mr. Joseph Reaves to Miss Lizzie Hilliard, all of Dodge county, Ga.

In Bainbridge, Ga., January 9, 1873, by Rev. S. D. Clements, Mr. B. D. Ainsworth of Thomasville, Ga., to Miss Ella A. Lester, daughter of Rev. R. Lester, of the South Georgia Conference.

On the 25th of December, 1872, by the Rev. P. C. Harris, Mr. H. W. Waldin, of Houston county, Ga., to Miss M. A. Williams, of Decatur. *Southern Presbyterian and Index* please copy.

In Richmond county, on the 5th of December, 1872, by Rev. W. Ewing Johnston, Mr. John M. Day to Miss Sarah J. Vause, all of Richmond county.

In Richmond county, on the 19th of December, 1872, by Rev. W. Ewing Johnston, Mr. Thomas H. Weeks to Miss Laura J. Elmore, all of Richmond county.

In Richmond county, on the 24th of December, 1872, by Rev. W. Ewing Johnston, Mr. Robert Cartledge to Miss Sarah Brazell, all of Richmond county.

By Rev. W. F. Robison, in Columbus, Dec. 29, 1872, Mr. H. L. Stewart to Miss Mary J. Day.

By Rev. W. F. Robison, Dec., 29, 1872, Mr. Robt. D. Knowls to Miss Nancy Jimmison.

On Jan. 1st, 1873, by Rev. W. R. Robison, Mr. S. R. Wentworth to Miss M. T. McMickins.

By Rev. W. F. Robison, in the Methodist Church, at Hamilton, Ga., Mr. T. A. Cantrell, of Columbus, to Mrs. E. W. Powers, of the former place.

In Baldwin county, Ga., on the 7th inst., by Rev. J. W. Stipe, Mr. J. H. Brooks of Talbot county, Ga., to Miss Anna M. Moore, of the former place.

Issue of January 29, 1873

On the 18th Jan. 1873, by the Rev. H. Andrews, Mr. C. V. Fulton of McIntosh county, Ga., to Miss Harriet Clifford Townsend, also of McIntosh.

On Dec 8th, 1872, by Rev. L. F. Burtz, Mr. J. P. Dobbs to Miss Martha Ann Wood, both of Cherokee county, Ga.

By Rev. L. F. Burtz, Jan. 2d, 1873, Mr. Thomas J. Meek to Miss Mary F. Braswell, both of Cherokee county, Ga.

By Rev. L. F. Burtz, Jan. 12th, 1873, Mr. John Dickson to Mrs. Mary Jane Barrett, at the residence of the officiating minister, all of Cherokee county, Ga.

By Rev. W. A. Dodge, Jan. 9th 1873, Mr. Augustus Rogers, of Milton county, Ga., to Miss Maggie Hallman, of Forsyth county, Ga.

Dec. 12th, 1872, by Rev. R. A. Timmons, Mr. James A. Roden to Miss Fannie A. Porter, all of Talladega county, Ala.

Dec. 17th, 1872, by Rev. R. A. Timmons, Mr. C. A. Orr, of Oxford, Ala., to Miss Fannie Turner, of Owen Spring, Talladega county, Ala.

Jan. 19th, 1873, by Rev. R. A. Timmons, Mr. B. W. Linder, of Munford, Ala., to Miss Nannie I. Morril, of Chulifinnee, Ala.

On Dec. 19th, by Rev. John N. Wilcox, Mr. Robert J. Ellison to Miss Josephine Herrington, all of Burke county, Ga.

SOUTHERN CHRISTIAN ADVOCATE MARRIAGE NOTICES 1867-1878

On Jan. 16th 1873, by Rev. John N. Wilcox, Mr. Wm. V. Bell, of Richmond county, to Miss Nancy Roberson, of Burke county, Ga.

On Jan. 16th 1873, by Rev. John N. Wilcox, Mr. C. B. Heath to Miss Margaret V. Chester, all of Burke county, Ga.

Issue of February 5, 1873

On the 8th Dec., by Rev. J. M. Tolbert, at the residence of the bride's father, Mr. Thompson C. Witt to Miss Rebecca T. Feagle.

On the 19th of Dec., by Rev. J. M. Tolbert, at the residence of the bride's mother, Peter Clemens to Miss Mary E. Bryant.

On the 9th of Jan., by Rev. J. M. Tolbert, at the residence of the bride's father, Ambrose Cook to Miss Pamelia Harris.

On the 19th of Dec., 1872, by the Rev. G. A. Hough, Mr. John P. Haigler to Miss Allie U. Gaskin, all of Orangeburgh county, S. C.

By Rev. R. H. Howren, Jan. 16, 1873, Mr. Henry Bradshaw to Miss Louisa Thomas, of Gadsden county, Fla.

By Rev. Joseph M. Gable, Jan. 23d, 1873, Mr. Henry S. Sauls to Miss Nancy E. Shirley, third daughter of James Shirley, Esq., all of Cobb county, Ga.

In Montezuma, Ga., Jan. 23d, 1873, by Rev. T. B. Russell, Mr. M. A. Bush to Miss Sallie A. Norris.

In Dooly county, Ga., Jan. 26th, 1873, by Rev. T. B. Russell, Mr. James B. Prater to Miss Mary A. J. Smith.

In Dooly county, Ga., Jan. 26th, 1873, by Rev. T. B. Russell, Mr. Henry G. Lamar to Miss Martha A. E. Smith.

Issue of February 12, 1873

In Quitman, Ga., on the 30th Jan., 1873, by Rev. S. S. Sweet, Henry M. McIntosh, Esq., of Quitman, to Miss Annie White, of Covington, Ga.

On the 30th Jan., 1873, in Brooks county, Ga., by Rev. S. S. Sweet, R. J. Stansell, of Thomas county, to Miss Susan Albritton, of Brooks county, Ga.

In East Macon, on the 30th Jan., 1873, by Rev. John W. Burke, Mr. William H. Gugel to Miss Virginia E. Powers.

On the 16th Dec., 1872, at the residence of the bride's father, by E. G. Murrah, Mr. C. D. Goolsby, of Jasper county, Ga., to Miss Ella Bradley, of Monticello, Ga.

By E. G. Murrah, on 16th Jan. 1873, at the residence of the bride's mother, Mr. A. R. Barker to Miss F. M. Hickman, all of Jasper county, Ga.

By E. G. Murrah, on 23rd Jan. 1873, at the residence of the bride's father, Mr. B. H. Sanders, of Eatonton, Ga., to Miss Anna E. Leverett, of Jasper county, Ga.

At the residence of Mr. Robert Shields, Feb. 5th, 1873, by Rev. W. P. Pledger, Mr. E. A. Shields, of Columbus, Ga., to Mrs. Sophia M. Sheilds [sic] of Madison, Ga.

At the residence of the bride's father, on the 30th of Jan., by Robert L. Wiggins, Mr. William M. Pounds, of Talbot county, to Miss Susan K. Scott, of Harris county, Ga.

On the 30th Dec., 1872, by Rev. W. R. Branham, Jr., at the residence of the bride's father, Rev. Jas. O. Andrew to Miss Mary C. Gray.

On the 4th Feb., 1873, by Rev. W. R. Branham, Jr., at the residence of the bride's mother, Wm. H. Stembridge to Miss Louisa J. Robinson.

In Baldwin county, Jan. 22d, by Rev. A. J. Jarrell, Mr. D. P. Brown to Miss Christiana Moore.

On Dec. 25th, 1873, by Rev. P. C. Harris, Mr. W. H. Waldin, of Bibb county, to Miss M. A. Williams, of Decatur.

In Crawford county, on the 28th Jan., 1873, by The Rev. G. W. Persons, Mr. W. B. Gasset to Miss Aminda Wilder.

Jan. 22d, 1873, by Rev. J. T. Kilgo, Mr. B. E. Lyles to Miss A. Rosalie McMeekin, all of Fairfield, S. C.

On Jan. 2d, 1873, by Rev. L. Cannon, Robert Drose to Miss C. Driggers, all of Charleston county, S. C.

On Dec. 26th, 1872, by Rev. L. Cannon, Adolphus Ward, of North Carolina, to Miss Low Sanders, of Charleston county, S. C.

Jan. 23d, 1873, at the residence of Mr. A. C. Rhineheart, by Rev. Jas. N. Myers, Mr. John Maddox, of Walker county, Ga., to Miss Mattie Rea, daughter of Rev. W. T. Rea.

On 30th Jan. 1873, by Rev. Geo. W. Stone, at the residence of the bride's father, Mr. Joseph A. Stewart, of Conyers, Ga., to Miss Carrie J. Robinson, of Newborn, Ga.

By Rev. W. Lane, on the 16th Jan., 1873, Mr. L. L .Evans to Miss Mary Richardson, both of Smithville, Ga.

On the 23d Jan. 1873, at the residence of the bride's father, Judge John A. Simonton, by Rev. F. A. Kimbell, Mr. William T. Harris, eldest son of Hon. H. R. Harris, to Miss Leila G. Simonton, all of Greenville, Meriwether county, Ga.

In Knoxville, Ga., Jan. 19th, 1873, at the bride's uncle, Judge J. W. Avant, by Rev. I. L. Avant, Mr. A. J. Culverhouse, of Crawford county, Ga., to Miss Jinnie Rogers, of Washington county, Ga.

At Jasper, Hamilton county, Fla., on Wednesday the 5th of Feb., 1873, by Rev. S. S. Moore, Mr. Robert S., son of Judge Henry J. Stewart, to Miss Pauline DeGraffenreid.

By Rev. H. H. Porter, January 30th, 1873, Henry J. Stautt, of Walker county, to Miss R. F. Smith, of Chattooga county, niece of Rev. W. T. Rea.

Issue of February 19, 1873

At the residence of Rev. J. W. Burke, in Macon, Ga., by Rev. J. S. Key, D. D., at the same time and by the same ceremony, N. E. Harris, Esq., of Sparta, Ga., to Miss Fannie T. Burke, and Rev. B. H. Sasnett, of the North Georgia Conference, to Miss Mamie B. Burke.

On the 9th January 1873, by Rev. J. H. Zimmerman, Mr. Young G. Shuler, of Orangeburgh county, to Miss Julia L. Hutto, of Charleston county, S. C.

On the 6th February, at the residence of Mr. Thomas J. Stewart, Mr. John R. Chiles to Miss Catherine L. Stewart, all of Jones county, Ga.

By Rev. Geo. G. N. MacDonell, February 6th, 1873, in Wesley Church, Savannah, Mr. E. Frank Courvoisie, to Miss Hattie M. Neidlinger, both of Savannah, Ga.

By Rev. Henry M. Mood, on the 9th February, Mr. George L. Dantzler to Miss Mary L. Waldrop, both of Cokesbury, S. C.

On the 28th January, by Rev. Wm. C. Power, Mr. Warren K. Williams, of North Carolina, to Miss Mary E. Proctor, of Marion, S. C.

At the residence of Mr. John Pughesley, near Sandersville, January 29, by Rev. J. F. Mixon, Mr. Benj. W. Bryant, of Lowndes county, Ala., to Mrs. Ella G. Hopkins, of Sandersville, Ga.

By Rev. George C. Leavel, on Wednesday, Feb. 5th, 1873, at the residence of Dr. C. J. Allred, Mr. Henry Griner to Miss Amanda Townsend, all of Marion county, Fla.

January 31st, 1873, by Rev. P. M. Ryburn, Mr. W. P. Coyle, of Madison county, Fla., to Miss Florence M. Fife, of Atlanta, Ga.

On the 19th December 1872, by Rev. J. A. Turner, at the residence of the bride's father, Mr. Charles Kilgore to Miss Nancy Josie Smith, all of Jasper county.

On the 19th January 1873, by Rev. J. A. Turner, at the residence of the bride's father, Mr. N. G. Cook, son of Rev. Wesley Cook, to Miss Molisia Turner, of Jasper county.

February 3d, by Rev. F. M. Morgan, at the residence of Captain M. Bray, Miss Caroline Morgan, formerly of Sumter, S. C., to Mr. J. H. Sleight, of Oconee county, S. C.

On February 4th 1873, by Rev. A. A. James, at the residence of the bride's mother, Mr. Reuben T. Gee to Miss Gertrude Gist.

By Rev. John J. Little, on the evening of the 16th January last, Mr. John M. Satterwhite to Miss Laura A. Delamer, all of Harris county, Ga.

By Rev. R. J. Harwell, February 10, Mr. W. A. Bailey to Miss Jennie Williams, all of Troup county, Ga.

On Tuesday evening, February 11, 1873, at the Methodist Church in Albany, Ga., by Rev. R. J. Corley, Hon. Thos. R. Lyon to Miss Mittie Sutton.

December 18, 1872, by Rev. J. B. Traywick, Mr. Marshall Blackman to Miss Martha Major, all of Anderson co., S. C.

On January 1, 1873, by Rev. W. Hutto, Thomas Fochee to Miss Sallie Clemm.

SOUTHERN CHRISTIAN ADVOCATE MARRIAGE NOTICES 1867-1878

<u>Issue of February 26, 1873</u>

By Rev. L. A. Darsey, Jan. 2d, 1873, Mr. Rufus W. Bass to Miss Missouri Hollman, all of Burke county, Ga.

On the 16th Jan., 1873, by Rev. L. A. Darsey, Mr. Edward Dukes to Miss Lizzie Stewart, of Burke county, Ga.

On the 23d Jan. 1873, by Rev. L. A. Darsey, Mr. Wm. T. H. Lynch to Miss Rebecca A. Harald, of Burke county, Ga.

At the residence of Mr. Columbus Wimberly, Burke county, Ga., by Rev. L. A. Darsey, Feb. 6th 1873, Mr. John L. Cowart, of Emanuel county, Ga., to Mrs. Fannie Strozier.

By Rev. L. A. Darsey, Feb. 13th, 1873, Mr. Turner Dukes to Miss Gertrude Attaway, all of Burke county, Ga.

At the residence of James Young in Bulloch county, Ga., Feb. 13th 1873, Mr. Homer Blitch, of Savannah, to Miss Mollie Williams, of Bulloch county, Ga.

At the residence of Mrs. L. G. Dinkins, by Rev. A. S. Dickinson, Feb. 6th 1873, Mr. J. B. Knox to Miss Lula M. Dinkins, all of Brundidge Pike county, Ala.

In the Methodist Church, at Lake City, Fla., Feb. 2d, 1873, by Rev. Jas. P. DePass, Dr. Thos. W. Carter to Mrs. Margaret C. Dozier.

On the 13th Feb. 1873, at the residence of Mr. Thos. H. Varner, by Rev. T. H. Timmons, Mr. Solomon T. Zellars to Miss Sallie A. Petty, all of Campbell county, Ga.

Feb. 19th 1873, at the residence of the bride's father, by Rev. A. C. Thomas, Rev. James S. Embry, of the North Georgia Conference, to Miss Mary E. Mays, of Warren county, Ga.

On the 20th of Feb. 1873, by Rev. Jas. O. Branch, Sandford M. Northington, of Sandersville, Ga., to Miss Sarah H. Shackelford, of Macon, Ga.

<u>Issue of March 5, 1873</u>

On the 13th Feb., by Rev. W. Hutto, Mr. John Clemm to Miss Emma Caldwell, both of Abbeville county, S. C.

By Rev. N. D. Morehouse, on 29th January, Mr. Geo. M. Willett to Mrs. Melina H. Dawson, both of Savannah, Ga.

By Rev. N. D. Morehouse, on 19th February, Mr. Wm. H. Shearouse to Miss M. J. Burgstiner, all of Effingham county, Ga.

On the 26th of January by Rev. W. E. Johnston, Mr. Nathan Stephens to Miss Frances Day, all of Richmond county, Ga.

On the 12th of February by Rev. W. E. Johnston, Mr. William Thomas Jenkins to Miss C. C. Elsmore, all of Richmond county, Ga.

On the 12th of February, 1873, by Rev. A. G. Worley, at the residence of Colonel T. R. Willis, Mr. Wm. G. Turner to Miss Mattie C. Marshall, all of Wilkes county, Ga.

January 30, 1873, by Rev. J. E. Watson, Mr. D. R. Christenbury of Mecklenburg co., N. C., to Miss E. F. Chreighton, of York county, S. C.

January 30, 1873, by Rev. J. E. Watson, Mr. W. S. Chreighton, son of Mr. J. P. Chreighton, to Miss Cynthia A. Sturgis, daughter of Col. T. W. Sturgiss, all of York county, S. C.

On the 14th of January, by Rev. R. N. Wells, Mr. W. P. Bookter, of Richland, S. C., to Miss Sallie Davis, of Fairfield, S. C.

In Barnesville, on the 23d inst., by Rev. J. P. Duncan, at the residence of A. Stafford, Miss Susan Ridley Duncan to Col. J. F. Redding, of Barnesville.

Near Branchville, S. C., on Thursday, the 6th of February 1873, by Rev. D. J. Simmons, Mr. Abraham Dukes to Miss Martha McAlhaney.

At Woodlawn, near Augusta, on the 20th inst., by Rev. T. A. Seals, Mr. George S. Hall and Miss Maggie E. Julien.

By Rev. E. G. Murrah, at the residence of the bride's father, on 5th February, in Jasper county, Ga., Mr. A. W. Ellis to Miss A. R. Shaw, all of Jasper county, Ga.

By Rev. E. G. Murrah, on 13th February, Mr. Jackson Jones to Miss Tresa Barr, all of Jasper county, Ga.

By Rev. E. G. Murrah, on the 25th February, Mr. J. T. Tolbert to Miss Zenobia Maxwell, all of Oglethorpe county, Ga.

Issue of March 12, 1873

By Rev. Thos. B. Lanier, at Bartow, Mr. N. T. Harmon to Miss Bettie Evans, all of Jefferson county, Ga.

On the 13th Feb. 1873, by Rev. J. M. Lowrey, Mr. Wm. G. Armor to Miss Lula H. Hutcheson, both of Green county, Ga.

On Feb. 20, at Donaldsville, by Rev. J. W. Murray, Mr. Calvin Martin to Miss Anna P. Rowland, all of Abbeville county.

In Macon, on the 3d March, by Rev. J. W. Burke, Louis nelson to Aurelia Russell, daughter of Jacob W. Russell.

Near Jonesboro, Ga., Feb. 26th 1873, by Rev. J. W. Stipe, Mr. J. W. Cox, of Maynardville, Tenn., to Miss I. J. Mann, of Clayton county, Ga.

On the 27th of Feb., 1873, at the residence of the bride's father, by Rev. W. Ewing Johnston, Mr. Stephen Deas to Miss Martha J. Gay, all of Richmond county, Ga.

In Macon, on the 3d inst., by Rev. J. W. Burke, Isaac Watts to Emaline Ryalls.

Issue of March 19, 1873

On the 26th February, in Effingham county, Ga., by Rev. H. D. Morehouse, George W. Helmly to Miss Ellen c. Shearouse.

On the 18th of February by Rev. J. L. Sifly, Mr. J. S. Albergotti to Miss Amelia S. Moss, both of Orangeburg, S. C.

By Rev. W. F. Roberts, Feb. 20, 1873, Mr. A. W. Clements, of Montgomery county, Ga., to Miss Elizabeth P. Cook, of Coffee county, Ala.

On March 4th 1873, by Rev. W. F. Roberts, Mr. Samuel H. Barber, of Douglass, Coffee county, Ga., to Miss Abbie B. McRae, of Telfair county, Ga.

On March 6th, by Rev. F. Auld, Mr. John J. Street to Miss Josephine Strauss, all of Orangeburg, S. C.

At the residence of the bride's father, near Villula, Ala., February 8, 1873, by Rev. j. A. Pace, brother of the bride's groom, Mr. Francis H. Pace to Miss Virginia M. Rune.

Issue of March 26, 1873

On the 26th of Feb., 1873, by Rev. W. H. Thomas, at the residence of Dr. Daniel Lott, in the village of Waycross, Ware county, Ga., Mr. Josiah Simons, of Clinch county, Ga., to Miss Fannie Lott, of Ware county, Ga.

On the 28th of Jan., by Rev. Wm. C. Power, Mr. Warren K. Williams of North Carolina, to Miss Mary E. Proctor, of Marion district, S. C.

By Rev. Wm. C. Power, on the 13th of Feb., 1873, Dr. Alex. W. Ellerbe of Cheraw, S. C., to Miss Mary E. Ellerbe, of Marion dist., S. C.

On Wednesday evening, March 12th 1873, by Rev. R. W. Bigham, at the residence of Dr. Hamilton, near Dalton, Ga., Capt. R. K. Bowie, of Newton county, to Miss Julia Hamilton.

On the 11th March 1873, at the residence of Mr. Jas. H. Gossett, by Rev. John B. Wilson, Mr. Ninian W. Leach to Miss Lavonia Rains, both of Union county, S. C.

On the 12th of March, 1873, by the Rev. F. A. Kimbell, at the residence of the bride's father, Hon. Henry R. Harris, of Greenville, Ga., Mr. John T. Wimbish, of LaGrange, to Miss Ella L. Harris.

Feb. 18th 1873, at the residence of Major Zachry, near Oxford, Ga., by Rev. I. L. Hopkins, Mr. George W. Gruber, of Charleston, S. C., to Miss Mary J. Bradley, of Newton county, Ga.

By Rev. D. J. Simmons, on the 6th of March, 1873, Mr. Irvin Metze to Miss Lovey Dukes, of Orangeburg county, S. C.

Issue of April 2, 1873

In Kingston, Ga., March 20, 1873, by the Rev. J. T. Lin, Mr. S. H. Landrum, of Atlanta, to Miss Emma Reynolds, daughter of Rev. J. A. Reynolds, of North Georgia Conference.

Issue of April 9, 1873

By Rev. Thos. B. Lanier, March 26th, 1873, at the house of the bride, Mr. Nisbet R. Morgan to Miss Margaret Berry, all of Effingham county, Ga.

On the 27th March, 1873, by Rev. F. Auld, Mr. James R. Vaughn to Miss Amanda L. Inabnit, both of Orangeburg county, S. C.

March 4th, at the residence of the bride's father, in Crawford county, by Rev. S. E. Bassett, Mr. Charles Van Valkenburg to Miss Josie E. Dent.

On the 25th of March, 1873, by Rev. R. B. Tarrant, at the residence of the bride's uncle, Jno. R. Milhouse, Esq., in Orangeburg county, S. C., Mr. C. D. C. Adams, formerly of Charleston, S. C., to Miss Mary Augusta Cleckley, formerly of Columbus, Ga.

By the Rev. W. A. Florence, on the 20th of March 1873, at the bride's residence, in Greene county, Ga., Mr. William Whitaker, of N. Y., to Mrs. Elladecia Florence

On the 27th of March, 1873, at the residence of the bride's father, by Rev. J. E. Broadax, Mr. James J. Patrick to Miss Mollie E. Hunter, all of Muscogee county, Ga.

In Cuthbert, Ga., March 23d, 1873, by Rev. B. F. Breedlove, Mr. J. R. Wooten to Miss Rebecca Taylor.

By Rev. W. A. Fariss, at the bride's father, on the 11th Dec., 1872, Wm. Z. holland, of S. C., to Miss Mollie A. Bradley, of Georgia.

Issue of April 16, 1873

On 27th March 1873, by Rev. W. F. Robison, at the residence of the bride's father, Rev. J. C. McGehee, of Harris county, Ga., Mr. John D. McPhail of Columbus, to Miss ellen D. McGehee.

In Gibson, April 3d, by Rev. J. B. Purvis, Rev. J. C. Raybun, of Glascock county, to Miss Susan A. Louge, of the former place.

On the 3d of April, 1873, by the Rev. J. E. Sentell, Mr. Lawrence F. Lawson to Miss Mary A. Jones, both of Brooks county, Ga.

At the bride's residence, March 9, 1873, by Rev. D. J. McMillan, Mr. J. J. Wakelin, of Columbus, Ohio, to Mrs. M. N. Chapman, of Pickens county, S. C.

By Rev. J. W. Stipe, Feb. 18, 1873, Mr. R. M. Winter to Miss Jennie Wood, all of Jonesboro, Ga.

In Orangeburg, S. C., April 1st, 1873, by Rev. D. J. Simmons, Mr. Warren C. Fairy to Miss Dorcas E. Collier.

April 3d, 1873, at the residence of the bride's father, in Randolph county, Ga., Rev. Barnard H. Lester to Miss Alzoah Standley, daughter of Chas. Standley, Esq.

Issue of April 23, 1873

On the 10th April 1873, by Rev. S. S. Sweet, S. G. Watson to Miss Emma Slaughter, all of Brooks county, Ga.

April 10th, 1873, by Rev. W. H. Hunt, Mr. Havey Simons to Miss Mary E. Duren, all of Columbia county, Fla.

n the evening of the 16th April 1873, by the Rev. James Jones of the South Georgia Conference, in First Street Methodist E. Church, South, macon ,Ga., Mr. Thomas P.

Kingsberry, of Washington City, D. C., to Miss Mary Lena Brewer, of the city of Macon, Ga., daughter of Mrs. Caroline E. Brewer and grand-daughter of Mr. T. A. Brewer, of Vineville, and also of the Rev. James Jones.

Issue of April 30, 1873

April 24, in Opelika, Ala., at the residence of the bride's father, by the Rev. Wm. M. Motley, Mr. Thos. S. Matthews, to Miss Bessie Houser.

Issue of May 7, 1873

On the 24th April, 1873, by Rev. F. Auld, Mr. Jerome McMichael to Miss Elizabeth W., daughter of Dr. Donald W. Barton, all of Orangeburg county, S. C.

By Rev. Jno. M. Bowden, on the 27th of April 1873, Mr. Jno. A. Tatum, of Troup county, to Mrs. Lizzie Baker, of Meriwether county, Ga.

At the residence of the bride's father, April 23d, 1873, by Rev. W. P. Lovejoy, Mr. Wm. G. Howard, of Madison ,Ga., to Miss Mary F. Reid, of Eatonton, Ga.

In Sandersville, Ga., April 30th, 1873, by Rev. J. F. Mixon, Mr. Benjamin J. Tarbutton to Miss Mary H. Bags.

By Rev. T. J. Simmons, in Resaca, Ga., March 25th 1873, at the residence of John Hill, Esq., Mr. William L. Stevens, of Virginia, to Miss Elizabeth Hughey, of the former place.

On the 15th of April, by Rev. Wm. C. Power, Marcus Stackhouse, Esq., to Miss Mary S. Lester, both of Marion dist., S. C.

By Rev. J. K. Little, at the residence of James Crockett, March 28th, 1873, Mr. W. C. Crenshaw to Miss Mary A. Clanton, all of Lancaster, S. C.

On the 24th April, 1873, by Rev. D. D. Cox, Mr. James S. Baker to Miss Arah R. Eady, all of West Point, Ga.

Issue of May 14, 1873

April 22, 1873, at the residence of the bride's father, by Rev. A. C. Thomas, Mr. C. M. Bethune, of Talboton, Ga., to Miss Eugenia T. Gunn, of Camak, Ga.

In Orangeburg county, S. C., by Rev. J. S. Beasley, April 23d, 1873, Mr. David Stivender to Mrs. Margaret Rucker; the former aged 82 years, the latter about 70.

In Swainsboro, Emanuel county, Ga., by Rev. L. B. Bouchelle, Mr. John C. Coleman to Miss Martha S. Moring.

On the 29th of April, 1873, by Rev. Geo. C. Leavel, at the Methodist Church, Mr. W. P. Trantham to Mrs. Sue F. Crowson, all of Ocala, Florida.

In Webster county, April 20, by Rev. J. T. Ainsworth, Mr. Joshua C. Roberts to Miss Millisson G. Goars.

In the Methodist Church, Bainbridge, Ga., April 17, 1873, by Rev. S. D. Clements, Mr. A. T. Reid to Miss Mollie Dennard.

At the residence of Mr. W. W. McAfee, Atlanta, Ga., March 25, 1873, by Rev. P. M. Ryburn, Mr. G. A. Bonner to Miss M. E. McGuire, both of Carroll county, Ga.

By Rev. P. M. Ryburn, May 1, 1873, Mr. J. H. Mashburn to Miss Amanda Jenkins, both of Atlanta, Ga.

By Rev. P. M. Ryburn, May 8, 1873, Mr. Leonard F. Hagan to Miss Mary P. Hamilton, both of Atlanta, Ga.

Issue of May 21, 1873

On the 6th May 1873, by Rev. A. G. Dempsey, Mr. John L J. Pool, of Clayton county, to Miss E. L. M. Stubbs, of DeKalb county.

On the 7th May, 1873, by Rev. A. R. Danner, at the bride's father's residence, Mr. George K. Guery to Miss Elizabeth A. Goodwin, all of Ridgeville, S. C.

On April 8th, 1873, by Rev. W. F. Roberts, Mr. A. N. Curry to Miss Mattie W. Wilcox, all of Coffee county, Ga.

By Rev. A. J. Dean, April 29th, 1873, Charles J. Tucker, Esq., to Miss Emma G. Graham, all of Lumpkin, Ga.

In Marietta Ga., on the 8th May, 1873, by Rev. Wm. A. Rogers, Mr. Wm. C. Mansfield to Miss Zoe Sevier Rogers.

In Marietta Ga., May 6th, 1873, by Rev. Geo. W. Yarborough, Mr. James F. Nutting, of Atlanta, to Miss Cattie Morris, of Marietta, Ga.

In Columbia county, Florida, April 16th, 1873, by Rev. A. Peeler, M. D., Mr. Simeon E. C. Collins to Miss M. Lenna Gunnin.

In Columbia county, Florida, by Rev. A. Peeler, M. D., May 11th, 1873, Mr. James R. Lites to Miss Ann E. Gunnin.

Issue of May 28, 1873

On the 13th of April, by Rev. G. H. Pooser, Mr. A. J. Braid to Miss Sarah J. Williamson, of Beaufort county, S. C.

In Stewart county, Ga., May 8, 1873, by W. J. Rea, Esq., Mr. Enoch J. Leviner, formerly of Marlborough District, S. C., to Mrs. Mary J. May, of Stewart county.

In the Baptist Church at Glennville, Ala., on the 15th of May, by Rev. J. S. Jordan, Mr. George M. Jordan, of Eufaula, Ala., to Miss Eliza Price, of the former place.

At the residence of the bride's father, April 20, 1873, by Rev. R. H. Barnett, Mr. J. F. Long to Miss Mary H. Frenzot.

May 15, 1873, at the residence of the bride's father, in Wilkes county, Ga., by Rev. Thomas H. Gibson, Mr. Wiley T. Corbin to Miss S. Gebrella Combs.

April 10, by Rev. F. T. J. Brandon, in Athens, Ala., Mr. J. C. Hickey, of Texas, to Miss Annie E. Garrison, formerly of Georgia.

On 8th May 1873, by Rev. Wm. Hutto, Mr. John Jester to Miss Nannie Pert, all of Abbeville co., S. C.

Issue of June 4, 1873

On the 15th May, 1873, at the residence of the bride, by Rev. E. F. Gates, Mr. Chares [sic] Moore, to Miss Emily Raifield Armor, all of Tampa, Fla.

By Rev. J. B. Wardlaw, on 21st May, at the residence of the bride's brother-in-law, C. R. Keen, Esq., of Macon county, Ga., Mr. C. A. Greer, of Eufaula, Ala., to Miss S. D. Dabbs, late of Danville, Virginia.

On the 4th of March 1873, by Rev. W. F. Quillian, Mr. James C. Quillian, to Miss Luvicy Pierce, both of Hall county, Ga.

At the residence of the bride's mother, on the 25th May 1873, by Rev. James H. Jordan, Dr. Walter P. Stubbs, of Macon, Ga., to Miss Julia E. Simmons, of Houston county.

Issue of June 11, 1873

On May 21st, 1873, by Rev. J. H. McMullan, Mr. E. B. Benson to Miss Alice E. Adams, all of Hart county, Ga.

In Warren county, Ga., May 22d, 1873, by Rev. Wesley F. Smith ,Mr. W. f. Gregory and Miss Mattie Kensey.

On the 28th of May, 1873, in the Methodist Episcopal Church, South, at Brunswick, Ga., by Rev. J. O. A. Cook, Joseph E. Lambright and Miss Julia S. Dart.

June 1st, 1873, at the residence of Mr. Samuel Perkins, of Fulton county, Ga., Mr. S. D. Atkison, of Madison, Ga., to Miss Jennie Johnson, of Greensboro, Ga.

By Rev. John Calvin Johnson, at the parsonage in Watkinsville, Clarke county, Ga., May 29, 1873, Mr. Alexander W. Ashford to Miss Loula Knight, daughter of Rev. John W. Knight, of the North Georgia Conference.

By Rev. John Calvin Johnson, June 1st, 1873, Mr. James Collins, of Jackson county, to Miss Anna Dickson, of Clarke county, Ga.

Issue of June 18, 1873

On the 4th of June, 1873, by Rev. F. A. Branch, Mr. J. Dill Marshall to Miss Tiny Houser, all of Fort Valley, Ga.

On 28th May, 1873, in Elberton, Ga., by Rev. J. H. Grogan, Rev. W. F. Quillian, of the No. Ga. Conf., to Miss Lucy Vail.

June 4th, 1873, in the Methodist Church in Eatonton, by Rev. W. P. Lovejoy, Mr. Michael B. Dennis to Miss Mattie Cowles, all of Eatonton, Ga.

June 8th, 1873, at the residence of the bride's mother, by Rev. T. H. Timmons, Mr. O. R. Longino, of Palmetto, Ga., to Miss E. C. Smith, of Douglass county, Ga.

At the residence of the Rev. B. B. Ransome, by Rev. J. May, on the 4th June, 1873, in Dallas county, Ark., Capt. Robert Atkinson, of Columbia county, Ark., to Mrs. E. A. Gordon, of the former county.

Issue of June 25, 1873

May 29th 1873, 9 o'clock, A. M. at the residence of Major Burton, by Rev. S. D. Clements, Mr. L. Oscard Jackson, to Miss Estelle Bruton, all of Bainbridge, Ga.

On the 3d June 1873, by Rev. F. Auld, Mr. Wm. B. Sally to Miss Anna R., youngest daughter of the late W. T. McKewn, all of Orangeburg, S. C.

By Rev. Geo. C. Leavel, June 8, 1873, Mr. J. J. Luffman to Miss Lindy G. McCully, both of Marion county, Fla.

By Rev. Geo. C. Leavel, June 10, 1873, at the residence of Capt. S. O. Howes, Ocala, Fla., Dr. R. J. Kendrick, of Sumpter county, Fla., to Mrs. I. C. Henderson, of Marion county, Fla.

Issue of July 2, 1873

In Newberry, S. C., June 18th 1873, by Rev. J. L. Shuford, Rev. A. M. Chrietzberg, of the South Carolina Conference, to Miss Hattie E. (fifth) daughter of Dr. James Kilgore, deceased.

At the residence of Mr. Jas. Wilsons, on the 19th July 1873, by the Rev. E. M. Bounds, Rev. Junius Jordan, to Mrs. P. A. Welborn, of Eufaula, Ala.

At the residence of the bride's father, by Rev. Alex. P. Wright, on the 18th of June 1873, in Lawton, Ga., Mr. Nash J. Brossius, of Virginia, to Miss Mary E. Meynardie, of Charleston, S. C.

At Marshallville, Macon county, Ga., on the 22d of June, 1873, by Rev. F. A. Branch, Thomas S. Martin to Miss Aurelia E. Johnson.

By the Rev. J. W. Barr, on the 24th June 1873, at the residence of the bride's father, M. M. Padgett, Esq., Mr. J. T. Taylor, of Staunton, Va., to Miss E. O. Padgett, of Edgefield county.

Issue of July 9, 1873

On the evening of the 26th ult., at the residence of the bride's mother, by the Rev. J. M. Potter, Mr. J. B. Brazier to Miss Virginia S. Smith, all of Stewart county, Ga.

On June 18, by Rev. J. R. Littlejohn, Mr. N. W. H. Gilbert, of Houston county, to Mary D. Bacon, of Hogansville, Ga.

June 26, by Rev. Geo. W. Yarbrough, Mr. David R. Carlton, of Union Point, Ga., and Miss Annie M. Wynn, of Putnam co., Ga.

By the Rev. S. R. Weaver, at the bride's step-father's, Mr. Lee, in Randolph county, Mr. J. H. Lyle, of Springvale, to Miss M. E. Carter.

Near Twiggsville, Twiggs county, Ga., on the 15th of June, 1873, by John S. Evans, Esq., Mr. Levy Sauls to Miss Queen Newby, all of Twiggs co., Ga.

Issue of July 16, 1873

By Rev. R. F. Evans, July 2d, 1873, in Chattahoochee county, Ga., at the residence of Miles Greene, his daughter, Mary V. L. Green, to Mr. Josiah Evans, son of Rev. Josiah Evans, deceased.

In Thomson, Ga., June 19th 1873, by Rev. J. M. Lowry, Mr. John W. Willingham to Miss Susan A. Smith, all of Thomson, Ga.

By Rev. J. B. McFarland, June 22d, 1873, Mr. Ira W. Moore to Miss Ann J. Heartsfield, both of Walker county, Ga.

In Elbert county, Ga., June 24th, 1873, by Rev. F. G. Hughes, Rev. Thos. J. Adams to Miss Eliza C. Tucker.

At the residence of the bride's father, on the evening of the 3d July 1873, by Rev. P. G. Reynolds, Mr. C. T. Farrar to Miss Rosa V. Dawn, all of Whitfield county, Ga.

Issue of July 23, 1873

By Rev. W. J. Cotter, on the 15th inst., Mr. Thos. Swindall to Mrs. M. E. Cook, all of Troup county, Ga.

At half past one o'clock, on the 10th inst., at the residence of the bride's mother, in Coweta county, Ga., by Rev. Thomas H. Timmons, Mr. G. W. Vance, of Newnan, Ga., to Miss R. A. Strong, of Coweta county, Ga.

On the 3d July, by the Rev. J. R. Rowan, Mr. J. C. Ireland to Miss Mattie L. Davis, second daughter of the Rev. C. C. Davis, all of Cobb county, Ga.

At the Methodist Church in Cuthbert, Ga., June 24, 1873, by Rev. B. F. Breedlove, Mr. R. H. Cobb to Miss Eliza Hillman.

In the Methodist Church at Spartanburg, S. C., July 8, 1873, by Rev. A. M. Shipp, D. D., President Wofford College, Rev. H. F. Chrietzberg, of Charleston, S. C., to Miss Adria E. Kirby, of Spartanburg, S. C.

Issue of July 30, 1873

On the 12th of July, 1873, by Rev. E. H. Giles, at the bride's fathers, Mr. Thos. Hawkins to Miss Alace A. Wood, all of Hillsboro, Fla.

In Talbotton, Ga., July 10th 1873, by Rev. R. W. Dixon, Rev. J. Harvey Hammet, of Summerville, S. C., to Miss Fannie T. Matthews, of Talbotton, Ga.

At Fort Myers, Monroe county, Fla., June 23d, 1873, by Rev. Josiah Bulloch, Mr. Charles W. Thompson to Miss Laura J. Hendry, eldest daughter of Capt. F. A. Hendry, all of the same county.

By Rev. D. J. Weems, July 10th 1873, at Mr. Wm. Smith's, Mr. P. C. Yates to Miss Susie Smith.

On the 6th July, 1873, by Rev. G. H. Pooser, Mr. J. H. Heape to Miss Julia F. Benton, of Beaufort county, S. C.

On the 15th July 1873, by Rev. G. H. Pooser, Mr. W. S. Tillinghast, Attorney at Law, Beaufort county, to Miss S. English Patterson, of Barnwell county, S. C.

Issue of August 6, 1873

By Rev. George C. Leavel, on Wednesday, July 23d, 1873, at the residence of the bride's father, John F. Collins, Mr. Thomas H. Arick to Miss Annie E. Collins, all of Marion county, Fla.

June 12, 1873, at the residence of the bride's brother, in the town of Florence, by Rev. A. Hamby, D. H. Hamby, to Mrs. Sue McP. Corry, all of Darlington county, S. C.

By the Rev. B. W. Williams, near Homer, July 19, at the residence of Mr. Wm. Slayton, Mr. Reuben C. Higginbothan to Miss Margaret J. Slaton.

By Rev. J. B. Wardlaw, at the residence of the bride's brother, Mr. Rodolph Batton, near Oglethorpe, Ga., on the 27th of July 1873, by the Rev. Philip L. Henderson, Mr. G. W. Smith to Miss Ida Batton, all of Macon county.

At the residence of the Mrs. Zachry, near West Point, Ga., on the 10th of June, 1873, by the Rev. Philip L. Henderson, Mr. Geo. H. Black, of LaFayette, Ala. to Miss Mary Emma Zachry, of the former place.

At the residence of the bride's father, H. H. Brown, Esq., on the 19th of June, 1873, by the Rev. Philip L. Henderson, Mr. Zach Schuessler to Miss Ella Ida Brown, all of LaFayette, Ala.

By Rev. J. R. Traywick, July 22, 1873, Mr. Thaddeus S. Teague to Miss Stella C. Fuller, of Laurens county, S. C.

By Rev. J. L. Gibson, July 23d, 1873, at the bride's father, in Dooly county, Ga., Mr. G. H. Turnison of Greensboro, Ga., Miss L. E. Patrick.

Issue of August 13, 1873

On the evening of the 28th day of July, 1873, by Rev. R. R. Dagnall, Mr. J. L. Gregorie, of Chicago, Ill., to Miss Rosa Bella, of Abbeville county, S. C.

Issue of August 20, 1873

On the 31st July 1873, by Rev. W. Lane, Mr. Jos. F. Johnson, of Union Springs, Ala., to Miss Mary E. Bennett, of Smithville, Ga.

By Rev. T. H. Timmons, on Tuesday morning, August 12, 1873, at the residence of Mrs. Burch, in Palmetto, Mr. H. B. Lane, of Franklin, Ga., to Miss M. E. Jones, of Palmetto, Ga.

On the 7th inst., in Quitman, Ga., by Rev. S. S. Sweet, Dr. D. L. Ricks to Miss S. M. McElveen.

At the residence of Charles Davis, the bride's brother, by Rev. J. C. Crisp, on the 22d of May 1873, in Union county, S. C., F. C. Browne to Miss Lucy Davis.

At the Methodist Parsonage, Pacolet circuit, South Carolina Conference, by Rev. J. C. Crisp, on the 7th August, 1873, A. C. Elmore to Miss E. G. Burgess, both of Union county, S. C.

In the Methodist Church at Cartersville, Ga., on the 20th inst., by Rev. L. J. Davies, Mr. Julien M. Stoy to Miss Ida E., daughter of Mr. Walter Cameron, all of Augusta, Ga.

Issue of August 27, 1873

On 6th Aug., at Mrs. J. O. Miller's, by Rev. J. B. Campbell, Mr. Wiley K. Bell to Miss Nannie Miller, all of Darlington county, S. C.

On 14th Aug. 1873, at the bride's mother, by Rev. J. B. Campbell, Mr. James Parrott to Miss Lizzie DeWitt, both of Darlington county, S. C.

On the 8th of July 1873, by the Rev. Wm. R. Johnson, Mr. Spartan Goodlett to Miss Annie B. Davis, all of Apalachicola, Fla.

On the 13th of July 1873, by the Rev. Wm. R. Johnson, Mr. D. W. C. Willis to Miss Emma M. Marks, all of Apalachicola, Fla.

On the 14th of Aug., 1873, by Rev. Wm. R. Johnson, Mr. William Roberts, to Miss Emma E. Capps, all of Apalachicola, Fla.

Issue of September 3, 1873

At the residence of the bride's father, on 19th August, by Rev. Geo. W. W. Stone, J. W. Jones of Atlanta, to Miss Eudora R. Brickell, of Newton co., Ga.

August 6, 1873, at 4 o'clock P. M., by Rev. S. D. Clements, Mr. W. W. Wright to Miss Florence M. Maxwell, all of Bainbridge, Ga.

Issue of September 10, 1873

Near Jeffersonville, Twiggs county, Ga., on the 26th Aug. 1873, by John S. Evans, Esq., Mr. Elbert T. Sauls to Miss Isadore Sauls, all of Twiggs county, Ga.

On Aug. 26th 1873, in Gwinnett county, Ga., at the residence of M. Pink Copeland, by Rev. B. T. Thomas, Mr. Samuel Cox to Mrs. Mary Jones.

September 4th 1873, by Rev. F. M. Kennedy, D. D., Mr. Edward W. Waterhouse to Miss Mattie Loula Brinn, all of Macon, Ga.

On the 20th Aug. 1873, by Rev. C. C. Fishburne, Mr. E. R. Beaty to Miss B. J. Collins, both of Conwayboro, S. C.

On the 26th Aug. 1873, by Rev. C. C. Fishburne, Mr. J. P. Williams, of Bull Creek, S. C., to Miss Olivia Outland, of Georgetown, S. C.

Issue of September 17, 1873

In Columbia county, Ga., at the residence of the bride's residence [sic], on the 2d of September, by Rev. R. A. Conner, Rev. Dr. Thomas H. Bryans, of Thompson, McDuffie county, to Miss Eliza Parks, of the former place.

On the 4th of September, at the residence of the bride's father, by Rev. R. A. Conner, Mr. Alpheus Reville to Miss Alice Langston, daughter of Wm. J. Langston, all of Columbia county, Ga.

By Rev. P. G. Reynolds, Sept. 4th, 1873, at the residence of the bride's father, Mr. W. C. Brodwick to Miss Emma Fraker, all of Whitfield county, Ga.

By Rev. E. M. Bounds, at Eufaula, Ala., Miss F. Rosalie Jordan, daughter of Rev. Junius Jordan, to J. Henry Simonton, Esq., of Abbeville, Ala.

On the 3d of September, by the Rev. John H. Harris, Mr. Richard F. G. Roberts to Miss Catherine E. Ogletree, all of Henry county, Ga.

Issue of September 24, 1873

At Tampa, Tuesday morning, 9th Sept., 1873, at the residence of Rev. E. F. Gates, by Rev. E. F. Gates, Rev. E. H. Giles, P. E. of Tampa District, to Miss Melville B. Wells.

In Macon, on the 14th Sept. 1873, by Rev. J. W. Burke, Mr. J. W. Newton to Miss Ella Beavers.

At the residence of the bride's father in Orangeburg county, S. C., Sept. 11th 1873, by Rev. D. J. Simmons, Mr. James J. Fairy to Miss Ella A. Fersner.

On 16th Sept. 1873, by Rev. W. C. Bass, C. L. Willingham to Miss Lila M., daughter of the late Wm. A. Ross, all of Macon, Ga.

On 16th Sept. 1873, by Rev. B. E. Ledbetter, Mr. B. F. Crisler to Miss Mary M. Teasley, daughter of Hon. W. A. Teasley, all of Canton, Ga.

In Fernandina, Florida, on the 16th of Sept. 1873, by Rev. Dr. Thomas K. Leonard, Rev. Thomas W. Tomkins, of the Florida Conference, to Miss Anna Gertrude, daughter of the late Col. T. Timanus.

By Rev. T. J. Simmons, near Tilton, Ga., Sept. 2d, 1873, Mr. L. H. Sebastian to Miss Sallie Moore.

Issue of October 1, 1873

On the 4th September, at the residence of the bride's father, by Rev. A. R. Danner, Mr. John E. Easterling to Miss Martha Wilson, daughter of Wade Wilson, all of Colleton county, S. C.

On the 18th September, at the residence of the bride's father, By Rev. A. R. Danner, Mr. Wm. J. K. Westbury to Miss Melissa Josephine Murray, daughter of Dr. Joseph Murray, all of Charleston county.

On the 18th of September, 1873, by Rev. L. Wood, Mr. Robt. N. Dukes of williamsburg, to Miss Anna Morris, of Timmonsville, S. C.

By Rev. John Calvin Johnson, on the 18th Sept., 1873, Mr. Jacob M. Dicken to Miss Viola M. Banton, all of Clarke county, Ga.

By Rev. John Calvin Johnson, on the 18th September, 1873, Mr. Wm. R. Clemmons, of Morgan county, Ga., to Miss Tocora Dicken, of Clarke county, Ga.
On the 16th September, by Rev. Wm. W. Mood, at Hodges, Abbeville co., S. C., Mr. G. T. Reid to Miss L. Josie Stokes, grand daughter of General G. W. Hodges.

SOUTHERN CHRISTIAN ADVOCATE MARRIAGE NOTICES 1867-1878

Issue of October 8, 1873

Sept. 24th, 1873, by Rev. R. R. Johnson, Mr. P. D. Hamrick, of Jonesboro, Ga., to Miss S. E. Mann, near Jonesboro, Ga.

In the Methodist Church, Kingston, Ga., Sept. 3d, 1873, by Rev. J. T. Lin, Mr. John Hardin to Miss Mary A. Roper, all of Bartow county, Ga.

At the Hon. Mark Hardin's on Sept. 23d, 1873, by Rev. J. T. Lin, Mr. Robert Dehome(?), of Atlanta, to Miss Ann F. Hardin, of Bartow county, Ga.

At the residence of the bride's father, near Perry, Ga., Oct. 1st, 1873, by Rev. S. H. J. Sistrunk, Mr. J. B. Shine to Miss Mollie Barker.

Issue of October 15, 1873

By Rev. John M. Bowden, on the 14th of Sept., 1873, Mr. George T. McLaughlin to Miss Alice F. McCarter, all of Meriwether county, Ga.

Oct. 2d, 1873, by Rev. J. H. Zimmerman, Mr. Allison E. McCoy, to Miss Olivia L. Wiggins, all of Charleston county, S. C.

Sept. 25th, 1873, by Rev. E. J. Pennington, Mr. Henry J. Stall to Miss Susannah E. Pennington, eldest daughter of the officiating minister, all of Summerville, S. C.

August 21st, 1873, by Rev. J. B. Traywick, Mr. Frane Medlock to Miss Lou Nash, both of Laurens county, S. C.

By Rev. B. A. Johnson, on the 5th of October, 1873, Mr. George P. Martin to Miss Sarah A. Bruce, all of Warren county, Ga.

On the 30th September 1873, by Rev. L. Wood, Mr. W. D. Rollins to Miss Addie E. Garner, all of Timmonsville, S. C.

In Macon, on the 9th inst., by Rev. John W. Burke, Mr. James A. Burke to Miss Sarah C. Davidson, all of Macon.

Sept. 26, 1873, by Rev. John Murphy, at his residence, Mr. R. F. Harper of Fayette county, Ga., to Miss Martha A. Hoffman, of Macon county, Ala.

At Frost's Mill, S. C., October 1st, 1873, by Rev. W. D. Kirkland, Mr. S. J. Thomas to Miss Rachel Martin.

In Columbia, S. C., October 2d, 1873, by Rev. W. D. Kirkland, Mr. H. c. Beard to Miss Eliza C. Joy, all of Columbia, S. C.

In Talbotton, Ga., Sept. 21, 1873, by Rev. R. W. Dixon, Edward H. Harvey to Mrs. Susan T. Claiborn, both of Talbotton, Ga.

In Talbot county, Ga., Sept. 25, 1873, by Rev. R. W. Dixon, David R. Bryan to Miss Anna M. Couch, both of Talbot county, Ga.

Issue of October 22, 1873

Oct. 18th 1873, by Rev. C. w. Smith, Mr. W. J. Jarvis to Miss Lula A. Harris, all of Macon, Ga.

SOUTHERN CHRISTIAN ADVOCATE MARRIAGE NOTICES 1867-1878

Issue of October 29, 1873

On the 13th October 1873, in Washington, Ga., by Rev. Thomas H. Gibson, Mr. William Garner to Miss Georgia G. Nance.

In the Presbyterian Church in Dalton, Ga., Oct. 16, 1873, by Rev. A. W. Gaston, Mr. Wm. C. Huff, of Red Clay, to Miss Lida Emmonds, daughter of W. S. Emmonds, Esq., of the former place.

At the parsonage, Newnansville, Fla., by Rev. R. H. Barnett, Solomon O. Zetrour to Miss Minnie F. Bridges, daughter of Rev. J. M. Bridges, October 9th 1873.

In the M. E. Church, South, in Forsyth, Ga., Oct. 21, 1873, by Rev. D. J. Myrick, Dr. R. F. Wright to Miss Mary E. Lampkin, both of Forsyth, Ga.

By Rev. John W. McRoy, October 21, 1873, Dr. T. D. Cleckley to Miss Eugenia R. Jennings, daughter of the late John S. Jennings, of Orangeburg county, S. C.

On the morning of the 23d October, by Rev. C. J. Toole, Mr. R. A. Johnson, of Bibb county, Ga., to Miss Missouri Simmons, of Houston county, Ga.

By Rev. I. Munden, October 21st, 1873, in Jefferson county, Fla., Mr. Oscar B. Lane, of Quitman, Ga., to Miss Emma C. Young.

19th October 1873, by Rev. John R. Parker, Mr. J. M. Keith of Harmony Grove, Ga., to Mrs. Amanda Nix, of Jackson county, Ga.

Issue of November 5, 1873

By Rev. Jno. M. Bowden, on the 12th of Oct. 1873, Mr. Jno. W. Hardaway to Miss Josephine Duke, all of Hogansville, Ga.

On the 26th of Oct., 1873, by Rev. Jno. M. Bowden, Mr. Eleazer Mobley to Miss Aldora Moreland, all of Hogansville, Ga.

In Archer, Alachua county, Fla., October 22d, 1873, by Rev. Jno. Penny, Mr. Thomas W. Davis, of Marion county, Fla., to Miss Marion H. Weston.

On the 23d October 1873, by Rev. W. H. Graham, Mr. David K. Ellis to Miss Louisa F. Hunt, all of Upson county, Ga.

At James P. Lyle's of Springvale, the bride's father's, Oct. 9th, 1873, Mr. Joseph Kimble of Stewart county, to Miss Laura Lyle.

Oct. 28th by Rev. R. F. Jones, Mr. S. S. McCollum to Miss J. P. Harris, all of Coweta county, Ga.

By Rev. W. R. Branham, Jr., on 30th October 1873, W. T. Forrar, of Jones county, to Miss Matilda E. Lowe, of Baldwin county, Ga.

On 28th Oct. 1873, at the residence of Mr. John Davis, by Rev. E. L .Loveless, L. A. Dowdell, Esq., of Auburn, Ala., to Miss Nannie N. Davis, of Lee county, Ala.

In Warren county, Ga., Oct. 21st, 1873, by Rev. Wesley F. Smith, Mr. W. L. Trynum, of Atlanta, to Miss S. T. Ivy, of the former place.

By Rev. J. R. Mayson, at the residence of Wm. Guest, in McDonough, Ga., Mr. James B. Turner to Miss Sallie Guest, Oct. 15th, 1873.

By Rev. Thos. B. Lanier at Bartow, Ga., Oct. 21st, 1873, Mr. John A. McMillen to Miss Hattie F. Johnson.

On 26th Oct. 1873, in Dalton, Ga., by Rev. F. A. Kimbell, Mr. M. C. Arwood to Miss Tabitha J. Smith.

On 27th Oct. 1873, by Rev. F. A. Kimbell, Mr. John R. Simonton to Miss Sallie V. Cozart, all of Atlanta, Ga.

On 29th Oct. 1873, by Rev. F. A. Kimbell, Mr. James Haggie to Miss Sallie Emmerson, of Tunnell Hill, Whitfield county, Ga.

Oct. 21st, 1873, by Rev. A. J. Dean, Mr. James A. McLester, of Stewart county, Ga., to Miss Laura A. Battle, of Lumpkin, Ga.

Issue of November 12, 1873

On the 22d of October, by Rev. W. F. Roberts, Mr. James Boyd to Miss Mary L. McRae, both of Telfair county, Ga.

At the residence of the bride's brother-in-law, Mr. James M. McGehee in Quitman county, Ga., by Rev. G. T. Embry, Mr. J. R. Minter of Marion county, Ga., to Miss Mary M. Lowe, of Quitman county, Ga.

In the Methodist Church, Griffin, Ga., October 28th ult., by Rev. John W. Heidt, Mr. M. A. Johnson to Miss Clara Logan, daughter of Col. J. H. Logan, all of Griffin.

In Newnan, Ga., by Rev. John W. Heidt, October 15th ult., Dr. Wm. D. Walton, of Washington, Ga., to Miss Rowena Reese, daughter of Dr. Reese, of Newnan, Ga.

At Salem Church, Monroe county, Ga., on the evening of the 23d of October 1873, by Rev. J. J. Singleton, Mr. T. P. Winsor to Miss L. O. V. Evans, daughter of Judge James H. Evans.

By Rev. Jas. O. Branch, Nov. 4th 1873, Mr. Wm. R. Cox to Miss Lizzie L. Jones, all of Macon, Ga.

By Rev. J. Anderson, D. D., in the Methodist Church, Monticello, on the 29th October, Rev. H. E. Partridge, of the Florida Conference, to Miss Sallie A. Neilson, of Monticello.

By Rev. W. S. Baker, October 23d, Mr. Columbus M. Brannan to Miss Hellen A. Tarpley, all of Irwinton, Ga.

By Rev. W. S. Baker, October 28th, Mr. S. F. B. Lester, of Savannah, to Miss E. J. Stubbs, of Irwinton, Ga.

By Rev. J. R. Little, October 1st, Mr. J. J. Hull to Miss Sue Boyd, eldest daughter of Mr. and Mrs. J. B. Boyd, all of Lancasterville, S. C.

On the 20th of October, 1873, by Rev. Albert Gray, Rev. Miles W. Lewis to Miss Amie C. Champion, both of Greene county, Ga.

By Rev. J. Lewis, Jr., at Athens, Ga., November 4th 1873, Mr. George P. Raney, of Tallahassee, Fla., to Miss Mary Elizabeth Lamar, of Athens, Ga.

By Rev. J. Lewis, Jr., at Athens, Ga., November 4th 1873, Rev. James M. Bell to Miss Sarah L. Winfery.

In the M. E. Church, South, in Palmetto, Ga., Nov. 5th 1873, by Rev. T. H. Timmons, Mr. John L. Askew, of Chambers co., Ala., to Miss L. V. Meriwether, of Coweta county, Ga.

In the M. E. Church, South, in Palmetto, Ga., Nov. 5th 1873, by Rev. T. H. Timmons, Mr. I. W. Johnson, of Oglethorpe, to Miss Vollie White, of Coweta.

By Rev. L. P. Neese, Mr. Thos. H. Dozier, of Columbia county, Ga., to Miss Ida C. Wilkes, of Lincolnton, Ga., on 22d of October.

Mr. W. W. Sims, of Coweta county, Ga., to Miss Ellen E. Cunningham, of Lincoln county, Ga., on 30th October 1873,

Near Branchville, S. C., Oct. 30th 1873, by Rev. D. J. Simmons, Mr. Franklin Fairy to Miss Laura Berry, daughter of Capt. J. R. Berry.

Issue of November 19, 1873

On the 15th October, 1873, at the Methodist Church, by Rev. E. F. Gates, Mr. Charles E. Harrison to Miss Arianna E. Givens, daughter of John T. Givens, all of Tampa, Fla.

In Quincy, Fla., Oct. 28th 1873, by Rev. H. E. Partridge, Mr. Benjamin Irby, of Va., to Miss Sallie V. Munroe, of Quincy; and Dr. Chas. A. Hentz to Miss Leila Munroe, both of Quincy, Fla.

Nov. 4th, 1873, by Rev. H. P. Pitchford, Mr. John C. Mickler, of West Union, to Miss Dora J., daughter of Wesley Pitchford, of Walhalla, S. C.

In Washington, Ga., November 6th, 1873, by Rev. P. A. Heard, Dr. J. e. Pope of Athens, Ga., to Miss Mattie Wylie, of Washington, Ga.

In Georgetown, Ga., Oct. 30th 1873, by Rev. J. B. McGehee, James H. Guerry, Esq., to Miss Lizzie Helen Goode.

In Glennville, Ala., Oct. 23d, 1873, by Rev. J. S. Key, Mr. Americus C. Mitchell, Jr., to Miss Susie S. Dawson, youngest child of the late Rev. Dr. Thos. H. Dawson.

In St. Luke's church, Columbus, Ga., Oct. 29th 1873, by Rev. J. S. Key, Mr. Louis M. Lynch, to Miss Amelia E. Ligon.

By Rev. T. J. Simmons, Oct. 26th, 1873, Mr. William Cooper to Miss Elizabeth V. West, all of Whitfield county, Ga.

By Rev. T. J. Simmons, Oct. 30th, 1873, Mr. Henry Smith to Miss Clarisa Morehead.

In Elberton, Ga., Oct. 29th 1873, by Rev. F. G. Hughes, Mr. W. H. Heard to Miss Jennie F. Harper.

Oct. 26th, 1873, by Rev. J. H. Grogan, Rev. G. F. Quillian, of Elberton, Ga., to Miss Ella Smith, of Oglethorpe county, Ga.

In Elbert county, Ga., Nov. 5th 1873, by Rev. Geo. W. Yarbrough, Rev. Benj. W. Williams, of the North Georgia Conference, to Mrs. Laura H. Smith, of Elbert county, Ga.

On 4th of Nov. 1873, in Opelika, Ala., by Rev. Wm. M. Motley, of the Ala. Conf., Lorenso S. Brown, of Baltimore, to Miss Ruth McDaniel, late of Tuscalosa, Ala.

By Rev. A. C. Thomas, on Nov. 6th, 1873, Mr. Samuel S. Shields, of Warren county, Ga., to Miss Mollie E. Brooks, of Taliaferro county, Ga.

On 9th of Nov., 1873, near Thomasville, Ga., by Rev. Dr. Leonard, Mr. Benjamin W. Mauldin to Miss Clara A., daughter of Mr. George S. Faison, of Thomas county, GA.

In Athens, Ga., on 8th Nov., 1873, by Rev. H. W. Speer, Mr. Joseph E. Sitton to Miss Lizzie Handrup.

Issue of November 26, 1873

On 13th November, by Rev. J. B. Wardlaw, Dr. Robert Y. Halley, formerly of Tazwell, Marion county, Ga., to Miss Lucy Gains, of Macon co., Ga.

Near Cokesbury, Abbeville county, S. C., on the 13th November, by Rev. Wm. W. Mood, Mr. John M. Sadler of Laurens county, S. C., and Miss Anna Williams, of Abbeville county, S. C.

On the 11th instant, near Bainbridge, Georgia, by Rev. H. F. Hoyt, R. Joseph Binford, of New Orleans, La., to Miss Harriet C. Munnerlyn.

By Rev. W. W. Stewart, on 6th November 1873, Robert McCorcle to Miss Melissa Spinks, all of Marion county, Ga.

By Rev. W. W. Stewart, on 16th November 1873, Charles Wommack, to Miss Fannie Donnan, all of Marion county, Ga.

November 6th, near Twiggsville, Twiggs county, Ga., by John S. Evans, Esq., Mr. Randal Railey to Miss Georgean Garvis, all of Twiggs county, Ga.

In Midway, Oct. 30th, by Rev. A. J. Jarrell, Mr. Wm. B. Adams of Sandersville, Ga., to Miss Mattie H. Wells, of Midway.

On Tuesday, November 11, 1873, by Rev. H. J. Ellis, Miss Addie A. Bassett, of Troup county, Ga., to Mr. Jas. P. Baker, of Chambers county, Ala.

By Rev. W. G. Hanson, November 6, R. N. Taylor to Miss Lizzie Swann, all of Pike county, Ga.

By Rev. W. G. Hanson, November 20, J. D. Dunn, of Griffin, Ga., to Miss Narcissa Green, of Zebulon, Ga.

Issue of December 3, 1873

On Nov. 11th, by Rev. J. R. Littlejohn, Mr. J. S. Haley, of Putnam county, Ga., to Miss Amelia J. Ellis, of Hayneville, Ga.

On Nov. 19th, 1873, by Rev. J. R. Littlejohn, Mr. C. E. Brown to Miss Bessie J. Walker, both of Houston county, Ga.

On Nov. 20th, 1873, by Rev. J. R. Littlejohn, Dr. J. P. Newman to Miss Ann E. Holleyman, both of Houston county, Ga.

In Fort Valley, Ga., on 26th Nov., 1873, by Rev. W. M. Hayes, Col. B. H. Robinson, of Blakely, Ga., to Miss Addie A. Jones, of Fort Valley, Ga.

On 17th Nov., 1873, in Fernandina, Fla., by Rev. Thos. W. Tomkies, Mr. Wm. O. McDowell, of New York City, to Miss Josephine, daughter of the late Col. Henry Timanus.

By Rev. J. B. Payne, on 1st Oct. 1873, in Thomaston, Ga., Mr. Robert A. Mathews, of Harris county, Ga., to Miss Sallie Thompson, of Thomaston, Ga.

By Rev. J. B. Payne, in Thomaston, Ga., Rev. Joseph Holmes, of Barnesville, Ga., to Miss Annie Floyd, of Madison, Ga.

On 20th Nov., 1873, by Rev. C. A. Conaway, Mr. John B. Crowley to Miss Mary E. Thomas, all of Oglethorpe county, Ga.

Nov. 4th, 1873, in Rome, Ga., by Rev. W. M. Crumley, Mr. M. J. Wimpy, of Rome, to Miss Georgia Crews, of Bartow county, Ga., daughter of S. S. Crews.

In Cave Spring, Ga., Nov. 13th, 1873, by Rev. B. B. Quillian, Mr. J. E. Childress, of Rutherford county, Tenn., to Miss Sue D. Irwin, daughter of G. W. Irwin, of the former place.

Nov. 18th, 1873, by Rev. J. L. Sifly, Mr. Francis P. Largley, of Charleston, S. C., to Miss Bell Moorer, of Orangeburg county, S. C.

By Rev. J. R. Little, Nov. 6th, 1873, Mr. James S. McCardell to Miss Sallie L., daughter of Mr. and Mrs. Andrew J. McIlwain, all of Lancaster, S. C.

On 20th Nov., 1873, at St. James' Church, Augusta, Ga., by Rev. J. E. Evans, Mr. L. C. Strong, of Savannah, Ga., to Miss Flewellin Evans, daughter of Rev. J. E. Evans, No. Ga. Conf.

By Rev. Thos. B. Lanier, at Capt. McCrone's, Bethany, Ga., Nov. 16th, 1873, Mr. H. W. J. Ham, of Eastman, Ga., to Miss Anna E. Cook, of Jefferson county, Ga.

By Rev. Thos. B. Lanier, at Bartow, Ga., Nov. 18th, 1873, Mr. Samuel C. Evans to Miss Lula L. Carswell, all of Jefferson county, Ga.

Oct. 14th, 1873, by Rev. J. B. Traywick, Mr. Thos. Bellotte, of Pendleton, S. C., to Miss Mary Milam, of Laurens, S. C.

Nov. 5th, 1873, by Rev. J. B. Traywick, Mr. Barnette S. Langston to Miss Mary Mills, both of Laurens, S. C.

In Columbia, South Carolina, Nov. 25th, 1873, by Rev. Sidi H. Browne, Mr. H. Bascom Browne to Miss Mollie M. Moody.

By Rev. J. B. C. Quillian, Nov. 13th, 1873, Mr. S. A. Anderson, of Marietta, Ga., to Miss Nannie A. M., daughter of Hon. E. H. Lindley, of Powder Springs, Ga.

In Troup co., Ga., Nov. 25th, 1873, by Rev. W. J. Cotter, Mr. J. J. Adams to Miss M. S. J. Smith.

By Rev. W. J. Cotter, Nov. 27th, 1873, Mr. S. B. Bailey to Miss L. R. Embry.

By Rev. Jno. M. Bowden, Nov. 16th, 1873, Mr. R. Drisco Winslett to Miss Sebell Dewbery, all of Troup county, Ga.

Issue of December 10, 1873

November 18, 1873, by Rev. Geo. G. N. MacDonell, Mr. Henry Y. Righton to Miss Mary Ella Doty, all of Savannah, Ga.

By Rev. Geo. G. N. MacDonell, November 26, 1873, in Whitesville, Ga., Mr. Andrew H. Charlton, of Savannah, Ga., to Miss Mary P. Maner, daughter of the late Samuel Maner, Esq., of South Carolina.

November 26, by Rev. J. W. Stipe, Mr. J. M. Bagbey to Miss Ella Wood, all of Jonesboro.

In Bibb county, Nov. 27, 1873, by Rev. Wesley F. Smith, Mr. Wm. J. Thomas to Miss Sallie E. Hill, all of Bibb county.

In Warrenton county, December 3d, 1873, by Rev. Wesley F. Smith, Mr. Robt. L. Felts to Miss Laura L. Rogers, all of Warren county.

In York county, S. C., Nov. 22d, 1873, by Rev. J. F. England, Mr. D. C. Anderson to Miss Annie Crook. Columbia and Wilmington papers please copy.

By the Rev. John H. Harris, november 20, 1873, Mr. E. P. Hammond to Miss Fannie Ware, all of Newton county, Ga.

Near Cumming, Ga., on 16th October, by Rev. W. A. Dodge, Mr. Henry B. Moor to Miss N. E. Hutchens, all of Forsyth county, Ga.

On the 27th of November, by Rev. L. R. Bell, Mr. Seaborn T. Pearson, of Hackneyville, Ala., to Miss Leonora D. Dean, all of Tallapoosa county, Ala.

On 27th November, by Rev. C. P. Murdock, Mr. W. W. Nally to Miss Ella L. Raysor, all of Jefferson county, Fla.

By Rev. J. O. A. Connor, Nov. 23d, 1873, at the residence of Mr. J. S. Funches, Mr. Paul Gramling to Miss Eugenia F. Funches, daughter of Mrs. Rachel E. Funches, all of Orangeburgh co., S. C.

By Rev. J. O. A. Connor, Nov. 27, 1873, Mr. J. T. Dukes to Miss J. A. F. E. Huff, daughter of Mrs. Mary Huff, all of Orangeburgh co., S. C.

By Rev. T. F. Lunsford, Nov. 20, 1873, Dr. E. B. Welder to Miss Fannie Harp, daughter of Rev. M. Harp, all of Fayette county, Ga.

By Rev. C. A. Mitchell, October 12, 1873, Mr. John W. Smith to Mrs. S. B. Stroud, both of Crawford county, Ga.

By Rev. C. A. Mitchell, Nov. 25, 1873, Mr. Wm. H. Spier, of Barnesville, Ga., to Mrs. Mary A. Grove, of Monroe county, Ga.

By Rev. C. A. Mitchell, November 27, 1873, Capt. J. Monroe Ponder, of Forsyth, Ga., to Miss Anna M. Norwood, of Culloden, Ga.

Issue of December 17, 1873

On the 27th Nov., by Rev. T. A. Seals, Col. Wm. M. Mitchell, of Lynchburg, Va., to Miss Lucy E. Reaney, of Augusta, Ga.

Dec. 4th, in Union county, S. C., by Rev. Samuel A. Weber, Mr. John R. Willie to Miss L. Josephine Smith, daughter of William Smith, Esq., all of Union.

By Rev. W. W. Wadsworth, at the residence of Mr. G. B. Crenshaw, on 23d Nov., 1873, Mr. Newton W. Johnson to Miss N. Ellen Howard, all of Newton county, Ga.

On 3d Dec., by Rev. W. W. Wadsworth, Mr. William D. Chambless, of Atlanta, Ga., to Miss S. Loulie Pace, daughter of Judge C. D. Pace, Covington, Ga.

On 2d Dec., 1873, at the residence of Wm. Dorns, Esq., by Rev. G. M. Boyd, Mr. Benjamin F. Hutchings, of Anderson county, S. C., to Miss Mary Jeanette Dearing, of Edgefield county.

By Rev. W. W. Stewart, on Dec. 2d, 1873, Horace A. Harris, of Americus, Ga., to Miss Elmina, daughter of Daniel James, of Marion county, Ga.

At the residence of Col. D. R. Barton, in Orangeburg county, S. C., Dec. 4th, 1873, by Rev. D. J. Simmons, Mr. Alonzo J. Izlar to Miss Virginia McMichael.

By Rev. J. B. Wardlaw, Dec. 9th, 1873, Mr. Rufus A. Smith of Lee county, Ga., to Miss Joannie Cloud, of Macon county, Ga.

At the residence of the bride's mother, on 4th of Dec., by Rev. D. M. Banks, Mr. D. M. Rowe to Miss Lou Hurt, both of Hurtville, Russel county, Ala.

On the 9th of Nov., 1873, by Rev. M. F. Malsby, in Jasper county, Ga., Mr. John H. Smith, of Newton county, Ga., to Miss Carrie Ivy.

By Rev. M. F. Malsby, on the 20th Nov., 1873, Mr. J. G. Nix to Miss Tunny Yarborough, all of Newton county, Ga.

By Rev. M. F. Malsby, on 30th Nov., 1873, in the M. E. Church at Social Circle, Ga., Mr. George P. Johnson to Miss Mary F. Malsby, all of Social Circle.

By Rev John Calvin Johnson, on Nov. 2d, 1873, Mr. Richard S. Jones, of Morgan county, Ga., to Miss Sallie J. Ward, of Clarke county, Ga.

By Rev John Calvin Johnson, on Dec. 4th, 1873, Mr. Marcellus D. Browning to Miss Haseltine J. Brittain, all of Clarke county, Ga.

At the residence of the bride's father, Nov. 20th, 1873, by the Rev. Geo. C. Clarke, Mr. John Gamage to Miss Esther Parker, all of Terrell county, Ga.

At the residence of the bride's father, Nov. 25th, 1873, by the Rev. Geo. C. Clarke, Mr. J. R. Christian, editor of the Thomasville "Times," to Miss A. H. Evans, of Terrell county, Ga.

At the residence of the bride's father, Dec. 3d, 1873, by Rev. Geo. C. Clarke, Mr. Laurence A. Houser, of Perry, Ga., to Miss Viola Bryan, of Terrell county, Ga.

At the residence of the bride's father, Dec. 7th, 1873, by Rev. Geo. C. Clarke, Mr. W. C. Marshall to Miss Susan Gammage, all of Terrell county, Ga.

In Wesley Church, Savannah, Ga., Dec. 9th, 1873, by Rev. Geo. G. N. MacDonell, Mr. R. Osbourne Hext, of Burke county, Ga., to Miss Emma C. Wright, of Savannah, Ga.

Issue of December 24, 1873

In Brothersville, Richmond county, Ga., Nov. 27, by Rev. R. A. Conner, Mr. Samuel B. Clark to Miss Evelina Allen, both of the former place.

December 16, 1873, in Twiggs county, Ga., by Rev. C. W. Smith, Dr. A. Mathis of Sandersville, to Miss Nannie G. Gibson, of Twiggs county.

In Perry, Ga., on the 10th December 1873, by Rev. W. Knox, Mr. Edwin Martin, Editor of the Houston Journal, to Miss Maggie D. Mann, of Perry, Ga.

In the M. E. Church, South, in West Point, Ga., Dec. 9th 1873, by Rev. D. D. Cox ,Dr. Henry G. Henderson to Miss Mary A. Oslin, daughter of Dr. J. W. Oslin, all of West Point, Ga.

On the 4th of December 1873, by Rev. T. J. Mellard, Mr. Sidney F. Vogt to Miss Anna Weatherford, daughter of Middleton E. Weatherford, Esq., all of Charleston county, S. C.

By Rev. Joseph M. Gable, Dec. 11, 1873, Mr. C. B. Hunton to Mrs. Julia Hodge, both of Cobb county, Ga.

By Rev. A. J. Dean, Nov. 9th, 1873, B. F. Harrell, Esq., to Miss Maggie A. Yarborough, all of Lumpkin, Ga.

By Rev. A. J. Dean, Dec. 3d, 1873, B. B. Willett, of Stewart county, Ga., to Miss Mattie Stanley, of Lumpkin, Ga.

Dec. 11th, 1873, by Rev. I. O. A. Conner, Mr. Perry Patrick to Miss Olivia Bouzard, all of Orangeburg county, S. C.

Dec. 3d, 1872, at Butler, Ga., by Rev. Thos. T. Christian, Mr. David H. Marchant to Miss Julia A. Bond, daughter of Rev. W. M. D. Bond, of the South Georgia Conference.

On the 9th of Dec., 1873, by Rev. T. H. Timmons, Major John H. Odoin[?] of Hogansville, Ga., to Miss Sallie E. Menifer, of Palmetto, Ga.

On the 10th Dec., by Rev. J. N. Dupree, Rev. Wm. C. Rowland to Miss Charlotte I. Lockhart, all of Tallapoosa county, Ala.

Nov. 27th, 1873, by Rev. W. P. Lovejoy, Mr. A. A. Denham to Miss Katie B. Harwell, all of Eatonton, Ga.

On the 18th of Dec., 1873, at the residence of Mrs. Kellam, by Rev. J. J. Morgan, Mr. David S. Blackshear, of Laurens county, to Miss Pauline H. Howard, daughter of Col. T. C. Howard, of Kirkwood, Ga.

On the 16th of Dec. 1873, by Rev. R. B. G. Walters, Mr. R. B. G. Walters to Miss Lummie A. Jossie, of Washington county, Ga.

Issue of January 7, 1874

On the 23d November, by Rev. G. G. Smith, at the residence of Mrs. Sarah Brannon, Marietta, Ga., Isaac McConnell, of Weatherford, Texas, to Mrs. Sarah E. Campbell, of Marietta, Ga.

On the 3d December, by the Rev. G. G. Smith, at the residence of Thos. W. Reed, Cobb county, Ga., Mr. W. T. Robertson, of Oakley Mills, to Miss Leona Reed, daughter of T. W. Reed.

On the 22d December, in Barnesville, by Rev. G. G. Smith, Mr. Oliver H. Greene, of Macon, Ga., to Miss Mary C. Hanson, daughter of Rev. J. B. Hanson, of Barnesville, Ga.

By Rev. G. G. Smith, on the 9th October, at the residence of H. B. Wallis, near Marietta, Ga., Mr. J. P. Moore, of Cobb county, to Miss S. Ollie Wallis, of Marietta, Ga.

At the residence of Henry S. Speer, Atlanta, Ga., Dec. 28, 1873, by Rev. C. J. Oliver, Mr. Fletcher B. Speer, to Miss Nancy Bean, all of Atlanta, Ga.

On the 18th December, 1873, at the residence of John H. Eley, Esq., by Rev. J. H. Kilpatrick, Mr. Bertram Moore to Miss Mattie Eley, and Mr. z. T. Walker to Miss Fannie Eley, all of Greene co., Ga.

Nov. 27th, at Sandersvile, Ga., by Rev. J. F. Mixon, Mr. John A. Robison, of Washington county, to Miss Lou Brantly, of the former place.

In Macon county, Ga., Dec. 22, 1873, by Rev. N. A. Hornaday, Mr. Alexander Pierson to Susannah Hewitt.

In Macon county, Ga., Dec. 22, 1873, by Rev. N. A. Hornaday, Mr. Alexander F. Green to Julia Passmore.

In Macon, on the 18th ult., by Rev. John W. Burke, Mr. William Streyer to Miss Eliza S. Gibson, all of this city.

On the 23d Dec., at the residence of Dr. D. W. Hammond, in Macon, by Rev. S. S. Sweet, W. A. McNeil, Esq., of Quitman, Ga., to Miss Viola Johns, of Macon, Ga.

Dec. 17th, 1873, at the residence of Gen. Arthur, of Lexington, by Rev. A. J. Cauthen, Rev. G. T. Harmon, of the South Carolina Conference, to Miss Maggie Seibles.

Dec. 28, 1873, in Crawford county, Ga., by Rev. T. B. Russell, Mr. Thos. W. young to Miss Winnie Gassett.

On the 28th December, by Rev. S. S. Sweet, B. F. Bowers, Esq., to Mrs. A. Davidson, all of Macon, Ga.

By Rev. C. E. Dowman, Dec. 21st, 1873, Mr. J. P. Sewell, of Fulton county, Ga., to Miss Mary Ann Lee, of Campbell county, Ga.

Dec. 18, 1873, by Rev. J. F. England, Rev. T. P. England, of the North Carolina Conference, to Miss M. F. Jackson, of Gaston county, N. C.

By Rev. E. G. Murrah, in Monticello, Ga., on the 23d November, Mr. O. P. Hickmon to Miss Elizabeth Turner.

On the 21st Dec., 1873, by Rev. W. H. Graham, Mr. F. E. Caraway, to Miss Elizabeth McFall, all of Monroe county, Ga.

December 18, 1873, by Rev. D. Kelsey, in McDuffie county, Ga., Mr. Wm. T. Martin, of Columbia co., Ga., to Miss Mary C. Printup.

In Columbia co., Ga., Dec. 23d, by Rev. D. Kelsey, Mr. Aquilla M. Flint to Miss Cordelia W. Agerton.

By Rev. H. Dorman, Dec. 23d, 1873, S. H. Hendry, of Harris county, Ga., to Miss A. Florence, of Meriwether county, Ga.

December 11, 1873, by Rev. W. H. Hunt, Mr. Wm. W. Anderson to Miss Louisa A. Herb, all of Columbia county, Fla.

On the 18th December 1873, by Rev. Alexander P. Wright, Mr. Wm. S. Fender to Miss Jennie Sims, all of Lowndes county, Ga.

By Rev. J. D. Rodgers, Dec. 24, 1873, Wm. L. Ingram to Miss Mary A. DeLacy, all of Gadsden co., Fla.

December 16, 1873, by Rev. S. D. Clements, Mr. James M. Wooldridge, of Jamestown, to Miss Lovie E. Dozier, of Muscogee county, Ga.

By Rev. L. R. Bell, on the 23d December, Mr. Jos. G. Pearson, to Miss Alice A. Freeman, daughter of Dr. J. S. Freeman, all of Tallapoosa county, Ala.

By Rev. John Penny, Dec. 24, 1873, Rev. James D. McDonell, of Fernandina, to Miss Mattie, the eldest daughter of Capt. B. W. Wimberly, of Bronson, Levy county, Fla.

Issue of January 14, 1874

In Meriwether county, Ga., January 1st, 1874, by Rev. H. J. Ellis, Mr. Hugh K. Ector to Miss Laconia Biggers.

By Rev. W. Heidt, on the 5th Dec., Mr. Marcus S. Baker to Miss Fannie A. Newsom, daughter of the late Frederick Newsom, all of Savannah, Ga.

On the 18th Dec., by Rev. E. J. Knight, Capt. Chas. F. Cone, of Hamilton county, Fla., to Miss Lula Dellegall, of Suwanee county, Fla.

On the 23d Dec.,1873, by Rev. E. J. Knight, Mr. Andrew D. Knight to Miss Elizabeth Cheshire, daughter of Rev. A. Cheshire, all of Hamilton county, Fla.

By Rev. John Calvin Johnson, Dec. 17, 1873, at Watkinsville, Clarke county, Ga., Mr. Washington B. Jackson, of Athens, Ga., to Miss Naomi A. Langford, of the former place.

By Rev. A. J. Dean, Dec. 23d, 1873, Rev. J. T. Lowe, President Lumpkin Female College, to Miss A. J. Kirksey, all of Lumpkin, Ga.

On the 31st Dec., 1873, by Rev. Jas. Hunnicutt, Mr. Wm. H. Parks to Miss Mary O. Smith, daughter of Rev. Geo. E. Smith, all of Coweta county, Ga.

Dec. 17th, 1873, by Rev. T. B. Russell, in Fort Valley, Ga., Mr. Jos. H. Quinker to Miss Ella E. Sanford.

Jan. 1st, 1874, by Rev. P. G. Reynolds, Mr. D. H. Findlay to Miss Lullie E. Goodwyn, all of Calhoun county, Ga.

In Weston, Ga., on Dec. 14, 1873, by Rev. J. T. Ainsworth, Mr. J. M. Saville to Miss Plen Brawner.

By Rev. T. Alonzo Harris, on the 23d Dec., 1873, at the residence of Judge P. W. Hutcheson, Sr., Mr. C. C. Feagin, of Sumter county, Ga., to Miss Mary A. Johnson of Oglethorpe county, Ga.

On the 21st Dec., 1873, in Baker county, Fla., by Rev. F. M. Smith, Mr. Benj. D. Mann to Miss Cinderella Taylor, daughter of Lewis Taylor.

Issue of January 21, 1874

Dec. 18, 1873, by Rev. T. S. L. Harwell, Mr. Henry Brasell, of Troup county, Ga., to Miss Florence Culpepper, of Meriwether county, Ga.

In Graniteville, S. C., Nov. 30, 1873, by Rev. L. C. Loyal, Mr. Wm. C. Prater to Miss Sarah E. S. Syfrett.

Jan. 13, 1874, in Graniteville, S. C., by Rev. L. C. Loyal, Mr. James Baker to Miss Margaret Walker Wright.

At the house of Isaac Herbert, Esq., in Newberry county, S. C., on Dec. 18, 1873, by Rev. Thos. G. Herbert, Mr. John Eidson, of Edgefield county, S. C. to Miss Annie Herbert.

Jan. 11, 1874, by Rev. C. P. Murdock, Mr. W. L. Adams of Hamilton county, Fla., to Miss Mary J. Dallas, of Madison county, Fla.

By Rev. R. A. Conner, on the 18th Dec., 1873, at the residence of Gen. Stephen Drane, in McDuffie county, Ga., Mr. Chas. A. Hatcher, of Columbia county, Ga., to Miss Louisa V. Hamrick of the former place.

In Hamilton, Ga., Jan. 8, 1874, by Rev. D. R. McWilliams, Mr. w. M. Middlebrook, of Atlanta, to Miss Sallie Turner, of Hamilton.

Jan. 1st, by Rev. G. H. Pooser, Mr. Javan Pye to Miss Henrietta M. Sanders, all of Beaufort county, S. C.

Jan. 6, 1874, by Rev. W. P. Lovejoy, Mr. Ralph Jones to Miss S. B. morton, all of Putnam county, Ga.

On the 7th Jan., 1874, by Rev. J. O. A. Cook, Rev. Herbert P. Myers, fo the So. Ga. Conf., to Miss Renna F. Darling, of Blackshear, Ga.

In Decatur, Ga., by Rev. F. B. Davies, Dec. 30th, 1873, Mr. James D. Collins, of Atlanta, to Miss Alice E. Clara, of the former place.

On the 8th Jan., 1874, by Rev. L. A. Darsey, Mr. Bishop B. Blackwell, Attorney at Law, to Miss Ella M. Stewart, youngest daughter of Hon. H. J. Stewart, all of Jasper, Fla.

By Rev. W. G. Hanson, Nov. 25th, 1873, Mr. James Hudgins, of Upson county, Ga., to Miss Mattie Bragg, of Pike county, Ga.

By Rev. W. G. Hanson, Nov. 27th, 1873, W. N. Norton to Miss F. C. Kendall, all of Spalding county, Ga.

On the 11th Jan. 1874, in Winterville, Ga., by Rev. T. Alonzo Haris, Mr. William R. Argo to Miss Maggie S. Winter, daughterof D. H. Winter, both of Clarke county, Ga.

Dec. 23d, 1873, by Rev. F. F. Reynolds, Rev. R. L. Campbell to Miss M. E. Mattox.

Nov. 25th, 1873, in Marion county, Fla., by Rev. Jas. P. DePass, Mr. George F. MacDonald to Miss Tallula W. Gunnels.

By the Rev. E. Heidt, on the 5th of Jan. 1874, Mr. Marcus S. Baker to Miss Fannie A., daughter of the late Frederick Kernson, all of Savannah, Ga.

On the 13th of Jan. 1874, by Rev. J. Chambers, at the residence of the bride's father, Mr. James J. Bagwell to Miss Frances Bulllard, all of Campbell county, Ga.

By Rev. N. D. Morehouse, on 10th Dec., 1873, Mr. G. h. Berry to Miss Maggie Rahn, all of Effingham county, Ga.

In Sumpter county, Ga., Jan. 13th, 1874, by Rev. Geo. C. Thompson, Mr. J. W. Bower, of Irwinton, Ga., to Miss Maggie Kitchens, of Sumpter county, Ga.

On the 15th of Jan., 1874, by Rev. C. W. Smith, Rev. John W. Glenn, of the So. Ga. Conference, to Miss Fannie Stevens, of Badlwin county, Ga.

Issue of January 28, 1874

On the 6th of January, by Rev. W. Ewing Johnston, Mr. James M. Seals to Mrs. Fannie A. Moss, all of Richmond county, Ga.

On the 19th of January, 1874, by Rev. W. Ewing Johnston, Mr. DeWitt C. Willer to Miss Mary Daniels, all of Richmond county, Ga.

On the 13th of January, 1874, by Rev. W. P. Ocain, Mr. T. A. Zone to Miss S. J. Carsway, both of Suwannee county, Fla.

On the 31st December, 1873, by Rev. R. R. Dagnall, Mr. T. Cox, of Williamston, S. C., to Miss Lottie M. Hellams, of Laurens county, S. C.

In Marietta, Ga., Jan. 13, 1874, by Rev. W. F. Glenn, Mr. W. J. Marchman to Miss Mollie Henderson.
In Marietta, Ga., Jan. 20, 1874, by Rev. W. F. Glenn, Mr. S. C. Thompson, of Atlanta, to Miss Emma G. Rude, of Marietta.

On the 14th January 1874, by Rev. W. T. Hamilton, Mr. H. McCorkle to Miss Lucinda A. Smith, all of McDuffie county, Ga.

At the residence of Mr. R. S. Neal, Columbia co., Ga., on the 15th of January, 1874, by Rev. W. T. Hamilton, Dr. H. C. Rhensy, of Burke county, Ga., to Miss L. D. Gordon, formerly of Opelika, Ala.

By Rev. G. W. Persons, on the 18th instant, Mr. Walter J. Short, of Columbia county, Ga., to Miss Sallie F. Hampton, daughter of Jacob Hampton, of Houston county, Ga.

Jan. 11, by Rev. M. C. Blackburn, of the Trinity Conference, Mr. Jas. A. L. McFarland to Miss Cornelia B. Webster, all of Pilot Point, Texas.

On the 15th inst., by Rev. J. H. Zimmerman, at the residence of Mrs. Sarah Thomas, Mr. J. W. Gardner to Miss L. F. J. Thomas, all of Charleston co., S. C.

In the Methodist Church, in Quitman, Ga., by Rev. S. S. Sweet, Jas. H. Wade, Esq., to Miss Jennett Newlove, both of Quitman, Brooks co., Ga.

Issue of February 4, 1874

Jan. 5th, 1874, by Rev. B. L. Hume, Mr. Wm. H. Jones to Miss Sarah E. Glenn, all of Morgan county,Ga.

By Rev. B. L. Hume, Jan. 22d, 1874, Mr. James L. Morgan, of Humbolt, Tenn., to Miss Lucinda R. Jones, of Morgan county,Ga.

Jan. 21st, 1874, in Wilkes county, Ga., by Rev. T. H. Gibson, Mr. N. E. Lyon to Miss Sallie E. Pleaston[?].

Near Branchville, S. C., Jan. 22d, 1874, by Rev. D. J. Simmons, Mr. Charles J. Felder to Miss Elizabeth J. McAlhaney, youngest daughter of Mr. Benj. B. McAlhaney.

On the 11th Jan. 1874, by Rev. S. J. Hill, Mr. Rufus O. Dixon to Miss Antoinette Stuckey, all of Bishopville, S. C.

In Jackson county, Ga., Jan. 29th 1874, by Rev. J. M. Venable, Mr. W. D. Seymour to Miss Josie H. Morgan.

On Jan. 15th, 1874, by Rev. W. D. Kirkland, Mr. Wm. H. Squier to Miss M. Grace Kennedy, all of Columbia, S. C.

On Jan. 28th, 1874, by Rev. W. D. Kirkland, Mr. George C. Homanstine to Miss Mary C. Smith, all of Columbia, S. C.

In Macon, on the 29th ult., by Rev. John W. Burke, Mr. F. W. DeLane to Miss Mary S. Munson.

Issue of February 11, 1874

Jan. 1st, 1874, Mr. Wylie Willis to Miss Kate Sullivan, both of Laurens county, S. C., by Rev. J. M. Traywick.

Jan. 15th, 1874, Mr. Melvin Shell to Miss Emma Switzer, daughter of Capt. J. R. Switzer, both of Laurens county, S. C., by Rev. J. B. Traywick.

Jan. 15th, 1874, Mr. Quincy Willis to Miss Ella Leak, both of Laurens county, S. C., by Rev. J. B. Traywick.

Jan. 28th, 1874, Mr. John W. Greer, of the city of Greenville, S. C., to Miss P. Alice Sullivan, daughter of Hon. Chas. P. Sullivan, of Laurensville, S. C., by Rev. J. B. Traywick.

By Rev. H. Rece, on the 17th of Dec., 1873, Mr. R. J. Beckum to Miss Elizabeth Penington, both of Jefferson county, Ga.

By Rev. M. H. Rece, on the 8th of January 1874, Mr. James W. Gay of Richmond county, to Miss E. A. Daniel of Jefferson county, Ga.

Jan. 27th, at the residence of Mr. W. C. Bailey, by Rev. W. W. Wadsworth, Mr. J. W. Lewis of Missouri, to Miss lucy Meriwether, of Jasper county, Ga.

By Rev. J. W. Simmons, of Columbus, Ga., Mr. J. R. Cunningham, of Griffin, to Miss Carrie E. Hunt, daughter of Mr. Thos. S. Hunt, of Spalding county, Ga.

Jan. 20th, in Russell county, Ala., by Rev. J. W. Simmons, Mr. James Benson, of columbus, to Miss Martha Brown.

Jan. 22d 1874, on the Upper Orange ct., South Carolina Conference, by Rev. A. R. Danner, Mr. Leonidas C. Murph, to Miss Alice V. Inabnet, daughter of Rev. John Inabnet.

On the 4th February 1874, by Rev. G. W. Hardaway, Mr. William J. Smith of Baldwin county, Ga., to Miss Harvie J. Butts, of Hancock county, Ga.

Issue of February 18, 1874

On the 22d Jan. 1874, by Rev. W. M. Watts, Mr. Louis L. Vann to Miss Rebecca A. Jourdan, all of Thomas county, Ga.

On the 27th Jan. 1874, by Rev. W. M. Watts, Mr. Jas. L. Whiddon to Miss Eliza Pugh, all of Thomas county, Ga.

On the 5th Feb., 1874, by Rev. J. H. Zimmerman, at the residence of Mrs. Frances Moorer, Mr. John E. Moorer to Miss Ella J. Moorer, all of Orangeburgh county, S. C.

By Rev. Geo. C. Leavel, Jan. 27th, 1874, Dr. W. R. O. Veal to Miss Nettie A. Smith, all of Marion county, Fla.

Feb. 3d, 1874, by Rev. Geo. C. Leavel, Mr. Wm. C. Jeffords to Miss Mary R. Gates, all of Marion county, Fla.

Dec. 18th, 1873, by Rev. A. McCorquodale, Mr. Jas. S. Beasly to Miss Adwina Dubose.

On Dec. 24th 1873, by Rev. A. McCorquodale, Mr. George Bishop to Miss E. Lewis.

On Jan. 11th 1874, by Rev. A. McCorquodale, Robt. Y. McLeod, M. D., to Mrs. M. E. Rodgers, all near Bishopville, S. C.

Jan. 15th, 1874, by Rev. W. J. Jordan, Mr. G. H. Dawson to Miss L. E. Anderson, all of Tatnall county, Ga.

Jan. 21st, 1874, by Rev. W. J. Jordan, Mr. G. W. Hollman to Miss Susan Padget, all of Tatnall county, Ga.

By Rev. W. F. Robison, on the 10th of Feb. 1874, Mr. John Fale, of Hawkinsville to Miss Camilla A. Shepard, all of Houston county, Ga.

On the 29th January, 1874, in the Methodist Church, Lancaster, S. C., by Rev. R. L. Harper, Mr. W. D. Lemmond to Miss Sallie A. Mayes.

On the 28th Dec., 1873, by Rev. D. C. Oliver, Mr. Justain Henderson to Miss Ann O. Saville, all of Banks county, Ga.

SOUTHERN CHRISTIAN ADVOCATE MARRIAGE NOTICES 1867-1878

On the 22d Jan., 1874, by Rev. D. C. Oliver, Mr. Milton A. Wilbanks to Miss S. Addie Simmons, all of Banks county, Ga.

On the 5th Feb., 1874, by Rev. Wm. W. Mood, Mr. John M. moore of Charlotte, N. C., to Miss M. Janie Hill, daughter of Col. Richard S. Hill, of Anderson, S. C.

In Newnan, Ga., Jan. 27th, 1874, by Rev. Alex. M. Thigpen, Col. Peter Francisco Smith to Miss Lizzie Hill, daughter of Mr. A. B. Hill.

Feb. 11th, 1874, in LaGrange, Ga., by Rev. P. L. Heard, Mr. Gustavus A. Hornady to Miss Louisa Kate Beall.

Issue of February 25, 1874

Feb. 10, by Rev. S. J. Hill, at the house of Captain Isham Moore, Mr. john H. Dixon of Bishopville, S. C., to Miss Sallie Sanders of Roften Creek.

On 1st inst., by Rev. W. H. Potter, John Major Baker, Esq., to Miss Camila Ann Tremble.

By Rev. W. Hutto, Mr. Charles Cook to Miss Sallie Melichamp, on the 4th inst., in Georgetown county, S. C., and Mr. Wm. H. Rowe to Miss Sarah W. Small, all of Williamsburg county, S. C.

By Rev. J. S. Bryan, Feb. 11, 1874, Mr. A. P. Dixon of Meriwether county, Ga., to Miss Fannie E. Owen, of Harris county, Ga.

In Elbert county, Ga., Jan. 27th, 1874, by Rev. F. G. Hughes, J. B. C. Jordan to Miss Dora A. Adams.

In Elberton, Ga., January 28th, 1874, by Rev. F. G. Hughes, Thomas J. Blackwell to Miss Mamie A. Jones.

At Heardmont Academy, Elbert county, Ga., Feb. 3d, 1874, by Rev. F. G. Hughes, Francis B. Cleveland to Miss Ida L. McCalla.

Feb. 4th, at the residence of Mr. James L. Maddux, by Rev. W. W. Wadsworth, Mr. Lucian Benton to Miss Willie Flournoy, all of Jasper county, Ga.

By Rev. D. M. Banks, on the 10th of February, Miss Sallie H. Banks, daughter of Dr. N. P. Banks, to Mr. Jas. B. Tarver, all of Enon, Bullock county, Ala.

On the 12th of February, by the Rev. John M. Marshall, Mr. Robert S. Hendry to Miss Laura T. Martin, both of Liberty county, Ga.

By Rev. R. H. Howren, on the 15th January, Mr. H. T. Caulk to Miss Jane Hadden, all of Madison county, Fla.

On the 17th February, 1874, by Rev. Thos. J. Adams, Mr. Henry B. Jones to Miss Elizabeth C. McKinley, the former of Taliaferro, and the latter of Hancock county, Ga.

By Rev. John H. Wilcox, Jan. 1st, 1874, Mr. H.V. Lester to Miss Mary Bell, both of Burke co., Ga.

Issue of March 4, 1874

In Quitman, Ga., Feb. 18th, by Rev. Walker Lewis, Mr. John Nugent, of Quitman, to Miss Hannah Spann, of Savannah.

In Brooks county, Ga., Feb. 19th, 1874, by Rev. Walker Lewis, Mr. Wm. B. Elenburg, of Brooks county, to Miss Mary E. Golding, of the same county.

On Feb. 8th, 1874, by Rev. S. G. Jones, Mr. J. W. Wright to Miss C. A. Lewis, all of Paulding county, Ga.

Feb. 17th, 1874, at the residence of Rev. J. Coggins, by Rev. Wm. T. Taylor, Mr. A. J. Tully to Miss L. S. Coggins, all of Wakulla county, Fla.

On the 10th of Feb., 1874, by Rev. W. F. Roberts, Mr. G. Q. Williams, of Appling county, Ga., to Miss Sudie E. Willcox, of Telfair county, Ga.

By Rev. John Calvin Johnson, on 19th Feb. 1874, Mr. George T. Murrell, of Oxford, Ga., to Miss Leila W. Morton, of Clarke county, Ga.

On the 28th Jan., 1874, by Rev. W. W. Stewart, Mr. Samuel S. Monk to Miss Mattie N. Minter, all of Marion county, Ga.

On the 15th Feb., 1874, by Rev. W. W. Stewart, Rev. A. J. Harvey of the Baptist Church, to Miss Mollie F. Brown, both of Buena Vista, Ga.

By Rev. Albert Gray, in Greensboro', Ga., Jan. 13th, 1874, Mr. O. T. Hightower to Miss Mary S. Tunison, both of Greensboro', Ga.

On the 18th of February, 1874, at Union Point, by Rev. J. H. Kilpatrick, Mr. William T. Flynt, of Taliafero county, Ga., to Miss Lilla W. Moore, eldest daughter of Dr. W. A. Mooe [sic, for Moore].

Issue of March 11, 1874

February 28, 1874, by Rev. J. M. Boyd, Mr. James M. McConnell to Miss Jane Tinkler, both of Fairfield county, S. C.

Near Georgetown, S. C., February 19, 1874, by Rev. L. Wood, Mr. Hugh G. Taylor to Miss Sarah M. Butts.

By Rev. J. E. Penny, February, 16, 1874, Rev. W. Bowman, of the South Carolina Conference, to Miss Carrie C. Nash, of Laurens county, S. C.

On the 24th of February, in Auburn, Ala., by Rev. E. L. Loveless, Mr. W. R. Kline to Miss M. O. Rosseau.

February 19, 1874, by Rev. S. D. Clements, Mr. Jesse W. Kimbrough to Miss Julie E. Davidson, all of Muscogee.

In Roswell, Ga., February 10th, by Rev. Joshua M. Parker, Mr. C. W. Fraser, of Mississippi, to Mrs. E. A. Fraser, of Roswell.

SOUTHERN CHRISTIAN ADVOCATE MARRIAGE NOTICES 1867-1878

<u>Issue of March 18, 1874</u>

In Savannah, Ga., March 4th 1874, by Rev. A. M. Wynn, Dr. Thomas T. Seibels, to Miss Lavinia Banks.

March 5th 1874, at the residence of Mrs. Hardy in Hot Springs, Ark., by Rev. I. Z. T. Morris, Mr. Haleford Wakelin, of Hot Springs, Ark., to Miss Maria E. Wiseman, of Cleveland, Ohio.

By Rev. Louis B. Bouchelle, March 3d, 1874, Mr. Wm. L. Henderson, of Oxford, Ga., to Miss M. Eugenia Bullard, of Burke county, Ga.

By Rev. Isaac Munden, Jan. 28th, 1874, Mr. T. W. Cato to Miss America Thomas, all of Alachua county, Fla.

By Rev. Isaac Munden, Feb. 26th, 1874, Mr. Spencer Downing to Miss Mary Bradshaw, both of Alachua county, Fla.

By Rev. N. D. Morehouse, on 12th of Feb., in Effingham county, Ga., at the residence of Dr. Jenkins, Geo. N. Hendry, of Thomas county, Ga., to Miss Gertrude Jenkins.

March 4th 1874, by Rev. A. J. Cauthen, Dr. J. H. B. Moseley, of Lowndesville, to Miss Annie J. Bruce, daughter of J. Bruce, of Abbeville county, S. C.

Feb. 17th, 1874, by Rev. A. J. Cauthen, Thos. Mauldin to Miss Amelia Craft, of Anderson county, S. C.

By Rev. A. J. Cauthen, Feb. 26th, 1874, Caleb Clinkscales to Miss Ella Bowman, of Abbeville, S. C.

By Rev. A. J. Cauthen, Feb. 26th, 1874, Dr. O. R. Horton of Belton, to Miss Lollie Latimer, daughter of J. M. Latimer, Jun., near Lowndesville, S. C.

March 5th, 1874, by Rev. E. S. Tyner, Mr. D. F. Burnett, to Miss R. J. Paul, all of Madison county, Fla.

In Effingham county, Ga., on the 11th Feb., 1874, by Rev. E. Heidt, Rev. J. S. Jordan, of the South Georgia Conference, to Miss Tallulah G. Heidt, daughter of the officiating clergyman.

By Rev. J. L. Lupo, on the 25th of Feb., 1874, Mr. R. B. Lang to Miss Alice M. Franks, all of Lincolnton, Ga.

<u>Issue of March 25, 1874</u>

By Rev. W. Hutto, 10th March, 1874, Richard Cribb to Miss Kizzie Cribb, all of Williamsburg co., S. C.

By Rev. N. D. Morehouse, 12th March, at No. 2, C. R. R., James E. Marlow to Miss Clara E. Harrel, all of Savannah, Ga.

March 3d, 1874, by Rev. H. C. Christian, at the residence of Eli Hill, in the town of LaFayette, Walker county, Ga., Rev. Marcus H. Edwards to Miss Lizzie E. Hill. Nashville *Advocate* please copy.

March 12th, 1874, by Rev. Wm. H. LaPrade, Mr. Judson Crabb to Miss Mary A. Noyes, both of Cedar Town, Ga.

At the residence of Rev. W. H. Ellison, D. D., in clayton, Ala., March 12th, 1874, by Rev. S. A. Pilley, Dr. J. T. Floyd to Miss Jennie M. Ellison.

On the 12th of March, in the Methodist Church at Yorkville, S. C., by Rev. D. D. Dantzler, assisted by Rev. H. H. Dixon, Mr. G. H. Oleary to Miss Alice Walker, daughter of Mr. W. M. Walker, all of Yorkville, S. C.

On the 12th of March 1874, by Rev. W. Ewing Johnston, Mr. Wm. New to Miss Harriet Cornelia Henry, all of Richmond county, Ga.

Feb. 26th, 1874, by Rev. P. F. Kistler, near Bamberg, S. C., Mr. Edward Berry, of Branchville, S. C., to Miss Henrietta Simmons, daughter of Rowland Simmons, Esq.

In Macon, on the 19th inst., by Rev. J. W. Burke, George W. Causey to Miss Sarah L. Crocroft.

Issue of April 1, 1874

By Rev. N. D. Morehouse, on 29th January 1874, Christopher Conaway, of Effingham county, Ga., to Miss Laura M. Douglass, of Chatham county, Ga.

By Rev. J. J. Singleton, on the 17th of March 1874, Mr. Calvin J. Ward, to Miss Ella Dantzler, both of Bartow county, Ga.

At the residence of P. E. Lowe, Welborn, Fla., Feb. 25th, 1874, by Rev. Jno. J. Taylor, Mr. B. J. Worrell, of Jacksonville, Fla., to Miss Isabel S. McClellan, daughter of the late Capt. G. E. McClellan, of Suwannee county, Fla.

In Quitman, Ga., March 4th, by Rev. Walker Lewis, Mr. Kinchen H. Williams to Miss Sallie P. Seaman, both of Brooks county, Ga.

At the residence of the bride's mother, March 19th, 1874, by Rev. D. J. McMillan, Rev. J. C. C. Newton, of the Kentucky Military Institute, to Miss Lettie E. Lay, of Pickens county, S. C.

On the 25th March 1874, by Rev. J. W. Glenn, Mr. Wm. J. Fields, of Burke county, Ga., to Miss Cornelia A. Palmer, of Richmond, Bath.

Nov. 26th, 1873, by Rev. D. R. McWilliams, Mr. G. M. Kilpatrick to Miss Ella L. Stanford, both of Waverly Hall, Ga.

At Mt. Zion Church, Waverly Hall, Ga., Feb. 4th, 1874, by Rev. V. E. Manget, Mr. J. T. Blount, of Texas, to Miss Adele W. Darden, of Waverly Hall, Ga.

Issue of April 8, 1874

In Savannah, Ga., by Rev. H. H. Parks, March 23, 1874, Mr. Geo. H. Warner to Mrs. Talula Moore.

By Rev. H. H. Parks, March 25, 1874, in Savannah, Ga., Thos. F. Thompson to Miss Maggie Meldrim.

By Rev. H. H. Parks, March 26, 1874, in Savannah, Henry H. Gleason to Miss Louise Craft.

March 3d, 1874, by Rev. W. M. Motly, at the residence of W. C. Hart, Lee county, Ala., Mr. J. H. Lockhart to Miss Ella McT. Hurt.

March 19th, 1874, Dr. N. Gallie Coleman to Mrs. Mattie Forgy, daughter of Henry Fuller, both of Laurens county, S. C., by Rev. J. B. Traywick.

In Brooksville, Ga., by Rev. J. D. Rogers, Dr. Bethel McMulllen, of Old Tampa, Hillsboro county, Fla., to Miss N. H. Taylor, of the former place.

On the 22d January 1874, at the residence of the bride's father, in St. Louis, Mo., by Rev. L. M. Lewis, Mr. J. S. Thrasher, of Atlanta, Ga., to Miss M. Callie Collier.

Issue of April 15, 1874

Near Twiggsville, Twiggs county, Ga., March 12th, 1874, by John S. Evans, Esq., Mr. H.. J. Newby to Miss Willie Hunter, all of Twiggs county, Ga.

By Rev. A. J. Dempsey, March 10th, 1874, Mr. J. E. Nobell to Miss R. J. Caldwell, both of East Point, Ga.

By Rev. A. J. Dempsey, April 5th, 1874, Mr. A. E. Harrison to Miss Elizabeth Ganesis, both of Clayton county, Ga.

April 2d, 1874, by Rev. A. J. Cauthen, J. M. Young to Miss E. V. Cromer, of Abbeville, S. C.

On the 19th of Feb., by Rev. J. D. Rogers, at the residence of the bride's father, Spring Hill, Fla., Sheldon Stringer, M. D., of Brooksville, Fla., to Miss Mettie Lykes.

On the 12th of March, 1874, by Rev. J. D. Rogers, at the residence of Judge A. Mayo, Mr. H. N. Morton, of Crystal River, to Miss Emma E. Blain, all of Hernando county, Fla.

Issue of April 22, 1874

April 2d, 1874, by Rev. A. J. Cauthen, Mr. J. M. Young to Miss E. N. Cromer, of Abbeville county, S. C.

On the 8th of April 1874, by Rev. Joel Allen, Mr. James R. Watson to Miss Flora E. Lane, all of Marion county, S. C.

On April 2d 1874, by Rev. W. J. Green, Mr. W. G. Higgs, of Liverpool, Eng., to Miss Mattie A. Richards, of St. Marys, Ga.

On Tuesday night, April 14, 1874, by Rev. Thomas J. Adams, Mr. Gainham G. Edmond, son of Washington, to Miss Cattin Bell, Bell, of Crawfordville, Ga.

Issue of April 29, 1874

At Vining's, Ga., Feb. 26th, 1874, by Rev. Geo. W. Yarbrough, Samuel S. Yarbrough to Miss Ella V. Pace.

SOUTHERN CHRISTIAN ADVOCATE MARRIAGE NOTICES 1867-1878

Issue of May 6, 1874

On the 23rd April, 1874, in Live Oak, Fla., by Rev. T. S. Tyner, Mr. C. Nichols to Miss Nannie Ramsey, all of Gainesville, Fla. The N. O. *Advocate* please copy.

April 19th, by Rev. W. H. Hunt, Mr. James M. Allerson, near Live Oak, to Miss Ardella A. J. Williams, of Welborn, all of Suwannee county, Fla.

On April 16, by Rev. G. W. Hardaway, Mr. Wm. G. Hawkins, to Miss Sarah E. Tatum, all of Baldwin county, Ga.

By Rev. John Inabinet, on 30th April, Mr. Joel J. Hooker to Miss Belinsa C. Robinson, all of Orangeburg county, S. C.

Issue of May 13, 1874

By Rev. F. B. Davies, in Decatur, Ga., April 16th, 1874, Mr. J. J. Bowins, of Atlanta, Ga., and Miss Sarah Marshall, of Decatur, Ga.

On the 30th of April, at the residence of Mr. Henry Kemp's, by Rev. W. M. Watts, Mr. Geo. W. Turner to Miss Julia Allgood[?], all of Brooks county, Ga.

By J. W. Yarbrough, April 29th, 1874, A. H. Mallory to Miss Sudie A. Turnell.

By Rev. John Calvin Johnston, in Madison, Morgan county, Ga., on 30th April, 1874, Mr. Newton E. Rhodes, of Athens, Ga., to Miss Emma V. Bearden, of the former place.

In Columbia county, Ga., May 3d, 1874, by Rev. D. Kelsey, Mr. J. A. Simmons to Miss Lavinia Crawford.

By Rev. John W. McRoy, May 6th, 1874, Benjamin D. Moss, of Orangeburg, S. C., to Miss Mary E. Riley, of Barnwell county, S. C.

By Rev. Geo. G. N. MacDonell, April 23d, 1874, in Fernandina, Florida, Mr. Bernard M. Davis to Miss Ada Jane, eldest daughter of the late Col. George Dewson, of Fernandina, Fla.

Issue of May 20, 1874

May 5th, 1874, by Rev. B. L. Hume, Dr. C. P. Brown to Miss Mary E. Tomlin, all of Morgan county, Ga.

In Taylor county, Ga., by Rev. E. J. Rents, Mark A. Perry, Esq., to Miss Nancy McCants, May 10th, 1874.

In Columbia, S. C., May 6, 1874, by Rev. W. D. Kirkland, Mr. Wm. George, of Charleston, S. C., to Miss Sallie Foster, of St. Augustine, Fla.

May 6th, 1874, by Rev. W. S. Baker, Rev. J. J. Methvin, of Cleveland, to Miss E. L. Beall, of Irwinton, Ga.

Issue of May 27, 1874

In Opelika, Ala., on the morning of the 21st inst., by Rev. E. L. Lovelace, at the residence of the bride's mother, Mr. Harry C. Brown, of Talbotton, Ga. to Miss Susie A. Dowdell, of Opelika, daughter of the late Hon. James F. Dowdell.

Issue of June 3, 1874

In Talbotton, Ga., May 20th, 1874, by Rev. R. W. Dixon, Thomas N. Beall to Miss Jennie Worrill, daughter of Hon. E. H. Worrill, all of Talbotton, Ga.

In Thomasville, Ga., on May 21st, 1874, Mr. Lerbrus Dekle to Miss Mollie R. Cook.

May 21st, 1874, by Rev. J. J. Tooke, Mr. P. M. Adams to Miss Julia A. Morris, all of Reynolds, Taylor county, Ga.

By Rev. Isaac Munden, April 22d, 1874, Mr. Bunyan M. Hill of South Carolina, to Miss Eliza Ann M. Huggins, of Alachua county, Fla.

In Opelika, Ala., on the morning of the 14th May by Rev. E. L. Lovelace, at the residence of the bride's mother, Mr. Harry C. Brown, of Talbotton, Ga. to Miss Susie A. Dowdell, of Opelika, daughter of the late Hon. James F. Dowdell.

In Warren county, Ga., by Rev. Wesley F. Smith, May 13th, 1874, Mr. John C. Lowe to Miss Mattie V. Rogers, all of Warren county, Ga.

In Cuthbert, Ga., May 7th, 1874, by Rev. B. F. Breedlove, Mr. J. W. Bell to Miss F. L. Stewart.

On the 5th May, 1874, near Wrightsboro, Ga., by Rev. W. T. Hamilton, Mr. Albert L. Pearre to Miss E. C. Cody, all of McDuffie county, Ga.

On the 21st of May, 1874, by Rev. E. S. Tyner, Mr. N. D. Hughey to Miss Julia A. Loper, all of Madison county, Fla.

Issue of June 10, 1874

At Stockton, Ga., May 31st, 1874, by Rev. J. w. Talley, Rev. Nathan Talley to Miss Rachel Vanguson, all of that place.

By Rev. Sanford Leak, May 14th, 1874, Mr. Jasper Shell of Paulding county, Ga., to Miss Henrietta Bryce, of Carroll county, Ga.

May 31st, 1874, by Elder W. T. Godard, Mr. William A. King, of Brooks county, Ga., to Miss M. A. C. Grubbs, of Spalding county, Ga.

In Gadsden county, Fla., May 26th, 1874, by Rev. R. L. Honiker, Henry H. Spear to Miss Dee MacMillan.

Near Floyd Springs, Ga., May 21st, 1874, by Rev. W. H. Hickey, Mr. Joseph P. Phipps to Miss Annie Griffith, the former of Gordon county, and the latter of Floyd county, Ga.

At Waccamaw Lake, N. C., April 20th, 1874, by Rev. James W. Dickson, Mr. P. W. Fanning, of Wilmington, N. C., to miss Emily J. Moore, late of Colleton, S. C.

By Rev. Isaac Munden, May 19th, 1874, at the parsonage in Newnansville, Fla., Mr. J. T. Stokes, to Miss L. R. Laws.

By Rev. N. D. Morehouse, at the parsonage in Whitesville, on 24th May 1874, David Spier to Miss Julia Blitch, all of Effingham county, Ga.

On 27th May, 1874, by Rev. R. A. Eakes, Mr. Thomas A. Gramling, of Atlanta, Ga., to Miss Carrie O. Kellogg, of Cumming, Ga.

May 28th, 1874, by Rev. R. W. Bigham, in Gordon county, Ga., Rev. D. J. Weems of the North Georgia Conference, to Miss Lula L. Burch.

In St. Paul's Methodist Church, Atlanta, Ga., May 28th, 1874, by the pastor, Rev. W. P. Pledger, Mr. W. H. Clowe to Miss Jennie Bolin, all of Atlanta, Ga.

In St. Paul's Methodist Church, Atlanta, Ga., May 28th, 1874, by Rev. W. P. Pledger, Mr. H. H. Herrington, of Macon, Ga., to Miss Katie Wiker, of Atlanta, Ga.

Issue of June 17, 1874

On the 24th May, 1874, by Rev. J. D. Bunnels, in Banks county, Ga., Mr. Harwell P. Quillian to Miss Mary E. Oliver.

In Lincoln county, Ga., Mary 28th, by Rev. D. Kelsey, Dr. George M. Lane to Miss Mary Frances Dunn, eldest daughter of the late Rev. John S. Dunn.

June 3d 1874, in Polk county, Ga., by Rev. James W. Trawick, Wm. J. Waddy of Greenville, Ga., to Miss Mollie H. Ledbetter, daughter of Rev. L. L. Ledbetter, deceased.

Issue of July 1, 1874

On the 17th June by Rev. John W. Heidt, Rev. J. Sidney Bryan, of the North Georgia Conference, to Miss Ella Pope, daughter of Cadesman Pope, Esq., of Pike county, Ga.

By Rev. John Inabnit, on the 21st of June 1874, Capt. J. C. J. Wannamaker, of Lexington county, to Miss Minerva A. Robinson, of Orangeburg county, S. C.

On the 31st May 1874, at the residence of W. F. Boyd, Esq., by Rev. J. Claudius Miller, Mr. Wade A. Crouch to Miss Mary E. Bodie, all of Edgefield county, S. C.

In Polk County, Ga., by Rev. J. B. Traywick, on the 3d of June, Mr. J. W. Wadley, of Greenville, Ga., to Miss Mary H. Ledbetter, daughter of the late Dr. L. L. Ledbetter of the North Georgia Conference.

On the 18th of June at Live Oak, Fla., by Rev. A. A. Robinson, Mr. Joseph G. Wagner to Miss Sallie K. White, of Live Oak, Fla.

By Rev. A. W. Williams on the 11th of June 1874, in Clarke county, Ga., Mr. James d. Cleaton, of Harmony Grove, Ga., to Miss Clara E. Lampkin.

Issue of July 8, 1874

By Rev. W. Hutto, on April 23d, Mr. Benj. Chandler to Miss Alice Huggins, all of Williamsburg, S. C.

In Macon, Ga., on the 11th of June 1874, by the Rev. J. O. Branch, Mr. W. H. Whitehead to Miss M. Eunice Thomson, daughter of Dr. M. S. Thomson, of Macon, Ga.,

By Rev. Geo. C. Leavel, June 24th 1874, in the Methodist Church, Ocala, Florida, Mr. C. H. White to Miss Aurora M. Crutchfield, all of Marion county, Florida.

Issue of July 15, 1874

May 28th, by Rev. J. E. Watson, Mr. Elijah T. Nun, son of e. J. and Sarah E. Nun, to Miss E. R. Daniel, daughter of Mr. J. J. and Harriet Daniel.

On the 2d July 1874, by Rev. E. S. Tyner, Mr. J. L. Williams to Miss Laura N. Smith, daughter of Mr. D. H. Smith, all of Madison county, Fla.

On the 5th of July 1874, by Rev. O. L. Smith, Mr. John E. Rosser to Mrs. Julia E. Foster, all of Covington, Ga.

In Columbus, Ga., July 2d, 1874, by Rev. R. W. Dixon, John Mehaffey to Miss Laura E. Ford, of Columbus, Ga.

June 28th 1874, by Rev. R. R. Johnson, Mr. C. M. Shields, of Henry county, To Miss J. N. Porter, of Clayton county. GA.

May 28th, 1874, in Talbotton, by Rev. L. B. Payne, Mr. U. C. Tignor, of Talbot county, to Miss I. C. Kaigler, of Talbotton.

Issue of July 22, 1874

July 2d 1874, at Midway, by Rev. W. R. Branham, Mr. Thos. Hyer to Miss Laura Clarke.

On July 2d 1874, by Rev. W. R. Branham, Professor I. S. Hopkins to Miss Mary R. Hinton, all of Oxford, Ga.

Issue of July 29, 1874

July 14, 1874, by Rev. T. W. Dyer, Rev. Henry D. Moore, President of the Alabama Conference Female College, at Tuskegee, to Miss Carrie M. Tait, daughter of Hon. Felix Tait, of Wilcox county, Ala.

In Louisville, Ga., July 15, 1874, by Rev. H. D. Murphy, Judge Wm. H. Watkins to Mrs. E. A. Roberson.

Issue of August 5, 1874

July 16th 1874, by Rev. James Spence, L. A. H. Tippins, of Tatnall county, Ga., to Miss Ella E. Lanier, of Liberty county, Ga.

By Rev. C. C. Davis, at Fairbourn, Ga., Mr. James M. Milles, of Atlanta, Ga., to Miss Mary E. Chambers, youngest daughter of Rev. Joseph Chambers, of the North Georgia Conference.

In Cartersville, Ga., on the 29th of July 1874, by Rev. L. J. Davies, Mr. John S. Hollinshead, of Bartow county, Ga., to Miss Mary M. Parrott, daughter of the late Judge Jr. Parrott, of Cartersville, Ga.

Issue of August 12, 1874

On the 15th July, by Rev. J. S. Jordan, Mr. E. J. Coleman of Emanuel county, to Miss Hattie Lake, of Laurens county, Ga.

July 23d 1874, by Rev. Luther M. Smith, D. D., Mr. N. T. Burks, of Henderson, Texas, to Miss Mary Palmer, of Oxford, Ga.

By Rev. J. L. Lupo, on the 21st of July 1874, Dr. Thos. S. Humphries to Miss Attha O. Hollenshead, both of Lincoln county, Ga.

Issue of August 19, 1874

By Rev. J. H. B. McRae, June 21st 1874, Mr. W. C. Watson to Miss S. E. Greaves, of Brooks county, Ga.

By Rev. J. H. B. McRae, July 30th 1874, Mr. J. W. Allen to Miss N. Austin, all of Brooks county, Ga.

In Dalton, Ga., July 29th 1874 by Rev. Jno. T. Norris, Mr. C. E. Lucky of Knoxville, Tenn., to Miss Julia O. Sims, of Dalton, Ga.

At the parsonage, Mary 30th, 1874, by Rev. R. M. Lockwood, Octavius Hopkins to Mary Kele, daughter of Dr. J. Holmes, all of Darien, Ga.

At the M. E. Church on "The Ridge" on Sunday evening, July 26th 1874, by Rev. R. M. Lockwood, Davis S. Sinclair, Esq., to Miss Emma C. Bealer, both of Darien.

At the residence of Mr. Perry Peacock, by Squire Clagorn, of Schley county, Ga., Mr. Mathew R. Wood, of Washington county, Ga., to Miss Mollie D. Scarboro, of Schley county, Ga.

Issue of August 26, 1874

At Centerville, Ga., on the 12th May 1874, by Rev. G. H. Mallette, assisted by Rev. S. S. Moore, Mr. John W. Beaton to Mrs. Jane E. Sparks, consort of the late Rev. J. G.Sparks, of the Alabama Conference.

Issue of September 2, 1874

On the 20th Aug., 1874, by Rev. Wm. M. Mood, Mr. David White to Miss Melissa N. McMillan, all of Anderson, South Carolina.

In Branchville, S. C., Aug. 9th 1874, by Rev. D. J. Simmons, Mr. W. H. Easterlin to Miss Hattie A. Howell.

Aug. 18th 1874, at the lower Sulphur Springs, Suwanee county, Fla., by the Rev. A. A. Robinson, Judge Henry C. Rippey to Mrs. Sarah C. Mitchell.

In Quincy, Fla., Aug. 11th 1874, by Rev. H. M. Partridge, Mr. Geo. Wilder, of Galveston, Texas, to Miss Bettie Keenan, of Quincy.

In Gadsden county, Fla., Aug. 19th 1874, by Rev. H. E. Partridge, Rev. Jno. M. Bridges, of the Florida Conference, to Mrs. Martha A. Hines, of Gadsden county, Fla.

In Columbus, Ga., Aug. 4th 1874, by Rev. E. H. McGehee, Mr. T. E. Harris to Miss Clara C. McGehee, daughter of Rev. J. B. McGehee, P. E., of the Columbus District.

By Rev. A. C. Mixon, July 16th 1874, Mr. A. J. Belcher to Miss Leonora G. Nix, all of Newton county, Ga.

By Rev. A. C. Mixon, August 8th 1874, Mr. Wm. B. O. Eason to Miss Louisa Rakestraw, all of Newton county, Ga.

Issue of September 9, 1874

Sept. 1st 1874, at the residence of Rev. J. A. Palmer, by Rev. Dr. Sappington, Wm. G. Cotton to Mrs. Sarah Sherman, all of Troup county, Ga.

By Rev. J. S. Beasley, Sept. 2d, 1874, Mr. H. Z. Graham to Miss Lizzie Whitehead, all of Williamsburg county, S. C.

Issue of September 23, 1874

On September 13, 1874, at Grace Church, in White county, Ga., by Rev. Robt. P. Martin, Mr. E. P. Edge to Miss A. D. Marshall, all of White county.

East Macon, on the 17th inst., by Rev. J. W. Burke, Mr. John J. Poole to Miss H. Laura Yearty.

By Rev. Geo. C. Leavell, Thursday, September 3d, 1874, Dr. Patrick Todd to Mrs. Mary E. Brown, all of Marion county, Florida.

By Rev. W. C. Dunlap, on 3d of Sept., 1874, Mr. E. G. Harris, of Hampton, Ga., to Miss Mary Springer, of Carroll county, Ga.

In Houston county, Ga., on the 1st Sept., 1874, by Rev. S. S. Sweet, Joseph H. Shinholser, Esq., of Bibb county, Ga., to Miss Clifford N. Haywood, of Houston county, Ga.

August 27th 1874, by Rev. R. R. Johnson, Mr. Sidney H. Smith, of Henry county, GA., to Miss Susan A. Andrew, of Newton county, Ga.

On the 6th Sept 1874, by Rev. J. Rufus Felder, Mr. Daniel D. Bateman to Miss Mary C. Birch, daughter of the late John L. Birch, all of Perry, Houston county, Ga.

Near Ringgold, Ga., on the 2d of September 1874, by Rev. J. B. McFarland, Mr. Wm. Martin to Miss Mary McSpadden, all of Catoosa county.

By Rev. J. J. Harris, August 31st 1874, Mr. R. H. Wade of Tehuacana, Limestone county, Texas, to Miss A. A. Walker, of Pickens county, Ga.

At Yemassee, S. C., August 13th, by Rev. W. P. Mouzon, Mr. John P. Sellers to Mrs. Henrietta M. Jamison.

In Forsyth, Ga., September 15, 1874, by Rev. D. D. Cox, Mr. J. W. Banks of Forsyth, to Miss Ella K. Woodruff, of Columbus, Ga.

On the 10th September 1874, by Rev. D. D. Dantzler, Mr. Chas. B. Lattimore, of Shelby, N. C., to Miss Martha Jane Jackson, of York county, S. C.

Issue of September 30, 1874

On the 28th of July 1874, by Rev. W. J. Green, Mr. J. a. Peoples, of Camden county l,GA., to Miss Mary A. Mann, of St. Mary's, Ga.

On Sept. 10th 1874, by Rev. W. J. Green, Mr. Lucien M. Vocelle, to Miss Jane E. Vance of St. Mary's, Ga.

On the 2d Sept. 1875, in Cassville, Ga., by the Rev. Hezekiah Best, Mr. A. S. Hough, of Madison, Ga., to Miss Mary F. Brown, daughter of the late Col. Geo. W. Brown, of the former place.

Issue of October 7, 1874

Sept. 29, 1874, in Wilkes county, Ga., by Rev. Thos. H. Gibson, Mr. George W. Florence to Miss Lizzie Cooper.

Sept. 2d, 1874, by Rev. J. L. Shuford, Rev. Hugh W. Whitaker, of the South Carolina Conference, to Miss Carrie Sleigh, of Newbury county, S. C.

By Rev, E. S. Tyner, of the evening Sept. 24, 1874, Mr. A. H. McCardel, of Boston, Ga., to Miss Ella N. Tooke, of Madison county, Fla.

Issue of October 14, 1874

On the 17th of Sept. 1874, at Mountville, Ga., by Rev. Jno. M. Bowden, Mr. James A. Cox, to Miss Ella V. Fischer, all of Troup county, Ga.

On the 1st of Oct., 1874, by Rev. Geo. K. Quillian, Mr. Robert F. Quillian to Miss India J. Chapman, both of Hall county, Ga.

On the 4th of October 1874, by Rev. Dr. Leonard, Mr. Emory Lassiter to Miss Henrietta McNair, both of Decatur county, Ga.

In Marietta, Ga., Oct. 1st, 1874, by Rev. W. F. Glenn, Dr. J. A. Griffith to Miss Lita Goss.

On the 1st Oct 1875, by Rev. John Inabinet, Mr. J. P. Walsh to Miss Admira R. Riley, all of Orangeburg, S. C.

In St. Louis, Mo., Sept. 8th 1874, by Rev. R. P. Farris, D. D., F. Thornton Gamewell, to Belle G. Cooper, both formerly of Camden, S. C.

In Warren county, Ga., Oct. 6th 1874, by Rev. Wesley F. Smith, Mr. Wm. C. Wright to Miss Fannie E. Gresham, of Warren.

In Greenville county, S. C., Sept. 10th 1874, by Rev. J. Finger, Mr. J. W. McCullough to Miss Janie K. Sullivan.

Issue of October 21, 1874

Oct 7th 1874, by Rev. E. S. Tyner, Mr. James M. Grover to Miss Kate M. Wyche, all of Madison county, Fla.

By Rev. E. S. Tyner, Oct. 7th 1874, Mr. Geo. T. Redd to Miss Lizzie Harrington, all of Madison county, Fla.

By the Rev. E. S. Tyner, Oct. 8th 1874, Mr. P. J. Poppel to Miss E. A. Seaver, of Madison county, Fla.

On the 14th Oct., 1874, by Rev. T. H. Timmons, Mr. Frank W. Eberhart to Miss Mattie T. Bridges, daughter of Capt. N. C. Bridges, all of Coweta county, Ga.

On the 6th October 1874, by Rev. S. J. Bethea, Mr. R. L. Lame to Miss R. C. Gaddy, all of Marion county, S. C.

On the 7th October by Rev. Jas. S. Hunnicutt, Mr. Lewis C. Grady to Miss Fannie Carmichael, daughter of Robt. Carmichael, all of Coweta county, Ga.

On the 11th October 1874 by Rev. J. J. Morgan, Mr. Thos. A. Hagin to Miss Lizzie Graham, all of Bulloch county, Ga.

By Rev. L. P. Neese, on the 8th October 1874, Mr. Thomas More to Miss Alice V. Sims, both of Fulton county, Ga.

Issue of October 28, 1874

By Rev. F. A. Branch, on the 20th of October, Mr. Lewis A. Rumph to Miss Jennie R. Moore, eldest daughter of Mr. Benning Moore, all of Houston county, Ga.

On the 20th October, by Rev. F. A. Branch, Mr. Samuel H. Rumph to Miss Clara E. Moore, youngest daughter of Mr. Benning Moore, all of Houston county, Ga.

In Athens, Ga., Oct. 15, 1874, by Rev. P. A. Heard, Rev. Jos. R. Ivie to Miss Lizzie Wright.

By Rev. Wm. Hutto, Oct. 1, 1874, Mr. Thomas A. Burress to Miss Nancy Cribb, all of Williamsburg, S. C.

By Rev. C. A. Mitchell, Oct. 15, 1874, Mr. Isaac H. Askin of Monroe county, Ga., to Mrs. M. Mattie Hogan, of Upson county, Ga.

By Rev. J. P. Wardlaw, in Valdosta, Ga., Sept. 2d, 1874, Miss Alice Cashon to Mr. C. M. Williams, of Tatnall county.

By Rev. J. P. Wardlaw, in Valdosta, Ga., October 7th 1874, Miss Anna S. Howell to Mr. Cowper L. Shelton.

Sept. 17, 1874, in Charleston county, S. C., by Rev. L. Cannon, Mr. E. A. Droze to Miss Alice Driggers.

October 5th, 1874, in Charleston county, S. C., by Rev. L. Cannon, Mr. John Hollin to Miss Susan Grooms.

Near Luthersville, on the 15th Oct., 1874, by Rev. W. J. Cotter, Mr. J. M. Powledge, to Miss Mollie Fuller, daughter of J. W. Fuller, Esq.

Issue of November 4, 1874

In Roswell, Ga., Oct. 21, 1874, by Rev. R. S. Paden, Sanders C. Webb, of Coweta county, Ga., to Miss Matilda C. Coker, of Roswell, Ga.

Oct. 4, 1874, by Rev. T. G. Herbert, Rev. D. D. Dantzler, of the South Carolina Conference, to Miss Fanny Goggans, daughter of Daniel Goggans, Esq., of Newberry county, S. C.

On 15th October, 1874, by Rev. H. Tyler, Prof. S. M. Bobo to Mrs. Mary E. Webb, all of Hartwell, Ga.

Oct. 22, 1874, by Rev. H. Tyler, Mr. A. J. Palmer to Miss Mary E. Palmer, all of Anderson county, S. C.

By Rev. J. W. Stipe, Oct. 20th, 1874, Mr. L. W. Harris, of Coweta county, Ga., to Miss R. J. Shackelford, of Heard county, Ga.

Oct. 22d, 1874, in Wilkes county, Ga., by Rev. Thos. H. Gibson, Mr. B. Frank Powell, to Miss C. A. Prather.

Oct. 7, 1874, by Rev. W. P. Lovejoy, Mr. J. T. LaFavor to Miss Elma Gibson.

Oct. 22d, 1874, by Rev. W. P. Lovejoy, Mr. J. T. Callaway, of Albany, Ga., to Miss Anna Adams, of Eatonton, Ga..

Oct. 22d, 1874, by Rev. W. P. Lovejoy, Mr. W. G. Little to Miss Carrie Adams, of Eatonton, Ga.

At Gibson, Ga., Oct. 1st, by Rev. J. F. Mixon, Rev. J. W. Domingos, of the South Georgia Conference, to Miss H. A. Lassiter, formerly of Warren county, Ga.

Near Valdosta, Lowndes county, by Rev. J. P. Wardlaw, on the 21st of October, Mr. Wm. Zeigler to Miss Columbia Shelton.

By Rev. Wm. Seymour, Oct. 18, 1874, Mr. David L. Hancock to Miss Lucinda C. Finch, all of Jackson county, Ga.

In Bartow county, Ga., on the 27th of October, by Rev. L. J. Davies, Hon. E. C. Palmer, of St. Paul, Minnesota, to Mrs. C. A. Rowland, daughter of Dr. Hollinshed, of Fort Valley, Ga.

On the 27th October, in Culloden, Ga., by Rev. B. J. Johnson, Mr. Chas. H. Redding, of Clinton, Ga., to miss Clara E. Jackson, daughter of Wilkins W. Jackson, of Culloden, Ga.

On the 28th October, 1874, by Rev. W. W. Mood, Mr. Wm. C. Scott to Miss Ida Scott, all of Anderson, S. C.

By Rev. Jas. W. Trawick, in Polk county, Ga., Oct. 27th, 1874, Mr. J. E. Good, of Cartersville, Ga., to Miss Fannie Wood.

By Rev. R. W. Bingham, Oct. 28, 1874, at the residence of Col. H. Washburn, Whitefield county, Ga., Mr. W. C. Wade, of Scriven, to Miss Hattie F. Washburn.

Issue of November 11, 1874

In Russell county, Ala., Oct. 29th, 1874, by Rev. J. B. McGehee, Captain Jourdan H. Mitchell, to Miss Mary Lou Upshaw.

In Griffin, Ga., Oct. 29th, 1874, by Rev. Jno. W. Heidt, Col. Wm. J. Anderson, of Fort Valley, to Miss Celia Goodrich, of the former place.

On the 1st of November, 1874, by Rev. J. W. Domingos, Mr. Green B. Brown to Miss Susan E. Doolittle, both of Washington county, Ga.

On the 15th of Oct. 1874, by Rev. W. F. Robison, Mr. L. W. Malsby of Monroe county, Ga., to Miss Sarah K. McMurray, of Houston county.

On the 21st Oct., 1874, by Rev. R. W. Lovett, Rev. Edwin J. Burch, of the South Georgia Conference, to Miss Lula J. Roberts, daughter of Elijah Roberts, of Scriven county, Georgia.

In Talbotton, Ga., Oct. 22d, 1874, by Rev. R. W. Dixon, Walter P. Watts to Miss Mittie Beall, of Talbotton, Ga.

On the 15th Oct., 1874, by Rev. W. A. Florence, Mr. John W. Bacon, of Lexington, Ga., to Mrs. Carrie E. Thompson, of Oxford, Ga.

On 29th October 1874, by Rev. E. S. Tyner, Mr. Herman Bodenstein to Miss Susan Ganey, all of Madison county, Fla.

On the 29th October 1874, by Rev. J. W. Domingos, Mr. George W. Tates, of Edinburg, Scotland, to Miss Christiana Webster, of Washington county, Georgia.

By Rev. J. B. Payne on the 29th of Oct., 1874, Mr. Wylie Redding of Pike county, GA., to Miss Sally E. White, of upson county, Ga.

By Rev. J. Lewis, Jr., Athens, Ga., Nov. 3d, 1874, Mr. Bourke Spalding to Miss Ella P. Barrow.

Issue of November 25, 1874

On the 19th Oct., 1874, Mr. N. B. Ousley to Miss Lizzie A. Holt, both of Bibb county, Ga.

Oct. 14th, 1874, by Rev. P. M. Ryburn, Mr. Luther S. Turner to Miss Susie B. McKinley, all of West Point, Ga.

On 11th Nov., by Rev. W. M. Lockwood, at No. 1. M. & B. R. R., Mr. George S. Washington to Mrs. Mancy S. Myers, daughter of Rev. W. H. Thomas, of the South Georgia Conference.

Nov. 12th, 1874, at the residence of Mr. R. A. Gowman, by the Rev. A. Nettles, Mr. J. D. Compton, of Charleston, S. C., to Miss Sue R. Bowman, of Orangeburg county, S. C.

In Crawford county, Ga., Nov. 4th, 1874, by Rev. E. J. Rentz, John H. Neisler, of Taylor county, Ga., to Miss Mary A. Walker.

In Butler, Ga., Nov. 10th, 1874, by Rev. E. J. Rentz, E. W. Jeter to Miss Mollie J. Walden.

Oct. 22, at the residence of Col. A. P. Mooty, West Point, Ga., by Rev. P. M. Ryburn, Mr. A. C. Miller to Miss Nora M. Taylor, of Tallapoosa county, Ala.

Nov. 8, at the residence of Mr. J. S. Baker, West Point, Ga., by Rev. P. M. Ryburn, Mr. Thos. J. Eady to Miss Fannie Baker, both of West Point, Ga.

On the 13th Oct., 1874, by Rev. J. J. Harris, Dr. A. H. Stearns, of Jasper, to Miss Rosalie E. Stephens, of Talking Rock.

By Rev. J. J. Harris, on the 14th of Oct., near Walesca, Cherokee county, Ga., James H. Stone, of Bartow county, Ga., to Miss Julia Word, of Cartersville, Ga.

At the Methodist Church in Wadesboro, N. C., Oct. 27th, 1874, by Rev. O. J. Brent, Mr. James Plunkett, to Miss Emma L. Coppedge.

On the 11th Nov., 1874, by Rev. E. S. Tyner, Mr. Edward M. Glass, of Jacksonville, Fla., to Miss Missouri A. Rowe, of Madison county, Fla.

Oct. 24th, 1874, by Rev. J. N. Myers, at the residence of Rev. C. C. Morgan, Mr. Bascom Williams of Hall county, Ga., to Miss H. P. Morgan, of Forsyth county, Ga.

Nov. 12th, 1874, by Rev. D. J. Weems, Mr. N. A. Tensley, of Dalton, Ga., to Miss Mary E. Berry, of Murray county, Ga.

Nov. 12th, 1874, in Edgewood church, by Rev. J. R. Mayson, Mr. Jesse Y. Carroll to Miss Annie Bessent, only daughter of Mrs. P. G. Bessent, all of Atlanta, Ga.

Near Cave Spring, Ga., Nov. 15th, 1874, by Rev. B. B. Quillian, Mr. J. W. Milligan to Miss Eva Fain.

In Fort Valley, Ga., Nov. 11th, 1874, by Rev. T. B. Russell, Mr. George D. Anderson to Miss Anna E. Houser.

Nov. 1st, 1874, by Rev. W. W. Wadsworth, in Jasper county, Ga., Rev. Jno. H. Mashburn, of the North Georgia Conference, to Miss Josie Holloway.

Nov. 12th, 1874, by Rev. W. W. Wadsworth, Mr. Alex. G. McDonald to Miss Balzona Chambers, all of Jasper county, Ga.

By Rev. John Calvin Johnson, Nov. 4th, 1874, Mr. William T. Cochran to Mrs. Martha W. Wilkins, both of Oglethorpe county, Ga.

By Rev. John Calvin Johnson, Nov. 5th, 1874, Mr. Doctor M. Wilson to Miss Susan M. Royal, all of Athens, Ga.

In Thomas county, Ga., Oct. 15th, 1874, Mr. L. H. Player to Miss Susan S. Reynolds.

In Thomasville, Ga., Oct. 27th, 1874, by Rev. E. H. McGehee, Rev. Jno. D. Clark, of Randolph county, Ga., to Miss Sarah F. McKinnon.

In Thomas county, Ga., Nov. 5th, 1874, by Rev. E. H. McGehee, Mr. Geo. W. Wood to Mrs. Martha A. Tate.

On Nov. 4th, 1874, by Rev. J. W. Glenn, Mr. James Billingslea, of Greensboro, Ga., to Mrs. Mattie A. Tippin, of Uniontown, Ala.

On Nov. 5th, 1874, by Rev. J. W. Glenn, Mr. Frank W. Wimberly to Miss Bettie B. Jones, all of Uniontown, Ala.

By Rev. L. P. Neese, Nov. 12th, 1874, D. F. Neese to Miss Avie A. Mansell, all of Milton county, Ga.

On 10th Nov., 1874, by Rev. C. A. Conaway, Mr. J. F. H. Jackson, of Clarke county, Ga., to Miss Mattie A. Jarrell, of Oglethorpe county, Ga.

On Nov. 13th, 1874, by Rev. C. A. Conaway, Mr. Henry Myer to Miss Mary E. Fleeman, all of Oglethorpe county, Ga.

In Lawtonville, Beaufort county, S. C., Nov. 4th, 1874, by Rev. L. C. Loyal, William Cuyler Johnston, Jr., to Laura Catharine, eldest daughter of William M. Oneal, Esq., all of the above place.

In Langley, Aiken county, S. C., Nov. 12th, 1874, by Rev. L. C. Loyal, Rev. William Richard Puckett to Georgia Emma Weatherbee, all of the above place.

At Albany, Ga., Nov. 11th, 1874, by Rev. George J. Griffiths, William B. Freeman, to Miss Eliza Patterson, both of Dougherty county, Ga.

At Albany, Ga., Nov. 11th, 1874, by Rev. George J. Griffiths, David Woodin to Mrs. Susanna Freeman, both of Dougherty county, Ga.

On the 5th Nov. 1874, by Rev. Dr. Leonard, at the residence of Mr. Alexander Pope, Mr. Charles F. Logue to Miss Mary F. Pope, of Decatur county, Ga.

Nov. 12, 1874, by Rev. Jas. O. Branch, at the residence of the bride's mother, Macon ,Ga., Rev. Robert L. Honiker, of the South Georgia Conference, to Miss Mary Lelia Dougherty.

Nov. 5th, 1874, in Wilkes county, Ga., by Rev. T. H. Gibson, Mr. E. S. Carlyon to Miss Nora E. Bradley.

Nov. 5th, 1874, by Rev. David Roberts, Mr. J. J. Ritter to Miss H. H. Roberts, youngest daughter of the officiating minister, all of Jefferson county, Fla.

In Branchville, S. C., Nov. 8th, 1874, by Rev. D. J. Simmons, Mr. Angus M. Haton to Miss Maggie M. Reeves.

Nov. 18th, 1874, by Rev. T. P. Cleveland, Mr. J. Fletcher Colbert, of Madison county, Ga., to Miss Minnie L. Arnold, of Coweta county, Ga.

In Roswell, Ga., Nov. 12th, 1874, by Rev. R. S. Paden, Mr. James A. South, to Miss Mary E. Coker, all of Roswell, Ga.

Near Marietta, Ga., Nov. 2d, 1874, by Rev. William A. Parks, Mr. R. B. Garwood, of Florida, to Miss Fannie A. Sewell, daughter of Rev. Isaac Sewell.

Issue of December 2, 1874

Nov. 5th, 1874, by Rev. Thomas J. Adams, Mr. Thomas J. Stephens to Miss Ida Johnson, both of Crawfordville, Ga.

Nov. 8th, 1874, by Rev. Thomas J. Adams, Mr. John H. Stone to Miss Anna R. Lewis, both of Baytown, Ga.

Nov. 18, 1874, by Rev. Thomas J. Adams, Mr. Edmund H. Ogletree to Miss Lucy Ann Moore, both of Taliaferro county, Ga; also Mr. Wm. Cary to Miss Martha E. Moore, the former of Wilkes county, Ga.

Nov. 19, 1874, by Rev. Thomas J. Adams, Mr. Moses Jones to Miss Sallie E. Fielding, the former of Lincoln county, and the latter of Crawfordville, Ga.

Nov. 26, 1874, at the residence of Judge J. N. Burkett, by Rev. C. J. Toole, Mr. Henry D. Clark, of Bibb county, to Miss Hattie V. Mason, of Twiggs county, Ga.

By Rev. W. J. Cotter, in Meriwether county, Ga., on the 23d November, Mr. M. T. Justiss to Miss M. A. A. Chaffin.

On the 19th November, 1874, by Rev. Robert L. Wiggins, Dr. J. H. Williford to Miss E. C. Gunnells, all of Terrell county, Ga.

Nov. 12th, 1874, by Rev. W. W. Graham, Mr. J. M. McNamee of Opelika, to Miss Rowena Frazier, of Smith's Station, Ala.

In Thomasville, Ga., November 17th, 1874, by Rev. E. H. McGehee, Mr. Baker A. Bass to Miss Ella McKinnon.

Nov. 17, 1874, by Rev. H. W. Ledbetter, Mr. A. P. Birch, of Opelika, Ala., to Miss Julia B. Glenn, of Glennville, Ala.

By Rev. John Calvin Johnson, Nov. 19, 1874, Mr. Wm. P. Price to Miss Sallie Lowe, all of Clarke county, Ga.

On the 11th of Nov., 1874, by Rev. T. W. Tomkies, Mr. Henry D. Holland to Miss Cornelia H. Douglas, both of Jacksonville, Fla.

In Newnan, Ga., Nov. 10, 1874, by the Rev. James Stacy, Mr. B. F. Melson to Miss Ellen J. Pinson, daughter of J. J. Pinson, Esq.

Issue of December 9, 1874

On Thursday morning, 3d Dec., 1874, at the Wesleyan Female College, Macon, Ga., by Rev. E. H. Myers, D. D., Miss Fannie A., eldest daughter of the officiating minister, to S. W. Hitch, Esq., Solicitor of the Brunswick circuit, Ga.

Nov. 12th, 1874, by Rev. M. F. Malsby, Mr. J. L. G. Woods, of Henry county, Ga., to Miss S. V. Barnes, of Jasper county, Ga.

Nov. 3d, 1874, by Rev. J. W. Glenn, Mr. Isaac F. Farmer to Miss Bettie Stratford, all of Louisville, Ga.

In Louisville, Ga., Nov. 12th, 1874, by Rev. J. W. Glenn, Mr. Wm. C. D. Roberts, of Louisville, to Miss Alice E. Gobert, of Jefferson county, Ga.

Nov. 26th, 1874, by Rev. J. H. Zimmerman, Mr. Samuel R. Shuler to Miss Irene E. Moorer, all of Orangeburg county, S. C.

In Hancock county, Ga., by Rev. H. J. Ellis, Rev. J. W. Stipe, of the North Georgia Conference, to Miss Kittie Evans.

Oct. 8th, 1874, by Rev. M. F. Malsby, Mr. W. G. Kelley to Miss S. W. Shaw, all of Jasper county, Ga.

On 25th Nov., 1874, in Griffin, Ga., by Rev. John W. Heidt, Mr. James J. White to Miss Cleora Johnson, all of Griffin.

Issue of December 16, 1874

Dec. 3, 1874, by Rev. S. A. Weber, Miss Mollie Prince, of Williamston, to Mr. Lawrence Fouche, of Ninety-Six, S. C.

Dec. 6, 1874, by Rev. S. A. Weber, Miss Mettie West, of Greenville, to Mr. T. Cox, of Williamston, S. C.

In Attapulgus, Ga., November 24, 1874, by Rev. D. Leonard, Mr. Peter T. Stoner, of Texas, to Miss Mary R. Donalson, eldest daughter of Geo. W. Donalson.

On Nov. 18, 1874, by Rev. J. B. Dell, Mr. S. C. Jenkins to Miss Ophelia Herrington, all of Screven county, Ga.

Nov. 26, 1874, near Suspension, Ala., at the residence of Mrs. Fontaine, by Rev. D. M. Banks, Miss Clara F. McQueen to Mr. D. W. McIver, of Tuskegee, Ala.

In Bainbridge, Ga., Nov. 18, 1874, by Rev. R. L. Honiker, Geo. R. Mayton, to Miss Ollie S. Bates.

Near Bainbridge, Ga., Dec. 1st, by Rev. R. L. Honiker, Capt. Wm. P. Jackson, of the steamer Emily, to Miss Lunie A. Collins.

On the 4th of December, 1874, by Rev. W. H. Thomas, Mr. Wm. H. McDonald, to Miss Margaret E. Hilliard, both of Waycross, Ga.

On 23d of November, 1874, by Rev. W. H. Thomas, Mr. S. Allen to Miss L. Sumerall, both of Dupont, Ga.

Issue of December 23/30, 1874

In Irwinton, Ga., Nov. 26, 1874, by Rev. A. M. Williams, Mr. W. S. Van Landingham to Miss Fannie Rutland.

In Rome, Ga., Nov. 24, 1874, by Rev. W. M. Crumley, Mr. S. M. Cox, to Miss M. E. DeJournett.

In Chattooga county, Ga., Nov. 25th, 1874, by Rev. L. S. Munford, of Cartersville, Ga., to Miss M. H. Jones, youngest daughter of Hon. R. W. Jones, of Chattooga county, Ga.

November 19, by Rev. W. R. Branham, Adiel S. Florence to Miss Mary A. Snow, all of Social Circle, Ga.

In Oxford, Ga., December 1, 1874, by Rev. W. R. Branham, Mr. Menendas Johnson, of Key West, Fla., to Miss M. Ophelia Lovejoy, of the former place.

On Dec. 1st, 1874, by Rev. A. W. Rowland, Mr. Oscar P. Rowland, of Covington, Ga., to Miss Alice V. Shy, of Jasper county, Ga.

By Rev. George C. Leavel, on Thursday, Nov. 25, 1874, Mr. Samuel Pyles to Miss Mary D. Barnes, all of Marion county, Fla.

By Rev. George C. Leavel, Nov. 25, 1874, Dr. John A. Ferguson to Miss Maggie Agnew, all of Marion county, Fla.

In Troup county, Ga., Dec. 17th, at the residence of Mr. Jesse Haralson, Mr. Charles M. Sanders to Miss Exa Cofield.

Dec. 15, 1874, by Rev. R. R. Johnson, Mr. J. A. Johnson to Miss B. V. Smith, near Jonesboro, Ga.

Dec. 2, 1874, by Rev. B. L. Hume, Mr. John House to Miss Eliza Allen, all of Morgan county, Ga.

Dec. 12, by Rev. B. L. Hume, Mr. John W. Richardson, Sr., to Miss Amanda Allen.

Dec. 11, 1874, by Rev. B. L. Hume, Mr. John J. Perkins to Miss Anna Nunn.

Dec. 17, 1874, by Rev. B. L. Hume, Mr. C. W. Allen to Miss Emma J. Johnson, all of Morgan county, Ga.

Dec. 16, 1874, by Rev. W. W. Graham, Mr. C. N. Bickerstaff to Miss Emma J. Boykin, all of Russell county, Ala.

Nov. 12, 1874, by Rev. J. W. McRoy, Mr. J. D. Baxter, of Orangeburg county, to Miss V. R. Walker, of Barnwell county, S. C.

By Rev. John W. Bowden, on the 26th of November, 1874, Mr. Riley O. Turner to Miss Ludie F. Willingham, all of Meriwether county, Ga.

By Rev. John W. Bowden, on the 10th of December, 1874, near Mountville, Troup county, Ga., Mr. Wm. C. Cox to Miss Emma E. Davis.

By Rev. John W. Bowden, on the 17th of December, 1874, Mr. J. O. Norwood of Hogansville, to Miss Anna White, of LaGrange, Ga.

Dec. 3d, 1874, by Rev. A. J. Cauthen, Mr. Preston Allen to Miss Mary Lockhart, near Lowndesville, S. C.

By Rev. A. J. Cauthen, Dec. 10, 1874, Mr. E. Smith to Miss Sue Pressley, Lowndesville, S.C.

By Rev. A. J. Cauthen, Dec. 11, 1874, Mr. ---- Harkness to Miss Mollie Pettigrew, of Abbeville county, Lowndesville, S. C.

In Twiggs county, Ga., Nov. 29, 1874, by Rev. B. H. Sasnett, Col. Joseph D. Jones to Miss Hattie Wimberly, of Twiggs county, Ga.

In Jefferson county, Nov. 18, 1874, by Rev. J. W. Glenn, W. H. Baston to Miss Adella E. Denny.

By Rev. D. M. Banks, Dec., 8, Mr. H. J. Banks to Miss Sallie K. Tarver, both of Enon, Ala.

Nov. 23, 1874, by Rev. L. Cannon, Mr. William Campbell to Miss Elizabeth Driggers, all of Goose Creek parish, Charleston county, S. C.

In Troup co., Ga., Dec. 9th, by Rev. H. J. Ellis, Mr. J. R. Freeman, to Miss M. L. Haynes.

In Troup co., Ga., Dec. 10th, 1874, by Rev. H. J. Ellis, Mr. J. R. Wilson to Miss Alice A. Darden.

In Orangeburg county, S. C., Dec. 10, 1874, by Rev. A. R. Danner, Mr. Jos. A. Wolfe to Miss Frederick A. Geiger.

Dec. 6th, 1874, at the residence of Mrs. Mary Sullings, by Rev. L. W. Rast, Mr. Leander S. Moorer to Miss Julia B. Wannamaker, all of Orangeburg county, S. C.

In Spalding county, Dec. 17, by Rev. J. W. Simmons, Mr. A. F. Huckaby to Miss Ida E. Hunt.

In Girard Church, Ala., by Rev. J. W. Simmons, Mr. John R. Garrett to Miss Ellen Gifford, Nov. 29, 1874.

In Trinity Church, Ala., Nov. 12, by Rev. J. W. Simmons, Mr. Absolom Younge to Miss Mary Eason.

At Rich Hill, Spartanburg county, S. C., Dec. 11, 1874, by Rev. M. H. Pooser, Mr. John L. Heidtman of Orangeburg, S. C., to Miss Annie M., eldest daughter of the officiating minister.

On Dec. 17, 1874, by Rev. J. D. Gunnells, Willis H. Stephens of Madison county, to Miss Elizabeth Hutcherson, of Franklin county, Ga.

On 10th inst., by Rev. W. T. Read, Mr. John A. Fife to Miss Lucinda T. Edwards, both of Henry county, Ga.

On 18th Dec., 1874, by Rev. M. L. Underwood, Mr. F. L. Comer, of Cleaveland, Ga., to Miss N. E. Lattner.

In Columbia co., Ga., Nov. 17, 1874, by Rev. D. Kelsey, Mr. Wm. Harrison Briggs, of South Carolina, to Miss Mary Saluda Hamilton.

Dec. 1st, 1874, by Rev. D. Kelsey, Mr. James L. Fulcher to Mrs. Sarah A. Flint.

In Harlem, Ga., Dec. 14, 1874, by Rev. D. Kelsey, Mr. H. H. Williams to Miss E. E. Pearre, of McDuffie county, Ga.

Dec. 9, 1874, at the residence of Mr. S. J. Arnold, in Coweta county, GA., by Rev. T. H. Timmons, Mr. Walter E. Overby, of Stewart county to Miss Sallie B. Sims, step-daughter of Rev. John M. Marshall.

Dec. 3d, by Rev. J. F. Mixon, Mr. James H. Palmer to Mrs. Laura A. Brantley, both of Washington county, Ga.

Dec. 15th, 1874, by Rev. J. F. Mixon, Mr. William H. Renfroe of Sandersville, Ga., to Miss Martha A. Stubbs, of Washington county, Ga.

In Attapulgus, Ga., on the 17th of Dec., 1874, by Rev. Dr. Leonard, Mr. James Duncan Lester, to Miss Frances R., youngest daughter of Mr. William B. Smith, of Decatur county, Ga.

Dec. 4, 1874, by Rev. W. H. Hunt, Mr. John C. Henry, of Lake City, Columbia county, to Miss Olivia Mizelle, of White Springs, Hamilton county, all of Florida.

On 17th Dec., 1874, near Vienna, Ga., by Rev. N. B. Ousley, Mr. J. w. Edward,s of Macon, Ga., to Miss Penn Bryan, of the former place.

By Rev. D. R. McWilliams, at the residence of Mr. H. W. Pitts, on the 17th Dec., 1874, Mr. Thos. Pace, of Cedartown, to Mrs. Mary P. Marshall, of Harris county, Ga.

On the 2d Dec., 1874, by Rev. H. R. Felder, at the residence of Mr. S. P. Salter, of Houston county, Ga., Mr. R. G. Owen, of Cuthbert, Ga., to Miss Anna L. Lane, of Houston county, Ga.

On the 16th Dec., 1874, by Rev. Wm. M. Crymes, Dr. C. E. French, of Stewart county, Ga., to Miss Rebecca T. Smith, of Webster county, Ga. also at the same time and place by Rev. Wm. M. Crymes, Mr. Wm. K. Bostick to Miss Sallie Smith, daughters of the Hon. Jubilee Smith.

On 17th Dec., 1874, by Rev. Wm. M. Crymes, Mr. Richard Jackson to Miss Sarah Anderson.

Issue of January 6, 1875

Dec. 26, 1874, by Rev. C. H. Pritchard, J. P. Pritchard, of Lowndesville, S. C., to Miss L. Laval Ewart, of Spartanburg, S.C.

On the 17th of December, 1874, by Rev. J. N. Patterson, Mr. James B. Hunter to Miss Melissa T. Johnson, all of Union Springs, Ala.

In Albany, Ga., at the residence of Mr. I. J. Brinson, Esq., by Rev. Geroge J. Griffiths, Miss Annie Lollie Thorne, daughter of Joseph Thorne, Esq., of Albany, Ga., to Mr. Homer O. Powers, of the Southwestern Railway.

In McIntosh county, Ga., on the 23d Dec., by Rev. H. Andrews, Mr. Laura M. Nelson to Mr. Charles A. Space, of Darien.

By Rev. Atticus G. Haygood, Mr. Henry Emery of Atlanta, to Miss Lizzie Branham, daughter of Rev. W. R. Branham, Sr., of Oxford.

Dec. 17, 1874, by Rev. J. O. A. Connor, L. J. Kiser, of Orangeburg county, S. C., to Miss Emma C. Way, daughter of Aaron Way, of Charleston county, S. C.

By Rev. O. A. Connor, Dec. 17, 1874, Mr. O. B. Whetsel to Miss Ann R. Snell, all of Orangeburg county, S. C.

By Rev. J. O. Connor, Oct. 24, 1874, Mr. W. T. Bowman to Miss M. C. Murray, all of Colleton Orangeburg county, S. C.

Dec. 17, 1874, by Rev. H. C. Fentress, Mr. Frank Smith of Telfair county, GA., to Miss Ellen Clements, of Montgomery county, Ga.

By Rev. F. M. T. Brannon, Dec. 17, Jephtha A. Spradling, of Coweta county, to Miss Telitha C. White, of Meriwether county, Ga.

By Rev. F. M. T. Brannon, Dec. 22, Jonathan H. Read, of Troup county, to Miss Sallie E. North, of Coweta county.

By Rev. F. M. T. Brannon, Dec. 24, Robert E. Latimore, of Meriwether county, to Miss Mattie E. McLain, of Coweta, Ga.

By Rev. M. H. Eakes, Dec. 23d, 1874, Mr. Wyly R. Brogdan to Mrs. Julia Wilson.

By Rev. M. H. Eakes, Dec. 23d, 1874, Mr. A. T. Pattillo to Miss Era Woodward.

In Union Springs, Ala., on the 19th of December, 1874, by Rev. J. A. Peterson, Mr. John F. Bonnell, of Georgia, to Miss Belle McAndrew.

On 17th December, 1874, at the residence of Mr. W. W. Waldrop, by Rev. D. D. Dantzler, Mr. John A. Werts to Miss Nora Kinard, daughter of the late Middleton Kinard, of Newberry county, S. C.

At Wacahoota, Fla., Dec. 6, 1874, by Rev. John C. Reynolds to Miss Mollie White, all of Muscogee county, Ga.

Dec. 2d, 1874, at the residence of Mr. S. Turrentine, by Rev. S. D. Clements, Mr. Wm. Bozwell to Miss Rebecca R.Morgan, all of Harris county, Ga.

By Rev. Geo. C. Clarke, at the residence of Mr. Geo. W. Currie, Mr. B. F. Hawes, of Lumpkin, Ga., to Miss Henrietta Irwin, of Dawson, Ga.

By Rev. G. C. Clarke, Dec, 22d, 1874, Mr. Wm. G. Aven, of Webster county, to Miss Emma G. Moore, of Dawson, Ga.

Issue of January 13, 1875

In Edgewood, Ga., by Rev. J. R. Mayson, Dec., 29th, 1874, Mr. Henly E. Bain to Miss Ella E. Cook.

On the 31st of Dec., 1874, by Rev. Wm. C. Power, Mr. Edward M. Fore to Miss Maggie E., eldest daughter of Charles Haselden, Esq., all of Marion District, S. C.

By Rev. J. H. Elder, Dec. 24th, 1874, Mr. Willie J. Elder to Miss A. O. Murphy, both of Spalding county, Ga.

On the 24th Dec., 1875, by Rev. J. H. Elder, Mr. H. H. Callaway to Miss M. E. Starr, both of Spalding county, Ga.

In Hardeeville, S. C., Dec. 13th, 1874, by Rev. J. R. Coburn, Mr. R. W. Tindall of Sumter, S. C., to Miss Meta W. Coburn, daughter of the officiating minister.

In Atlanta, Ga., Dec. 31st, 1874, by Rev. W. C. Dunlap, Mr. A. L. Hendrix to Miss Josie B. Terry, both of that city.

Dec. 23d, 1874, by Rev. D. L. Whitaker, Mr. J. H. Rainey to Miss Katie B. Hall, all of Anderson county, S. C.

Jan. 5th, 1875, by Rev. R. R. Johnson, Mr. J. J. Brogdon, of Gwinnett county, Ga., to Miss F. H. Wi---, of Lawrenceville, Ga.

Dec. 24th, 1874, by Rev. William Hutto, Mr. Eugene M. Parlor to Miss Mary M. Evans, all of Orangeburg county, S. C.

On the 22d Dec., 1874, by Rev. Jos. S. Key, D. D., Rev. Howard W. Key, of the South Georgia Conference, to Miss Ozella Biggers, daughter of Hon. James B. Biggers, of Harris county, Ga.

At Cedar Town, Ga., Dec. 23d, 1874, by Rev. W. H. LaPrade, W. Ed. Wood to Miss Ella Vann.

In Jefferson county, Fla., on the 14th of Dec., 1874, by Rev. W. D. Core, Alfred William Raysor to Miss Petnah Adelia Nalley.

In Decatur, Ga., Dec. 15th, 1874, by Rev. W. R. Foote, Mr. T. H. Hughes to Miss Mollie McCrary, of the Orphan's House.

By Rev. J. J. Reynolds, Nov. 5th, 1874, Mr. George Gordon to Miss Sarah Wodford, all of Darlington county, S. C.

By Rev. J. J. Reynolds, Nov. 12th, 1874, Mr. Simeon Fields to Miss Nora Wilson, all of Darlington county, S. C.

By Rev. J. T. Webb, on Sunday, 3d of January, 1875, Mr. Walner L. Kennon to Miss Rebecca Wells, daughter of Berry Wells, of Lowndes county, Ga.

In Camilla, Ga., on the 24th of Dec., 1874, by Rev. E. H. McGehee, Rev. Joseph P. Wardlaw of the South Georgia Conference, to Miss A. Simmie Coachman.

Dec. 29th, 1874, by Rev. J. B. Wardlaw, Capt. Fletcher T. Snead to Mary L. Wardlaw, daughter of the officiating minister, all of Oglethorpe, Ga.

On the 8th of Dec., 1874, by Rev. Jno. J. little, Mr. B. B. Cotton to Miss Carrie R. Pierce, daughter of Dr. Pierce of Whitesville, Ga.

On the 24th of Dec., 1874, by Rev. James R. Smith, Mr. James D. McCord, Junior, to Miss Mollie Owen, all of Jackson, Butts county, Ga.

Issue of January 20, 1875

By Rev. J. H. Wilkins, Jan. 7th, 1875, Mr. James Lee[?] of Ware county, Ga., to Miss Margaret Booth, of Clinch county, Ga.

In Branchville, S. C., Dec. 24th, 1874, by Rev. D. J. Simmons, Mr. Stephen S. Walters and Miss Eliza J. Patrick.

In Troup county, on the 22d Dec., by Rev. W. J. Connor, Mr. J. C. Mallory and Miss M. H. Hodnett.

Near Grantville, Ga., on the 12th inst., by W. J. Cotter, Mr. Purnell Hearn, to Tennessee, and Mrs. M. A. R. Kelley, of Twiggs county, Ga.

By Rev. John Calvin Johnson, Dec. 23d, 1874, Mr. Joseph R. Palmer and Miss Florence S. Huggins, all of Athens, Ga.

By Rev. John Calvin Johnson, Dec. 24th, 1874, Mr. William H. Broach, of Walton county, Ga., to Miss Sarah B. McLeroy, of Clarke county, Ga.

By Rev. John Calvin Johnson, Dec. 31st, 1874, Mr. Reuben H. McAlpin and Mrs. Leonora V. Hand, all of Athens, Ga.

By Rev. R. H. Howren, Mr. George N. Footman and Miss Amanda H. Fisher, all of Leon county, Fla.

By Rev. R. H. Howren, Dec. 22d, 1874, Mr. George VanHorn and Miss Lenora B. Elliott, all of Leon county, Fla.

By Rev. A. J. Dean, Jan. 7th, 1875, Mr. Machinus Goode and Miss Mollie Humber, all of Stewart county, Ga.

By Rev. J. H. Zimmerman, Jan. 7th, 1875, Mr. Jas. A. Green and Miss Geneva J. Cummins, all of Colleton county, S. C.

By Rev. C. C. Cary, Jan. 1st, 1875, Mr. William A. Rorie, of Wilkes county, Ga., and Miss Nannie G. Dorough, daughter of Mr. J. P. Dorough, of Oglethorpe county, Ga.

In LaGrange, Ga., Dec. 10th, 1874, by Rev. Wm. Park, Mr. L. M. Park, of New York, to Miss Addie Bigham, daughter of Hon. B. H. Bigham.

In Greenville, Ga., Dec. 17th, 1874, by Rev. Wm. Park, Mr. Wm. M. Marchman, of Troup county, and Miss Mary B. Marchman.

In Talladega county, Ala., Dec. 24th, 1874, by Rev. Wm. Park, Mr. James P. Burk and miss Ellen F. Hitchcock[?].

Issue of January 27, 1875

Jan. 7th, 1875, by Rev. Thos. B. Lanier, Mr. B. E. Gaines to Miss Ella V. Hodges, all of Bulloch county, Ga.

Jan. 14th, 1875, by Rev. E. S. Tyner, Mr. H. A. Blackburn, of Live Oak, Fla., to Miss Jennie V. Dickinson, of Madison, Fla.

On Dec. 28th, 1874, by Rev. D. Tiller, Mr. W. A. McLeane, of Darlington county, S. C., to Miss Lizzie Pierce, of Kershaw county, S. C.

Jan. 3rd, 1875, by Rev. Robt. P. Martin, Mr. S. P. Clack to Miss Mollie J. Whitworth, all of Gwinnett county, Ga.

Jan. 14th, 1875, by Rev. J. E. Sentell, Mr. M. C. Wilkinson, of Quitman, Ga., to Miss M. F. Werdon, of Boston, Ga.

Jan. 12th, 1875, in Atlanta, Ga., by Rev. W. H. Potter, Mr. A. C. Harmon, of Savannah, Ga., to Miss M. Della Potter.

Jan. 12th, 1875, at the residence of Mr. James Dasher, by Rev. Alex. P. Wright, Mr. T. P. Creech, to Miss M. E. Harrison, all of Valdosta, Ga.

On 20th Dec., 1874, by Rev. N. D. Morehouse, William G. Dugger to Miss Loanza Nease, all of Effingham county, Ga.

Jan. 12th, 1875, by Rev. W. W. Graham, Mr. W. B. Revell to Miss Katie Jefferson, all of Russell county, Ala.

Jan. 13th, 1875, by Rev. Jno. M. Bowden, at the residence of A. G. Grier, Esq., by Rev. J. H. Martin, Hon. Stephen Collins, of Macon, Ga., to Miss M. C. Wilson.

On the 14th Jan., 1875, by Rev. Jno. M. Bowden, Mr. Benjamine A. Shaw to Miss Martha J. Patton, all of Campbell county, Ga.

On the 17th Jan. 1875, by Rev. J. S. Bryan, Mr. H. W. Verstille, of Columbus, Ga., to Miss Sarah A. White, of Coweta county, Ga.

By Rev. Jno. W. McRoy, Jan. 20th, 1875, Daniel M. Westbury to Miss Izorah E. Smoke, all of Orangeburg county, S. C.

Dec. 23d, 1874, by Rev. S. Leake, Mr. J. B. Cothran to Miss Lizzie Mitchell, grand-daughter of Rev. C. Trussel.

In Macon, Ga., Dec. 3d, 1874, by Rev. G. G. N. MacDonell, Mr. A. M. Massengale, of Warren county, Ga., to Miss Hattie E. Brinn, of Macon, Ga.

SOUTHERN CHRISTIAN ADVOCATE MARRIAGE NOTICES 1867-1878

Issue of February 3, 1875

By the Rev. E. Morris, of the P. M. Church, Jan. 5th, 1875, Mr. G. M. Dodson to Miss P. O. Arnold, all of Henry county, Ga.

By the Rev. E. Morris, of the P. M. Church, Jan. 6th, 1875, Mr. J. J. Askew, to Miss Anna H. Dodson, all of Henry county, Ga.

At the residence of Judge John Collier, in Atlanta, Jan. 14th, 1875, by Rev. T. P. Cleveland, Mr. A. Rudolph, of Gainesville, Ga., and Miss B. E. Latimer, of Atlanta.

At the residence of Mr. C. H. Durant, near Lynchburg, S. C., on Wednesday evening, Jan. 20th, 1875, by Rev. S. A. Weber, Miss Maggie Bruce Murchison to Mr. Moses B. McDonald.

By Rev. G. W. Hardaway, Jan. 26th, 1875, Mr. Mr. George M. Reed, of Columbia county, Ga., to Miss Mollie A. Dooly, of McDuffie county, Ga.

In Alafia, Fla., Dec. 22d, 1875, by Rev. H. H. Giles, Mr. Hugh Gallagher to Miss Rosa B. Anderson.

In Washington, Ga., by Rev. W. P. Rivers, Jan. 21st 1875, Mr. A. Barnett to Miss Ida hill.

By Rev. George C. Leavel, at Orange Springs, Fla., Jan. 19th, 1875, Mr. William Cox to Miss Lula Pearson, all of Marion county, Fla.

By Rev. A. G. Dempsey, Dec. 23d, 1874, Mr. J. S. Farmer to Miss A. V. Chapman, all of Clayton county, Ga.

By Rev. A. G. Dempsey, Dec. 24th, 1874, Mr. J. M. Mercer to Miss B. A. Allen, all of Fulton county, Ga.

By Rev. A. G. Dempsey, Jan. 13th, 1875, Mr. Samuel Taliafero to Miss Emma Gilbert, all of Fulton county, Ga.

By Rev. A. G. Dempsey, Jan. 17th, 1875, Mr. J. F. Knight to Miss L. M. Davis, all of Fulton county, Ga.

Issue of February 10, 1875

On Jan. 20th, 1875, by Rev. E. S. Tyner, Mr. W. S. Hamilton, of Jefferson county, Fla., to Miss Eliza E. Paul, of Madison county, Fla.

By Rev. Thos. B. Lanier, Jan. 14th, 1875, Mr. W. S. Reeves to Miss Mollie A. Ward, all of Burke county, Ga.

In Columbus, Ga., Jan. 28th, 1875, by Rev. J. B. McGehee, Mr. Cyrus L. Raiford, of Muscogee, to Miss Emma L. Marshall, of Brandon, Miss.

By Rev. G. T. Embry, in Vienna, Ga., Jan. 21st, 1875, Mr. Bryant A. Wood, to Miss W. L. Lilley.

Jan. 21st, 1875, by Rev. G. T. Embry, near Vienna, Ga., Mr. Jas. H. Swearingen to Miss M. J. C. Lasseter.

In Palmetto, Ga., Jan. 20th, 1875, by Rev. W. P. Pledger, Rev. B. E. L. Timmons, of the North Georgia Conference, to Miss Lucy C. H. Menifee.

On the 27th Jan., 1875, by Rev. J. E. Sentell, Mr. W. A. Jones to Miss E. J. McRae, both of Brooks county, Ga.

By Rev. Joseph M. Gable, Jan. 26th, 1875, Mr. Cicero J. Manning, of Cobb county, Ga., to Miss Mary E. Manning of South Carolina.

In Fayetteville, N. C., Jan. 27th, 1875, at the Methodist Church, by Rev. E. W. Thompson, Mr. R. T. Gray, Associate Editor of the *Raleigh Christian Advocate*, to Miss Caro, daughter of E. J. Lilly.

In Dougherty county, Ga., on 21st Jan. 1875, by Rev. George J. Griffiths, Mr. Samuel Pendry to Miss George E. Clarke, both of Dougherty county, Ga.

Issue of February 17, 1875

By Rev. W. A. Dodge, Dec. 23, 1874, Mr. Walter Dickinson, of Alabama, to Miss Virginia Orr, of Atlanta, Ga.

By Rev. W. A. Dodge, Dec. 24, 1874, Mr. Theodore C. Wilkie, of Atlanta, Ga., to Miss Sallie Goldsmith, of Stone Mountain, Ga.

By J. S. Evans, Esq., near Tarversville, Twiggs county, Ga., Feb. 4th, 1875, Mr. John W. Mercer to Miss Laurea A. Wood, all of Twiggs county, Ga.

By J. S. Evans, Esq., near Twiggsville, Twiggs county, Ga., Feb. 9th, 1875, Mr. John Floyd to Miss Ellen Sauls, all of Twiggs county, Ga.

By Rev. John H. Mashburn, Jr., Feb. 9th, 1875, Mr. G. W. Haynes, of Alabama, to Miss Eugenie Holloway, of Jasper.

By Rev. R. W. Bigham, at the residence of Dr. Pilcher, near Warrenton, Ga., Jan. 21st, 1875, Mr. Thomas M. Parham to Miss Mary Anna Cheeley.

By Rev. H. H. Parks, Jan. 16th, 1875, Oscar L. Reese, Esq., of Carrolton, Ga., to Miss Mollie Fannie Reed, daughter of Mr. I. Alex. Reed, of LaGrange, Ga..

By Rev. H. H. Parks, Feb. 5th, 1875, Mr. Jas. E. Hudson, of Troup county, Ga., to Miss Ella Baugh, of LaGrange.

By Rev. H. H. Parks, Feb. 5th, 1875, Mr. Wm. E. Stratford, of Russell county, Ala., to Miss Mattie E. Godwin, daughter of Mr. Wm. T. Godwin, of LaGrange, Ga.

By Rev. E. H. Myers, D. D., at Savannah, Ga., Jan. 13th, 1875, Mr. Clayton Pierce miller, of Savannah, to Miss Sarah Ellen Strobhart, daughter of the late H. N. Strobhart, Esq., of Hardeeville, S. C.

By Rev. W. C. Bass, D. D., at the Brown House, Macon, Ga., Feb. 9th, 1875, Capt. Robert E. Park, to Miss Ella H., daughter of Gen. S. W. Holt.

By Rev. Thos. W. Munnerlyn, Jan. 21st, 1875, Mr. S. C. Wolfe, of Charlotte, N. C., to Miss Addy M. Mobley, of Rock Hill, York county, S. C.

By Rev. Thos. W. Munnerlyn, Jan. 27th, 1875, Mr. James Poage to Mrs. Margaret Barnes, all of York county, S. C.

By Rev. W. E. Johnston, Jan. 7th, 1875, Mr. Moses M. Mulkey to Miss Elizabeth P. Byrd, all of Richmond county, Ga.

By Rev. W. E. Johnston, Feb. 4th, 1875, in Richmond county, Ga., Mr. Stephen Shaw to Miss Elizabeth Riley.

By Rev. James S. Embry, in DeKalb county, Ga., Jan. 28th, 1875, Mr. John W. Pace of Milton county, Ga., to Miss S. E. A. Hardeman, of DeKalb county, Ga.

By Rev. A. J. Cauthen, Feb. 9th, 1875, Mr. W. H. Hartzog, of Blackville and Miss A. B. Attaway, near Barnwell village, S. C.

By Rev. D. J. Myrick, Feb. 3d, 1875, near Subligna, Ga., Mr. William D. Hix to Miss Susan V. High, both of Chattooga, Ga.

Issue of February 24, 1875

In Polk co., Ga., Feb. 4th, 1875, by Rev. Wm. H. LaPrade, Mr. Jno. D. Hightower to Miss Rosa Darden.

At Cedar Town, Ga., Feb. 10th, 1875, by Rev. Wm. H. LaPrade, Dr. L. S. Ledbetter to Miss Lula Dodds.

By Rev. Dr. Smith, of Smithville, Ga., Feb. 4th, 1875, Mr. Whitfield Williams to Miss Sarah Elizabeth Sealy, all of Lee county, Ga.

On Feb. 10th, 1875, by the Rev. H. F. Chrietzberg, Mr. Benjamin N. Pearce to Miss Sallie S. D. Tiller, youngest daughter of Capt. Joseph L. Tiller, all of Kershaw county, S. C.

In Spalding, Macon county, Ga., Feb. 4th, 1875, by Rev. E. H. McGehee, Capt. R. W. Westbrook to Miss L. E. McKenzie.

Dec. 24th, 1875, by Rev. B. F. Fariss, Mr. J. M. Seago to Miss Florrie K. Styles, all of Richmond county, Ga.

By Rev. B. F. Fariss, Feb. 3rd, 1875, Mr. Wm. Rufus Buzhardt to Miss Georgie F. Seago, all of Richmond county, Ga.

Feb. 11th 1875, near Thomasville, Georgia, by Rev. R. L. Honiker, Charles B. Stubbs, of Macon, Ga., to Miss Mattie J. Mithell [sic], of Thomas county, Ga.

By Rev. Geo. C. Leavel, at Old Town, Fla., Feb. 8th, 1875, Mr. B. A. Weathers to Miss M. J. Ferguson, all of Marion county, Fla.

By Rev. Geo. C. Leavel, Feb. 11th, 1875, Mr. P. C. Sessions to Miss Anna R. Brown, all of Marion county, Fla.

On Feb. 4th, 1875, by Rev. W. W. Wadsworth, in Baldwin county, Ga., Mr. Edward S. Vinson to Miss Annie A. Morris.

At the residence of Mr. P. B. Haralson, near Atlanta, Ga., Feb. 16th, 1875, by Rev. T. H. Timmons, Mr. Joseph R. Davis, of Gainesville, Ga., to Miss Nannie M. Thompson.

By Rev. J. A. Kennedy, Feb. 4th, 1875, Mr. Wm. D. Dickinson, to Miss Josephine Zetrouer, youngest daughter of the late John R. Zetrouer, all of Alachua county, Fla.

By Rev. W. Hutto, Jan. 21st, 1875, D. H. Grooms to Miss Anna J. Neal, all of Charleston county, S. C.

By Rev. W. Hutto, Jan. 9th, 1875, Mr. Willis DeHay to Miss Amelia D. Carson, all of Orangeburg county, S. C.

In Greenville, S. C., Jan. 24th, 1875, by Rev. O. A. Darby, Prof. Harvey T. Cooke to Miss Corrie A. Carpenter.

Feb. 17th, 1875, in Wilkes county, Ga., by Rev. Thos. H. Gibson, Mr. M. Thomas Rogers to Miss Sallie c. Darden.

Dec. 27th, 1874, by Rev. B. S. Clements, Mr. W. P. Vardamon, to Mrs. E. A. Bonner, both of Meriwether county, Ga.

By Rev. John Calvin Johnson, 19th Jan., 1875, Mr. William R. Tuck to Miss Mattie Macon, all of Clarke county, Ga.

By Rev. John Calvin Johnson, on 17th Feb., 1875, Mr. Thomas W. Bearden, of Morgan county, Ga., to Miss Mattie Cochran, of Oglethorpe county, Ga.

Issue of March 3, 1875

In Cartersville, Ga., Feb. 16th, Mr. Chas. H. Johnson, of Griffin, to Miss Bettie Hardy, of Cartersville.

By Rev. J. F. Mixon, Jan. 19th, 1875, Mr. Thomas Clegg to Miss Erin O'Kelly, both of Pleasant Valley, Walton county, Ga.

By Rev. D. R. McWilliams, Feb. 9th, 1875, Mr. A. J. Deane, of Mississippi, to Miss Nellie Burt, of Marion county, Ga.

By Rev. J. L. Melton, Feb. 4th, 1874 [sic], Mr. John W. Garlington to Miss Missouri A. T. Sanders, all of Tallapoosa county, Ala.

By the Rev. W. M. D. Bond, Dec. 16th, 1874, Mr. Charles Marshall to Miss Eliza Houser, all of Houston county, Ga.

By Rev. R. H. Howren, Feb. 11th, 1875, Mr. Jesse J. Rogers to Miss Lou Thomas, all of Jefferson county, Fla.

By Rev. C. W. Smith, Feb. 21st, 1875, Mr. Franklin C. Davis, of Newton county, Ga., to Miss Eliza M. Stevens, of Baldwin county, Ga.

By Rev. T. F. Pierce, Feb. 14th, 1875, Mr. G. C. Samuels to Miss Lizzie Dunnaway, all of Wilkes county, Ga.

By Mr. McCorkle, Jan. 17th, 18754, Mr. Samuel A. Waler, of Wilkes county, Ga., to Miss Amelia J. Willis, of McDuffie county, Ga.

By Rev. S. D. Clements, Jan. 28th, 1875, Mr. F. W. Cook to Miss Julia V. Murphy, all of Jefferson county, Ga.

By Rev. F. B. Davies, Feb. 17th, at Longwood, Newton county, Mr. W. C. Smith, of Lithonia, to Miss Sallie E. Perry, Newton county, Ga.

Issue of March 10, 1875

In Macon, Ga., Feb. 21st, 1875, by Rev. S. S. Sweet, Mr. Ermenegelio Savis to Miss Sarah Shepherd.

In Quitman, Ga., Feb. 25th, 1875, by Rev. S. S. Sweet, Mr. Sidney E. Ives, of Macon, Ga., to Miss Nellie C. Ives, of Quitman, Ga.

By Rev. T. S. L. Harwell, Feb. 21st, 1875, Mr. T. M. C. Buffington to Miss Dora E. Gaddy, all of Cobb county, Ga.

By Rev. W. T. Hamilton, on 16th Feb., 1875, Mr. John B. Willingham, of McDuffie county, Ga., to Miss Betie J. Farmer, of Jefferson county, Ga.

In Bartow, Ga., Feb. 23d, 1875, by Rev. Thos. B. Lanier, Mr. W. J. Evans to Miss Lillia B. Carswell, all of Jefferson county, Ga.

By Rev. Thos. B. Lanier, at Bethany, Ga., Feb. 23d, 1875, Mr. William J. Parker to Miss Emma J. McCrone, all of Jefferson county, Ga.

By Rev. F. M. T. Brannon, Feb. 25th, 1875, Mr. E. W. Russell of Newnan, Ga., to Miss M. A. E. J. Partridge, adopted daughter of Judge Jesse Partridge, of Meriwether county, Ga.

Feb. 14th, 1875, by Rev. Jno. T. Whitaker, Mr. Jas. A. Cardwell to Miss Charlie V. Thedford, all of Harris county, Ga.

On the 25th Feb., 1875, in Monroe county, Ga., by Rev. Jno. A. Reynolds, Mr. A. T. Nobles to Miss Zach Owens.

By Rev. J. F. England, Feb. 18th, 1875, Mr. Charles T. Crook to Miss Nannie Prather, all of York county, S. C.

Feb. 25th, 1875, by Rev. I. G. Parks, Dr. C. C. Garriett to Miss M. E. A. Quillian, daughter of Rev. J. B. C. Quillian, of the No. Ga. Conference, all of Douglasville, Ga.

Near Marietta, Ga., Feb. 17th, 1875, by Rev. W. F. Glenn, Mr. Willie Ray, of Atlanta, Ga., to Miss Annie Elliott.

By Rev. W. J. Cotter, Feb. 17th, 1875, Mr. A. P. Camp, son of the late Rev. H. Camp, of Coweta county, Ga., to Miss Mittie Dunlap, of Meriwether county, Ga.

Issue of March 17, 1875

By Rev. Walter Manning, March 4th, 1875, Mr. J. P. Groover to Miss Lizzie Gable, daughter of Rev. Joseph M. Gable, all of Cobb county, Ga.

By Rev. S. A. Pilley, at the residence of B. B. McKinny, Louisville, Ala., Feb. 16th, 1875, Frank W. Eidson to Miss Fannie Flournoy.

By Rev. B. E. L. Timmons, in Cave Spring, Ga., Feb. 16, 1875, Mr. J. R. Barron to Miss Fannie Tiley.

By Rev. William Hutto, January 21st, 1875, Mr. Robert Sweatman to Miss Mary Grooms, all of Charleston county, S. C.; also, Dr. M. J. Dantzler, of Orangeburg, S. C., to Miss Dora E. Shingler, of Charleston county, S. C.

By Rev. W. B. Bell, March 3d, 1875, Mr. John A. Ledford to Miss Eveline Logan, both of White county, Ga.

By Rev. J. B. Littlejohn, Feb. 25th, 1875, Mr. T. U. Sessions to Miss Lizzie Weston, both of Terrell county, Ga.

Issue of March 24, 1875

March 4th, 1875, by Rev. W. F. Quillian, Mr. Samuel Lovingood, of Elbert county, GA., to Miss Ella A. Smith, of Wilkes county, Ga.

In Fairburn, Ga., March 11th, 1875, by Rev. Jno. M. Bowden, Col. Leonard S. Roan to Miss Willie E. Strickland.

March 4th, 1875, by Rev. E. S. Tyner, Mr. Owen P. Raines to Miss Mary F. Stanton, all of Madison county, Fla.

At Social Circle, Walton county, Ga., January 16th, 1875, by Rev. Luther M. Smith, D. D., Rev. Miles W. Arnold, of the North Georgia Conference, to Mrs. Elizabeth S. Nowell.

March 4th, 1875, by Rev. S. A. Weber, assisted by Rev. S. Lander, Miss Ida E. Clinkscales, of Williamston, to Mr. E. K. Hardin, Principal of the Batesburg Female High School, Leesville, S. C.

By Rev. W. J. Cotter, March 9th, 1875, Mr. J. C. Willingham to Miss Jennie J. Justiss, both of Merriwether county, Ga.

Issue of March 31, 1875

By Rev. L. P. Neese, at Cumming, Ga., Feb. 18th, Mr. Chapel Hughes to Miss Julia Johnston, all of Cumming, Ga.

By Rev. L. P. Neese, at Cumming, Ga., March 14th, Col. J. A. Sawyer, of Dahlonega, Ga., to Miss Elena Dobson, of Boston, Mass.

By Rev. E. S. Tyner, March 17th 1875, Mr. R. J. Bryan to Miss N. C. Gramling, all of Madison county, Fla.

By E. S. Tyner, March 18th 1875, Mr. W. F. Howard to Miss Mary I. Leslie, all of Madison county, Fla.

By Rev. W. F. Glenn, in Marietta, Ga., March 16th, 1875, Mr. Thos. E. Veal, of Atlanta, to Miss E. C. Lowry.

Issue of April 7, 1875

By Rev. T. S. L. Harwell, March 14th, 1875, Mr. J. F. Brinkley, formerly of Warren county, Ga., to Miss Mollie Chalker, of Cobb county, Ga.

By Rev. J. T. Payne, at Millhaven, March 25th, 1875, Theo. N. Winn, Esq., to Mrs. Laura G., relict of Col. William B. Gaulden, both of Liberty county, Ga.

In the Baptist Church, at Jewell's Mills, Hancock county, Ga., March 25th, 1875, by Rev. T. J. Veasy, Mr. Thaddeus Walker to Miss Mary Willie Enlow, all of Hancock county, Ga.

Dec. 20th, 1874, by Rev. J. O. A. Radford, Mr. B. F. Stidham, of Flowery Branch, Ga., to Miss Josie Morgan, of Paulding county ,Ga.

In Macon, Ga., March 20th, 1875, by Rev. W. C. Bass, D. C., Rev. W. B. Bonnell and Miss Alice J. Wright, eldest daughter of Rev. Arminius Wright.

By Rev. Thos. W. Munnerlyn, March 23d, 1875, Mr. John A. Kidd to Miss Mary Jane Daniels, all of York county, S. C.

March 30th, 1875, in Cokesbury, S. C., by the Rev. Manning Brown, Rev. A. W. Barnett, M. D., of Eufaula, Ala., to Miss Adella A. Conner, of the former place.

Issue of April 14, 1875

By Rev. J. M. Marshall, March 30th, 1875, in Hinesville, Ga., Mr. J. M. Dugger, of Atlanta, to Miss Sallie D. Harris, of the former place.

By Rev. J. M. Marshall, March 31st, 1875, in Liberty county, Ga., Mr. W. V. Gill, of Barnwell county, S. C., to Miss Pattie Farmer, of the former county and state.

By Rev. W. T. Laine, April 1st, 1875, Mr. James M. Campbell to Miss A. V. Mitchell.

By the Rev. Edward Bradley, of Nashville, in Shelbyville, Tenn., March 30th, 1875, at the Church of the Redeemer (Episcopal), Miss Mary Louie, eldest daughter of col. Jas. L. Scudder, to Mr. Bascom Myrick, of Forsyth, Ga.

By Rev. H. R. Felder, in Spalding, Macon co., Ga., March 7th, 1875, Mr. B. D. Shumate to Miss Michael J. Horn.

By Rev. H. R. Felder, in Perry, Ga., March 31st, 1875, Mr. John H. Powers to Miss Corinne Smith.

By Rev. T. J. Phillips, April 1st, 1875, Mr. John M. Thomas to Miss Maggie Stokes, all of Gadsden county, Fla.

By Rev. E. S. Tyner, March 31st, 1875, Mr. J. Christopher Pillans to Miss M. Hoyt Beggs, all of Madison county, Fla.

By Rev. J. S. Jordan, March 23d, 1875, Mr. J. Harmon Morgan, of Scriven county, to Miss Rosie A. Hodges, of Bulloch.

By Rev. R. R. Johnson, March 31st, 1875, Mr. Hamilton Maffett to Miss Sarah A. Ivie, all of Laurenceville, Ga.

By Rev. W. Ewing Johnson, March 5th, 1875, Mr. Joseph H. Green to Miss Sarah J. Brown, all of Richmond county, Ga.

By Rev. John W. Heidt, March 30th, 1875, in Wilkes county, Ga., Mr. Charles E. Irvin to Miss Mollie Fortson, all of Wilkes county.

Issue of April 21, 1875

April 8th, 1875, by Rev. R. F. Evans, Mr. Jos. C. Walker to Miss S. E. Hudson, daughter of J. R. Hudson, all of Camilla, Ga.

April 13th, 1875, by Rev. R. F. Evans, Mr. Thomas Lake, A. & G. R. R., to Miss S. K. McMath, of Camilla, Ga.

March 30th, 1875, by Rev. Geo. G. N. MacDonell, Miss Clara F. Kerr, formerly of Abbeville, S. C., to Mr. J. M. Boakman, of Kentucky.

April 8th, 1875, by Rev. Geo. G. N. MacDonell, Miss Julia M. Walker, of Savannah, Ga., to Mr. John H. Groves, of Atlanta, Ga.

By Rev. J. B. Payne, March 14th, 1875, Thomas P. Butts to Miss Nannie Lewis, both of Upson county, Ga.

By Rev. J. B. Payne, March 30th, 1875, Wm. E. McAndrew to Miss Susan Newman, both of Upson county, Ga.

By Rev. J. J. Harris, near Wallesca, Ga., April 8th, 1875, Mr. Sebron R. Jackson, to Mrs. Mary Conner, all of Cherokee county, Ga.

By Rev. W. A. Dodge, Feb. 4th, 1875, Mr. P. H. Owens to Miss Ruth Webb, all of Atlanta, Ga.

By Rev. W. A. Dodge, March 1, 1875, Mr. Elijah L. Wood to Mrs. Georgia E. Hanye, all of Atlanta, Ga.

By Rev. W. A. Dodge, March 4th, 1875, Mr. William Warwick to Mrs. Martha Jane Edna, all of Atlanta, Ga.

By Rev. W. A. Dodge, March 11th, 1875, John Beiser to Miss Mary E. Wilmoth, all of Atlanta, Ga.

By Rev. W. A. Dodge, April 7th, 1875, Mr. Wm. M. Crim to Miss Cecillia C. Adamson, both of Atlanta, Ga.

On the 31st of March, 1875, by Rev. W. G. Booth, Mr. John C. Neal, of Thomas county, Ga., to Miss Mattie Bryan, daughter of the Rev. D. H. Bryan, of Jefferson county, Florida.

April 14th, 1875, by Rev. E. P. Bonner, Mr. Ambrose J. Avery to Miss Mattie S. Magruder, all of Columbia county, Ga.

At Monticello, Fla., by Rev. E. L. T. Blake, March 15th, 1875, Rev. J. Lewis, Jr., to Miss Sallie W. Lamar.

Issue of April 28, 1875

By Rev. J. J. Morgan, April 18th, 1875, Mr. Simeon Brinson to Miss Hattie Russell, all of Decatur county, Ga.

By Rev. F. Pasco, April 18th, 1875, Mr. Solomon S. Green to Miss Ann Causey, all of Volusia county, Fla.

By Rev. B. E. L. Timmons, April 18th 1875, in Cave Spring, Ga., Mr. R. N. Smith to Miss Nannie Tilly.

By Rev. E. S. Tyner, April 18th, 1875, Mr. J. F. Cooper to Miss Mary Caraway, all of Madison county, Fla.

By Rev. Arminius Wright, in Mulberry street church, Macon, Ga., April 20th 1875, Mr. John L. Hardeman, and Miss Fannie E. Ross.

By Rev. A. C. Gantt, April 29th, 1875, Mr. Wm. C. Hutson and Miss Lizzie F. Dutart, both of Cainhoy, St. Thomas Parish, Charleston county, S. C.

Issue of May 5, 1875

On the 18th April 1875, at the First M. E. Church, South, Key West, Fla., Dr. R. D. Murray, Surgeon U. S. Marine Hospital Service, to Miss Lillie Bell Fulwood, the bride's father officiating.

In Savannah, Ga., April 2d, 1875, by the Rev. A. M. Wynn, Mr. Mark Anthony, of Americus, Ga., to Miss Minnie W. Wynn, daughter of Rev. A. M. Wynn.

On the 14th of April, in Burke county, Ga., by the Rev. J. O. A. Clark, Mr. William C. Palmer to Miss Mary E. Rheney.

By Rev. T. B. Russell, Feb. 3d, 1875, in Marshallville, Ga., Mr. Henry Willis, of Oglethorpe, Ga., to Miss Mary E. Nixon, of the former place.

Issue of May 12, 1875

By Rev. W. Hutto, April 22d, 1875, George M. Norris to Miss Henrietta H. Connor, all of Charleston county, S. C.

By Rev. A. M. Wynn, in Savannah, on the 15th ult., John D. Charlton to Miss Mattie Butler, all of Savannah.

By Rev. C. A. Mitchell, April 15th, 1875, Mr. Charles B. Andrews, to Miss Mary Carrie Harwell, both of Upson county, Ga.

By Rev. F. A. Branch, in the Methodist Church, Hayneville, Ga., May 5th, 1875, Mr. R. O. Pate, of Hawkinsville, Ga., to Miss Minnie E. Brown, daughter of Capt. John G. Brown, of the former place.

By Rev. R. W. Dixon, in Cuthbert, Ga., May 5th, 1875, Samuel J. Williams, of Bullock county, Ga., to Miss Imogene McHan, daughter of Rev. W. B. McHan, deceased, of Cuthbert, Ga.

At the residence of Mrs. D'Antignac, in Augusta, May 5, 1875, by Rev. Clement A. Evans, Miss Mary Lou Walker, daughter of Maj. John W. Walker, and Mr. Isaac W. Beason, all of the same place.

Issue of May 19, 1875

By Rev. A. G. Gantt, May 5th, 1875, in St. John's Berkley, Charleston county, S. C., Mr. R. R. Lindsay to Miss Eudora Harvey.

By Rev. A. Thornburgh, at Payne's Chapel, in Walker county, Ga., May 3, 1875, Mr. Jesse B. Faucette to Miss Victoria Coxwell, all of Walker county, Ga.

By Rev. J. T. Kilgo, on the 28th of April, Mr. J. T. Donaldson to Miss M. A. Kinsey, all of Marlboro, S. C.

By Rev. D. J. Myrick, May 11th, 1875, Rev. John T. Richardson, of the North Georgia Conference, to Miss Clandy B. Fowler, of Catoosa county, Ga.

Issue of May 26, 1875

By Rev. F. G. Hughes, near Union Point, Ga., on the 11th May 1875, Luther R. Jackson to Miss Emma A. Carlton.

By Rev. Wm. C. Power, April 28th, 1875, Mr. Richard Jordan, of Horry county, S. C., to Miss Pattie K. Evans, daughter of Nathan Evans, Esq., of Marion, S. C.

By Rev. J. B. Platt, May 12th, 1875, Mr. Ludwig Hatje to Miss Margaret Carpenter, all of Manning, S. C.

By Rev. J. P. Wardlaw, May 6th, 1875, near Butler, Ga., Mr. W. D. Grace to Mrs. Nannie W. Loyd.

By Rev. J. J. Tooke, May 20th, 1875, in Macon county, Ga., George K. Looper, Esq., of Dawson county, Ga., to Miss Eleanor K. Neisler, daughter of Mr. Daniel Neisler.

Issue of June 2, 1875

May 11th, 1875, at the residence of Mrs. Miller, in Talbot county, by Rev. John S. Searcy, Mr. G. H. Jordan, or Butler, Ga., to Miss Cornelia Weaver, daughter of Judge Weaver, of Talbot.

By Rev. T. B. Russell, in Macon county, Ga., May 18th, 1875, Mr. Thomas Butler Harris to Miss Mary Ida Hooks.

By Rev. J. H. Grogan, Mr. J. C. Swearengin, of South Carolina, to Miss lucy Brewer, of Elbert county, Ga.

By the Rev. J. H. Zimmerman, May 19th, 1875, at the Methodist Church in Ridgeville, S. C., Mr. John W. Harbinson to Miss Frances R. Lemacks, all of Colleton county, S. C.

On May 12th, by Rev. E. H. Myers, D. D., Mr. Frederick M. Houser and Miss Mary Tallulah Houston, all of Savannah Ga.

At White Springs, Fla., May 2d, 1875, by Rev. John A. Moseley, Miss Lelia F. Collier to Mr. Charles Hussey.

Issue of June 9, 1875

By Rev. H. H. Parks, May 19th, 1875, at St. James Church, Augusta, Ga., Mr. Wm. P. Parks to Miss Jennie C. Simons.

In Macon, Ga., June 2d, 1875, by Rev. Arminius Wright, Dr. Herschel V. Johnson and Miss Carrie Belle Roberts.

By Rev. G. S. Johnston, May 13th, 1875, Mr. Wm. E. Edge, of Opelika, Ala., to Miss Minta A. Brannan, eldest daughter of Mr. S. M. Brannan, of Mt. Airy, Harris county, Ga.

By Rev. J. M. Bowden, April 27th, 1875, Mr. William T. Hearn to Miss Frances Pool, all of Campbell county, Ga.

By Rev. Manning Brown, at the Methodist Church in Newberry, May 28th, 1875, Mr. J. Clarke Wardlaw, of Walhalla, S. C., to Miss Bettie Moorman, of the former place.

By Rev. Alex. P. Wright, June 1st, 1875, Mr. James B. Turner, of Henry county, GA., to Miss Eda E. Webb, of Calhoun county, Ga.

Issue of June 16, 1875

By Rev. M. L. Banks, May 27th, 1875, in Orangeburg county, S. C., Mr. John W. Fanning to Miss Anna R. Winningham.

By Rev. P. A. Heard, June 2d, 1875, Dr. J. S. Todd, of Atlanta, to Miss Julia H. Beall, of LaGrange, Ga.

By Rev. G. H. Pooser, in Laurens county, S. C., May 26th, 1875, Mr. Wilbur F. Pooser of Orangeburgh county, S. C., to Miss S. Eugenia, daughter of the late Rev. John G. Humbert.

At Waynesboro, Ga., May 11th, 1875, by Rev. J. O. A. Clark, Richard H. Milledge to Miss Rosa H. Gresham.

Issue of June 23, 1875

By Rev. A. J. Dean, June 8th, 1875, Mr. James E. Cargill, of Columbus, Ga., to Miss Mollie S. Battle, of Lumpkin, Ga.
By Rev. A. J. Dean, June 10th, 1875, Mr. Patrick H. Morris, of Eufaula, Ala., to Mrs. Pauline E. Seymour, of Lumpkin, Ga.

On the 13th of June 1875, at Easley Station, S. C., by Rev. J. Q. Stockman, Mr. Herman Pechner, formerly of Richmond, Va., to Miss Mamie Dickson, of Pickens county, S. C.

By Rev. J. B. Wilson, June 8th, 1875, Mr. W. A. McWhirter to Miss Anna K. Fowler, all of Union county, S. C.

By Rev. W. H. Fleming, D. D., June 20th, 1875, Rev. J. Walter Dickson, of the South Carolina Conference, to Miss Annie M. Ichorb, of Yorkville.

By Rev. A. Gamewell Gantt, June 3d, 1875, Mr. Thos Greer, of Georgetown county, to Miss Addria V. Anderson, of Camhoy, Charleston county, S. C.

By Rev. J. B. McFarland, at Subligna, Ga., June 8th, 1875, Mr. F. F. Starr to Miss Florence Towe, both of Chattooga county, Ga.

Issue of June 30, 1875

By Rev. E. S. Tyner, March 30th, 1875, near Madison C. H., Fla., Col. Hunter Pope, of Madison, Fla., to Miss Mamie L. Sams, daughter of Elder W. M. Sams, of Decatur, Ga.

By Rev. E. S. Tyner, June 6th, 1875, Mr. J. B. Watts to Miss E. Roberta Taylor, all of Madison county, Fla.

By Rev. Jas. A. Rosser, June 9th 1875, at the residence of Mr. Henry Parish, in Berrien County, Ga., Mr. Norman Campbell, of Brooks, to Miss Martha Wilks, of Tattnall county, Ga.

By Rev. H. R. Felder, June 10th, 1875, in Montezuma, Ga., Mr. John H. robinson to Miss Fannie C. Carmichael, all of Montezuma.

Buy Rev. G. T. Harmon, near Mars Bluff, S. C., June 10th 1875, Mr. Jonathan L. Bailey and Miss S. Malinda Jones.

By Rev. Geo. G. N. MacDonell, June 13th, 1875, Mr. James C. Keel to Miss Mattie Jordan, both of Macon, Ga.

By Rev. Geo. C. Leavel, June 17th, 1875, Mr. George Pasteur to Miss Jane Forbes, all of Marion county, Fla.

By Rev. John W. McRoy, at George's Station, S. C., June 17th, 1875, James B. Berry, Esq., of Branchville, and Miss Sallie E. Street, of George's, S. C.

By Rev. Dr. Rowell, May 20th, 1875, Mr. Wm. J. Huggins to Mrs. S. A. Bishop, all of Richland Fork, S. C.

In Wadesboro, N. C., June 22d, 1875, by Rev. F. M. Kennedy, D. D., Rev. Oscar J. Brent, of the North Carolina Conference, to Miss Julia L. Marshall, of Wadesboro.

Issue of July 7, 1875

By Rev. J. B. Jecoat [sic, for Jefcoat], June 17th, 1875, Mr. W. R. Norton to Miss Mattie Stewart, all of Orange county, Fla.

By Rev. H. Dorman, June 15th, 1875, Mr. Elias D. Hines to Miss Martha O. Barnes, all of Harris county, Ga.

By Rev. John M. Bowden, in Fairburn, Ga., June 15th, 1875, Mr. James E. Cummings, of Atlanta, Ga., to Miss Callie E. King, of the former place.

At the residence of Mr. John L. Oliver, on Sunday morning, the 6th inst., by Rev. Thos. T. Christian, Mr. A. F. Green, of Athens, Tenn., and Miss Vashti Oliver, daughter of mr. W. B. F. Oliver, of Americus.

By Rev. T. T. Christian, June 23d, Dr., A. F. Tullis to Miss Jennie Ainsworth, daughter of Rev. James T. Ainsworth, of the South Georgia Conference.

By Rev. R. W. Dixon, in the Methodist Church, in Cuthbert, Ga., June 17th, 1875, Idus L. Fielder, Esq., to Miss Julia D. Toombs, all of Cuthbert, Ga.

By Rev. John W. Burke, in East Macon, July 1st, 1875, Mr. A. W. S. Mazo to Miss Hattie Fulford.

By Rev. T. J. Clyde, June 24th, 1875, at the residence of Dr. J. W. Summers, Orangeburg county, S. C., Mr. Harrison Holton to Miss Lucy A. Allison, all of Charleston, S. C.

By Rev. R. A. Conner, June 29th, 1875, in Augusta, Ga., Mr. James M. Whitaker, of Columbia county, to Miss Lula P. Hicks, of the former place.

Issue of July 14, 1875

By Rev. H. H. Parks, June 23d, 1875, Thos. H. Whitaker, Esq., of LaGrange, Ga., to Miss Dinque Reid, of Troup county, Ga.

By Rev. John R. Parker, July 1st, 1875, Rev. R. R. Johnson, of the North Georgia Conference, to Miss M. L. West, of Lawrenceville, Ga., formerly of Tallahassee, Fla.

By Rev. J. J. Tooke, in Taylor county, Ga., July 1st, 1875, Mr. R. T. Ingraham to Miss Lou Cooper, daughter of Mr. A. G. Cooper.

By Rev. C. C. Fishburne, July 1st, 1875, at China Grove, S. C., Mr. Allard B. Hemmingway to Miss Minnie E. Britton.

Issue of July 21, 1875

By Rev. J. J. Giles, at the residence of Mr. Perry collins, June 29th, 1875, Col. H. J. McGee to Miss Kate M. Collins, all of Tatnall county, Ga.

Issue of July 28, 1875

By Rev. E. S. Tyner, July 8th, 1875, Mr. J. Q. Hunter, of Columbia county, Fla., to Miss Mit Ellison, of Madison county, Fla.

By Rev. W. J. Cotter, in Troup county, July 1st, 1875, Mr. E. E. Reid to Miss Mollie Simms.

By Rev. W. J. Cotter, in Meriwether county, July 15th, 1875, Mr. C. J. Jackson to Mrs. P. A. Robertson.

By Rev. Alex. M. Thigpen, in Newnan, Ga., June 24th, 1875, Mr. Samuel T. Shields and Miss Lucy Word.

By Rev. A. Gamewell Gantt, July 6th, 1875, Mr. Joe H. Hutson, of Charleston county, S. C., to Miss Mary E. Grier, of Georgetown county, S. C.

By Rev. A. Gamewell Gantt, July 6th, 1875, Mr. Chas A. Robins, of North Carolina, to Miss M. Adella Grier, of Georgetown county, S. C.

By Rev. W. H. Lawton, July 15th, 1875, the Rev. W. S. F. Wightman, to Miss Carrie Louisa Lawton, daughter of the officiating clergyman.

By Rev. J. O. A. Cook, July 7th, 1875, Rev. Wesley Lane, of the South Georgia Conference, to Miss Mary A. Hardaway, daughter of Judge Robert H. Hardaway, of Thomasville, Ga.

Issue of August 4, 1875

By Rev. E. S. Tyner, July 8th, 1875, Mr. John Q. Hunter, of Columbia county, Fla., to Miss Mit Ellison, of Madison county, Fla.

By Rev. E. S. Tyner, July 22d, 1875, Mr. A. J. Stephens to Miss Fannie McCall, all of Madison county, Fla.

By Rev. E. F. Gates, June 17th, 1875, at the Methodist Church, Tampa, Fla., Mr. James F. Hendry, of Fort Myers, to Miss Julia I. Frierson of Tampa, Fla.

Issue of August 11, 1875

By Rev. W. P. Smith, July 29th, 1875, Mr. F. M. Crawford, of Hart county, to Miss Mary L. Freeman, of Franklin county.

Issue of August 18, 1875

In Edgewood, August 5th, 1875, by Rev. H. J. Ellis, Mr. B. J. McCain, of Atlanta, to Miss Tallula V. Cook, of Edgewood, Ga.

Issue of August 25, 1875

By Rev. T. W. Tomkies, July 8th, 1875, Mr. M. R. Bowden, to Miss T. P. Timanus, all of Jacksonville, Fla.

By Rev. Walter Manning, August 5th, 1875, Mr. J. L. Banister to Miss L. H. Johnson, of Cobb county, Ga.

By Rev. F. B. Davies, in Oxford, Ga., August 11th, 1875, Mr. James S. Hargrove, of Newton county, to Miss Ella Gaither, of Oxford, Ga.

By Rev. W. M. C. Conly, August 12th, 1875, at the residence of Mrs. N. Laslie, in Telfair county, Mr. James Mullen of Mullengar, to Miss Catharine Watson, of Telfair county.

By Rev. S. Waldon, August 4th, 1875, at the residence of George Hamilton, of Polk county, Fla., Mr. C. W. Gillett, of Manatee county, Fla., to Miss Mary A. Farabee, of Polk county, daughter of Rev. Dr. Farabee.

Issue of September 8, 1875

In Georgetown, S. C., August 26th, 1875, by Rev. L. wood, Mr. Rodolph Richter to Miss Mary Bryant.

By Rev. L. B. Bouchelle, Mr. M. G. Wood, of Washington county, Ga., to Miss E. Lou Wells, of Emanuel county, Ga.

At Bethel Church, Orangeburg circuit, July 19th, 1875, by Rev. D. D. Dantzler, Mr. john M. Ayers to Mrs. Sarah Hair, all of Orangeburg co., S. C.

In Macon, Ga., August 29th, 1875, by Rev. John W. Burke, Mr. W. R. Calvert and Miss Mollie R. King.

By Rev. W. C. Bass, September 2d, 1875, Daniel C. Driggars, Esq., and Miss Mary E. Lumpkin, all of Bibb county, Ga.

By Rev. B. S. Key, in Homerville, Ga., August 26th, 1875, Mr. J. N. Welch to Miss Lizzie R. Anderson, all of Homerville, Ga., formerly of Savannah, Ga.

SOUTHERN CHRISTIAN ADVOCATE MARRIAGE NOTICES 1867-1878

Issue of September 15, 1875

By Rev. H. H. Parks, September 2d, 1875, in Atlanta, Ga., Hon. W. W. Turner, of LaGrange, Ga., to Miss Mattie E. Coker, of Atlanta, Ga.

By Rev. J. Bradford, September 1st, 1875, in the Methodist Church, Camilla, Ga., Frank Exley, of Savannah, Ga., to Miss Alice B. Crum, of Camilla, Ga.

Issue of September 22, 1875

In Macon, September 12th, 1875, by Rev. J. W. Burke, Mr. A. Tissereau to Miss Fannie Smith.

By Rev. Jno. M. Bowden, September 9th, 1875, Mr. Jno. H. Huff to Miss Leila H. Hearn, of Fairburn, Ga.

By Rev. John Calvin Johnson, September 9th, 1875, Mr. James A. Nichols, of Clarke county, Ga., to Miss Emma R. Collins, of Oconee county, Ga.

Issue of September 29, 1875

By Rev. Wm. McCall, September, 4th, 1875, Mr. Thomas Redding, of Madison, Fla., to Miss Ida Stripling, from Houston, Texas.

By Rev. O. w. Ransom, September 6th, 1875, Mr. Thos. S. Browning to Miss Kanses E. Watts.

By Rev. W. J. Wardlaw, September 14th, 1875, Mr. James A. Brightwell, to Miss Georgia C. Campbell, all of Oglethorpe county, Ga.

By Rev. A. Thornburgh, September 16th, 1875, Mr. Carles [sic] Cumpton to Miss Emma P. Kerkis, all of Walker county, Ga.

By Rev. E. S. Tyner, September 20th, 1875, Mr. Chas. G. Hines to Miss Fannie Mosely, all of Madison, Fla.

Issue of October 6, 1875

By Rev. T. H. Timmons, September 23d, 1875, Mr. W. T. B. Simmons to Miss Sarah C. Reed, all of Atlanta, Ga.

Issue of October 13, 1875

By Rev. F. B. Davies, at Social Circle, Ga., September 23d, 1875, Mr. Josiah P. Freeman, to Miss Emma G. Snow.

By Rev. T. A. Seals, September 9th, 1875, Mr. Henry C. McGaughy to Miss Martha A. Brown, all of Whitfield county, Ga.

By Rev. T. A. Seals, September 30th, 1875, Rev. Geo. C. Rankin, of the Holston Conference, Methodist E. Church, South, and Miss Fanny Lou Denton, of Dalton, Ga.

By Rev. G. H. Pooser, September 30th, 1875, at Jackson station, Port Royal R. R., S. c., Mr. John S. Tanner to Miss Patience Peacock, both of Washington county, Ga.

By Rev. Alex. P. Wright, September 28th, 1875, Mr. T. E. Shadgett, of Arlington, to Miss Lillie B. Lewis, of Early county, Ga.

By Rev. Alex. P. Wright, September 30th, 1875, Mr. Giles T. Webb to Miss Sallie W. Pullen, all of Early county, Ga.

By Rev. R. W. Barber, September 29th, 1875, Mr. J. f. J. Caldwell, of Newberry, to Miss R. C. Connor, of Cokesbury, S. C.

By Rev. E. S. Tyner, September 30th, 1875, Mr. C. H. Fretwell to Miss E. R. Stephens, all of Madison county, Fla.

By Rev. M. H. Eakes, September 16th, 1875, Mr. Z. T. Roberts, of Gwinnett county, Ga., to Miss Fanny Lenoir, of Milton county, Ga.

By Rev. M. H. Eakes, October 7th, 1875, Mr. J. R. Brantly, of Senoia, Ga., to Miss Dora Howell, of Gwinnett county, Ga.

Issue of October 20, 1875

By Rev. J. B. Jefcoat, September 30th, 1875, Mr. Jesse T. Lamp to Miss Sarah S. Buchan, all of Orange county, Fla.

By Rev. J. W. Christian, October 5th, 1875, Mr. Wiley E. Jones, of Randolph county, Ala., to Miss Ida E. Spikes, of Fredonia, Chambers county, Ala.

by Rev. J. D. Gray, October 10th, 1875, in the Methodist Church at Sunnyside, Ga., Dr. John P. Starr to Miss Alice Griffin.

By Rev. Arminius Wright, in Macon, Ga., October 14th, 1875, Mr. Wiley Barnes and Miss Rosa Hammond, daughter of Dr. D. W. Hammond.

By Rev. Arminius Wright, in Macon, Ga., October 14th, 1875, Mr. I. H. Johnson and Miss Sallie C. Hinton, only daughter of Rev. J. W. Hinton, D. D.

Issue of October 27, 1875

By Rev. E. J. Burch, October 14th, 1875, Mr. Samuel M. Clark to Miss Helen M. Fleming, all of Louisville, Ga.

By Rev. D. J. Simmons, in Summerville, S. C., October 13th, 1875, Mr. Joseph H. Abbey to Miss Mary Ann Cooke.

By Rev. J. H. Baxter, near White Sulphur Springs, Merriwether county, Ga., October 17th, 1875, Rev. James Jones, of the North Georgia Conference, to Mrs. Catharine E. Christian.

By Rev. John N. Hudson, October 16th 1875, Mr. T. E. J. Cowart, of Lee, to Miss M. V. Clarke, of Sumter county, Ga.

By Rev. J. T. Ainsworth, November 30th, 1875, Mr. R. T. Connally, of Chattanooga, to Miss Alice Black of Sumter county, Ga.

Issue of November 3, 1875

By Rev. W. A. Rogers, October 21st, 1875, Mr. James R. May, of Colleton, to Miss Fannie Strother, of Sumter, S. C.

By Rev. C. D. Rowell, October 19th, 1875, Mr. J. D. Jones, of Georgia, to Miss G. M. Garner, of Richland county, S. C.

By Rev. C. D. Rowell, October 20th, 1875, Mr. W. J. Ledingham, of Richland county, to Miss Mary A. Rowell, eldest daughter of C. D. and M. E. Rowell, of South Carolina Conference.

By Rev. J. Q. Stockman, October 13th, 1875, Mr. F. A. Lewis, of Seneca City, S. C., to Miss Mattie M. Erwin, of Brevard, N. C.

By Rev. J. Q. Stockman, October 7th, 1875, Mr. James Clayton to Miss Charlotte Hughes, of Pickens county, S. C.

By Rev. A. Gray, in Monticello, Ga., October 17th, 1875, Mr. Virgil A. Chapin to Mis Louisa E. Charping, both of Monticello, Ga.

By Rev. R. W. Barber, October 19th, 1875, Mr. J. S. Fair, of Newberry, to Miss Hannie Herndon, of Cokesbury, S. C.

By Rev. T. B. Russell, October 21st, 1875, Mr. Edward P. Chambers, of Eufaula, Ala., to Miss Georgia C. Riley, of Winchester, Macon county, Ga.

By Rev. C. C. Davis, October 20th, 1875, Mr. Joseph A. Tribble to Miss Lucy Thurman, all of Fulton county, Ga.

By Rev. J. H. Cline, October 21st, 1875, Mr. J. C. Harman, of Meriwether county, to Miss Jennie C. Marchman, of Troup county.

By Rev. J. D. Rogers, October 7th, 1875, Mr. Charles E. Wells to Miss Eliza Smith, in Hernando county, Fla.

By Rev. T. J. Phillips, October 4th, 1875, Mr. Z. F. Stokes, of Gadsden county, Fla., to Miss Sallie L. Scott, of Leon county, Fla.

By Rev. L. J. Davies, in Griffin, Ga., October 19th, 1875, Mr. William E. Baker, of Pike county, to Miss Alice McWilliams, of Griffin, Ga.

By Rev. L. A. Darsey, October 21st, 1875, Mr. Bartlett Adams, of Eastport, Me[?]., to Miss Lizzie Packard, of St. Mary's Ga.

At Orangeburg, S. C., October 28th, 1875, by Rev. H. A. C. Walker, Rev. George J. Griffiths, D. D., of the South Georgia Conference, to Miss Anna W. Wightman, daughter of Rev. John Wesley Wightman, D. D., of the Kentucky Conference.

By Rev. T. J. Clyde, October 14th, 1875, Mr. J. Olin Jones, to Miss C. R. Fogler, all of Orangeburg county, S. C.

By Rev. H. R. Felder, in Montezuma, Macon county, Ga., October 19th, 1875, Mr. C. A. Bedingfield to Miss P. B. Dawson.

SOUTHERN CHRISTIAN ADVOCATE MARRIAGE NOTICES 1867-1878

By Rev. H. R. Felder, October 27th, 1875, Mr. D. R. Wimberly, of Houston county, Ga., to Miss Julia Byrom, of Byromville, Dooly county, Ga.

By Rev. H. R. Felder, October 27th, 1875, Mr. C. W. Reynolds to Miss M. L. Smith, all of Macon county, Ga.

By Rev. T. H. Timmons, October 27th, 1875, at Payne's Chapel, Mr. W. N. Sheridan to Miss Turissa R. Ragan, all of Atlanta, Ga.

Issue of November 10, 1875

By Rev. W. W. Wadsworth, October 12th, 1875, in Jones county, Ga., Mr. James W. Turk, of Clinton, to Miss Cordelia Singleton.

By Rev. W. W. Wadsworth, October 15th, 1875, Mr. John H. Lanham to Mrs. Emma E. Ellison, of Milledgeville, Ga.

By Rev. W. W. Wadsworth, October 31st, 1875, at the residence of Mr. Wynne, in Midway, Ga., Mr. James Jeff Pinckard to Mrs. Garphelia Gamble, both of Macon, Ga.

By Rev. John Calvin Johnson, November 2d, 1875, Mr. William P. Nichols to Miss Callie Swan, all of Clarke county, Ga.

By Rev. Alex. P. Wright, October 31st, 1875, Mr. S. B. Timmons to Miss F. E. Johnson, daughter of Thomas G. Johnson, all of Early county, Ga.

By Rev. P. F. Kistler, October 28th, 1875, in Bamberg, S. C., Mr. W. G. Sease, of Summerville, S. C., to Miss Minnie F. Kistler.

By Rev. Wm. H. LaPrade, October 28th, 1875, in Polk county, Ga., Mr. A. Aubyn Camp to Miss Laura Hutchings.

By Rev. S. S. Sweet, October 31st, 1875, Dr. Oliver Toole, of Whiteville, Ga., to Miss Kittie S. Redding, daughter of the late Abner Redding, of Bibb county, Ga.

By Rev. J. J. Morgan, October 24th, 1875, Mr. Thomas S. Funderburke to Mrs. Georgia A. O'Neal, all of Decatur county, Ga.

By Rev. B. H. Sasnett, November 4th, 1875, in Washington county, Ga., Mr. John G. Harrison, to Miss Annie E. Palmer.

By Rev. R. M. Saunders, October 28th, 1875, in Norfolk, Va., Judge David W. Gwynn, of Tallahassee, Fla., to Miss Francina A. Nash, of Norfolk.

Issue of November 17, 1875

By Rev. Jas. R. Smith, October 5th, 1875, Mr. W. J. Barrett to Miss Lula L. Carter, all of Pike county, Ga.

By Rev. J. Walter Dickson, October 28th, 1875, Mr. W. I. Garrison to Mrs. Mary J. Alexander, both of York county, S. C.

By Rev. J. Walter Dickson, November 2d, 1875, Mr. C. G. Parish, of Yorkville, S. C., to Miss Laura Eva Fitchett, of York county, S. C.

By Rev. W. F. Quillian, October 28th, 1875, Mr. Leonidas F. Finger, of Gainesville, Ga., to Miss Mattie J. Quillian, of White county, Ga.

By Rev. J. T. Ainsworth, October 21st, 1875, in Schley county, Ga., Mr. R. H. Slappy to Miss Emma Stewart.

By Rev. Alex. P. Wright, November 4th, 1875, Mr. G. D. Oliver, of Arlington, Ga., to Miss M. A. Fudge, of Colquitt, Ga.

By Rev. J. W. McRoy, November 4th, 1875, Mr. J. N. Westbury, of Colleton, to Miss Ida J. Myers, of Orangeburg county, S. C.

By Rev. S. J. Hill, October 9th, 1875, Mr. J. F. Kelly, of Darlington, to Miss A. R. Dixon, of Bishopville, S. C.

By Rev. S. S. Sweet, October 11th 1875, Mr. John D. Ham, of Macon, to Miss Laura Riley, of Hamilton, Ga.

Issue of November 24, 1875

By Rev. J. W. McRoy, November 11th, 1875, Donald N. Staley, of Barnwell, to Miss Sallie Fairy, of Orangeburg county, S. C.

By Rev. John M. Bowden, November 10th, 1875, Mr. Delone N. Dorsett to Mrs. Mary A. Harvy, all of Fairburn, Ga.

By Rev. Wm. C. Power, November 7th, 1875, Mr. Joseph W. Kimball, of Johnsonville, S. C., to Miss Eliza McIntosh, of Marlboro, S. C.

By Rev. T. J. Phillips, November 10th, 1875, Dr. W. K. Anders, of Bladen county, N. C., to Miss Ella J. Cromartie, of Leon county, Fla.

By Rev. J. B. McFarland, at Mt. Vernon church, November 4th, 1875, Mr. C. T. Claibern to Miss Julia Parker, both of Whitfield county, Ga.

By Rev. Wm. C. Power, November 3d, 1875, near Florence, S. C., Mr. David H. Hamby, to Miss Kate C., daughter of Peter A. Brunson, Esq., all of Darlington District, S. C.

By Rev. W. A. Rogers, November 10th, 1875, Mr. C. L. Stuckey to Miss Janie Dixon, both of Bishopville, S. C.

By Rev. Thos. G. Herbert, November 4th, 1875, Dr. Lucius Bellinger Bates to Miss Sallie E. McCants, all of Newberry county, S. C.

By Rev. H. Tyler, November 4th, 1875, in Anderson, S. C., Mr. S. W. Milford to Miss M. B. Palmer, both of Anderson.

By Rev. Albert Gray, November 11th, 1875, Mr. John A. Penn to Miss Mary T. Grubbs, both of Jasper county, Ga.

By Rev. W. W. Dunham, November 9th, 1875, in Petersburg, Va., R. N. Littlejohn, of Charlotte, N. C., to Miss Maggie L. Blanks, of the former city.

By Rev. T. E. Wannamaker, in Allendale, S. C., November 11th, 1875, Mr. S. P. Maner, Jr., to Miss Anna B. Martin, daughter of the late Capt. J. V. Martin.

SOUTHERN CHRISTIAN ADVOCATE MARRIAGE NOTICES 1867-1878

Issue of December 1, 1875

By Rev. S. R. Weaver, November 24th, 1875, at the residence of Mrs. Bennett, Henry county, Ala., Dr. R. S. Wimberly, of Florence, Ga., and Mrs. L. H. Greer, of Henry co., Ala.

By Rev. W. Lane, in the Methodist church in Ellaville, Ga., on the 16th November, Mr. Charley Deusler to Miss Jennie Lasseter, both of Dawson, Ga.

November 9th, 1875, by Rev. A. Gamewell Gantt, Mr. H. W. Browning, of Charleston county, S. C., to Miss Anna S. Berry, of Orangeburg county, S. C.

November 18th, 1875, by Rev. A. Gamewell Gantt, at the residence of Mr. John C. Bradley, Mr. Geo. E. Parker, of North Carolina, to Miss Edith R. Ward, of Charleston, S. C.

In LaGrange, Ga., on the 25th ult., by Rev. Jno. W. Burke, F. G. Hancock, Esq., of Atlanta, to Miss Eula Ferrell, of LaGrange.

By Rev. J. V. M. Morris, in Bulloch county, Ga., on the 11th of November, 1875, Mr. J. B. Cone to Miss Mitt. A. Hodges.

By Rev. D. J. Weems, November 4th, 1875, Rev. Floyd M. Oswalt, of Forestville, Ga., to Miss Mattie Asles, of Floyd county, Ga.

By Rev. D. J. Simmons, near Ridgeville, Colleton county, S. C., November 14th, 1875, Mr. Smith Rhodes to Miss Annie Pendarvis.

By Rev. Walter Knox, November 23d, 1875, Mr. Thomas M. Bailey to Miss Fannie E. Dozier, both of Talbot county, Ga.

By Rev. Thomas Battle, November 18th, 1875, Mr. Robert N. Watson to Miss Kitty Harmon, all of Meriwether county, Ga.

By Rev. F. M. T. Brannan, November 18th, 1875, Mr. J. R. Pennington to Miss Leila Battles, all of Monroe county, Ga.

By Rev. M. H. Pooser, November 16, 1875, Mr. Joel Inabinet to Mrs. Chloe Ann Harrison, all of Edgefield county, S. C.

By Rev. M. H. Pooser, November 16, 1875, Mr. Harmon Martin to Mrs. Martha M. K.k Gibson, all of Edgefield county, S. C.

In Randolph county, Ga., by Rev. R. W. Dixon, November 10, 1875, Edward B. Ridgeway, of Cuthbert, Ga., to Miss Mary C. Knowles, of Randolph county, Ga.

In Cuthbert, Ga., by Rev. R. W. Dixon, November 24th, 1875, Samuel E. Freeman, of Fort Gaines, Ga., to Miss B. Gertrude Tackets, of Cuthbert, Ga.

At Albany, Ga., November 17th, 1875, by Rev. George J. Griffiths, D. D., Mr. Hezekiah D. Thomas to Mrs. Marian C. Oglesby, nee Greer, both of Dougherty county, Ga.

By Rev. W. W. Graham, at Mt. Zion Church, November 23d, 1875, Mr. W. H. Gibson to Miss Ella Byrd, all of Lee county, Ga.

Issue of December 8, 1875

By Rev. T. B. Russell, November 25th, 1875, in Fort Valley, Ga., Mr. Frank C. Houser to Miss Leola E. Greene.

By Rev. T. B. Russell, near Fort Valley, Ga., December 1st, 1875, Mr. Jas. Taylor Harris to Miss Laura Estelle Deschamps, the latter formerly of Sumter, S. C.

By Rev. A. J. Cauthen, November 28th 1875, Mr. R. E. Way of Blackville, to Miss -- Glenn, of Charleston, S. C.

By Rev. John W. McRoy, at Reevesville, S. C., November 25th, 1875, William F. Street to Miss Elizabeth B. Heaton.

By Rev. A. W. Harris, November 28th, 1875, in the Methodist E. Church, Mr. E. D. Souter to Miss E. A., daughter of Rev. Wm. Peeler, all of Green Cove Springs, Fla.

By Rev. Geo. H. Wells, December 1, 1875, Dr. H. Baer to Miss Adela B., daughter of Mr. A. C. Phin, of Charleston, S. C.

By Rev. J. J. Singleton, November 25th, 1875, Mr. Thomas B. Merks to Miss Sarah A. Gaines, both of Bartow county, Ga.

By Rev. J. J. Singleton, November 30th, 1875, Mr. T. F. Colbert to Miss C. E. Templeton, both of Bartow county, Ga.

By Rev. N. D. Morehouse, November 8th, 1875, Mr. Samuel Houton to Miss Mary Lasiter, both of Alexander, Ga.

By Rev. N. D. Morehouse, November 17th, 1875, Mr. Wm. W. Walker, of Savannah, Ga., to Miss Margaret R. Jones, of Burke county, Ga.

By Rev. E. S. Tyner, November 18th, 1875, Mr. R. A. Ivey of Live Oak, Fla., to Miss E. J. Williams, of Brooks county, Ga.

By Rev. E. S. Tyner, November 25th, 1875, Mr. Thos. A. Beggs to Miss Ella S. Armstrong, all of Madison county, Fla.

By Rev. H. W. Key, November 18th, 1875, Mr. Miles Wade, of Alabama, to Miss Maddie V. Biggers, of Muscogee, Ga.

November 18th, at the residence of Wilson U. Sterns, Russell county, Ala., by Rev. John W. Solomon, Dr. Thomas B. Campbell, of Macon county, Ala., to Miss Julia M. Sterns.

Also, at the same time and place, by Rev. John W. Solomon, Mr. John C. Abney to Miss Eugenia O. Sterns.

By Rev. S. J. Hill, November 24th, 1875, Mr. Robert Muldraw, of Bishopville, to Miss Mary M. Muldraw, of St. Lukes.

By Rev. S. J. Hill, December 1st, 1875, Rev. E. M. Merritt, of the South Carolina Conference, to Miss Amanda Durant, of Bishopville.

By Rev. S. J. Hill, December 1st, 1875, Mr. David Dixon to Miss Blandina Durant, all of Bishopville.

Issue of December 15, 1875

By Rev. E. J. Rents, November 25th, 1875, at Mr. J. Bateman's. Mr. W. T. Montfort to Miss E. H. Rutherford, all of Butler, Ga.

By Rev. E. J. Rents, December 8th, 1875, at Mr. J. E. Montfort's. Mr. Hugh Neisler to Miss Sallie E. Montfort, all of Taylor county, Ga.

By Rev. D. D. Dantzler, December 2d, 1875, Mr. James E. Boone to Miss Rosa L. Crum, all of Orangeburg, S. C.

By Rev. D. D. Dantzler, December 2d, 1875, at the residence of the bride's brother, Mr. Willie Rives, Mr. Wliliam C. Crum to Miss Octavia M. S. Rives, all of Orangeburg, S. C.

By Rev. T. F. Pierce, November 25th, 1875, Rev. W. W. Lampkin, of the North Georgia Conference, to Miss Fannie M. Booker, of Wilkes county, Ga.

By Rev. T. F. Pierce, November 25th, 1875, Mr. T. L. Rees, of McDuffie county, to Miss A. G. Booker, of Wilkes county, Ga.

By Rev. Thomas B. Lanier, November 21st, 1875, Mr. John W. Carpenter to Miss Talula Huchins, all of Burke county, Ga.

By Rev. Thomas B. Lanier, December 1st, 1875, Mr. Peter A. Porter to Miss Amelia K. Berry, all of Effingham county, Ga.

By Rev. W. F. Robison, November 23d, 1875, Mr. Hatsel S. Holdridge, of Macon, to Miss Laura P. Havis, of Perry, Ga.

By Rev. W. F. Robison, December 1st, 1875, Mr. John W. Gaddy and Miss Mary E. Avant, both of Perry, Ga.

By Rev. W. F. Robison, December 2d, 1875, Mr. Hardy D. Cross and Mrs. Sallie E. Waddell, both of Houston county, Ga.

By Rev. A. H. Quillian, November 25th, 1875, November 25th, 1875, in Walsenburg, Huerfano county, Colorado, Robert A. Quillian, Esq., to Miss Isabella Campbell.
By Rev. W. A. Rice, November 28th, 1875, Dr. J. P. Holmes, of Macon, Ga., to Miss Ella S. Merritt, of Marianna, Fla.

By Rev. George J. Griffiths, D. D., November 24th, 1875, at Albany, Ga., Mr. Gideon Wallace, of Worth county, to Mrs. Nannie DeVan, formerly Carter, of Albany, Ga.

By Rev. S. S. Sweet, December 9th, 1875, in Macon, Ga., Mr. Wm. C. Leak to Miss ella L. Whitehurst.

By Rev. W. I. Greene, November 30th, 1875, in Fort Valley, Ga., Mr. Walter R. Anderson to Miss Mary T. Haddock.

By Rev. G. S. Johnston, November 28th, 1875, in Hamilton, Ga., Mr. Wm. O. Moss to Miss Emma J. Bedell, both of Harris county, Ga.

By Rev. W. B. Foote, December 9th, 1875, Rev. H. J. Ellis, of the North Georgia Conference, to Miss Susie Smith, of Oak Bowery, Ala.

By Rev. R. B. Tarrant, November 28th, 1875, Mr. John Glover to Miss Lou Ehney, all of Orangeburg county, S. C.

By Rev. R. B. Tarrant, December 2d, 1875, at the residence of the officiating minister, Mr. Wm. Livingstone to Miss Florella Summers, all of Orangeburg, S. C.

By Rev. A. J. Dean, December 9th, 1875, Rev. J. E. Godfrey, of Atlanta, to Mrs. Sarah M. Simmons, of Stewart county, Ga.

Issue of December 22-29, 1875

By Rev. W. J. Cotter, November 28th, 1875, Mr. J. M. O'Neal, to Miss R. Carden.

By Rev. W. J. Cotter, December 14th, 1875, Mr. G. M. Field, to Miss M. C. Sewell.

By Rev. W. J. Cotter, December 14th, 1875, Mr. J. T. Barrow, to Miss C. R. Sewell.

By Rev. A. M. Williams, in Laurens county, Ga., December 2d, 1875, at the residence of the bride's grand-mother, Mr. J. Daniel Smith to Miss Sallie R. Rheney.

By Rev. T. H. Timmons (Rev. C. J. Oliver participating in the ceremony) December 12th, 1875, in Atlanta, Ga., Mr. J. H. Hawes to Miss Julia Green, all of Atlanta, Ga.

By Rev. Bishop Keener, December 8th, 1875, in Oxford, Ga., Rev. J. Rembert Smith, of the North Georgia Conference, to Carrie Palmer, eldest daughter of the late Prof. James E. Palmer. Richmond *Christian Advocate* please copy.

By Rev. D. J. Simmons, December 9th, 1875, Mr. Charles W. Sanders, of Green county, Ala., to Miss Ellen A. Smith, of Charleston county, S. C.

By Rev. W. G. Johnson, December 14th, 1875, Prof. R. J. Smith, of Putnam county, to Miss Sarah M. Barron, of Jones county, Ga.

Issue of January 5, 1876

By Rev. E. S. Tyner, December 23d, 1875, Mr. Frank Hadden to Miss F. A. Caule of Madison county, Fla.

By Rev. Jas. W. Traywick, December, 26th, 1875, in Polk county, Ga., Rev. J. W. Lee, of the North Georgia Conference, to Miss Emma E. Ledbetter, daughter of Rev. Lewis L. Ledbetter deceased.

By Rev. J. H. Zimmerman, December 9th, 1875, at the residence of Dr. J. Murray, Mr. Lawrence W. Westbury to Miss Sarah M. V. Murray, all of Colleton county, S. C.

By Rev. J. H. Zimmerman, December 23d, 1875, Mr. Lewis A. Hilton to Miss Emma J. Bell, all of Colleton county, S. C.

By Rev. J. H. Zimmerman, December 31st, 1875, Mr. J. A. Way to Miss Arcena R. Cummings, all of Colleton county, S. C.

By Rev. S. E. Bassett, December 21st, 1875, in Crawford county, Mr. Eugene A. Wright of Houston county to Miss Ella Vinson.

By Rev. S. E. Bassett, December 23d, 1875, in Crawford county, Hon. W. G. Vinson to Mrs. J. E. T. Pope, all of Crawford county.

By Rev. J. R. Mayson, November 20th, 1875, at the residence of Rev. J. P. Howell, Mr. Thomas J. Hines of Chambers county, Ala., to Miss Mary J. Howell, of Troup county, Ga.

By Rev. J. R. Mayson, at Midway Church, December 24th, 1875, Mr. Andrew W. Maffett to Miss Susan D. Boykin, all of Troup county, Ga.

By Rev. John Inabinet, December 23d, 1875, Mr. D. A. W. Murph to Miss Frazier Wolf, all of Orangeburg county.

By Rev. W. Ewing Johnston, December 22d, 1875, in Richmond county, Mr. John D. Greiner to Miss Ella Hatfield.

By Rev. W. Ewing Johnston, December 23d, 1875, Mr. John H. Tinley to Miss Catherine L. Tinley, all of Richmond county, Ga.

By Rev. W. Ewing Johnston, December 26th, 1875, Mr. Adolphus Sanders to Miss Sarah Cowley, all of Richmond county, Ga.

By Rev. W. M. Watts, December 22d, 1875, Mr. Jas. H. Jordan to Miss Anna Ansley, all of Thomas county, Ga.

By Rev. F. B. Davies, December 7th, 1875, at Social Circle, Mr. William Park to Miss Josie E. Colton.

By Rev. T. B. Russell, December 23d, 8175, in Marshallville, Ga., Mr. J. W. Frederick to Miss Carrie E. Walker.

By Rev. E. S. Tyner, December 15th, 1875, Mr. John S. Dozier to Miss Mary E. Waller, all of Madison county, Fla.

By Rev. J. W. Humbert, December 22, 1875, Rev. A. Coke Smith, of the South Carolina Conference, to Miss Kate, daughter of the late Gen. H. H. Kinard, of Newberry, S. C.

By Rev. E. P. Bonner, December 23d, 1875, Mr. H. F. Norvill to Miss A. J. Spires, all of Columbia county, Ga.

By Rev. C. Trussell, December 15th, 1875, Rev. H. M. Newton, of Whitesburg, Ga., to Miss Sallie Morgan, of Rock Mart, Ga.

By Rev. R. W. Dixon, December 9th, 1875, William A. Campbell, of Macon, Ga., to Miss S. Cebie Perkins, of Cuthbert, Ga.

By Rev. R. W. Dixon, December 28th, 1875, James A. Allison to Miss Docia B. Key, both of Cuthbert, Ga.

By Rev. Josiah W. Jordan, December 14th, 1875, Mr. Simeon G. Smith to Miss Eunice E. Tignor, both of Talbot county, Ga.

By Rev. Josiah W. Jordan, December 23d, 1875, Mr. James W. Dewberry to Miss Mary F. Smarr, all of Monroe county, Ga.

By W. T. Laine, December 16, 1875, Mr. J. A. Hunt to Miss Parisade Carroll.

By W. T. Laine, Wm. H. Young to Miss Demarius Matthews.

By Rev. W. H. Graham, December 14th, 1875, Benjamin B. Sotory to Miss C. P. Rains, both of Upson county, Ga.

By Rev. W. H. Graham, December 20th, 1875, Jesse McRay of Merriwether to Miss Querny Pugh of Upson county, Ga.

By Rev. W. H. Graham, December 23d, 1875, Mr. J. H. Bailey to Miss Mary S. Minter, all of Upson county, Ga.

By Rev. Thos. F. Pierce, December 23d, 1875, Mr. Tunis W. Powell, of High Shoals, Morgan county, to Miss Fannie Davenport, of Point Peter, Oglethorpe county, Ga.

By Rev. O. L. Smith, December 21st, 1875, Mr. James T. Van Horn to Columbus, Ga., and Miss Addie L. Spence of Covington, Ga.

By Rev. T. H. Timmons, of Paynes' Chapel, in Atlanta, Ga., December 21st, 1875, Mr. John A. Wright to Miss Mary E. Fagan.

By Rev. R. M. T. Brannon, near Greenville, Ga., December 15th, 1875, Mr. Charles R. Carter of Barnesville, Ga., to Miss Julia E. Ector, daughter of the late Col. Walton Ector.

By Rev. D. F. C. Timmons, December 19th, 1875, Mr. Thomas P. Clegg to Miss Ophelia Edmunds, all of Walton county, Ga.

By Rev. D. F. C. Timmons, December 26th, 1875, Mr. John D. Malsby of Atlanta, Ga., to Miss A. H. Cary of Monroe, Ga.

By Rev. J. T. Ainsworth, December 14th 1875, December 14th, 1875, Mr. Anson Slapy of Mashalville, Ga., to Miss Jennie Stewart of Schley county, Ga.

By Rev. Dr. Leonard, in the Methodist Church, Attapulgus, Ga., December 21st, 1875, Mr. George Pierce Wood of Decatur county, Ga., to Miss Annie Giles, daughter of Col. Thomas R. Smith, of Attapulgus, Decatur county, Ga.

By Rev. G. H. Pattillo, in the Methodist Church, Sparta, Ga., December 21st, 1875, Mr. Henry Harris to Miss S. Amelia Williams.

By Rev. G. H. Pattillo, in the Methodist Church, Sparta, Ga., December 21st, 1875, Mr. Thomas R. Lamar to Miss J. Bettie Larson.

By Rev. Junius Jordan, near Eufaula, Ala., December 16th, 1875, Mr. Frank R. Powell to Miss Carrie Dudley.

By Rev. W. R. Stilwell, December 16th, 1875, Mr. P. T. Carmical to Miss E. T. Fambrough, all of Coweta county, Ga.

By Rev. W. G. Hanson, October 10, 1875, in Cherokee county, Ga., Mr. J. V. Kinnett to Miss M. A. Wheeler.

By Rev. W. G. Hanson, November 10th, 1875, Mr. B. P. Christopher of Cherokee county, Ga., to Mrs. Mary Whitmore, of Roswell, Ga.

By Rev. W. G. Hanson, near Dalton, Ga., December 15th, 1875, Mr. W. N. Hathorne to Miss Lizzie Bivings.

By Rev. B. B. Ross, at the residence of Mr. Isaac Ross, December 21st, 1875, Mr. Thomas L. Frazer to Miss Ella N. Ross, both of Opelika, Ala.

By Rev. R. H. Howren, December 21st, 1875, Mr. L. Wooten to Miss Mary C. Russell, all of Waukeenah, Fla.

By Rev. R. H. Howren, October 27, 1875, Mr. S. Merrit to Miss M. Oder, all of Jefferson county, Fla.

By Rev. T. H. Timmons, December 29th, 1875, at the residence of Mr. Wealch, in Atlanta, Ga., Mr. Bartlet Goodwin to Louisa Elizabeth Holcomb, all of Atlanta, GA.

By Rev. W. L. Wooton, in Lincoln county, Ga., December 21st, 1875, Mr. Samuel A. Fortson of Wilkes county, Ga., to Miss Mollie E. Barksdale of Lincoln county, Ga.

By Rev. W. M. Watts, On December 2d, 1875, Mr. B. W. McManes to Miss Ella R. Hayes, all of Cairo, Thomas county, Ga.

By Rev. W. M. Watts, On December 8th, 1875, Dr. T. Jeff Brown of Amouie, Fla., to Miss Sallie M. Powell, of Cairo, Thomas county, Ga.

By Rev. J. E. Sentell, December 12th, 1875, Mr. W. U. Ansley to Miss Bettie E. Pearson, all of Thomas county, Ga.

By Rev. J. Finger, December 21st, 1875, Mr. J. L. Crenshaw of Pickens county, S. C., to Miss Amanda M. Martin, of Anderson county, S. C.

By Rev. J. Finger, December 21st, 1875, Mr. J. W. Evatt to Miss Matilda M. Newton of Anderson county, S. C.

By Rev. N. D. Morehouse, December 9th, 1875, Mr. Needham Buxton of Burke county, Ga, to Miss Anna E. Oliver, of Scriven county, Ga.

By Rev. L. W. Rast, December 6th, 1875, Mr. John Stack to Miss Julia Golson, daughter of J. P. Golson, all of Orangeburg county, S. C.

By Rev. W. J. Green, December 9th, 1875, Mr. A. J. Lyle of Leon county, Fla., to Miss Susan E. Dickey, of Thomas county, Ga.

Issue of January 12, 1876

By Rev. Dr. M. M. Michau, December 29th, 1875, in Hamilton county, Fla, Mr. J. A. Ivey of Suwannee county, Fla., to Miss C. P. --y.

By Rev. E. S. Tyner, December 30, 1875, Mr. G. W. Jarvis to Miss R. A. Edwards, all of Madison county, Fla.

By Rev. Clement C. Cary, December 16th, 1875, Mr. Benjamin J. Kinney to Miss Mamie L. David, all of Lincoln county, Ga.

By Rev. Clement C. Cary, December 23d, 1875, Mr. James M. Tankersley to Miss --llie Ann Albea, all of Lincoln county, Ga.

By Rev. W. W. Graham, December 23, 1875, Mr. P. R. Rutledge of Lee county, Ala., to Miss Lizzie Jones, of Russell county, Ala.

By Rev. W. W. Graham, December --, 1875, at Wesley Chapel, Mr. George T. Burke to Miss Lizzie Watson, all of Butler county, Ala.

December 28th, 1875, at "Refuge," Decatur county, Ga., the home of the bride's father, Hon. Charles J. Munnerlyn, by Rev. H. L. Ho--, Mr. I. B. English to Macon, Ga., to Miss Mary H. Munnerlyn.

By Rev. W. W. Stewart, December 28th, 1875, Mr. W. S. Williams to Miss Stella Brooks, daughter of Capt. Robert Brooks of Talbot county, Ga.

By Rev. W. W. Stewart, January 5th, 1876, Mr. E. R. Richards, of Macon, to Miss Sallie W. Ellison, daughter of Col. W. H. Ellison, of Talbot county, Ga.

By Rev. C. Trussell, December 15th, 1875, Mr. Henry M. Newton, of Whitesburg, Ga., to Miss Sallie J. Morgan, of Pauldin county, Ga.

By Rev. A. J. Stokes, December 18th, 1875, at Mullins, S. C., W. A. Oliver, M. D., to Miss Jennie McDuffie, daughter of Neal C. McDuffie.

By Rev. A. J. Stokes, December 12th, 1875, near Midway, S. C., Mr. G. L. Salley, of Orangeburg, S. C., to Miss Mattie S. Stokes, daughter of Capt. Jefferson Stokes.

By Rev. A. J. Stokes, December 31st, 1875, at Camden, S. C., Mr. James Nelson, of Kershaw county, to Miss Emma J. Capers, daughter of the late Rev. Samuel W. Capers.

By Rev. W. Hutto, December 2d, 1875, Mr. Ellis Kizer, of Colleton, to Miss Rosa Shuler, of Charleston county, S. C.

By Rev. W. Hutto, December 5th, 1875, Mr. Jesse Hilton to Miss Mary E. Elzif, all of Charleston, S. C.

By Rev. R. B. Tarrant, December 12th, 1875, at the residence of Mr. Philip Martin, Mr. Henry Inabinet to Miss Cornelia Phillips, all of Orangeburg county.

By Rev. R. B. Tarrant, December 21st, 1875, Mr. John A. Summers to Miss Florence Phillips, all of Orangeburg.

By Rev. W. T. Capers, D. D., December 22d, 1875, at the Columbia Female College, Mr. Alexander N. Talley, Jr., to Miss Elizabeth Whitner Jones, daughter of Rev. S. B. Jones, S. C.

By Rev. H. R. Felder, December 21st, 1875, at Byromville, Dooley county, Ga., Mr. W. H. Clarke, of Atlanta, to Miss Annie Byrom, of Byromville, S. C.

By Rev. H. R. Felder, December 9th, 1875, at the residence of Mr. L. E. Veal, Mr. Wm. Minor of Montezuma, to Miss Anna Moreland, of Dooley county, Ga.

By Rev. W. F. Robison, December 9th, 1875, Dr. Chas. T. Jackson, of Houston county, Ga., to Miss Lula Alexander, of Forsyth, Ga.

By Rev. M. Puckett, December 19th, 1875, at the Jasper parsonage, Mr. Wm. Conner to Miss Ann Harris, daughter of Rev. J. J. Harris, of the North Georgia Conference.

By Rev. C. W. Key, December 23d, 1875, Hon. S. C. Lamkin, of Columbia county, to Miss Josephine B. Jackson, of Augusta, Ga.

Issue of January 19, 1876

By Rev. Joseph M. Gable, December 23d, 1875, Mr. Dennis J. Manning to Miss Florence F. Baxter, all of Cobb county, Ga.

By Rev. Jno. M. Bowden, December 23d, 1875, Mr. Jno. Hearn to Miss Georgia V. Johnson, of Fairburn, Ga.

By Rev. R. L. Wiggins, January 6th 1875, in Hayneville, Houston county, Ga., Mr. A. Fredrick Walker, of Marshallville, Ga., to Miss Mattie S. Pitts, of the former place.

By Rev. W. T. Hamilton, December 23d, 1875, Dr. C. R. Giles, of Jefferson, Ga., to Miss Ida J. Williams of Thompson, Ga.

By Rev. W. T. Hamilton, January 5th, 1876, Rev. Geo. E. Bonner, of the North Georgia Conference, to Miss C. E. Langston, of Columbia county, Ga.

By Rev. H. A. C. Walker, January 4th 1876, in Spartanburg, S. C., his son, Rev. Arthur C. Walker, to Miss Virginia Kirkland, daughter of the late Rev. Wm. C. Kirkland.

By Rev. A. J. Stokes, December 30th, 1875, in Camden, S. C., Mr. Jas. R. Nelson to Miss Emma D. Capers, youngest daughter of the late Rev. Samuel Wragg Capers, of the South Carolina Conference.

By Rev. H. J. Ellis, January 6th, 1876, in Troup county, Ga., Mr. W. R. Bradfield to Miss Willie Florence Pitman.

By Rev. W. F. Quillian, December 21st, 1875, Mr. Robert P. Blackwell to Miss Katie H. Vail, all of Elberton, Ga.

By Rev. T. Alonso Harris, December 21st, 1875, William H. Dean to Miss Fannie S. Thompson, both of Clarke county, Ga.

By Rev. J. W. Farmer, December 29th, 1875, Mr. D. W. Folesom, of Lowndes county, Ga., to Miss E. L. Hughes, of Liberty county, Ga.

By Rev. J. B. McGehee, December 23d, 1875, in Talbot, Mr. John Gammage, to Miss Isabella C. Stewart, eldest daughter of Rev. W. W. Stewart.

By Rev. J. B. McGehee, January 5th, 1876, Mr. Owen McGarrigle, to Miss Sallie E. Brewer.

By Rev. J. B. McGehee, January 12th, 1876, Mr. S. Cincinnatus McBryde, of Taylor, to Miss Lena R. McBryde, of Talbot.

By Rev. A. W. Rowland, December 21st, 1875, Mr. Allen C. Smith, of Newton county, to Miss Amanda Sinford of Jasper county, Ga.

By Rev. Rev. A. W. Rowland, December 23d, 1875, Mr. William Binford, of Jasper county, to Miss Lula Smith, of Newton county, Ga.

By Rev. J. H. D. McRae, November 30th, 1875, Mr. Daniel Tant to Miss Winnie Williams, all of Brooks county, Ga.

By Rev. J. H. D. McRae, December 24th, 1875, Mr. Joel H. Morris, of Florida, to Mrs. Martha A. McMullen, of Georgia.

By Rev. R. W. Dixon, in Georgetown, Ga., Mr. Thomas A. Shelton to Miss Mary A. Davidson, of Georgetown, Ga.

By Rev. W. A. Faris, December 23d, 1875, Mr. James N. Potts to Miss M. A. Freeman, all of Jackson county, Ga.

By Rev. W. A. Faris, January 6th, 1876, Mr. James C. Jarrett to Miss C. C. LeMasters, all of Jackson county, Ga.

Issue of January 26, 1876

By Rev. Landy Wood, January 16th, 1876, in Georgetown, S. C., Mr. Sherod Henrey Barnes to Miss Sarah E. McDonald, daughter of Mr. H. T. McDonald.

By Rev. P. H. Moss, January 5th, 1876, Mr. E. G. Chaffin to Miss S. A. Barron, all of Troy, Ala.

By Rev. Jere. S. Williams, January 18th, 1875, at Enon, Ala., Mr. John J. Banks, son of Rev. D. M. Banks, to Miss Mattie A. Cotton, daughter of the late Rev. J. L. Cotton, D. D.

By Rev. R. B. Lester, December 14th 1875, in Sumter county, Ga., Mr. James w. Lester to Miss Emma O. Critenden.

By Rev. A. J. Cauthen, January 13th, 1876, Dr. J. W. Folk, of Jalapa, Newberry county, to Miss H. A. Fogle, of Barnwell county.

By Rev. E. S. Tyner, January 13th, 1876, Mr. H. R. Morrow to Miss Mary J. Dale, all of Madison county, Fla.

By Rev. L. Wood, January 11th 1876, in Georgetown, S. C., Mr. George B. Nesmith, of Black Mingo, to Mrs. Esther A. Nesmith, of the former place.

By Rev. W. P. Lovejoy, January 4th 1876, Mr. R. M. Dowdle to Miss Alice Jones.

By Rev. George J. Griffiths, D. D., January 13th, 1876, Mr. Robert N. McKennon to Miss Georgia A. Vann, all of Thomas county, Ga.

By Rev. John Inabnet, January 12th, 1876, Mr. Henry F. Frank, of Columbia, S. C., to Mrs. Narcissa S. Beckham, of Lexington, S. C.

By Rev. S. S. Sweet, January 19th, 1876, at the residence of R. B. Hall, Esq., in Macon, Ga., Mr. William H. Hodges, of Houston county, to Miss Mary Taylor Hall, of Macon.

By Rev. D. J. McMillan, December 23d, 1875, Mr. H. H. Horton, of Lancaster county, to Miss M. A. Stover, of Kershaw county, S. C.

By Rev. John M. Bowden, January 16th, 1876, Mr. R. F. Duke to Miss Mary F. Miller, of Campbell county, Ga.

By Rev. John M. Bowden, January 16th, 1876, Mr. James D. Goodman to Miss Helen E. Vickers, of Fairburn, Ga.

By Rev. J. C. Ley, December 25th, 1875, Mr. M. J. Beckham to Miss Cora A. Fifer.

By Rev. J. C. Ley, January 12th, 1876, Mr. R. B. Hunter to Miss F. A. Dansby.

By Rev. J. C. Ley, January 13th, 1876, Mr. M. C. Scott to Miss Carrie S. Gradick.

By Rev. J. W. Simmons, January 12th, 1876, Mr. Louis O. Trimble to Mrs. Carrie Sawyer, all of Brunswick, Ga.

By Rev. J. W. Simmons, January 13th, 1876, Mr. John S. Burns to Miss Katie S. Gray, all of Brunswick, Ga.

By Rev. J. D. Anthony, January 13th, 1876, in the Methodist Church, in Sandersville, Ga., Mr. John C. Pace, Jr., to Miss F. Alice Laveigne, daughter of J.T. and M. T. Laveigne, all of Sandersville.

By Rev. J. D. Anthony, January 11th, 1876, Col. William Fish, of Oglethorpe, Ga., to Miss Mamie P. Hines, of Sandersville, Ga.

By Rev. J. D. Gray, January 16th, 1876, in Henry county, Ga., Mr. Sidney P. Mann to Miss Mary V. Fife.

By Rev. Wm. W. Hardy, January 9th, 1876, Mr. John Kimble to Miss Lydia Finley, all of Henry county, Ga.

By Rev. E. S. Tyner, January 18th, 1876, Mr. F. A. Avant, of Laurinburg, N. C., to Miss Prusia A. Florid, of Madison county, Fla. St. Louis *Christian Advocate* please copy.

Issue of February 2, 1876

By Rev. W. D. Kirkland, January 20th, 1876, Mr. Charles A. Sutherlin to Miss Jane Willis, all of Greenville, S. C.

By Rev. Geo. C. Leavel, at the residence of Mr. James Carter, January 19th, 1876, Mr. James Gregory to Miss Georgia Dallas, all of Marion county, Fla.

By Rev. A. Coke Smith, January 19th, 1876, Mr. Archibald McCraney to Miss Friday, all of Columbia, S. C.

By Rev. J. L. Gibson, January 23d, 1876, at the residence of Maj. L. L. Hardin, Mr. J. s. Gibson to Miss M. F. Hardin, all of Macon county, Ga.

By Rev. G. T. Harmon, January 18th, 1876, Mr. Samuel S. Dusenbury to Miss Cornelia Dusenbury, all of Horry county, S. C.

By Rev. J. W. Burke, in Bibb county, Ga., January 23d, 1876, Capt. David M. Currett to Miss Sarah C. Rogers.

By Rev. D. D. Dantzler, January 25th, 1876, at the residence of Mr. Newton Sistrunk, Mr. David W. Snell to Miss Jubie C. Oliver, all of Orangeburg county, S. C.

By Rev. J. R. Mayes, December 30th, 1876, at the residence of Anderson Mayo, Esq., Hernando county, Fla., Mr. Virgil Alberson of Hernando, Fla., to Miss N. A. Blane, of Fairfield, S. C.

By Rev. Dr. Whitefoord Smith, Spartanburg, S. C., January 19th, 1876, Mr. Charles S. Walker, of Owensboro', Ky. (formerly of South Carolina), to Miss Mary E. Boyd, daughter of Dr. J. J. Boyd, of Spartanburg.

By Rev. Landy Wood, in the Methodist Church, Georgetown, S. C., January 4th, 1876, Mr. Edward N. Jeannerett, of Charleston, to Miss Sallie E. Anderson, of Georgetown.

By Rev. Landy Wood, at the residence of Mr. John Ballune, Georgetown, S. C., January 20th, 1876, Mr. Edwin T. Foster to Miss Orietta D. Wilson.

Issue of February 9, 1876

By Rev. J. C. Stoll, in Marion county, S. C., January 20, 1876, Mr. W. Kirkland Fort to Miss Laura L. Edwards, all of Marion county, S. C.

By Rev. J. V. M. Morris, Columbus, Ga., January 13th, 1876, Mr. Joel Moore to Miss Ellen Shavers.

By Rev. J. V. M. Morris, Columbus, Ga., January 13th, 1876, Mr. James I. Treadway to Miss Lizzie Pickran.

By Rev. W. T. Capers, at the residence of Dr. C. H. Miot, Columbia, S. C., January 27th, 1876, Mr. Wesley L. Gregg of Marion, S. C., to Miss Hattie Heron, youngest daughter of the late Jacob Bell, Esq., of Columbia.

By Rev. C. W. Key, January 27th, 1876, Mr. J. H. Boyd, of McDuffie county, to Miss Maggie C. Jackson, of Augusta, formerly of Talbotton, Ga.

By Rev. Cornelius Newton, January 23d, 1876, Dr. M. C. Wallace of Marlboro county, S. C., to Miss Annie L. English, of Sumter county, S. C.

By Rev. Jas. Mahoney, of the North Carolina Conference, December 28th, 1875, at the Methodist Episcopal Church, South, Fernandina, Fla., Mr. Jas. C. Thomson, of Pikeville, Tenn., to Miss Lizzie Flowers, of Fernandina, Fla.

By Rev. W. D. Kirkland, January 27th, 1876, Mr. Henry A. Garrett to Miss Sue E. Smith, all of Greenville, S. C.

By Rev. T. E. Wannamaker, January 19th 1876, Mr. C. W. Tucker to Miss Emma R. Wannamaker, daughter of the officiating minister.

By Rev. P. G. Reynolds, at the residence of the bride's grand father, Col. Harlin, January 25th, 1876, Mr. G. M. Boyd to Miss M. J. Humphrey, all of Gordon county, Ga.

By Rev. I. C. Harris, January 27th, 1876, Mr. Wm. B. Gibson, of Dawson, to Miss Ursula A. Coward, of Terrell county, Ga.

Issue of February 16, 1876

By Rev. I. O. Connor, February 3, 1876, Mr. Wesley Whetsel, of Orangeburg county, S. C., to Miss Lizzie Collier, daughter of Mr. John Collier, of Colleton county, S. C.

By Rev. E. S. Tyner, February 3, 1876, Mr. William M. King, to Miss S. V. Geer, all of Madison county, Fla.

By Rev. J. D. Rogers, December 29, 1875, Mr. George McKendree, to Miss Francis Lyons, all of Hernando county, Fla.

By Rev. J. D. Rogers, January 27, 1875, Mr. Thos J. McPherson, to Miss Martha A. Cook, all of Hernando county, Fla.

By Rev. A. J. Dean, January 13, 1876, Mr. M. A. Halliday, to Miss S. L. Ball, both of Stewart county, Ga.

By Rev. A. J. Dean, January 30, 1876, Mr. W. Horton Branch, of Mitchel county, Ga., to Miss Sallie E. Thornton, of Lumpkin, Ga.

By Rev. John M. Carlisle, assisted by Rev. W. K. Greeden, Rev. D. D. Dantzler, of the South Carolina Conference to Miss Frances G. Cook, of Bennettsville, S. C.

By Rev. Jere S. Williams, February 3, 1876, Mr. James H. Alston, of Barbour county, Ala., to Miss Mary E. Turman, of Bulloch county, Ala.

By Rev. Landy Wood, at the residence of Mr. John Ballune, Georgetown, S. C., January 20, 1876, Mr. Edwin T. Porter, to Miss Orietta D. Wilson.

By Rev. Landy Wood, at the residence of Mr. S. K. Gasque, Georgetown, S. C., February 3, 1876, Mr. Everett Thompson, of Georgetown county, to Miss Margaret J. Wall, daughter of Mr. Jas. Wall of Williamsburg county, S. C.

By Rev. J. B. McGehee, in Talbotton, Ga., January 27, 1876, Mr. Junius G. Oglesby, of Atlanta, Ga., to Miss Eugenia H. Cottingham.

By Rev. W. L. Pegues, January 20, 1876, Rev. E. T. Hodges, of the South Carolina Conference, to Miss Hattie G. Pegues, of Marlboro, S. C.

By Rev. J. O. A. Cook, January 27, 1876, Mr. Jno. W. Carmine, to Miss Susan E. Taylor, all of Thomasville, Ga.

By Rev. J. O. A. Cook, January 27, 1876, Mr. Samuel L. Moore, to Miss Cornelia Wind, all of Thomasville, Ga.

By Rev. J. L. Sifly, January 20, 1876, in Colleton county, S. C., Mr. Edgar Skinner, of Charleston, S. C., to Miss Mary Ann Durant, second daughter of the late Rev. H. H. Durant, of the South Carolina Conference.

By Rev. C. V. Neidlinger, December 23, 1875, Mr. Eugene P. Jaudon, to Miss Marietta M. Morgan, all of Effingham county, Ga.

By Rev. C. V. Neidlinger, November 16, 1875, Mr. B. W. Bebee, to Miss Ella M. Waldhour, all of Effingham county, Ga.

By Rev. M. H. Pooser, January 16, 1876, Mr. W. Smith Crouch, to Miss Ida Wills, daughter of J. D. Wills, Esq., all of Edgefield county, S. C.

By Rev. J. C. Holmes, January 4, 1876, Mr. Edward Cowan, to Miss Lula Kendrick, all of Cobb county, Ga.

By Rev. J. C. Holmes, January 5, 1876, Mr. A. P. McLain, to Miss Henrietta Orr, of Cobb county, Ga.

By Rev. J. C. Holmes, December 6, 1875, Mr. J. Gladden to Miss Ella Davenport.

By Rev. J. C. Holmes, December 23, 1875, Mr. J. Westbrooks to Miss Ella Cowan.

By Rev. Jere S. Williams, February 8, 1876, Col. A. M. George, of Cuthbert, Ga., to Mrs F. M. Burke of Spring Hill, Barbour county, Ala.

By Rev. J. B. Jeffcoat, February 1, 1876, G. F. Dinkel, to Miss Mary F. Slaughter, all of Orange county, Fla.

By Rev. W. T. Laine, February 6, 1876, in Fulton county, Ga., Mr. A. F. Davidson, to Miss M. L. Dobbins.

By Rev. J. L. Williams, January 19th, 1876, Mr. T. A. Braswell, of Hawkinsville, to Miss Lizzie Calhoun, of Jesup, Ga.

By Rev. A. Wyrick, November 7th, 1875, Mr. James W. Edwards to Miss Catharine Annie Morris, all of Jefferson county, Fla.

Issue of February 23, 1876

By Rev. Jno. M. Bowden, February 13, 1876, Mr. Adam P. King, to Miss Margaret A. Miller, of Campbell county, Ga.

By Rev. Clement C. Gary, February 8, 1876, in Washington, Ga., Mr. I. Newton Zellards, of Lincoln county, Ga., to Miss Clara E. Anderson, of Wilkes county, Ga.

By Rev. J. B. McFarland, February 10, 1876, in Walker county, Ga., Mr. John Schmitt, to Miss Sarah E. Thompson.

By Rev. J. J. Morgan, December 14, 1875, Dr. Jas O'Neal, to Miss Dessie Funderburke, all of Decatur county, Ga.

By Rev. M. L. Banks, February 8, 1876, Mr. Jas. H. Vidal, of Charleston, S. C., to Miss Mary C. Oliver, of Orangeburg county, S. C.

By Rev. Landy Wood, February 10, 1876, at the residence of Mr. Edwin Blakely, Georgetown county, S. C., Mr. David R. Newton, to Miss Sarah A. D. Blakely, daughter of the late Wm. J. Blakely.

By Rev. Landy Wood, February 10, 1876, at the residence of Mr. Edwin Blakely, Georgetown county, S. C., Mr. W. S. J. Lewis to Miss Ella Newton.

By Rev. Jas. F. Dorman, February 3, 1876, Mr. Alexander McDaniel, to Miss Octavia Freeman, all of Tallapoosa county, Ala.

by Rev. John Inabinet, February 19, 1876, Mr. A. T. Hydrick, to Miss Viola C. Riley, all of Orangeburg, S. C.

Issue of March 1, 1876

By Rev. Dr. R. W. Hubert, in Warren county, Ga., December 11, 1875, Mr. Adolphus D. Kitchens, to Miss Emma Gresling.

By Rev. Dr. R. W. Hubert, in Warren county, Ga., December 16, 1875, Mr. W. H. Banner to Miss Hattie R. Heath.

By Rev. Dr. R. W. Hubert, in Warren county, Ga., December 23, 1875, Mr. C. W. Gresling to Miss Vandella S. Kitchens.

By Rev. Dr. R. W. Hubert, in Warren county, Ga., January 13, 1876, Mr. Redding Caton to Miss Mary McDonald.

By Rev. Dr. R. W. Hubert, in Warren county, Ga., January 26, 1876, Mr. J. R. Spence to Miss Emily McCrary.

By Rev. Dr. R. W. Hubert, in Warren county, Ga., January 27, 1876, Mr. L. A. Brake to Miss Sarah McSwain.

By Rev. Dr. R. W. Hubert, in Augusta, Ga., January 15, 1876, Mr. H. J. Burkhalter, to Miss Lizzie Anderson.

By Rev. John M. Carlisle, assisted by Rev. W. K. Breeden, Rev. D. Z. Dantzler, of the South Carolina Conference, to Misss Frances G. Cook, of Bennettsville, S. C.

By Rev. S. D. Clements, December 12, 1875, Mr. Ephraim Ponder to Miss Mattie Perkins, all of Jefferson county, Ga.

By Rev. S. D. Clements, February 20, 1876, in Macon, Ga., Mr. Wm. T. Harvey, to Miss Mary E. Land.

By Rev. W. M. Watts, February 13, 1876, Mr. A. E. Patterson, to Miss Lavinia Swift, all of Mosely Hall, Fla.

By Rev. J. J. Giles, at the residence of Rev. Wm. Harden, February 9, 1876, Mr. Rober tA. Giles to Miss Anna L. Hardin, all of Tattnal county, Ga.

By Rev. Thos. F. Pierce, January 26, 1876, Dr. George P. Bass, of Putnam county, Ga., to Miss Minnie Cox, of Morgan county, Ga.

By Rev. Thos. F. Pierce, February 2, 1876, Dr. Robert Willingham, of Lexington, Ga., to Miss Emma Pharr, of Washington, Ga.

By Rev. R. B. Tarrant, January 20, 1876, Mr. Cephas Livingston, to Miss Camilla Gibson, all of Orangeburg county, S. C.

By Rev. R. B. Tarrant, January 23, 1876, Mr. G. Asbury Summers, to Miss Carrie Ehney, all of Orangeburg county, S. C.

By Rev. R. H. Felder, February 13, 1876, Mr. T. H. Marshall, to Miss Henrietta Epting, all of Macon county, Ga.

By Rev. A. Gray, January 6, 1876, Mr. Charles N. Pitts, to Miss Julia Bowdoin, both of Jasper county, Ga.

By Rev. A. Gray, January 18, 1876, Mr. John W. Bradley, of Jones county, Ga., to Miss Mollie Greer, of Jasper county, Ga.

By Rev. A. Gray, January 25, 1876, Mr. James Wamack to Miss Evaline Pitts, both of Jasper county, Ga.

By Rev. A. Gray, February 3, 1876, Mr. P. P. Kelley, of Jasper county, Ga., to Miss Katie E. Peurifoy, of Putnam county, Ga.

By Rev. A. Gray, Mr. John T. Faulkner, to Miss Sallie E. Slaughter, both of Jasper county, Ga.

By Rev. D. J. Simmons, at the residence of Mr. Lewis A. Zeigler, February 3, 1876, Mr. Hugh E. Phillips, of Barnwell county, S. C., to Miss Marcilla J. Woolf, of Orangeburg county, S. C.

By Rev. W. L. Wootten, Jr., February 17, 1876, Mr. Z. T. Page to Miss Clara B. Roundtree.

By Rev. W. I. Greene, February 8, 1876, Mr. J. O. Lilly to Miss Lizzie Slappey, daughter of the late Mr. Reuben H. Slappey.

By Rev. E. J. Burch, February 17, 1876, Mr. W. H. Jones, to Miss julia E. Palmer, all of Jefferson county, Ga.

By Rev. Dr. G. L. McCleskey, January 16, 1876, Mr. A. D. Clotfelter to Miss Dicy L. O'Kelly, all of Clarke county, Ga.

By Rev. J. H. D. McRae, January 23, 1876, Mr. Robert Stancil, to Miss Susie Ward, both of Brooks county, Ga.

By Rev. J. H. D. McRae, January 27, 1876, Mr. Henry W. Eady, to Miss Laura J. Mercer, both of Brooks county, Ga.

Issue of March 8, 1876

By Rev. C. D. Mann, at the residence of Mr. H. R. Gaston, February 10, 1876, Mr. James Huggins to Miss Lenora Gaston, all of Oconee county, S. C.

By Rev. G. W. Thomas, at Red Clay, Ga., Mr. Joseph A. Ross of Whitefield county, Ga., to Miss Maggie A. England.

By Rev. H. C. Smart, February 17, 1876, Mr. Samuel G. Solomons to Miss Lillie M. Box, all of Beaufort county, S. C.

By Rev. A. J. Dean, February 9, 1876, Mr. John P. West, of Upson county, Ga., to Miss Estelle Stokes, of Lumpkin, Ga.

By Rev. A. J. Dean, February 15, 1876, Mr. Job C. Patterson, of Perote, Ala., to Miss Sarah C. Stubbs, of Lumpkin, Ga.

By Rev. R. L. Wiggins, February 17, 1876, near Haynesville, Ga., Mr. Charles T. Clarke, of Randolph county, to Miss Hattie Albritton, of Houston county, Ga.

By Rev. R. L. Wiggins, February 23, 1876, near Henderson, Ga., Rev. Thomas K. Armstrong, of Montgomery, Ala., to Miss Carrie F. Johnston, of Houston county, Ga.

By Rev. S. Leake, January 20, 1876, Mr. Harry Taylor, of Cobb county,k Ga., to Miss Mary J. Tomson, of Marietta, Ga.

By Rev. S. Woodbery, February 10, 1876, near Quincy, Fla., Mr. Wm. H. Gunn, of Liberty county, Fla., to Miss Erwine S. Wyatt.

By Rev. B. W. Key, February 25, 1876, in St. Mary's, Ga., Mr. Walter Scott, to Miss Wilmer C. Halzendorf.

By Rev. B. Sanders, February 29, 1876, Mr. Larkin Harrison, to Miss Sarah C. McLucas, of Fayette county, Ga.

By Rev. W. P. Mouzon, February 28, 1876, Dr. Daniel F. Moorer, to Miss Ada Appleby, only daughter of the late Dr. M. T. Appleby, all of Colleton county, S. C.

By Rev. J. T. Wightman, D. D., February 24, 1876, in Charleston, S. C., Mr. S. S. D. Muckenfuss to Miss Mary A. Babb [Barr?], all of Charleston.

Issue of March 15, 1876

By Rev. W. M. Potter, March 7, 1876, near Madison, Ga., Mr. J. T. Comer, of Athens, Ga., to Miss Alice Townsend.

By Rev. W. T. Hamilton, February 29, 1876, at the residence of Judge Wm. Johnston, Mr. John M. Curtiss, to Mrs. Mary A. Collins, all of Thomson, Ga.

By Rev. W. F. Quillian, February 17, 1876, Mr. R. J. Wood, of Alabama, to Mrs. M. J. Pyson, of Carrollton, Ga.

Issue of March 22, 1876

By Rev. William Hutto, February 8, 1876, Mr. Fred D. Edwards to Miss Lovey C. Shuler, all of Orangeburg, S. C.

By Rev. William Hutto, February 24, 1876, Mr. Danie D. Snell to Miss Emma L. JHutto, of Charleston, S. C.

By Rev. W. M. D. Bond, March 12, 1876, Mr. Rober tA. Brown to Miss Mahalia Pardue, all of Macon, Ga.

By Rev. C. W. Smith, March 9, 1876, Mr. Frederick A. Winter, of richmond county, GA., to Miss Mary E. Holmes, of Bibb county, Ga.

By Rev. N. Athon, January 6, 1876, Mr. W. R. Dowd to Miss M. A. Overby, all of Stewart county, Ga.

By Rev. W. A. Fariss, March 2, 1876, Mr. A. J. Williamson to Miss Josie Freeman, both of Jackson county, Ga.

By Rev. A. M. Williams, March 9, 1876, in Laurens county, Ga., Mr. Benjamin F. Mason to Miss Almida F. Walker.

By Rev. Landy Wood, February 24, 1876, in Georgetown, S. C., Mr. John D. Huggins, of Nichols, Marion county, to Miss Josephine E. Anderson, daughter ofthe late J. B. Anderson, of Georgetown, S. c.

By Rev. J. W. Simmons, March 12, 1876, in the Methodist Church in Brunswick, Mr. Wm. R. Dart to Miss Cordelia Gray.

By Rev. J. W. Simmons, March 15, 1876, in Brunswick, Mr. Wm. H. Bunkley, of Cumberland Island, to Miss M. C. Wilder, daughter of James Wilder.

By Rev. J. W. Simmons, March 15, 1876, in Brunswick, Ga., Mr. Miles Jones, of Darien, Ga., to Miss Dora E. Ballard, of Camden county Ga.

Issue of March 29, 1876

By Rev. W. H. Speer, at the residence of Mr. C. W. Boyd, March 2, 1876, John W. Daniel, M. D., to Miss Penina J. Boyd, all of Franklin, Ga.

By Rev. D. J. McMillan, February 2, 1876, Mr. W. T. B. Duncan, to Miss R. E. Robertson, both of Lancaster county, S. C.

By Rev. D. J. McMillan, March 2, 1876, Mr. Samuel Cremager, to Miss Clara Floyd, both of Lancaster county, S. C.

By Rev. D. J. McMillan, March 5, 1876, Mr. Benjamin Truesdel, of Kershaw, S. C., Miss Laura T. Horton, of Lancaster county, S. C.

By Rev. E. S. Tyner, in the Methodist Church, at Rocky Springs, Madison county, Florida, March 19, 1876, Mr. Wade H. Redding, of Live Oak, Fla., to Miss Sallie Alvis, of Madison county, Fla.

By Rev. C. C. Fishburne, February 1, 1876, near Bird's Station, Mr. Wm. Brownlee to Miss Mary J. Waymer, both of Colleton county, S. C.

By Rev. J. H. Zimmerman, March 22, 1876, at the residence of L. R. Beckwith, in Orangeburg Co., S. C., Dr. S. J. Brabham, of Barnwell co., S. C., to Miss Sallie F. Beckwith, second daughter of the late L. B. Beckwith, Esq.

By Rev. W. H. Hunt, March 19, 1876, Mr. James W. Dicks, to Miss Frances D. Raulason, all of Columbia county, Fla.

Issue of April 5, 1876

By Rev. J. D. Gunnells, March 19, 1876, Mr. David P. Carson to Miss J. M. Alexander, both of Franklin county, Ga.

By Rev. Geo. E. Bonner, March 21, 1876, Mr. D. Duncan to Miss Emily Price, all of Rabun county, Ga.

By Rev. Jas. L. Bartlette, at the residence of Mr. Jas. White in Sumter county, S. C., March 22, 1876, Rev. W. A. Rogers, of the South Carolina Conference, to Miss Annie Anderson, formerly of Alabama.

SOUTHERN CHRISTIAN ADVOCATE MARRIAGE NOTICES 1867-1878

Issue of April 12, 1876

By Rev. W. L. Wooten, Jr., in Augusta, Ga., April 2, 1876, Mr. Wm. Oliver Melton, to Mrs. Mary Rausson.

By Rev. W. A. Rogers, March 26, 1876, Mr. L.J. Bradford, to Miss Possie Barfield, all of Sumter county, S. C.

By Rev. W. H. Potter, D. D., in the 1st Methodist Church, Athens, Ga., March 30, 1876, Mr. Frederick B. lucas, to Miss Susie H. Taylor, all of Athens. Ga

By Rev. J. McAlpin Harding, February 28, 1876, at the residnce of Mr. Ed. P. Herrick, Athens, Penn., Mr. C. T. Connors, of Lancaster, S. C., to Miss Ellen R. Tompkins, of Binghamton, N. Y.

Issue of April 19, 1876

By Rev. J. W. Simmons at Frederica, St. Simon's Island, April 11, 1876, Wm. C. Taylor, of Glynn county, Ga., to Miss L. V. Stevens, of the former place.

By Rev. H. B. Frazee, April 12, 1876, Mr. Jas. J. Wester to Miss Sarah J. Messman, all of Jacksonville, Fla.

By Rev. H. B. Frazee, near Jacksonville, Fla., April 11, 1876, Mr. George W. Brown, of Savannah, Ga., to Miss Onarine L. Pickett.

By Rev. J. Walter Dickson, April 2, 1876, Mr. John f. Beard to Miss Eliza L. Dean, all of Columbia, S. C.

By Rev. A. J. Dean, March 23, 1876, Mr. A. W. Gibson, of Macon, Ga., to Miss Charlotte E. Hightower, of Lumpkin, Ga.

Issue of April 26, 1876

By Rev. J. A. Clifton, April 13, 1876, Mr. William Bodie, of Edgefield co., S. C., to Miss Sallie Mitchell, of Lexington co., S. C.

By Rev. W. J. Cotter, in Troup co., Ga., April 11, 1876, Mr. M. S. Wood, to Miss R. E. Clyatt.

By Rev. W. J. Cotter, in Coweta co., Ga., April 16, 1876, Mr. C. J. Haynes, to Miss G. A. Carmical.

By Rev. A. M. Thigpen, near Cedar Town, Ga., March 23, 1876, Mr. James M. Watters, to Miss Sarah Cornelia Wynne, daughter of Mrs. M. E. Whitehead.

By Rev. J. B. Wilson, April 15, 1876, Dr. S. S. Linder, to Miss Florence E. Smith, all of Union co., S. C.

By Rev. R. L. Honiker, April 19, 1876, Mr. William A. Dickenson, to Miss julia McElvey, all of Bainbridge, Ga.

By Rev. D. C. Crook, in Barbour co., Ala., April 18, 1876, James H. Drake, of Portsmouth, Va., to Miss Lizzie M. Ott, of Alabama.

SOUTHERN CHRISTIAN ADVOCATE MARRIAGE NOTICES 1867-1878

Issue of May 2, 1876

By Rev. John W. Heidt, Dec. 22, 1875, Mr. Polk Bohannon to Miss Nannie Brannon; and April 23, 1876, Mr. James R. Cotton to Miss Katty Brannon--both daughters of Rev. F. M. T. Brannon.

By Rev. C. P. Murdock, in the Methodist Church, Williamsburg, Fla., April 16, 1876, Mr. J. W. Buchanan, of Columbia County, Fla., to Miss M. A. Murdock, of Jefferson county, Fla.

By Rev. A. J. Cauthen, April 20, 1876, Mr. H. N. Hutto to Miss Lina Wray of Barnwell county, S. C.

By Rev. J. T. Kilgo, April 12, 1876, Mr. Hugh McCollum to Miss Rachel Galloway, all of Marlboro county, S. C.

By Rev. G. W. Gatlin, April 20, 1876, Mr. Thomas M. Britton to Mis sJ. Fowler McConnell, all of Williamsburg, S. C.

By Rev. J. T. Ainsworth, in Cairo, Ga., April 20, 1876, Mr. William J. Dickey to Miss Lizzie J. Everett.

Issue of May 9, 1876

By Rev. G. J. Griffiths, D. D., in Boston, Ga., April 23, 1876, Mr. William M. Brooks, to Miss Mary C. Watts, eldest daughter of Rev. W. M. Watts, of the Florida Conference. All of Boston, Georgia.

By Rev. G. J. Griffiths, D. D., in Boston, Ga., April 23, 1876, Mr. Samuel G. Vanlanding-ham, of Cairo, Ga., to Miss Fannie E. Watts, second daughter of Rev. W. M. Watts, of the Florida Conference.

By Rev. J. S. Embry, April 30, 1876, Mr. Adolphus T. Logan, to Miss Sarah M. Peeples, all of Murray county, Ga.

Issue of May 16, 1876

By Rev. H. F. Chrietzberg, May 2d, 1876, Mr. Eugene C. Zemp to Miss Mary G. Blakeney, all of Kershaw county, S. C.

By Rev. Jno. T. Whitaker, April 9th, 1876, Mr. John A. Williams, of Meriwether county, to Miss Annie M. O. Smith, of Harris county, Ga.

By Rev. Albert Gray, April 27th, 1876, Mr. W. M. Carter, of Barnesville, Ga., to Mrs. M. E. Brown, of Monticello, Ga.

By Rev. Albert Gray, May 2d, 1876, Mr. J. W. Roberts, to Miss Anna M. Nolen, both of Jasper county, Ga.

By Rev. A. M. Wynn, in Savannah, April 5th, 1876, Capt. Chas. F. Stubbs to Miss Annie M. Goodwin.

By Rev. J. W. Burke, in Macon, May 4th, 1876, Otho B. Gilbert to Miss Emma P. Jones.

Issue of May 23, 1876

By Rev. W. W. Mood, May 14, 1876, Mr. Jackson Smith to Miss Lizzie Holiday, all of Anderson county, S. C.

By Rev. Dr. W. R. Hubert, May 11, 1876, Mr. W. J. Howell, of Hancock co., to Miss Sarah J. Culpepper, of Warren co., Ga.

By Rev. A. M. Williams, May 14, 1876, Mr. Jacob M. Jones, to Miss Louisa Brett, all of Laurens co., Ga.

By Rev. H. R. Felder, May 3, 1876, at the residence of Mr. Lee, in Montezuma, Ga., Mr. Jno. S. Byrom, to Mrs. E. B. White.

By Rev. N. D. Morehouse, May 14, 1876, Mr. J. N. Carpenter, to Mrs. Julia A. Whitfield, all of Burke co., Ga.

By Rev. A. Clark, May 11, 1876, in Wayne county, Ga., Mr. Wiliam R. Causey, to Miss Mary E. Purdom.

By Rev. C. A. Evans, in St. John's Church, Augusta, Ga., May 16, 1876, Mr. W. F. Eve, to Miss Ida A. Evans, all of Augusta, Ga.

Issue of May 30, 1876

By Rev. W. W. Oslin, May 22, 1876, at the residence of R. J. Hester, of Oconee county, Ga., Mr. Richard B. Aycock, of Oglethorpe county, Ga., to Miss Della Hillsman, of Madison, Ga.

By Rev. W. F. Quillian, May 18, 1876, Mr. Ernest G. Kramer to Miss Nellie Mandeville, all of Carrollton, Ga.

By Rev. W. Knox, May 12, 1876, at the Ridge, near Darien, Ga., Mr. G. T. Stein to Miss H. B. Thompson.

By Rev. Thos. B. Lanier, May 17, 1876, Dr. D. M. Sanford, of Forsyth, Ga., to Miss Mary E. Jones, daughter of Hon. J. B. Jones, Herndon, Burke county, Ga.

By Rev. Thos. B. Lanier, May 18, 1876, Mr. Mongin S. Lake, of Savannah, Ga., to Miss Augusta Paris Perkins, daughter of S. E. Perkins, of Perkinsville, Burke county, Ga.

By Rev. F. L. Allen, Feb. 15, 1876, Rev. John C. Huckabee, of the Texas Conference, to Miss Martha A. Dorrough, of Bastrop co., Texas.

Issue of June 6, 1876

By Rev. B. F. Fariss, May 18, 1876, Rev. Selwyn S. Smith, of Oxford, Ga., to Miss Sallie A. Stewart, of Harlem, Ga.

By Rev. J. R. Littlejohn, May 3, 1876, Mr. N. A. Thompson, of Marion co., to Miss Ella C. Glass[?], of Sumter co., Ga.

By Rev. H. R. Felder, May 14, 1876, Mr. Jno. B. Lamar, to Miss E. C. Lovejoy, all of Montezuma, Ga.

By Rev. G. W. Thomas, April 26, 1876, at the residence of Adam Chastain, in Catoosa co., Ga., Mr. A. B. Baker to Miss Georgia Chastain, both of Catoosa co., Ga.

By Rev. G. W. Thomas, April 26, 1876, at the residence of Adam Chastain, Mr. Luther B. Bates of Whitfield co., Ga., to Miss Fannie Baker, of Catoosa co., Ga.

Issue of June 13, 1876

By Rev. E. S. Tyner, June 1, 1876, Mr. J. A. Jackson to Miss Jane G. Stephens, all of Madison county, Fla.

By Rev. W. H. Hollinshead, May 25, 1876, in the Methodist Church at Marshallville, Ga., Mr. Wal-- J. Walker, to Miss Lou E. Crocker[?].

By Rev. Josiah W. Jordan, May 28, 1876, at Union Church, Crawford county, Ga., Mr. H. F. Sanders to Miss Maggie L. Danielly, both of Crawford county, Ga.

Issue of June 20, 1876

By Rev. O. L. Smith, D. D., June 7, 1876, Mr. E. H. Bowden, of Union Point, to Miss Fanny King, of Covington, Ga.

By Rev. T. G. Herbert, Mr. John S. Swygert, to Miss Mary E. Wicker, of Newberry co., S.C.

By Rev. B. W. Key, in St. Mary's, Ga., June 7, 1876, Mr. N. F. Pratt, of St. Mary's, Ga., to Miss Mary I. Barr, of Columbus, Ga.

By Rev. David E. Starr, in Clayton county, Ga., May 11, 1876, Mr. John T. Lambert, to Miss Ida Peacock, both of Clayton county, Ga.

By Rev. J. Rembert Smith, June 11, 1876, Mr. Henry C. Shields, to Miss Mary Olena Bond.

By Rev. H. C. Fentress, May 28, 1876, Mr. J. T. Hinson, of Hazlehurst, Ga., to Miss Nancy Lott, of Coffee county, Ga.

By Rev. A. J. Dean, June 11, 1876, Mr. H. B. Everette, to Miss L. A. Boynton, of Lumpkin, Ga.

Issue of June 27, 1876

By Rev. T. H. Timmons, May 25, 1876, Mr. T. A. Pope, of Atlanta, Ga., to Miss Lena A. Turner, of Cobb county, Ga.

By Rev. George William Walker, at Winnsboro, S. C., June 15, 1876,, Mr. L. F. Cooper to Miss Mattie Kistler, neice of Rev. Paul F. Kistler.

By Rev. John S. Johnson, June 15, 1876, at the residence of Mrs. Fannie Simpson, Mr. Owen N. Geise to Miss Sallie Smith, all of Terrell county, Ga.

By Rev. C. J. Oliver, near Atlanta, Ga., Miss N. C. Elliott, of Fulton county, Ga., to Mr. S. N. Ray, of Macon county, Ga.

Issue of July 4, 1876

By Rev. R. T. Nabors, June 21, 1876, in Washington Street Church, Houston, Texas, Rev. I. Z. T. Morris, of Texas Conference, to Miss Belle Waters, of Houston, Texas.

By Rev. E. S. Tyner, June 22, 1876, Mr. John Finlayson, of Jefferson co., Fla., to Miss Lizzie Hines, of Madison co., Fla. N. O. Christian Advocate please copy.

By Rev. C. E. Dowman, June 20, 1876, Mr. Henry D. Duer, to Miss Julia S., daughter of Hon. C. H. DuPont, all of Gadsden co., Fla.

By Rev. W. P. Mouzon, June 22, 1876, at the residence of Mr. H. B. Harbeson, Mr. Jno. B. Hucks, formerly of Georgetown, S. C., to Miss Eliza Ann Liston, of Colleton co., S. C.

By Rev. M. L. Underwood, June 22, 1876, Mr. James O. Lee, to Miss Lizzie Akin, all of Douglas co., Ga.

By Rev. W. L. Pledger, June 5, 1876, Mr. M. Waterman Hunter, to Miss Charlotte Waterman, all of Timmonsville, S. C.

Issue of July 11, 1876

By Rev. W. F. Cook, June 29, 1876, in Atlanta, Ga., Dr. J. L. Scruggs, of Livingston, Ala., to Mrs. Fannie C. Gary, of the former place.

By Rev. W. F. Cook, July 4, 1876, in Atlanta, Ga., Mr. J. O. Wynn, to Miss Lizzie J. Echols, all of Atlanta.

By Rev. A. Nettles, June 22, 1876, Mr. Calhoun Hatchel, to Miss Ella Ray, all of Marion county, S. C.

By Rev. John Kershaw, June 20, 1876, at Cokesbury, Rev. Richard D. Smart, of Beaufort county, to Miss Ella, eldest daughter of Col. D. Wyatt Aiken, of Cokesbury, S. C.

By Rev. D. W. Core, June 24, 1876, in Putnam county, Fla., Mr. Charles Harrod Gautier, to Miss Osgood Amanda Green.

Issue of July 18, 1876

By Rev. J. W. Jordan, July 9, 1876, in Ellaville, Ga., Mr. M. R. Murphy, to Miss Minnie G. Tidwell.

By Rev. D. D. Cook, June 25, 1876, Mr. Joseph R. Boone, of Gainesville, to Mrs. Mary E. Heath, of Hall county, Ga.

By Rev. Joseph Carr, July 5, 1876, Mr. Andrew J. Kiser, of Atlanta, To Miss Ida C. Jackson, daughter of Mr. Wm. Jackson, of Palmetto, Ga.

Issue of July 25, 1876

By Rev. H. J. Harvey, July 14, 1876, Mr. Joshua D. Sullivan, of Macon ,Ga., to Miss Fannie S. Jobson, of Augusta, Ga.

On the 6th of July, by Rev. E. P. Bonner, Mr. Thomas K. Blalock to Miss Susan M. Bening, all of Columbia co., Ga.

By Rev. H. R. Felder, July 4th, 1876, in the Methodist church at Montezuma, GA., Mr. I. C. Jarnagin to Miss Ida B. Lester, all of Montezuma, Macon co,. Ga.

Issue of August 8, 1876

By Rev. U. Sinclair Bird, in St. Mary's, Ga., Rev. Lowndes A. Darsey, of the south Georgia Conference, to Miss Eliza S., daughter of Mrs. Mary B. DuBose, of St. Mary's, Ga.

By Rev. J. S. Jobson, at the residence of Mr. Jesse Tucker, June 21, 1876, Mr. H. T. Powell and Miss E. C. Register, all of Terrell county.

By Rev. J. W. Rogers, in Reedy Creek church, on the line of Warren and Glasscock counties, on the 23d of July 1876, Col. John Smith Johnson, of Warren county, to Miss Sarah J. Stapleton, of Glasscock county.

By Rev. W. T. Laine, July 16, 1876, Mr. James W. Weeks to Miss Eugenie Nash.

By Rev. A. J. Dean, July 4th 1876, Mr. George M. Carroll, of Thomas county, Ga., to Miss Susan A. Thornton, of Lumpkin, Ga.

By Rev. John B. Wilson, on the 20th July, Mr. G. C. Harris to Miss S. E. Brakefield, all of Union county, S. C.

By Rev. John B. Wilson, on the 27th July at the residence of the bride's father, Mr. Jesse L. Swink to Miss Maggie A. Bishop, all of Union county, S. C.

In Georgetown, S. C., July 27th, 1876, by the Rev. Landy Wood, Mr. James K. Hawkins, late of Sag Harbor, Long Island, N. Y., to Miss Caroline, daughter of Mr. Leffert R. Cornell, of Flat Bush, L. I., N. Y.

By Rev. T. A. Seals, in Dalton, Ga., 27th July, Mr. Jno. B. Boyd of Gordon county, to Miss Orie Barrett, of Dalton.

Issue of August 15, 1876

By Rev. S. D. Clements, July 13, 1876, Mr. Jas. E. Lowery, to Miss Gertrude Heath, all of Macon, Ga.

By Rev. J. S. Jordan, August 3, 1876, Mr. Harry F. W. Hibner of Macon, Ga., to Miss Addie A. Keebler, of Effingham county, Ga.

By Rev. W. W. Oslin, July 27, 1876, Mr. Albinus Bishop, to Miss Mattie A. Thrasher, all of Oconee county, Ga.

By Rev. C. C. Cary, in Oglethorpe county, Ga., August 2, 1876, Mr. James W. Arnold, of Wilkes county, to Miss Hattie Dillard, eldest daughter of Fielding Dillard, Esq.

Issue of August 22, 1876

By Rev. W. W. Lumpkin, on the 10th August, Mr. T. S. Edwards to Miss M. V. Harris, all of Walker county, Ga.

By Rev. T. P. England, on the 26th of July 1876, Rev. J. F. England, of the South Carolina Conference, to Miss Emily C. Healan, of Lenoire, Caldwell county, N. C.

By Rev. J. J. Singleton, on the 1st of August, 1876, Mr. Iverson A. Jones to Miss Josie Hyer.

Issue of August 29, 1876

By Rev. A. P. Wright, July 30, 1876, Mr. V. B. Baughn, to Miss Mattie E. Sheffield, all of Colquitt, Miller county, Ga.

By Rev. J. W. Burke, in Macon, Ga., August 22, 1876, Mr. S. F. Coffin, to Miss Elizabeth Smith, late of Laurens county, Ga.

By Rev. Landy Wood, at the Methodist Parsonage, Georgetown, S. C., August 10, 1876, Mr. Nelson Britt, to Miss Eliza Ann Byrdie.

By Rev. Landy Wood, at the residence of Capt. K. Moss, Georgetown, S. C., August 10, 1876, Mr. James Phillips, of Dublin, Harford county, Md., to Miss Lydia Anna Watts, of Georgetown, S. C.

Issue of September 5, 1876

By Rev. Wm. W. Hardy, August 17th, 1876, Mr. William Davis to Miss Carrie Evans, both of Monroe county, Ga.

By Rev. E. S. Tyner, August 28, 1876, in Ochlawila Baptist Church, Mr. Chas. B. McNair to Miss Lizzie B. Wyche, all of Madison county, Fla.

By Rev. J. Penny, on the 22d June 1876, at the residence of the bride's great grandmother, Mrs. E. Duskin, near Micanopy, Mr. T. L. Cooper, of Marion co., Fla., to Miss Ruth A. E. Binnicker, of Alachua co., Fla.

Issue of September 12, 1876

By Rev. R. M. Lockwood, August 14, 1876, in the Methodist Church, Bainbridge, Ga., Morse C. Lanier, Esq., of Gadsden county, Fla., to Virginia Augusta, daughter of J. Berrien Oliver, Esq., of New York.

By Rev. W. R. Branham, Jr., August 24, 1876, Mr. J. Lamb Johnston, of Charleston, S. C., to Miss Hattie P. Williams, of Nacoochee Valley.

By Rev. N. D. Morehouse, July 27, 1876, in Alexander, Burke county, Ga., James F. Rackley, to Miss Julia P. Brickett, all of Scriven county, Ga.

Issue of September 19, 1876

By Rev. A. G. Peden, September 5, 1876, Mr. George H. Huguley, of Upson county, to Miss Annie L. Pope, daughter of Mr. C. Pope, of Pike county, Ga.

By Rev. Landy Wood, August 31, 1876, in Georgetown, S. C., Mr. Charles F. Kinsey, of Quakertown, Bucks county, Pa., to Miss Emma Aquila Davis, of Georgetown, S. C.

Issue of September 26, 1876

By Rev. Robert P. Martyn, September 14, 1876, Mr. J. S. Blakey, to Miss H. M. Parks, daughter of W. W. Parks, all of Gwinnett county, Ga.

By Rev. J. A. Mood, at the Laurens Parsonage, August 31, 1876, Mr. J. T. Langston, of Laurens county, to Miss Sallie L. Fitch, of Union, S. C.

By Rev. J. M. Bowden, in Fairburn, Ga., Sept. 14, 1876, Mr. Owen H. Cochren, to Mrs. Virginia A. Howard.

Issue of October 3, 1876

By Rev. F. G. Hughes, September 14, 1876, Mr. J. T. Dargan, of Dallas, Texas, to Miss Teresa P. Carlton, of Green county, Ga.

By Rev. Jno. M. Bowden, September 24, 1876, Mr. George W. Tarrance, to Mrs. Charity A. Martin, of Campbell county, Ga.

By Rev. G. H. Pooser, September 10, 1876, at Altman Station, Port Royal Railroad, S. C., Mr. W. E. Boyd, to Miss Annie E. Barnett, all of Beaufort county, S. C.

By Rev. John O. Wilson, September 13, 1876, Mr. Wenston J. Rogers, to Miss M. Bettie Muldrow, all of Darlington, S. C.

By Rev. P. W. Edge, September 29, 1876, Mr. James H. Land, to Miss Mary C. Jones, all of Twiggs county, Ga.

By Rev. J. M. Austin, September 20, 1876, in Quitman, Brooks county, Ga., Mr. Henry B. Giles, to Miss Flora E. Irvine, all of Quitman, Ga.

Issue of October 10, 1876

By Rev. H. J. Ellis, September 28, 1876, in Troup county, Ga., Mr. Henry H. Towns, to Miss S. M. J. Glantors, all of Troup county.

By Rev. J. A. Moseley, September 11, 1876, Mr. Henry P. Bradford, to Miss Mary F. Thomas, all of Lowndes county, Ga.

By Rev. G. W. Thomas, September 14, 1876, in Ringgold, Ga., Mr. John Langwith, to Miss Rosa Roper, all of Catoosa county, Ga.

By Rev. G. W. Thomas, September 20, 1876, in Catoosa county, Ga., Mr. John S. Cleveland, of Tennessee, Miss Kissie Holston, of Catoosa county, Ga.

By Rev. A. J. Cauthen, September 12, 1876, Mr. Winfield Clark, to Miss Eunice Smith, of Orangeburg county, S. C.

By Rev. P. F. Kistler, September 26, 1876, Mr. Daniel Utsey, formerly of Charleston, S. C., to Mrs. Cornelia Barnes, of Barnwell county, S. C.

By Rev. Wm. W. Mood, September 19, 1876, Mr. A. Clark, to Miss Mattie F. Wilcox, all of Anderson, S. C.

Issue of October 17, 1876

By Rev. J. Walter Dickson, October 8, 1876, in Columbia, S. C., Mr. T. J. Carling, of New York, to Miss Ella F. Miller, of Columbia, S. C.

By Rev. Dr. Leonard, in the Methodist Parsonage, Camilla, Ga., October 5, 1876, Mr. Robert R. Terrell, Jr., of Albany, Ga., to Miss Ida T. Spence, of Mitchell county, Ga.

By Rev. J. W. Murray, Oct. 5, 1876, Mr. Philip A. Murray, to Miss Sallie A. Mulloy, of Chesterfield county, S. C.

By Rev. E. S. Tyner, Sept. 27, 1876, Mr. John A. Wilson, to Mrs. E. J. Thomson, both of Madison county, Fla.

By Rev. E. S. Tyner, Oct. 5, 1876, Mr. Albert Loper, to Miss Laura Redd, both of Madison county, Fla.

By Rev. Julius T. Curtiss, Oct. 10, 1876, Mr. Jno. L. Smith, of Union Point, to Miss Julia C. Phillips, youngest daughter of Capt. Wm. Phillips, of Augusta, Ga.

Issue of October 24, 1876

By Rev. J. H. D. McRae, September 3, 1876, Mr. C. C. McRae, to Miss L. A. Allen,the former of Brooks, the latter of Colquitt county, Ga.

By Rev. John O. Wilson, October 16, 1876, at Darlington, S. C., Mr. Henry E. P. Sanders, to Mrs. Elizabeth H. Haynesworth.

By Rev. J. M. Austin, October 10, 1876, in the Methodist Church, Valdosta, Ga., Mr. Jas. F. Staples, to Miss Sue M. Ashley.

By Rev. Walter L. Yarbrough, October 10, 1876, Mr.Wm. J. Burton, of Alabama, to Miss Emma J. Hix, of Chattooga county, Ga.

By Rev. W. L. Pegues, September 21, 1876, Timmonsville, S. C., Mr. Benton K. Brockington, to Miss Alice E. Sykes.

Issue of October 31, 1876

By Rev. F. M. T. Brannon, October 19, 1876, Mr. Wm. M. White, to Miss Willie Sewell, all of Merriwether county, Ga.

By Rev. W. R. Foote, October 12, 1876, Mr. George t. Mitchell, of Floyd county, Ga., to Mrs. F. Jane Bramlett, of Kirkwood, Ga.

By Rev. W. J. Cotter, October 15, 1876, Mr. G. W. Clower, to Miss M. C. Bellamy, all of Grantville, Ga.

By Rev. D. E. Starr, October 17, 1876, Rev. W. W. Hardy, to Miss Nancy A. Foster, all of Henry county, Ga.

By Rev. John R. Pate, October 19, 1876, Mr. William R. Fullerton, to Mrs. Ann B. Burnett, both of Upson county, Ga.

By Rev. W. F. Glenn, October 12, 1876, at the residence of Maj. Wm. Barnette, of Hickory, Miss., Mr. W. E. Gilbert, of Marietta, Ga., to Miss Lucy F. Harper, of the former place.

By Rev. Dr. Leonard, October 11, 1876, in Camilla, Ga., Mr. William D. Lewis, of Bainbridge, Ga., to Miss Sarah Emma Lewis, of Camilla, Ga.

By Rev. Dr. Leonard, October 19, 1876, at the residence of Rev. Joseph J. Bradford, Mr. John C. Wilson, of Camilla, Ga., to Miss Louisa C. Bradford, of Mitchell county, Ga.

Issue of November 7, 1876

By Rev. T. H. Timmons, near Atlanta, Ga., Oct. 25, 1876, Mr. A. Y. Owings, to Miss Susie A. Fagan.

By Rev. J. A. Clifton, Oct. 26, 1876, Mr. Franklin Smith of Lexington co., S. C., to Miss Mattie Holstein, of Edgefield co., S. C.

By Rev. J. B. McGehee, in Talbot co., Ga., Oct. 25, 1876, Mr. A. P. Small of Macon, Ga., to Miss Ella Deane Mathews, daughter of Dr. Wm. P. Mathews.

By Rev. T. A. Seals, in the Methodist Episcopal Church, South, in Dalton, Ga., Oct. 19, 1876, Mr. J. W. Chambers, of Marietta, to Miss Bettie Prater, of Dalton.

By Rev. T. A. Seals, in Dalton, Ga., Oct. 31, 1876, Mr. Charles E. Cook of Kentucky, to Miss Annie T. Christian, of Dalton.

By Rev. L. M. Little, assisted by Rev. R. N. Wells, in Sumter, S. C., at the Circuit Parsonage, Oct. 26, 1876, Mr. S. J. Mitchell, to Miss A. E. Little.

By Rev. R. B. Tarrant, Oct. 18, 1876, Mt. J. Franklin Cope, to Miss Carrie E. Carson, all of Orangeburg co., S. C.

By Rev. H. H. Parks, in Augusta, Ga., Oct. 13, 1876, Mr. Francis P. Olmstead, to Mrs. Louisa Ann McLin, both of Newnansville, Fla.

By Rev. H. H. Parks, at Belair, Ga., Oct. 18, 1876, Mr. Charles J. Clifford to Miss J. Adella Batchelor, both of Richmond Co., Ga.

By Rev. H. H. Parks, in St. James Church, Augusta, Ga., Oct. 26, 1876, Mr. John McCann, Jr., to Miss Maggie E. Brodie, both of Augusta, Ga.

By Rev. LeRoy F. Beaty, Oct. 12, 1876, in Edgefield co., S. C., Mr. Marion L. Wheeler, of Newberry co, S. C., to Miss Ida L. Fellers, of Edgefield co., S. C.

By Rev. J. P. Wardlaw, Oct. 15, 1876, in Trinity Church, Brownsville, Ala., Mr. Joseph E. Gammon, to Miss Fannie Tatum, all Columbus, Ga.

By Rev. G. W. Walker, Oct. 19, 1876, in the Methodist Church, Winnsboro, S. C., Mr. C. L. Refo, to Miss Maria L. Williams.

By Rev. R. B. Lester, Oct. 24, 1876, Mr. James H. Anderson, of Macon, Ga., son of Gen. Charles D. Anderson, to Miss Louisa J. Austin, daughter of Dr. Davis N. Austin, of Fort Valley, Ga.

By Rev. Eli Smith, Oct. 19, 1876, Mr. William M. Smith to Miss Mattie J. Thompson, all of Jackson co., Ga.

By Rev. John O. Wilson, Oct. 31, 1876, Mr. John J. Dargan, of Sumter, S. C., to Miss Theodosia G. Williamson, of Darlington, S. C.

Issue of November 14, 1876

By Rev. R. W. Hubert, M. D., in Elim Church, in Warren co., Ga., Nov. 5, 1876, Dr. John Atwell, to Miss Gussie Hall.

By Rev. J. B. Wilson, Oct. 29, 1876, at the residence of Mr. Lewis Fraser, Mr. H. b. Fraser, to Miss Marinda Bowyer, the former of Baker co., Fla., and the latter of Marlboro co., S.C.

By Rev. B. W. Key, at the residence of Mr. D. R. Proctor, Mr. George Mizell, to Miss S. Gertrude Proctor, both of Camden co., Ga.

By Rev. Walker Lewis, in Dawson, Ga., Nov. 5, 1876, Mr. J. W. Norman, to Miss Hattie J. Jobson.

On Nov. 7, 1876, in the Methodist Church in Fort Valley, Ga., Dr. W. B. Mathews, to Miss Mary E. Anderson. Also, at the same time, M. Claude Green, to Miss Annie E. Anderson, both daughters of Gen. C. D. Anderson. Revs. Green, Lester, and Sessions officiating.

Issue of November 21, 1876

By Rev. J. R. Pate, November 9, 1876, Mr. William H. Byers, to Miss M. A. C. Barnett, both of Upson county, Ga.

By Rev. C. A. Conaway, November 12, 1876, Mr. Z. F. Stanton, to Miss M. J. Cosby, all of Gwinnett county, Ga.

By Rev. Eli Smith, November 3, 1876, Mr. C. L. Walker, of Fulton county, Ga., to Miss Agnes Irby, of Hall county, Ga., also at the same time Mr. John T. Irby of Hall county, Ga., to Miss Nannie C. Waters, of Marietta, Ga.

By Rev. M. H. Galloway, in Irwin county, Ga., Rev. R. M. Booth, of the South Georgia Conference, to Miss Loupine Clements.

By Rev. W. T. McMichael, November 7, 1876, at the residence of Capt. William Chambers, of Jones county, Ga., Mr. Henry Bonner, to Miss Fannie D. Finney.

By Rev. W. T. McMichael, November 7, 1876, at the residence of Mr. Nathan Morris, Mr. Joel Godard, to Miss Lula Morris.

By Rev. J. W. Domingos, November 2, 1876, Mr. James Pope, to Miss Emily J. Speight, both of Dooly county, Ga.

By Rev. J. W. Domingos, November 2, 1876, Mr. Willoughby Manning, of Houston county, Ga., to Mrs. Nancy Ragan, of Dooly county, Ga.

By Rev. T. H. Timmons, November 8, 1876, in Payne's Chapel Church, Atlanta, Ga., Mr. Duncan McDonald, to Miss Mary L. Hindman, all of Fulton county, Ga.

By Rev. R. W. Rogers, October 24, 1876, in Pike county, Ga., Mr. William W. Wilson, to Miss Charlotte McDaniel.

By Rev. R. W. Rogers, November 12, 1876, in Pike county, Ga., Mr. Thos. B. Perdue, to Miss Ellen W. Nelson.

By Rev. E. L. T. Blake, November 2, 1876, Mr. A. E. Phillips, to Miss Eugenia, eldest daughter of Thos. J. Rawls, Esq.-- all of Tallahassee, Fla.

By Rev. Geo. C. Thompson, November 10, 1876, in the Presbyterian Church, Blackshear, Ga., Mr. Saml. T. Memry, to Miss Hester A. Brantly.

By Rev. R. W. Dixon, November 8, 1876, in the Methodist Church in Cuthbert, Ga., Mr. Carlton J. Smith, to Miss Mattie B. Flewellen, all of Cuthbert, Ga.

By Rev. R. W. Dixon, November 9, 1876, in Georgetown, Ga., Mr. William A. Barnett of Eufaula, Ala., to Miss Addie V. Mercer, of Georgetown, Ga.

By Rev. R. W. Dixon, November 9, 1876, in Randolph county, Ga., Mr. Jared B. McWilliams, of Cuthbert, Ga., to Miss Mattie L. Dozier, of Randolph county, Ga.

By Rev. W. P. Rivers, October 15, 1876, Mr. B. Goodwyn, to Miss Belle Pound, of Barnesville, Ga.

By Rev. W. P. Rivers, November 2, 1876, Mr. D. A. Stroud, to Miss Lula V. Blalock, of Upson county, Ga.

By Rev. W. P. Rivers, November 14, 1876, Mr. B. R. King, to Miss Alice E. Beckham, of Barnesville, Ga.

By Rev. J. W. G. Watkins, November 12, 1876, at Damond Hill Church, Madison county, Ga., Mr. J. A. Pitner, of Athens, Ga., to Miss Corall Reese, of Muscogee county, Ga.

Issue of November 28, 1876

By Rev. D. D. Cox, in Gainesville, Ga., November 16, 1876, Mr. E. M. Chapman, to Miss Talulah Watkins, all of Gainesville, Ga.

By Rev. J. W. Murray, November 16, 1876, at Chesterfield C. H., Dr. E. H. McBride to Miss Annie E. Murray, all of Chesterfield co., S. C.

By Rev. R. H. Howren, October 4, 1876, Mr. Benjamin Morris, to Miss Mollie Roach, all of Jefferson co,. Fla.

By Rev. R. H. Howren, October 19, 1876, Mr. W. Cash to Miss S. Mixon, all of Jefferson co,. Fla.

By Rev. E. S. Tyner, Nov. 14, 1876, Mr. Thomas T. Ellison, to Miss Rosell W. Morrow, daughter of Prof. H. E. Morrow, all of Moseley Hall, Fla.

By Rev. W. I. Greene, in Fort Valley, Ga., Nov. 15, 1876, Mr. Wm. M. Reese, to Miss Julia J. Houser.

By Rev. John R. Parker, at Col. H. C. Kellogg's, Forsyth co., Ga., Nov. 16, 1876, Mr. Thomas A. Gramling, of Atlanta, Ga., to Miss Addie J. Kellogg.

By Rev. J. S. Embry, Nov. 16, 1876, at the residence of Mr. Jacob Hopkins, Mr. Moses Holland, to Miss Florence G. Peeples, all of Murray co., Ga.

By Rev. W. W. Stewart, Nov. 19, 1876, at the residence of Mrs. E. Leonard, Major N. P. Carreker, to Mrs. Lizzie L. Hill, all of Talbot co., Ga.

By Rev. W. P. Rivers, Nov. 15, 1876, Mr. John M. Zorn, of Upson co., to Mrs. A. M. Nottingham of Monroe co., Ga.

By Rev. W. H. LaPrade, at Rome, Ga., Nov. 12, 1876, Mr. John Fincher, to Miss virginia D. Matthis.

By Rev. W. H. LaPrade, at South Rome, Nov. 14, W. Jerome Ray, Esq., of Monroe, Ga., to Miss A. G. Harris.

By Rev. J. M. Austin, Nov. 15, 1876, Mr. Joseph Mabbit to Miss Ida C. Raysor, all of Quitman, Brooks co., Ga.

By Rev. G. G. Smith, in LaGrange, Ga., Sept. 11, 1876, Dr. J. A. Chapple, to Mrs. Annie W. Ware, both of LaGrange, Ga.

By Rev. G. G. Smith, at the residence of A. H. Cox, Esq., Oct. 31, 1876, Mr. James H. Sledge, of LaGrange, Ga., to Miss Mary Louise Cox, of Troup co., Ga.

By Rev. J. W. Burke, in Macon, Ga., Nov. 21, 1876, Mr. C. A. Dewberry, to miss Sarah Ann Munson.

By Rev. W. R. Foote, Jr., at the residence of Mr. L. M. Moore, Mr. Wm. A. Cook, to Miss Emma G. Moore, both of Baldwin co,. Ga.

By Rev. F. P. Brown, Nov. 9, 1876, Mr. George W. Simons, to Miss Susan F. Langford, both of McDuffie, co,. Ga.

By Rev. F. P. Brown, Nov. 19, 1876, Mr. George W. Stokes, of Barnwell co., S. C., to Miss Josephine E. Moore, of McDuffie, co,. Ga.

Issue of December 5, 1876

By Rev. H. J. Ellis, November 21, 1876, in Troup county, Ga., Mr. Sam. Gates, of Meriwether county, Ga., to Miss Bessie Hill, of Troup county, Ga.

By Rev. H. J. Ellis, November 9, 1876, in Troup county, Ga., Mr. J. Vinson Wright, to Miss Mollie Perry.

By Rev. J. Rembert Smith, November 23, 1876, in McDonough, Ga., Mr. Geo. S. Hanes, of Jonesboro, Ga., to Miss Josie Strange, of the former place. (Baptist Index please copy.)

By Rev. D. D. Dantzler, November 23, 1876, Mr. W. Laurance Segrest, to Miss A. Elizabeth Foures, all of Orangeburg county, S. C.

By Rev. Jno. M. Bowden, November 26, 1876, Mr. Thomas E. Penington, to Miss Alice I. Wilkerson, of Campbell county, Ga.

By Rev. Jno. M. Bowden, November 26, 1876, Mr. George C. Andrew to Miss Mary E. Shannon, of Campbell county, Ga.

By Rev. Isaac J. Newberry, November 26, 1876, Mr. W. S. Lipscomb, of Spartanburg county, S. C., to Miss Ella A. Littlejohn, of Union county, S. C.

By Rev. E. J. Rentz, November 23, 1876, at the residence of Rev. W. B. Merritt, of Marion county, Ga., Mr. John B. Holley to Miss Lizzie J. Merritt.

By Rev. R. A. Conner, November 23, 1876, in Oglethorpe county, Ga., Rev. E. B. Rees, M. D., of Columbia co., Ga., to Miss Katie E. Dozier, daughter of Augustus Dozier of the former place.

By Rev. W. T. Hamilton, November 14, 1876, Mr. J. T. Neal, to Miss Mollie M. Burr, all of Thomson, Ga.

By Rev. A. J. Dean, November 2, 1876, Mr. D. M. Geesling to Miss Elmira V. Hurley, all of Stewart county, Ga.

By Rev. A. J. Dean, November 16, 1876, Mr. Jordan T. Jackson, of Alabama, to Miss Sarah Wheeler, of Stewart county, Ga.

By Rev. A. J. Dean, November 28, 1876, Mr. A. L. Raleigh, of Eufaula, Ala., to Miss Lizzie Singer, of Lumpkin, Ga.

By Rev. Wm. H. LaPrade, November 22, 1876, in Chattooga county, Ga., Mr. John C. Bailey, of Floyd county, Ga., to Miss Ida E. Morton, of Chattooga county, Ga.

By Rev. R. W. Dixon, November 21, 1876, in Randolph county, Ga., Mr. John C. Ward, to Miss Alice Gomiley, all of Randolph county, Ga.

By Rev. R. W. Dixon, November 21, 1876, in Randolph county, Ga., Mr. Joseph C. Goldwin to Miss Willie F. Ward, all of Randolph county, Ga.

By Rev. C. W. Felder, November 16, 1876, Mr. P. B. Mouzon, to Miss Sallie M. Brailsford, daughter of T. W. Brailsford, Sr., all of Clarendon county, S. C.

By Rev. A. M. Williams, November 9, 1876, in Laurens county, Ga., Mr. Milton C. Jackson, to Miss Subeliann Jones.

By Rev. A. M. Williams, November 23, 1876, in Johnson county, Ga., Mr. Arthur B. Fort, to Miss Mollie A. Lovett.

By Rev. J. W. Hinton, D. D., November 21, 1876, at the residence of F. T. Snead, Esq., Oglethorpe, Ga., Rev. W. L. Wootten, Jr., of the North Georgia Conference, to Miss Lizzie W. Snead.

By Rev. H. S. Andrews, November 19, 1876, in McIntosh county, Ga. Mr. Duke M. McIntosh, to Miss Mady M. Space, all of McIntosh county, Ga.

By Rev. J. W. Burke, November 26, 1876, in Macon, Ga., Mr. J. W. Newton, to Miss Martha A. Murfee.

By Rev. J. B. Wilson, November 16, 1876, Mr. Ira S. Harris to Miss Ceredia Auretta Pryor, all of Union county, S. C.

By Rev. J. B. Wilson, November 19, 1876, Mr. N. C. Rollins to Miss Harriet White, all of Union county, S. C.

By Rev. J. B. Wilson, November 23, 1876, Mr. L. M. Parsons, of Spartanburg, S. C., to Miss Vickie Harlan, of Union county, S. C.

By Rev. E. S. Tyner, November 26, 1876, at the residence of Mr. Coleman Roe, Mr. J. e. Ragans, to Miss N. A. E. Roe, all of Madison county, Fla.

By Rev. J. H. Wilkins, November 23, 1876, in Lowndes county, Ga., Mr. Riley Newborne to Miss Elizabeth Anderson, of Clinch county, Ga.

Issue of December 12, 1876

By Rev. J. W. Humbert, November 30, 1876, Mr. R. McKibbin Dailey, to Miss Mary P. Mason, of Beaufort county, S. C.

By Rev. W. J. Cotter, November 26, 1876, Meriwether county, Ga., Mr. J. C. Barnes to Miss C. B. Powledge.

By Rev. J. B. McFarland, November 30, 1876, Mr. A. S. Hawkins, to Miss Hattie A. McFarland, all of Walker county, Ga.

By Rev. T. H. Timmons, November 30, 1876, in Atlanta, Ga., Mr. William H. Smith, to Miss Samantha O. Hendrix, all of Atlanta, Ga.

By Rev. J. J. Harris, November 29, 1876, Mr. J. T. Kilgo, to Miss Lydia A. Douglass, all of Milton county, Ga.

By Rev. W. F. Glenn, November 21, 1876, in Marietta, Ga., Mr. Daniel White, to Miss Melissa Bowles.

By Rev. D. L. Anderson, November 23, 1876, Mr. Geo. M. Lazenby, of Columbia county, Ga., to Miss Sallie E. Dyson, of Wilkes county, Ga.

By Rev. D. L. Anderson, November 26, 1876, Mr. Robert Chafin to Miss Mary Drinkard, all of Wilkes county, Ga.

By Rev. J. D. Gunnels, November 23, 1876, at the residence of Leroy Parks, Banks county, Ga., Mr. William C. Ward, to Miss Permelia O. Ledbetter.

By Rev. H. R. Felder, November 8, 1876, Mr. John W. Jones, of Houston county, Ga., to Miss Hattie Glozier, of Macon county, Ga.

By Rev. H. R. Felder, November 16, 1876, Mr. C. C. Lilly to Miss Clifford Hardie, all of Montezuma, Ga.

By Rev. G. W. Gatlin, November 23, 1876, Mr. Thomas P. Steele, M. D., to Miss Eliza Ann McConnell, all of Williamsburg, S. C.

By Rev. Thomas T. Christian, December 5, 1876, Rev. J. W. Weston, of the South Georgia Conference, to Miss Lillian L. Adams, of Sumter county, Ga.

By Rev. Thomas T. Christian, December 6, 1876, Col. Macellus Castlen, of Monroe county, Ga., to Miss Juliet Harrison, of Americus, Ga.

By Rev. C. W. Smith, December 5, 1876, in Macon, Ga., Mr. James Greene, to Miss Sudie C. Hollingsworth.

Issue of December 19-26, 1876

By Rev. S. Donelly, December 7, 1876, Mr. Saml. T. Fleming, of Archer, Fla., to Miss rosa D. Smith, of Wacahoota, Fla.

By Rev. S. H. J. Sistrunk, December 14, 1876, Mr. W. C. Epting, of Montezuma, Ga., to Mrs. Nancy E. Elliott, of Houston county, Ga.

By Rev. R. D. Gentry, December 7, 1876, Dr. Joseph O. Hayns[?], to Miss Georgia H. Temple, all of Bradford county, Fla.

By Bishop McTyeire, December 7, 1876, Prof. J. M. Webb, of Calleoka, Tenn,. to Miss Lily eldest, daughter of Dr. A. M. Shipp, of Vanderbilt University.

By Rev. Jno. M. Bowden, November 30, 1876, Mr. Jno. W. Bates, of Carroll county, Ga., to Miss Martha A. Smith, of Campbell county, Ga.

By Rev. J. M. Carlisle, November 30, 1876, Mr. Edwin S. Carlisle to Miss Annie A. Breeden, daughter of J. L. Breeden, Esq., all of Bennettsville, S. C.

By Rev. P. F. Kistler, December 7, 1876, near Bamberg, S. C., Mr. D. F. Hooten, to Miss Julia P. Bamberg.

By Rev. O. L. Smith, D. D., December 6, 1876, in Newton county, Ga., Mr. C. B. Rosser, to Miss Ada Sams.

By Rev. T. Ward White, November 28, 1876, in Hale county, Ala., Dr. W. P. Matthews, of Talbot county, Ga., to Mrs. M. A. E. Lipscomb.

By Rev. F. M. T. Brannan, December 3, 1876, at the residence of A. Thomson, Mr. W. T. Rosser, to Miss Mattie M. Means, all of Meriwether county, Ga.

By Rev. J. L. Sifley, November 8, 1876, in Colleton county, S. C., Mr. H. Benjamin Ackerman, to Miss Margaret A. E. Peirce, eldest daughter of Dr. Geo. Peirce, evangelist.

By Rev. W. A. Florence, December 5, 1876, in Monroe, Ga., Mr. Myron Ellis, of Meriwether county, Ga., to Mrs. Sarah H. Sheats, of Monroe, Ga.

By Rev. J. S. Jobson, December 14, 1876, in Terrell county, Ga., Mrs. Mary V. Jones, to Mr. Noel W. Pace, of Calhoun county, Ga.

By Rev. Geo. G. Smith, in the M. E. Church, Grantville, Ga., Mr. Jno. F. Lovejoy, to Miss Mary L. Cotter, daughter of Rev. W. J. Cotter, of North Georgia Conference.

By Rev. R. A. Seale, December 13, 1876, Mr. Geo. Reidel, to Miss A. E. Seago, all of Richmond county, Ga. Savannah papers please copy.

By Rev. Geo. W. Yarbrough, November 30, 1876, in Dirt Town Valley, Rev. Walter L. Yarbrough, of the North Georgia Conference, to Miss Lura Morton.

By Rev. J. B. Kilpatrick, December 14, 1876, in White Plains, Green county, Ga., Mr. William L. Tappan, to Miss Willie Jernigan, youngest daughter of S. J. Jernigan, Esq., all of White Plains, Ga.

Issue of January 2, 1877

By Dr. W. I. Greene, on the 5th December, 1876, Dr. E. V. Steedman, of South Carolina, to Mrs. C. P. Stewart, of Houston county, Ga.

SOUTHERN CHRISTIAN ADVOCATE MARRIAGE NOTICES 1867-1878

By Dr. W. I. Greene, on the 7th December, 1876, at the residence of Mr. Blewster, Mr. E. Bridges to Miss Bell Hammock, all of Houston county, Ga.

By Dr. W. I. Greene, on the 12th December, 1876, Mr. John W. Gurr to Miss Carrie Goodin, all of Houston county, Ga.

By Dr. W. I. Greene, December 20th, 1876, Mr. Jesse F. Kinard, of Sumter county, to Miss Carrie Hampton, of Houston county, Ga.

By Rev. J. J. Workman, December 19th, 1876, Samuel D. Elrod, of Anderson county, S. C., to Miss Elizabeth L. Martin, of Abbeville county, S. C.

By Rev. R. W. Dixon, December 21st, 1876, in Georgetown, Ga., John E. Fuller, of Geneva, Ga., to Miss Sue F. Dozier, of the former place.

By Rev. J. F. Mixon, December 3d, 1876, at Independence Church, Broad River circuit, Mr. A. H. Hendricks to Miss Alice Gibson, both of Wilkes county, Ga.

By Rev. C. C. Cary, December 21, 1876, in Clarke county, Ga., Mr. Nathan Davis and Miss Nannie Puryear.

By Rev. Dr. Leonard, December 19th, 1875, Mr. Samuel W. Livingston, of Newton, to Miss Lucia O. Norris, of Baker county, Ga.

By Rev. W. W. Oslin, December 20th, 1875, Mr. Alfred L. King, of Oconee county, to Miss Lula Ritch, daughter of Jere. Ritch, Esq., of Jackson county, Ga.

By Rev. W. M. Watts, on the 23d November, 1876, Mr. Wm. D. Sutley to Miss Rebecca Gray, all of Madison county, Fla.

By Rev. Jos. B. Lanier, December 20, 1876, at Mr. Reuben Chance's, Lawtonville, Burke county, Ga., Dr. M. D. Lanier, of Milledgeville, to Miss Sylvetta Lovett.

By Rev. J. S. Jordan, December 20, 1876, at the residence of Mr. J. F. Berry, Effingham county, Ga., Mr. Wm. W. Enicks, of Scriven county, to Miss Anna J. Rahn, of Effingham county.

By Rev. A. M. Williams, in Mulberry Street Methodist Church, Macon, Ga., December 19, 1876, Mr. John M. Brown, of Spalding county, Ga., to Miss Lucy B. Spain, of Macon.

By Rev. J. T. McBryde, in Americus, Ga., Rev. A. M. Williams, of the South Georgia Conference, to Miss Lorena L. Brown.

By Rev. W. H. Hunt, December 10th, 1876, Mr. A. J. Hunt to Miss Callie Clement, all of Columbia county, Fla.

By Rev. Leroy F. Beaty, December 7th, 1876, Mr. F. Thos. Kelley to Miss Lucy E. Lake, all of Newberry county, S. C.

By Rev. J. B. Payne, November 28, 1876, Mr. John M. Murphy, of Tennessee, to Miss Dolly Ann Ingram, of Thomaston, Ga.

By Rev. J. B. Payne, November 29, 1876, Mr. J. C. McMichael, of Barnesville, to Miss Anna M. Sandich, of Thomaston, Ga.

By Rev. P. F. Kistler, December 20th, 1876, near Buford's Bridge, S. C., Mr. Wilson R. Williams, of Allendale, to Miss Mamie Brabham.

By Rev. Wm. B. Neal, November 16th, at Chapel Hill church, Mr. James N. Woddail, to Miss Elizabeth A. Zuber, all of Macon county, Ala.

By Rev. Wm. B. Neal, December 7th, Mr. E. A. Torbet to Miss Prince Ella Buchannan, all of Russell county, Ala.

By Rev. H. A. C. Walker, December 12, 1876, Mr. C. G. Dantzler to Miss Laura A. Moss, daughter of Wm. C. Moss, Esq., all of Orangeburg county, S. C.

By Rev. John M. Bowden, December 13, 1876, Mr. Edmon B. Hopkins to Miss Lenora Wilkerson, all of Campbell county, Ga.

By Rev. John M. Bowden, December 20, 1876, Dr. James T. Davenport to Miss Mary A. Latham, all of Campbell county, Ga.

By Rev. C. W. Smith, December 21, 1876, Mr. Josiah Lumsden to Mrs. J. H. Powers, all of Bibb county, Ga.

By Rev. D. D. Dantzler, December 3, 1876, Mr. J. W. H. Dukes, Sr., to Miss Mary Funches, all of Orangeburg county, S. C.

By Rev. D. D. Dantzler, December 12, 1876, Mr. Benj. S. Crum, to Miss Emma A. Bowman, daughter of Dr. O. N. Bowman, of Orangeburg county, S. C.

By Rev. S. S. Sweet, December 5, 1876, at the residence of M. H. Cutter, in East Macon, Ga., Mr. Hubbard Reynolds to Miss Mississippi Bryan.

By Rev. W. E. Johnston, December 21, 1876, in Richmond county, Ga., Mr. Wm. b. moss to Miss Nettie E. Hargraves, all of Richmond county.

By Rev. W. P. Rivers, November 21, 1876, Mr. John T. Dozier to Miss Anna Davis, of Upson county, Ga.

By Rev. W. P. Rivers, November 21, 1876, Mr. John Cherry, of Bibb county, to Miss Fannie Dozier, of Upson county, Ga.

By Rev. Joseph J. Seally, November 16, 1876, near Newnansville, East Fla., Mr. Albert Strickland to Miss Giles Hague.

By Rev. Joseph J. Seally, December 6, 1876, near Newnansville, East Fla., Mr. J. B. Huggins to Miss M. E. Downing.

By Rev. Joseph J. Seally, December 14, 1876, near Newnansville, East Fla., Mr. H. L. Riviere to Miss Sallie A. Downing.

By Rev. T. W. Moore, in the city of Jacksonville, Fla., December 27, 1876, Mr. James S. Hull of Live Oak, to Miss Mary N. Bradley of Jacksonville.

By Rev. Thomas H. Timmons, in Paynes Chapel, Atlanta, Ga., December 21, 1876, Mr. Edwin T. Paynes, to Miss Anna P. Holmes, all of Atlanta, Ga.

<u>Issue of January 9, 1877</u>

By Rev. W. F. Roberts, December 7, 1876, Mr. Lawrence N. Ryals to Miss Caroline Morrison, of Montgomery county, Ga.

By Rev. Geo. G. N. MacDonell, January 2, 1877, Mr. John W. Walthall to Miss Josephine Brown, both of Bibb county, Ga.

By Rev. J. O. A. Clark, December 20, 1876, at the residence of Mr. Henry Mitchell, Mr. A. Curtis Brown to Miss Mary A. T. Mitchell.

By Rev. A. Clark, December 19, 1876, Mr. John S. Clark to Miss Sudie T. Kellam, all of Liberty county, Ga.

By Rev. Levi Bedenbaugh, December 12, 1876, at the residence of Dr. J. C. Delapierriere, near Fiat Shoals, Ga., Dr. John Taylor, of Lutherville, Ga,. to Miss Rosa Delapierriere, all of Merriwether county, Ga.

By Rev. J. S. Jobson, December 27, 1876, at the residence of Mr. J. B. F. Harrell, Mr. P. T. Smith to Miss Nannie E. Register, all of Terrell county, Ga.

By Rev. J. R. Little, November 15, 1876, Mr. John Farabee, formerly of Mt. Pleasant, Sullivan's Island, S. C., to Miss Kate Hodges, of Marlboro county, S. C.

By Rev. J. R. Little, December 19, 1876, Mr. Wm. K. Hilliard to Miss Nannie, second daughter of Mr. Henry J. Rogers, Sr., of Marlboro county, S. C.

By Rev. M. H. Pooser, November 19, 1876, Mr. Wm. G. Walker to Mrs. Ann L. Foy, all of Edgefield county, S. C.

By Rev. M. H. Pooser, December 21, 1876, at the residence of G. W. Coleman, Esq., Mr. Richard C. Griffith to Miss Mary A. Campbell, all of Edgefield county, S. C.

By Rev. W. F. Glenn, December 14, 1876, in Jefferson, Jackson county, Ga., Mr. W. J. Davenport, of Oglethorpe county, GA., to Miss Loula Glenn of the former place.

By Rev. D. J. Myrick, January 2, 1877, in Griffin, Ga., Rev. J. H. Daniel, of Heard county, Ga., to Miss Emma McDowell, of Griffin, Ga.

By Rev. J. S. Jordan, December 25, 1876, in Effingham county, Ga., Rev. T. I. Nease, of the South Georgia Conference, to Miss Emma Nease.

By Rev. D. Blalock, December 27, 1876, Mr. J. W. Miles to Miss S. E. Branda.

By Rev. J. B. McGehee, December 7, 1876, in Talbot county, Ga., Rev. W. F. Lloyd of the South Georgia Conference, to Miss Jessie Grace.

By Rev. J. B. McGehee, December 19, 1876, in Taylor county, Ga., Mr. Charles J. Grace to Miss V. A. Lloyd.

By Rev. J. B. McGehee, December 26, 1876, at Howard, Ga., Mr. S. S. Bowen, of Mississippi, to Miss Stella Matthews.

By Rev. J. B. McGehee, December 27, 1876, in Talbot, Ga., Mr. Wm. I. Lumpkin to Mrs. Sarah M. Bussey.

By Rev. J. J. Singleton, December 19, 1876, Mr. Reese Kerr to Miss Mary Dantzler, both of Bartow county, Ga.

By Rev. J. J. Singleton, December 21, 1876, Mr. Creed H. Cunyers to Miss Villa D. Leeke, both of Bartow county, Ga.

By Rev. Geo. H. Wells, on Tuesday evening December 21, 1876, at Fair View, Mr. G. W. Wannamaker to Miss Lilly E. Bates, daughter of Dr. R. W. Bates, all of Orangeburg county, S. C.

By Rev. W. W. Lumpkin, December 21, 1876, at Mount Zion Church, Mr. Johnie D. Cooper to Miss Mary L. Combs, all of Wilkes county, Ga.

By Rev. D. F. C. Timmons, December 18, 1876, Mr. Wm. L. Wood to Miss Carrie P. Jackson, all of Walton county, Ga.

By Rev. D. F. C. Timmons, December 19, 1876, at the residence of Mrs. G. S. Cowan, Mr. C. L. Hayes to Miss Olivia E. Carter, all of Monroe, Walton county, Ga.

By Rev. J. T. Lowe, December 21, 1876, Mr. Jno. H. Cates to Miss Lou Walton, all of Monroe county, Ga.

By Rev. D. J. Simmons, December 20, 1876, at the residence of Dr. G. I. Odom, in Orangeburg county, S. C., Mr. John A. McCreary, of Barnwell county, S. C. to Miss Cornelia A. Odom.

By Rev. Dr. Leonard, January 2, 1877, in Camilla, Ga., Mr. Daniel B. Henderson to Miss Sallie Cullens.

By Rev. E. P. Bonner, November 23, 1876, Mr. Leroy Miles to Miss Mary Epps, all of Columbia county, Ga.

By Rev. E. P. Bonner, December 21, 1876, Mr. J. M. Ivy, of Columbia county, Ga., to Miss E. E. Thomas, of Richmond county, Ga.

By Rev. E. P. Bonner, December 25, 1876, Mr. Olonzo Grover to Miss Ella J. Gray, all of Columbia county, Ga.

By Rev. C. A. Conaway, November 26, 1876, Mr. J. C. Carter to Miss Nannie Hancock.

By Rev. C. A. Conaway, December 18, 1876, Mr. S. O. Callaway to Miss Mattie E. Tiller, second daughter of Capt. J. S. Tiller, of Point Peter, Oglethorpe county, Ga.

Issue of January 16, 1877

By Rev. T. A. Harris, December 24, 1876, in Winterville, Ga., Mr. J. H. F. Mosemann to Miss Martha E. Thompson.

By Rev. T. A. Harris, December 26, 1876, Mr. C. h. Anthony to Miss Susie Dotsey, both of Clark county, Ga.

By Rev. E. S. Tyner, December 14, 1876, Mr. John Jarvis to Miss Mary E. Paul, all of Madison county, Fla.

By Rev. E. S. Tyner, January 4, 1876, Mr. John H. Bailey to Miss Mary C. Smith, all of Madison county, Fla.

By Rev. E. S. Tyner, January 7, 1876, Mr. J. A. Cottenham to Miss Eliza B. Dutton, all of Madison county, Fla.

By Rev. F. B. Davies, December 24, 1876, Dr. Alphonzo H. Rogers to Miss Eleanor E. Lowe, all of Warren county, Ga.

By Rev. T. H. Stewart, December 31, 1876, at Rehobath Church, Sumter county, Ga., Mr. J. A. Rawlins, of Lancaster, Texas, to Miss Georgia Rogers, of Sumter county, Ga.

By Rev. W. A. Rogers, December 20, 1876, Mr. James Bennett, of Lancaster, S. C., to Miss Octavia Crosswell, of Bishopville, S. C.

By Rev. Jno M. Bowden, December 21, 1876, Mr. Seabron Longino to Miss Margaret Davenport, all of Campbell county, Ga.

By Rev. Jno M. Bowden, December 21, 1876, Mr. Jno. F. Goodman to Miss Emma J. Harvey, all of Campbell county, Ga.

By Rev. Wm. Hutto, June 22, 1876, Mr. Arthur Dantzler to Miss Rebecca Dantzler, all of Orangeburg, S. C.

By Rev. Wm. Hutto, September 28, 1876, Mr. Samuel Hutto, to Miss Laura E. Thirston, the former of Orangeburg, the latter of Charleston county, S. C.

By Rev. Wm. Hutto, January 3, 1877, Mr. Edwin Dantzler to Miss Mary J. Williams, all of Charleston county, S. C.

By Rev. Wm. Hutto, December 21, 1876, Mr. J. D. Murray to Miss Virginia E. Livingston, all of Charleston county, S. C.

By Rev. R. F. Williamson, December 5, 1876, Mr. Willie Little to Miss Amanda P. Wommack, all of Schley county, Ga.

By Rev. R. F. Williamson, December 5, 1876, Mr. James F. Woods to Miss Julia Wommack, all of Schley county, Ga.

By Rev. R. F. Williamson, December 7, 1876, Mr. C. R. Tondee to Miss E. D. Chapman, all of Schley county, Ga.

By Rev. R. F. Williamson, December 19, 1876, Mr. J. C. Strange to Miss Emma Massey, all of Schley county, Ga.

By Rev. R. F. Williamson, December 21, 1876, Mr. Z. T. Mott to Miss E. A. Strange, all of Schley county, Ga.

Issue of January 23, 1877

By Rev. D. J. Simmons, January 7, 1877, Mr. James Milhouse to Miss Laura Davis, daughter of Mr. D. D. Davis, all of Orangeburg county, S. C.

By Rev. S. R. Weaver, December 23, 1877, in the church in Bluffton, Ga., Mr. M. N. Killabrew, of Alabama, to Miss R. M. Lee, of Clay county, Ga.

By Rev. D. M. Banks, January 9, 1877, at the residence of Maj. E. W. Tarver, Enon, Ala., Mr. John F. Cone, of Notasulga, to Miss Laura G. Tarver.

By Rev. H. R. Felder, December 31, 1876, in Spaulding, Macon county, Ga., Mr. Morgan E. Chastain to Miss Vic R. McKenzie.

By Rev. H. R. Felder, December 24, 1876, Col. R. G. Ozier to Miss Olivia McLendon, all of Montezuma, Ga.

By Rev. H. R. Felder, January 7, 1877, Maj. James D. Fredrick to Miss Dora A. Keen, all of Marshalville, Macon county, Ga.

By Rev. R. B. Lester, January 9, 1877, Mr. Robert Law, of Bainbridge, Ga., to Miss Clara E. Jones, daughter of Henry Wilks Jones, Esq., of Burke county, Ga.

By Rev. J. M. Potter, January 7, 1877, at the Methodist E. Church, South, in Chickasawhatchie, Ga., Mr. T. F. Collier to Miss Mittie Woolbright, all of Terrel county, Ga.

By Rev. J. T. Welch, December 19, 1876, Mr. Timothy L. cob to Miss Amanda Bradford, both of Lowndes county, Ga.

By Rev. J. S. Jordan, January 2, 1877, in Bulloch county, Ga., Mr. W. A. Hodges, of Bulloch, to Miss Emma S. Slater.

By Judge H. C. Ward, December 14, 1876, Mr. W. H. Barr to Miss N. A. E. Evans, all of Twiggs county, Ga.

By Rev. J. W. Weston, January 11, 1877, in Fort Gaines, Ga., Mr. Wm. Armstrong, of Clay county, Ga., to Miss Elizabeth McLenden, of Fort Gaines, Ga.

By Rev. F. B. Davies, January 16, 1877, Mr. john F. Johnson to Miss Fanny Norris, all of Warren county, Ga.

By Rev. T. R. Kendall, December 19, 1876, Mr. Robert Christian, of Clinton, Jones county, Ga., to Miss Lizzie Gibson, of Crawford county, Ga.

By Rev. F. M. T. Brannan, January 7, 1877, in Grantville, Ga., Mr. Thos. Moore to Miss Samanthia Sewell.

By Rev. J. Finger, December 12, 1876, in the Methodist Church at Williamston, S. C., Mr. Thomas Gilstrap to Miss Mary McDugle, of Greenville county, S. C.

Issue of January 30, 1877

By Rev. Jas. D. Mauldin, December 21, 1876, Mr. W. M. Wells to Miss E. V. Mercer, all of Scriven county, Ga.

By Rev. Jas. D. Mauldin, January 14, 1877, Mr. John W. Beckum to Miss Alice S. Arrington, all of Jefferson county, Ga.

By Rev. J. J. Singleton, January 18, 1877, Mr. John D. Lanier to Miss Rachael M. Clayton.

By Rev. Dr. Harlan, January 9, 1877, Mr. Jno. DeJournette, Jr., to Miss Mary Fields, all of Whitfield county, Ga.

By the bride's father, January 3, 1877, Mr. John E. Goodwin to Miss Margaret E. Carson, at Cedar Hill, Waccamow, S. C.

By Rev. W. W. Stewart, January 21, 1877, at the residence of Mrs. M. L. Miller, Mr. W. H. Crawford to Miss A. B. Miller, all of Talbot county, Ga.

By Rev. W. M. Crumley, January 16, 1877, in Trinity Church, Atlanta, Ga., Mr. William A. Gregg to Miss Lizzie L. Jones, daughter of Col. O. H. Jones, all of Atlanta, Ga.

By Rev. J. H. D. McRae, December 19, 1876, Mr. S. L. Morse to Miss Fannie Rosser, all of Brooks county, Ga.

By Rev. J. H. D. McRae, January 2, 1877, at the Rev. John Dilk's, Mr. J. W. Joyce to Miss Caddie Harrington, all of Brooks county, Ga.

By Rev. J. H. D. McRae, January 11, 1877, Mr. J. W. Baker to Miss Julia Rogers, all of Brooks county, Ga.

By Rev. J. A. Porter, January 10, 1877, Mr. Lewis a. Nelson to Miss Rosa Louise Crafts, both of Charleston, S. C.

By Rev. A. J. Cauthen, January 24, 1877, Mr. Lewis Russ to Miss Laura Hutto, all of Barnwell county, S. C.

Issue of February 6, 1877

By Rev. W. C. Patterson, December 5, 1876, Mr. W. B. Robertson to Miss Minnie H. Porter, grand-daughter of the officiating minister, all of Lancaster, S. C.

By Rev. W. C. Patterson, December 26, 1876, Mr. J. M. Yoder, of Newton, N.C., to Miss Mary S. Tillman, eldest daughter of J. L. Tillman, of Lancaster, S. C.

By Rev. D. J. Simmons, January 16, 1877, Mr. Austin Livingston to Miss Mary A. Bonnett, all of Orangeburg county, S. C.

By Rev. A. Nettles, January 21, 1877, at the residence of the bride's brother-in-law, Mr. J. E. Gregg to Miss Sallie A. Davis, all of Marion, S. C.

By Rev. Theo. E. Smith, November 15, 1876, in Cartersville, at the Presbyterian Church, Mr. W. C. Leigh, of Newnan, Ga., to Miss Ellan Leigh Remington, of Cartersville, Ga.

By Rev. R. M. Walker, January 14, 1877, at Swainsboro, Ga., Mr. C. J. Jenkins to Miss Mary E. McLeod.

By Rev. W. T. McMichael, January 18, 1877, in Jones county, Ga., Mr. James A. Roberts to Miss Annie Stripling.

By Rev. W. T. McMichael, January 25, 1877, in Clinton, Jones county, Ga., Mr. Wiley H. Holsenback to Miss Helen Morgan.

By Rev. J. D. Rogers, January 11, 1877, Mr. Pleasant A. Tucker to Miss Edna R. Shirley, daughter of Jonathan Shirley, all of Hernando county, Fla.

By Rev. J. D. Rogers, January 17, 1877, Mr. William D. Boulden, of Sumter county, Fla., to Miss Helen M. Pemberton, of Hernando county, Fla.

By Rev. J. D. Rogers, January 4, 1877, Mr. A. Judson Hayman to Miss Elizabeth Barnes, daughter of Rev. J. F. Barnes, of Hernando county, Fla.

By Rev. J. D. Rogers, January 5, 1877, at the residence of H. w. Hancock, Mr. Nathan J. High to Mrs. Nancy J. Whidden, all of Manatee county, Fla.

By Rev. J. D. Rogers, January 9, 1877, Mr. James S. Strickland, of Hillsboro, Fla., to Mrs. Mary E. Strickland, of Hernando county, Fla.

By Rev. L. W. Rast, January 11, 1877, Mr. William Wages to Miss Harriet Simpson, all of Lexington, S. C.

By Rev. L. W. Rast, January 11, 1877, at Mr. Jonathan Kaigler's, Mr. Richard Rucker to Miss Sallie Knight, all of Lexington county, S. C.

By Rev. D. F. Spigener, January 16, 1877, Mr. F. Marion Rast, of Lexington county, S. C., To Miss Emma Rickenbaker, all of Orangeburg co., S. C.

By Rev. L. W. Rast, November 30, 1876, at Miss Barbara Pound's, Mr. John Richter to Miss Louisa Pound, all of Orangeburg, S. C.

Issue of February 13, 1877

By Rev. D. Cran Oliver, November 19, 1876, Mr. W. A. Chambers to Miss M. A. Gillespie, all of Banks county, Ga.

By Rev. D. Cran Oliver, December 15, 1876, Mr. B. H. Parks to Miss Margaret Gillespie, all of Banks county, Ga.

By Rev. D. Cran Oliver, December 22, 1876, Mr. J. S. Verner to Miss Georgia E. Gunnells, all of Banks county, Ga.

By Rev. D. Cran Oliver, December 26, 1876, Mr. J. J. Moore to Miss Mary H. Sanders, all of Madison county, Ga.

By Rev. D. Cran Oliver, January 4, 1877, Mr. Howell Garrison to Miss Sallie Gillespie, all of Banks county, Ga.

By Rev. D. Cran Oliver, January 18, 1877, Mr. S. K. Mason to Miss Mattie Holbrooks, all of Banks county, Ga.

By Rev. D. Cran Oliver, February 1, 1877, Mr. D. P. Kesler of Franklin county, Ga., to Miss L. C. Ward, of Banks county, Ga.

By Rev. J. W. Hinton, D. D., February 7, 1877, Mr. Davis H. Howes, of Macon ,Ga., To Miss Susie M. Wright, of Washington county, Ga., daughter of Col. H. G. Wright.

By Rev. B. F. Breedlove, at the residence of Mr. W. Shepard, in Jefferson county, Ga., Dr. S. F. Hunt to Miss A. E. McCroan.

By Rev. J. D. Rogers, January 25, 1877, Mr. Wm. A. Jones to Miss Martha L. jones, daughter of Mr. Hilliard Jones, of Hernando county, Fla.

By Rev. C. E. Dowman, January 31, 1877, in Quincy, Fla., Mr. John T. Howard to Miss Roseta R. Jones.

By Rev. J. E. Watson, February 4, 1877, Mr. Geo. L. Bouknight to Miss Mary Bickley, all of Lexington county, S. C.

By Rev. W. J. Flanders, January 7, 1877, Mr. J. R. Flanders, of Emanuel county, Ga., to Miss Nancy Smith, of Johnson county, Ga.

By Rev. J. E. Watson, February 7, at the residence of the Maj. Sanders Swygert, Mr. John H. Swygert to Miss Anna Swygert, all of Lexington county, S. C.

By Rev. Wm. W. Mood, January 25, 1877, Mr. William Lawson to Miss Harriet Austin, all of Union county, S. C.

By Rev. W. W. Oslin, January 30, 1877, at the residence of Sam'l Thomson, Esq., Mr. S. D. Dunevent, of Morgan county, Ga., to Miss Anna Eblin, of Oconee county, Ga.

By Rev. W. S. Baker, January 17, 1877, in Jeffersonville, Ga., Rev. C. J. Toole, of the South Georgia Conference, to Miss Loula P. Jones, daughter of Elias Jones deceased.

By Rev. C. B. Stewart, January 25, 1877, Mr. White Terry to Miss Ellen Thomason, all of Greenville county, S. C.

By Rev. Wm. Hutto, January 18, 1877, Mr. Watts S. Banister to Miss Carrie C. Breland, all of Charleston county, S. C.

By Rev. Wm. Hutto, January 18, 1877, Mr. John M. Myers to Miss Caroline M. Thomas, all of Orangeburg county, S. C.

By Rev. W. C. Patterson, February 1, 1877, Mr. J. M. Smith to Miss Missouri Dunlap, all of York county, S. C.

By Rev. R. L. Wiggins, December 7, 1876, in Houston county, Ga., Mr. Perry Smoak to Miss Sallie means, daughter of Dr. Means.

By Rev. W. R. Steeley, January 21, 1877, Charles W. Mims, Esq., of Twiggs county, Ga., to Miss M. S. Coley, of Pulaski county, Ga.

Issue of February 20, 1877

By Rev. H. R. Felder, February 7, 1877, in Albany, Ga., Maj. D. J. Owen of Alapaha, Ga., to Miss Fannie A. Sutton, of Albany, Ga.

By Rev. A. G. Haygood, January 1, 1877, Mr. M. A. Malone, son of Rev. J. D. Malone, to Miss S. G. Jones, all of Social Circle, Ga.

By Rev. John Finger, January 26, 1877, in Timmonsville, S. C., Mr. I. J. Wilson to Miss H. Berry Moore.

By Rev. E. M. Whitney, January 24, 1877, Mr. James L. Keen to Miss Leona J. Linder, daughter of Dr. J. T. Linder, all of Laurens county, Ga.

By Rev. Jos. S. Key, January 23, 1877, in St. Paul Church, Columbus, Ga., Rev. Walter H. Johnson to Miss Florence Verstille, of Columbus, Ga.

By Rev. Wm. H. Trammell, February 8, 1877, Dr. W. H. Groves, of Whitfield county, Ga., to Miss Josie Coleman, only daughter of L. C. Coleman, Esq., of Lincoln county, Ga.

By Rev. Wm. Hutto, February 6, 1877, Mr. Hamilton A. K. Felder, of Orangeburg, S. C., to Miss Mary G. Thomas, of Charleston county, S. C.

By Rev. D. J. McMillan, December 6, 1876, Mr. W. L. Kelley, of Darlington, S. C., to Mrs. M. A. Truesdel, of Lancaster county, S. C.

By Rev. D. J. McMillan, December 7, 1876, Mr. Robt. S. Floyd to Miss Sallie E. Reeves, both of Lancaster county, S. C.

By Rev. D. J. McMillan, January 24, 1877, Mr. S. J. Barrett of Bishopville, S. C., to Miss Y. P. McKnight, of Clarendon county, S. C.

By Rev. T. A. Harris, January 28, 1877, Mr. J. M. F. Watson to Miss Bettie M. Towns, both of Clarke county, S. C.

By Rev. J. K. McCain, February 8, 1877, Dr. B. O. Bennett to Miss Lamira M. Leonard, all of Reidville, Spartanburg county, S. C.

By Rev. W. F. Glenn, January 30, 1877, in Cherokee county, Ga., Rev. W. D. Anderson of the North Georgia Conference to Miss Leila Latimer.

By Rev. E. Davis, January 30, 1877, Mr. H. P. Howell to Miss D. Ann Talley, daughter of Dr. J. W. Talley, all of Mill Town, Berrien county, Ga.

By Rev. M. S. Andrews, D. D., January 30, 1877, Mr. Wiley F. Williams to Miss Fannie P. Hightower, daughter of Daniel P. Hightower of Lee county, Ala.

By Rev. W. H. Speer, in Franklin, Ga., Mr. F. M. Tomlin to Miss S. B. Hutchins, both of Franklin, Ga.

By Rev. W. H. Speer, January 14, 1877, at the residence of James Brown, Mr. A. J. Addington to Miss S. E. Brown, both of Fannin county, Ga.

By Rev. W. H. Speer, January 25, 1877, at the Morris House in Morganton, Ga., Mr. W. S. Dobbs to Miss M. J. Logan, of Morganton, Ga.

By Rev. Wm. C. Power, January 17, 1877, Mr. Peter McIntosh of Richmond county, N. C., to Miss Minnie Floyd, of Marion District, S. C.

Issue of February 27, 1877

By Rev. W. M. D. Bond, February 14, 1877, Mr. Berryman T. Thompson, of Newnan, GA., to Miss Susan J. Longino, of Campbell county, Ga.

By Rev. E. S. Tyner, January 25, 1877, Mr. J. G. R. Freeman to Miss M. Williams, all of Madison county, Fla.

By Rev. E. S. Tyner, February 4, 1877, Mr. Joseph Bennett to Mrs. Ella Bennett, all of Madison county, Fla.

By Rev. A. J. Dean, February 25, 1877, Mr. G. W. Haynes, of Dougherty county, Ga., to Miss Fannie Larry, of houston county, Ga.

By Rev. B. E. L. Timmons, February 14, 1877, Rev. O. C. Simmons, of the North Georgia Conference, to Miss Carrie E. Moore, daughter of Mr. J. C. Moore of Floyd county, Ga.

By Rev. J. H. D. McRae, February 15, 1877, Mr. G. W. Austin to Miss Julia J. Benton, all of Dixie, Ga.

By Rev. J. M. Potter, February 15, 1877, in Lee county, Ga., Mr. J. F. Cox to Miss A. H. Moreland.

By Rev. Jno. M. Bowden, February 13, 1877, Mr. Thomas L. Bowden to Miss annie E. Meatcham, all of Meriwether county, Ga.

Issue of March 6, 1877

By Rev. J. H. Zimmerman, January 25, 1877, at the residence of the bride's grand-father, Mr. P. J. Felkel to Miss David Ann Hungerpeler, all of Orangeburg county, S. C.

By Rev. M. L. Underwood, February 21, 1877, at the residence of Mr. Geo. A. Mitchell, in Floyd county, Ga., Mr. J. L. Chupp, of DeKalb county, Ga., to Miss Nonie A. Bramlette.

By Rev. Whitefoord S. Martin, February 22, 1877, Dr. J. E. Garner to Miss Mollie McGowin, both of Union county, S. C.

By Bishop McTyeire, February 21, 1877, Prof. Samuel G. Sanders, of Georgetown, Tex., to Miss Mary W. Shipp, second daughter of Dr. Shipp, of Vanderbilt University.

By Rev. T. H. Stewart, February 15, 1877, Mr. J. A. McDonald to Miss Cornelia W. Page, all of Sumter county, Ga.

By Rev. T. H. Stewart, February 18, 1877, Mr. George D. Rogers to Miss Julia Gauff, all of Sumter county, Ga.

By Rev. G. H. Pooser, January 18, 1877, Mr. John P. Brunner to Miss Georgiana Sweat, all of Colleton county, S. C.

By Rev. H. J. Ellis, February 15, 1877, in Troup county, Ga., Mr. George W. Davis to Miss Laura A. Smith.

By Rev. J. K. McCain, February 25, 1877, Mr. David Mostillo to Miss Lizzie Dickson, all of Greenville county, S. C.

Issue of March 13, 1877

By Rev. A. J. Jarrell, February 21, 1877, in St. James' Methodist Church, Augusta, Ga., Mr. Benj. D. Jones to Miss Bessie A. Crump.

By Rev. J. V. M. Morris, March 5, 1877, in Columbus, Ga., Mr. James Cato to Miss C. S. Ballington, all of Columbus, Ga.

By Rev. M. L. Banks, February 18, 1877, at Wesley Chapel Church, Orangeburg county, S. C., Mr. Jerome B. Cooper to Miss Emma J. Clarke.

By Rev. W. P. Pledger, February 27, 1877, at Glenwood, Douglas county, Ga., Rev. Marion L. Underwood of the North Georgia Conference to Miss Florence A. Brockman.

By Rev. J. R. Littlejohn, February 20, 1877, Mr. G. L. Smith of Marion county, Ga., to Miss Mary J. Carr, of Sumter county, Ga.

By Rev. J. R. Littlejohn, February 22, 1877, Mr. Smith Davenport of Webster county, Ga., to Mrs. Martha R. Alexander, of Marion county, Ga. *Christian Index* please copy.

By Rev. J. R. Littlejohn, February 28, 1877, Mr. George H. Williams to Miss Fannie Moore, both of Sumter county, Ga.

By Rev. John F. Neal, March 6, 1877, Dr. James P. Peeler of Madison county, Fla., to Miss Julia V. Goodbread of Live Oak, Fla.

Issue of March 20, 1877

By Rev. A. W. Jackson, March 1, 1877, Mr. Samuel Willowman to Miss Minnie Leroy, all of Greenville county, S. C.

By Rev. C. A. Conaway, March 8, 1877, Mr. A. R. Dawson to Miss Annie F. Anthony, all of Clarke county, Ga.

By Rev. T. J. Phillips, March 8, 1877, Mr. John Waters of Leon county, Fla., to Miss Amanda Townsend of Jefferson county, Fla.

By Rev. W. G. Hanson, March 6, 1877, Mr. W. T. Keith to Miss Mary E. England, all of Red Clay, Ga.

By Rev. A. R. Danner, February 22, 1877, Mr. John A. Geiger to Miss Texas M. Inabinet, all of Orangeburg county, S. C.

By Rev. W. H. Hunt, March 8, 1877, Mr. S. W. Kennedy of Suwannee county, Fla., to Miss Flora K. Godbold, of Columbia county, all of Florida. The *Marion Star* will please copy.

By Rev. B. H. Sasnett, January 9, 1877, near Sparta, Ga., Mr. J. T. Laveigne Jr., of Beaufort county, S. C., to Miss Sarah E. Grant, daughter of Jeff and Winifred Grant of Hancock county, Ga.

By Rev. D. J. Simmons, March 4, 1877, in Orangeburg county, S. C., Mr. J. M. Cope to Miss Maggie Salley, daughter of Mr. Nathaniel Salley.

By Rev. J. F. Sifly, March 1, 1877, Mr. Oren B. Dukes to Miss Angie R. Risher[?], all of Colleton county, S. C.

Issue of March 27, 1877

By Rev. W. F. Cook, March 7, 1877, Mr. Ed. Cahn to Miss Mary E. Wilson, all of Atlanta, Ga.

By Rev. W. F. Cook, March 8, 1877, Mr. W. H. Greene to Miss Sallie Guiharin, all of Atlanta, Ga.

March 7th, 1877, by Rev. O. W. Ransom, Mr. Arthur Speer to Miss Alice roper, daughter of Col. W. C. Roper, all of Orange county, Fla.

On the 15th of March, 1877, by Rev. Wm. C. Power, Rev. Whitefoord Smith Martin, of the S. C. Conference, to Miss Vernelle C. Brockington, daughter of Dr. James S. Brockington, of Kingstree, S. C.

In Monroe county, Ga., by Rev. J. t. Lower, Mr. Walter T. Ross, of Macon, Ga., to Miss Maggie F. Redding, daughter of J. T. Redding, Esq., of Monroe county, Ga.

Issue of April 3, 1877

By Rev. M. H. Pooser, March 8, 1877, Mr. T. Jeff Darby to Miss E. Catharine, daughter of T. J. Bailey, Esq., all of Chester county, S. C.

By Rev. R. D. Gentry, March 15, 1877, in Wakulla county, Fla., Mr. Archibald G. Morrison to Miss Lodoiska Whetstone, all of Wakulla county, Fla.

By Rev. John W. McRoy, March 15, 1877, Mr. William G. Davis to Miss Eller J. Davis, all of Marion county, S. C.

By Dr. W. J. Greene, February 22, 1877, Mr. Virgil Fagan to Miss Eula Stewart, both of Houston county, Ga.

By Dr. W. I. Greene, February 27, 1877, Mr. Jno. Claxton of Ft. Valley, Ga., to Miss Mary Brown, near Hayneville, Ga.

By Rev. T. G. Herbert, March 15, 1877, Mr. Leonidas M. Holland of Fairfield county, S. C., to Miss Eliza Aiken Crooks, daughter of Maj. Thos. Crooks of Newberry county, S. C.

By Rev. T. G. Herbert, March 1, 1877, Mr. Jacob Dominick to Miss Alice Lake, all of Newberry county, S. C.

Issue of April 10, 1877

By Rev. John W. McRoy, April 1st, 1877, in the Methodist Church, at Britton's Neck, Laurence Dozier to Miss Elizabeth Stevenson, adopted daughter of the late Samuel Stevenson, all of Marion county, S. C.

By Rev. John W. McRoy, April 1st, 1877, at the residence of J. G. Jordan, Mr. A. P. Hix to Miss Mary E. Pace, all of Marion county, S. C.

By Rev. J. H. D. McRae, March 1, 1877, Mr. Merkkum Dukes to Miss Maxey More, all of Brooks county, Ga.

By Rev. J. H. D. McRae, March 14, 1877, Mr. John H. Vick to Miss Donie Dodd, all of Brooks county, Ga.

By Rev. A. Gray, March 6th, 1877, Mr. John C. Speights to Miss S. J. Dozier, both of Jasper county, Ga.

Issue of April 17, 1877

By Rev. W. D. Payne, April 6, 1877, Mr. B. H. Fincher to Mrs. Susie Buchanan, all of Atlanta, Ga.

By Rev. J. H. D. McRae, April 1, 1877, Mr. R. T. Moore to Miss Angie Hurst, all of Brooks county, Ga.

By Rev. J. H. D. McRae, April 5, 1877, Mr. J. W. Baker to Miss Amanda Dukes, all of Brooks county, Ga.

By Rev. John W. McRoy, April 5, 1877, at the residence of Mr. Edward Collins, in Marion, S. C,. Mr. H. D. Hemingway of Conwayboro, S. C., to Miss Laura Legette of Marion county, S. C.

By Rev. W. G. Hanson, March 22, 1877, near Vernell's Station, Ga., Mr. John H. Speer, to Miss Harriet McGaughey, all of Whitefield county, Ga.

Issue of April 24, 1877

By Rev. R. B. Lester, April 3, 1877, at the residence of Jno. D. Munnerlyn, Esq., Mr. J. Hope McKenzie to Miss May Lawson, all of Waynesboro, Ga.

By Rev. A. M. Marshall, in Putnam county, Ga., Mr. James Wright of Madison, Ga., to Miss Kate Baldwin.

By Rev. J. B. McFarland, April 12, 1877, Mr. James R. Camp to Miss M. Crumpton, all of Walker county, Ga.

By Rev. R. F. Williamson, April 10, 1877, at the residence of Maj. E. S. Baldwin, Capt. R. J. Redding of Atlanta, Ga., to Mrs. Lizzie Worrel, of Sumter county, S. C.

By Rev. A. A. Barnett, April 3, 1877, Mr. J. Letcher Bryan to Miss Alice Maddox, all of Orange county, Fla.

By Rev. G. H. Pooser, April 3, 1877, near 41 Station, S. C. R. R., at the residence of Mr. James Fickling, the bride's brother, Rev. P. J. Oeland of Spartanburg county, S. C., to Miss Christian B. Fickling of Beaufort, S. C.

By Rev. G. H. Pooser, April 11, 1877, Mr. John T. Browning of Charleston county, S. C., to Mrs. M. S. Kingman of Colleton county, S. C.

By Rev. J. B. Payne, February 1, 1877, in Thomaston, Ga., Mr. Charles T. Fox to Miss J. H. Pritchard, both of Thomaston, Ga.

By Rev. J. L. Gibson, April 17, 1877, in Montezuma, Ga., Mr. Thomas Brantly to Miss Victoria V. Vinson.

Issue of May 1, 1877

By Rev. G. W. Gatlin, April 12, 1877, Mr. A. M. Chandler to Miss Julia McConnell, all of Williamsburg county, S. C.

By Rev. W. F. Quillian, April 22, 1877, in the Methodist Church, Carrollton, Ga., Mr. Albert F. Sharp to Miss Katie Blalock, all of Carrollton, Ga.

Issue of May 8, 1877

By Bishop Pierce, April 22, 1877, at the parsonage on Richmond circuit, Mr. J. W. Keener of Augusta, Ga., to Miss S. A. Seale, daughter of Rev. R. A. Seale.

By Rev. Samuel Woodbery, April 5, 1877, at Lake city, in the Methodist church, Mr. Joseph F. Lines of Quincy, Fla., to Miss Kate L. Stewart, of Lake City, Fla.

By Rev. S. S. Sweet, May 2, 1877, in Macon, Ga., Mr. Rufus J. Phelts to Miss Emma C. Daniels.

By Rev. J. J. Harris, April 29, 1877, Mr. Wm. n. Wilson of Cherokee county, Ga., to Miss Mary J. James, of Forsyth county, Ga.

Issue of May 15, 1877

By Rev. W. C. Patterson, March 29th, 1877, Mr. John Steele to Miss Mary J. Madison.

By Rev. W. C. Patterson, March 31st, 1877, Mr. Robert Johnson to Miss Lou S. Patton.

By Rev. S. B. Jones, D. D., assisted by Rev. J. M. Carlisle, May 28, 1877, near Pendleton, S. C., the Rev. J. E. Carlisle, of the S. C. Conference, to Miss Emma L. Jones, daughter of the principal officiating minister.

By Rev. T. H. Stewart, May 1st, 1877, Mr. K. C. Bullard, of Telfair county, Ga., to Miss Joanna Hudson, of Schley county, Ga.

By Rev. U. Sinclair Bird, in the Methodist Church at Fernandina, April 18th, 1877, Miss Ida Josephine Lefils to Mr. M. M. Davis.

By Rev. Geo. T. King, April 15th, 1877, Mr. Edmund Lenning of British Columbia, to Miss Opelia P. Simmons, daughter of Col. W. H. Simmons, of Jasper, Pickens county, Ga.

By Rev. Walter Knox, April 30th, 1877, Capt. Rudolph M. Hjelmstram, of the Brig Kate Upton, to Miss Eleanor Hazzard, of McIntosh county, GA.

By Rev. J. C. Davis, April 29th, 1877, at the residence of Rev. N. L. Swett, Mr. A. B. Coward, of Chesterfield county, S. C., to Miss M. E. Swett, of Marlborough county, S. C.

Issue of May 22, 1877

By Rev. D. J. Simmons, May 1, 1877, Mr. Lawton Jeffcoat to Miss Elvira Phillips, daughter of Mr. W. F. Phillips, of Orangeburg county, S. C.

By Rev. W. M. D. Bond, May 13, 1877, near Palmetto, Ga., Millard Congore to Miss Bella Horton, all of Coweta county, Ga.

By Rev. W. M. D. Bond, May 13, 1877, near Palmetto, Ga., Levi Odom to Miss Nannie Black, all of Coweta county, Ga.

By Rev. J. W. G. Watkins, May 10, 1877, Mr. James H. Black to Miss Lou J. Bell, daughter of Rev. J. C. Bell of White county, Ga.

Issue of May 29, 1877

By Rev. R. H. Howren, April 12, 1877, Mr. Milton Tucker to Miss Fannie Tucker, all of Jefferson county, Fla.

By Rev. W. H. LaPrade, May 15, 1877, at Cedar Town, Ga., Mr. Chas. H. Whiteley of Rome, Ga., to Miss Mary Joe Downer, of Cedar Town, Ga.

By Rev. R. M. Lockwood, in the Methodist Episcopal Church, Bainbridge, Ga., Mr. Wilbur F. Moss, Esq., of Eastman, Ga., to Miss Fannie Dallam, daughter of the officiating minister.

By Rev. A. M. Williams, May 15, 1877, in Pulaski county, Ga., Mr. Benton H. Pitts of Hayneville, Houston county, Ga., to Miss Martha C. Sparrow, of the former place.

By Rev. W. P. Mouzon, May 6, 1877, in Trinity Church, Bamberg, S. C., Mr. Jeff D. Copeland to Miss Minnie C. Hartzog, daughter of Henry Hartzog.

By Rev. J. L. Sifley, April 26, 1877, at Hendersonville, S. C., Mr. S. Anderson Marvin to Miss Mary J. Sanders, both of Colleton, S. C.

By Rev. J. L. Sifley, April 29, 1877, in Colleton, S. C., Mr. Richard Duett, of Beaufort, S. C., to Mrs. Hariet Carter, of Colleton, S. C.

Issue of June 5, 1877

By Rev. L. P. Neese, April 19, 1877, Mr. Daniel Buran to Miss Mary Guthrie, all of Campbell county, Ga.

By Rev. L. P. Neese, May 1, 1877, Mr. Samuel A. Wilson to Miss Mary V. Hornsbey, all of Campbell county, Ga.

By Rev. L. P. Neese, May 22, 1877, Mr. Richard P. McLarin[?] to Miss Sallie C. Swann, all of Campbell county, Ga.

By Rev. L. P. Neese, May 23, 1877, Mr. V. Q. Williams, of Bartow county, Ga., to Miss M. Q. Jefferson, of Cherokee county, Ga.

By Rev. W. H. Potter, May 24, 1877, Mr. Henry C. McGinty to Miss Jane Edge, all of Athens, Ga.

Issue of June 12, 1877

By Rev. R. L. Harper, May 29, 1877, Mr. Francis Sims to Miss Alice O'Brien, all of Charleston, S. C.

By Rev. A. C. Davidson, May 27, 1877, in Sharon, Ga., Mr. J. P. Sturdivant to Miss S. Fannie Brooke, daughter of Judge W. T. Brooke, all of Taliaferro county, Ga.

By Rev. S. D. Parker, Esq., April 17, 1877, Mr. Isaac Murray to Miss Amand Shiver, both of Worth county, Ga.

By Rev. S. D. Parker, Esq., December 5, 1876, Mr. J. L. Boone to Miss Sallie L. Watson, both of Worth county, Ga.

Issue of June 19, 1877

By Rev. Atticus G. Haywood, D. D., in Atlanta, Ga., at the residence of Wm. A. Rawson, Esq., Mr. William A. Haygood of Atlanta, Ga., to Miss Mamie F. Holt, formerly of Stewart county, Ga.

By Rev. F. A. Branch,, June 19, 1877, in St. Luke church, Columbus, Ga., Mr. Robert A. Carson to Miss Ida C. Brannon, daughter of A. M. Brannon, of Columbus, Ga.

SOUTHERN CHRISTIAN ADVOCATE MARRIAGE NOTICES 1867-1878

Issue of June 26, 1877

By Rev. R. E. Brewer, June 20, 1877, at the residence of the late A. W. McDade, Esq., Colonel Howard Pope Park of Greenville, Ga., to Miss Sannie J. McDade, of Mt. Meigs, Ala.

By Rev. H. S. Andrews, assisted by Rev. J. Sloeman Ashmore, June 13, 1877, Mr. Wesley Ashmore to Miss Lettie M. Andrews, all of Liberty county, Ga.

Issue of July 3, 1877

By Rev. D. J. Simmons, June 12, 1877, Mr. J. Howel Easterlin to Miss Eliza J. Carson, daughter of Mr. D. N. Carson, of Orangeburg county, S. C.

By Dr. Thomas Boring, June 18, 1877, in the Methodist Church, at Dixie, the Rev. J. H. D. McRae of Brooks county, Ga., to Miss S. J. Newton of Scriven county, Ga.

By Rev. J. M. Potter, June 25, 1877, Rev. J. J. Sessions to Miss Kareen Elizabeth Wimberly, daughter of Capt. J. S. Wimberly, all of Calhoun county, Ga.

By Rev. H. J. Ellis, June 20, 1877, in Troup county, Ga., Mr. John D. Wells of Atlanta, Ga., to Miss Hattie Lockhart of Troup county, Ga.

By Rev. W. F. Smith, June 18, 1877, in Lithonia, Ga., Mr. A. J. Almand to Miss S. C. E. Bond, only daughter of Dr. W. P. Bond, all of the former place.

By Rev. J. S. Jobson, June 24, 1877, at the residence of Mr. H. S. Bell in Dawson, Ga., Mr. A. B. Lowrey of Gravilla, Ala., to Miss Georgia A. Reddick of the former place.

By Rev. W. M. Watts, June 10, 1877, Mr. J. C. C. Robarts, to Miss Nora Niblack, all of Columbia county, Fla.

Issue of July 10, 1877

By E. S. Tyner, June 12, 1877, Mr. W. B. Davis of Madison, Fla., to Miss E. M. Moriarty, of Schley county, Ga.

By Rev. W. P. Pledger, June 28, 1877, in Washington, Ga., Mr. Theoderic M. Green to Miss Metta Andrews, daughter of the late Judge Garnett Andrews.

By Rev. C. B. Hurt, June 26, 1877, in Russel county, Ala., Mr. L. E. Irby to Miss Mary Roberts Laney.

By Rev. J. C. Davis, June 21, 1877, at the residence of E. D. Smith, Mr. J. K. Smith to Miss Mary G. Smith, all of Marlborough county, S. C.

Issue of July 17, 1877

By Rev. J. W. Burke, in Macon, Ga., Prof. Wm. Cheatham, to Miss Jennie Lunsford.

By Rev. A. J. Hughes, July 10, 1877, Mr. W. D. Gregory, to Miss Mattie S. Summerour, all of Cahutta Springs, Murray county, Ga.

SOUTHERN CHRISTIAN ADVOCATE MARRIAGE NOTICES 1867-1878

Issue of July 24, 1877

By Rev. A. W. Clisby, July 17, 1877, in Macon, Ga., Rev. Francis Milton Kennedy, D. D., Editor of the SOUTHERN CHRISTIAN ADVOCATE, to Mrs. Louise Clisby Wise, eldest daughter of the senior editor of the *Telegraph and Messenger*.

By Rev. Clement C. Cary, July 10, 1877, July 10, 1877, in the Methodist Church, at Winterville, Ga., Mr. Isham H. Pittard to Miss Sue R. Pittard, both of Oglethorpe county, Ga.

Issue of July 31, 1877

By W. O. Hampton, July 15, 1877, Calvin A. Jones to Miss Jennett Bunch, all of Duval county, Fla.

By Rev. John W. Burke, July 25, 1877, near Macon, Mr. J. M. R. Riggins, of Texas, to Miss Sarah A. E. Andrews, of Bibb county, Ga.

Issue of August 7, 1877

By Rev. W. G. Hanson, at Pleasant Grove, M. E. Church, South, Mr. George Beamgard to Miss Ollie Bird, all of Whitfield county, Ga.

By Rev. J. E. Watson, July 28,1877, at the residence of Capt. Thos. Boyd, Mr. W. H. Hough, of Newberry, to Miss Mary Jacobs, of Lexington, S. C.

By Rev. Saml. Woodbery, July 25, 1877, Mr. John A. Cody, of St. Marks, Fla., to Miss Victoria Wright, of Lake City, Fla.

Issue of August 14, 1877

By Rev. W. A. Florence, July 19, 1877, in Elbert county, Ga., Mr. Robert A. Turner to Miss Harriet C. Maxwell.

By Rev. J. B. Wardlaw, July 31, 1877, Mr. William E. McFail, of Atlanta, Ga., to Miss Florence L. Girardeau, of Liberty county, Ga.

By Rev. W. Lane in the Methodist Church, in Cairo, Ga., August 1, 1877, Mr. Jas. E. Evans to Miss Bettie Hayes, both of Cairo.

Issue of September 4, 1877

By Rev. I. F. Cary, August 19, 1877, in Center village, Ga., Mr. Jas. C. Beaton, formerly of Nansemond county, Ga., to Miss Florence S., eldest daughter of Mr. John Holsendorf, of the former place.

Issue of September 11, 1877

By Rev. J. J. Singleton, September 2, 1877, Mr. S. D. Hendrix to Miss M. L. Gaines, both of Bartow county, Ga.

Issue of September 18, 1877

By Rev. W. G. Hanson, August 29, 1877, Mr. Wm. P. Miler to miss Mary J. Bender, all of Whitfield county, Ga.

By Rev. R. H. Howren, September 5, 1877, at Waukeenah, Fla., Mr. J. V. W. Cobb to Miss Susan C. Russell, daughter of Dr. J. S. Russell.

By Rev. W. L. Wootten, August 26, 1877, at the residence of Dr. W. P. Anderson, Mr. E. T. Harris to Miss Annie L. Anderson, all of Wilkes county, Ga.

Issue of September 25, 1877

By Rev. W. F. Robison, August 19, 1877, in Weston, Ga., Mr. W. G. Burch, of Texas, to Miss A. M. Reddick, of the former place.

By Rev. W. C. Collins, September 15, 1877, near Centerville, Fla., Mr. Irvine W. Grambling to Miss Emma E. Manning, all of Leon county, Fla.

By Rev. N. D. Morehouse, August 23, 1877, Mr. W. H. Goff to Miss E. E. Perkins, all of Burke county, Ga.

Issue of October 2, 1877

By Rev. F. P. Brown, September 19, 1877, Mr. A. C. Ivy of Fort Mills, York county, S. C., to Miss Georgia E. Moore, of McDuffie county, Ga.

By Rev. C. L. Pattillo, September 15, 1877, in Gwinnett county, Ga., Mr. J. P. Pharr to Miss M. L. Pattillo, all of Gwinnett county, Ga.

By Rev. D. D. Cox, September 20, 1877, in Atlanta, Ga., Mr. J. H. Goodwin to Miss Emma A. McAfee, all of Atlanta.

Issue of October 9, 1877

By Rev. J. A. Clifton, September 30, 1877, at Bethlehem Church, Edgefield county, S. C., Mr. McPherson Wright to Miss Telula Cogburn.

By Rev. W. P. Pledger, September 10, 1877, in Washington, Ga., Mr. Gilbert Y. Lowe to Miss Beatrice Gertrude Booker.

By Rev. C. D. Rowell, September 19, 1877, Mr. Henry Kinsler to Miss Sallie Geiger, all of Lexington county, S. C.

By Rev. John C. Ley, assisted by Rev. H. E. Partridge, Sept. 17, 1877, in the First Methodist Church in Key West, Rev. H. B. Somelian, our Cuban Missionary, to Miss Sarah Reid, of Key West, Fla.

By Rev. C. E. Dowman, September, 15, 1877, in the Methodist Church, Quincy, Fla,. Mr. H. Warren Scott, of Gadsden county, Fla., to Miss Sallie Lee Hentz, daughter of Dr. C. A. Hentz, of the former place.

Issue of October 16, 1877

By Rev. W. C. Collins, October 3, 1877, near Oak Dale, Fla., Mr. Flavius T. Cristie to Miss Janie Heir, all of Leon county, Fla.

By Rev. J. L. Shuford, October 2, 1877, Mr. John E. Brown, of Sumter, S. C., to Mrs. Sarah A. Smith, widow of the late Rev. Williamson Smith, of the S. C. Conference.

By Rev. M. L. Underwood, October 4, 1877, in the Methodist Church at Forrestville, Ga., Mr. Thos. D. Walker to Miss Sarah J. Quarles.

Issue of October 23, 1877

By Rev. H. D. Murphy, October 2, 1877, Mr. J. R. Murphy to Miss Belle C. Tarver, daughter of Judge A. E. Tarver, all of Jefferson county, Ga.

By Rev. Alex. M. Thigpen, October 9, 1877, in Whitefield county, Ga., Rev. Isaac H. Parks, of No. Ga. Conf. to Miss Jimmie Tarver.

By Rev. J. R. Mayson, at the residence of Mr. J. D. Smith, Atlanta, Ga., Mr. T. J. Dempsey of Dubois, Dodge county, Ga., to Miss America Smith, of Atlanta, Ga.

By Rev. W. D. Kirkland, October 7, 1877, Mr. E. Calhoun Bailey to Miss L. Elizabeth Dennis, all of Mars Bluff, S. C.

By Rev. W. D. Kirkland, October 7, 1877, Mr. Jno. W. Liles to Miss Plumer Grimsley, all of Mars Bluff, S. C.

By Rev. W. D. Kirkland, October 10, 1877, Mr. Tilman D. Howard to Mrs. Mary Worrell, all of Mars Bluff, S. C.

By Rev. W. C. Dunlap, October 17th, Mr. H. W. Young to Miss Sarah E. Reese, both of McDuffie county, Ga.

By Rev. J. L. Sifly, September 27, 1877, Mr. Henry W. Ackerman to Miss Lizzie W. Willis, eldest daughter of Hon. R. A. Willis, all of Colleton, S. C.

Issue of October 30, 1877

By Rev. W. D. Kirkland, October 21, 1877, Mr. John Redder to Miss anna M. Taylor, all of Mars Bluff, S. C.

By Rev. Calder Bainaird, October 3, 1877, Mr. Wm. G. Riley of Beaufort, to Miss Maggie H. Boineau, of Colleton county, S. C.

By Rev. Jno. M. Bowden, October 18, 1877, Mr. David E. Clementes to Miss Annie T. Brannon, all of Henry county, Ga.

By Rev. Jno. M. Bowden, October 21, 1877, Mr. William W. Hightower of Monroe county, Ga., to Miss Zipporah M. Glass, of Henry county, Ga.

By Rev. G. H. Pooser, September 12, 1877, at Ridgeville, S. C., Mr. Lewis W. Hilton to Mrs. A. A. C. Brownlee, all of Colleton county, S. C.

By Rev. J. B. McFarland, October 17, 1877, Mr. A. S. Fricks to Miss Julia M. Connally, all of Walker county, Ga.

By Rev. J. V. M. Morris, October 7, 1877, in Brownsville, Lee county, Ala., Mr. L. W. Warrill to Miss Cornelia E. McBryde.

By Rev. J. V. M. Morris, October 7, 1877, in Trinity Church, Brownsville, Ala., Mr. J. B. West to Mrs. V. A. Meeks.

By Rev. J. V. M. Morris, October 11, 1877, in Columbus, Ga., Mr. Benj. Allen to Miss Mattie Bencher.

By Rev. J. V. M. Morris, October 18, 1877, in Girard, Ala., Mr. C. H. West to Miss Mary J. Grubbs.

By Rev. J. W. Baker, October 23, 1877, at the residence of Dr. J. B. Dillard, in Belton, Ga., Mr. W. W. House to Miss Lou A. Dillard, all of Banks county, Ga.

By Rev. J. A. Clifton, October 18, 1877, in Edgefield county, S. C., Mr. William Rushton to Miss Susan E. Hamilton.

Issue of November 6, 1877

October 25, 1877, at the residence of Mr. David H. Riley, the bride's step father, near Perry, Houston county, Ga., by the Rev. T. B. Russell, Mr. Frank Jeter, of Macon, Ga., to Mrs. Bessie J. Riley.

By Rev. Wm. W. Mood, October 17, 1877, Mr. Leon Gwinn to Miss Lilly Davis, all of Spartanburg county, S. C.

By Rev. E. S. Tyner, October 15, 1877, Mr. T. P. Edwards to Miss Mollie P. Langford, all of Madison county, Fla.

By Rev. E. S. Tyner, October 18, 1877, Mr. J. D. Linch to Miss Bettie E. Jones, all of Madison county, Fla.

By Rev. J. M. Austin, October 25, 1877, Col. Mark A. Huson to Mrs. Sue A. Loyless, all of Dawson, Ga.

By Rev. M. L. Underwood, October 28, 1877, Mr. Benjamin Penn to Miss Martha E. R. Sharp, all of Floyd county, Ga.

By Rev. J. B. Wilson, October 21, 1877, Mr. Worth Gault to Miss Dora Holmes, all of Union county, S. C.

By Rev. J. B. Wilson, October 21, 1877, Mr. G. T. Willis, of Greenville, S. C., to Miss Julia Hollis, of Limestone Springs, S. C.

By Rev. J. B. Wilson, October 24, 1877, at the Baptist Church at Limestone Springs, S. C., Mr. Charles Rauchfuss, of New York City, to Miss Julia C. Clarke, of Limestone Springs, S. C.

By Rev. R. W. Barber, assisted by Rev. R. D. Smart, October 24, 1877, Hon. F. A. Conner, of Cokesbury, S. C., to Mrs. S. J. Springs, of Rock Hill, S. C.

By Rev. R. W. Barber, October 18, 1877, Mr. Thomas Farris, of Arkansas, to Miss Clementine Farris, of York county, S. C.

By Rev. L. A. Darsey, October 24, 1877, at the residence of W. D. Grace, Esq., Mr. Joseph S. Brown to Miss Savannah S. Lloyd, all of Taylor county, Ga.

By Rev. L. A. Darsey, September 23, 1877, Mr. Wm. W. Downs to Miss Missouri Barber, all of Talbot county, Ga.

By Rev. A. M. Williams, October 21, 1877, near Hawkinsville, Ga., Mr. Matthew F. Jones, of Port Royal, S. C., to Miss M. Josephine Bagby.

By Rev. A. M. Williams, October 24, 1877, in Hawkinsville, Ga., Mr. James W. Bowyer to Miss Mary Burch, daughter of Rev. E. A. Burch.

By Rev. N. D. Morehouse, October 30, 1877, Hon. J. A. Robson, of Sandersville, Ga., to Miss Georgia A. Shewmake, of Burke county, Ga.

By Rev. W. T. Capers, D. D., October 11, 1877, at the residence of Rev. H. B. Browne, Sampit, Georgetown county, S. C., Mr. Robert D. Ham, of Georgetown, to Miss E. Florence Moody, of Columbia, S. C.

Issue of November 13, 1877

By Rev. F. M. T. Brannon, October 30, 1877, Mr. Pleasant W. Stafford to Miss Nelia C. Stewart, all of Coweta county, Ga.

By Rev. C. Raiford, November 4, 1877, Mr. Benjamin F. McIntosh to Miss Emma S. McMurry, all of Thomas county, Ga.

By Rev. L. J. Davies, November 1, 1877, in Forsyth, Ga., Mr. Wm. Barkly Fleck, of Macon, Ga., to Miss Talitha C. Bennett, of the former place.

By Rev. Wm. Hutto, October 25, 1877, Mr. S. W. Harllee, of Colleton county, S. C., to Miss Emma A. Jaudon, of Charleston, S. C; also, at the same time and place, by the same, Mr. Hamilton Harllee, of Colleton county, S. c., to Miss Amelia A. Jaudon, of Charleston, S.C.

By Rev. Alex. M. Thigpen, November 6, 1877, near Ringgold, Ga., Rev. George W. Thomas, of North Georgia Conference, to Miss Mary F., daughter of Mr. T. J. Payne, of Catoosa county, Ga.

By Rev. J. B. Traywick, October 16, 1877, Mr. Augustus Hough, of Greenville, S. C., To Miss Claudia Sullivan, daughter of Jefferson Sullivan of Laurens county, S. C.

By Rev. J. B. Traywick, at the residence of Mrs. Lou Puckett, Mr. Whitefield B. Wharton to Miss Mattie Puckett, both of Laurens county, S. C.

By Rev. J. B. Traywick, Mr. Patrick Todd, of Laurens county, S. C., to Miss Annie Roberts, of Greenwood, S. C.

By Rev. W. A. Rogers, October 31, 1877, Mr. M. P. Crawford to Miss Lizzie Twitty, all of Lancaster, S. C.

By Rev. Geo. C. Clarke, November 7, 1877, in the Methodist Church, Talbotton, Ga., Mr. Charles W. Kimbrough to Miss Elizabeth Worrill, youngest daughter of Hon. E. H. Worrill, all of Talbotton.

By Rev. J. P. Wardlaw, October 24, 1877, near Buena Vista, Ga., Mr. William S. Wells to Miss Eula J. McMichael.

By Rev. J. P. Wardlaw, October 25, 1877, near Buena Vista, Ga., Mr. Samuel U. Fulford to Miss Emma Wells.

Issue of November 20, 1877

By Rev. Clement C. Cary, November 7, 1877, in Oglethorpe county, Ga., Mr. H. Towns Comer to Miss Mamie Dillard, daughter of Mr. Fielding Dillard.

By Rev. J. A. Clifton, October 18, 1877, in Edgefield county, S. C., Mr. William Rushton to Miss Susan E. Hamilton.

By Rev. W. R. Branham, Jr., November 8, 1877, in Edgewood Church, Mr. Jas. P. McDonald to Miss Annie Akers.

By Rev. W. R. Branham, Jr., November 8, 1877, at the residence of Mr. Saunders in Edgewood, Mr. John C. Besier to Miss S. F. Crawford.

By Rev. W. P. Harrison, October 18, 1877, in Atlanta, Ga., Mr. Richard M. Morrow, of Selma, Ala., to Miss Lois E. Winter, daughter of James L. Winter, Esq., of Atlanta.

By Rev. W. P. Harrison, November 1, 1877, Mr. Hugh V. Barrow, of Hogansville, Ga., to Miss Mary E. McLin, daughter of J. G. McLin, of Atlanta, Ga.

By Rev. Wm. W. Mood, November 5, 1877, Mr. John R. Green to Miss Tabitha Hembree, all of Spartanburg county, S. C.

By Rev. J. R. Littlejohn, November 1, 1877, at the residence of Jesse Salter, Mr. M. C. Mims of Dougherty county, to Miss Laura Platt, of Sumter county, Ga.

By Rev. W. J. Wardlaw, October 30, 1877, at the residence of Patrick Bass, Mr. D. R. Bradley to Miss Eliza Bass, all of Sumter county, Ga.

By Rev. W. J. Wardlaw, November 7, 1877, at the residence of Mr. Alexander Bass, Mr. John A. Dorman to Miss Jonna C. Bass, both of Sumter county, Ga.

Issue of November 27, 1877

By Rev. M. L. Banks, November 14, 1877, at Upper St. Matthew parsonage, Orangeburg county, S. C., Mr. Whitfield W. Wannamaker to Miss Ella Lou Banks.

By Rev. W. C. Lovett, November 14, 1877, Mr. Harmon H. Clark to Miss Y. C. Willis, all of Bibb county, Ga.

By Rev. W. G. Booth, October 20, 1877, in the M. E. Church, in Concord, Gadsden county, Fla., Mr. Orin Roberson to Miss Florence Laing, all of Gadsden county, Fla.

By Rev. W. B. Neal, November 15, 1877, Mr. Jephtha M. Hardwick to Miss L. Parker, all of Tallapoosa county, Ala.

By Rev. B. F. Breedlove, November 8, 1877, at the residence of Mr. W. C. Salter, in Jefferson county, Ga., Mr. R. H. Malone to Miss C. A. Tarver.

By Rev. G. T. King, October 14, 1877, Mr. John A. Allen, of Pickens county, Ga., to Miss Almira Bradley, of Gilmer county, Ga.

By Rev. G. T. King, November 15, 1877, Mr. Maddox M. Simmons to Miss Emily McCutchen, all of Pickens county, Ga.

By Rev. E. H. McGehee, November 7, 1877, in Decatur county, Ga., Mr. Jno. G. Allen, of Columbus, Ga., to Miss Lillias Dickerson.

By Rev. E. H. McGehee, November 14, 1877, in Newton, Baker county, Ga., Prof. William N. Sheats of Gainesville, Fla., to Miss Mary S. Williams.

In the city of Augusta, November 15th, 1877, by Rev. C. W. Key, his grand-daughter, Miss Mollie R. Massengale to Mr. Wm. H. Houser, of Houston county, Ga.

By Rev. F. M. T. Brannon, Dr. Wm. T. Brown of Whitesburg county, to Miss Hattie m. Wilson, of Merriwether county, Ga.

By Rev. H. J. Ellis, November 7, 1877, in Troup county, Ga., Mr. James G. Perry to Miss Anna Estes.

By Rev. Wm. W. Mood, November 11, 1877, Mr. S. Tucker Littlefields to Miss Lucenia Rhodes, all of Spartanburg county, S. C.

By Rev. Geo. W. Yarbrough, in Pike county, Ga., Rev. Richard W. Rogers, of the North Georgia Conference, to Miss Fannie Eubank.

By Rev. J. W. Domingos, November 13, 1877, Mr. Geo. L. Collins, of Montezuma, Macon county, Ga., to Miss Nettie A. Richardson, of Twiggs county, Ga.

By Rev. H. J. Ellis, November 13, 1877, in West Point, Ga., Mr. Thos. A. Lovelace, of Troup county, to Miss sallie E. A. Lovelace, of West Point, Ga.

By Rev. L. P. Neese, October 1, 1877, Dr. A. H. Wilson to Miss Carrie A. Hornsby, all of Campbell county, Ga.

By Rev. L. P. Neese, October 28, 1877, Mr. Wm. H. Maxwell to Miss E. R. Guice, all of Fairburn, Ga.

By Rev. L. P. Neese, November 15, 1877, Mr. J. S. McLendon to Miss M. E. Tanner, all of Atlanta, Ga.

By Rev. Landy Wood, November 15, 1877, at the Methodist Church, Conwayboro, S. C., Mr. James C. Collins, late of Georgetown, S. C., to Miss Emma j. Parker, daughter of Mr. Wm. L. Parker, late of Magnolia, N. C.

Issue of December 4, 1877

By Rev. A. W. Walker, November 1, 1877, Mr. Barnett Smith to Miss Lucy Major, both of Pickens, S. C.

By Rev. A. W. Walker, November 4, 1877, Mr. William Major, of Anderson, S. C., to Miss Sallie Byars, second daughter of Rev. D. D. Byars, of the S. C. Conference.

By Rev. A. W. Walker, November 15, 1877, Mr. Jessee Ellis to Mrs. Cynthia Day, both of Pickens, S.C. *Christian Neighbor* please copy.

By Rev. W. G. Hanson, November 20, 1877, Mr. William A. Bowdoin to Miss Jennie Webb, all of Monroe county, Ga.

By Rev. Wm. L. Wootten, November 18, 1877, in Wilkes county, Ga., Dr. Gilbert H. Wootten, of Texarkana, to Mrs. Amelia T. Jordan.

By Rev. Wm. Hutto, November 8, 1877, Mr. Alonzo A. Hart to Miss Anna J. Murry, all of Charleston county, S. C.

By Rev. J. O. A. Connor, November 20, 1877, Mr. D. Benson Connor, son of the officiating minister, to Miss Annie A. Stokes, daughter of Dr. Peter Stokes, all of Colleton county, S.C.

By Rev. A. W. Jackson, November 22, 1877, Mr. Daniel McBramlet to Miss Barbary E. Fowler, all of Greenville county, S. C.

By Rev. J. L. Sifley, November 7, 1877, Mr. C. W. Butler to Miss Hattie Johnson, all of Colleton, S. C.

By Rev. J. L. Sifley, November 22, 1877, at Walterboro, S. C., Mr. J. R. Hunter to Miss A. W. West, all of Colleton, S. C.

By Rev. Geo. C. Thompson, November 15, 1877, in St. Marys, Ga., Mr. Robert S. Bessent to Miss Annie E. Rudolph.

By Rev. S. D. Clements, October 30, 1877, Mr. B. C. Kimbrough to Miss Ida R. Hunley, all of Hamilton, Ga.

By Rev. S. D. Clements, November 22, 1877, Mr. James W. Sparks to Miss Katie L. Kilpatrick, of Waverly Hall, Ga.

By Rev. Leroy F. Beaty, November 29[?], 1877, Mr. L. R. Claxton, of Fairfield, S. c., to Miss Sallie A. Tedards, of Greenwood, S. C.

By Rev. R. A. Seale, November 21, 1877, Mr. Daniel M. Rountree to Miss Mary E. Collins.

By Rev. Jno. M. Bowden, November 25, 1877, Mr. Daniel P. Shields, of Clayton county, Ga., to Miss Ella E. Bond, of Henry county, Ga.

By Rev. J. M. Gable, November 15, 1877, Mr. Isaac Sewell, Jr., to Miss Maggie Mayes, all of Cobb county, Ga.

By Rev. J. M. Gable, November 18, 1877, Mr. Thomas Hardman to Miss L. E. Wells, all of Cobb county, Ga.

By Rev. G. H. Pooser, November 18, 1877, Mr. A. H. Aultman, of Marion, S. C., to Miss Anna E. Browning, of Charleston county, S. C.

By Rev. W. A. Rogers, November 22, 1877, Mr. Henry D. Twitty to Miss Lizzie Bailey, all of Lancaster, S. C.

By Rev. W. L. Pegues, November 22, 1877, at the residence of Mr. Thos. Smoot, Mr. G. Trueluck to Miss Maggie Smoot.

By Rev. W. L. Pegues, November 22, 1877, at the residence of Mr. Thos. Smoot, Mr. Wm. Flowers to Miss Ada Wood.

Issue of December 11, 1877

By Rev. G. T. Embry, December 4, 1877, Mr. Thomas M. Freeman to Miss L. F. Zant, both of Dooly county, Ga.

By Rev. A. C. Davidson, November 22, 1877, Mr. Pulaski E. Battle, of Sharon, Taliaferro county, Ga., to Miss Ellen T. Adams, of Wilkes county, Ga.

By Rev. F. B. Davies, November 28, 1877, Mr. Robert L. Felts to Miss Annie D. Rogers, all of Warren county, Ga.

By Rev. Walker Lewis, November 20, 1877, in Macon, Ga., Mr. Richard H. Brinn to Miss Annie E. Smith.

By Rev. W. W. Stewart, November 29, 1877, Mr. Jas. D. Kendall to Miss Mary Lumsden, all of Talbot county, Ga.

By Rev. W. Ewing Johnston, November 28, 1877, in Burke county, Ga., Mr. Edwin W. Hack, of Richmond county, Ga., to Miss Bessie M. Jones.

By Rev. T. S. L. Harwell, November 15, 1877, Mr. M. J. Harwell, of Troup county, Ga., to Miss N. J. Brown, of Coweta county, Ga.

By Rev. J. R. Mayson, November 21, 1877, Rev. W. A. Candler, of North Georgia Conference, to Miss Nettie Curtright, of LaGrange, Ga.

By Rev. J. O. A. Clark, November 21, 1877, Mr. James G. West, of Savannah, Ga., to Miss Isabel Davant, eldest daughter of Col. R. J. Davant, of Whitesville, Effingham county, Ga.

By Rev. F. M. Kennedy, December 5, 1877, in Mulberry Street Methodist Church, Macon, Ga., Mr. Asa S. Bates, of Butler, Ga., to Miss Mamie M. Clancy, of Macon, Ga.

By Rev. J. E. Sentell, November 29, 1877, Mr. Millard McRae, of Telfair county, Ga., to Miss Mary L. Clements, of Montgomery county, Ga.

By Rev. J. E. Sentell, December 4, 1877, Mr. J. H. Ryals to Miss Christian F. McRae, both of Telfair county, Ga.

By Rev. Josiah W. Jordan, November 29, 1877, Mr. E. D. Jordan to Miss Clara E. Anderson, all of Monroe county, Ga.

By Rev. T. B. Russell, November 28, 1877, in Marshalville, Ga., Mr. John D. Rambo, of Columbus, Ga., to Miss Mary E. Caskill.

By Rev. T. B. Russell, November 29, 1877, at Hebron Church, Mr. S. Bushrod Sanford to Miss Lizzie J. Pooser, both of Crawford county, Ga.

By Rev. W. P. Lovejoy, September 21, 1877, Mr. B. P. Strozier to Miss Leonora Hailes, both of Greene county, Ga.

By Rev. W. P. Lovejoy, October 4, 1877, Dr. Joseph E. Crossby to Mrs. Susan R. Smith, all of Greene county, Ga.

By Rev. W. P. Lovejoy, November 21, 1877, Dr. W. F. Hailes to Miss Cora Smith, daughter of Mr. Walker Smith, of Greene county, Ga.

By Rev. W. P. Lovejoy, November 27, 1877, Prof. T. N. Barker, of Atlanta, Ga., to Miss Dora Lovejoy, of Oxford, Ga.

Issue of December 18, 1877

By Rev. J. W. Burke, December 6, 1877, in East Macon, Ga., Mr. G. T. Powers, of Floyd county, Ga., to Miss Mattie I. Rogers.

By Elder Jas. A. Griffin, November 29, 1877, in Chattahoochee, Ga., Mr. W. F. Cook to Miss Gertrude Patterson.

By Rev. E. P. Bonner, December 11, 1877, Mr. William J. Smith to Miss Nora P. Ramsey, all of Columbia county, Ga.

By Rev. C. W. Smith, December 12, 1877, in Macon, Ga., Mr. Z. L. Bashlor, to Miss J. L. Maxey.

By Rev. W. C. Bass, December 6, 1877, at Oxford, Ga., Howard E. W. Palmer, Esq., to Miss Emma Stone, second daughter of Prof. G. W. W. Stone, of the former place.

By Rev. R. B. Lester, November 15, 1877, Dr. Ausier Preskitt to Miss Lillie May Syms, all of Burke county, Ga.

By Rev. R. B. Lester, December 2, 1877, Mr. John F. Smith to Mrs. Dora R. Dorsey, all of Burke county, Ga.

By Rev. R. B. Lester, December 5, 1877, at the residence of Wiley Smith, Esq., Mr. Asa Brown Miss Ellen M. Wimberly, both of Jefferson county, Ga.

By Rev. H. B. Treadwell, December 9, 1877, in Brunswick, Ga., Mr. Benj. F. Treadwell to Miss D. A. Moore, all of Brunswick Ga.

By Rev. J. W. Humbert, December 6, 1877, Mr. J. H. Williams to Miss Sallie L. Brooks, daughter of Mr. J. L. Brooks, all of Newberry county, S. C.

By Rev. W. T. McMichael, November 11, 1877, at the residence of Mrs. Pitts, in Jones county, Ga., Mr. James M. Middlebrooks to Miss Martha D. Pitts.

By Rev. Wm. H. Trammell, November 15, 1877, Mr. George Tankersly to Miss Ella J. Tankersly, all of McDuffie county, Ga.

By Rev. W. C. Dunlap, December 9, 1877, Mr. L. C. Smith to Miss Margaret McLean, both of McDuffie county, Ga.

By Rev. Clement C. Cary, November 29, 1877, in Athens, Ga., to Miss Amy L. Brusse, of Athens, Ga.

By S. D. Parker, December 4, 1877, in Worth county, Ga., Mr. Samuel F. Whitten, of Alexander City, Ala., to Miss Mary A. Chesnutt, of Worth county, Ga.

By Rev. Geo. C. Leavel, November 20, 1877, Mr. W. H. Towles, of Taylor county, Fla., to Miss Eliza E. McMullen, of Hillsborough county, Fla.

By Rev. John Calvin Johnson, November 15, 1877, Mr. David M. McCleskey, of Clarke county, Ga., to Miss Elizabeth E. Espy, of Jackson county, Ga.

By Rev. John Calvin Johnson, November 28, 1877, Mr. Joseph E. Bradberry to Miss Mary E. Wier, all of Clarke county, Ga.

Issue of December 25, 1877

By Rev. Jas. E. Godfrey, December 6, 1877, in Randolph county, Ga., Mr. John R. Tompkins, of Stewart county, Ga., to Miss Selma Monger, of Randolph county, Ga.

By Rev. Jas. E. Godfrey, December 21, 1877, at Lumpkin, Ga., Mr. A. L. Haws, of Newton, to Miss Mattie Davis, of Lumpkin, Ga.

By Rev. A. Gray, December 9, 1877, Mr. William J. Talmadge to Miss H. Z. Key, both of Monticello, Ga.

By Rev. A. Gray, December 13, 1877, Mr. James L. Pennington, of Social Circle, Ga., to Miss Amma L. Weaver, of Hearnville, Putnam county, Ga.

By Rev. W. H. Thomas, December 18, 1877, Mr. J. J. Richards, of St. Mary's, Ga., to Miss Rosa B. Grovenstene, of Waycross, Ga.

By Rev. D. D. Dantzler, December 11, 1877, at the residence of Mr. M. Miller, Mr. Daniel G. Bozard to Miss Elizabeth R. Funches, all of Orangeburg county, S. C.

By Rev. I. Alexander, in Gregg county, Texas, Mr. Willie C. Holt, of Smith county, to Miss Susie W. Fisher, of Gregg county, Texas.

Issue of January 8, 1878

By Rev. J. F. Mixon, November 15, 1877, Mr. John O. Scott of Abbeville, S. C., to Miss Lula C. Smith, of Wilkes county, Ga.

By Rev. John R. Parker, assisted by Rev. T. P. Cleveland, December 13, 1877, Mr. Jno. R. Brown to Miss Addie M. Langston, all of Gainesville, Ga.

By Rev. H. H. Parks, December 11, 1877, at the residence of Geo. Myrick, Midway, Ga., Mr. J. G. Beasley, of Russell county, Ala., to Miss Goodwyn Myrick, daughter of the late Dr. J. W. Myrick.

By Rev. H. H. Parks, December 18, 1877, at the residence of Mr. Calhoun, Atlanta, Ga., Mr. H. V. Sanford, of Milledgeville, Ga. (firm of Mapp & Sanford) to Miss Mary Martin, formerly of Norcross, Ga.

By Rev. John W. Burke, December 20, 1877, in Macon, Ga., Mr. Edward a. Bright to Miss Mary Lee Hudson, all of this city.

By Rev. John M. Marshall, December 27, 1877, at Attapulgus, Ga., Dr. G. M. Jones to Miss M. E. Stanford.

By Rev. L. P. Neese, December 19, 1877, Mr. W. F. Milam to Miss M. C. Stephens, all of Fayette county, Ga.

By Rev. L. P. Neese, December 20, 1877, Mr. John H. Elder, of Atlanta, Ga., to Miss Mary E. Black, of Campbell county, Ga.

By Rev. L. P. Neese, December 25, 1877, Mr. Wm. A. Shell to Miss S. E. Brown, of Campbell county, Ga.

By Rev. Geo. E. Gardner, November 13, 1877, in Atlanta, Ga., Mr. Jno. B. Whitaker to Miss Emma Holtzclaw.

By Rev. Geo. E. Gardner, December 16, 1877, Mr. J. A. Ivy to Miss Carrie Harbuck, both of Fulton county, Ga.

By Rev. Geo. E. Gardner, December 19, 1877, Mr. Albert D. Maier to Miss Lula Holland, both of Atlanta, Ga.

By Rev. Geo. E. Gardner, December 25, 1877, Mr. C. P. Baldwin, of Bartow county, Ga., to Miss M. C. Berry, of Atlanta, Ga.

By Rev. Geo. E. Gardner, December 26, 1877, Rev. Wm. E. Goode, of Florida, to Miss Jennie Cohron, daughter of Rev. Joseph Cohron, of Atlanta, Ga.

December 19, 1877, Rev. Wm. H. Ariail[?], of the South Carolina Conference, to Miss Hattie Yeargin, of Laurens county, S. C., by Rev. J. B. Traywick.

December 20, 1877, Mr. Henry Wharton to Miss Ida Harris, both of Laurens county, S. C., by Rev. J. B. Traywick.

By Rev. Landy Wood, December 26, 1877, at the residence of the late Levin H. Joiner, Conwayboro, S. C., Mr. John Enzor to Miss Ellinor Noble, daughter of the late Rev. Alfred M. Noble, all of Horry county, Ga.[sic]

By Rev. Landy Wood, December 27, 1877, at the residence of the Thos. S. Beatty, Horry county, S. C., Mr. John A. Todd to Miss Mary Louise Beatty, daughter of the late James Beaty.

By Rev. M. H. Pooser, December 6, 1877, Mr. J. Randolph Davis to Miss Kattie Harden, second daughter of Jno. Harvey Harden, Esq., all of Chester county, S. C.

By Rev. T. R. Kendall, November 8, 1877, Mr. Edward Dorsey to Miss Mattie Clowers, all of Henry county, Ga.

By Rev. T. R. Kendall, November 26, 1877, Col. Thos. K. Noland to Miss Annie M. Lemon, all of McDonough, Ga.

By Rev. T. R. Kendall, December 6, 1877, Mr. Geo. C. Carpenter, of Burke county, Ga., to Miss Sallie G. Read, of Hampton, Ga.

By Rev. T. R. Kendall, December 27, 1877, Mr. Z. P. Manson, of Hampton, Ga., to Miss A. F. Crawford, of Henry county, Ga.

By Rev. John T. Duncan, December 25, 1877, Mr. Edward Bronson to Miss Sarah F. Lanier, all of Orange county, Fla.

By Rev. T. A. Seals, December 16, 1877, in the Methodist Church, Madison, Ga., Dr. Barton E. Anderson, of Morgan county, to Miss Annie Saffold, of Madison.

By Rev. J. P. Wardlaw, December 11, 1877, near Buena Vista, Ga., Mr. O. C. Bullock to Miss Minnie Deane, all of Marion county, Ga.

By Rev. J. P. Wardlaw, December 23, 1877, near Buena Vista, Ga., Mr. Robert S. Simpson, of Harris county, Ga., to Miss Mattie Munro, of Marion county, Ga.

By Rev. N. C. Ware, December 13, 1877, Mr. George M. Gunry to Miss Maggie Bohler, all of Columbia county, Ga.

By Rev. Dr. Spalding, in Atlanta, Ga., Dr. J. C. Pendleton to Miss Bertha Swift.

By Rev. T. B. Russell, December 19, 1877, in Marshalville, Ga., Mr. Calvin P. Brown, of Hawkinsville, Ga,. to Miss Nellie C. Sperry, of former place.

By Rev. John M. Marshall, December 20, 1877, in Attapulgus, Ga., Mr. Junius H. Gregory to Miss Hattie Grinnell Marshall, daughter of the officiating minister.

By Rev. Wm. C. Power, December 20, 1877, Mr. James K. Davidson of Springfield, Mass., to Miss S. Kate Reid ,daughter of the late W. L. J. Reid, of Cheraw, S. C.

By Rev. Wm. C. Power, December 20, 1877, in Cartersville, Ga., Mr. James P. Ramsau to Miss Jennie C. Kingsberry.

By Rev. J. M. Kenney, December 20, 1877, Rev. Ellison D. Stone, of Athens, Ga., to Miss Emma C. Bradford, of Clarkesville. Milledgeville paper will please copy.

By Rev. G. W. Persons, December 19, 1877, at the residence of Mrs. Judge Culverhouse, Crawford county, Ga., Mr. William G. Lowman of Fort Valley, to Mrs. L. V. McManus, daughter of Mrs. Culverhouse.

By Rev. W. W. Stewart, December 13, 1877, Mr. Raleigh Turner to Miss Lizzie F. Marone, all of Talbot county, Ga.

By Rev. H. R. Felder, November 15, 1877, in Dougherty county, Ga., Mr. Lewis R. Cox to Miss M. E. Reynolds, of Bainbridge, Ga.

By Rev. H. R. Felder, December 4, 1877, at the residence of Dr. Pattillo, in Dougherty county, Ga., Mr. Thos. U. Peed to Miss M. E. Avery.

By Rev. H. R. Felder, December 6, 1877, in the Baptist Church, in Americus, Ga., Mr. W. J. Thornton, of Atlanta, Ga., to Miss Ida Felder, of Americus; at the same time and place, Mr. A. L. Reese to Miss J. L. Walker, of Americus.

By Rev. J. H. Zimmerman, December 16, 1877, in Orangeburg county, S. C., Mr. Wm. W. Oliver to Miss C. E. Haigler.

By Rev. George W. Duval, December 19, 1877, Mr. John T. Scruggs to Miss Etta M. Herrin, both of Chattooga county, Ga.

By Rev. R. R. Dagnall, December 11, 1877, at the residence of Mrs. N. H. Rogers, Mr. W. J. Douglass to Miss Mary E. Beard, all of Union county, S. C.

By Rev. Morgan Bellah, December 20, 1877, at the residence of Morgan Hoard, in Barnesville, Ga., Mr. Henry S. Head to Miss Adella Howard.

By Rev. J. E. Sentell, December 20, 1877, Mr. W. K. Bussey to Miss Mary C. Clark, both of Dodge county, Ga.

By Rev. L. Wood, December 6, 1877, at Vaux Hall, Waccamaw, S. C., Mr. Frank W. Lachicotte, of Waverly, to Miss S. Lilian Stokes, eldest daughter of the Rev. G. W. Stokes, formerly of the S. C. Conference.

By Rev. W. A. Rogers, December 20, 1877, Charles Spencer, Esq., of Sumter county, S. C., to Mrs. Abbie A. Rogers, of Pennsylvania.

By Rev. J. T. Kilgo, assisted by Rev. W. A. Rogers, December 29, 1877, Mr. john C. Campbell of Marlboro, S. C., to Miss Anna M. Kilgo, daughter of the principal officiating minister.

By Rev. J. W. Domingos, December 25, 1877, Mr. William G. Sullivan, of Crawfordvillle, Ga., to Miss Winnnie Lester, of Jeffersonville, Ga.

By Rev. John H. Grogan, December 11, 1877, Jno. T. Osborn, Esq., of Elberton, Ga., to Miss Lula Stovall, of Elbert county, Ga.

By Rev. F. A. Branch, December 19, 1877, at the residence of Mr. A. Gamewell, near Columbus, Ga., Mr. Augustus C. Bowles to Miss Ella Gammell.

By Rev. T. T. Christian, November 20, 1877, Mr. J. W. Walters of Sumter county, Ga., to Miss Sallie Ella Littlejohn, daughter of the Rev. J. R. Littlejohn, of the S. G. Conference.

By Rev. J. R. Littlejohn, December 19, 1877, Mr. Z. F. Markey to Miss Anna H. Rylander, daughter of M. M. Rylander, all of Sumter county, Ga.

By Rev. J. R. Littlejohn, December 20, 1877, Mr. John Salter, of Sumter county, Ga., to Miss J. A. McCoy, of Opelika, Ala.

Issue of January 15, 1878

By Rev. J. J. Sealey, December 24, 1877, in Tampa, Fla., Mr. Varanus W. Olds, to Miss Mary L. Givens, all of Tampa, Fla.

By Rev. J. W. R. Alexander, December 27, 1877, Rev. McKinzie Mazingo to Miss Mary Talivar, all of Darlington county, S. C.

By Rev. J. D. Rogers, January 3, 1878, at the residence of the bride's stepfather, Mr. Warren A., Pace, Mr. John G. Martin, of Marion county, to Miss Maggie A. Fussel, of Putnam county, Fla.

By Rev. E. P. Bonner, December 23, 1877, Mr. John S. Smith to Miss M. E. Epps, all of Columbia county, Ga.

By Rev. E. P. Bonner, January 3, 1878, Judge Thomas N. Hicks to Miss Mattie O. Jones, all of Columbia, Ga.

By Rev. R. H. Reid, December 19, 1877, Mr. J. White Westmoreland, of Laurens county, S. C., to Miss Julia Leonard, of Reidville.

Issue of January 22, 1878

By Rev. S. A. Weber, September 30, 1877, in Orangeburg, S. C., Mr. E. S. Griffin to Miss Eva Sistrunk.

By Rev. S. A. Weber, November 15, 1877, in Orangeburg, S. C., Mr. Sherrod A. Reeves to Miss Julia Ransdale.

By Rev. S. A. Weber, November 29, 1877, in Orangeburg, S. C., Mr. Alfred Jones to Miss Corrie Wannamaker.

By Rev. S. A. Weber, November 27, 1877, in Orangeburg, S. C., Mr. I. Pembroke Brunson to Miss Nora Nettles.

By Rev. S. A. Weber, December 27, 1877, in Orangeburg, S. C., Mr. Lewis Cummings, of Charleston, S. C., to Miss Rosa Cummings, of Orangeburg.

By Rev. W. T. McMichael, December 19, 1877, at the residence of Mrs. Sheats, in Jones county, Ga., Mr. James W. Stubbs to Miss E. R. Pitts.

By Rev. F. P. Brown, December 20, 1877, Mr. Alfred L. Johnson, of McDuffie county, to Miss Mamie F. Fuller, of Warren county, Ga.

By Rev. W. W. Stewart, January 10, 1878, in the Providence Methodist Church, Mr. Robert C. Fryer, of Barnesville, to Miss Mattie B. Owen, of Talbot county, Ga.

By Rev. R. Johnson, December 20, 1877, Mr. J. M. Barrow to Mrs. E. M. Peacock, of Upson county, Ga.

By Rev. R. R. Johnson, January 3, 1878, Mr. L. N. Pritchard, of Thomaston, Ga., to Miss Hennie Moore, of Talbot county, Ga.

By Rev. R. R. Johnson, January 9, 1878, Mr. Robt Hartman to Miss E. E. Johnson, of Thomaston, Ga.

By Rev. R. R. Johnson, January 9, 1878, Mr. Wm. S. February, of Jonesboro, Tenn., to Miss Georgia C. Caraway, of Thomaston, Ga.

By Rev. R. L. Wiggins, November 29, 1877, near Perry, Ga., Mr. Sol Laidler to Miss Loula Turrentine.

By Dr. A. Peeler, January 10, 1878, Mr. Thomas E. Jones, of Terrell county, Ga., to Mrs. A. G. Poe, of Alachua county, Fla.

By Rev. R. B. Bryan, January 3, 1878, Mr. R. B. Wells, of Burke county, Ga., to Miss Mollie Smith, of Washington county, Ga.

By Rev. R. B. Bryan, January 10, 1878, Mr. Thos. B. Smith to Miss Mary Winifred Moye, both of Washington county, Ga.

By Rev. Geo. H. Wells, January 3, 1878, in Darlington county, S. c., Mr. Geo. W. Wiggins to Miss S. C. S. Purvis.

By Rev. Geo. H. Wells, assisted by the bride's father, January 10, 1878, in the Methodist Church in Timmonsville, S. C., Milton C. Littlejohn, M. D., of Union county, S. C., to Miss Loula C. Newbery, daughter of Rev. I. J. Newbery, of S. C. Conference.

By Rev. J. W. Weston, January 1, 1878, in Webster county, Ga., Mr. Urban L. Weston, of the Dawson *Journal*, to Miss Mittie Davenport, of Webster county.

By Rev. E. Wadsworth, D. D., January 8, 1878, in Mobile, Ala., Rev. Andrew J. Lamar, of the Alabama Conference, to Miss Mattie Elsworth, only daughter of John Elsworth, Esq.

By Rev. W. W. Lampkin, December 27, 1877, Mr. J. W. Brand to Miss Georgia H. McCormick, all of Heard county, Ga.

By Rev. John Inabinet, December 20, 1877, Mr. M. W. Robinson to Miss Cora C. Houske, all of Orangeburg, S. C.

By Rev. Atticus G. Haygood, December 20, 1877, in Oxford, Ga., Rev. Wm. C. Lovett, of the South Georgia Conference, to Miss Mamie Smith, daughter of the late Rev. J. Blakley Smith.

By Rev. O. L. Smith, January 3, 1878, A. B. Simms, Esq., of Covington, Ga., to Miss Sarah S. T. Jackson, of Greene county, Ga.

By Rev. J. L. Shuford, January 8, 1878, Mr. W. J. Witherspoon to Mrs. Susan Davis, all of Clarendon, S. C.

By Rev. G. S. Johnston, November 29, 1877, Mr. B. L. Mitchell to Miss S. F. Neisler, both of Taylor county, Ga.

By Rev. J. F. Sifley, December 20, 1877, in Orangeburg county, S. C., Mr. Lawrence N. Riley to Miss Henrietta A. Smoke.

By Rev. L. A. Darsey, December 11, 1877, Mr. Samuel Jessup to Miss Emma Jenkins.

By Rev. L. A. Darsey, December 24, 1877, Mr. Andrew J. McGee, of Taylor county, Ga., to Miss Sallie E. Parker, of Talbot county, Ga.

By Rev. L. A. Darsey, January 10, 1878, in the Methodist Church, in Geneva, Ga., Charles Dozier, Esq., to Miss Kate Fuller, all of Talbot county, Ga.

Issue of February 5, 1878

By Dr. W. I. Greene, January 17, 1878, M. L. Blewster to Mrs. Mattie Pool, all of Houston county, Ga.

By Dr. W. I. Greene, January 17, 1878, at the residence of Mr. Elbert Fagan, Mr. R. G. Blewster to Miss Mollie Fagan, all of Houston county, Ga.

By Dr. W. I. Greene, January 24, 1878, Mr. John Goodin to Miss Blasingame, all of Houston county, Ga.

By Rev. O. A. Darby, January 24, 1878, in the chapel of the Williamston Female College, Mr. George E. Prince, of Williamston, S. C., to Miss Mattie Lander, daughter of Rev. Saml. Lander of the S. C. Conference.

By Rev. Robt. P. Martyn, December 13, 1877, Mr. B. T. Thomas, Jr., to Miss Emma J. Clark, all of Gwinnett county, Ga.

By Rev. Dr. Leonard, January 18, 1878, near Boston, Ga., Mr. George W. English, of Decatur county, Ga., to Miss Mary Grant Weldon, of Thomas county, Ga.

SOUTHERN CHRISTIAN ADVOCATE MARRIAGE NOTICES 1867-1878

By Rev. John W. McRoy, January 24, 1878, Mr. W. P. McGill to Miss Georgeanna A. Nusum, all of Williamsburg county, S. C.

By Rev. W. J. Cotter, January 6, 1878, Mr. W. R. Mills to Miss M. A. Lovingood, all of Elbert county, Ga.

By Rev. W. J. Cotter, January 15, 1878, Mr. G. B. Conwell to Miss S. V. Hall, all of Elbert county, Ga.

By Rev. P. S. Twitty, January 24, 1878, in the Methodist Church, at Perry, Ga., Mr. Samuel D. Rodgers to Miss Ida A. Cater.

By Rev. F. A. Kimbell, January 22, 1878, at the residence of Mr. W. E. Hange, Mr. James T. Dunlap to Miss Mary Alice Small, all of Atlanta, Ga.

By Rev. G. H. Pooser, January 3, 1878, at Ridgeville, S. C., Mr. J. G. Magwood, of Charleston, S. C., to Miss Ennie J. Ferrill, of Colleton county, S. C.

By Rev. G. H. Pooser, January 20, 1878, at Byrd's Station, S. C. R. R., Mr. Irving P. Rump to Miss Ida J. Crawford, all of Colleton county, S. C.

By Rev. G. H. Pooser, January 22, 1878, near Graham's T. O. S. C. R. R., Mr. John H. Babers, of Barnwell county, S. C., Miss Victoria L. Jennings, of Orangeburg county, S. C.

By Rev. A. J. Cauthen, January 16, 1878, Mr. Hezekiah Ritter, of Barnwell, S. C., to Miss Emma Kittrell, of Orangeburg, S. C.

By Rev. R. P. Franks, January 10, 1878, Mr. B. C. Kay to Miss Kittie L. Latimer, both of Abbeville county, S. C.

By Rev. R. P. Franks, January 15, 1878, Mr. Joseph Martin to Mrs. Sallie Christopher, both of Abbeville county, S. C.

By Rev. S. D. Clements, January 15, 1878, Mr. Matthew Carlisle, Jr., to Miss Mary Walker, all of Talbot county, Ga.

By Rev. S. D. Clements, January 16, 1878, Mr. J. H. Mobley to Miss Willie F. Webster, all of Hamilton county, Ga.

By Rev. W. A. Candler, January 13, 1878, in the Sixth Church, Atlanta, Ga., Mr. W. A. Smith to Miss L. A. Brown.

By Rev. H. M. Quillian, January 20, 1878, at the residence of the bride's grandfather, Mr. Tilford McConnell, Mr. George M. Brand, of Logansville, Ga., to Miss Ida P. McConnell, of Gwinnett county, Ga.

By Rev. E. J. Burch, January 16, 1878, Mr. Elliot Mingledorff to Miss Julia Biddenback, all of Effingham county, Ga.

By Rev. R. B. Lester, January 17, 1878, Mr. George E. Thomas to Miss Julia Adella Rheney, all of Burke county, Ga.

By Rev. Jno. Finger, January 1, 1878, Mr. D. T. W. Terry to Miss S. J. Thomason, all of Greenville county, S. C.

SOUTHERN CHRISTIAN ADVOCATE MARRIAGE NOTICES 1867-1878

By Rev. J. D. Gray, January 17, 1878, in Eatonton, Ga., Mr. C. J. Booker to Miss Carrie Lou Pearson.

By Rev. W. F. Robison, January 10, 1878, in Bartow county, Ga., Mr. S. A. Gilreath to Miss Della Loveless, both of Bartow county, Ga.

By Rev. E. P. Bonner, January 22, 1878, Mr. John Eubank to Miss Dora Smalley, all of Columbia county, Ga.

By Rev. O. L. Smith, January 20, 1878, Mr. Charles J. Howell, of Columbus, Ga., to Miss Sallie A. E. Henderson, of Oxford, Ga.

By Rev. M. L. Banks, December 19, 1877, in Orangeburg county, S. C., Mr. John Fletcher Houser to Mrs. Virginia Clarke.

By Rev. M. L. Banks, January 8, 1878, in Orangeburg county, S. C., Mr. Norman Jacob Robinson to Miss Margaret Cornelia Stack.

By Rev. M. L. Banks, January 17, 1878, in Orangeburg county, S. C., Mr. Richard Sineth to Miss Mahala B. Wannamaker.

By Rev. B. E. L. Timmons, January 9, 1878, Mr. W. F. Comer of Floyd county, Ga., to Miss Katie Carsochan, of Rome, Ga.

By Rev. B. E. L. Timmons, January 13, 1878, Mr. John A. Summers, of rome Ga., to Miss E. A. Thompson, of Polk county, Ga.

By Rev. L. P. Neese, January 10, 1878, Mr. John A. Brown to Miss Charlotte Hearn, all of Campbell county, Ga.

By Rev. J. W. Burke, December 29, 1878, at the National Hotel, Macon, Ga., Dr. S. F. Salter, of Atlanta, Ga., to Mrs. Ella E. Palmer, of Burke county, Ga.

By Rev. L. J. Davies, January 23, 1878, at the Methodist Church, Forsyth, Ga., Mr. Gus. Watkins, of Forsyth, Ga., to Miss Georgia Hammond, eldest daughter of Hon. A. D. Hammond, of Forsyth, Ga.

By Rev. L. J. Davies, January 23, 1878, at the Methodist Church, Forsyth, Ga., Mr. E. T. Murphey, of Barnesville, Ga., to Miss Alice Hammond, daughter of Hon. A. D. Hammond, of Forsyth, Ga.

By Rev. L. J. Davies, January 23, 1878, in Forsyth, Ga., Mr. W. A. Cooper, of Griffin, Ga., to Miss Sallie Phelps, daughter of Mrs. Eugenia Phelps, of Forsyth, Ga.

By Rev. C. C. Hines, January 24, 1878, Mr. S. J. Banneau to Miss Fannie J. Davis, of Decatur county, Ga.

By Rev. R. B. Lester, January 17, 1878, in Waynesboro, Ga., Dr. Chas. E. Ward to Mrs. Julia K. Wilson, all of Burke county, Ga.

By Rev. John R. Parker, January 30, 1878, Mr. William C. English to Miss M. C. Fitzpatrick, daughter of Rev. H. H. Fitzpatrick, all of Warrenton, Ga.

Issue of February 12, 1878

By Rev. N. D. Morehouse, December 20, 1877, Col. William Warnock to Miss Margaret Murphy, all of Burke county, Ga.

By Rev. M. L. Underwood, January 31, 1878, Mr. Nelson Adams to Miss Jennie McKeehan, all of Catoosa county, Ga.

By Rev. Dr. R. W. Hubert, January 31, 1878, near Warrenton, Mr. John B. Anderson to Miss Laura V. English, all of Warren county, Ga.

By Rev. J. A. Clifton, January 24, 1878, Mr. M. M. Quattlebaum, of Lexington county, S. C., to Miss Ella Whittle, of Edgefield county, S. C.

By Rev. John M. Marshall, January 31, 1878, in Decatur county, Ga., Mr. James M. White to Miss Amanda Collins.

By Rev. John M. Marshall, January 31, 1878, in Decatur county, Ga., Mr. B. D. Wilson to Miss Euphemia G. Chestnut.

By Rev. I. O. A. Connor, December 18, 1877, in Orangeburg county, S. C., Mr. I. J. May, of Colleton county, S. C. to Miss Fannie S. Connor, daughter of the officiating clergyman.

By Rev. W. H. Trammell, January 31, 1878, Mr. S. E. Kelly, of Columbia county, Ga., to Miss Fannie A. Ramsey, of Lincoln county, Ga.

Issue of February 19, 1878

By Rev. Millard Law, January 17, 1878, in Los Angeles, Cal., Rev. A. M. Campbell, of the Los Angeles Conference, to Miss Josie E. Peel.

By Rev. J. M. Potter, Feb. 7, 1878, Mr. James L. Dozier, of Ducker Station, to Miss Emma J. Jones, daughter of Willis Jones, Esq., of Lee county, Ga.

By Rev. L. F. Burtz, Dec. 20, 1877, Mr. William Saterfield to Miss Malinda V. Dobbs, all of Cherokee county, Ga.

By Rev. L. F. Burtz, Feb. 7, 1878, Mr. Milton J. Owens to Miss Kate Austin, both of Cobb county, Ga.

By Rev. Morgan Callaway, at "The Anchorage," Nov. 14, 1877, Mr. W. T. Lang, of Manchester, England, to Miss Amulet Pope, of Washington, Ga.

By Rev. W. W. Wadsworth, in Hall county, Ga., Jan. 16, 1878, Mr. W. R. Winburn, to Miss Ellen Thompson.

By Rev. W. W. Wadsworth, Feb. 3, 1878, at the Methodist Church, in Gainesville, Ga., Mr. W. M. Redwine to Miss Emma Florence Hooker.

By Rev. Charles S. Vedder, Jan. 31, 1878, at the Huguenot Church, Charleston, S. C,. Minor C. Galluchat, of Manning, S. C., to Miss Thomassa Thompson, of Augusta, Ga.

By Rev. Geo. G. Smith, Midway, Ga., Mr. Robert Adams to Miss Eudocia Hammond, daughter of John Hammond, Esq.

By Rev. W. L. Yarbrough, Jan. 27, 1878, Mr. John F. McCloud to Miss Henrietta Hix, all of Chattooga county, Ga.

By Rev. W. G. Booth, in Gadsden county, Fla., Dec. 20, 1877, Mr. Willie Smith to Miss Hattie Hinson.

By Rev. W. G. Booth, at Concord, Gadsden co., Fla., Jan. 30, 1878, Mr. Joshua Stokes to Mrs. Margaret Tucker.

By Rev. W. G. Booth, at Concord, Gadsden co., Fla., Jan. 31, 1878, Mr. Walter Nicholson to Miss Ellendor Thomson.

By Rev. W. G. Booth, at Gadsden co., Fla., Jan. 31, 1878, Mr. Henry Whittle to Miss Claudia Thomson.

By Rev. William D. Anderson, December 12, 1877, in Cherokee county, Ga., Rev. Jno. M. Lowrey, of the No. Ga. Conference, to Miss Ella O. Latimer.

By Rev. William D. Anderson, January 13, 1878, in Cedar Town, Ga., Mr. Gussie Adams to Miss Bettie Watts.

Issue of February 26, 1878

By Rev. A. Johnston, January 27, 1878, Mr. Samuel Hale, of Walker county, Ga., to Miss Josie Harper, of Chattooga county, Ga.

By Rev. Geo. W. Duval, Jr., February 7, 1878, Mr. T. S. Littlejohn, of Walker county, Ga., to Miss Lizzie Watson, of Chattooga county, Ga.

By Rev. Geo. W. Duval, Jr., January 10, 1878, Mr. John W. Carroll to Miss Sarah Roberts, both of Chattooga county, Ga.

By Rev. Geo. W. Duval, Jr., February 17, 1878, Mr. James Simmons to Miss Sarah Taylor, both of Chattooga county, Ga.

By Rev. J. R. Littlejohn, January 24, 1878, Mr. William P. Page to Miss Georgia Windsor, daughter of Mr. Alexander Windsor, all of Sumter county, Ga.

By Rev. Wm. H. LaPrade, February 13, 1878, at LaGrange, Ga., Mr. Thos. H. Lippitt, of Worth county, Ga., to Miss Mary D. Bacon, of LaGrange.

By Rev. Wm. H. LaPrade, February 14, 1878, at LaGrange, Ga., Mr. William B. Cotter, of LaGrange, to Miss Louise M. Tuggle, of Mobile, Ala.

By Rev. T. B. Russell, January 30, 1878, in Fort Valley, Ga., Mr. H. W. Scovill to Miss M. C. Bateman.

By Rev. Wm. W. Mood, February 3, 1878, Mr. Wm. F. O'Sheals to Miss Janie Dunnaway, all of Spartanburg county, S. C.

By Rev. W. D. Kirkland, February 7, 1878, Mr. Horace Thorpe to Miss Frances Ferrell, all of Mars Bluff, S. C.

By Rev. Geo. H. Wells, February 13, 1878, Mr. E. J. McLaughlin to Miss Catharine M. C. Turner, daughter of Mr. Adam Turner, all of Darlington county, S. C.

By Rev. John O. Wilson, February 14, 1878, in Charleston county, S. C., Mr. Arnold A. Browning to Miss Mattie O. Willson.

By Rev. G. H. Pooser, February 10, 1878, at Ridgeville, S. c., Mr. Augustus H. Mood to Miss Florence A. Moorer, all of Colleton county, S. C.

By Rev. Geo. C. Clarke, February 19, 1878, Mr. Joseph Wells, of Terrell county, Ga., to Miss Fannie Oustian, of Randolph county, Ga.

By Rev. Wesley F. Smith, February 13, 1878, in Lithonia, Ga., Mr. F. G. McKenney, of Thomaston, Ga., to Miss Mollie A. Hunt, daughter of Dr. Hunt, of the former place.

By Rev. J. H. Zimmerman, January 14, 1878, Mr. H. D. H. Felkel to Miss I. C. Huffman, all of Orangeburg county, S. C.

Issue of March 5, 1878

Married by Rev. S. A. Weber, February 17, 1878, in Orangeburg county, S. C., Mr. Preston Saunders to Miss Lucia Smoke.

Issue of March 12, 1878

By Rev. B. F. Breedlove, February 19, 1878, at the Methodist Church, in Talbotton, Ga., Mr. F. B. Jossey, of Macon, Ga., to Miss C. W. Leonard, of Talbotton.

By Rev. Wm. Thomas, February 14, 1878, Mr. Andrew J. Ellerbe to Miss Annie D. Ellerbe, all of Chesterfield county, S. C.

By Rev. George J. Griffiths, D. D., February 19, 1878, near Bainbridge, Ga., Mr. William H. Davis, of Mitchell county, Ga., to Miss Hattie E. Crawford.

By Rev. W. W. Duncan, January 31, 1878, Mr. J. S. Wannamaker, of Orangeburg, S. C., to Miss Pattie Duncan, second daughter of Maj. D. R. Duncan, of Spartanburg, S. C.

By Rev. J. M. Potter, February 21, 1878, in Webster county, Ga., Mr. R. Z. Bowman to Mrs. Ella V. Leverett.

By Rev. L. A. Darsey, February 19, 1878, Mr. John C. Jackson to Miss Bettie mitchell, both of Harris county, Ga.

By Rev. R. B. Tarrant, February 7, 1878, Mr. Charles M. Odom, of Orangeburg county, S. C., to Miss Anna T. Milhous, of Barnwell county.

By Rev. R. B. Tarrant, January 31, 1878, at Mr. J. W. Martin's, Mr. Davis Austin to Miss Missouri Crout, all of Orangeburg county.

By Rev. Walker Lewis, February 13, 1878, in Macon, Ga., Mr. F. M. Jenkins to Miss M. F. Clark.

By Rev. S. N. Tucker, February 21, 1878, in Macon, Ga., Mr. Frank H. McGee to Miss Susie J. Pace

By Rev. J. Walter Dickson, February 14, 1878, Mr. Julian B. Friday, of Columbia, S. C., to Miss Cora A. Smith, eldest daughter of Hon. James M. Smith, of Bamberg, S. C.

By Rev. J. Walter Dickson, February 24, 1878, Mr. Thos. J. Spigener to Miss Henrietta C. Ross, both of Richland county, S. C.

By Rev. J. T. Kilgo, January 15, 1878, Mr. W. J. Ledingham to Mrs. T. A. McInTyre, daughter of Dr. Ashley LeGette, all of Marion county, S. C.

By Rev. Albert M. Williams, February 20, 1878, Mr. Mr. Van Bell to Miss Sallie E.Powell, all of Hawkinsville, Ga.

By Rev. A. Gamewell Gantt, February 20, 1878, Mr. T. Middleton Harvey to Miss Kate A. Harvey, all of Charleston county, S. C.

By Rev. Geo. E. Gardner, February 3, 1878, in Atlanta, Ga., Mr. A. M. Turner to Miss Fannie J. Smith, all of Atlanta.

By Rev. M. L. Banks, February 9, 1878, in Orangeburg county, S. c., Mr. Edgar Geddings Bomar to Mrs. Mary Keitt Sullins.

By Rev. J. B. Fitzpatrick, February 27, 1878, Rev. C. E. Dowman, of the Florida Conference, to Miss Julia Monroe, daughter of Wm. Monroe, Esq., of Quincy, Fla.

By Rev. Miles D. Norton, February 21, 1878, at Dallas, Ga., Mr. Thomas Clonts, of Atlanta, Ga., to Miss Jennie Foot, of Dallas, Ga.

By Rev. W. M. Watts, February 27, 1878, in the Methodist Church at Waukeenah, Fla,. Mr. R. D. Johnson to Miss Eliza J. Edwards, all of Jefferson county, Fla.

Issue of March 19, 1878

By Rev. T. P. Phillips, March 6, 1878, at Smith's Chapel Academy, Mr. W. T. ElRoy to Miss Rosey Hammonds, all of Anderson county, S. C.

By Rev. W. H. Hunt, March 5, 1878, Mr. John R. Hernder to Miss Williametta E. Gadbold, all of Columbia county, Fla.

By Rev. J. E. England, February 20, 1878, near Rehobothville, Morgan county, Ga., Mr. George P. Arrington to Miss Lucy A. Avert, daughter of J. W. and F. A. Avret [sic].

By Rev. J. A. Moseley, February 13, 1878, Mr. Mark Rigell, of Sumter county, Fla., to Mrs. Lizzie Sparkman, of Columbia county, Fla.

By Rev. J. W. Domingos, February 7, 1878, Mr. Andrew A. Cowart, of Wilkinson county, Ga., to Miss Carrie E. Rutherford, of the same county.

By Rev. J. W. Domingos, February 24, 1878, Mr. Adam A. Long, of Warren county, Ga., to Miss Dora R. Gallemore, of Twiggs county, Ga.

By Rev. J. W. Domingos, March 10, 1878, Mr. Charles E. Taylor, of Long Street, Pulaski county, Ga., to Mrs. Mary J. Phillips, of the same county.

By Rev. O. A. Thrower, January 3, 1878, at the hotel in Cave Spring, Ga., Mr. Jno. Weatherley to Miss Ida Morrison.

By Rev. O. A. Thrower, February 23, 1878, near Cave Spring, Ga., Mr. Fletcher Tilley to Miss Willie Ford, daughter of A. S. Ford, Esq.

By Rev. O. A. Thrower, March 6, 1878, in South Rome, Ga., Mr. Wm. J. Burnett to Miss Mattie Wright, daughter of N. F. Wright, Esq.

By Rev. W. H. Trammell, February 26, 1878, Mr. James A. Crook to Miss Fannie Martin, all of Lincoln county, Ga.

By Rev. S. G. Chiles, January 15, 1878, Mr. Thomas J. Pinson to Miss Sallie Johnson, all of Worth county, Ga.

By Rev. S. G. Chiles, February 21, 1878, Mr. M. E. Jenkins, of Worth county, Ga., to Miss Maggie Jones, of Mitchell county, Ga.

By Rev. Jno. A. Mood, February 28, 1878, Mr. George A. Platt to Miss Abbie McRay, all of Graniteville, Aiken county, S. C.

Issue of March 26, 1878

By Rev. J. B. Wilson, March 7, 1878, Mr. J. N. Littlejohn to Miss Minnie Littlejohn, both of Union county, S. C.

By Rev. R. W. Dixon, March 13, 1878, in Dawson, Ga., Mr. P. L. Odum, of Newton, Ga., to Miss Ellen M. Peeples, of Dawson, Ga.

By Rev. J. P. Wardlaw, January 8, 1878, near Buena Vista, Ga., Mr. Aaron Renew to Miss Susan Corley.

By Rev. J. P. Wardlaw, February 20, 1878, in Buena Vista, Ga., Mr. R. J. Jordan to Miss Susan F. Williams.

By Rev. R. W. Dixon, March 19, 1878, near Dawson, Ga., Mr. D. J. Ray, of Conyers, Ga., to Miss Mollie W. Geise, of Terrell county, Ga.

Issue of April 2/3, 1878

By Dr. Leonard, March 20, 1878, Mr. Hezekiah Roberts, of Brooks county, Ga., to Miss Moselle Peacock, daughter of Mr. Delamar C. Peacock, of Thomas county, Ga.

By Rev. J. D. Gray, March 25, 1878, at Eatonton, Ga., Mr. William A. Ammons, of Memphis, Tenn., to Miss Sallie Armor, of Green county, Ga.

By Rev. W. F. Quillian, February 27, 1878, in Payne Chapel Church, Atlanta, Ga., Mr. W. B. Arbery to Miss M. E. Goodman.

By Rev. William D. Anderson, March 7, 1878, in Cedar Town, Ga., Mr. W. M. Phillips to Mrs. Angie Colville.

By Rev. J. N. Myers, March 10, 1878, Mr. J. M. Johnson, of Gordon county, GA., to Miss C. C. Chastain, of Whitfield county, Ga.

By Rev. A. A. Robinson, March 7, 1878, at Fort Myers, Fla., Mr. Howell A. Parker to Miss Mary G. Verdier.

By Rev. J. H. Wilkins in Clinch county, Ga., at Mr. Morris Bram's, Mr. O. T. Mattox to Miss Julia A. Lightfoot, all of Clinch county, Ga.

By Rev. L. P. Neese, March 13, 1878, Mr. Wesley T. Stipe to Miss Elizabeth L. Pendington, all of Campbellton county, Ga.

Issue of April 9, 1878

By Rev. T. P. Phillips, March 26, 1878, Mr. J. C. Gant to Mrs. J. C. King, at the residence of Mr. Pickrel, all of Anderson county, S. C.

By Rev. J. Rembert Smith, March 26, 1878, in Buford, Ga., Mr. John R. McGaughey, of Decatur county, Ga., to Miss Fannie Vance, of the former place.

By Rev. N. T. Burks, March 21, 1878, at the Southwestern University Chapel, Walter Davis, Esq., of Waco, Tex., to Miss Anna Lane, of Georgetown, Tex., daughter of Rev. J. S. Lane, of the N. W. Texas Conference.

By Rev. George W. Duval, Jr., March 10, 1878, Mr. W. S. Young of Dalton, Ga., to Miss Sarah Simmons of Chattooga county, Ga.

By Rev. A. W. Jackson, March 10, 1878, Mr. J. B. Garrison to Miss Cate Payne, all of Greenville county, S. C.

By Rev. R. R. Johnson, March 26, 1878, Mr. J. F. Means to Miss E. E. Hightower, of Thomaston, Ga.

By Rev. A. C. Davidson, M. D., March 24, 1878, in the Presbyterian Church, Sharon, Ga., Mr. Leonard M. Thompson to Miss Hattie R. Brooks, both of Sharon.

By Rev. W. M. Watts, April 2, 1878, at Lloid's Sta., No. 2 J. P. & M. R. R., Mr. L. P. Giles to Miss Arizona E. Freeman, all of Jefferson county, Fla.

By Rev. J. W. Domingos, March 31, 1878, Mr. William C. Solomon to Miss Mattie L. Renfro, both of Twiggs county, Ga.

Issue of April 16, 1878

By Rev. Geo. G. N. MacDonell, March 28, 1878, Mr. Charles F. Bennett to Miss Mary M. Freeney, both of Macon, Ga.

By Rev. C. W. Smith, April 10, 1878, in Bibb county, Ga., Capt. George F. Cherry to Miss Susie V. Paul, of Bibb county, Ga.

By Rev. W. F. Robison, April 7, 1878, in Bartow county, Ga., Mr. Jas. C. Lanier to Miss Mary E. Sproul, both of Bartow county, Ga.

By Rev. J. E. Sentell, March 21, 1878, Rev. S. G. Chiles of So. Ga. Conf., to Miss n. E. Watson, of Worth county, Ga.

By Rev. J. J. Morgan, April 4, 1878, Mr. Wm. J. Pelot to Miss Ella R. Boring, daughter of Dr. I. M. Boring, all of Atlanta, Ga.

By Rev. W. G. Hanson, March 28, 1878, Mr. John L. Harkins to Miss Hannah S. Kiker, all of Gordon county, Ga.

By Rev. W. G. Booth, April 4, 1878, at Salem Church, Mr. George W. Saxon, of Tallahassee, Fla., to Miss Sallie R. Ball, of Gadsden county, Fla.

Issue of April 23, 1878

By Rev. W. T. Caldwell, April 7, 1878, Mr. Edward Herndon, of Atlanta, Ga., to Miss Annie J. Freeman, of Troup county, Ga.

By Rev. J. B. Wilson, March 28, 1878, Mr. Charles Littlejohn to Miss Eugenia A. Littlejohn, of Union county, S. C.

By Rev. J. W. Domingos, April 11, 1878, Mr. James S. Burke to Miss Lula E. Sinquefield, both of Wilkinson county, Ga.

By Rev. John R. Parker ,March 31, 1878, in Warrenton, GA., in the Methodist Church, Mr. Peter F. Smith to Miss Emma E. Brinson.

By Rev. James R. Smith, M. D., April 3, 1878, in Stanfordville, Putnam county, Ga., Mr. J. L. Whaley, of Jones county, Ga., to Miss Ione Odom, eldest daughter of B. B. Odom, Esq.

Issue of April 30, 1878

By Rev. Dr. Ross C. Houghton, April 21, 1878, at Union M. E. Church, St. Louis, Mo., Mr. Robt. DeJournette, of Rome, Ga., to Miss Victoria Clover, of Columbus, Ohio.

By Rev. D. M. Banks, April 18, 1878, at the residence of Dr. C. H. Hurt, of Hurtsville, Russell county, Ala., Mr. Clarence Glenn, of Eufaula, Ala., to Miss Lucy Cotter, daughter of the late James L. Cotter, D. D.

By Rev. John Inabinet, April 18, 1878, Mr. N. A. Whetstone to Miss Julia E. Dash, all of Orangeburg, S. C.

By Rev. O. A. Thrower, April 8, 1878, at Livingston, Ga., Mr. S. W. Kirton to Miss Julia E. Erwin, all of Floyd county, Ga.

By Rev. M. D. Norton, April 4, 1878, Hon. M. L. Garrett of Brownsville, Ga., to Miss Mollie Skeen of Fairburn, Ga.

By Rev. R. F. Evans, April 18, 1878, Mr. Joseph T. Collier to Miss Anna G. Redding, both of Dooly county, Ga.

Issue of May 7, 1878

By Rev. J. B. Payne, April 23, 1878, at the house of Rev. J. B. Hanson the bride's father, Judge J. W. Thomas of Athens, Ga., to Mrs. Mary C. Green, of Pike county, Ga.

By Rev. C. L. Pattillo, April 25, 1878, in Dawsonville, Ga., at the residence of Col. M. L. Smith, Mr. W. A. Allen of Gilmer county, Ga., to Miss Flora Smith, of Dawsonville, Ga.

By Rev. M. L. Underwood, April 7, 1878, Mr. A. M. Harris to Miss Elizabeth Kittles, all of Catoosa county, Ga.

By Rev. M. L. Underwood, April 30, 1878, at the residence of Dr. A. S. Fowler, of Ringgold, Ga., Mr. J. D. Rooney to Miss Alfaretta Brownlow.

Issue of May 14, 1878

By Rev. C. W. Smith, D. D., May 4, 1878, Mr. Joel T. Walker of Houston county, GA., to Miss Ella Mathis, of Jones county, Ga.

By Rev. L. P. Neese, May 6, 1878, Mr. Luther N. B. Cook to Miss Lizzie Dailey, of Campbell county, Ga.

By Rev. E. J. Rentz, April 30, 1878, at M. E. Church, Camilla, Ga., Mr. Henry C. Curry, of Bainbridge, Ga., to Miss Emma McElveen, of Camilla, Ga.

By Rev. W. H. F. Roberts, April 25, 1878, Mr. Calvin C. Wheeler to Miss Hattie Montford, all of Jefferson county, Fla.

By Rev. G. W. Thomas, April 16, 1878, in Catoosa county, Ga., Mr. Shadrach Inman to Miss J. B. Russell, all of Catoosa county, Ga.

Issue of May 21, 1878

By Rev. Geo. E. Gardner, May 8, 1787, in Atlanta, Ga., Mr. Wm. C. Dickson to Miss Louella Sample, all of Atlanta.

By Rev. A. W. Jackson, May 26, 1878, Mr. L. A. Saybt to Miss Bettie Ward, all of Greenville, S. C.

By Rev. A. W. Jackson, May 9, 1878, Mr. W. F. Walker to Miss Harriet McElrath, all of Greenville, S. C.

By Rev. James C. Stoll, May 7, 1878, at St. Luke's Church, Sumter county, S. C., Rev. James W. Wolling of the South Carolina Conference, to Miss Lida Green, of Sumter county, S. C.

By Rev. James Kirton, April 7, 1878, Mr. S. Walter Morris of Williamsburgh county, S. C., to Miss E. Gullielma Hovis, formally [sic] of Appling county, Ga.

Issue of May 28, 1878

By Rev. W. H. Hunt, May 8, 1878, Rev. J. A. Moseley, of Hamilton county, to Miss C. J. Smallwood, of Columbia county, all of Florida.

By Rev. J. B. Platt, April 25, 1878, in Charleston county, S. C., Mr. Thomas L. Connor to Miss Minny E. Wiggins.

By Rev. T. B. Russell, May 16, 1878, Mr. Wm. G. Edwards in Miss Maggie F. Houser, eldest daughter of Mr. John H. Houser, all of Houston county, Ga.

By Rev. J. N. Myers, May 12, 1878, Mr. James A. Teasley to Miss Jennie Brown, all of Murray county, Ga.

By Rev. J. N. Myers, May 12, 1878, Mr. William Brown to Miss Emma Teasley, all of Murray county, Ga.

By Rev. R. W. Dixon, May 16, 1878, in Georgetown, Ga., Mr. H. W. Mann of Perry, Ga., to Miss Olva Morris, of Georgetown, Ga.

By Rev. Robt. T. Martyn, May 15, 1878, near Dawson, Ga., Mr. John H. Shoemaker, of the Selma Rome and Dalton R. R., to Miss Willie A. Land, of Whitfield county, Ga.

By Rev. P. F. Kistler, May 21, 1878, Mr. J. C. McDaniel of Columbia, S. C., to Miss Mary Ann Shuler, daughter of Dr. Wm. M. Shuler, of Colleton county, S. C.

By Rev. A. J. Cauthen, May 16, 1878, at Graham, S. C., Mr. A. S. Jennings to Miss Emmie B. Cauthen, daughter of the officiating minister.

By Rev. Jno. R. Parker, May 16, 1878, Mr. W. H. Todd to Miss A. R. Langford, daughter of Rev. Uriah Langford, all of Warren county, Ga.

By Rev. J. Rembert Smith, May 19, 1878, in Buford, Ga., Mr. J. Newton Verner, of Gwinnett county, Ga., to Miss Mollie Cain, of the former place.

Issue of June 4, 1878

By Rev. W. H. Hunt, May 22, 1878, Mr. William B. Aycock, of Wayne county, Ga., to Miss Virginia W. King, of Columbia county, Fla.

Issue of June 11, 1878

By Rev. W. M. Whiting, May 21, 1878, in Eastman, Ga., Mr. G. F. Harrison to Miss Mollie Bishop, daughter of Judge James Bishop.

By Rev. Lewis W. Rast, May 26, 1878, Mr. Jacob V. Reed to Miss Drusilla Rucker, all of Orangeburg county, S. C.

By Rev. W. O. Hampton, May 21, 1878, Mr. James E. Smith to Miss Ella McAlpin, all of Hamilton county, Fla.

By Rev. H. H. Parks, May 23, 1878, in Atlanta, Ga., Mr. Jno. E. Caldwell to Miss Emma E. Wilson.

By Rev. H. H. Parks, May 28, 1878, in Atlanta, Ga., Mr. Walter G. McClellan to Miss Ida B. Osborne.

By Rev. John O. Willson, May 23, 1878, Mr. S. R. James Smith to Miss S. Lula Murchison, all of Kershaw county, S. C.

By Rev. G. W. Duval, May 19, 1878, Mr. J. B. Rodgers, of Rome, Ga., to Miss Florence Wiley, of Chattooga county, Ga.

Issue of June 18, 1878

By Rev. S. D. Clements, May, 26, 1878, Mr. Robt. G. Johnson, of Muscogee county, Ga., to Miss Mary L. Bruce, of Harris county, Ga.

By Rev. D. Z. Dantzler, Rev. J. B. Platt, assisting, May 30, 1878, Dr. Fred W. Dantzler, of Orangeburg county, S. C., to Miss Victoria Connor, of Charleston county, S. C.

By Rev. Robt. P. Martyn, June 4, 1878, in Varnells, Whitfield county, Ga., Mr. Lee Wright, of Charleston, Tenn., to Miss Irene Wilson, of the former place.

By Rev. H. M. Quillian, May 23, 1878, Mr. Frank T. Pentecost to Miss Ophelia T. Born, all of Lawrenceville, Ga.

By Rev. M. Calloway, D. D., June 11, 1878, in Oxford, Ga., Mr. Ulla G. Hardeman to Miss M. K. Deavors, daughter of Rev. A. J. Deavors, of the North Georgia Conference.

By Rev. J. P. Wardlaw, May 22, 1878, in the Methodist Church, Buena Vista, Ga., Mr. H. M. Stokes to Miss M. C. Carr, all of Marion county, Ga.

By Rev. J. D. Rogers, May 30, 1878, Mr. F. M. Coleman, of Silver Springs, Fla., to Miss Kezia C. Caldwell of Alachua county, Fla.

Issue of June 25, 1878

By Rev. A. C. Mixon, June 12, 1878, Mr. John S. Wright to Miss Althea White, all of Newton county, Ga.

By Rev. E. L. T. Blake, June 9, 1878, in Tallahassee, Fla., Mr. W. f. Powell, of Live Oak, to Miss Rhoda M. Galloway, of Tallahassee.

By Rev. R. A. Conner, June 6, 1878, in Thomson, Ga., in the Methodist Church, Mr. M. Burke Hatcher, of Harlem, to Miss Fannie, eldest daughter of Mr. and Mrs. B. S. Embree, of the former place.

By Rev. N. B. Ousley, June 12, 1878, William S. Humphries, Esq., of Quitman, Ga., to Miss Sallie E. Ousley, of Lowndes county, Ga.

Anderson, Isabella C. (Spigener) 126
Anderson, J. 161
Anderson, J. B. 235
Anderson, James H. 37, 245
Anderson, John B. 287
Anderson, Josephine E. (Huggins) 235
Anderson, Josephus 12, 128, 134
Anderson, Julia F. (Coley) 16
Anderson, L. E. (Dawson) 173
Anderson, Laura V. (English) 287
Anderson, Leila (Latimer) 261
Anderson, Lizzie (Burkhalter) 232
Anderson, Lizzie R. (Welch) 212
Anderson, Louisa A. (Herb) 169
Anderson, Louisa J. (Austin) 245
Anderson, M. J. (Wilkins) (Patrick) 72
Anderson, Mag. G. (Wilson) 13
Anderson, Marietta R. (Peacock) 59
Anderson, Mary A. (Hemphill) 37
Anderson, Mary C. (Scott) 76
Anderson, Mary E. (Mathews) 246
Anderson, Mary E. (Robinson) 83
Anderson, Mary T. (Haddock) 220
Anderson, Melvina (Cartwright) 30
Anderson, Nannie A. M. (Lindley) 164
Anderson, Robert J. 16
Anderson, Rosa B. (Gallagher) 199
Anderson, Rosa M. (Bass) 43
Anderson, S. A. 164
Anderson, Sallie E. (Jeannerett) 229
Anderson, Sallie P. (Marable) 81
Anderson, Sallie S. (White) 70
Anderson, Sarah (Jackson) 194
Anderson, Susie O. (Stephens) 117
Anderson, Thos. J. 44

Anderson, W. D. 261
Anderson, W. P. 270
Anderson, W. W. 45
Anderson, Walter R. 220
Anderson, William D. 288, 291
Anderson, Wm. J. 60, 187
Anderson, Wm. W. 169
Andrew, George C. 248
Andrew, James A. 37
Andrew, James O. 145
Andrew, Mary C. (Gray) 145
Andrew, Mary E. (Shannon) 248
Andrew, Susan A. (Glenn) 37
Andrew, Susan A. (Smith) 184
Andrews, Amanda (Gorton) 79
Andrews, Charles B. 207
Andrews, E. A. (Cotton) 90
Andrews, Garnett 268
Andrews, H. 143, 195
Andrews, H. S. 249, 268
Andrews, J. G. 90
Andrews, Josephine (-Broome) 39
Andrews, Lettie M. (Ashmore) 268
Andrews, Lilly H. (Williams) 2
Andrews, M. S. 46, 59, 261
Andrews, Mary Carrie (Harwell) 207
Andrews, Mattie (Hogan) 70
Andrews, Metta (Green) 268
Andrews, R. W. 2
Andrews, Rosa Lydia (Daniel) 88
Andrews, S. L. (Colyer) 91
Andrews, Sarah A. E. (Riggins) 269
Ansley, Anna (Jordan) 222
Ansley, Bettie E. (Pearson) 224
Ansley, W. U. 224
Anthony, Annie F. (Dawson) 263
Anthony, Arcadia (Davis) 16
Anthony, C. H. 255
Anthony, E. J. (Alexander) 17
Anthony, G. L. W. 5, 27, 38, 45
Anthony, Geo. L. W. 1
Anthony, J. D. 228
Anthony, James D. 17
Anthony, Mark 207

Anthony, Minnie W. (Wynn) 207
Anthony, S. 19
Anthony, Susie (Dotsey) 255
Anthony, Wm. L. 16
Appleby, Ada (Moorer) 234
Appleby, Julia (Heaton) 80
Appleby, M. T. 234
Arbery, M. E. (Goodman) 291
Arbery, W. B. 291
Archer, (Daganheart) 110
Archer, Florence C. (Mulligan) 59
Archer, Jno. B. 59
Archer, W. D. 110
Argo, Maggie S. (Winter) 171
Argo, William R. 171
Ariail, Hattie (Yeargin) 280
Ariail, Wm. H. 280
Arick, Annie E. (Collins) 156
Arick, Thomas H. 156
Arington, Amanda E. (Smith) 72
Arington, Julia (Hicks) 46
Armfield, Ellen E. (Fitzgerald) 7
Armistead, T. A. 100
Armor, Emily Raifield (Moore) 153
Armor, Lula H. (Hutcheson) 148
Armor, Sallie (Ammons) 291
Armor, Wm. G. 148
Armstrong, Alexander 42
Armstrong, Carrie F. (Johnston) 234
Armstrong, David C. 126
Armstrong, Elizabeth (McLenden) 257
Armstrong, Ella I. (Willett) 42
Armstrong, Ella S. (Beggs) 219
Armstrong, Emma (Miller) 125
Armstrong, Harriet L. (Ray) 43
Armstrong, J. K. 74, 75
Armstrong, James M. 52, 140
Armstrong, Susie R. (Harris) 126
Armstrong, Thomas K. 234
Armstrong, Wm. 257
Arnold, Asbury H. 79
Arnold, C. W. 118
Arnold, Charles W. 117
Arnold, Daniel W. 123

Arnold, Elizabeth S. (Nowell) 204
Arnold, Ellen A. (Simms) 79
Arnold, F. M. 78
Arnold, Hattie (Dillard) 241
Arnold, Henry 131
Arnold, J. N. 109
Arnold, James W. 241
Arnold, Julia (Walker) 10
Arnold, Keran J. (Hames) 123
Arnold, L. (Smith) 32
Arnold, Lewis 140
Arnold, M. E. (Pugeley) 66
Arnold, M. W. 57
Arnold, Maggie (Burnsides) 78
Arnold, Martha W. (Young) 117
Arnold, Mattie (Wiseman) 118
Arnold, Miles W. 204
Arnold, Minnie L. (Colbert) 190
Arnold, Monterey (Houston) 11
Arnold, P. O. (Dodson) 199
Arnold, S. G. (Post) 57
Arnold, S. J. 194
Arnold, Sallie A. (Botts) 140
Arnold, Samuel J. 11
Arnold, Sarah C. (Moss) 109
Arnold, Wm. 66
Arnold, Zephie (Evans) 131
Arnow, Josephine (Flowers) 29
Arrington, Alice S. (Beckum) 257
Arrington, E. (Williams) 19
Arrington, George P. 290
Arrington, Lucy A. (Avert) 290
Arrington, R. R. 19
Arthur, 168
Arthur, Mary (Harrison) 66
Arthur, Z. J. 66
Arwood, M. C. 161
Arwood, Tabitha J. (Smith) 161
Ash, E. Jane (Ledford) 124
Ashford, Alexander W. 153
Ashford, Jennie (Kirkpatrick) 119
Ashford, Loula (Knight) 153
Ashford, W. T. 119
Ashley, Sue M. (Staples) 244
Ashmore, J. (Hardy) 70
Ashmore, J. Sloeman 268

Ashmore, Lettie M. (Andrews) 268
Ashmore, Wesley 268
Askew, Anna H. (Dodson) 199
Askew, J. J. 199
Askew, John L. 162
Askew, L. V. (Meriwether) 162
Askew, Mollie C. (Burgess) 3
Askew, N. I. (Bellah) 94
Askin, Isaac H. 47, 186
Askin, Lou (Williams) 47
Askin, M. Mattie (Hogan) 186
Asles, Mattie (Oswalt) 218
Athon, N. 234
Athons, N. 83
Atkins, Marian F. (King) 131
Atkins, Wm. T. 131
Atkinson, E. A. (Gordon) 153
Atkinson, Robert 153
Atkinson, Sallie A. (Davenport) 24
Atkison, Jennie (Johnson) 153
Atkison, S. D. 153
Atson, Corra (Colley) 83
Attaway, A. B. (Hartzog) 201
Attaway, Emma (Barnett) 138
Attaway, Gertrude (Dukes) 147
Atwater, Antoinett E. (Respress) 106
Atwater, Jas. W. 106
Atwell, Gussie (Hall) 246
Atwell, John 246
Atwell, Sarah (Bradley) 72
Auld, F. 19, 54, 69, 84, 87, 92, 103, 108, 149, 150, 151, 154
Aultman, A. H. 276
Aultman, Anna E. (Browning) 276
Aultman, Laura (Long) 139
Austell, Ophelia M. (Gorman) 58
Austin, Davis 289
Austin, Davis N. 245
Austin, G. W. 262
Austin, Harriet (Lawson) 260
Austin, J. M. 9, 11, 35, 52, 57, 62, 137, 243, 244, 248, 272
Austin, Julia J. (Benton) 262
Austin, Kate (Owens) 287

Austin, Louisa J. (Anderson) 245
Austin, Mary J. (Zeigler) 87
Austin, Missouri (Crout) 289
Austin, N. (Allen) 183
Autry, Cordelia A. (Jones) 120
Avant, F. A. 228
Avant, I. L. 27, 43, 47, 54, 56, 77, 79, 87, 93, 111, 122, 134, 139, 145
Avant, J. L. 35
Avant, J. W. 145
Avant, Mary E. (Gaddy) 220
Avant, Prusia A. (Florid) 228
Avary, J. C. 58
Avary, Mattie A. (Flanigan) 48
Avary, Sallie (Howard) 58
Aven, Emma G. (Moore) 196
Aven, Wm. G. 196
Avera, B. F. 35
Avera, Missouri (Lewis) 35
Averett, George W. 136
Averett, Mattie J. (Wattles) 136
Avert, F. A. 290
Avert, J. W. 290
Avert, Lucy A. (Arrington) 290
Avery, Ambrose J. 206
Avery, Elizabeth 50
Avery, James 50
Avery, Laura J. (Carter) 50
Avery, M. E. (Peed) 281
Avery, Mattie S. (Magruder) 206
Avinger, A. P. 94
Avinger, M. E. (Shuler) 94
Avret, Mary L. T. (Day) 140
Avry, Ann (Byrun) 15
Avry, James V. 15
Aycock, Della (Hillsman) 238
Aycock, Nancy E. (Pattillo) 106
Aycock, Richard B. 238
Aycock, Virginia W. (King) 295
Aycock, William B. 295
Ayers, John M. 212
Ayers, Sarah (Hair) 212
Babb, A. S. 115
Babb, Ella (Simmons) 115
Babb, Mary A. (Muckenfuss) 234
Babcock, Mary Norton (Matthews) 120

Babcock,, John W. 120
Babers, John H. 285
Babers, Victoria L. (Jennings) 285
Bacon, Carrie E. (Thompson) 188
Bacon, Hattie (Henderson) 23
Bacon, John W. 188
Bacon, Mary D. (Gilbert) 154
Bacon, Mary D. (Lippitt) 288
Baer, Adela B. (Phin) 219
Baer, H. 219
Bagbey, Ella (Wood) 165
Bagbey, J. M. 165
Bagby, M. Josephine (Jones) 273
Baggarly, F. W. 2
Baggents, Amanda (Morgan) 80
Baggents, James F. 80
Baggett, Mary A. (McEachern) 81
Baggett, Rebecca (Griffith) 27
Baggett, W. F. 27
Baggs, Mary J. L. (Sheppard) 53
Bags, Mary H. (Tarbutton) 151
Bagwell, Frances (Bullard) 171
Bagwell, James J. 171
Bailey, C. J. 115
Bailey, E. Calhoun 271
Bailey, E. Catharine (Darby) 264
Bailey, Fannie E. (Dozier) 218
Bailey, H. H. 48
Bailey, Ida E. (Morton) 249
Bailey, J. A. 108
Bailey, J. H. 223
Bailey, J. P. 94
Bailey, Jennie (Williams) 146
Bailey, John C. 249
Bailey, John H. 256
Bailey, Jonathan L. 210
Bailey, L. Elizabeth (Dennis) 271
Bailey, L. R. (Embry) 165
Bailey, Lizzie (Twitty) 276
Bailey, M. N. (Sharp) 124
Bailey, Margaret R. (McCay) 110
Bailey, Martha Julia (Newton) 39
Bailey, Mary C. (Smith) 256
Bailey, Mary S. (Minter) 223

Bailey, Mattie (Embry) 115
Bailey, N. A. (Sewell) 108
Bailey, S. B. 165
Bailey, S. Elizabeth (McKay) 74
Bailey, S. Malinda (Jones) 210
Bailey, Sallie (Robertson) 48
Bailey, T. J. 264
Bailey, Thomas M. 218
Bailey, W. A. 146
Bailey, W. C. 173
Baily, Bethia (Jenkins) 136
Baily, Correna (Marbutt) 6
Baily, F. C. H. (Brown) 66
Baily, F. O. 66
Baily, Joseph 136
Baily, Louis 6
Baily, Malodia M. (Wilkinson) 137
Baily, William C. 137
Bain, Ella E. (Cook) 196
Bain, Henly E. 196
Bainaird, Calder 271
Bains, C. J. 31
Bains, S. E. (Stripling) 31
Baker, A. B. 239
Baker, A. S. 141
Baker, Addie A. (Bassett) 163
Baker, Alice (McWilliams) 215
Baker, Allen 136
Baker, Amanda (Dukes) 264
Baker, Arah R. (Eady) 151
Baker, Camila Ann (Tremble) 174
Baker, Fannie (Bates) 239
Baker, Fannie (Eady) 188
Baker, Fannie A. (Kernson) 171
Baker, Fannie A. (Newsom) 169
Baker, Frances M. (Seay) 80
Baker, Georgia (Chastain) 239
Baker, J. S. 188
Baker, J. W. 258, 264, 272
Baker, James 170
Baker, James P. 163
Baker, James S. 58, 151
Baker, John Major 174
Baker, John T. 80
Baker, Julia (Rogers) 258
Baker, Julius 19
Baker, Lizzie (Tatum) 151
Baker, Lizzie (Wade) 141
Baker, M. C. (Pyles) 136
Baker, Marcus S. 169, 171

Baker, Margaret Walker (Wright) 170
Baker, Martha M. J. (Smith) 72
Baker, Mattie (Manson) 24
Baker, N. M. (Sewell) 19
Baker, Nannie (Stone) 58
Baker, Nannie S. (Miller) 110
Baker, Samuel 72
Baker, W. S. 20, 31, 33, 84, 161, 179, 260
Baker, William E. 215
Baldwin, Andrew J. 108
Baldwin, B. J. 7, 100
Baldwin, Berta (Crouch) 108
Baldwin, C. P. 280
Baldwin, Clara S. (Hardaway) 108
Baldwin, E. Burke 108
Baldwin, E. S. 265
Baldwin, Kate (Wright) 265
Baldwin, M. C. (Berry) 280
Balkcom, Alexander 108
Balkcom, Josephene E. (Warren) 108
Ball, S. L. (Halliday) 230
Ball, Sallie R. (Saxon) 292
Ballad, Mary K. (Hux) 79
Ballar, Nancy (Burke) 12
Ballar, Rob't Pollok 12
Ballard, David 41
Ballard, Dora E. (Jones) 235
Ballard, Edward D. 44
Ballard, Leona (Pope) 41
Ballard, Maggie (Johnston) 44
Ballew, Cattie (Gruber) 64
Ballew, D. L. 6
Ballew, Joseph B. 64
Ballew, Nannie M. (Franks) 6
Ballington, C. S. (Cato) 262
Ballune, John 229, 230
Bamberg, Julia P. (Hooten) 251
Banister, Carrie C. (Breland) 260
Banister, J. L. 212
Banister, L. H. (Johnson) 212
Banister, Watts S. 260
Banks, D. M. 81, 140, 166, 174, 192, 193, 227, 257, 293
Banks, Ella K. (Woodruff) 184
Banks, Ella Lou (Wannamaker) 274
Banks, H. J. 193
Banks, J. W. 184
Banks, John J. 227

Banks, Lavinia Seibels 176
Banks, M. L. 130, 209, 231, 262, 274, 286, 290
Banks, Mattie A. (Cotton) 227
Banks, N. P. 174
Banks, Sallie F. (Franklin) 81
Banks, Sallie H. (Tarver) 174
Banks, Sallie K. (Tarver) 193
Bankston, G. Josephine (Johnson) 133
Bankston, Henry 31
Bankston, Nancy E. (Hellings) 31
Banneau, Fannie J. (Davis) 286
Banneau, S. J. 286
Banner, Hattie R. (Heath) 232
Banner, W. H. 232
Banton, Viola M. (Dicken) 158
Barber, Abbie B. (McRae) 149
Barber, Jas. R. 65
Barber, Lou (Wood) 65
Barber, Missouri (Downs) 272
Barber, R. W. 214, 215, 272
Barber, Samuel H. 149
Barco, A. T. 23
Barefield, Jane (Joiner) 21
Barentine, Adam (Liles) 79
Barentine, D. 79
Barfield, Frances E. (Ogletree) 117
Barfield, H. H. 16
Barfield, John J. 64
Barfield, Martha A. L. (McGehee) 64
Barfield, Possie (Bradford) 236
Barfield, W. P. (Carrol) 16
Barfield, William N. 117
Barineau, Lizzie E. (Howren) 27
Barineau, S. J. 27
Barker, A. R. 144
Barker, Dora (Lovejoy) 278
Barker, F. M. (Hickman) 144
Barker, G. W. 80
Barker, Mollie (Shine) 159
Barker, R. P. (Riley) 92
Barker, S. E. (Bates) 92
Barker, T. N. 278
Barkesdale, B. R. 25
Barkesdale, E. C. (Crawford) 25

Barksdale, Mollie E. (Fortson) 224
Barn, L. B. 47
Barnes, (Grant) 119
Barnes, A. H. 56
Barnes, C. B. (Powledge) 250
Barnes, Cornelia (Utsey) 243
Barnes, Elizabeth (Peddy) 33
Barnes, Elizabeth (Hayman) 259
Barnes, Fannie (Low) 56
Barnes, J. C. 250
Barnes, J. F. 259
Barnes, Laura M. (Evans) 18
Barnes, Margaret (Poage) 201
Barnes, Martha O. (Hines) 210
Barnes, Mary D. (Pyles) 192
Barnes, Norie (Denham) 22
Barnes, Rebecca (Felkel) 53
Barnes, Rosa (Hammond) 214
Barnes, S. V. (Woods) 191
Barnes, Sam. 119
Barnes, Sarah E. (McDonald) 227
Barnes, Sherod Henrey 227
Barnes, W. H. H. 22
Barnes, Wiley 214
Barnett, A. 199
Barnett, A. A. 265
Barnett, A. W. 205
Barnett, Addie V. (Mercer) 247
Barnett, Adella A. (Conner) 205
Barnett, Annie E. (Boyd) 243
Barnett, Elizabeth D. (Colquitt) 51
Barnett, Emma (Attaway) 138
Barnett, Ida (Bohannan) 95
Barnett, Ida (Hill) 199
Barnett, John E. 138
Barnett, M. A. C. (Byers) 246
Barnett, R. H. 152, 160
Barnett, T. R. 71, 81
Barnett, William A. 247
Barnette, Wm. 244
Barnhart, Anna (Stephens) 104
Barnhart, John E. 104
Barr, 52
Barr, H. D. 129
Barr, J. W. 154

Barr, Mary A. (Muckenfuss) 234
Barr, Mary I. (Pratt) 239
Barr, N. A. E. (Evans) 257
Barr, Sue M. (McCulley) 129
Barr, Tresa (Jones) 148
Barr, Victoria (Leonard) 38
Barr, W. H. 257
Barrett, Carrie C. 103
Barrett, Daniel D. 113
Barrett, Elizabeth A. (Wallace) 103
Barrett, Emma (Rose) 61
Barrett, Lula L. (Carter) 216
Barrett, Mary J. (Webster) 113
Barrett, Mary Jane (Dickson) 143
Barrett, Orie (Boyd) 241
Barrett, S. J. 261
Barrett, Sallie (Smith) 113
Barrett, W. J. 216
Barrett, Y. P. (McKnight) 261
Barrington, S. J. (Bartley) 33
Barron, Fannie (Tiley) 203
Barron, J. R. 203
Barron, S. A. (Chaffin) 227
Barron, Sarah M. (Smith) 221
Barrow, C. R. (Sewell) 221
Barrow, E. M. (Peacock) 283
Barrow, Ella P. (Spalding) 188
Barrow, Hugh V. 274
Barrow, J. M. 283
Barrow, J. T. 221
Barrow, Jennie (Turner) 118
Barrow, Mary E. (McLin) 274
Barrow, Pope 115
Barrow, Thomas A. 118
Barry, Eliza J. (Allison) 100
Barry, Mary (Persons) 60
Barry, Mattie (Brown) 60
Barry, Osgood A. 100
Bars, (Waters) 73
Barsey, L. E. (Harnage) 60
Bartlett, Florence (Alden) 124
Bartlett, Hattie M. (Evans) 139
Bartlett, P. M. 124
Bartlette, Jas. L. 235
Bartley, Anna (Cole) 8
Bartley, C. G. 11
Bartley, M. L. 33
Bartley, O. G. 8

Bartley, S. J. (Barrington) 33
Barton, Agness (Smith) 28
Barton, Cynthia A. (Hood) 28
Barton, D. R. 166
Barton, Donald W. 151
Barton, E. (Oglevie) 29
Barton, Elizabeth W. (McMichael) 151
Barton, Eugenia C. (Etta) 63
Barton, Fannie R. 103
Barton, James T. 140
Barton, Mary (Raysor) 107
Barton, Mary S. (Rivers) 16
Barton, Nannie S. (Hodges) 84
Barton, Robt. T. 16
Barton, Savannah A. (Lawrence) 8
Barton, Theophilus F. 107
Barton, Thos. B. 28
Barwick, Elizabeth E. (Leavel) 78
Basford, Mary A. (Benson) 58
Bashlor, J. L. (Maxey) 278
Bashlor, Z. L. 278
Baskin, James 134
Baskin, Joseph E. 82
Baskin, Laney (Stuckey) 82
Baskin, Rhoda (Bledsoe) 134
Bass, Alexander 274
Bass, Ann E. (Coleman) 40
Bass, Baker A. 191
Bass, Carrie Grabilla (Moate) 40
Bass, E. W. (Truett) 6
Bass, Eliza (Bradley) 274
Bass, Ella (McKinnon) 191
Bass, George P. 232
Bass, Jonna C. (Dorman) 274
Bass, Josian 134
Bass, Margaret M. (Sterling) 68
Bass, Mary (Inman) 76
Bass, Mattie W. (McCoy) 134
Bass, Milton 40, 68
Bass, Minnie (Cox) 232
Bass, Missouri (Hollman) 147
Bass, Patrick 274
Bass, Rosa M. (Anderson) 43
Bass, Rufus W. 147
Bass, W. B. 43
Bass, W. C. 13, 44, 57, 60, 62, 122, 135, 158, 200, 205, 212, 278

Bass, Wm. C. 57
Bassett, Addie A. (Baker) 163
Bassett, S. E. 150, 221, 222
Baston, Adella E. (Denny) 193
Baston, W. H. 193
Batchelor, J. Adella (Clifford) 245
Bateman, Daniel 55
Bateman, Daniel D. 184
Bateman, J. 220
Bateman, Jane (Whitehead) 55
Bateman, M. C. (Scovill) 288
Bateman, Mary C. (Birch) 184
Bateman, Mittie (Mathews) 87
Bates, Annie (Redfearn) 50
Bates, Asa S. 277
Bates, Bettie J. (Brown) 7
Bates, Eliza C. (Dibble) 66
Bates, Eugenia (Herrington) 56
Bates, F. A. (Crawford) 60
Bates, Fannie (Baker) 239
Bates, J. B. 92
Bates, J. F. 56
Bates, J. K. 50
Bates, Jno. W. 251
Bates, Lilly E. (Wannamaker) 255
Bates, Lou (Hoyl) 49
Bates, Lucius Bellinger 217
Bates, Luther B. 239
Bates, M. W. 60
Bates, Mamie M. (Clancy) 277
Bates, Martha A. (Smith) 251
Bates, Mary A. (Pemberton) 68
Bates, Minnie B. (Wannamaker) 141
Bates, Ollie S. (Mayton) 192
Bates, R. J. 7
Bates, R. W. 66, 68, 255
Bates, S. E. (Barker) 92
Bates, Sallie E. (McCants) 217
Bates, Sarah E. (Hughes) 3
Bates, W. T. C. 141
Bates, Wilson M. 3
Battey, Grace (Bayard) 79
Battle, Elizabeth (Brooks) 105
Battle, Ellen T. (Adams) 277
Battle, Laura A. (McLester) 161

Battle, Mollie S. (Cargill) 209
Battle, Pulaski E. 277
Battle, Thomas 218
Battles, Leila (Pennington) 218
Batton, Ida (Smith) 156
Batton, Rodolph 156
Batts, Sophia (Scott) 10
Baugh, Ella (Hudson) 200
Baughn, Mattie E. (Sheffield) 242
Baughn, V. B. 242
Baxley, Nancy J. (Thornton) 35
Baxter, A. M. 90
Baxter, Bettie (Knowles) 57
Baxter, Eunice (Strickland) 90
Baxter, Fannie P. (Thrasher) 126
Baxter, Florence F. (Manning) 226
Baxter, George 131
Baxter, Ida W. (Hays) 85
Baxter, J. D. 193
Baxter, J. H. 110, 112, 113, 118, 214
Baxter, James H. 126
Baxter, S. M. 141
Baxter, V. R. (Walker) 193
Baxter, Virginia E. (Wells) 85
Bayard, Grace (Battey) 79
Bayard, N. G. 79
Baynard, A. C. 142
Bayne, A. F. 58
Bayne, Bettie H. (Singleton) 58
Bazemore, Anna (Parish) 139
Bazemore, J. M. 139
Bazemore, Nannie (Turrentine) 19
Beale, 70
Beale, C. Augusta (Hopkins) 70
Beale, Elvira L. (Johnson) 140
Beale, William B. 140
Bealer, Emma C. (Sinclair) 183
Beall, A. A. 20
Beall, Annie L. (Hayes) 76
Beall, E. E. (Mansfield) 33
Beall, E. L. (Methvin) 179
Beall, Emma D. (Patterson) 84
Beall, Jennie (Worrill) 180
Beall, Julia H. (Todd) 209
Beall, Louisa Kate (Hornady) 174
Beall, M. E. (Ridley) 53

Beall, Mattie J. (Hughes) 20
Beall, Mittie (Watts) 188
Beall, Robert 76
Beall, Sue J. (Johnson) 109
Beall, Thomas N. 180
Beall, Walter F. 109
Beamgard, George 269
Beamgard, Ollie (Bird) 269
Bean, Emma B. (Mays) 39
Bean, Nancy (Speer) 168
Beard, Eliza L. (Dean) 236
Beard, H. C. 159
Beard, John F. 236
Beard, Laura (Best) 10
Beard, Mary E. (Douglass) 281
Beard, Wm. H. 10
Bearden, Emma V. (Rhodes) 179
Bearden, Fannie J. (Herbert) 107
Bearden, Mattie (Cochran) 202
Bearden, Thomas W. 202
Beardin, Aaron E. 76
Beardin, Eliza J. (Langford) 76
Beasley, Goodwyn (Myrick) 279
Beasley, J. G. 279
Beasley, J. S. 151, 184
Beasly, Adwina (Dubose) 173
Beasly, Jas. S. 173
Beason, Isaac W. 207
Beason, Mary Lou (Walker) 207
Beaton, Florence S. (Holsendorf) 269
Beaton, James C. 269
Beaton, Jane E. (Sparks) 183
Beaton, John W. 183
Beatty, Mary Louise (Todd) 280
Beatty, Thos. S. 280
Beaty, Ann E. (Causcy) 28
Beaty, B. J. (Collins) 157
Beaty, B. Lewis 13
Beaty, E. R. 157
Beaty, F. C. (Guiton) 30
Beaty, Fannie C. (Grissette) 13
Beaty, James 280
Beaty, James L. 17
Beaty, Julia E. (McCracken) 28
Beaty, LeRoy F. 245, 252, 276
Beaty, M. C. 13
Beaty, Mary B. (Cobb) 17

Beaty, Mary E. (Burroughs) 13
Beaty, Sallie H. (Walker) 114
Beaty, Samuel S. 13
Beavers, Elbert 15
Beavers, Ella (Newton) 158
Beavers, Mary N. (Simes) 15
Bebee, B. W. 230
Bebee, Ella M. (Waldhour) 230
Beck, 40
Beckham, Alice E. (King) 247
Beckham, Cora A. (Fifer) 228
Beckham, M. J. 228
Beckham, Narcissa S. (Frank) 227
Beckman, Dora A. (Hancock) 15
Beckman, J. S. 15
Beckum, Alice S. (Arrington) 257
Beckum, Elizabeth (Penington) 172
Beckum, John W. 257
Beckum, R. J. 172
Beckwith, G. C. (Tucker) 45
Beckwith, L. B. 235
Beckwith, L. R. 235
Beckwith, S. E. M. (Davis) 31
Beckwith, Sallie F. (Brabham) 235
Becton, J. W. 141
Becton, Martha (Rodgers) 141
Bedell, Ann (Manes) 48
Bedell, Emma J. (Moss) 220
Bedell, Georgia A. (Clower) 59
Bedell, Laura P. (Murphy) 107
Bedell, Mary E. (Lynch) 55
Bedenbaugh, Levi 254
Bedingfield, C. A. 215
Bedingfield, P. B. (Dawson) 215
Bee, Jos. 120
Bee, Sallie (Bunch) 120
Beggs, Ella S. (Armstrong) 219
Beggs, M. Hoyt (Pillans) 205
Beggs, Thos. A. 219
Beington, Annie N. (Richardson) 78
Beington, C. W. 78
Beiser, John 206

Beiser, Mary E. (Wilmoth) 206
Belcher, A. J. 183
Belcher, Leonora G. (Nix) 183
Bell, Catharine (Black) 46
Bell, Cattin (Edmond) 178
Bell, Emma J. (Hilton) 221
Bell, F. L. (Stewart) 180
Bell, George 46
Bell, George C. 8
Bell, Georgia (Wimberly) 21
Bell, Gilford E. 66
Bell, H. P. 119
Bell, H. S. 268
Bell, Isabella J. (Stephens) 68
Bell, J. 21
Bell, J. C. 266
Bell, J. W. 180
Bell, Jacob 229
Bell, James M. 162
Bell, James S. 68
Bell, Josephine (Brinn) 84
Bell, L. B. 86
Bell, L. R. 165, 169
Bell, Leak C. (Price) 92
Bell, Lou J. (Black) 266
Bell, Louisa M. (Crymes) 66
Bell, M. 55
Bell, M. Emma (Jarrel) 7
Bell, Mary (Lester) 174
Bell, Mary A. (Shuford) 77
Bell, Mary C. (Cox) 55
Bell, Mary J. (Lowrance) 129
Bell, Mary R. (Gardner) 119
Bell, Mattie P. (Duncan) 8
Bell, Nancy (Roberson) 144
Bell, Nannie (Miller) 157
Bell, Sallie E. (Powell) 290
Bell, Sarah (Johnson) 7
Bell, Sarah L. (Winfery) 162
Bell, Savannah (Brown 82
Bell, Van 290
Bell, W. B. 204
Bell, W. S. 7
Bell, Wiley K. 157
Bell, Wm. V. 144
Bella, Rosa (Gregorie) 156
Bellah, I. S. 94
Bellah, Morgan 4, 67, 84, 281
Bellah, N. I. (Askew) 94
Bellah, S. J. 133
Bellah, Samuel 17
Bellamy, M. C. (Clower) 244
Bellotte, Mary (Milam) 164

Bellotte, Thos. 164
Bencher, Mattie (Allen) 272
Bender, Mary J. (Miler) 269
Bening, Susan M. (Blalock) 240
Benn, Martha (Lumpkin) 112
Benn, Wm. 112
Bennett, 218
Bennett, Anna Maria (Holland) 55
Bennett, B. O. 261
Bennett, Charles F. 292
Bennett, Dallas M. 55
Bennett, Ella (Bennett) 261
Bennett, Florence (Maudeville) 57
Bennett, J. A. R. 57
Bennett, James 256
Bennett, Joseph 261
Bennett, Lamira M. (Leonard) 261
Bennett, Mary E. (Johnson) 156
Bennett, Mary M. (Freeney) 292
Bennett, Octavia (Crosswell) 256
Bennett, Talitha C. (Fleck) 273
Benning, Carrie A. (Carter) 107
Benning, Pattie M. (Crawford) 93
Benning, Thomas E. 93
Benson, Alice E. (Adams) 153
Benson, B. K. 58
Benson, Callie (Cary) 90
Benson, E. B. 153
Benson, J. C. 15
Benson, James 173
Benson, Martha (Brown) 173
Benson, Mary A. (Basford) 58
Benson, Myra F. (Webb) 78
Benson, Sallie (Laidler) 15
Benton, Julia F. (Heape) 155
Benton, Julia J. (Austin) 262
Benton, Lucian 174
Benton, Sarah A. (Johnston) 60
Benton, Willie (Flournoy) 174
Berling, Mary Jane (Valentine) 78
Bernard, Bettie (Weatherly) 15
Bernard, Hugh R. 15
Berry, A. F. 84

Berry, Amelia K. (Porter) 220
Berry, Ann Elizabeth (Devereaux) 42
Berry, Anna S. (Browning) 218
Berry, Annie E. (Copeland) 84
Berry, Edward 177
Berry, G. H. 171
Berry, Georgia A. (Good) 74
Berry, Henrietta (Simmons) 177
Berry, Indiana V. (Griffin) 21
Berry, J. E. 42
Berry, J. F. 252
Berry, J. R. 162
Berry, James B. 210
Berry, John 21
Berry, Laura (Fairy) 162
Berry, M. C. (Baldwin) 280
Berry, Maggie (Rahn) 171
Berry, Margaret (Morgan) 149
Berry, Mary E. (Tensley) 189
Berry, Sallie E. (Street) 210
Berry, Sarah J. (Rahn) 122
Berry, Susan A. (Porter) 9
Berry, Susie M. (Smith) 50, 51
Besier, John C. 274
Besier, S. F. (Crawford) 274
Bessent, Annie (Carroll) 189
Bessent, Annie E. (Rudolph) 276
Bessent, P. G. 189
Bessent, Robert S. 276
Besson, Sallie (Graves) 12
Besson, W. Eugene 12
Best, Hezekiah 185
Best, Laura (Beard) 10
Bethea, Bettie H. (McLaurin) 71
Bethea, H. R. (Smith) 102
Bethea, S. J. 185
Bethea, Thomas H. 71
Bethune, C. M. 151
Bethune, Eugenia T. (Gunn) 151
Bethune, Susan V. (Hester) 72
Betts, Amanda D. (Sims) 142
Betts, Margaret J. (Kilgore) (Stanton) 73
Betts, Wm. O. 142
Betts, Z. B. 73
Bevens, Ella T. (Rush) 97
Beverly, Nathan 44

Beverly, Parthenia A. (Stafford) 44
Bickerstaff, C. N. 193
Bickerstaff, Emma J. (Boykin) 193
Bickley, Caroline (Mickler) 57
Bickley, Mary (Bouknight) 260
Bickley, Sallie A. E. (Phillips) 86
Bickley, Simon P. 86
Biddenback, Julia 285
Bigby, Alemeta A. (Stevens) 22
Bigby, Benj. O. 22
Bigby, J. S. 112
Bigby, Lizzie (McClendon) 112
Biggers, James B. 196
Biggers, Joseph L. 118
Biggers, Julia F. (Henderson) 24
Biggers, Laconia (Ector) 169
Biggers, Maddie V. (Wade) 219
Biggers, Minerva (Cox) 118
Biggers, Ozella (Key) 196
Biggs, Daniel V. 103
Biggs, Ellen N. (Culpepper) 45
Biggs, M. E. (Goodwin) 142
Biggs, Stella Florence (Weaver) 103
Bigham, Addie (Park) 197
Bigham, B. H. 197
Bigham, R. W. 6, 37, 38, 47, 56, 63, 88, 91, 112, 141, 149, 181, 200
Bigham, S. J. (Davies) 141
Bilbro, Mittie (Pope) 53
Biles, Pauline C. (Keep) 129
Billingslea, James 189
Billingslea, Mattie A. (Tippin) 189
Billingsley, Helon (Wall) 35
Billue, Martha (Walker) 39
Billue, R. S. 39
Binford, Harriet C. (Munnerlyn) 163
Binford, Lula (Smith) 226
Binford, R. Joseph 163
Binford, William 226
Bingham, R. W. 187
Binnicker, Ruth A. E. (Cooper) 242
Binns, Mary (Fouch) 107
Binson, Laurah A. (Purrnal) 128
Birch, A. P. 191
Birch, John L. 184

Birch, Julia B. (Glenn) 191
Birch, Mary C. (Bateman) 184
Bird, Almira (Wicker) 5
Bird, Frances A. (Edwards) 102
Bird, J. I. E. 78
Bird, J. L. 4
Bird, J. W. 52
Bird, John 81
Bird, L. C. (Keebler) 3
Bird, M. R. (Hogan) 52
Bird, Ollie (Beamgard) 269
Bird, S. Louisa (Johnson) 4
Bird, Sarah J. (Bradly) 73
Bird, Susie (Bradly) 73
Bird, Tallulah (Norris) 81
Bird, U. Sinclair 241, 266
Bird, W. S. 78
Bird, Wm. 102
Bish, Henry 71
Bish, Ophelia (Dye) 71
Bishop, Albinus 241
Bishop, E. (Lewis) 173
Bishop, George 173
Bishop, James 295
Bishop, Kate (Hadley) 16
Bishop, Maggie A. (Swink) 241
Bishop, Mattie A. (Thrasher) 241
Bishop, Mollie (Harrison) 295
Bishop, Olive E. (Bower) 87
Bishop, R. 55
Bishop, S. A. (Huggins) 210
Bishop, Sarah (Dawkins) 55
Bivings, Jas 13
Bivings, Lizzie (Hathorne) 224
Bivins, D. B. 52
Bivins, Eugenia J. (Reed) 52
Bivins, Roxey (Speet) 135
Black, Alice (Connally) 214
Black, C. A. 65
Black, Catharine (Bell) 46
Black, E. Eliza (Gibson) 88
Black, E. P. (Holloway) 65
Black, Geo. H. 156
Black, James H. 266
Black, Joseph 46
Black, Lou (Collier) 106
Black, Lou J. (Bell) 266
Black, Mary E. (Elder) 279
Black, Mary Emma (Zachry) 156
Black, Nannie (Odom) 266
Black, S. A. (Colquitt) 27
Black, S. W. (Dukes) 96
Black, Susan W. (Munroe) 78
Black, Thomas 106

Black, W. S. 32, 35, 37, 59, 83, 101
Blackburn, Benjamin F. 49
Blackburn, Emma J. (Sloan) 49
Blackburn, H. A. 198
Blackburn, Jennie V. (Dickinson) 198
Blackburn, M. C. 172
Blackman, Marshall 146
Blackman, Martha (Major) 146
Blackmon, Homer 31
Blackmon, Johnnie Beatrice (Locke) 31
Blackmon, L. B. (Burton) 18
Blackshear, David S. 167
Blackshear, Pauline H. (Howard) 167
Blackstock, Joseph 50
Blackstock, Sallie (Davis) 50
Blackwar, Anastatia (Napier) 42
Blackwell, Bishop B. 170
Blackwell, Ella M. (Stewart) 170
Blackwell, Katie H. (Vail) 226
Blackwell, Mamie A. (Jones) 174
Blackwell, Martha (Sapp) 7
Blackwell, Robert P. 226
Blackwell, Thomas J. 174
Blain, Emma E. (Morton) 178
Blake, Annie (Cromartie) 12
Blake, Belle (Tillman) 138
Blake, E. L. T. 125, 206, 247, 296
Blake, James 138
Blakely, Edwin 231
Blakely, Sarah A. D. (Newton) 231
Blakely, Wm. J. 231
Blakeney, Hennie J. (DuBose) 35
Blakeney, J. M. 35
Blakeney, Mary G. (Zemp) 237
Blakey, H. M. (Parks) 242
Blakey, J. S. 242
Blalock, Alice G. (Floyd) 1
Blalock, D. 254
Blalock, Katie (Sharp) 265
Blalock, Lula V. (Stroud) 247
Blalock, Lyman H. 1
Blalock, Maggie E. (Tanner) 99

Blalock, Mary Ellen (Mathews) 125
Blalock, Mattie (Hightower) 26
Blalock, Susan M. (Bening) 240
Blalock, Thomas K. 240
Blane, N. A. (Alberson) 229
Blanks, Maggie L. (Littlejohn) 217
Blanten, Benjamin G. 100
Blanten, Lela (Marshall) 100
Blanton, Mary L. (Ellis) 120
Blanton, Sallie E. (DeLamar) 71
Blar, Fannie (Dantzler) 127
Blasingame, (Goodin) 284
Blease, Sallie (Pearson) 37
Bledsoe, Camilla (Green) 62
Bledsoe, F. M. 95
Bledsoe, Isaac 13
Bledsoe, Minnie (Goode) 95
Bledsoe, Rhoda (Baskin) 134
Bledsoe, Sallie (Rice) 13
Bledsoe, William H. 62
Blewster, 252
Blewster, M. L. 284
Blewster, Mattie (Pool) 284
Blewster, Mollie (Fagan) 284
Blewster, R. G. 284
Blitch, Homer 147
Blitch, John G. 114
Blitch, Julia (Spier) 180
Blitch, Laura (Spear) 67
Blitch, Laura M. (Young) 114
Blitch, Mollie (Williams) 147
Blocker, Lizzie (Greer) 31
Blount, Adele W. (Darden) 177
Blount, D. E. 60
Blount, E. H. 92
Blount, Fannie (Campbell) 60
Blount, Ida M. (Graves) 51
Blount, J. T. 177
Blount, James R. 51
Blount, Mary J. (Smith) 92
Blow, B. F. 52
Blow, Mollie A. A. (Knapp) 52
Blue, Ellen F. (Jones) 77
Blue, O. R. 77
Blum, Albert 33
Blum, Sarah (Weeks) 33
Blume, E. (Randall) (Bryan) 26

Boulware, Mary A. (Sample) 57
Bounds, E. M. 154, 158
Boutell, G. H. 131
Boutell, S. A. (Dale) 131
Boutwell, Geo. C. 128
Boutwell, Hattie B. Lidden 128
Bouzard, Olivia (Patrick) 167
Bowden, Annie E. (Meatcham) 262
Bowden, C. P. (Range) 91
Bowden, E. H. 239
Bowden, Fanny (King) 239
Bowden, J. M. 84, 104, 105, 209, 243
Bowden, James T. 89
Bowden, John H. 137
Bowden, John M. 64, 71, 87, 123, 151, 159, 160, 165, 185, 198, 204, 210, 213, 217, 226, 227, 228, 231, 243, 248, 251, 253, 256, 262, 271, 276
Bowden, John W. 193
Bowden, Jos. M. 140
Bowden, M. R. 212
Bowden, Malissa (Faulkner) 89
Bowden, Nancy F. (Phelps) 99
Bowden, T. P. (Timanus) 212
Bowden, Thomas L. 262
Bowden, W. H. 91
Bowdoin, Jennie (Webb) 275
Bowdoin, Julia (Pitts) 232
Bowdoin, William A. 275
Bowdon, Eliza M. (Akers) 74
Bowdon, John M. 74
Bowen, Eliza (Reeves) 132
Bowen, Georgia A. (Johnson) 54
Bowen, Jane P. (Tapper) 30
Bowen, Mary A. (Moseley) 11
Bowen, Mary C. (Fletcher) 121
Bowen, S. S. 254
Bowen, Stella (Matthews) 254
Bowen, Thomas J. 132
Bower, Isaac O. 87
Bower, J. W. 171
Bower, Maggie (Kitchens) 171
Bower, Olive E. (Bishop) 87
Bowers, A. (Davidson) 168
Bowers, B. F. 168
Bowie, Julia (Hamilton) 149
Bowie, R. K. 149

Bowie, Sallie (Satterfield) 96
Bowins, J. J. 179
Bowins, Sarah (Marshall) 179
Bowles, Augustus C. 282
Bowles, Ella (Gammell) 282
Bowles, Melissa (White) 250
Bowman, Carrie C. (Nash) 175
Bowman, Ella (Clinkscales) 176
Bowman, Ella V. (Leverett) 289
Bowman, Emma A. (Crum) 253
Bowman, John S. 124
Bowman, M. C. (Murray) 195
Bowman, Mary E. (Winn) 135
Bowman, O. N. 253
Bowman, P. G. 80
Bowman, R. Z. 289
Bowman, Robert 135
Bowman, Ruth R. (Gorden) 124
Bowman, Sue R. (Compton) 188
Bowman, W. 7, 13, 74, 175
Bowman, W. S. 33
Bowman, W. T. 195
Bowyer, James W. 273
Bowyer, Marinda (Fraser) 246
Bowyer, Mary (Burch) 273
Box, Lillie M. (Solomons) 233
Boyd, Annie E. (Barnett) 243
Boyd, C. W. 235
Boyd, Eliza (Williams) 106
Boyd, Fannie (Rudolph) 23
Boyd, G. M. 166, 229
Boyd, J. B. 161
Boyd, J. H. 229
Boyd, J. J. 229
Boyd, J. M. 2, 175
Boyd, J. William 106
Boyd, James 161
Boyd, Jane (Brown) 72
Boyd, John B. 241
Boyd, John F. 89
Boyd, Joseph 112
Boyd, Leola (Miller) 89
Boyd, M. J. (Humphrey) 229
Boyd, M. J. 51
Boyd, Maggie (Stone) 51
Boyd, Maggie C. (Jackson) 229

Boyd, Mary E. (Walker) 229
Boyd, Mary L. (McRae) 161
Boyd, Orie (Barrett) 241
Boyd, Penina J. (Daniel) 235
Boyd, Sallie (Keller) 43
Boyd, Sue (Hull) 161
Boyd, Thos. 269
Boyd, W. E. 243
Boyd, W. F. 181
Boyd, Wier 23
Boyer, Marabo H. 80
Boyer, Vivianna B. (Skrine) 80
Boykin, Bettie H. (O'Neal) 83
Boykin, Emma J. (Bickerstaff) 193
Boykin, Henrietta (Anderson) 8
Boykin, Paul G. 8
Boykin, Roxy A. (Shepherd) 8
Boykin, S. C. 83
Boykin, Susan D. (Maffett) 222
Boyleston, Carrie (Riley) 43
Boyleston, Geo. 43
Boynto, Charles E. 14
Boynto, Myra A. (Haygood) 14
Boynton, 132
Boynton, L. A. (Everette) 239
Boynton, Miriam (Tigner) 132
Bozard, Daniel G. 279
Bozard, Elizabeth R. (Funches) 279
Bozeman, C. M. 56
Bozeman, Celia Lester (Lucas) 99
Bozeman, Elenora (Ryan) 30
Bozeman, F. H. 99
Bozeman, Mollie (Jelks) 113
Bozeman, Sallie E. (Bohannon) 56
Bozwell, Rebecca R. (Morgan) 195
Bozwell, Wm. 195
Brabham, Mamie (Williams) 253
Brabham, S. J. 235
Brabham, Sallie F. (Beckwith) 235
Brach, F. A. 115
Bradberry, Joseph E. 279
Bradberry, Mary E. (Wier) 279

Braddy, Mollie S. (Harden) 22
Bradfield, W. R. 226
Bradfield, Willie Florence (Pitman) 226
Bradford, Amanda (Cob) 257
Bradford, Ann E. (Hall) 76
Bradford, Daniel W. 76
Bradford, Emma C. (Stone) 281
Bradford, Henry P. 243
Bradford, J. 213
Bradford, Joseph J. 245
Bradford, Joshua 139
Bradford, L. J. 236
Bradford, Louisa C. (Wilson) 245
Bradford, Mary F. (Thomas) 243
Bradford, Possie (Barfield) 236
Bradley, Almira (Allen) 274
Bradley, D. R. 274
Bradley, Edward 205
Bradley, Eliza (Bass) 274
Bradley, Elizabeth (Donehoo) 129
Bradley, Ella (Goolsby) 144
Bradley, Frank M. 102
Bradley, George M. 129
Bradley, J. M. 47
Bradley, James W. 72
Bradley, John C. 218
Bradley, John W. 233
Bradley, Martha E. (Rainey) 102
Bradley, Mary (Shuptrine) 47
Bradley, Mary J. (Gruber) 149
Bradley, Mary N. (Hull) 253
Bradley, Mary S. (Warnell) 35
Bradley, Mollie (Greer) 233
Bradley, Mollie A. (Holland) 150
Bradley, Nora E. (Carlyon) 190
Bradley, Sallie (Butler) 128
Bradley, Sarah (Atwell) 72
Bradley, Thos. 128
Bradly, Eli 73
Bradly, Sarah J. (Bird) 73
Bradly, Susie (Bird) 73
Bradly, W. H. 73
Bradshaw, Henry 144
Bradshaw, Louisa (Thomas) 144
Bradshaw, Mary (Downing) 176
Bradwell, Lizzie L. (Clifton) 24

Bradwell, S. D. 24
Brady, Susan A. L. (Dennis) 97
Bragall, G. A. (Newsom) 79
Bragdon, Mattie A. (Strickland) 35
Bragg, Mattie (Hudgins) 170
Braid, A. J. 152
Braid, Sarah J. (Williamson) 152
Brailsford, Sallie M. (Mouzon) 249
Brailsford, T. W. 249
Brake, L. A. 232
Brake, Sarah (McSwain) 232
Brakefield, S. E. (Harris) 241
Bram, Morris 291
Bramblett, Geo. W. 59
Bramblett, Sallie L. (Walker) 59
Bramlett, Alfred H. 142
Bramlett, Augusta W. 93
Bramlett, F. Jane (Mitchell) 244
Bramlett, Georgia A. (Hill) 93
Bramlett, J. N. 37
Bramlett, Maria L. (King) 37
Bramlett, Mary B. (Zellner) 142
Bramlette, Nonie A. (Chupp) 262
Branam, Amanda J. (Fitts) 142
Branam, Thos. J. 142
Branch, F. A. 36, 103, 111, 115, 153, 154, 186, 207, 267, 282
Branch, Isabella (Dawkins) 53
Branch, J. O. 181
Branch, Jas. O. 129, 147, 161, 190
Branch, Sallie E. (Thornton) 230
Branch, W. Horton 230
Brand, George M. 285
Brand, Georgia H. (McCormick) 284
Brand, Ida P. (McConnell) 285
Brand, J. W. 284
Branda, S. E. (Miles) 254
Brandan, A. O. (Wiley) 90
Brandon, Anna C. (Fullwood) 26
Brandon, Carrie (Woodward) 15

Brandon, D. Ann (Clower) 67
Brandon, F. T. J. 152
Brandon, Frank 15
Brandon, John W. 26
Braney, Sallie R. (Kelsey) 129
Braney, Solomon 129
Branham, Lizzie (Emery) 195
Branham, W. R. 21, 54, 78, 145, 160, 182, 192, 195, 242, 274
Brannan, Columbus M. 161
Brannan, F. M. T. 108, 218, 218, 251, 257
Brannan, Hellen A. (Tarpley) 161
Brannan, Minta A. (Edge) 209
Brannan, R. M. T. 113
Brannan, S. M. 209
Branning, D. J. 33
Branning, D. L. 33, 62
Brannon, A. M. 267
Brannon, Annie T. (Clementes) 271
Brannon, F. M. T. 65, 103, 104, 195, 203, 237, 244, 273, 275
Brannon, Ida C. (Carson) 267
Brannon, Katty (Cotton) 237
Brannon, Nannie (Bohannon) 237
Brannon, R. M. T. 223
Brannon, Sarah 168
Brant, Susan C. (Clem) 130
Brantley, Laura A. (Palmer) 194
Brantley, Mittie M. (Culver) 45
Brantley, S. J. (Johnson) 24
Brantley, Wm. D. 45
Brantly, Dora (Howell) 214
Brantly, Hester A. (Memry) 247
Brantly, J. R. 214
Brantly, Lou (Robison) 168
Brantly, Thomas 265
Brantly, Victoria V. (Vinson) 265
Branton, Catharine (Cox) 21
Brasell, Florence (Culpepper) 170
Brasell, Henry 170
Braswell, Elijah 5
Braswell, Lizzie (Calhoun) 231
Braswell, Mary F. (Meek) 143

Bush, M. A. 144
Bush, Sallie A. (Norris) 144
Bushart, D. P. 25
Bushart, Mary E. S. (Meadors) 25
Bussey, Mary C. (Clark) 281
Bussey, Sarah M. (Lumpkin) 254
Bussey, T. E. (Ware) 83
Bussey, W. D. 87
Bussey, W. K. 281
Bussy, H. T. 33
Butler, C. W. 276
Butler, Ellas C. (McDonald) 48
Butler, F. S. (Johnson) 66
Butler, Hattie (Johnson) 276
Butler, J. S. 102
Butler, James 128
Butler, Lizzie F. (Perkerson) 85
Butler, M. A. (Rives) 64
Butler, M. E. (Garrett) 63
Butler, Martha A. T. (Jones) 81
Butler, Mattie (Charlton) 207
Butler, Nancy M. (Mashburn) 58
Butler, Sallie (Bradley) 128
Butler, Sarah A. (Cox) 116
Butler, Sumner E. 85
Butler, Wm. O. 116
Butts, Harvie J. (Smith) 173
Butts, Jesse B. 42
Butts, Mary L. (Hunt) 64
Butts, Mildred O. (Burt) 42
Butts, Nannie (Lewis) 206
Butts, Sarah M. (Taylor) 175
Butts, Thomas P. 206
Buxton, Anna E. (Oliver) 224
Buxton, Leonora N. (Heath) 40
Buxton, Needham 224
Buzhardt, Carrie E. (Traywick) 2
Buzhardt, Georgie F. (Seago) 201
Buzhardt, Wm. Rufus 201
Byars, D. D. 275
Byars, Sallie (Major) 275
Byas, Agnes (Jones) 9
Byers, M. A. C. (Barnett) 246
Byers, William H. 246
Bynum, Fannie (Reynolds) 30
Bynum, John 30
Bynum, P. (Lavendor) 46

Byrd, 285
Byrd, Andrew 26
Byrd, Daniel 26
Byrd, Elizabeth P. (Mulkey) 201
Byrd, Ella (Gibson) 218
Byrd, John 41, 113
Byrd, Julia M. (Westbury) 26
Byrd, Lavinia (McNealy) 41
Byrd, Martha E. (Hodges) 58
Byrd, Mary J. (Foster) 113
Byrd, Sarah (Westbury) 26
Byrdie, Eliza Ann (Britt) 242
Byrom, Annie (Clarke) 225
Byrom, E. B. (White) 238
Byrom, Jno. S. 238
Byrom, Julia Wimberly 216
Byrum, Nancy J. (Helms) 37
Byrun, Ann (Avry) 15
Cade, Sallie C. (Slaughter) 49
Cade, Saml. R. 49
Cady, E. L. (Hair) 26
Cagle, Elijah 100
Cahn, Ed. 263
Cahn, Mary E. (Wilson) 263
Cain, Annie E. (Legg) 95
Cain, Jas. A. 47
Cain, Lee America (Warren) 47
Cain, Mollie (Verner) 295
Cain, Robt. L. 95
Cakely, Hattie L. (Pledger) 78
Cakely, James R. 78
Caldwell, A. G. 133
Caldwell, Emma (Clem) 147
Caldwell, Emma E. (Wilson) 295
Caldwell, J. F. J. 214
Caldwell, Jno. E. 295
Caldwell, Kezia C. (Coleman) 296
Caldwell, M. J. 140
Caldwell, R. C. (Connor) 214
Caldwell, R. J. (Nobell) 178
Caldwell, Sallie E. (Glenn) 140
Caldwell, W. T. 2, 21, 40, 45, 119, 125, 127, 293
Calhoun, 279
Calhoun, E. M. J. (Riley) 133
Calhoun, Edwin B. 126
Calhoun, Lizzie (Braswell) 231
Calhoun, Nannie (McBee) 126

Calhoun, Susan (Riley) 13
Callaway, Anna (Adams) 187
Callaway, H. H. 196
Callaway, J. T. 187
Callaway, M. E. (Starr) 196
Callaway, Mattie E. (Tiller) 255
Callaway, Morgan 56, 287
Callaway, S. O. 255
Callaway, S. P. 76
Callier, Mattie C. (Martin) 47
Calloway, M. 296
Caloway, Secludy (Dunn) 128
Calvert, Mollie R. (King) 212
Calvert, W. R. 212
Cambbell, Martha (Wilks) 210
Cameron, Henry C. 123
Cameron, Ida E. (Stoy) 157
Cameron, Laura (Follendore) 123
Cameron, M. A. (Ware) 119
Cameron, Walter 157
Cammer, Eliza (Dyer) 71
Cammer, William H. 71
Camp, A. Aubyn 216
Camp, A. P. 203
Camp, Annie C. (Whorton) 23
Camp, Berryman S. 2
Camp, C. D. 23
Camp, Caroline (Kayler) 49
Camp, H. 203
Camp, J. L. 126
Camp, J. M. (Stone) 126
Camp, James R. 265
Camp, Julia A. (Porter) 71
Camp, Laura (Hutchings) 216
Camp, M. (Crumpton) 265
Camp, Mary M. (Nance) 2
Camp, Mittie (Dunlap) 203
Camp, Richard 49
Campbell, 28
Campbell, A. E. (Dell) 28
Campbell, A. M. 81, 287
Campbell, A. V. (Mitchell) 205
Campbell, Anna M. (Kilgo) 282
Campbell, Daniel 142
Campbell, Elbert L. 82
Campbell, Elgivia E. (Redwine) 2
Campbell, Elizabeth (Driggers) 193
Campbell, Eudora J. (Peacock) 82

Carroll, Annie (Bessent) 189
Carroll, Annie V. (Lovejoy) 48
Carroll, George M. 241
Carroll, Jesse Y. 189
Carroll, John W. 288
Carroll, Judge 48
Carroll, Nancy M. (Lewis) 16
Carroll, Parisade (Hunt) 222
Carroll, Sarah (Roberts) 288
Carroll, Susan A. (Thornton) 241
Carroll, Thos. T. 110
Carsochan, Katie (Comer) 286
Carson, Amelia D. (DeHay) 202
Carson, Carrie E. (Cope) 245
Carson, D. N. 268
Carson, David P. 235
Carson, Eliza J. (Easterlin) 268
Carson, Hattie A. (Weeks) 120
Carson, Ida C. (Brannon) 267
Carson, J. M. (Alexander) 235
Carson, Jacob 120
Carson, Margaret E. (Goodwin) 258
Carson, Robert A. 267
Carsway, S. J. (Zone) 171
Carswell, Lillia B. (Evans) 203
Carswell, Louis L. 116
Carswell, Lula L. (Evans) 164
Carswell, Mary A. (Sexton) 116
Carter, A. (Humphries) 46
Carter, Amanda (Nelson) 11
Carter, Carrie A. (Benning) 107
Carter, Charles R. 223
Carter, Charlotte E. (Perry) 31
Carter, Edward A. 62
Carter, Elisa (Major) 59
Carter, Ella H. 68
Carter, Emma (Gedell) 73
Carter, Hannah L. (McNiell) 51
Carter, Hariet (Duett) 267
Carter, Helen (Lee) 95
Carter, J. C. 255
Carter, James 228

Carter, James H. 107
Carter, Jane E. (Rawls) 18
Carter, Jane T. (Speer) 55
Carter, Jessie L. (Bond) 31
Carter, Julia E. (Ector) 223
Carter, Kate L. (McCamy) 40
Carter, Laura J. (Avery) 50
Carter, Lou A. (Lee) 93
Carter, Lula L. (Barrett) 216
Carter, M. 95
Carter, M. E. (Brown) 237
Carter, M. E. (Lyle) 154
Carter, Margaret C. (Dozier) 147
Carter, Nannie (Hancock) 255
Carter, Nannie (Wallace) (DeVan) 220
Carter, Olivia E. (Hayes) 255
Carter, S. Augusta (Lawson) 62
Carter, S. W. 50
Carter, Thos. W. 147
Carter, W. C. 55
Carter, W. M. 237
Cartledge, Robert 143
Cartledge, Sarah (Brazell) 143
Cartwright, Melvina (Anderson) 30
Carwell, C. Van (Murphy) 67
Carwell, H. 67
Cary, A. H. (Malsby) 223
Cary, Amy L. (Brusse) 278
Cary, C. C. 197, 241, 252
Cary, Callie (Benson) 90
Cary, Clement C. 90, 224, 269, 274, 278
Cary, I. F. 269
Cary, Martha E. (Moore) 190
Cary, Wm. 190
Casey, Ann (Holly) 4
Casey, Salina A. (McCrary) 76
Cash, S. (Mixon) 247
Cash, W. 247
Cashon, Alice (Williams) 186
Caskill, Mary E. (Rambo) 277
Cassady, Bettie (Strange) 94
Cassady, Elbert S. 94
Cassidy, J. J. 115
Castlen, Juliet (Harrison) 250
Castlen, Macellus 250
Caswell, Lou E. (McDade) 137

Caswell, M. M. 79, 80
Catchings, Lavinia (Watson) 111
Cater, Ida A. (Rodgers) 285
Cates, Jno. H. 255
Cates, Lou (Walton) 255
Cathcart, Ida J. (Kennedy) 121
Catlin, A. E. (Churchill) 41
Cato, America (Thomas) 176
Cato, C. S. (Ballington) 262
Cato, James 262
Cato, T. W. 176
Caton, Mary (McDonald) 232
Caton, Redding 232
Caule, F. A. (Hadden) 221
Caulk, H. T. 174
Caulk, Jane (Hadden) 174
Causey, Ann (Green) 206
Causey, Ann E. (Beaty) 28
Causey, Asa 28
Causey, George W. 177
Causey, Mary E. (Purdom) 238
Causey, Sarah L. (Crocroft) 177
Causey, Wiliam R. 238
Causseaux, Edney (Ferrell) 136
Causseaux, Eliza (Anderson) 136
Causseaux, Elizabeth (Ferrell) 136
Causseaux, S. K. 136
Causseaux, Wm. W. 136
Cauthen, A. J. 1, 6, 41, 42, 62, 72, 76, 119, 123, 142, 168, 176, 178, 193, 201, 219, 227, 237, 243, 258, 285, 295
Cauthen, Emmie B. (Jennings) 295
Center, Marion (Gibson) 63
Center, T. R. 63
Chadwick, M. K. 3
Chadwick, Salina (Harris) 3
Chaffin, E. G. 227
Chaffin, M. A. A. (Justiss) 190
Chaffin, S. A. (Barron) 227
Chafin, Mary (Drinkard) 250
Chafin, Robert 250
Chairs, Clara (McQueen) 11
Chairs, Livinia J. (Jones) 51
Chairs, Thos E. 11
Chalker, Mollie (Brinkley) 204
Chamberlain, Jane (Fallin) 69
Chamberlain, R. 69

Chamberlain, Virginia (Montgomery) 72
Chambers, A. M. (Foster) 49
Chambers, Balzona (McDonald) 189
Chambers, Bettie (Prater) 245
Chambers, Edward P. 215
Chambers, Fannie C. (Gramling) 50
Chambers, Georgia C. (Riley) 215
Chambers, J. 51, 60, 61, 99, 171
Chambers, J. W. 245
Chambers, Joseph 182
Chambers, M. A. (Gillespie) 259
Chambers, Martha B. (Dunn) 44
Chambers, Mary E. (Milles) 182
Chambers, W. A. 259
Chambers, William 246
Chambers, William M. 44
Chambless, Fannie O. (Hill) 134
Chambless, S. Loulie (Pace) 166
Chambless, William D. 166
Champion, Amie C. (Lewis) 161
Chance, Abram 84
Chance, Dio (Davis) 25
Chance, Florence M. (Reeves) 21
Chance, Frances (Reeves) 133
Chance, L. D. J. 133
Chance, Reuben 252
Chance, Virginia E. (Oliver) 84
Chance, Willoby 25
Chancellor, L. A. E. (Allen) 49
Chancellor, Wm. F. 49
Chandler, A. M. 265
Chandler, Alice (Huggins) 181
Chandler, Benj. 181
Chandler, Julia (McConnell) 265
Chandler, Marietta (Jones) (Dodge) 64
Chandler, W. A. (Elliott) 99
Chapin, Louisa E. (Charping) 215
Chapin, Virgil A. 215
Chapman, A. V. (Farmer) 199
Chapman, Anna E. (Thomas) 62

Chapman, Colin M. (Cook) 122
Chapman, Dora C. (Swearingen) 15
Chapman, E. D. (Tondee) 256
Chapman, E. M. 247
Chapman, Eugenia A. (McNeil) 22
Chapman, India J. (Quillian) 185
Chapman, Louisa (Sinquefield) 114
Chapman, M. N. (Wakelin) 150
Chapman, Robert D. 22
Chapman, Sarah W. (Sistrunk) 41
Chapman, Talulah (Watkins) 247
Chapman, Thomas 62
Chapman, William P. 15, 114
Chapple, Annie W. (Ware) 248
Chapple, J. A. 248
Charles, Sallie A. E. (Henderson) 286
Charlton, Andrew H. 165
Charlton, John D. 207
Charlton, Mary P. (Maner) 165
Charlton, Mattie (Butler) 207
Charping, Louisa E. (Chapin) 215
Chase, Horace G. 101
Chase, Martha L. (Gardner) 101
Chastain, Adam 239
Chastain, C. C. (Johnson) 291
Chastain, Georgia (Baker) 239
Chastain, James T. 23
Chastain, Morgan E. 257
Chastain, N. E. C. (Miller) 23
Chastain, Vic R. (McKenzie) 257
Chasteen, Mary Ann (Stanley) 129
Cheak, P. W. (Scarborough) 57
Cheatham, Jennie (Lunsford) 268
Cheatham, John T. 109
Cheatham, Sarah E. (Clark) 109
Cheatham, Wm. 268
Cheeley, Mary Anna (Parham) 200

Cheney, Francis G. (Love) 11
Cherry, Fannie (Dozier) 253
Cherry, George F. 292
Cherry, J. T. 78, 87, 111
Cherry, Jane E. (Vinson) 87
Cherry, John 253
Cherry, Susie V. (Paul) 292
Cheshire, A. 169
Cheshire, Elizabeth (Knight) 169
Chesnutt, Mary A. (Whitten) 278
Chester, Margaret V. (Heath) 144
Chestnut, Euphemia G. (Wilson) 287
Childress, J. E. 164
Childress, Sue D. (Irwin) 164
Childs, J. E. J. (Alsabrook) 77
Chiles, Catherine L. (Stewart) 146
Chiles, John R. 146
Chiles, Mary Emma (Raysor) 125
Chiles, N. E. (Watson) 292
Chiles, S. G. 83, 125, 291, 292
Chipley, Bessie (Coxe) 124
Chipley, Irvine 124
Chisholm, Jno. B. 88
Chisholm, Mary A. (Evans) 88
Chitty, Emma F. (Gould) 96
Choate, A. C. (Pennick) 116
Choate, A. E. 116
Chreighton, Cynthia A. (Sturgis) 148
Chreighton, E. F. (Christenbury) 148
Chreighton, J. P. 148
Chreighton, W. S. 148
Chrietzberg, A. M. 154
Chrietzberg, Adria E. (Kirby) 155
Chrietzberg, Belle P. (Perkins) 61
Chrietzberg, Bond E. 61
Chrietzberg, H. F. 155, 201, 237
Chrietzberg, Hattie E. (Kilgore) 154
Christenbury, D. R. 148
Christenbury, E. F. (Chreighton) 148
Christian, A. H. (Evans) 166
Christian, A. P. (Connally) 20

318

Coleman, Hattie (Lake) 182
Coleman, John C. 151
Coleman, Josie (Groves) 260
Coleman, Kezia C. (Caldwell) 296
Coleman, L. C. 260
Coleman, Ludie C. (Meriman) 122
Coleman, M. W. 122
Coleman, Martha S. (Moring) 151
Coleman, Mattie (Forgy) (Fuller) 178
Coleman, N. Gallie 178
Coleman, N. H. 127
Coleman, Statie (Sessions) 65
Coleman, W. L. 40
Coley, Julia F. (Anderson) 16
Coley, M. S. (Mims) 260
Colley, Corra (Atson) 83
Colley, Josiah 83
Collier, Anna G. (Redding) 293
Collier, Dorcas E. (Fairy) 150
Collier, J. W. 27
Collier, John 44, 199, 229
Collier, John W. 132
Collier, Joseph T. 293
Collier, Lamar 44
Collier, Lelia F. (Hussey) 208
Collier, Lizzie (Whetsel) 229
Collier, Lou (Black) 106
Collier, Luta (Zachry) 44
Collier, M. C. (Lowman) 27
Collier, M. Callie (Thrasher) 178
Collier, Mittie (Woolbright) 257
Collier, Sallie E. (Wright) 132
Collier, T. F. 257
Collins, (Aldrich) 135
Collins, Alice E. (Clara) 170
Collins, Amanda (White) 287
Collins, Anna (Dickson) 153
Collins, Annie E. (Arick) 156
Collins, B. J. (Beaty) 157
Collins, Bertie Dozier 98
Collins, Edward 265
Collins, Emma J. (Parker) 275
Collins, Emma R. (Nichols) 213

Collins, Geo. L. 275
Collins, James 153
Collins, James C. 275
Collins, James D. 170
Collins, Jeremiah 135
Collins, John F. 156
Collins, John G. 46
Collins, Kate M. (McGee) 211
Collins, Lunie A. (Jackson) 192
Collins, M. C. (Wilson) 198
Collins, M. Lenna (Gunnin) 152
Collins, Marian G. (Shaw) 124
Collins, Mary A. (Curtiss) 234
Collins, Mary E. (Rountree) 276
Collins, Nancy E. (Slagle) 39
Collins, Nettie A. (Richardson) 275
Collins, Perry 211
Collins, Rosa R. (Smallwood) 137
Collins, Sarah E. (Waller) 46
Collins, Simeon E. C. 152
Collins, Stephen 198
Collins, Thomas R. 137
Collins, W. C. 270
Collins, W. J. 44
Collins, Wm. A. 98
Colquit, Bettie (Winfrey) 78
Colquit, H. H. 78
Colquitt, A. M. (England) 110
Colquitt, Elizabeth D. (Barnett) 51
Colquitt, J. A. 27
Colquitt, James H. 51
Colquitt, S. A. (Black) 27
Colson, Elizabeth (Weaver) 4
Colson, Laura R. (Frazer) 135
Colson, M. J. 135
Colton, Josie E. (Park) 222
Colville, Angie (Phillips) 291
Colyer, M. T. 91
Colyer, S. L. (Andrews) 91
Combs, Lucy J. (Smith) 141
Combs, Mary L. (Cooper) 255
Combs, S. Gebrella (Corbin) 152
Comer, Alice (Townsend) 234
Comer, F. L. 194
Comer, H. Towns 274

Comer, J. T. 234
Comer, Katie (Carsochan) 286
Comer, Mamie (Dillard) 274
Comer, N. E. (Lattner) 194
Comer, W. F. 286
Comfort, D. 116
Compton, J. D. 188
Compton, Sue R. (Bowman) 188
Conaway, C. A. 125, 164, 189, 246, 255, 263
Conaway, Christopher 177
Conaway, Laura M. (Douglass) 177
Conder, Amanda V. (Wentz) 35
Conder, Eli 35
Cone, Chas. F. 169
Cone, J. B. 218
Cone, John F. 257
Cone, Laura G. (Tarver) 257
Cone, Lula (Dellegall) 169
Cone, Mitt. A. (Hodges) 218
Coney, J. D. 96
Congore, Bella (Horton) 266
Congore, Millard 266
Conley, W. M. C. 110
Conly, W. M. C. 212
Conn, Henrietta (Miller) 104
Conn, Wm. Thos. 104
Connally, A. P. (Christian) 20
Connally, Alice (Black) 214
Connally, D. W. 20
Connally, Julia M. (Fricks) 271
Connally, M. A. (Witcher) 20
Connally, Molly (Silvey) 26
Connally, R. T. 214
Connally, Susan J. (Wardlaw) 20
Connally, Wm. 26
Conner, Adella A. (Barnett) 205
Conner, Ann (Harris) 225
Conner, F. A. 272
Conner, I. O. A. 167
Conner, M. Fannie (Hatcher) 134
Conner, Mary (Jackson) 206
Conner, R. A. 6, 23, 30, 32, 35, 51, 58, 73, 134, 157, 167, 170, 211, 249, 296
Conner, S. J. (Springs) 272
Conner, Wm. 225

Connerly, Joanna (Brett) 115
Connerly, W. P. H. 115
Connor, Annie A. (Stokes) 276
Connor, D. Benson 276
Connor, Eddie (Simmons) 34
Connor, Fannie S. (May) 287
Connor, Henrietta H. (Norris) 207
Connor, I. O. 229
Connor, I. O. A. 287
Connor, J. O. 195
Connor, J. O. A. 165, 195, 276
Connor, Julia (Westberry) 70
Connor, Minny E. (Wiggins) 294
Connor, O. A. 195
Connor, R. C. (Caldwell) 214
Connor, Thomas L. 294
Connor, Victoria (Dantzler) 295
Connor, W. J. 197
Connor, Wesley 34
Connors, C. T. 236
Connors, Ellen R. (Tompkins) 236
Conwell, G. B. 285
Conwell, S. V. (Hall) 285
Coogler, Mary M. (McConnell) 101
Cook, 67
Cook, Ambrose 144
Cook, Anna E. (Ham) 164
Cook, Anna M. (Green) 53
Cook, Annie T. (Christian) 245
Cook, Charles 174
Cook, Charles E. 245
Cook, Colin M. (Chapman) 122
Cook, D. D. 240
Cook, Donie E. (Trice) 84
Cook, Edwin A. 87
Cook, Elizabeth P. (Clements) 149
Cook, Ella E. (Bain) 196
Cook, Emma G. (Moore) 248
Cook, Emmie (Kirkland) 42
Cook, F. W. 202
Cook, Frances G. (Dantzler) 230, 232
Cook, Gertrude (Patterson) 278
Cook, J. O. A. 5, 22, 26, 69, 76, 81, 83, 104, 135, 153, 170, 211, 230

Cook, J. W. 44
Cook, James M. 66
Cook, James O. A. 31
Cook, Julia V. (Murphy) 202
Cook, Lizzie (Dailey) 294
Cook, Luther N. B. 294
Cook, M. E. (Swindall) 155
Cook, Martha A. (McPherson) 230
Cook, Molisia (Turner) 146
Cook, Mollie R. (Dekle) 180
Cook, N. G. 146
Cook, Pamelia (Harris) 144
Cook, R. A. (Hudson) 62
Cook, R. M. 62
Cook, Sallie (Williams) 66
Cook, Sallie (Melichamp) 174
Cook, Sallie E. (Joiner) 87
Cook, Saml. A. 53
Cook, Susan A. (Dicken) 115
Cook, Susie E. (Jelks) 76
Cook, Tallula V. (McCain) 212
Cook, Thomas 122
Cook, W. F. 35, 36, 75, 79, 82, 84, 91, 97, 106, 131, 240, 263, 278
Cook, Wesley 146
Cook, Wm. A. 248
Cooke, Corrie A. (Carpenter) 202
Cooke, Harvey T. 202
Cooke, John H. 13
Cooke, Mary Ann (Abbey) 214
Cooke, Savannah A. (Morris) 13
Cookroy, Anna M. (Davis) 17
Cookroy, Wm. R. 17
Coombs, James 126
Coombs, L. D. (Edmondson) 39
Coombs, Mary S. (Wimberly) 126
Coon, John 13
Coon, Sarah (Burns) 13
Coon, Sue L. (Lomas) 82
Cooper, A. G. 211
Cooper, Belle G. (Gamewell) 185
Cooper, Elizabeth V. (West) 162
Cooper, Emma J. (Clarke) 262
Cooper, J. F. 207
Cooper, J. J. 84
Cooper, Jerome B. 262
Cooper, Johnie D. 255

Cooper, L. F. 239
Cooper, Lewis S. 14, 15
Cooper, Lizzie (Florence) 185
Cooper, Lou (Ingraham) 211
Cooper, Lou B. (Proctor) 84
Cooper, Mary (Caraway) 207
Cooper, Mary A. (Lewis) 14, 15
Cooper, Mary E. (Richardson) 114
Cooper, Mary L. (Combs) 255
Cooper, Mattie (Kistler) 239
Cooper, O. L. (Hared) 40
Cooper, Ruth A. E. (Binnicker) 242
Cooper, Sallie (Phelps) 286
Cooper, T. L. 242
Cooper, Talula (Smith) 14
Cooper, W. A. 286
Cooper, William 162
Cope, Carrie E. (Carson) 245
Cope, J. Franklin 245
Cope, J. M. 263
Cope, Maggie (Salley) 263
Copeland, Annie E. (Berry) 84
Copeland, Jeff D. 267
Copeland, M. Pink 157
Copeland, Mary (McKay) 64
Copeland, Minnie C. (Hartzog) 267
Copeland, Sallie (Paten) 128
Copeland, Winnie F. (Little) 71
Coppage, L. B. (Tidwell) 2
Coppage, W. N. 2
Coppedge, Emma L. (Plunkett) 188
Corbin, S. Gebrella (Combs) 152
Corbin, Wiley T. 152
Cordry, M. L. (Little) 73
Core, D. W. 240
Core, W. D. 196
Corley, Annie E. (Bryant) 77
Corley, R. J. 29, 48, 118, 127, 146
Corley, Susan (Renew) 291
Cornell, Caroline (Hawkins) 241
Cornell, Leffert R. 241
Cornwell, Agnes (Cornwell) 117

Cornwell, Eli 44
Cornwell, Martha (Ilchers) 44
Cornwell, Martin 117
Cornwell, R. M. (Allen) 42
Cornwell, W. D. 42
Cornwell, William 117
Corpening, Jane (Johnson) 6
Corpening, Virginia (Dunvant) 49
Corry, Sue McP. (Hamby) 156
Cosby, George C. 112
Cosby, Julia (Freeman) 112
Cosby, M. J. (Stanton) 246
Cothran, J. B. 198
Cothran, Lizzie (Mitchell) 198
Cottenham, Eliza B. (Dutton) 256
Cottenham, J. A. 256
Cottenham, Mary O. (Sneed) 16
Cotter, A. B. (Fairchild) 123
Cotter, G. Hal. 123
Cotter, James L. 293
Cotter, Louise M. (Tuggle) 288
Cotter, Lucy (Glenn) 293
Cotter, Mary L. (Lovejoy) 251
Cotter, W. J. 1, 16, 18, 57, 65, 88, 92, 99, 105, 111, 115, 116, 123, 155, 164, 165, 186, 190, 197, 203, 204, 211, 221, 236, 244, 250, 251, 285
Cotter, William B. 288
Cottingham, Eliza M. (Tignor) 61, 62
Cottingham, Eugenia H. (Oglesby) 230
Cottingham, Jas. D. 62
Cotton, B. B. 197
Cotton, Carrie R. (Pierce) 197
Cotton, E. A. (Andrews) 90
Cotton, Eliza J. (Harwell) 87
Cotton, J. L. 227
Cotton, James R. 237
Cotton, Katty (Brannon) 237
Cotton, L. A. (Poer) 90
Cotton, Mattie A. (Banks) 227
Cotton, Sarah (Sherman) 184
Cotton, Thomas S. 87
Cotton, Wm. G. 184
Cottrell, Joseph B. 12, 31
Cottrell, Z. D. 80

Couch, Anna M. (Bryan) 159
Couch, Mary A. (Lee) 111
Couch, William S. 111
Courtney, Jonas 74
Courtney, Sallie (Roberts) 74
Courvoisie, E. Frank 146
Courvoisie, Hattie M. (Neidlinger) 146
Covington, Celestia A. (Houston) 27
Covington, D. A. 27
Cowan, Edward 230
Cowan, Ella (Westbrooks) 231
Cowan, G. S. 255
Cowan, Lula (Kendrick) 230
Coward, A. B. 266
Coward, M. E. (Swett) 266
Coward, Ursula A. (Gibson) 229
Cowart, Andrew A. 290
Cowart, Carrie E. (Rutherford) 290
Cowart, Fannie (Strozier) 147
Cowart, G. A. 121
Cowart, J. H. 36
Cowart, John L. 147
Cowart, M. A. (Redding) 121
Cowart, M. V. (Clarke) 214
Cowart, Salatha A. (Kimbrough) 36
Cowart, T. E. J. 214
Cowey, Martha J. (Mann) 67
Cowles, Mattie (Dennis) 153
Cowles, Nellie D. (Wyche) 37
Cowles, William T. 37
Cowley, Sarah (Sanders) 222
Cox, A. H. (Moreland) 262
Cox, A. H. 248
Cox, Annie Adelia (Bull) 37
Cox, B. B. 21
Cox, C. W. 10
Cox, Catharine (Branton) 21
Cox, D. D. 37, 55, 80, 119, 151, 167, 184, 247, 270
Cox, Ella V. (Fischer) 185
Cox, Emma E. (Davis) 193
Cox, I. J. (Mann) 148
Cox, J. F. 262
Cox, J. W. 148
Cox, James A. 185
Cox, Jessie 4
Cox, John 10

Cox, John H. 109
Cox, Katie (Fry) 66
Cox, L. E. (Kittles) 115
Cox, L. M. B. (Robinson) 34
Cox, Lewis R. 281
Cox, Lizzie L. (Jones) 161
Cox, Lottie M. (Hellams) 171
Cox, Lula (Pearson) 199
Cox, M. E. (DeJournett) 192
Cox, M. E. (Reynolds) 281
Cox, M. E. (Wall) 10
Cox, M. T. (West) 48
Cox, Martha E. (Vivins) 4
Cox, Mary (Jones) 157
Cox, Mary A. (Robinson) 57
Cox, Mary C. (Bell) 55
Cox, Mary Louise (Sledge) 248
Cox, Mary M. (Furlow) 109
Cox, Mettie (West) 191
Cox, Minerva (Biggers) 118
Cox, Minnie (Bass) 232
Cox, Mollie E. (Palmer) 88
Cox, Ophelia F. (Puryear) 123
Cox, P. Duncan 5
Cox, R. 34
Cox, S. M. 192
Cox, Samuel 157
Cox, Sarah A. (Butler) 116
Cox, Sarah V. (Griner) 75
Cox, T. 171, 191
Cox, T. Allana (Fulcher) 5
Cox, Thos. J. 75
Cox, William 199
Cox, William C. 193
Cox, William H. 57
Cox, William R. 115, 161
Coxe, 129
Coxe, Bessie (Chipley) 124
Coxe, J. T. 124
Coxwell, Victoria (Faucette) 208
Coyl, E. 9
Coyl, Louisa (Scott) 9
Coyle, Florence M. (Fife) 146
Coyle, W. P. 146
Cozart, Ann M. 132
Cozart, Annie M. (Smith) 72
Cozart, Lou C. (Harralson) 81
Cozart, Sallie V. (Simonton) 161
Cozart, Susie E. (Fraser) 132
Cozbey, Emma (Moore) 142

Crowder, Martha E. (Doster) 30
Crowder, R. 30
Crowder, Rebecca A. (Yarborough) 6
Crowell, C. A. 24, 66
Crowley, E. M. 39
Crowley, John B. 164
Crowley, Martha (McDonald) 39
Crowley, Mary E. (Thomas) 164
Crowson, Sue F. (Trantham) 151
Crum, Alice B. (Exley) 213
Crum, Benj. S. 253
Crum, Emma A. (Bowman) 253
Crum, Octavia M. S. (Rives) 220
Crum, Rosa L. (Boone) 220
Crum, William C. 220
Crumley, A. J. (Tindal) 27
Crumley, M. G. 27
Crumley, M. M. 43
Crumley, W. M. 37, 164, 192, 258
Crump, Bessie A. (Jones) 262
Crump, John B. 9
Crumpton, M. (Camp) 265
Crutchfield, Aurora M. (White) 181
Crymes, A. C. 4
Crymes, Louisa M. (Bell) 66
Crymes, Mattie (Wilson) 4
Crymes, Thomas 73
Crymes, W. M. 66
Crymes, Wm. M. 54, 194
Culbreath, Abbie (Merchant) 96
Culbreath, James 96
Cullens, Sallie (Henderson) 255
Culler, Agnes C. (Horger) 69
Culler, Anna M. (Houser) 97
Culler, W. V. 97
Culp, Benj. F. 15
Culp, Selina A. (Moon) 15
Culpepper, Ellen N. (Biggs) 45
Culpepper, Florence (Brasell) 170
Culpepper, Sarah J. (Howell) 238
Culpepper, William H. 45
Culver, Benjamin C. 127
Culver, L. E. 45
Culver, Missouri M. (Moore) 125

Culver, Mittie M. (Brantley) 45
Culver, Sallie T. (Davis) 127
Culverhouse, 281
Culverhouse, A. J. 145
Culverhouse, Jinnie (Rogers) 145
Culverhouse, L. V. (McManus) (Lowman) 281
Cumly, Ella (Maunds) 69
Cummings, Alice E. (Owens) 142
Cummings, Arcena R. (Way) 221
Cummings, Callie E. (King) 210
Cummings, James E. 210
Cummings, Jane N. (Ackermon) 117
Cummings, Lewis 283
Cummings, Richard 117
Cummings, Rosa (Cummings) 283
Cummins, Geneva J. (Green) 197
Cumpton, Carles 213
Cumpton, Emma P. (Kerkis) 213
Cunard, Nancy E. T. (Myears) 46
Cunard, Newton 46
Cunningham, Carrie E. (Hunt) 173
Cunningham, Ellen E. (Sims) 162
Cunningham, J. R. 173
Cunningham, Julia A. (Boston) 96
Cunningham, L. (Crawford) 105
Cunningham, W. B. 96
Cunningham, Wm. M. 54
Cunyers, Creed H. 255
Currett, David M. 228
Currett, Sarah C. (Rogers) 228
Currie, Geo. W. 196
Curry, A. N. 152
Curry, Ann (Hellams) 27
Curry, Emma (McElveen) 294
Curry, Harvey 27
Curry, Henry C. 294
Curry, Mary (Way) 79
Curry, Mattie W. (Wilcox) 152
Curry, W. L. 19
Curtis, 68
Curtiss, John M. 234
Curtiss, Julius T. 244
Curtiss, Mary A. (Collins) 234

Curtright, Nettie (Candler) 277
Curtwright, Flem (Gerding) 116
Cuthbert, Lucius 105
Cuthbertson, M. W. 15
Cuthbertson, Nettie F. (Wadsworth) 15
Cutter, Emma C. (White) 44
Cutter, M. A. (Davis) (Cannon) 81
Cutter, M. H. 81, 253
Cutter, P. B. D. 44
Cuyler, D. M. (Hood) 40
Cuyler, Estelle (Smith) 40
D'Antignac, 207
Dabbs, S. D. (Greer) 153
Dabney, Janes (Hayes) 106
Dadisman, L. M. 22
Dadisman, Susan (Snellings) 22
Daganheart, (Archer) 110
Dagnall, E. W. 98
Dagnall, Laura (Nicholas) 128
Dagnall, Lizzie C. (Senter) 98
Dagnall, Lizzie J. (Eubanks) 106
Dagnall, Mary E. (Hellams) 27
Dagnall, R. R. 27, 106, 123, 156, 171, 281
Dagnall, R. S. 55
Dailey, Lizzie (Cook) 294
Dailey, Mary P. (Mason) 250
Dailey, R. McKibbin 250
Dalden, Lizzie S. (Patterson) 12
Dale, F. J. (White) 18
Dale, Mary J. (Morrow) 227
Dale, S. A. (Boutell) 131
Dallas, Georgia (Gregory) 228
Dallas, Mary J. (Adams) 170
Dallis, Leslie W. 111
Dallis, Low (Leslie) 111
Damon, Louisa M. (Edmondson) 99
Dampier, M. F. (Dean) 119
Dana, Fannie S. (White) 52
Dana, Orlando N. 52
Dandridge, Mary E. A. (Verdier) 18
Danels, R. C. (Wimbush) 4
Danforth, J. R. 11
Daniel, A. E. (Lang) 126
Daniel, C. C. 126
Daniel, E. A. (Gay) 173
Daniel, E. B. 90

Davies, F. B. 59, 79, 85, 95, 96, 108, 113, 114, 122, 141, 170, 179, 203, 212, 213, 222, 256, 257, 277

Davies, L. J. 4, 7, 12, 16, 74, 125, 157, 182, 187, 215, 273, 286

Davies, S. J. (Bigham) 141

Davies, T. J. 31

Davis, A. B. C. 74

Davis, A. E. (Adams) 40

Davis, A. W. 124

Davis, Ada Jane (Dewson) 179

Davis, Adrian (Jones) 65

Davis, Alice (Evans) 63

Davis, Angeline S. (Hutto) 106

Davis, Ann E. (Harris) 37

Davis, Anna (Dozier) 253

Davis, Anna (Lane) 292

Davis, Anna M. (Cookroy) 17

Davis, Annie B. (Goodlett) 157

Davis, Arcadia (Anthony) 16

Davis, Augustus A. 59

Davis, Benjamin B. 8

Davis, Bernard M. 179

Davis, Bettie E. (Walker) 90

Davis, C. C. 155, 182, 215

Davis, Carrie (Evans) 242

Davis, Charles 156

Davis, D. D. 256

Davis, Dio (Chance) 25

Davis, E. 261

Davis, E. H. (Stewart) 40

Davis, E. M. (Moriarty) 268

Davis, Edwin T. 10

Davis, Eliza M. (Stevens) 202

Davis, Elizabeth (Nichols) 8

Davis, Elizabeth S. (Hays) 131

Davis, Eller J. (Davis) 264

Davis, Emily (Freeman) 83

Davis, Emma Aquila (Kinsey) 242

Davis, Emma E. (Cox) 193

Davis, F. B. 93

Davis, Fannie (McCaskill) 38

Davis, Fannie J. (Banneau) 286

Davis, Fannie Virginia (Lane) 116

Davis, Franklin C. 202

Davis, George W. 262

Davis, H. G. 3

Davis, Hannah E. 81

Davis, Hattie E. (Crawford) 289

Davis, Hattie E. (Wilder) 74

Davis, Henrietta (Nettles) 106

Davis, I. L. 36

Davis, Ida Josephine (Lefils) 266

Davis, J. C. 266, 268

Davis, J. O. 81

Davis, J. Randolph 280

Davis, J. W. 37

Davis, James E. 17

Davis, John 160

Davis, John W. 121

Davis, Joseph R. 201

Davis, Julia E. (Martin) 1

Davis, Kattie (Harden) 280

Davis, L. B. 50, 51

Davis, L. M. (Knight) 199

Davis, Laura (Milhouse) 256

Davis, Laura A. (Smith) 262

Davis, Lilly (Gwinn) 272

Davis, Lucy (Browne) 156

Davis, M. A. (Cutter) (Cannon) 81

Davis, M. M. 266

Davis, M. T. (Lowery) 124

Davis, Maria C. (Boland) 74

Davis, Marion H. (Weston) 160

Davis, Martha F. (Hayes) 3

Davis, Mary (Davis) 121

Davis, Mary J. (Kearing) 54

Davis, Mattie (Haws) 279

Davis, Mattie L. (Ireland) 155

Davis, Mattie T. (Jones) 10

Davis, Meriam (Freeman)36

Davis, Milton 83

Davis, Nannie (Puryear) 252

Davis, Nannie M. (Thompson) 201

Davis, Nannie N. (Dowdell) 160

Davis, Nathan 252

Davis, O. J. 81

Davis, Olivia (Hodges) 29

Davis, R. M. 31

Davis, R. W. 103

Davis, S. E. M. (Beckwith) 31

Davis, Sade Q. (Payne) 18

Davis, Sallie (Blackstock) 50

Davis, Sallie (Bookter) 148

Davis, Sallie A. (Gregg) 258

Davis, Sallie T. (Culver) 127

Davis, Sophia A. G. (Lowrey) 1

Davis, Susan (Witherspoon) 284

Davis, Thomas 63

Davis, Thomas W. 160

Davis, W. B. 268

Davis, W. Richardson 116

Davis, Walter 292

Davis, William 242

Davis, William A. 18

Davis, William G. 264

Davis, William H. 289

Davis, William L. 90

Davis, William S. 131

Davis, Young M. E. 106

Dawkins, Dorcas (Kersey) 102

Dawkins, Emily (Goodman) 93

Dawkins, Geo. 53

Dawkins, Isabella (Branch) 53

Dawkins, John 102

Dawkins, Sarah (Bishop) 55

Dawn, Rosa V. (Farrar) 155

Dawson, A. R. 263

Dawson, Annie F. (Anthony) 263

Dawson, Annie T. (Mitchell) 32

Dawson, G. H. 173

Dawson, L. E. (Anderson) 173

Dawson, Lou (Jones) 46

Dawson, Melina H. (Willett) 147

Dawson, P. B. (Bedingfield) 215

Dawson, Sallie J. (Edge) 80

Dawson, Susie S. (Mitchell) 162

Dawson, Thomas H. 32, 162

Day, A. A. 119

Day, Cynthia (Ellis) 275

Day, Frances (Stephens) 147

Day, John M. 143

Day, Julius C. 80

Day, Mary J. (Stewart) 143

Day, Mary L. T. (Avret) 140

Day, Richard H. P. 140

Day, Sarah E. (Stewart) 80

Day, Sarah J. (Vause) 143

DeCamps, Evadna (Ingraham) 34

DeGraffenreid, Pauline (Stewart) 145

DeHay, Amelia D. (Carson) 202

DeHay, Willis 202

Dickinson, M. K. (Lester) 29

Dickinson, Mattie A. (Crawford) 29

Dickinson, Virginia (Orr) 200

Dickinson, Walter 200

Dickinson, Wm. D. 202

Dicks, Frances D. (Raulason) 235

Dicks, James W. 235

Dickson, Anna (Collins) 153

Dickson, Annie M. (Ichorb) 209

Dickson, Clara C. (Harris) 104

Dickson, David 104

Dickson, J. Walter 209, 216, 236, 243, 289, 290

Dickson, James W. 180

Dickson, John 143

Dickson, Lizzie (Mostillo) 262

Dickson, Louella (Sample) 294

Dickson, Loutie (Ward) 117

Dickson, Mamie (Pechner) 209

Dickson, Mary Jane (Barrett) 143

Dickson, Sallie E. (Clarke) 40

Dickson, Virginia (Eady) 127

Dickson, Wm. C. 294

Dilk, John 258

Dill, C. E. 46

Dill, Maggie (McBryde) 46

Dillard, Fielding 241, 274

Dillard, Hattie (Arnold) 241

Dillard, J. B. 272

Dillard, James F. 97

Dillard, Lizzie (Hutcherson) 97

Dillard, Lou A. (House) 272

Dillard, Mamie (Comer) 274

Dillard, Mary E. (Hall) 22

Dillard, Mattie A. (Bobo) 6

Dillon, Mary Talulah (Thomas) 104

Dinkel, G. F. 231

Dinkel, Mary F. (Slaughter) 231

Dinkins, L. G. 147

Dinkins, Lula M. (Knox) 147

Dishroon, O. N. (Gilreath) 138

Dishroon, W. V. 138

Dismuke, Alice (Munroe) 69

Dismuke, Geo. W. 69

Dixon, A. P. 174

Dixon, A. R. (Kelly) 217

Dixon, Antoinette (Stuckey) 172

Dixon, Blandina (Durant) 219

Dixon, C. C. (Durant) 137

Dixon, David 219

Dixon, Ellen (Acock) 46

Dixon, Fannie E. (Owen) 174

Dixon, H. H. 177

Dixon, J. L. 123

Dixon, J. Lee 22

Dixon, James 46

Dixon, Janie (Stuckey) 217

Dixon, Janie T. (Campbell) 21

Dixon, John H. 174

Dixon, Mattie A. (Heys) 76

Dixon, R. W. 11, 21, 39, 43, 64, 66, 96, 129, 134, 155, 159, 180, 182, 188, 207, 210, 218, 222, 227, 247, 249, 252, 291, 294

Dixon, Rufus O. 172

Dixon, S. P. 137

Dixon, Sallie (Sanders) 174

Dixon, Sarah C. (Smith) 80

Dixon, Sophronia (Potter) 62

Dixon, Turner 76

Dixon, Wm. K. 137

Doar, Alice (Croft) 94

Doar, Edwin D. 94

Dobbins, C. C. (Herrington) 24

Dobbins, John 64

Dobbins, M. L. (Davidson) 231

Dobbins, Mattie E. (Ramply) 112

Dobbins, P. A. (Carmichael) 64

Dobbins, W. D. 112

Dobbs, J. P. 143

Dobbs, M. J. (Logan) 261

Dobbs, Malinda V. (Saterfield) 287

Dobbs, Martha Ann (Wood) 143

Dobbs, W. S. 261

Dobson, Elena (Sawyer) 204

Dobson, Elizabeth (Skinner) 2

Dodd, Donie (Vick) 264

Dodds, Lula (Ledbetter) 201

Dodge, Marietta (Chandler) (Jones) 64

Dodge, W. A. 5, 36, 39, 64, 69, 143, 165, 200, 206

Dodson, Anna H. (Askew) 199

Dodson, G. M. 199

Dodson, P. O. (Arnold) 199

Doggett, 98

Doggett, Maria C. (Pasco) 98

Doke, Zemton (Mizell) 133

Domingos, H. A. (Lassiter) 187

Domingos, J. W. 187, 188, 246, 275, 282, 290, 292, 293

Dominick, Alice (Lake) 264

Dominick, Jacob 264

Donaldson, J. T. 208

Donaldson, M. A. (Kinsey) 208

Donaldson, Maggie A. (Newman) 2

Donalson, Geo. W. 191

Donalson, Mary R. (Stoner) 191

Donehoo, Elizabeth (Bradley) 129

Donelly, S. 250

Donnan, Fannie (Wommack) 163

Doolittle, Susan E. (Brown) 187

Dooly, Mollie A. (Reed) 199

Dorman, Antionette M. (Harrison) 89

Dorman, H. 169, 210

Dorman, Hiram 89, 131

Dorman, Jas. F. 231

Dorman, John A. 274

Dorman, Jonna C. (Bass) 274

Dorns, Wm. 166

Dorough, J. P. 197

Dorough, Mattie Z. (Brawner) 73

Dorough, Nannie G. (Rorie) 197

Dorough, Rebecca G. (Parish) 41

Dorough, T. T. 73

Dorrough, Martha A. (Huckabee) 238

Dorsett, Delone N. 217

Dorsett, Mary A. (Harvy) 217

Dorsey, Dora R. (Smith) 278

Dorsey, E. L. 107

Dorsey, Edward 280

Dorsey, Mattie (Clowers) 280

Edding, Laura S. (Renolds) 102
Edge, A. D. (Marshall) 184
Edge, Albert A. 80
Edge, E. P. 184
Edge, Jane (McGinty) 267
Edge, Minta A. (Brannan) 209
Edge, P. W. 243
Edge, Sallie J. (Dawson) 80
Edge, Wm. E. 209
Edison, Elizabeth (Boling) 126
Edmond, Cattin (Bell) 178
Edmond, Gainham G. 178
Edmond, Washington 178
Edmondson, Joseph A. 99
Edmondson, L. D. (Coombs) 39
Edmondson, Louisa M. (Damon) 99
Edmondson, Mattie R. (Dart) 140
Edmondson, Z. Y. 39
Edmunds, Ophelia (Clegg) 223
Edna, Martha Jane (Warwick) 206
Edwards, 17
Edwards, Caroline Mc. P. (Kilgore) 1
Edwards, Catharine Annie (Morris) 231
Edwards, Eliza J. (Johnson) 290
Edwards, Emma J. (Miller) 36
Edwards, Frances A. (Bird) 102
Edwards, Fred D. 234
Edwards, Geo. W. 28
Edwards, Indiana E. (Johnson) 133
Edwards, J. A. 36
Edwards, J. W. 194
Edwards, James W. 231
Edwards, Julia W. (Shuler) 98
Edwards, Laura L. (Fort) 229
Edwards, Lizzie E. (Hill) 176
Edwards, Lovey C. (Shuler) 234
Edwards, Lucinda T. (Fife) 194
Edwards, M. (Bugg) 117
Edwards, M. A. (McCants) 17
Edwards, M. V. (Harris) 241
Edwards, Maggie F. (Houser) 294

Edwards, Marcus H. 176
Edwards, Mollie P. (Langford) 272
Edwards, Penn (Bryan) 194
Edwards, R. A. (Jarvis) 224
Edwards, Sallie (Millican) 28
Edwards, Sarah A. E. (Trible) 80
Edwards, T. P. 272
Edwards, T. S. 241
Edwards, Thomas A. 1
Edwards, Wm. A. 88
Edwards, Wm. G. 294
Ehney, Carrie (Summers) 232
Ehney, Lou (Glover) 221
Eidson, Annie (Herbert) 170
Eidson, Fannie Flournoy 203
Eidson, Frank W. 203
Eidson, John 170
Eidson, Rob. 126
ElRoy, W. T. 290
Elder, A. O. (Murphy) 196
Elder, Andrew J. 5
Elder, D. H. 42
Elder, Eugenia (Osborn) 24
Elder, H. T. 65
Elder, J. B. 117
Elder, J. H. 196
Elder, John H. 279
Elder, Martha (Campbell) 96
Elder, Mary E. (Black) 279
Elder, Mollie (Foster) 81
Elder, Nancy C. (Graham) 42
Elder, Robert 81
Elder, S. A. (Marshall) 65
Elder, Sarah Susan (Elder) 5
Elder, Willie J. 196
Elenburg, Mary E. (Golding) 175
Elenburg, Wm. B. 175
Eley, Fannie (Walker) 168
Eley, John H. 61, 168
Eley, Mary (Moore) 61
Eley, Mattie (Moore) 168
Elfe, Mary R. (Henly) 33
Ellerbe, Alex. W. 149
Ellerbe, Andrew J. 289
Ellerbe, Annie D. (Ellerbe) 289
Ellerbe, Mary E. (Ellerbe) 149
Ellerby, A. (Williams) 140
Ellerby, R. M. 140
Ellia, A. R. (Shaw) 148
Elliott, Annie (Ray) 203

Elliott, Lenora B. (VanHorn) 197
Elliott, Mattie (Nolan) 29
Elliott, N. C. (Ray) 239
Elliott, Nancy E. (Epting) 251
Elliott, W. A. (Chandler) 99
Elliott, W. P. 99
Ellis, A. W. 148
Ellis, Amelia J. (Haley) 163
Ellis, C. H. 18
Ellis, Cynthia (Day) 275
Ellis, David K. 160
Ellis, E. F. (Brunch) 40
Ellis, F. R. C. 113
Ellis, G. U. 133
Ellis, H. J. 79, 163, 169, 191, 193, 212, 220, 226, 243, 248, 262, 268, 275
Ellis, Henry J. 66
Ellis, James R. 120
Ellis, Jessee 275
Ellis, Louisa F. (Hunt) 160
Ellis, Mary L. (Blanton) 120
Ellis, Maryi E. (Green) 103
Ellis, Myron 251
Ellis, Ruth E. (Patterson) 71
Ellis, S. M. 103
Ellis, Sarah H. (Sheats) 251
Ellis, Susie Smith 220
Ellison, 23
Ellison, Emma E. Lanham 216
Ellison, Jennie M. (Floyd) 177
Ellison, Josephine (Herrington) 143
Ellison, Mit (Hunter) 211
Ellison, Robert J. 143
Ellison, Rosell W. (Morrow) 247
Ellison, Sallie W. (Richards) 225
Ellison, Susie (Williams) 3
Ellison, Thomas T. 247
Ellison, W. H. 16, 25, 34, 177, 225
Elmore, A. C. 156
Elmore, E. G. (Burgess) 156
Elmore, Laura J. (Weeks) 143
Elrod, Elizabeth L. (Martin) 252
Elrod, Samuel D. 252
Elroy, Rosey (Hammonds) 290
Elsmore, C. C. (Thomas) 147
Elsworth, John 284
Elsworth, Mattie (Lamar) 284

Felts, Annie D. (Rogers) 277

Felts, Laura L. (Rogers) 165

Felts, Robert L. 165, 277

Fender, Jennie (Sims) 169

Fender, Wm. S. 169

Fenegan, B. F. 132

Fenegan, Maggie (Platt) 132

Fentress, A. S. (Sessions) 71

Fentress, H. C. 71, 75, 97, 195, 239

Ferguson, John A. 192

Ferguson, Laura Eudora (Clifton) 30

Ferguson, M. J. (Weathers) 201

Ferguson, Maggie (Agnew) 192

Ferguson, Martha 30

Ferguson, Mary E. (Weems) 33

Ferguson, P. H. 33

Ferrand, Fannie (Miller) 51

Ferrell, A. M. 136

Ferrell, Edney (Causseaux) 136

Ferrell, Elizabeth (Causseaux) 136

Ferrell, Eula (Hancock) 218

Ferrell, Frances (Thorpe) 288

Ferrell, Frances A. (Lawrence) 35

Ferrell, Wm. B. 35

Ferrill, Ennie J. (Magwood) 285

Ferris, Ada M. (Britt) 100

Ferris, H. C. 100

Fersner, Ella A. (Fairy) 158

Few, Dudley (Little) 138

Few, M. O. (Stovall) 83

Fickling, Christian B. (Oeland) 265

Fickling, James 265

Field, G. M. 221

Field, M. C. (Sewell) 221

Fielder, A. D. 30

Fielder, Idus L. 210

Fielder, Julia D. (Toombs) 210

Fielder, L. J. (Wood) 30

Fielding, M. H. 41

Fielding, Sallie E. (Jones) 190

Fields, Cornelia A. (Palmer) 177

Fields, Mary (DeJournette) 257

Fields, Nora (Wilson) 196

Fields, Simeon 196

Fields, Wm. J. 177

Fife, Edward H. S. 126

Fife, Florence M. (Coyle) 146

Fife, John A. 194

Fife, Lucinda T. (Edwards) 194

Fife, Mary V. (Mann) 228

Fife, Sallie (Hand) 126

Fifer, Cora A. (Beckham) 228

Fike, C. L. 54

Fike, Mary A. (Goodwin) 54

Finch, Lucinda C. (Hancock) 187

Finch, Mary J. (Jobson) 121

Finch, William 121

Finche, Josephine (Sefers) 7

Fincher, B. H. 264

Fincher, John 248

Fincher, Joseph L. 86

Fincher, Martha A. (Hamlin) 86

Fincher, Susie (Buchanan) 264

Fincher, Virginia D. (Matthis) 248

Findlay, D. H. 170

Findlay, Lullie E. (Goodwyn) 170

Finger, J. 7, 185, 224, 257

Finger, John 260, 285

Finger, Leonidas F. 217

Finger, Mattie J. (Quillian) 217

Finlayson, John 240

Finlayson, Lizzie (Hines) 240

Finley, Lydia (Kimble) 228

Finney, Fannie D. (Bonner) 246

Fischer, Caroline E. (Horton) 44

Fischer, Ella V. (Cox) 185

Fischer, Wm. J. 44

Fish, Mamie P. (Hines) 228

Fish, William 228

Fishburne, C. C. 157, 211, 235

Fisher, Amanda H. (Footman) 197

Fisher, Cornelia (Guyton) 23

Fisher, Harris 59

Fisher, Julia E. (Guyton) 59

Fisher, Susie W. (Holt) 279

Fitch, Sallie L. (Langston) 243

Fitchett, Laura Eva (Parish) 216

Fitts, Amanda J. (Branam) 142

Fitzgerald, Ellen E. (Armfield) 7

Fitzgerald, W. H. 7

Fitzpatrick, H. H. 286

Fitzpatrick, J. B. 290

Fitzpatrick, Lizzie (Massey) 59

Fitzpatrick, M. C. (English) 286

Fitzpatrick, W. H. 59

Flagan, Missouri M. (Jordan) 50

Flagler, Alonzo W. 10

Flagler, Ella (Matthews) 10

Flanders, J. R. 260

Flanders, Nancy (Smith) 260

Flanders, W. J. 260

Flanigan, Jas. T. 48

Flanigan, Mattie A. (Avary) 48

Fleck, Talitha C. (Bennett) 273

Fleck, Wm. Barkly 273

Fleeman, Mary E. (Myer) 189

Fleming, Anna E. (Bobo) 32

Fleming, Benj. F. 126

Fleming, Donald 32

Fleming, Helen M. (Clark) 214

Fleming, Laura E. (Saulter) 126

Fleming, Martha (Wheeler) 37

Fleming, Rosa D. (Smith) 250

Fleming, Saml. T. 250

Fleming, W. H. 29, 34, 68, 69, 70, 209

Flemming, Jane (Simmons) 49

Fletcher, Annie A. (Anderson) 50

Fletcher, G. A. (Moss) 11

Fletcher, M. N. 71

Fletcher, Martha E. (Gee) 71

Fletcher, Mary C. (Bowen) 121

Fletcher, Sue C. (Turner) 131

Fletcher, Susannah (Wooten) 74

Fletcher, W. G. 121

Fletcher, Wm. E. 11

Flewellen, Mattie B. (Smith) 247

Flinn, C. J. 68

Flinn, H. J. G. (Harrell) 68

Flint, Aquilla M. 169

Flint, Cordelia W. (Agerton) 169
Flint, Sarah A. (Fulcher) 194
Flood, Amanda E. (Hinely) 12
Flood, T. S. 12
Florence, A. (Hendry) 169
Florence, Adiel S. 192
Florence, Cornelia J. (Jones) 54
Florence, Elladecia (Whitaker) 150
Florence, George W. 185
Florence, Lizzie (Cooper) 185
Florence, Mary A. (Snow) 192
Florence, W. A. 31, 82, 127, 150, 188, 251, 269
Florence, Wm. A. 54
Florid, Prusia A. (Avant) 228
Flournoy, Elizabeth M. (Fuller) 122
Flournoy, Emily P. (Williams) 94
Flournoy, Eva (Roby) 114
Flournoy, Fannie Eidson 203
Flournoy, J. M. 94
Flournoy, R. W. 74, 96
Flournoy, Sam A. 114
Flournoy, Willie (Benton) 174
Flowers, Ada (Wood) 276
Flowers, Emma J. (Rutledge) 34
Flowers, Jas. 34
Flowers, John C. 88
Flowers, John H. 29
Flowers, Josephine (Arnow) 29
Flowers, Laura E. (Brown) 88
Flowers, Lizzie (Thomson) 229
Flowers, Wm. 276
Floyd, A. G. 77
Floyd, Alice G. (Blalock) 1
Floyd, Annie (Holmes) 164
Floyd, Clara (Cremager) 235
Floyd, Eldridge M. 114
Floyd, Ella (Shuttles) 77
Floyd, Ellen (Sauls) 200
Floyd, Florida (Hammond) 132
Floyd, J. T. 177
Floyd, Jennie M. (Ellison) 177
Floyd, John 200
Floyd, Keneth 4

Floyd, Laura (Freeman) 16
Floyd, Mary F. (Lanier) 12
Floyd, Matthew J. 85
Floyd, Minnie (McIntosh) 261
Floyd, Missouri (Kirton) 4
Floyd, Robt. S. 261
Floyd, Sallie E. (Reeves) 261
Floyd, Sarah V. (Ruff) 85
Floyd, T. A. 16
Floyd, Valaria H. (Zittroner) 114
Flynt, Eugenia C. 83
Flynt, Hattie (Lester) 3
Flynt, Lilla W. (Moore) 175
Flynt, S. T. 3
Flynt, William T. 175
Fochee, Sallie (Clemm) 146
Fochee, Thomas 146
Fogle, H. A. (Folk) 227
Fogle, Julia C. (Kennerley) 117
Fogle, M. A. M. (Pfohl) 93
Fogler, C. R. (Jones) 215
Folesom, D. W. 226
Folesom, E. L. (Hughes) 226
Folk, H. A. (Fogle) 227
Folk, J. W. 227
Follendore, Laura (Cameron) 123
Folsom, L. A. 37
Folsom, Tempy Ann (Kennon) 68
Fontaine, 192
Foot, Jennie (Clonts) 290
Foote, W. B. 220
Foote, W. R. 5, 78, 83, 196, 244, 248
Footman, Amanda H. (Fisher) 197
Footman, George N. 197
Foran, A. M. (Pegg) 72
Forbes, Anna H. (Proctor) 43
Forbes, Jane (Pasteur) 210
Forbes, Jettie R. (Waterman) 101
Ford, A. S. 290
Ford, Laura E. (Mehaffey) 182
Ford, Willie (Tilley) 290
Fordham, Rachel A. (Metts) 48
Fore, Edward M. 196
Fore, Maggie E. (Haselden) 196
Foreman, Abraham 97
Foreman, Annie L. (Tyler) 106
Foreman, Josephine (Peacock) 97

Forgy, Mattie (Fuller) (Coleman) 178
Forrar, Matilda E. (Lowe) 160
Forrar, W. T. 160
Forrest, Daniel T. 23
Forrest, Susan F. (Hutto) 23
Forsythe, C. (Durst) 120
Forsythe, Collin 120
Fort, Arthur B. 249
Fort, Florida I. (Rawson) 76
Fort, Laura L. (Edwards) 229
Fort, Lucy E. (Bridges) 20
Fort, M. E. (Bridges) 22
Fort, Mollie A. (Lovett) 249
Fort, R. E. 22
Fort, W. Kirkland 229
Fortson, Mollie (Irvin) 205
Fortson, Mollie E. (Barksdale) 224
Fortson, Samuel A. 224
Fossett, W. (Lipsey) 84
Foster, A. H. 49
Foster, A. M. (Chambers) 49
Foster, Edwin T. 229
Foster, Joseph H. 61
Foster, Joseph M. 84
Foster, Julia E. (Rosser) 182
Foster, L. F. 113
Foster, Lottie (Brown) 61
Foster, Mary J. (Byrd) 113
Foster, Mollie (Elder) 81
Foster, Nancy A. (Hardy) 244
Foster, Orietta D. (Wilson) 229
Foster, Rebecca (Raven) 84
Foster, Sallie (George) 179
Foster, Wm. S. 7, 44
Fotte, W. R. 114
Fouch, George T. 107
Fouch, Mary (Binns) 107
Fouche, C. W. 55
Fouche, Lawrence 191
Fouche, Mollie (Prince) 191
Foures, A. Elizabeth (Segrest) 248
Fowdren, Laura C. (Willie) 37
Fowler, A. S. 293
Fowler, Anna K. (McWhirter) 209
Fowler, Barbary E. (McBramlet) 276
Fowler, Clandy B. (Richardson) 208
Fox, Charles T. 265
Fox, J. H. (Pritchard) 265

Foy, Ann L. (Walker) 254
Fraker, Emma (Brodwick) 158
Fraker, Mary E. (King) 37
Frank, Henry F. 227
Frank, Narcissa S. (Beckham) 227
Franklin, C. H. 81
Franklin, Elizabeth A. (Ivester) 67
Franklin, John R. 84
Franklin, Rosalie (Nathans) 84
Franklin, Sallie F. (Banks) 81
Franks, Alice M. (Lang) 176
Franks, Nannie M. (Ballew) 6
Franks, R. P. 285
Franks, William H. 6
Fraser, C. W. 175
Fraser, Colin M. 132
Fraser, E. A. (Fraser) 175
Fraser, H. B. 246
Fraser, Lewis 246
Fraser, Marinda (Bowyer) 246
Fraser, Susie E. (Cozart) 132
Frazee, H. B. 236
Frazer, Ella N. (Ross) 224
Frazer, Laura R. (Colson) 135
Frazer, Thomas L. 224
Frazier, Anna M. (Miller) 51
Frazier, Rowena (McNamee) 190
Frederick, Carrie E. (Walker) 222
Frederick, D. B. 88
Frederick, E. J. 87
Frederick, E. R. (Mellard) 88
Frederick, J. F. (Wilson) 87
Frederick, J. W. 222
Fredrick, Dora A. (Keen) 257
Fredrick, James D. 257
Free, A. C. 94
Free, Narcissus (Inabinet) 94
Freeman, A. H. 2
Freeman, Alice A. (Pearson) 169
Freeman, Annie J. (Herndon) 293
Freeman, Annie W. (Taliaferro) 94
Freeman, Arizona E. (Giles) 292

Freeman, B. Gertrude (Tackets) 218
Freeman, Eliza (Patterson) 190
Freeman, Emily (Davis) 83
Freeman, Emma G. (Snow) 213
Freeman, Emory C. (Jones) 132
Freeman, Fannie B. (Terry) 107
Freeman, Henry N. 94
Freeman, J. G. R. 261
Freeman, J. H. 36
Freeman, J. R. 193
Freeman, J. S. 169
Freeman, James F. 56
Freeman, John H. 109
Freeman, Josiah P. 213
Freeman, Josie (Williamson) 234
Freeman, Julia (Cosby) 112
Freeman, L. F. (Zant) 277
Freeman, Laura (Floyd) 16
Freeman, Leonora (Rosser) 60
Freeman, Louvinia G. (Matthews) 109
Freeman, M. (Williams) 261
Freeman, M. A. (Potts) 227
Freeman, M. L. (Haynes) 193
Freeman, M. S. 2
Freeman, Manda A. (Fuller) 2
Freeman, Mary A. H. (Johnson) 38
Freeman, Mary E. (Potts) 22
Freeman, Mary F. (Moye) 56
Freeman, Mary L. (Crawford) 212
Freeman, Mattie C. (Lamkin) 127
Freeman, Medora (McClendon) 2
Freeman, Meriam (Davis) 36
Freeman, Mildred A. (Taliaferro) 26
Freeman, Octavia (McDaniel) 231
Freeman, S. Leonard (Tutt) 123
Freeman, Samuel E. 218
Freeman, Susanna (Woodin) 190
Freeman, T. H. 68
Freeman, Thomas M. 277
Freeman, W. Capers 22
Freeman, William B. 190
Freeman, William J. 26

Freeney, Mary M. (Bennett) 292
French, C. E. 194
French, Rebecca T. (Smith) 194
Frenzot, Mary H. (Long) 152
Fretwell, C. H. 130, 214
Fretwell, E. R. (Stephens) 214
Fretwell, S. E. (Phillips) 130
Fricks, A. S. 271
Fricks, Julia M. (Connally) 271
Friday, (McCraney) 228
Friday, Cora A. (Smith) 289
Friday, Julian B. 289
Frierson, Julia I. (Hendry) 212
Fry, A. H. 66
Fry, Emma (Lane) 10
Fry, Frances A. (Niblock) 135
Fry, John 10
Fry, Katie (Cox) 66
Fryer, Catharine G. (Turner) 39
Fryer, Emma C. (Etheridge) 98
Fryer, H. C. 98
Fryer, J. R. 39
Fryer, Mattie B. (Owen) 283
Fryer, Robert C. 283
Fudge, Clara C. (Bostick) 9
Fudge, David L. 9
Fudge, M. A. (Oliver) 217
Fulcher, James L. 194
Fulcher, Sarah A. (Flint) 194
Fulcher, T. Allana (Cox) 5
Fulford, Emma (Wells) 273
Fulford, Hattie (Mazo) 210
Fulford, Samuel U. 273
Fulilove, Clara A. (Thrasher) 126
Fulilove, Seaborn J. 126
Fulkenberry, Clarissa A. (West) 4
Fulkenberry, John M. 4
Fuller, Elizabeth M. (Flournoy) 122
Fuller, F. 32
Fuller, Fanny (Trotter) 139
Fuller, Henry 178
Fuller, J. W. 186
Fuller, John E. 252
Fuller, John S. 2
Fuller, Kate (Dozier) 284
Fuller, M. (Lazenby) 32
Fuller, Mamie F. (Johnson) 283

Fuller, Manda A. (Freeman) 2
Fuller, Mattie (Coleman) (Forgy) 178
Fuller, Mollie (Powledge) 186
Fuller, Stella C. (Teague) 156
Fuller, Sue F. (Dozier) 252
Fuller, Wm. H. 122
Fullerton, Ann B. (Burnett) 244
Fullerton, William R. 244
Fullwood, Anna C. (Brandon) 26
Fulscher, Julia (Hughes) 83
Fulscher, Simpson 83
Fulsom, Susan J. (Cobb) 114
Fulton, C. V. 143
Fulton, Harriet Clifford (Townsend) 143
Fulton, John 66
Fulton, Loouilla A. (Holmes) 66
Fulwood, C. A. 3, 5, 42, 113
Fulwood, Charity (Mitchel) 130
Fulwood, Chas. A. 28, 99
Fulwood, Lillie Bell (Murray) 207
Fulwood, William 130
Funches, Elizabeth R. (Bozard) 279
Funches, Eugenia F. (Gramling) 165
Funches, J. S. 165
Funches, Mary (Dukes) 253
Funches, Rachel E. 165
Funderburk, D. A. C. 129
Funderburk, Lulie (Millhouse) 69
Funderburk, S. J. (Yates) 129
Funderburke, Dessie (O'Neal) 231
Funderburke, Georgia A. (O'Neal) 216
Funderburke, Thomas S. 216
Furlow, Charles 109
Furlow, H. W. (Gatewood) 19
Furlow, M. 19
Furlow, Mary M. (Cox) 109
Furlow, T. M. 19
Fussel, D. J. 141
Fussel, M. J. (Kelly) 141
Fussel, Maggie A. (Martin) 282
Futch, Elias H. 73
Futch, Rebecca J. (Whitehead) 73

Gable, (Tolbot) 49
Gable, J. M. 276
Gable, Joseph M. 63, 85, 129, 130, 138, 144, 167, 200, 203, 226
Gable, Josiah M. 43
Gable, Lizzie (Groover) 203
Gace, J. J. 7
Gadbold, Williametta E. (Hernder) 290
Gaddy, Dora E. (Buffington) 203
Gaddy, John W. 220
Gaddy, Mary E. (Avant) 220
Gaddy, R. C. (Lame) 185
Gadnall, R. R. 63
Gadsden, Anna A. (Brooks) 34
Gadsden, F. 34
Gafford, James 120
Gafford, Mary (Christian) 120
Gage, E. G. 18, 23, 42, 72, 75
Gailey, Jay O. 90
Gailey, Nellie G. (Adam) 90
Gaines, B. E. 198
Gaines, David R. 130
Gaines, E. P. 63
Gaines, Ella V. (Hodges) 198
Gaines, Emma (Martin) 68
Gaines, J. R. 7, 14, 18, 23, 30, 42, 44, 47, 51
Gaines, Lizzie (Quillian) 85
Gaines, M. L. (Hendrix) 269
Gaines, Martha J. (Johnson) 130
Gaines, Mary A. (Oslin) Sharp 63
Gaines, Sarah A. (Merks) 219
Gaines, Seletie F. (Dowds) 42
Gainey, Sarah (Taylor) 20
Gainey, Wesley 20
Gains, Lucy (Halley) 163
Gaither, Ella (Hargrove) 212
Gallagher, Hugh 199
Gallagher, Rosa B. (Anderson) 199
Gallemore, Dora R. (Long) 290
Galloway, M. H. 246
Galloway, Nettie (Munroe) 75
Galloway, Rachel (McCollum) 237

Galloway, Rhoda M. (Powell) 296
Galloway, Samuel 75
Galluchat, Minor C. 287
Galluchat, Thomassa (Thompson) 287
Gamage, Esther (Parker) 166
Gamage, John 166
Gamage, Sallie E. (Williams) 113
Gambell, Fannie (Paine) 50
Gambell, Julia (Smyth) 50
Gambell, L. 50
Gamble, Garphelia (Pinckard) 216
Gambrell, E. C. (Clinkscales) 89
Gambrell, James M. 89
Gambrell, Sallie A. P. (Johnson) 56
Gamewell, A. 282
Gamewell, Belle G. (Cooper) 185
Gamewell, F. Thornton 185
Gamewell, John N. 52
Gamewell, Kate L. (Bruns) 52
Gamewell, M. A. 48
Gamewell, W. A. 20, 32, 52, 59
Gamlin, V. C. (Renfro) 4
Gamlin, Z. D. 4
Gammage, Emily E. (Ludy) 68
Gammage, Isabella C. (Stewart) 226
Gammage, John 226
Gammage, Susan (Marshall) 166
Gammell, Ella (Bowles) 282
Gammon, Fannie (Tatum) 245
Gammon, Joseph E. 245
Ganann, George M. 85
Ganann, Hannah E. (Groverstine) 85
Ganesis, Elizabeth (Harrison) 178
Ganey, Susan (Bodenstein) 188
Gant, J. C. (King) 292
Gant, J. C. 292
Gantt, A. C. 207
Gantt, A. G. 113, 120, 135, 207
Gantt, A. Gamewell 209, 211, 218, 290
Gantt, Amanda M. (Reid) 132
Gantt, Emma C. (Browning) 113

337

Gardner, Carrie M. (Greene) 108
Gardner, Geo. E. 119, 280, 290, 294
Gardner, J. W. 172
Gardner, L. F. J. (Thomas) 172
Gardner, Martha L. (Chase) 101
Gardner, Mary R. (Bell) 119
Garlington, John W. 202
Garlington, Nannie J. (Crawley) 75
Garmany, Mary C. (Thomas) 83
Garner, Addie E. (Rollins) 159
Garner, G. M. (Jones) 215
Garner, Georgia G. (Nance) 160
Garner, J. E. 262
Garner, Mollie (McGowin) 262
Garner, William 160
Garrand, Willie M. (Harris) 100
Garrard, Anna F. (Leonard) 33
Garrard, Louis F. 33
Garrett, Elephair N. J. (Smith) 75
Garrett, Ellen (Gifford) 193
Garrett, Henry A. 229
Garrett, J. W. 63
Garrett, John R. 193
Garrett, M. E. (Butler) 63
Garrett, M. L. 293
Garrett, Mollie (Skeen) 293
Garrett, Sue E. (Smith) 229
Garriett, C. C. 203
Garriett, M. E. A. (Quillian) 203
Garrison, Annie E. (Hickey) 152
Garrison, Cate (Payne) 292
Garrison, Cora C. (Burtz) 81
Garrison, Howell 259
Garrison, J. A. 61
Garrison, J. B. 292
Garrison, Mary J. (Alexander) 216
Garrison, Nancy (Keplen) 61
Garrison, Sallie (Gillespie) 259
Garrison, Sarah M. (Cochran) 49
Garrison, W. I. 216
Gartin, Nannie S. (Higgins) 6

Gartrell, Emma C. (McGahagin) 44
Gartrell, W. J. 44
Garvin, Kate (Goudelock) 36
Garvis, Georgean (Railey) 163
Garwood, Fannie A. (Sewell) 190
Garwood, John W. 115
Garwood, Lou Bowie (Glover) 115
Garwood, R. B. 190
Gary, Clement C. 231
Gary, Fannie C. (Scruggs) 240
Gaskin, Allie U. (Haigler) 144
Gaskin, Rosa V. (Clarke) 104
Gaskins, Rosa (Clarke) 104
Gasque, S. K. 230
Gass, Henrietta P. (Lee) 20
Gasset, Aminda (Wilder) 145
Gasset, W. B. 145
Gassett, Winnie (Young) 168
Gaston, A. W. 160
Gaston, H. R. 233
Gaston, Lenora (Huggins) 233
Gates, Bessie (Hill) 248
Gates, E. F. 135, 153, 158, 162, 212
Gates, Mary R. (Jeffords) 173
Gates, Sam. 248
Gatewood, A. D. 19
Gatewood, H. W. (Furlow) 19
Gatlin, G. W. 111, 122, 237, 250, 265
Gatlin, M. Agnes (Ledingham) 111
Gauff, Julia (Rogers) 262
Gaulden, Laura G. (Winn) 204
Gaulden, William B. 204
Gault, Dora (Holmes) 272
Gault, Eliza J. (Johnson) 75
Gault, James 75
Gault, Worth 272
Gausey, 130
Gautier, Charles Harrod 240
Gautier, Osgood Amanda (Green) 240
Gay, 47
Gay, E. A. (Daniel) 173
Gay, James W. 173
Gay, Josephine (Johnson) 139

Gay, Julia L. (Bryan) 61
Gay, M. C. 61
Gay, Martha J. (Deas) 148
Gay, Nathaniel 128
Gay, S. Rebecca (Horton) 128
Gay, Susannah (Oseen) 118
Gay, Wm. F. 139
Gedell, Emma (Carter) 73
Gedell, Thomas 73
Gee, Gertrude (Gist) 146
Gee, Martha E. (Fletcher) 71
Gee, Reuben T. 146
Geer, S. V. (King) 230
Geesling, D. M. 249
Geesling, Elmira V. (Hurley) 249
Geiger, Frederick A. (Wolfe) 193
Geiger, J. L. (Spearman) 79
Geiger, John A. 263
Geiger, M. L. (Jordan) 79
Geiger, Sallie (Kinsler) 270
Geiger, Texas M. (Inabinet) 263
Geise, Mollie W. (Ray) 291
Geise, Owen N. 239
Geise, Sallie (Smith) 239
Gentry, Daniel C. 112
Gentry, Francis A. (Carden) 37
Gentry, R. D. 251, 264
Gentry, Rebecca D. (Thompson) 112
George, A. M. 231
George, Annie E. (Mell) 38
George, F. M. (Burke) 231
George, Kitty (Seay) 5
George, Mollie E. (Trapp) 90
George, Sallie (Foster) 179
George, Wm. 179
Gerding, Flem (Curtwright) 116
Gerding, Julius 116
German, Anna M. (Smith) 90
Gevers, Sallie (Nelson) 140
Gew, Mary J. (Marshall) 67
Gibbs, Martha D. (Johnson) 26
Gibson, A. W. 236
Gibson, Alice (Hendricks) 252
Gibson, Camilla (Livingston) 232
Gibson, Caroline (Perkins) 134
Gibson, Charlotte E. (Hightower) 236
Gibson, E. Eliza (Black) 88
Gibson, Eliza L. (Stuart) 23

Gibson, Eliza S. (Streyer) 168
Gibson, Ella (Byrd) 218
Gibson, Elma (LaFavor) 187
Gibson, Enoch 134
Gibson, G. W. 63
Gibson, J. Knight 88
Gibson, J. L. 156, 228, 265
Gibson, J. S. 228
Gibson, Lizzie (Christian) 257
Gibson, M. F. (Hardin) 228
Gibson, Maggie C. (Vaughn) 5
Gibson, Maliere (Vaughn) 95
Gibson, Marion (Center) 63
Gibson, Martha M. K. (Martin) 218
Gibson, Martha S. (Woods) 28
Gibson, Nannie G. (Mathis) 167
Gibson, T. F. 5
Gibson, T. H. 136, 172, 190
Gibson, Thomas H. 119, 124, 152, 160, 185, 187, 202
Gibson, Ursula A. (Coward) 229
Gibson, W. H. 218
Gibson, Wm. B. 229
Gifford, Ellen (Garrett) 193
Gilbert, A. L. 65
Gilbert, Carrie (Pearson) 25
Gilbert, Emma (Taliafero) 199
Gilbert, Emma P. (Jones) 237
Gilbert, Hattie (Horton) 104
Gilbert, K. M. (Livingston) 65
Gilbert, Lucy F. (Harper) 244
Gilbert, M. E. (Smith) 116
Gilbert, Mary D. (Bacon) 154
Gilbert, N. W. H. 154
Gilbert, Otho B. 237
Gilbert, W. E. 244
Gilbert, Wm. A. 25
Giles, Anna L. (Hardin) 232
Giles, Annie (Wood) 223
Giles, Arizona E. (Freeman) 292
Giles, C. R. 226
Giles, E. H. 13, 63, 101, 155, 158
Giles, Flora E. (Irvine) 243
Giles, H. H. 199
Giles, Henry B. 243

Giles, Ida J. (Williams) 226
Giles, J. J. 68, 116, 123, 211, 232
Giles, L. P. 292
Giles, Mary J. (Tranham) 13
Giles, Melville B. (Wells) 158
Giles, Robert A. 232
Gilkey, Adella J. (McJunkin) 20
Gilkey, J. Harvey 20
Gill, Pattie (Farmer) 205
Gill, W. V. 205
Gillam, Drusilla Ann (McRoy) 69
Gillespie, M. A. (Chambers) 259
Gillespie, Margaret (Parks) 259
Gillespie, Sallie (Garrison) 259
Gillett, C. W. 212
Gillett, Mary A. (Farabee) 212
Gillham, E. W. 63
Gillham, S. E. (McKee) 63
Gillis, B. H. Meredith 44
Gillis, Hugh M. 46
Gillis, Mary N. V. (Lewis) 46
Gillis, Mollie (Lewis) 44
Gilmer, M. E. (Johnson) 66
Gilmore, Ann Eliza (Wilhelm) 89
Gilreath, Della (Loveless) 286
Gilreath, Geo. H. 138
Gilreath, O. N. (Dishroon) 138
Gilreath, S. A. 286
Gilstrap, Mary (McDugle) 257
Gilstrap, S. A. (Dorsey) 107
Gilstrap, Thomas 257
Girardeau, Florence L. (McFail) 269
Gist, Gertrude (Gee) 146
Gittems, Sally (Skipper) 121
Givens, Arianna E. (Harrison) 162
Givens, John T. 162
Givens, Mary L. (Olds) 282
Givin, Sarah A. (Glowers) 100
Gladden, Ella (Davenport) 231
Gladden, J. 231
Gladney, Henrietta M. (Hart) 124
Glantors, S. M. J. (Towns) 243
Glass, Edward M. 188

Glass, Ella C. (Thompson) 238
Glass, Emma (Lee) 133
Glass, J. F. 45
Glass, Missouri (Ward) 45
Glass, Missouri A. (Rowe) 188
Glass, Newton A. 94
Glass, Ruth A. (Harris) 116
Glass, Tommie L. (Turner) 38
Glass, Virginia (Hightower) 94
Glass, Zipporah M. (Hightower) 271
Glaze, Fannie (Miller) 64
Glaze, Thos. W. 64
Glazier, Carrie E. W. (Seago) 54
Glazier, F. 54
Gleason, Henry H. 178
Gleason, Louise (Craft) 178
Glenn, (Way) 219
Glenn, Clarence 293
Glenn, Elizabeth (Taylor) 72
Glenn, Fannie (Stevens) 171
Glenn, J. N. 84
Glenn, J. W. 177, 189, 191, 193
Glenn, James B. 77
Glenn, John W. 171
Glenn, Julia B. (Birch) 191
Glenn, Loula (Davenport) 254
Glenn, Lucy (Cotter) 293
Glenn, Mattie I. (Robinson) 77
Glenn, Richard P. 72
Glenn, Sallie E. (Caldwell) 140
Glenn, Sallie Floyd (Johnson) 84
Glenn, Sarah E. (Jones) 172
Glenn, Susan A. (Andrew) 37
Glenn, W. F. 171, 185, 203, 204, 244, 250, 254, 261
Glisson, Amelia (Brown) 48
Glisson, Margaret (Rivers) 94
Glover, Eli S. 95
Glover, Henry 122
Glover, J. K. 115
Glover, Jennette (Keith) 122
Glover, John 221
Glover, Lou (Ehney) 221
Glover, Lou Bowie (Garwood) 115
Glover, Sarah A. (Hunter) 95

Glowers, John 100
Glowers, Sarah A. (Givin) 100
Glozier, Hattie (Jones) 250
Gnan, Ellen (Summerlin) 94
Goars, Millisson G. (Roberts) 151
Gober, Julia A. (Farris) 20
Gober, T. E. (Hamby) 138
Gobert, Alice E. (Roberts) 191
Gocto, Anna M. (Sims) 44
Gocto, Wm. R. 44
Godard, Joel 246
Godard, Lula (Morris) 246
Godard, W. T. 180
Godbold, Flora K. (Kennedy) 263
Goddard, Martha E. (Dumble) 62
Godfrey, Eliza Knight (Marshall) 30
Godfrey, J. E. 221
Godfrey, Jas. E. 279
Godfrey, Sarah M. (Simmons) 221
Godwin, Mattie E. (Stratford) 200
Godwin, Wm. T. 200
Goff, E. E. (Perkins) 270
Goff, W. H. 270
Goforth, Jane (Poteet) 88
Goforth, Preston T. 88
Goggans, Daniel 186
Goggans, Fanny (Dantzler) 186
Golding, Mary E. (Elenburg) 175
Goldsmith, Sallie (Wilkie) 200
Goldwin, Joseph C. 249
Goldwin, Willie F. (Ward) 249
Golson, J. P. 224
Golson, Julia (Stack) 224
Gomiley, Alice (Ward) 249
Good, Fannie (Wood) 187
Good, Georgia A. (Berry) 74
Good, J. E. 187
Good, J. T. 74
Goodall, James P. 127
Goodall, M. A. (Sams) 127
Goodbread, Julia V. (Peeler) 263
Goode, Jennie (Cohron) 280
Goode, Lizzie Helen (Guerry) 162
Goode, Machinus 197
Goode, Minnie (Bledsoe) 95

Goode, Mollie (Humber) 197
Goode, Sallie (Rutherford) 49
Goode, Wm. E. 280
Goodgion, Mary H. (Sullivan) 54
Goodgion, R. S. 54
Goodin, (Blasingame) 284
Goodin, Carrie (Gurr) 252
Goodin, John 284
Goodlett, Annie B. (Davis) 157
Goodlett, Spartan 157
Goodman, Emily (Dawkins) 93
Goodman, Emma J. (Harvey) 256
Goodman, Helen E. (Vickers) 228
Goodman, James D. 228
Goodman, James T. 93
Goodman, John 3
Goodman, John F. 256
Goodman, M. E. (Arbery) 291
Goodman, P. A. (Brunson) 23
Goodman, Sarah P. (Williams) 3
Goodrich, Celia (Anderson) 187
Goodrum, Charlie (Harris) 75
Goodrum, Thomas A. 75
Goodwin, Agnes (Brown) 131
Goodwin, Annie M. (Stubbs) 237
Goodwin, Bartlet 224
Goodwin, Clara C. (Saxon) 5
Goodwin, Elizabeth A. (Guery) 152
Goodwin, Emma A. (McAfee) 270
Goodwin, George T. 131
Goodwin, J. H. 270
Goodwin, John E. 258
Goodwin, Louisa Elizabeth (Holcomb) 224
Goodwin, M. E. (Biggs) 142
Goodwin, Margaret E. (Carson) 258
Goodwin, Mary A. (Fike) 54
Goodwin, Mary A. (Lavina) 53
Goodwin, Thomas 142
Goodwyn, B. 247
Goodwyn, Belle (Pound) 247
Goodwyn, Cattie (Pope) 56

Goodwyn, J. B. 56
Goodwyn, Lullie E. (Findlay) 170
Goolsby, C. D. 144
Goolsby, Carrie E. (White) 95
Goolsby, Ella (Bradley) 144
Goolsby, Francis C. 95
Gorden, Ruth R. (Bowman) 124
Gordon, Annie E. F. (Winter) 135
Gordon, E. A. (Atkinson) 153
Gordon, Ella A. (Ponder) 136
Gordon, George 196
Gordon, George M. 88, 135
Gordon, L. D. (Rhensy) 171
Gordon, Mary J. (Williams) 88
Gordon, Sarah (Wodford) 196
Gordys, G. M. 139
Gorman, J. M. 58
Gorman, Ophelia M. (Austell) 58
Gorton, Amanda (Andrews) 79
Gorton, Wm. B. 79
Gosden, Nancy J. (Landrum) 140
Goss, 7
Goss, I. J. M. 106
Goss, J. M. 2
Goss, Julia M. (Farabee) 126
Goss, Lita (Griffith) 185
Goss, S. Ellen (Craft) 7
Gossett, Jas. H. 149
Goudelock, Kate (Garvin) 36
Goudelock, Thomas 36
Gould, Emma F. (Chitty) 96
Gould, James 96
Gower, Fannie L. (Fain) 90
Gower, Mary E. (Simmons) 113
Gower, Thomas C. 113
Gowman, R. A. 188
Grace, Charles J. 254
Grace, Jessie (Lloyd) 254
Grace, Nannie W. (Loyd) 208
Grace, V. A. (Lloyd) 254
Grace, W. D. 208, 272
Gradick, Carrie S. (Scott) 228
Grady, Fannie (Carmichael) 186
Grady, Lewis C. 186
Graeser, Clarence A. 41

Greer, Addria V. (Anderson) 209
Greer, C. A. 153
Greer, John W. 172
Greer, L. H. (Wimberly) 218
Greer, Lizzie (Blocker) 31
Greer, Marian C. (Oglesby) (Thomas) 218
Greer, Mollie (Bradley) 233
Greer, P. Alice (Sullivan) 172
Greer, P. F. M. 31
Greer, S. D. (Dabbs) 153
Greer, Thos 209
Gregg, Hattie (Heron) 229
Gregg, J. E. 258
Gregg, Lizzie L. (Jones) 258
Gregg, Sallie A. (Davis) 258
Gregg, Wesley L. 229
Gregg, William A. 258
Gregorie, J. L. 156
Gregorie, Rosa (Bella) 156
Gregory, Florence (Munroe) 69
Gregory, Georgia (Dallas) 228
Gregory, Hattie Grinnell (Marshall) 281
Gregory, J. 69
Gregory, James 228
Gregory, Junius H. 281
Gregory, M. E. (Mood) 136
Gregory, Mattie (Kensey) 153
Gregory, Mattie S. (Summerour) 268
Gregory, Sue M. (Omberg) 97
Gregory, W. D. 268
Gregory, W. F. 153
Gregory, W. S. 136
Greiner, Corinne L. (Walker) 52
Greiner, Ella (Hatfield) 222
Greiner, John D. 222
Grenning, Lizzie (Lefler) 30
Grenning, Philip 30
Gresham, 28
Gresham, Eliza H. (Adams) 75
Gresham, Ella U. (Lassater) 35
Gresham, Fannie (Williams) 16
Gresham, Fannie E. (Wright) 185
Gresham, Frances E. (Reynolds) 28
Gresham, J. J. 35
Gresham, Rosa H. (Milledge) 209
Gresling, C. W. 232

Gresling, Emma (Kitchens) 232
Gresling, Vandella S. (Kitchens) 232
Grey, C. E. (Wiggins) 17
Grey, Charles G. 17
Grey, Lula (Hollis) 135
Grey, Mary T. (Howren) 141
Grey, Samuel H. 135
Grey, Wm. 141
Grier, A. G. 198
Grier, M. Adella (Robins) 211
Grier, Mary E. Hutson 211
Griffeth, Emma (Pyror) 113
Griffeth, J. F. 113
Griffeth, James 89
Griffin, 125
Griffin, Alice (Starr) 214
Griffin, E. S. 17, 282
Griffin, Eva (Sistrunk) 282
Griffin, Indiana V. (Berry) 21
Griffin, J. J. 21
Griffin, Jas. A. 278
Griffin, Lucy A. (Randall) 52
Griffin, Sallie M. (Smith) 17
Griffin, Z. B. (Coffee) (Reynolds) 125
Griffis, Daniel 5
Griffis, Lula (Howren) 5
Griffith, Annie (Phipps) 180
Griffith, Celestia A. (Thrasher) 24
Griffith, F. M. 2
Griffith, Fannie (Johnson) 12
Griffith, Francis P. 24
Griffith, Henrietta J. (Shines) 2
Griffith, J. A. 185
Griffith, J. R. 32, 49
Griffith, James 11, 17, 27, 40, 46
Griffith, Lita (Goss) 185
Griffith, Mary A. (Campbell) 254
Griffith, Rebecca (Baggett) 27
Griffith, Richard C. 254
Griffith, Sallie A. (White) 6
Griffiths, Anna W. (Wightman) 215
Griffiths, G. J. 237
Griffiths, George J. 128, 190, 195, 200, 215, 218, 220, 227, 289
Griggs, J. A. 34
Griggs, Jane (Haddock) 34
Griggs, Phoebe (Treadaway) 48

Grimsley, Plumer (Liles) 271
Griner, Amanda (Townsend) 146
Griner, Elizabeth C. (Crawford) 75
Griner, Henry 146
Griner, Sarah V. (Cox) 75
Grisham, Eliza O. (Pledger) 136
Grisham, James M. B. 136
Grisham, W. J. (House) 122
Grissette, Fannie C. (Beaty) 13
Grive, J. T. 9
Grive, N. E. (Darsey) 9
Groce, Florida H. (Hollingsworth) 10
Groce, Franklin L. 10
Grogain, Mollie (Moss) 79
Grogan, J. H. 22, 28, 41, 47, 78, 153, 162, 208
Grogan, John H. 282
Grooms, Anna J. (Neal) 202
Grooms, D. H. 202
Grooms, Mary (Sweatman) 204
Grooms, Susan (Hollin) 186
Groover, Alice C. (Joiner) 57
Groover, C. D. 57
Groover, J. P. 203
Groover, Lizzie (Gable) 203
Groover, M. J. (Harris) 7
Grove, Francis 21
Grove, Mary (Stroud) 21
Grove, Mary A. (Spier) 165
Grovenstene, Rosa B. (Richards) 279
Grover, Ella J. (Gray) 255
Grover, James M. 185
Grover, Kate M. (Wyche) 185
Grover, Martha C. (Brown) 51
Grover, Milton 51
Grover, Olonzo 255
Groverstine, Hannah E. (Ganann) 85
Groves, Betty A. (Harris) 100
Groves, C. J. 51
Groves, Ella (Graves) 51
Groves, John H. 206
Groves, Josie (Coleman) 260
Groves, Julia M. (Walker) 206
Groves, W. H. 260
Grubbs, M. A. C. (King) 180
Grubbs, Mary J. (West) 272

Grubbs, Mary T. (Penn) 217
Gruber, Cattie (Ballew) 64
Gruber, George W. 149
Gruber, Joseph A. C. 64
Gruber, Mary J. (Bradley) 149
Gruson, Emmette M. 64
Gruson, Meily M. (Hooks) 64
Guerry, Daniel 111
Guerry, James H. 162
Guerry, Lizzie Helen (Goode) 162
Guerry, Theodosia R. (Wootten) 111
Guery, Elizabeth A. (Goodwin) 152
Guery, George K. 152
Guest, Sallie (Turner) 161
Guest, Wm. 161
Gugel, Virginia E. (Powers) 144
Gugel, William H. 144
Guice, E. R. (Maxwell) 275
Guiharin, Sallie (Greene) 263
Guilds, Hannah (Harrell) 92
Guilds, Samuel 92
Guiton, F. C. (Beaty) 30
Guiton, Jasper 30
Gunn, Erwine S. (Wyatt) 234
Gunn, Eugenia T. (Bethune) 151
Gunn, Virginia (Woodsen) 128
Gunn, Wm. H. 234
Gunn, Zachary B. 128
Gunnells, E. C. (Williford) 190
Gunnells, Georgia E. (Verner) 259
Gunnells, J. D. 194, 235
Gunnels, J. D. 250
Gunnels, Tallula W. (MacDonald) 171
Gunnin, Ann E. (Lites) 152
Gunnin, M. Lenna (Collins) 152
Gunry, George M. 281
Gunry, Maggie (Bohler) 281
Gur, Harriet A. (Davidson) 82
Gur, Thos. M. 82
Gurr, Carrie (Goodin) 252
Gurr, John W. 252
Guthrie, Carrie E. (Craton) 43
Guthrie, Martin 48
Guthrie, Mary (Buran) 267

Guthrie, Mary F. (Pattillo) 48
Guthrie, W. S. 43
Guttenberger, Charley 5
Guttenberger, Emma (Peacock) 5
Guyton, Cornelia (Fisher) 23
Guyton, Julia A. (Smith) 74
Guyton, Julia E. (Fisher) 59
Guyton, M. J. 23
Guyton, Robert H. 74
Gwinn, Leon 272
Gwinn, Lilly (Davis) 272
Gwynn, D. W. 134
Gwynn, David W. 216
Gwynn, Emma (Nash) 134
Gwynn, Francina A. (Nash) 216
Hack, Bessie M. (Jones) 277
Hack, Edwin W. 277
Hadden, F. A. (Caule) 221
Hadden, Fanny (Worthy) 121
Hadden, Frank 221
Hadden, Jane (Caulk) 174
Hadden, Joel W. 121
Haddock, Jane (Griggs) 34
Haddock, Mary T. (Anderson) 220
Hadley, J. J. 16
Hadley, Kate (Bishop) 16
Haesler, B. 9
Haesler, Francis M. (Lawes) 9
Hafer, Elizabeth (Riley) 34
Hafer, J. A. 34
Hagan, Leonard F. 152
Hagan, Mary P. (Hamilton) 152
Haggie, James 161
Haggie, Sallie (Emmerson) 161
Hagin, Lizzie (Graham) 186
Hagin, Thos. A. 186
Hagins, Mary A. (Pledger) 124
Hague, A. 58
Hague, Antonette (Vardaman) 118
Hague, Arnold 118
Hague, Fanie P. (Thomas) 58
Hague, Giles (Strickland) 253
Haigler, Allie U. (Gaskin) 144
Haigler, C. E. (Oliver) 281
Haigler, John P. 144
Hailes, Cora (Smith) 277
Hailes, Leonora (Strozier) 277

Hailes, W. F. 277
Hair, E. L. (Cady) 26
Hair, G. W. 26
Hair, Malcom 66
Hair, Sarah (Ayers) 212
Hair, Sue (McMichael) 66
Hale, 112
Hale, Josie (Harper) 288
Hale, Rowena J. (Mobley) 1
Hale, Samuel 288
Haley, Amelia J. (Ellis) 163
Haley, J. S. 163
Hall, Ann E. (Bradford) 76
Hall, Anna G. (Boatright) 36
Hall, Charles A. 14
Hall, Eleanor E. (Zuber) 6
Hall, George S. 148
Hall, Gertrude (Jones) 85
Hall, Gussie (Atwell) 246
Hall, Harriet C. (Vance) 33
Hall, Isaac R. 22
Hall, Julia B. (Shoer) 14
Hall, Katie B. (Rainey) 196
Hall, Luther A. 36
Hall, Maggie E. (Julien) 148
Hall, Mary E. (Dillard) 22
Hall, Mary Taylor (Hodges) 227
Hall, N. J. (Smith) 18
Hall, Permelia (Vanlandingham) 31
Hall, R. B. 227
Hall, S. Gertrude (Jones) 86
Hall, S. V. (Conwell) 285
Hall, Sallie (Wright) 134
Hall, W. A. 31
Halley, Lucy (Gains) 163
Halley, Robert Y. 163
Halliday, M. A. 230
Halliday, S. L. (Ball) 230
Hallman, Maggie (Rogers) 143
Halsten, John 121
Halzendorf, Wilmer C. (Scott) 234
Ham, Anna E. (Cook) 164
Ham, E. Florence (Moody) 273
Ham, H. W. J. 164
Ham, John D. 217
Ham, Laura (Riley) 217
Ham, Robert D. 273
Hamby, A. 156
Hamby, Abthia L. (Turner) 104
Hamby, D. H. 156
Hamby, David H. 217
Hamby, Eliza (McLaughlin) 52
Hamby, J. M. 104

Hamby, Jos. T. 138
Hamby, Kate C. (Brunson) 217
Hamby, Noah 52
Hamby, Sue McP. (Corry) 156
Hamby, T. E. (Gober) 138
Hames, Josie (Strange) 248
Hames, Keran J. (Arnold) 123
Hames, M. L. (Kirkpatrick) 1
Hames, Sarah A. (Howell) 44
Hamilton, 149
Hamilton, Eliza E. (Paul) 199
Hamilton, George 212
Hamilton, James 80
Hamilton, Julia (Bowie) 149
Hamilton, Louisa A. (McFarland) 110
Hamilton, M. T. (Shy) 80
Hamilton, Madison S. 61
Hamilton, Mary (Lawson) 131
Hamilton, Mary P. (Hagan) 152
Hamilton, Mary Saluda (Briggs) 194
Hamilton, S. W. 12
Hamilton, Sallie L. (Green) 12
Hamilton, Susan E. (Rushton) 272, 274
Hamilton, W. S. 199
Hamilton, W. T. 4, 19, 38, 71, 82, 97, 98, 100, 171, 180, 203, 226, 234, 249
Hamilton, Wiley T. 18
Hamlet, J. W. 69
Hamlet, Susan B. (Hart) 69
Hamlin, Martha A. (Fincher) 86
Hammet, Fannie T. (Matthews) 155
Hammet, J. Harvey 155
Hammett, Lizzie E. (Stone) 115
Hammett, Wm. 115
Hammock, Bell (Bridges) 252
Hammond, 19
Hammond, A. D. 48, 286
Hammond, Alice (Murphey) 286
Hammond, D. W. 168, 214
Hammond, E. P. 165
Hammond, Elizabeth 9
Hammond, Eudocia (Adams) 287
Hammond, Fannie (Ware) 165

Hammond, Florida (Floyd) 132
Hammond, Geo. H. 132
Hammond, Georgia (Watkins) 286
Hammond, Herbert 9
Hammond, John 287
Hammond, Julia (Round) 9
Hammond, Mary (Holland) 48
Hammond, Mollie J. (Watts) 19
Hammond, Rosa (Barnes) 214
Hammonds, Rosey (Elroy) 290
Hampton, Carrie (Kinard) 252
Hampton, Jacob 171
Hampton, Louzana (Hay) 43
Hampton, Martha (Leatherwood) 1
Hampton, Sallie F. (Short) 171
Hampton, W. O. 269, 295
Hamrick, Louisa V. (Hatcher) 170
Hamrick, P. D. 159
Hamrick, S. E. (Mann) 159
Hancock, Annie (Wadley) 115
Hancock, David L. 187
Hancock, Dora A. (Beckman) 15
Hancock, Eula (Ferrell) 218
Hancock, F. G. 218
Hancock, Geo. H. 115
Hancock, H. W. 259
Hancock, J. W. 57
Hancock, Julia E. (Ives) 57
Hancock, Lucinda C. (Finch) 187
Hancock, Mattie A. (Lloyd) 51
Hancock, Nannie (Carter) 255
Hand, Leonora V. (McAlpin) 197
Hand, Sallie (Fife) 126
Handrup, Lizzie (Sitton) 163
Hanes, A. T. (Johnson) 74
Hanes, Geo. S. 248
Hange, W. E. 285
Hankins, A. Z. (Hawkins) 116
Hankins, Almira J. (Wright) 130
Hankins, S. M. 116
Hansel, Major 28
Hansel, Talulah (Pelham) 28

Hanson, J. B. 91, 99, 168, 293
Hanson, Jas. B. 67
Hanson, Mary C. (Green) 168
Hanson, Susan W. (Lambdin) 67
Hanson, W. G. 102, 103, 163, 170, 171, 223, 224, 263, 265, 269, 275, 292
Hanye, Georgia E. (Wood) 206
Harald, Rebecca A. (Lynch) 147
Haralson, Jesse 192
Haralson, P. B. 201
Harben, Lucia (Wilkinson) 62
Harben, T. B. 5
Harben, William M. 62
Harbeson, H. B. 240
Harbinson, Frances R. (Lemacks) 208
Harbinson, John W. 208
Harbuck, Carrie (Ivy) 280
Harcher, Fannie (Embree) 296
Hard, Anna M. (Miller) 139
Hard, B. W. 139
Hardaway, Clara S. (Baldwin) 108
Hardaway, G. W. 173, 179, 199
Hardaway, Jno. W. 160
Hardaway, Mary A. (Lane) 211
Hardaway, Robert H. 108, 211
Hardeman, Dollie (Whitaker) 6
Hardeman, Fannie E. (Ross) 207
Hardeman, Frances K. (Robinson) 122
Hardeman, J. 6
Hardeman, John L. 207
Hardeman, M. K. (Deavors) 296
Hardeman, S. E. A. (Pace) 201
Hardeman, Ulla G. 296
Harden, James A. 127
Harden, James R. 22
Harden, Jno. Harvey 280
Harden, Kattie (Davis) 280
Harden, Mary E. (Daniel) 127
Harden, Mollie S. (Braddy) 22
Harden, Wm. 232
Hardie, Clifford (Lilly) 250
Hardin, Ann F. (Dehome)(?) 159

Harris, Fannie T. (Burke) 146
Harris, G. 74
Harris, G. C. 241
Harris, H. R. 145
Harris, Henderson H. 8
Harris, Henry 223
Harris, Henry R. 149
Harris, Horace A. 166
Harris, I. C. 229
Harris, Ida (Wharton) 280
Harris, Ira S. 249
Harris, Isaac C. 64
Harris, J. J. 184, 188, 206, 225, 250, 266
Harris, J. P. (McCollum) 160
Harris, J. R. 69
Harris, J. W. J. 133
Harris, James 69
Harris, James B. 116
Harris, James Taylor 219
Harris, Jane (Lenard) 20
Harris, John C. 89
Harris, John H. 63, 84, 113, 126, 127, 158, 165
Harris, John L. 135
Harris, John P. 100
Harris, Josh H. 70
Harris, L. W. 187
Harris, Laura Estelle (Deschamps) 219
Harris, Leila G. (Simonton) 145
Harris, Lucinda E. (Ruff) 121
Harris, Lula A. (Jarvis) 159
Harris, M. E. (McMullan) 8
Harris, M. J. (Groover) 7
Harris, M. V. (Edwards) 241
Harris, Mariah (Wilson) 69
Harris, Mary (Oswalt) 46
Harris, Mary (Springer) 184
Harris, Mary Ida (Hooks) 208
Harris, Mary M. (Merk) 45
Harris, N. E. 146
Harris, N. J. 7
Harris, Nancy B. (Bonds) 31
Harris, P. C. 4, 143, 145
Harris, Pamelia (Cook) 144
Harris, R. J. (Shackelford) 187
Harris, Ruth A. (Glass) 116
Harris, S. Amelia (Williams) 223
Harris, S. E. (Brakefield) 241
Harris, Salina (Chadwick) 3
Harris, Sallie (Roundtree) 110

Harris, Sallie A. (Brown) 89
Harris, Sallie D. (Dugger) 205
Harris, Sallie E. (Simonton) 133
Harris, Susie R. (Armstrong) 126
Harris, T. A. 41, 57, 255, 261
Harris, T. Alonzo 37, 48, 170, 226
Harris, T. E. 183
Harris, T. P. 20
Harris, Thomas Butler 208
Harris, Thomas H. 45
Harris, W. H. 46
Harris, William T. 145
Harris, Willie M. (Garrand) 100
Harrison, A. E. 178
Harrison, A. L. 85
Harrison, Annie E. (Palmer) 216
Harrison, Antionette M. (Dorman) 89
Harrison, Arianna E. (Givens) 162
Harrison, C. A. (Abney) 74
Harrison, Charles E. 162
Harrison, Chloe Ann (Inabinet) 218
Harrison, Elizabeth (Ganesis) 178
Harrison, G. F. 295
Harrison, Gertrude A. (Street) 85
Harrison, J. C. 70
Harrison, J. R. 87
Harrison, John G. 216
Harrison, John T. 76
Harrison, Julia R. (Munsun) 119
Harrison, Juliet (Castlen) 250
Harrison, Larkin 234
Harrison, Louis L. 119
Harrison, M. E. (Creech) 198
Harrison, Mary (Arthur) 66
Harrison, Mary (Webb) 56
Harrison, Mollie (Bishop) 295
Harrison, Nancy E. (Lewis) 138
Harrison, R. M. 74
Harrison, Sanford T. 89
Harrison, Sarah C. (McLucas) 234
Harrison, W. P. 72, 131, 132, 274
Harrold, U. B. 93
Harry, Carrie (Talley) 125
Hart, Alonzo A. 276

Hart, Anna J. (Murry) 276
Hart, B. C. 61, 124
Hart, B. Fuller 54
Hart, Ellen Anna (Dennis) 54
Hart, Henrietta M. (Gladney) 124
Hart, Irene (Smith) 61
Hart, Louis 69
Hart, Susan B. (Hamlet) 69
Hart, Theodosia J. (Smith) 103
Hart, W. C. 178
Hartman, E. E. (Johnson) 283
Hartman, Robt 283
Hartsell, J. C. 6, 10, 16, 51
Hartwell, C. P. 98
Hartwell, J. B. 112
Hartwell, Julia C. (Jewett) 112
Hartwell, Mary W. (Hodges) 98
Hartzog, A. B. (Attaway) 201
Hartzog, Henry 267
Hartzog, Minnie C. (Copeland) 267
Hartzog, W. H. 201
Harvey, (Dumas) 113
Harvey, A. H. 40
Harvey, A. J. 175
Harvey, Amanda F. (Fell) 63
Harvey, Edward H. 159
Harvey, Elizabeth E. (Judge) 7
Harvey, Emma J. (Goodman) 256
Harvey, Eudora (Lindsay) 207
Harvey, H. J. 68, 95, 240
Harvey, Kate A. (Harvey) 290
Harvey, Louisa (Picket) 40
Harvey, Mary (Wimberly) 4
Harvey, Mary E. (Land) 232
Harvey, Mike 113
Harvey, Mollie F. (Brown) 175
Harvey, Susan T. (Claiborn) 159
Harvey, T. Middleton 290
Harvey, Wm. T. 232
Harvy, Mary A. (Dorsett) 217
Harwell, Eliza J. (Cotton) 87
Harwell, Ella T. (Shepard) 100
Harwell, Katie B. (Denham) 167

Hearn, Hattie C. (Pelot) 130

Hearn, Jno. 226

Hearn, Leila H. (Huff) 213

Hearn, M. A. R. (Kelley) 197

Hearn, Nettie (Thornton) 108

Hearn, Purnell 197

Hearn, Sam'l 136

Hearn, W. H. 130

Hearn, William T. 209

Heartley, Benjamin A. 134

Heartley, Eliza J. (Perkins) 134

Heartly, Augusta A. (King) 139

Heartsfield, Ann J. (Moore) 155

Heath, C. B. 144

Heath, Catharine (Mc-Grath) 105

Heath, E. P. 96

Heath, Elizabeth K. (Hilliard) 57

Heath, Gertrude (Lowery) 241

Heath, Hattie R. (Banner) 232

Heath, J. F. 63

Heath, John O. 105

Heath, Leonora N. (Buxton) 40

Heath, Lucy D. (Buford) 96

Heath, Margaret V. (Chester) 144

Heath, Mary E. (Boone) 240

Heath, Ocie Anna G. (Wing) 63

Heath, Oni May (Mizell) 68

Heath, Samuel J. 40

Heath, W. D. 49, 97, 110

Heaton, Elizabeth B. (Street) 219

Heaton, Joseph 80

Heaton, Julia (Appleby) 80

Hebert, M. C. (Patterson) 9

Heflin, Lee F. 95

Heflin, V. M. (Reynolds) 95

Heidt, E. 171, 176

Heidt, J. W. 109

Heidt, John W. 109, 132, 161, 181, 187, 191, 205, 237

Heidt, Lizzie (Morgan) 42

Heidt, Tallulah G. (Jordan) 176

Heidt, W. 169

Heidtman, Annie M. (Pooser) 194

Heidtman, John L. 194

Heilbron, Julius 48

Heilbron, Wilmer (Myers) 48

Heir, Janie (Cristie) 270

Heler, M. A. (Cromer) 112

Heler, M. A. 112

Hellams, Ann (Curry) 27

Hellams, Lottie M. (Cox) 171

Hellams, Mary E. (Dagnall) 27

Hellings, J. P. 31

Hellings, Nancy E. (Bankston) 31

Helmly, Ellen C. (Shearouse) 148

Helmly, George W. 148

Helms, H. J. 37

Helms, Nancy J. (Byrum) 37

Helton, E. A. (Allen) 131

Hembree, Tabitha (Green) 274

Hemingway, Ellen (Hemingway) 17

Hemingway, H. D. 265

Hemingway, J. A. 17

Hemingway, Laura (Legette) 265

Hemingway, Wm. C. 17

Hemmingway, Allard B. 211

Hemmingway, Minnie E. (Britton) 211

Hemphill, Emma B. (Luckie) 95

Hemphill, Martha A. (Fain) 33

Hemphill, Mary A. (Anderson) 37

Hemphill, Wm. A. 37, 95

Hemstead, Laura E. (Hayes) 54

Henderson, A. 70

Henderson, Ann O. (Saville) 173

Henderson, Daniel B. 255

Henderson, Frank 23

Henderson, Hattie (Bacon) 23

Henderson, Henry G. 167

Henderson, I. C. (Kendrick) 154

Henderson, Irene (Adair) 70

Henderson, Julia F. (Biggers) 24

Henderson, Justain 173

Henderson, M. Eugenia (Bullard) 176

Henderson, Mary A. (Oslin) 167

Henderson, Mollie (Marchman) 171

Henderson, Philip L. 156

Henderson, Sallie (Cullens) 255

Henderson, Sallie A. E. (Charles) 286

Henderson, W. 24

Henderson, Wm. L. 176

Hendon, E. M. (Johnson) 131

Hendricks, A. H. 252

Hendricks, Alice (Gibson) 252

Hendrix, A. L. 196

Hendrix, E. Augusta (Loomis) 105

Hendrix, Josie B. (Terry) 196

Hendrix, M. L. (Gaines) 269

Hendrix, S. D. 269

Hendrix, Samantha O. (Smith) 250

Hendry, A. (Florence) 169

Hendry, Anna E. (Hightower) 60

Hendry, F. A. 155

Hendry, Geo. N. 176

Hendry, Gertrude (Jenkins) 176

Hendry, James F. 212

Hendry, Julia I. (Frierson) 212

Hendry, Laura J. (Thompson) 155

Hendry, Laura T. (Martin) 174

Hendry, Robert E. 60

Hendry, Robert S. 174

Hendry, S. H. 169

Henly, 113

Henly, Mary R. (Elfe) 33

Henly, Robert L. 33

Henry, Charles M. 19

Henry, Fannie (McCain) 137

Henry, Harriet Cornelia (New) 177

Henry, John C. 194

Henry, M. T. (Hunter) 40

Henry, Olivia (Mizelle) 194

Henry, Samuel G. 137

Henry, Sue V. (Mattox) 55

Henry, Susan H. (Hunter) 19

Henry, W. T. 40

Hentz, C. A. 270

Hentz, Chas. A. 162

Hentz, Leila (Munroe) 162

Hentz, Sallie Lee (Scott) 270

Herard, Elizabeth A. (Roberts) 128

Herard, Jules A. 128

Herb, Louisa A. (Anderson) 169

Herbert, Annie (Eidson) 170

Herbert, Fannie J. (Bearden) 107

Herbert, G. E. 107

Herbert, Isaac 170

Herbert, T. G. 186, 239, 264

Herbert, Thos. G. 9, 84, 170, 217

Herman, P. L. 50

Hernder, John R. 290

Hernder, Williametta E. (Gadbold) 290

Herndon, Annie J. (Freeman) 293

Herndon, Edward 293

Herndon, Hannie (Fair) 215

Heron, Hattie (Gregg) 229

Herren, M. A. (Sewell) 11

Herrick, Ed. P. 236

Herrin, Etta M. (Scruggs) 281

Herring, A. H. 31

Herring, L. L. (Randle) 31

Herrington, A. (Prescott) 23

Herrington, Annie A. (Reeves) 23

Herrington, C. C. (Dobbins) 24

Herrington, Crawford T. 23

Herrington, Eugenia (Bates) 56

Herrington, H. B. 24

Herrington, H. H. 181

Herrington, Josephine (Ellison) 143

Herrington, Katie (Wiker) 181

Herrington, Mattie F. (Huggins) 19

Herrington, Ophelia (Jenkins) 191

Herrington, S. M. 19

Hester, Lidia T. (Crook) 45

Hester, R. J. 238

Hester, Sarah E.(Jackson) 5

Hester, Susan V. (Bethune) 72

Hester, Thomas G. 72

Hewell, Mollie (Shipp) 59

Hewitt, Susannah (Pierson) 168

Hewlett, Mary J. (Turner) 53

Hext, Emma C. (Wright) 167

Hext, R. Osbourne 167

Heys, Mattie A. (Dixon) 76

Heys, Wm. B. 76

Hibner, Addie A. (Keebler) 241

Hibner, Harry F. W. 241

Hickby, E. T. 140

Hickby, Georgia (Wardlaw) 140

Hickey, Annie E. (Garrison) 152

Hickey, J. C. 152

Hickey, W. H. 180

Hickman, F. M. (Barker) 144

Hickmon, Elizabeth (Turner) 168

Hickmon, O. P. 168

Hicks, E. D. 46

Hicks, Emma C. (Hudson) 64

Hicks, Julia (Arington) 46

Hicks, Lula P. (Whitaker) 211

Hicks, Mattie O. (Jones) 282

Hicks, Thomas N. 282

Higginbothan, Margaret J. (Slaton) 156

Higginbothan, Reuben C. 156

Higgins, Charity (McManus) 12

Higgins, Lawrence 6

Higgins, Malinda (Langford) 35

Higgins, Nannie S. (Gartin) 6

Higgins, W. E. 35

Higgs, Mattie A. (Richards) 178

Higgs, W. G. 178

High, Nancy J. (Whidden) 259

High, Nathan J. 259

High, Susan V. (Hix) 201

Hightower, Anna E. (Hendry) 60

Hightower, Catharine A. (Snead) 43

Hightower, Charlotte E. (Gibson) 236

Hightower, Daniel P. 261

Hightower, E. E. (Means) 292

Hightower, Elisha 18

Hightower, Fannie (Lee) 65

Hightower, Fannie P. (Williams) 261

Hightower, H. A. (Dickey) 120

Hightower, H. J. 65

Hightower, J. H. 120

Hightower, J. W. 26

Hightower, James W. 43

Hightower, Jno. D. 201

Hightower, Mary S. (Tunison) 175

Hightower, Mary S. P. (Slaughter) 18

Hightower, Mattie (Blalock) 26

Hightower, O. T. 175

Hightower, Rosa (Darden) 201

Hightower, Virginia (Glass) 94

Hightower, William W. 271

Hightower, Zipporah M. (Glass) 271

Hill, A. B. 174

Hill, Bessie (Gates) 248

Hill, Bunyan M. 180

Hill, Charles 110

Hill, Dicey (Trible) 33

Hill, Eli 176

Hill, Eliza Ann M. (Huggins) 180

Hill, Ella (Muse) 34

Hill, Eugenia T. (Morris) 26

Hill, Fannie (Pearson) 110

Hill, Fannie O. (Chambless) 134

Hill, G. E. (Strother) 100

Hill, Georgia A. (Bramlett) 93

Hill, H. H. 99

Hill, Henry 100

Hill, Ida (Barnett) 199

Hill, Isaac T. 26

Hill, J. J. (Lewis) 140

Hill, J. Jennie (Rogers) 75

Hill, James R. 134

Hill, James W. 140

Hill, Jemmie B. 131

Hill, John 151

Hill, L. L. 134

Hill, Laura M. (Lockwood) 55

Hill, Lizzie (Smith) 174

Hill, Lizzie E. (Edwards) 176

Hill, Lizzie L. (Carreker) 247

Hill, Louisiana (Zetrouer) 134

Hill, M. E. 18

Hill, M. Janie (Moore) 174

Hill, M. S. (Jeter) 66

Hill, Mary E. (Sledge) 99

Hill, Mary J. (Starke) 47

Hill, Mary P. (McCann) 18

Hill, Mattie M. (Wilkinson) 7

Hill, R. E. V. (Latimer) 99

Hill, Richard S. 174

Hill, S. J. 137, 172, 174, 217, 219

Hill, Sallie (Irwin) 91

Hill, Sallie E. (Thomas) 165

Hill, Sarah (Sheats) 78

Holley, Lizzie J. (Merritt) 248
Holleyman, Ann E. (Newman) 164
Holleyman, Mary A. (Parks) 118
Holleyman, W. F. 118
Holliday, Georgia (Strother) 56
Hollifield, A. Nelson 11
Hollin, John 186
Hollin, Susan (Grooms) 186
Hollingsworth, Florida H. (Groce) 10
Hollingsworth, Sudie C. (Greene) 250
Hollinshead, John S. 182
Hollinshead, Mary M. (Parrott) 182
Hollinshead, W. H. 239
Hollinshed, 187
Hollinshed, C. A. (Palmer) (Rowland) 187
Hollis, Julia (Willis) 272
Hollis, Lula (Grey) 135
Hollman, C. G. 26
Hollman, G. W. 173
Hollman, M. A. (Loller) 26
Hollman, Missouri (Bass) 147
Hollman, Susan (Padget) 173
Holloway, E. P. (Black) 65
Holloway, Eugenie (Haynes) 200
Holloway, Fannie M. (Jackson) 49
Holloway, Josie 189
Holly, Ann (Casey) 4
Holly, Franklin 4
Holman, Henrietta (McInis) 135
Holman, Maggie (Moss) 64
Holmes, Amanda M. (Morgan) 68
Holmes, Anna P. (Paynes) 253
Holmes, Annie (Floyd) 164
Holmes, C. J. 75
Holmes, Dora (Gault) 272
Holmes, E. A. (Mackay) 54
Holmes, E. P. (McGehee) 75
Holmes, Ella S. (Merritt) 220
Holmes, F. F. 46
Holmes, J. 183
Holmes, J. C. 230, 231
Holmes, J. P. 220
Holmes, Jennie H. (Evans) 25
Holmes, Joseph 164
Holmes, Kate (Mahone) 46

Holmes, Loouilla A. (Fulton) 66
Holmes, Mary E. (Winter) 234
Holmes, Mary Kele (Hopkins) 183
Holmes, N. L. 66
Holmes, Thomas E. 54
Holmes, Wm. T. 25
Holsenback, Helen (Morgan) 258
Holsenback, Wiley H. 258
Holsendorf, Florence S. (Beaton) 269
Holsendorf, John 269
Holstein, Mattie (Smith) 245
Holstern, Fannie E. (Massey) 44
Holston, Kissie (Cleveland) 243
Holt, Annie E. (Virgin) 118
Holt, Ella H. (Park) 200
Holt, Lizzie (Sheffield) 140
Holt, Lizzie A. (Ousley) 188
Holt, Mamie F. (Haygood) 267
Holt, S. W. 200
Holt, Susie W. (Fisher) 279
Holt, T. G. 140
Holt, Willie C. 279
Holt, Wm. S. 118
Holton, Harrison 210
Holton, Lucy A. (Allison) 210
Holtzclaw, Emma (Whitaker) 280
Holtzclaw, Ervin 115
Holtzclaw, R. Addie (West) 115
Holtzendorf, M. (Talley) 62
Holtzendorf, Robert 81
Holtzendorf, Stalina (Lovejoy) (Lamb) 81
Holzendorf, Georgia A. (Brown) 141
Homanstine, George C. 172
Homanstine, Mary C. (Smith) 172
Honiker, Mary Lelia (Dougherty) 190
Honiker, R. L. 180, 192, 201, 236
Honiker, Robert L. 190
Hood, Cynthia A. (Barton) 28
Hood, D. M. (Cuyler) 40
Hood, Green E. 28
Hook, J. C. P. 133
Hooke, Aurelia S. A. (Neese) 133
Hooker, Belinsa C. (Robinson) 179

Hooker, Emma Florence (Redwine) 287
Hooker, Joel J. 179
Hooks, Mary Ida (Harris) 208
Hooks, Meily M. (Gruson) 64
Hooper, Lou S. (Green) 26
Hooper, Wm. R. 26
Hooten, D. F. 251
Hooten, Julia P. (Bamberg) 251
Hoover, S. A. (Patterson) 71
Hopkins, C. Augusta (Beale) 70
Hopkins, Claude A. (Wynne) 70
Hopkins, Edmon B. 253
Hopkins, Ella G. (Bryant) 146
Hopkins, I. L. 149
Hopkins, I. S. 31, 35, 41, 104, 182
Hopkins, Jacob 247
Hopkins, Lambeth 70
Hopkins, Lenora (Wilkerson) 253
Hopkins, Mary Kele (Holmes) 183
Hopkins, Mary R. (Hinton) 182
Hopkins, Octavius 183
Hopson, J. S. 38
Hopson, Mary (Strickland) 38
Horger, A. J. 69
Horger, Agnes C. (Culler) 69
Horn, J. M. 97
Horn, M. C. (Vinson) 97
Horn, Michael J. (Shumate) 205
Hornaday, N. A. 168
Hornady, Gustavus A. 174
Hornady, Louisa Kate (Beall) 174
Horne, Mattie E. (Brock) 50
Horne, Sarah 50
Horne, Wm. E. 50
Horns, Mary E. (Bossill) 36
Hornsbey, Mary V. (Wilson) 267
Hornsby, Carrie A. (Wilson) 275
Hornsby, Julia V. (Smith) 77
Hornsby, Wm. D. 77
Horrid, Sarah (Stephens) 33
Horton, Bella (Congore) 266

Horton, Caroline E. (Fischer) 44
Horton, G. T. 104
Horton, H. H. 227
Horton, Hattie (Gilbert) 104
Horton, J. J. 128
Horton, Laura T. (Truesdel) 235
Horton, Lollie (Latimer) 176
Horton, M. A. (Stover) 227
Horton, O. R. 176
Horton, S. Rebecca (Gay) 128
Houck, Susan A. (Poppell) 102
Hough, A. S. 185
Hough, Augustus 273
Hough, Claudia (Sullivan) 273
Hough, G. A. 144
Hough, Mary (Jacobs) 269
Hough, Mary F. (Brown) 185
Hough, W. H. 269
Houghton, Ophelia (Mathews) 61
Houghton, Ross C. 293
Houghton, Wm. 61
House, Eliza (Allen) 192
House, John 192
House, Lou A. (Dillard) 272
House, Samuel 122
House, W. J. (Grisham) 122
House, W. W. 272
Houser, A. E. 137
Houser, Anna E. (Anderson) 189
Houser, Anna M. (Culler) 97
Houser, Bessie (Matthews) 151
Houser, Eliza (Marshall) 202
Houser, Fannie A. (Thigpen) 111
Houser, Frank C. 219
Houser, Frederick M. 208
Houser, I. N. (Rumph) 16
Houser, J. D. 16
Houser, John Fletcher 286
Houser, John H. 111, 294
Houser, Julia J. (Reese) 247
Houser, Laurence A. 166
Houser, Leola E. (Greene) 219
Houser, Maggie F. (Edwards) 294
Houser, Mary (Dejarnett) 88

Houser, Mary Tallulah (Houston) 208
Houser, Mollie R. (Massengale) 275
Houser, R. P. 88
Houser, Tiny (Marshall) 153
Houser, Viola (Bryan) 166
Houser, Virginia (Clarke) 286
Houser, Wm. H. 275
Houske, Cora C. (Robinson) 284
Houston, A. M. (Simms) 11
Houston, Celestia A. (Covington) 27
Houston, Mary Tallulah (Houser) 208
Houston, Monterey (Arnold) 11
Houston, R. V. 27
Houston, Sallie J. (McConnell) 20
Houton, Mary (Lasiter) 219
Houton, Samuel 219
Hovis, E. Gullielma (Morris) 294
Howard, Adella (Head) 281
Howard, Amanda (Winchester) 27
Howard, Anna F. (Thomas) 84
Howard, Annie S. (Jewett) 82
Howard, Ellis W. 82
Howard, John T. 259
Howard, Julia B. (Truslow) 129
Howard, Mary (Worrell) 271
Howard, Mary F. (Drew) 57
Howard, Mary F. (Reid) 151
Howard, Mary I. (Leslie) 204
Howard, N. Ellen (Johnson) 166
Howard, Pauline H. (Blackshear) 167
Howard, R. Fulton 27
Howard, Roseta R. (Jones) 259
Howard, Sallie (Avary) 58
Howard, T. C. 167
Howard, Tilman D. 271
Howard, Virginia A. (Cochren) 243
Howard, W. F. 204
Howard, W. H. 58
Howard, Wm. G. 151
Howe, Catharine (Murray) 115
Howe, M. V. (Hunt) 104

Howe, W. R. 104
Howel, Amanda (Wynn) 48
Howel, C. P. (Lefsy) 104
Howel, Martha Jane (Sheperd) 16
Howel, Sallie (Story) 84
Howell, Anna S. (Shelton) 186
Howell, Charles J. 286
Howell, D. Ann (Talley) 261
Howell, Dora (Brantly) 214
Howell, Elijah R. 44
Howell, Emma (Underwood) 17
Howell, G. V. (Allen) 31
Howell, H. P. 261
Howell, Harriet (Smith) 95
Howell, Hattie A. (Easterlin) 183
Howell, J. P. 222
Howell, James 17
Howell, John 71
Howell, Mary (Britt) 81
Howell, Mary J. (Hines) 222
Howell, Mattie (Cappel) 41
Howell, S. E. (Martin) 71
Howell, Sarah A. (Hames) 44
Howell, Sarah J. (Culpepper) 238
Howell, W. J. 238
Howell, W. P. 82
Howes, Davis H. 259
Howes, S. O. 154
Howes, Susie M. (Wright) 259
Howren, Lizzie E. (Barineau) 27
Howren, Lula (Griffis) 5
Howren, Mary T. (Grey) 141
Howren, R. H. 27, 34, 42, 67, 72, 77, 83, 115, 141, 144, 174, 197, 202, 224, 247, 266, 270
Howren, Robt. H. 5
Hoyl, Lou (Bates) 49
Hoyl, M. P. 49
Hoyl, Susan E. (Scoville) 66
Hoyl, Thos. I. 66
Hoyt, H. F. 163
Hoyt, Mary Catharine (Mood) 68
Hoyt, Oliver F. 68
Hubert, H. Virginia (Wilkie) 49
Hubert, Nannie H. (Thomas) 124
Hubert, R. W. 232, 246, 287
Hubert, W. R. 238

Huchins, Talula (Carpenter) 220

Huckabee, Harriet B. (Denby) 104

Huckabee, J. W. 104

Huckabee, John C. 238

Huckabee, Martha A. (Dorrough) 238

Huckaby, A. F. 193

Huckaby, Ida E. (Hunt) 193

Hucks, Eliza Ann (Liston) 240

Hucks, Jno. B. 240

Hudgens, Jennie (Crawford) 72

Hudgins, Caroline (Malony) 38

Hudgins, George E. 128

Hudgins, James 170

Hudgins, Mattie (Bragg) 170

Hudgins, P. E. 38

Hudgins, Rosa G. (Wannamaker) 128

Hudson, Alice (Turner) 139

Hudson, D. M. 134

Hudson, Ella (Baugh) 200

Hudson, Emma C. (Hicks) 64

Hudson, Eugenia (Farmer) 93

Hudson, J. E. 139

Hudson, J. R. 206

Hudson, James A. 61

Hudson, James E. 200

Hudson, Joanna (Bullard) 266

Hudson, John H. 74

Hudson, John I. 64

Hudson, John N. 214

Hudson, Mary A. (Adams) 74

Hudson, Mary E. (Ingrum) 61

Hudson, Mary Lee (Bright) 279

Hudson, R. A. (Cook) 62

Hudson, S. E. (Walker) 206

Huff, J. A. F. E. (Dukes) 165

Huff, James H. 71, 98

Huff, Jno. H. 213

Huff, Leila H. (Hearn) 213

Huff, Lida (Emmonds) 160

Huff, Mary 165

Huff, Mary E. (Ransome) 71

Huff, Sallie V. (Scurry) 90

Huff, Wm. C. 160

Huff, Wm. T. 90

Huffman, I. C. (Felkel) 289

Huggins, Alice (Chandler) 181

Huggins, Eliza Ann M. (Hill) 180

Huggins, Fannie L. 126

Huggins, Florence S. (Palmer) 197

Huggins, G. W. 133

Huggins, J. B. 253

Huggins, James 233

Huggins, John D. 235

Huggins, John I. 19

Huggins, Josephine E. (Anderson) 235

Huggins, Lenora (Gaston) 233

Huggins, M. E. (Downing) 253

Huggins, Mattie F. (Herrington) 19

Huggins, S. A. (Bishop) 210

Huggins, Sarah Waring (Porter) 133

Huggins, Wm. J. 210

Hughes, A. J. 90, 268

Hughes, Alice (Boozer) 72

Hughes, Chapel 204

Hughes, Charity E. (Lilly) 4

Hughes, Charlotte (Clayton) 215

Hughes, E. L. (Folesom) 226

Hughes, F. G. 34, 38, 54, 67, 108, 138, 155, 162, 174, 208, 243

Hughes, G. 23, 36, 39, 40, 53, 64, 91, 94

Hughes, G. F. 12

Hughes, George 141

Hughes, George W. 29

Hughes, Jas. E. 98

Hughes, Julia (Fulscher) 83

Hughes, Julia (Johnston) 204

Hughes, Lizzie (Nichols) 141

Hughes, M. A. (Rodgers) 90

Hughes, M. Eugenia (Clarke) 29

Hughes, Mattie J. (Beall) 20

Hughes, Mollie (McCrary) 196

Hughes, S. A. (Johnson) 65

Hughes, Sarah E. (Bates) 3

Hughes, T. H. 196

Hughey, Arie H. (Rutherford) 78

Hughey, Elizabeth (Stevens) 151

Hughey, N. D. 180

Hughey, W. Franklin 78

Hugueley, Maggie (Dowdell) 22

Huguley, Annie L. (Pope) 242

Huguley, George H. 242

Hull, Harriet M. (Williams) 16

Hull, J. J. 161

Hull, James S. 253

Hull, Mary N. (Bradley) 253

Hull, Sue (Boyd) 161

Humber, Anna E. (Mitchell) 33

Humber, Mollie (Goode) 197

Humbert, J. G. 29

Humbert, J. W. 222, 250, 278

Humbert, John G. 209

Humbert, S. Addie (Watson) 29

Humbert, S. Eugenia (Pooser) 209

Hume, B. L. 123, 172, 179, 192

Humphrey, Edward 107

Humphrey, M. J. (Boyd) 229

Humphrey, Rebecca J. (Pugh) 107

Humphries, A. (Carter) 46

Humphries, Attha O. (Hollenshead) 183

Humphries, J. F. 46

Humphries, Sallie E. (Ousley) 296

Humphries, Thos. S. 183

Humphries, William S. 296

Hundley, Margaret L. (-Sparkman) 125

Hundley, Z. F. 125

Hungerpeler, David Ann (Felkel) 262

Hunley, Ida R. (Kimbrough) 276

Hunnicutt, Jas. 169

Hunnicutt, Jas. S. 186

Hunnicutt, Mary J. (Turner) 56

Hunt, 289

Hunt, A. E. (McCroan) 259

Hunt, A. J. 252

Hunt, Annie (Morgan) 83

Hunt, Callie (Clement) 252

Hunt, Carrie E. (Cunningham) 173

Hunt, F. M. 10, 111

Hunt, Hellum 107

Hunt, Ida E. (Huckaby) 193

Hunt, J. A. 222

Hunt, Julia D. (Dubose) 119

Hunt, Louisa F. (Ellis) 160

Hunt, M. A. (Sears) 107

Hunt, M. V. (Howe) 104

Hunt, Mary L. (Butts) 64
Hunt, Mollie A. (McKenney) 289
Hunt, Parisade (Carroll) 222
Hunt, Patona E. (Hatcher) 138
Hunt, S. F. 259
Hunt, Sallie (Hogan) 16
Hunt, Thomas J. 16, 64, 173
Hunt, W. H. 42, 102, 111, 127, 131, 138, 140, 150, 169, 179, 194, 235, 252, 263, 290, 294, 295
Hunt, William F. 119
Hunt, William P. 138
Hunter, A. W. (West) 276
Hunter, Andrew 120
Hunter, Charlotte (Waterman) 240
Hunter, F. A. (Dansby) 228
Hunter, H. J. 16, 18, 34
Hunter, J. R. 276
Hunter, James B. 195
Hunter, John Q. 211
Hunter, Jos. B. 82
Hunter, Leonora A. (Townsend) 133
Hunter, Lou H. (Parks) 82
Hunter, M. T. (Henry) 40
Hunter, M. Waterman 240
Hunter, Mary E. E. (Roberts) 24
Hunter, Melissa T. (Johnson) 195
Hunter, Mit (Ellison) 211
Hunter, Mollie E. (Patrick) 150
Hunter, R. B. 228
Hunter, Sarah A. (Glover) 95
Hunter, Susan H. (Henry) 19
Hunter, T. C. 133
Hunter, W. Y. 24
Hunter, Willie (Newby) 178
Huntington, Chas. A. 107
Huntington, Elizabeth V. (Wyatt) 107
Hunton, C. B. 167
Hunton, Julia (Hodge) 167
Hurdle, Ceana J. (Walton) 35
Hurdle, William B. 35
Hurley, Elmira V. (Geesling) 249
Hurst, Angie (Moore) 264
Hurt, C. B. 268
Hurt, C. H. 293
Hurt, Ella McT. (Lockhart) 178
Hurt, Hallie L. (Smith) 22
Hurt, John T. 22

Hurt, Lou (Rowe) 166
Huson, Mark A. 272
Huson, Sue A. (Loyless) 272
Hussey, Charles 208
Hussey, Lelia F. (Collier) 208
Hutchens, N. E. (Moor) 165
Hutcherson, Elizabeth (Stephens) 194
Hutcherson, Lizzie (Dillard) 97
Hutcheson, Lula H. (Armor) 148
Hutcheson, P. W. 170
Hutcheson, S. Virginia (Johnson) 22
Hutchings, Benjamin F. 166
Hutchings, Dora C. (White) 46
Hutchings, Laura (Camp) 216
Hutchings, Mary Jeanette (Dearing) 166
Hutchins, C. L. 86
Hutchins, J. W. 73
Hutchins, Lula (Starr) 86
Hutchins, S. B. (Tomlin) 261
Hutchinson, Callie P. P. (O'Caine) 42
Hutchinson, E. Jennie (Stone) 93
Hutchinson, Rebecca F. (Marcum) 20
Hutchinson, S. P. 93
Hutson, Joe H. 211
Hutson, Lizzie F. (Dutart) 207
Hutson, Mary E. Grier 211
Hutson, Wm. C. 207
Hutto, Angeline S. (Davis) 106
Hutto, Emma (Whetsel) 80
Hutto, Emma L. J. (Snell) 234
Hutto, Gideon 106
Hutto, H. N. 237
Hutto, Julia L. (Shuler) 146
Hutto, Laura (Russ) 258
Hutto, Laura E. (Thirston) 256
Hutto, Lina (Wray) 237
Hutto, Narcissa A. (Matheney) 93
Hutto, Samuel 256
Hutto, Susan F. (Forrest) 23
Hutto, W. 73, 79, 80, 82, 91, 95, 98, 102, 103, 130, 141, 142, 146, 147, 174, 176, 181, 202, 207, 225
Hutto, Wesley 80

Hutto, William 68, 70, 72, 122, 153, 186, 196, 204, 234, 256, 260, 261, 273, 276
Hux, J. A. 79
Hux, Mary K. (Ballad) 79
Hydrick, A. T. 231
Hydrick, Viola C. (Riley) 231
Hyer, Josie 242
Hyer, Laura (Clarke) 182
Hyer, Thos. 182
Ichorb, Annie M. (Dickson) 209
Ilchers, Martha (Cornwell) 44
Inabinet, Anna (Walsh) 83
Inabinet, Chloe Ann (Harrison) 218
Inabinet, Cornelia (Phillips) 225
Inabinet, Henry 225
Inabinet, Joel 218, 222, 231, 284, 293
Inabinet, John 83, 94, 179, 185
Inabinet, Malechia 83
Inabinet, Narcissus (Free) 94
Inabinet, Texas M. (Geiger) 263
Inabnet, Alice V. (Murph) 173
Inabnet, John 173, 227
Inabnit, Amanda L. (Vaughn) 150
Inabnit, John 181
Ingham, George 89
Ingham, Maggie (Tomlin) 89
Ingraham, Evadna (DeCamps) 34
Ingraham, Lou (Cooper) 211
Ingraham, Peter 34
Ingraham, R. T. 211
Ingram, Dolly Ann (Murphy) 252
Ingram, Isaac 79
Ingram, Mary A. (DeLacy) 169
Ingram, Wm. L. 169
Ingrum, Mary E. (Hudson) 61
Inman, Benjamin 76
Inman, J. B. (Russell) 294
Inman, Mary (Bass) 76
Inman, Mary F. (Wells) 96
Inman, Shadrach 294
Irby, Agnes (Walker) 246
Irby, Benjamin 162
Irby, J. E. 30
Irby, John T. 246
Irby, L. E. 268

Irby, Mary Roberts (Laney) 268
Irby, Nannie C. (Waters) 246
Irby, Sallie V. (Munroe) 162
Ireland, J. C. 155
Ireland, Mattie L. (Davis) 155
Irvin, Charles E. 205
Irvin, Mollie (Fortson) 205
Irvine, Flora E. (Giles) 243
Irwin, B. S. 91
Irwin, G. W. 164
Irwin, Henrietta (Hawes) 196
Irwin, Sallie (Hill) 91
Irwin, Sue D. (Childress) 164
Isham, Ann E. (Albra) 93
Isham, Joseph 93
Ives, Julia E. (Hancock) 57
Ives, Nellie C. (Ives) 203
Ives, Sidney E. 203
Ivester, Andrew A. 67
Ivester, Elizabeth A. (Franklin) 67
Ivey, Anthony W. 92
Ivey, C. P. (--y) 224
Ivey, E. J. Williams 219
Ivey, J. A. 224
Ivey, Julia H. (Lester) 136
Ivey, M. T. (Martin) 4
Ivey, N. B. 62
Ivey, R. A. 219
Ivey, Rebecca M. (Peacock) 92
Ivey, Susan A. (Budington) 62
Ivey, Thomas E. 4
Ivie, Jos. R. 186
Ivie, Lizzie (Wright) 186
Ivie, Sarah A. (Maffett) 205
Ivy, A. C. 270
Ivy, C. M. (Withers) 90
Ivy, Carrie (Harbuck) 280
Ivy, Carrie (Smith) 166
Ivy, E. E. (Thomas) 255
Ivy, Flournoy 8
Ivy, G. W. 78, 82
Ivy, Georgia E. (Moore) 270
Ivy, J. A. 280
Ivy, J. M. 255
Ivy, Mattie (Knowles) 8
Ivy, S. T. (Trynum) 160
Izlar, Alonzo J. 166
Izlar, Anna A. (Felder) 87
Izlar, Josephine L. (Green) 114
Izlar, Virginia (McMichael) 166
Izlar, William V. 87

Jacks, C. 57
Jacks, Janie (Brightwell) 57
Jackson, A. W. 263, 276, 292, 294
Jackson, Anna E. (Leitner) 50
Jackson, Arthur M. 5
Jackson, Bettie (Mitchell) 289
Jackson, Bunnie E. (Norwood) 27
Jackson, C. J. 211
Jackson, Carrie P. (Wood) 255
Jackson, Chas. T. 225
Jackson, Clara E. (Redding) 187
Jackson, Drury B. 110
Jackson, Durant 73
Jackson, Emma A. (Carlton) 208
Jackson, Estelle (Bruton) 154
Jackson, Fannie M. (Holloway) 49
Jackson, H. P. 16, 140
Jackson, Ida C. (Kiser) 240
Jackson, J. A. 239
Jackson, J. E. (Adams) 40
Jackson, J. F. H. 189
Jackson, J. W. 12, 16, 24, 40
Jackson, James 5, 79
Jackson, James W. 104
Jackson, Jane G. (Stephens) 239
Jackson, John C. 289
Jackson, John S. 2, 3
Jackson, Jordan T. 249
Jackson, Josephine B. (Lamkin) 226
Jackson, L. E. (Burnet) 101
Jackson, L. Oscard 154
Jackson, Louisa E. (Nichols) 2, 3
Jackson, Lula (Alexander) 225
Jackson, Lunie A. (Collins) 192
Jackson, Luther R. 208
Jackson, M. F. (England) 168
Jackson, M. F. (Shands) 16
Jackson, Maggie C. (Boyd) 229
Jackson, Martha Jane (Lattimore) 184
Jackson, Mary (Conner) 206
Jackson, Mary A. E. (Brooks) 51
Jackson, Mary C. (Jones) 5
Jackson, Mary Louise (McRee) 104

Jackson, Mary S. (Schoolfield) 79
Jackson, Mattie A. (Jarrell) 189
Jackson, Milton C. 249
Jackson, N. E. (Kenny) 61
Jackson, Naomi A. (Langford) 169
Jackson, P. A. (Robertson) 211
Jackson, R. H. 27
Jackson, R. T. 49
Jackson, Richard 194
Jackson, Sarah (Anderson) 194
Jackson, Sarah (Wheeler) 249
Jackson, Sarah E. (Hester) 5
Jackson, Sarah L. (Weathers) 73
Jackson, Sarah S. T. (Simms) 284
Jackson, Sebron R. 206
Jackson, Subeliann (Jones) 249
Jackson, Susan J. (McRee) 110
Jackson, Washington B. 169
Jackson, Wilkins W. 187
Jackson, Wm. 240
Jackson, Wm. P. 192
Jackson, Wm. T. 51
Jacobs, Mary (Hough) 269
James, A. A. 146
James, Daniel 166
James, Elmina (Harris) 166
James, Margaret (Stevens) 1
James, Mary J. (Wilson) 266
Jamison, Henrietta M. (Sellers) 184
Jarnagin, I. C. 241
Jarnagin, Ida B. (Lester) 241
Jarrel, M. Emma (Bell) 7
Jarrell, A. J. 98, 99, 101, 145, 163, 262
Jarrell, Anna E. (Bryan) 21
Jarrell, Bettie S. (Morrell) 8
Jarrell, Joseph B. 8
Jarrell, Mattie A. (Jackson) 189
Jarrell, Nettie S. (Vincent) 46
Jarrell, W. B. 3, 8
Jarrell, Wm. H. 46
Jarrett, C. C. (LeMasters) 227
Jarrett, James C. 227
Jarvis, G. W. 224
Jarvis, John 255

355

Johnston, William Cuyler 189
Joiner, Alice C. (Groover) 57
Joiner, Emily S. (Skinner) 87
Joiner, Jane (Barefield) 21
Joiner, John 69
Joiner, Lessa J. (Brown) 85
Joiner, Levin H. 280
Joiner, Littleton 21
Joiner, Mary A. R. (Lester) 69
Joiner, Sallie E. (Cook) 87
Joiner, Tillmon D. 87
Jones, 91, 118
Jones, A. 88
Jones, A. G. (Poe) 283
Jones, A. Josephine (McDonald) 122
Jones, A. P. 64
Jones, Abram 80, 139
Jones, Addie A. (Robinson) 164
Jones, Adrian (Davis) 65
Jones, Agnes (Byas) 9
Jones, Alfred 283
Jones, Alice (Dowdle) 227
Jones, Amanda V. (Dermond) 58
Jones, Amelia F. (Jones) 127
Jones, Annie R. (Burnet) 139
Jones, Benj. D. 262
Jones, Bessie A. (Crump) 262
Jones, Bessie M. (Hack) 277
Jones, Bettie B. (Wimberly) 189
Jones, Bettie E. (Linch) 272
Jones, C. M. 69
Jones, C. R. (Fogler) 215
Jones, Calvin A. 269
Jones, Catharine E. (Christian) 214
Jones, Clara E. (Law) 257
Jones, Columbus F. 142
Jones, Cordelia A. (Autry) 120
Jones, Cornelia J. (Florence) 54
Jones, Corrie (Wannamaker) 283
Jones, David L. 120
Jones, Dora E. (Ballard) 235
Jones, E. J. (McRae) 200
Jones, E. L. 16
Jones, Elias 260
Jones, Eliza S. (Bostwick) 36

Jones, Elizabeth C. (McKinley) 174
Jones, Elizabeth Whitner (Talley) 225
Jones, Ella (Opry) 27
Jones, Ellen F. (Blue) 77
Jones, Emma J. (Dozier) 287
Jones, Emma L. (Carlisle) 266
Jones, Emma L. (Nebhut) 5
Jones, Emma P. (Gilbert) 237
Jones, Emory C. (Freeman) 132
Jones, Enoch C. 127
Jones, Eudora R. (Brickell) 157
Jones, Fannie D. (Smith) 60
Jones, Fanny (Parrott) 83
Jones, Florence (Vaughn) 84
Jones, Frances D. (McGregor) 57
Jones, Frank 9
Jones, G. M. (Garner) 215
Jones, G. M. 279
Jones, G. W. C. 60
Jones, Geo. T. 86
Jones, Georgia A. (Turner) 74
Jones, Gertrude (Hall) 85
Jones, H. C. 65
Jones, H. F. 65
Jones, Hattie (Glozier) 250
Jones, Hattie Wimberly 193
Jones, Henry B. 174
Jones, Henry Wilks 257
Jones, Hilliard 121, 259
Jones, Ida E. (Spikes) 214
Jones, Ida R. (Burch) 70
Jones, Iverson A. 242
Jones, J. B. 238
Jones, J. D. 215
Jones, J. Olin 215
Jones, J. W. 157
Jones, Jackson 148
Jones, Jacob M. 238
Jones, James 5, 16, 109, 150, 151, 214
Jones, Jennett (Bunch) 269
Jones, John 83
Jones, John F. 1
Jones, John W. 10, 250
Jones, Joseph D. 193
Jones, Joseph M. (Harrell) 45
Jones, Julia (Townsend) 121
Jones, Julia E. (Palmer) 233
Jones, Lavinia Y. 84
Jones, Lena (Miller) 64
Jones, Livinia J. (Chairs) 51

Jones, Lizzie (Rutledge) 225
Jones, Lizzie L. (Cox) 161
Jones, Lizzie L. (Gregg) 258
Jones, Lou (Dawson) 46
Jones, Lou (Tilly) 69
Jones, Louisa (Brett) 238
Jones, Loula P. (Toole) 260
Jones, Lucinda R. (Morgan) 172
Jones, Lucy 5
Jones, Lula (Bridwell) 88
Jones, M. A. (Morris) 77
Jones, M. E. (Lane) 156
Jones, M. E. (Scroggins) 10
Jones, M. E. (Stanford) 279
Jones, M. E. (Woodbery) 30
Jones, M. H. (Munford) 192
Jones, M. H. (Munroe) 69
Jones, M. Josephine (Bagby) 273
Jones, Maggie (Jenkins) 291
Jones, Mamie A. (Blackwell) 174
Jones, Margaret R. (Walker) 219
Jones, Marietta (Dodge) (Chandler) 64
Jones, Martha A. T. (Butler) 81
Jones, Martha L. (Jones) 259
Jones, Mary (Cox) 157
Jones, Mary 5
Jones, Mary A. (Lawson) 150
Jones, Mary A. (Watson) 109
Jones, Mary C. (Jackson) 5
Jones, Mary C. (Land) 243
Jones, Mary C. 76
Jones, Mary E. (Sanford) 238
Jones, Mary J. (Lee) 80
Jones, Mary V. (Pace) 251
Jones, Matthew F. 273
Jones, Matthew H. 81
Jones, Mattie O. (Hicks) 282
Jones, Mattie T. (Davis) 10
Jones, Miles 235
Jones, Minnie N. (Land) 103
Jones, Mitchel 58
Jones, Mollie F.(Mitchell) 1
Jones, Moses 190
Jones, O. H. 258
Jones, Palestine (Rentfrow) 142
Jones, R. F. 30, 56, 62, 95, 160
Jones, R. H. 90
Jones, R. W. 74, 192

Jones, Ralph 170
Jones, Richard S. 166
Jones, Robert F. E. 5
Jones, Robert H. 85, 86
Jones, Roseta R. (Howard) 259
Jones, S. 83
Jones, S. B. (Morton) 170
Jones, S. B. 69, 225, 266
Jones, S. C. (Jones) 83
Jones, S. G. (Malone) 260
Jones, S. G. 175
Jones, S. Gertrude (Hall) 86
Jones, S. Malinda (Bailey) 210
Jones, Sallie E. (Fielding) 190
Jones, Sallie E. (Slocumb) 109
Jones, Sallie J. (Ward) 166
Jones, Sallie L. (Ragan) 16
Jones, Sarah E. (Glenn) 172
Jones, Sarah E. (Northcutt) 86
Jones, Sophia (Johnson) 5
Jones, Subeliann (Jackson) 249
Jones, Susan B. (Porcher) 69
Jones, T. P. 51
Jones, T. S. 103
Jones, Thomas 51, 84
Jones, Thomas E. 283
Jones, Thomas J. 104
Jones, Timothy I. 77
Jones, Tresa (Barr) 148
Jones, Virginia S. (Johnston) 104
Jones, W. A. 200
Jones, W. B. 45
Jones, W. E. 64
Jones, W. H. 233
Jones, W. L. 27
Jones, W. P. 33
Jones, W. W. 101
Jones, Walter J. 122
Jones, Wiley E. 214
Jones, William A. 259
Jones, William B. 132
Jones, William H. 46, 172
Jones, Willis 287
Jones, Zachariah 64
Jones, Zachariah R. 5
Jordan, Amelia T. (Wooten) 276
Jordan, Anna (Ansley) 222
Jordan, Clara E. (Anderson) 277
Jordan, Cornelia (Weaver) 208
Jordan, Dora A. (Adams) 174

Jordan, E. D. 277
Jordan, Eliza (Price) 152
Jordan, F. Rosalie (Simonton) 158
Jordan, G. H. 208
Jordan, G. Marshall 114
Jordan, George M. 152
Jordan, Ira F. 50
Jordan, Isaac M. 111
Jordan, J. B. C. 174
Jordan, J. G. 264
Jordan, J. S. 152, 176, 182, 205, 241, 252, 254, 257
Jordan, J. W. 240
Jordan, James H. 153, 222
Jordan, John 101
Jordan, Josiah W. 222, 239, 277
Jordan, Julie E. (Thames) 111
Jordan, Junius 154, 158, 223
Jordan, Lizzie (Minnifee) 136
Jordan, Lou (Brown) 139
Jordan, M. L. (Geiger) 79
Jordan, Maggie L. (Johnson) 101
Jordan, Mattie (Keel) 210
Jordan, Missouri M. (Flagan) 50
Jordan, Nannie C. (Creswell) 114
Jordan, P. A. (Welborn) 154
Jordan, Pattie K. (Evans) 208
Jordan, R. J. 291
Jordan, Rebecca F. (Puc) 65
Jordan, Richard 208
Jordan, Susan F. (Williams) 291
Jordan, Tallulah G. (Heidt) 176
Jordan, V. A. 79
Jordan, W. J. 173
Jossey, C. W. (Leonard) 289
Jossey, F. B. 289
Jossie, Lummie A. (Walters) 167
Jourdan, Rebecca A. (Vann) 173
Joy, Eliza C. 159
Joyce, Caddie (Harrington) 258
Joyce, J. W. 258
Joyner, Indiana G. (Walton) 87
Joyner, M. R. 87
Judge, Elizabeth E. (Harvey) 7
Judge, T. A. 7

Julien, Maggie E. (Hall) 148
Justiss, Jennie J. (Willingham) 204
Justiss, M. A. A. (Chaffin) 190
Justiss, M. T. 190
Kaigler, I. C. (Tignor) 182
Kaigler, Jonathan 259
Kay, B. C. 285
Kay, Kittie L. (Latimer) 285
Kayler, Caroline (Camp) 49
Kaziah, Emoline (Stilwell) 37
Kaziah, R. P. 37
Kean, Robert B. 38
Kean, Sallie F. (Dozier) 38
Kearing, Mary J. (Davis) 54
Kearing, W. W. 54
Keebler, Addie A. (Hibner) 241
Keebler, E. A. 3
Keebler, L. C. (Bird) 3
Keefer, Annie E. (Worswick) 121
Keefer, William 121
Keel, James C. 210
Keel, Mattie (Jordan) 210
Keen, C. R. 153
Keen, Dora A. (Fredrick) 257
Keen, James L. 260
Keen, Leona J. (Linder) 260
Keenan, Bettie (Wilder) 183
Keener, 221
Keener, J. W. 265
Keener, John H. 50
Keener, Mary J. (Derrick) 50
Keener, S. A. (Seale) 265
Keep, Pauline C. (Biles) 129
Keep, Walter W. 129
Keith, Amanda (Nix) 160
Keith, J. M. 160
Keith, Jennette (Glover) 122
Keith, Mary E. (England) 263
Keith, W. T. 263
Keitt, Adelia (Ulmer) 88
Kellam, 167
Kellam, Sudie T. (Clark) 254
Keller, J. M. 43
Keller, Sallie (Boyd) 43
Kelley, F. M. (Pierce) 66
Kelley, F. Thos. 252
Kelley, Katie E. (Peurifoy) 233
Kelley, Lucy E. (Lake) 252

194, 223, 244, 245, 252, 255, 284, 291
Leonard, Anna F. (Garrard) 33
Leonard, C. W. (Jossey) 289
Leonard, D. 191
Leonard, E. 247
Leonard, Julia (Westmoreland) 282
Leonard, Lamira M. (Bennett) 261
Leonard, Laura E. (Mathews) 115
Leonard, Mattie J. (Matthews) 28
Leonard, Roderick 28
Leonard, S. Emma (Phelps) 96
Leonard, T. K. 23, 100
Leonard, Thomas K. 86, 103, 113, 118, 135, 137, 139, 140, 158
Leonard, Thomas W. 38
Leonard, Van 33
Leonard, Victoria (Barr) 38
Leroy, Benj. 94
Leroy, Emily S. (Wiggins) 94
Leroy, Emma (Newsom) 11
Leroy, H. H. 11
Leroy, Minnie (Willowman) 263
Leseuer, Mary C. (Perkins) 36
Leslie, Jennie (Crowder) 106
Leslie, Low (Dallis) 111
Leslie, Mary I. (Howard) 204
Lester, 246
Lester, Alzoah (Standley) 150
Lester, Avis M. (Clements) 27
Lester, Barnard H. 150
Lester, E. J. (Stubbs) 161
Lester, Ella A. (Ainsworth) 142
Lester, Emma O. (Crittenden) 227
Lester, Frances R. (Smith) 194
Lester, H. F. 136
Lester, H. V. 174
Lester, Hattie (Flynt) 3
Lester, Ida B. (Jarnagin) 241
Lester, J. W. 27
Lester, James Duncan 194
Lester, James W. 227
Lester, John A. 40
Lester, Julia H. (Ivey) 136

Lester, L. F. 29
Lester, M. K. (Dickinson) 29
Lester, Martha A. (Newton) 72
Lester, Mary (Bell) 174
Lester, Mary A. R. (Joiner) 69
Lester, Mary S. (Power) 151
Lester, R. 142
Lester, R. B. 27, 50, 76, 83, 90, 110, 227, 245, 257, 265, 278, 285, 286
Lester, S. F. B. 161
Lester, Sallie (Rogers) 40
Lester, Winnnie (Sullivan) 282
Lever, John 6
Lever, Nannie (Ruff) 6
Lever, Sue (Ruff) 1
Leverett, Anna E. (Sanders) 144
Leverett, Ella V. (Bowman) 289
Leviner, Enoch J. 152
Leviner, Mary J. (May) 152
Lewis, Amie C. (Champion) 161
Lewis, Anna R. (Stone) 190
Lewis, C. A. (Wright) 175
Lewis, E. (Bishop) 173
Lewis, Elisha 44
Lewis, Ella (Newton) 231
Lewis, F. A. 215
Lewis, J. 24, 49, 65, 86, 112, 122, 126, 129, 162, 188, 206
Lewis, J. J. (Hill) 140
Lewis, J. T. 16
Lewis, J. W. 79, 173
Lewis, Josiah 109
Lewis, L. M. 178
Lewis, Lillie B. (Shadgett) 214
Lewis, Lula (Trammell) 105
Lewis, Mary A. (Cooper) 14, 15
Lewis, Mary Hulit (Speer) 109
Lewis, Mary N. V. (Gillis) 46
Lewis, Mattie M. (Erwin) 215
Lewis, Miles W. 161
Lewis, Missouri (Avera) 35
Lewis, Mollie (Gillis) 44
Lewis, N. E. A. 3
Lewis, Nancy E. (Harrison) 138
Lewis, Nancy M. (Carroll) 16
Lewis, Nannie (Butts) 206
Lewis, Pleasant 138
Lewis, S. W. (Rogers) 3

Lewis, Sallie W. (Lamar) 206
Lewis, Sarah Emma (Lewis) 244
Lewis, W. S. J. 231
Lewis, Walker 105, 175, 177, 246, 277, 289
Lewis, William D. 244
Lewis, William F. 109
Lewis, Lucy (Meriwether) 173
Ley, J. C. 228
Ley, John C. 270
Lidden, Hattie B. Boutwell 128
Lightfoot, Ellen T. (Ross) 14
Lightfoot, Harriet A. (Lightfoot) 83
Lightfoot, John B. 83
Lightfoot, Julia A. (Mattox) 291
Lightfoot, Robert J. 14
Ligon, Amelia E. (Lynch) 162
Liles, Adam (Barentine) 79
Liles, F. L. 62
Liles, Jno. W. 271
Liles, Plumer (Grimsley) 271
Liles, Wm. A. 79
Lilley, W. L. (Wood) 199
Lilly, C. C. 250
Lilly, Caro (Gray) 200
Lilly, Charity E. (Hughes) 4
Lilly, Clifford (Hardie) 250
Lilly, E. J. 200
Lilly, J. O. 233
Lilly, John 4
Lilly, Lizzie (Slappey) 233
Lin, J. T. 110, 149, 159
Linch, Bettie E. (Jones) 272
Linch, J. D. 272
Linder, Anna (Tarply) 75
Linder, B. W. 143
Linder, Florence E. (Smith) 236
Linder, J. T. 260
Linder, Leona J. (Keen) 260
Linder, Nannie I. (Morril) 143
Linder, S. S. 236
Lindley, E. H. 164
Lindley, Nannie A. M. (Anderson) 164
Lindsay, Eudora (Harvey) 207
Lindsay, R. R. 207
Lindsay, Sarah A. (Murphey) 99
Lines, Joseph F. 265

Long, Susan (Moore) 62
Longino, E. C. (Smith) 153
Longino, Margaret (Davenport) 256
Longino, O. R. 153
Longino, Seabron 256
Longino, Susan J. (Thompson) 261
Loomis, Cornelia (Root) 60
Loomis, E. Augusta (Hendrix) 105
Loomis, John H. 105
Loomis, Lavinia C. (Bremer) 10
Looper, Eleanor K. (Neisler) 208
Looper, George K. 208
Loper, Albert 244
Loper, Julia A. 180
Loper, Laura (Redd) 244
Lord, J. W. 47
Lord, Mary A. (Trueluck) 47
Lott, Daniel 149
Lott, Fannie (Simons) 149
Lott, Nancy (Hinson) 239
Louge, Susan A. (Raybun) 150
Love, Eugene E. 11
Love, Francis G. (Cheney) 11
Love, J. C. 118
Lovejoy, A. R. 1, 45
Lovejoy, Annie V. (Carroll) 48
Lovejoy, Dora (Barker) 278
Lovejoy, E. C. (Lamar) 238
Lovejoy, Emma A. Rector 103
Lovejoy, James L. 73, 81
Lovejoy, John F. 251
Lovejoy, John S. 48
Lovejoy, M. Ophelia (Johnson) 192
Lovejoy, Mary L. (Cotter) 251
Lovejoy, Mary L. C. (Williams) 73
Lovejoy, Stalina (Lamb) (Holtzendorf) 81
Lovejoy, W. C. 34, 52, 60, 70
Lovejoy, W. P. 151, 153, 167, 170, 187, 227, 277, 278
Lovelace, E. L. 179, 180
Lovelace, Sallie E. A. (Lovelace) 275
Lovelace, Thos. A. 275
Loveless, Della (Gilreath) 286
Loveless, E. L. 160, 175
Lovett, Mamie Smith 284
Lovett, Mary E. (Oliver) 22

Lovett, Mollie A. (Fort) 249
Lovett, R. W. 22, 187
Lovett, Sylvetta (Lanier) 252
Lovett, W. C. 274
Lovett, Wm. C. 284
Lovett, Wm. R. 22
Loving, Nancy Ann (Williams) 25
Loving, W. P. 25
Lovingood, Ella A. (Smith) 204
Lovingood, M. A. (Mills) 285
Lovingood, Samuel 204
Low Fannie, (Barnes) 56
Low, J. M. N. 69
Low, Jas. M. N. 52
Low, Sallie A. (Parker) 42
Low, Samuel 56
Lowe, A. J. (Kirksey) 169
Lowe, Beatrice Gertrude (Booker) 270
Lowe, Caroline (Rickenbacker) 70
Lowe, Eleanor E. (Rogers) 256
Lowe, Emma T. (Scarborough) 31
Lowe, Gilbert Y. 270
Lowe, J. T. 11, 32, 104, 169, 255
Lowe, James T. 31, 99, 116
Lowe, John C. 180
Lowe, Juvernia R. (Moseley) 116
Lowe, Mary M. (Minter) 161
Lowe, Matilda E. (Forrar) 160
Lowe, Mattie V. (Rogers) 180
Lowe, P. E. 177
Lowe, Sallie (Price) 191
Lower, J. T. 264
Lowery, Gertrude (Heath) 241
Lowery, Jas. E. 241
Lowery, M. T. (Davis) 124
Lowman, George 27
Lowman, L. V. (Culverhouse) (McManus) 281
Lowman, M. C. (Collier) 27
Lowman, William G. 281
Lowrance, Mary J. (Bell) 129
Lowrance, W. W. 129
Lowrey, A. B. 268
Lowrey, Ella O. (Latimer) 288
Lowrey, Georgia A. (Reddick) 268
Lowrey, J. M. 1, 35, 148

Lowrey, Jno. M. 288
Lowrey, Sophia A. G. (Davis) 1
Lowry, E. C. 204
Lowry, J. M. 71, 155
Loyal, L. C. 51, 130, 170, 189
Loyal, Mary A. (Hilton) 130
Loyd, Jabez 39
Loyd, Juda C. M. (Pool) 39
Loyd, Nannie W. (Grace) 208
Loyless, Sue A. (Huson) 272
Lucas, Celia Lester (Bozeman) 99
Lucas, Frederick B. 236
Lucas, Susie H. (Taylor) 236
Luckey, R. H. 97
Luckie, Emma B. (Hemphill) 95
Lucky, C. E. 183
Lucky, Julia O. (Sims) 183
Lucy, Jennie E. (Wilson) 101
Lucy, Michael H. 101
Ludy, Emily E. (Gammage) 68
Ludy, W. H. 68
Luffman, J. J. 154
Lumpkin, 124
Lumpkin, Martha (Benn) 112
Lumpkin, Mary E. (Driggars) 212
Lumpkin, Sarah M. (Bussey) 254
Lumpkin, W. W. 241, 255
Lumpkin, Wm. I. 254
Lumsden, J. H. (Powers) 253
Lumsden, Josiah 253
Lumsden, Mary (Kendall) 277
Lundie, Mattie E. (Perkins) 5
Lundy, Alexander S. 71
Lundy, Matilda M. (Lee) 71
Lunquest, Cornelia (Cravey) 16
Lunquest, M. J. 16
Lunsford, Jennie (Cheatham) 268
Lunsford, T. F. 165
Lupo, J. L. 109, 111, 176, 183
Lupo, James L. 122
Lupo, Lula J. (Trunnell) 122
Lupo, Wesley 122
Luttrell, J. A. (Torly) 96
Luttrell, James 96

Lykes, Mettie (Stringer) 178
Lyle, A. J. 224
Lyle, J. H. 154
Lyle, James P. 160
Lyle, Laura (Kimble) 160
Lyle, M. E. (Carter) 154
Lyle, Mary E. (Venable) 138
Lyle, Susan E. (Dickey) 224
Lyles, A. Rosalie (Mc-Meekin) 145
Lyles, B. E. 145
Lynch, Amelia E. (Ligon) 162
Lynch, Colistia A. (Slayton) 95
Lynch, Geo. P. 95
Lynch, Geo. R. 55
Lynch, Louis M. 162
Lynch, Mary E. (Bedell) 55
Lynch, Rebecca A. (Harald) 147
Lynch, Wm. T. H. 147
Lynn, M. S. 123
Lynn, Rebecca (Jefferies) 123
Lyon, Mary D. (Wheeless) 110
Lyon, Mittie (Sutton) 146
Lyon, N. E. 172
Lyon, Sallie E. (Pleaston) 172
Lyon, Thos. R. 146
Lyons, Francis (McKendree) 230
Lysles, Fannie J. (Fant) 96
Mabbit, Ida C. (Raysor) 248
Mabbit, Joseph 248
MacDonald, George F. 171
MacDonald, Tallula W. (Gunnels) 171
MacDonell, G. G. N. 198
MacDonell, Geo. G. N. 30, 38, 42, 55, 116, 122, 130, 146, 165, 167, 179, 206, 210, 254, 292
MacMillan, Dee (Spear) 180
Mackay, E. A. (Holmes) 54
Macon, Mattie (Tuck) 202
Macon, Sarah (Stivender 117
Maddox, Alice (Bryan) 265
Maddox, John 145
Maddox, Mattie (Rea) 145
Maddux, Ellen (King) 45
Maddux, Emory A. 97
Maddux, Hettie (Peurifoy) 91
Maddux, James L. 174
Maddux, Jennie (Robinson) 57

Maddux, Jennie Lela (Watts) 29
Maddux, M. Arlone (Torrey) 97
Maddux, P. N. 91
Maddux, Thomas B. 29
Maddux, W. D. 57
Madison, Mary J. (Steele) 266
Maffett, Andrew W. 222
Maffett, Hamilton 205
Maffett, Sarah A. (Ivie) 205
Maffett, Susan D. (Boykin) 222
Maffit, Tillie C. (Crew) 131
Magruder, Matilda F. (Stovall) 93
Magruder, Mattie S. (Avery) 206
Magwood, Ennie J. (Ferrill) 285
Magwood, J. G. 285
Mahaffey, Emory V. M. 137
Mahaffey, Fannie K. (Mattox) 137
Mahone, Kate (Holmes) 46
Mahoney, Jas. 229
Maier, Albert D. 280
Maier, Lula (Holland) 280
Major, Elisa (Carter) 59
Major, Joseph W. 88
Major, Lucy (Smith) 275
Major, Maggie (Webb) 88
Major, Martha (Blackman) 146
Major, S. G. 59
Major, Sallie (Byars) 275
Major, William 275
Mallette, G. H. 183
Mallory, A. H. 179
Mallory, J. C. 197
Mallory, M. H. (Hodnett) 197
Mallory, S. A. (Mobley) 84
Mallory, Sudie A. (Turnell) 179
Malone, Anna (Oslin) 22
Malone, C. A. (Tarver) 274
Malone, J. D. 260
Malone, M. A. 260
Malone, Olivia Ann (Stokes) 34
Malone, P. J. 34
Malone, R. H. 274
Malone, S. G. (Jones) 260
Malone, W. J. 22
Malony, Caroline (Hudgins) 38
Malsby, A. H. (Cary) 223
Malsby, John D. 223
Malsby, L. W. 187
Malsby, M. F. 8, 10, 54, 63, 166, 191

Malsby, Mary F. (Johnson) 166
Malsby, Sarah K. (McMurray) 187
Mandeville, Alfred S. 94
Mandeville, Ann Eliza (Woodson) 94
Mandeville, Nellie (Kramer) 238
Mane, Siberia D. (Jernigan) 28
Maner, Anna B. (Martin) 217
Maner, Mary P. (Charlton) 165
Maner, S. P. 217
Maner, Samuel 165
Manes, Ann (Bedell) 48
Manes, E. 48
Manget, B. E. 113
Manget, V. E. 113, 177
Mankins, N. Lou (Green) 43
Manley, J. W. 48
Manley, Sarah C. (England) 48
Mann, A. T. 118
Mann, Benj. D. 170
Mann, C. D. 233
Mann, Cinderella (Taylor) 170
Mann, H. W. 294
Mann, I. J. (Cox) 148
Mann, J. R. 102
Mann, John W. 67
Mann, Maggie D. (Martin) 167
Mann, Martha J. (Cowey) 67
Mann, Mary A. (Peoples) 184
Mann, Mary E. (Brown) 100
Mann, Mary M. (Wallace) 102
Mann, Mary V. (Fife) 228
Mann, Olva (Morris) 294
Mann, S. E. (Hamrick) 159
Mann, Sidney P. 228
Manning, Cicero J. 200
Manning, Cordilia (Bryan) 29
Manning, Dennis J. 226
Manning, Emma E. (Grambling) 270
Manning, Florence F. (Baxter) 226
Manning, Houston 106
Manning, M. A. (McLean) 35
Manning, Mary E. (Manning) 200

Manning, Mattie R. (Stackhouse) 106
Manning, Nancy (Ragan) 246
Manning, Walter 203, 212
Manning, Willoughby 246
Mansell, Avie A. (Neese) 189
Mansfield, E. E. (Beall) 33
Mansfield, H. H. 33
Mansfield, Wm. C. 152
Mansfield, Zoe Sevier (Rogers) 152
Manson, 45
Manson, A. F. (Crawford) 280
Manson, Frank E. 24
Manson, Mattie (Baker) 24
Manson, Sue H. (Crockett) 30
Manson, Z. P. 280
Mapp, 279
Marable, Eva E. (Stovall) 24
Marable, Sallie P. (Anderson) 81
Marable, William H. 81
Marbut, E. 136
Marbut, Lodocey (Wharton) 136
Marbutt, Correna (Baily) 6
Marchant, David H. 167
Marchant, Julia A. (Bond) 167
Marchman, America (Stolvey) 107
Marchman, Civility (Stephens) 21
Marchman, Fannie J. (Buff) 15
Marchman, James 21
Marchman, Jennie C. (Harman) 215
Marchman, Mary B. (Marchman) 198
Marchman, Mollie (Henderson) 171
Marchman, Thomas 15
Marchman, W. J. 171
Marchman, Wm. M. 198
Marcum, Henry C. 20
Marcum, Martha (Roberts) 133
Marcum, Rebecca F. (Hutchinson) 20
Marcum, Welshin 133
Marden, Isaac 7
Market, Fannie A. (Greene) 92
Markey, Anna H. (Rylander) 282
Markey, Z. F. 282

Marks, Emma M. (Willis) 157
Markum, C. A. 47
Markum, Susan (Newmons) 47
Marlow, Clara E. (Harrel) 176
Marlow, James E. 176
Marone, Lizzie F. (Turner) 281
Marr, Donie W. (Shine) 141
Marr, Thomas J. 141
Marrow, David C. 115
Marrow, P. F. (Sawyer) 115
Marsh, Mary A. (Cobb) 19
Marsh, Wm. F. 19
Marsha, Achsah (Turner) 38
Marsha, E. W. 38
Marshall, A. D. (Edge) 184
Marshall, A. M. 117, 265
Marshall, Amanda M. (Sims) 75
Marshall, Charles 202
Marshall, Daniel 100
Marshall, Eliza (Houser) 202
Marshall, Eliza Knight (Godfrey) 30
Marshall, Emma L. (Raiford) 199
Marshall, Hattie Grinnell (Gregory) 281
Marshall, Henrietta (Epting) 232
Marshall, J. Dill 153
Marshall, J. M. 75, 205
Marshall, John G. 67
Marshall, John M. 174, 194, 279, 281, 287
Marshall, Julia L. (Brent) 210
Marshall, Lela (Blanten) 100
Marshall, Mary J. (Gew) 67
Marshall, Mary P. (Pace) 194
Marshall, Mattie C. (Turner) 147
Marshall, S. A. (Elder) 65
Marshall, Sarah (Bowins) 179
Marshall, Susan (Gammage) 166
Marshall, T. H. 232
Marshall, Tiny (Houser) 153
Marshall, W. C. 166
Marshall, W. J. 30
Martin, Addie (Lang) 128
Martin, Alonzo C. 78
Martin, Amanda M. (Crenshaw) 224

Martin, Angus 128
Martin, Anna B. (Maner) 217
Martin, Anna P. (Rowland) 148
Martin, Aurelia E. (Johnson) 154
Martin, Ben A. 73
Martin, Calvin 148
Martin, Carrie (Oslin) 96
Martin, Charity A. (Tarrance) 243
Martin, Cordelia (Johnson) 8
Martin, E. E. (Swindle) 66
Martin, E. M. (Williams) 24
Martin, Edwin 167
Martin, Eliza (Dantzler) 73
Martin, Elizabeth L. (Elrod) 252
Martin, Ellen (Newton) 91
Martin, Emma (Gaines) 68
Martin, Fannie (Crook) 291
Martin, George P. 159
Martin, H. J. 96
Martin, Harmon 218
Martin, J. H. 198
Martin, J. J. 66
Martin, J. S. 73
Martin, J. V. 217
Martin, J. W. 289
Martin, James L. 114
Martin, John 8
Martin, John G. 282
Martin, Joseph 285
Martin, Julia E. (Davis) 1
Martin, L. M. (Thomas) 139
Martin, Laura T. (Hendry) 174
Martin, M. A. (Simpson) 27
Martin, M. T. (Ivey) 4
Martin, Maggie A. (Fussel) 282
Martin, Maggie D. (Mann) 167
Martin, Martha M. K. (Gibson) 218
Martin, Mary (Summerville) 102
Martin, Mary (McSpadden) 184
Martin, Mary (Rush) 89
Martin, Mary (Sanford) 279
Martin, Mary C. (Printup) 169
Martin, Mattie C. (Callier) 47
Martin, Mollie E. (O'Connor) 73
Martin, Philip 225
Martin, R. M. 68
Martin, Rachel (Thomas) 159

Martin, Reuben 89
Martin, Robt. P. 139, 184, 198
Martin, S. E. (Howell) 71
Martin, Sallie (Christopher) 285
Martin, Sarah A. (Bruce) 159
Martin, Sarah E. (Livingston) 11
Martin, Susan F. (Ruff) 120
Martin, Thomas S. 154
Martin, Vernelle C. (Brockington) 263
Martin, Whitefoord S. 262
Martin, Whitefoord Smith 263
Martin, William 10, 50, 55, 133, 184
Martin, William H. 1, 47
Martin, William R. 102
Martin, William T. 169
Martin, Zilphia C. (Cann) 78
Martyn, Robert P. 242, 284, 295
Martyn, Robert T. 295
Marvin, E. M. 61
Marvin, Fannie (Wells) 33
Marvin, Mary J. (Sanders) 267
Marvin, S. Anderson 267
Mashburn, Amanda (Jenkins) 152
Mashburn, H. J. 48
Mashburn, J. H. 117, 130, 152
Mashburn, John H. 58, 189. 200
Mashburn, Mary J. (Johnson) 98
Mashburn, Nancy M. (Butler) 58
Mason, A. B. (Turner) 65
Mason, Almida F. (Walker) 234
Mason, Benjamin F. 234
Mason, Beulah A. (Booth) 137
Mason, F. E. 30
Mason, George W. 137
Mason, Hattie V. (Clark) 190
Mason, J. R. 113
Mason, Martha F. (O'Ferrell) 8
Mason, Mary P. (Dailey) 250
Mason, Mattie (Holbrooks) 259
Mason, S. K. 259
Massengale, A. M. 198

Massengale, Hattie E. (Brinn) 198
Massengale, Mollie R. (Houser) 275
Massengale, Sallie E. (Rush) 128
Massengale, T. R. 128
Massey, Amanda (Ward) 28
Massey, Emma (Strange) 256
Massey, Fannie E. (Holstern) 44
Massey, Lizzie (Fitzpatrick) 59
Massey, Mary S. (Massey) 39
Massey, Orren E. 44
Massey, Sarah Ann (Randall) 56
Massey, Thos. J. 39
Massey, Wayne (Subers) 108
Massey, Wm. 56
Massingale, George P. 70
Massingale, Julia B. H. (Smith) 70
Matheney, Narcissa A. (Hutto) 93
Matheney, W. H. 93
Mathew, 133
Mathews, 61
Mathews, E. M. 87
Mathews, Ella Deane (Small) 245
Mathews, Jas. N. 61
Mathews, Laura E. (Leonard) 115
Mathews, M. Valeria (Clayton) 3
Mathews, Mary (Pearson) 61
Mathews, Mary E. (Anderson) 246
Mathews, Mary Ellen (Blalock) 125
Mathews, Mary J. (Sibley) 1
Mathews, Mittie (Bateman) 87
Mathews, Ophelia (Houghton) 61
Mathews, Robert A. 115, 164
Mathews, Robert Greer 125
Mathews, Sallie (Thompson) 164
Mathews, W. B. 246
Mathews, Wm. C. 3
Mathews, Wm. P. 245
Mathis, A. 167
Mathis, Ella (Walker) 294
Mathis, James A. 120
Mathis, John B. 23

Mathis, Marietta A. A. (Mays) 23
Mathis, Nannie G. (Gibson) 167
Matthews, Bessie (Houser) 151
Matthews, Demarius (Young) 223
Matthews, Ella (Flagler) 10
Matthews, Fannie T. (Hammet) 155
Matthews, H. T. 120
Matthews, J. D. 56
Matthews, Louvinia G. (Freeman) 109
Matthews, M. A. E. (Lipscomb) 251
Matthews, Mary Norton (Babcock) 120
Matthews, Mattie J. (Leonard) 28
Matthews, Sallie S. (Allison) 81
Matthews, Samuel M. 10
Matthews, Sarah Emma (Mitchell) 56
Matthews, Stella (Bowen) 254
Matthews, Thos. S. 151
Matthews, W. P. 251
Matthews, Wm. C. 90
Matthews, Zimmie S. (Hardwick) 90
Matthis, Sabra (Clifton) 49
Matthis, Virginia D. (Fincher) 248
Mattox, E. 137
Mattox, E. A. A. (Bryant) 47
Mattox, Elijah 47
Mattox, Fannie K. (Mahaffey) 137
Mattox, Florida V. (Paxton) 111
Mattox, G. Crawford 55
Mattox, Julia A. (Lightfoot) 291
Mattox, M. E. 171
Mattox, Mary E. (Shepard) 67
Mattox, O. T. 291
Mattox, Sue V. (Henry) 55
Maudeville, Florence (Bennett) 57
Maul, Emeline E. (Walker) 94
Maul, Geo. 94
Maulden, James 10
Maulden, Nancy J. (Carmichael) (Kelly) 47
Maulden, Rhoda C. (Williams) 10
Maulden, Wm. E. 47

Mauldin, Amelia (Craft) 176

Mauldin, Benjamin W. 163

Mauldin, Clara A. (Faison) 163

Mauldin, Jas. D. 257

Mauldin, M. E. (Graham) 29

Mauldin, Thos. 176

Maunds, Ella (Cumly) 69

Maunds, Joseph H. 69

Maxey, J. L. (Bashlor) 278

Maxwell, E. R. (Guice) 275

Maxwell, Florence M. (Wright) 157

Maxwell, Gussie (Briant) 84

Maxwell, Harriet C. (Turner) 269

Maxwell, Penny (Hinson) 92

Maxwell, Wm. H. 275

Maxwell, Zenobia (Tolbert) 148

May, Fannie (Strother) 215

May, Fannie S. (Connor) 287

May, I. J. 287

May, J. 153

May, James R. 215

May, Mary J. (Leviner) 152

Mayer, L. C. (Kinard) 122

Mayer, O. B. 122

Mayes, A. J. 111

Mayes, J. R. 229

Mayes, Maggie (Sewell) 276

Mayes, Mary (Swain) 111

Mayes, S. D. 55

Mayes, S. F. (Brinkley) 55

Mayes, Sallie A. (Lemmond) 173

Maynard, Thomas P. 115

Mayo, A. 178

Mayo, Anderson 229

Mayo, George W. 98

Mayo, Mattie (McGregor) 98

Mays, Emma B. (Bean) 39

Mays, F. O. 39

Mays, Julia I. (Proctor) 90

Mays, Marietta A. A. (Mathis) 23

Mays, Mary E. (Embry) 147

Mayson, J. R. 67, 95, 116, 122, 137, 161, 189, 196, 222, 271, 277

Mayson, James 49

Mayson, Mattie (Tibert) 49

Mayton, Geo. R. 192

Mayton, Ollie S. (Bates) 192

Mazingo, Mary (Talivar) 282

Mazingo, McKinzie 282

Mazo, A. W. S. 210

Mazo, Hattie (Fulford) 210

McAfee, Emma A. (Goodwin) 270

McAfee, Maggie Love (Smith) 76

McAfee, Miller H. 76

McAfee, W. W. 152

McAffee, E. C. (Wells) 31

McAlhaney, Benj. B. 172

McAlhaney, Elizabeth J. (Felder) 172

McAlhaney, Martha (Dukes) 148

McAlpin, Daniel 78

McAlpin, Ella (Smith) 295

McAlpin, Leonora V. (Hand) 197

McAlpin, Lizzie (Watson) 8

McAlpin, Mary (Smith) 78

McAlpin, Reuben H. 197

McAndrew, Belle (Bonnell) 195

McAndrew, Susan (Newman) 206

McAndrew, Wm. E. 206

McBee, Nannie (Calhoun) 126

McBramlet, Barbary E. (Fowler) 276

McBramlet, Daniel 276

McBride, Annie E. (Murray) 247

McBride, E. H. 247

McBryde, Alexander 53

McBryde, Celia Ann (Clenny) 53

McBryde, Cornelia E. (Warrill) 271

McBryde, J. T. 252

McBryde, Lena R. (McBryde) 226

McBryde, Maggie (Dill) 46

McBryde, S. Cincinnatus 226

McCain, B. J. 212

McCain, Fannie (Henry) 137

McCain, J. K. 261, 262

McCain, James 49

McCain, John Kelly 137

McCain, Mary (Stone) 49

McCain, Tallula V. (Cook) 212

McCall, Claude (Weaver) 45

McCall, Fannie (Stephens) 212

McCall, James P. 45

McCall, John E. 44

McCall, M. J. G. 25

McCall, Mary A. (Wells) 44

McCall, Sarah J. (Eason) 53

McCall, Wm. 213

McCalla, Ida L. (Cleveland) 174

McCamy, Kate L. (Carter) 40

McCamy, Samuel B. 40

McCann, John 245

McCann, Maggie E. (Brodie) 245

McCann, Mary P. (Hill) 18

McCants, B. J. 107

McCants, J. A. 17

McCants, Leonora (McCants) 107

McCants, M. A. (Edwards) 17

McCants, Nancy (Perry) 179

McCants, Sallie E. (Bates) 217

McCantz, J. G. 138

McCantz, J. J. (Murrey) 138

McCardel, A. H. 185

McCardel, Ella N. (Tooke) 185

McCardell, James S. 164

McCardell, Sallie L. (McIlwain) 164

McCarter, Alice F. (McLaughlin) 159

McCarthy, Ella (McMichael) 114

McCarty, Mary Ann (Evans) 93

McCarty, P. D. 93

McCarty, W. A. 85

McCaskill, D. A. 38

McCaskill, Fannie (Davis) 38

McCay, Margaret R. (Bailey) 110

McCay, Thomas 110

McClane, C. E. (Dozier) 77

McClane, John P. 77

McClatchey, Adie (Reynolds) 34

McClatchey, D. F. 34

McClellan, G. E. 177

McClellan, Ida B. (Osborne) 295

McClellan, Isabel S. (Worrell) 177

McClellan, Walter G. 295

McClenaghan, H. 88

McClendon, Lizzie (Bigby) 112

McClendon, Medora (Freeman) 2

McClendon, S. Virginia (DeVaughn) 17

McClendon, W. W. 17

McCleskey, David M. 278

McCleskey, Elizabeth E. (Espy) 278

McCleskey, G. L. 233

McCloud, Henrietta (Hix) 288
McCloud, John F. 288
McClure, C. M. 81
McClure, J. D. 87
McClure, Mary (Taylor) 87
McCollough, Frances E. (Alexander) 134
McCollough, John 134
McCollum, A. S. 118
McCollum, Hattie (Everingham) 118
McCollum, Hugh 237
McCollum, J. P. (Harris) 160
McCollum, John H. 18
McCollum, Josephine T. (Walsh) 18
McCollum, Rachel (Galloway) 237
McCollum, S. S. 160
McColough, Mary E. (Templeton) 2
McConnell, E. J. 20
McConnell, Eliza Ann (Steele) 250
McConnell, H. A. (Hines) 77
McConnell, Ida P. (Brand) 285
McConnell, Isaac 168
McConnell, J. Fowler (Britton) 237
McConnell, James M. 175
McConnell, Jane (Tinkler) 175
McConnell, Julia (Chandler) 265
McConnell, Mary M. (Coogler) 101
McConnell, Sallie J. (Houston) 20
McConnell, Sarah E. (Campbell) 168
McConnell, Tilford 285
McConnell, Wm. 101
McCook, S. A. 136
McCorcle, Melissa (Spinks) 163
McCorcle, Robert 163
McCord, E. T. 117
McCord, Ellen C. (Spear) 117
McCord, James D. 197
McCord, Mollie (Owen) 197
McCorkle, 202
McCorkle, H. 171
McCorkle, Lucinda A. (Smith) 171
McCormick, Georgia H. (Brand) 284
McCorquodale, Allan 137

McCorquodale, A. 173
McCoy, Allison E. 159
McCoy, J. A. (Salter) 282
McCoy, Mattie W. (Bass) 134
McCoy, Olivia L. (Wiggins) 159
McCracken, B. B. 28
McCracken, Julia E. (Beaty) 28
McCraney, (Friday) 228
McCraney, Archibald 228
McCrary, B. F. 120
McCrary, C. F. 82
McCrary, E. B. 141
McCrary, E. V. (Dozier) 141
McCrary, Edna (Montgomery) 120
McCrary, Emily (Spence) 232
McCrary, G. I. A. 76
McCrary, Molie C. (Mitchell) 82
McCrary, Mollie (Hughes) 196
McCrary, Nancy E. (Smith) 46
McCrary, Salina A. (Casey) 76
McCreary, Cornelia A. (Odom) 255
McCreary, John A. 255
McCroan, A. E. (Hunt) 259
McCrone, 164
McCrone, Emma J. (Parker) 203
McCulley, Sue M. (Barr) 129
McCullough, J. W. 185
McCully, Lindy G. 154
McCurdy, Cornelia (Brinkley) 67
McCurdy, G. T. 67
McCurdy, Jas. G. 15
McCurdy, Sarah R. (Kinney) 15
McCutchen, Emily (Simmons) 274
McDade, A. W. 268
McDade, Lou E. (Caswell) 137
McDade, M. J. (Burch) 65
McDade, Sannie J. (Park) 268
McDade, W. D. 137
McDaniel, Alexander 231
McDaniel, Charlotte (Wilson) 246
McDaniel, Fannie E. (Lassiter) 129
McDaniel, J. C. 295
McDaniel, M. A. (Akers) 36

McDaniel, Mary Ann (Shuler) 295
McDaniel, Octavia (Freeman) 231
McDaniel, Ruth (Brown) 163
McDavid, Fannie M. (Sullivan) 13
McDavid, P. A. 13
McDonald, A. Josephine (Jones) 122
McDonald, Alex. G. 189
McDonald, Annie (Akers) 274
McDonald, Balzona (Chambers) 189
McDonald, Carrie O. (Mills) 119
McDonald, Cornelia W. (Page) 262
McDonald, D. A. (Roquemore) 39
McDonald, Duncan 246
McDonald, Ellas C. (Butler) 48
McDonald, H. T. 227
McDonald, J. A. 262
McDonald, Jas. D. 39
McDonald, Jas. P. 274
McDonald, John 19
McDonald, Lorenzo D. 119
McDonald, Maggie Bruce (Murchison) 199
McDonald, Margaret A. (Alexander) 19
McDonald, Margaret E. (Hilliard) 192
McDonald, Martha (Crowley) 39
McDonald, Mary (Caton) 232
McDonald, Mary L. (Hindman) 246
McDonald, Moses B. 199
McDonald, R. 122
McDonald, Sarah A. (Vinson) 23
McDonald, Sarah E. (Barnes) 227
McDonald, Virginia B. (Traylor) 118
McDonald, W. 133
McDonald, William 39
McDonald, William H. 192
McDonald, William J. 48
McDonell, James D. 169
McDonell, Mattie (Wimberly) 169
McDowell, Emma (Daniel) 254
McDowell, Georgia A. (Vinson) 77
McDowell, J. L. 20

McNair, Fannie E. (Stewart) 117
McNair, Henrietta (Lassiter) 185
McNair, Lizzie B. (Wyche) 242
McNair, N. A. (Patterson) 49
McNamee, J. M. 190
McNamee, Rowena (Frazier) 190
McNeal, J. H. 6
McNeal, M. E. (Livingston) 6
McNealy, A. 41
McNealy, Lavinia (Byrd) 41
McNeely, Eugenia (Tison) 25
McNeely, J. M. 25
McNeice, Susie (Webb) 139
McNeil, Eugenia A. (Chapman) 22
McNeil, Viola (Johns) 168
McNeil, W. A. 168
McNeill, Duncan 60
McNeill, Margaret A. (Sloan) 60
McNiell, Hannah L. (Carter) 51
McNiell, James 51
McPhail, Ellen D. (McGehee) 150
McPhail, John D. 150
McPherson, Martha A. (Cook) 230
McPherson, Thos J. 230
McQueen, Clara (Chairs) 11
McQueen, Clara F. (McIver) 192
McRacken, James 142
McRacken, Nina (Ross) 142
McRae, Abbie B. (Barber) 149
McRae, C. C. 244
McRae, C. F. 14
McRae, Christian F. (Ryals) 277
McRae, E. J. (Jones) 200
McRae, H. A. (Leak) 25
McRae, J. H. 47
McRae, J. H. B. 183
McRae, J. H. D. 7, 13, 19, 20, 23, 40, 55, 61, 75, 94, 133, 227, 233, 244, 258, 262, 264, 268
McRae, J. M. D. 47
McRae, L. A. (Allen) 244
McRae, Laura A. (McWhorter) 89
McRae, Mary L. (Boyd) 161
McRae, Mary L. (Clements) 277

McRae, Millard 277
McRae, S. J. (Newton) 268
McRae, Sarah J. (McKinnon) 33
McRae, Wiley B. 89
McRae, Wm. O. 33
McRary, Anne E. (Burns) 55
McRary, W. H. 55
McRay, Abbie (Platt) 291
McRay, Jesse 223
McRay, Querny (Pugh) 223
McRee, James I. 23
McRee, Mary Louise (Jackson) 104
McRee, Mollie Z. (Suber) 98
McRee, Richard B. 98
McRee, S. A. (Hinton) 23
McRee, Susan J. (Jackson) 110
McRoy, Drusilla Ann (Gillam) 69
McRoy, J. W. 18, 32, 39, 87, 93, 135, 193, 217
McRoy, John W. 34, 66, 69, 117, 135, 160, 179, 198, 210, 219, 264, 265, 285
McSpadden, Mary (Martin) 184
McStewart, C. 23
McStewart, Laura (Bryan) 23
McSwain, Annie C. (Nabers) 22
McSwain, D. 92
McSwain, E. T. 61
McSwain, Janie (McGowan) 61
McSwain, M. J. (Wallace) 92
McSwain, Nancy A. (Stokes) 78
McSwain, Nectar 78
McSwain, Sarah(Brake) 232
McSwain, W. A. 22
McTyeire, 251, 262
McTyeire, Georgia E. (Dean) 36
McWhirter, Anna K. (Fowler) 209
McWhirter, W. A. 209
McWhorter, Laura A. (McRae) 89
McWhorter, M. H. (Simmons) 131
McWhorter, M. L. (Powell) 38
McWhorter, S. W. 38
McWilliams, Alice (Baker) 215

McWilliams, D. R. 3, 9, 12, 60, 67, 128, 170, 177, 194, 202
McWilliams, Jared B. 247
McWilliams, Mattie L. (Dozier) 247
Mcgehee, E. H. 79
Mcroy, J. W. 116
Meaders, C. W. 130
Meaders, D. Albert 21
Meaders, John 107
Meaders, Mattie (Lambert) 107
Meaders, Mattie W. (Pitchford) 21
Meadors, C. 95
Meadors, Jos. N. 59
Meadors, Mary E. S. (Bushart) 25
Meadows, L. Q. 39
Meadows, Sarah J. (O'Conner) 39
Means, 260
Means, E. E. (Hightower) 292
Means, J. F. 292
Means, James 139
Means, Lizzie Powledge 108
Means, Lucretia (Lites) 139
Means, Mattie M. (Rosser) 251
Means, Sallie (Smoak) 260
Meashin, Ellen (Dent) 42
Meatcham, Annie E. (Bowden) 262
Medlock, Frane 159
Medlock, Lou (Nash) 159
Meek, Mary F. (Braswell) 143
Meek, Thomas J. 143
Meeks, L. J. (Smith) 71
Meeks, V. A. (West) 271
Mehaffey, John 182
Mehaffey, Laura E. (Ford) 182
Mein, Jane (Carrithers) 77
Meldrim, Maggie (Thompson) 177
Melichamp, Sallie (Cook) 174
Mell, Annie E. (George) 38
Mell, Wm. B. 38
Mellard, E. R. (Frederick) 88
Mellard, Emma C. (Brownlee) 138
Mellard, L. C. 65
Mellard, Laura (Livingston) 62
Mellard, Mattie C. (Clark) 65
Mellard, T. 138
Mellard, T. J. 62, 167

Miller, Sarah Ellen (Strobhart) 200
Miller, Tho. 101
Miller, W. Bennet 130
Miller, William B. 129
Miller, William R. 57
Miller, Willie (Williams) 129
Milles, James M. 182
Milles, Mary E. (Chambers) 182
Millhouse, Emma J. A. (Smack) 70
Millhouse, L. R. 69
Millhouse, Lulie (Funderburk) 69
Millican, Robert E. 118
Millican, Sallie (Brunson) 118
Millican, Sallie (Edwards) 28
Milligan, Eva (Fain) 189
Milligan, J. W. 189
Milligan, Jas. 57
Milling, J. E. (Pernell) 140
Millirous, J. A. 73
Millirous, Margaret (Potts) 73
Mills, C. W. 79
Mills, Carrie O. (McDonald) 119
Mills, Eliza C. (Stewart) 79
Mills, Grazilla M. (White) 69
Mills, John W. 5
Mills, M. A. (Lovingood) 285
Mills, Mary (Craton) 52
Mills, Mary (Langston) 164
Mills, W. R. 285
Mills, _. H. 52
Milner, R. W. 19
Milton, Mary J. (Thompson) 113
Milton, Robert 113
Mims, Charles W. 260
Mims, Laura (Platt) 274
Mims, M. C. 274
Mims, M. S. (Coley) 260
Mims, Olivia C. (Murray) 75
Mims, Peter J. 75
Mingledorff, Elliot 285
Minnifee, Lizzie (Jordan) 136
Minnifee, Samuel 136
Minor, Anna (Moreland) 225
Minor, Wm. 225
Minter, J. R. 161
Minter, Mary M. (Lowe) 161

Minter, Mary S. (Bailey) 223
Minter, Mattie N. (Monk) 175
Miot, C. H. 229
Mitchel, Charity (Fulwood) 130
Mitchell, A. E. (Little) 245
Mitchell, A. V. (Campbell) 205
Mitchell, Americus C. 162
Mitchell, Anna E. (Humber) 33
Mitchell, Annie T. (Dawson) 32
Mitchell, B. L. 284
Mitchell, Bettie (Jackson) 289
Mitchell, C. A. 8, 39, 74, 165, 186, 207
Mitchell, Chas. J. 135
Mitchell, F. Jane (Bramlett) 244
Mitchell, George A. 262
Mitchell, George T. 244
Mitchell, Georgia V. (Harp) 127
Mitchell, H. Addie (Stokes) 13
Mitchell, Henry 254
Mitchell, J. Andrew 122
Mitchell, J. H. 33
Mitchell, Janie F. (Stephens) 62
Mitchell, Jourdan H. 187
Mitchell, Lizzie (Cothran) 198
Mitchell, Lucy E. (Reaney) 166
Mitchell, M. A. (Quillin) 67
Mitchell, Mary A. T. (Brown) 254
Mitchell, Mary Lou (Upshaw) 187
Mitchell, Molie C. (McCrary) 82
Mitchell, Mollie F.(Jones) 1
Mitchell, N. C. (Adams) 73
Mitchell, Nellie M. (Spencer) 135
Mitchell, O. A. 28
Mitchell, R. R. 13
Mitchell, S. F. (Neisler) 284
Mitchell, S. J. 245
Mitchell, Sallie (Bodie) 236
Mitchell, Sallie B. (Lark) 122
Mitchell, Sallie J. (Neal) 18
Mitchell, Sarah C. (Rippey) 183
Mitchell, Sarah Emma (Matthews) 56

Mitchell, Susie S. (Dawson) 162
Mitchell, T. H. 67
Mitchell, W. B. 18
Mitchell, W. J. 140, 141
Mitchell, Wm. A. 32
Mitchell, Wm. M. 166
Mithell, Mattie J. (Stubbs) 201
Mixon, A. C. 8, 108, 119, 183, 296
Mixon, J. F. 39, 65, 141, 146, 151, 168, 187, 194, 202, 252, 279
Mixon, S. (Cash) 247
Mizell, A. Warren 68
Mizell, George 246
Mizell, L. T. 34, 51, 81, 98
Mizell, N. 133
Mizell, Oni May (Heath) 68
Mizell, S. Gertrude (Proctor) 246
Mizell, Zemton (Doke) 133
Mizelle, Olivia (Henry) 194
Moate, Carrie Grabilla (Bass) 40
Moate, John W. 40
Mobley, Addy M. (Wolfe) 200
Mobley, Aldora (Moreland) 160
Mobley, E. D. L. 1
Mobley, Eleazer 160
Mobley, H. W. 138
Mobley, J. H. 285
Mobley, James M. 45
Mobley, Jane (Robinson) 138
Mobley, Janie E. (Kramer) 56
Mobley, Janie F. (Kramer) 56
Mobley, Judge 56
Mobley, Kittie E. (Simpson) 28
Mobley, Reuben 28
Mobley, Rowena J. (Hale) 1
Mobley, S. A. (Mallory) 84
Mobley, Sallie (Kimbrough) 45
Mobley, Saml. 56
Mobley, W. L. 84
Mobley, Willie F. (Webster) 285
Monger, Selma (Tompkins) 279
Monk, Mattie N. (Minter) 175
Monk, Samuel S. 175
Monroe, Julia (Dowman) 290
Monroe, Wm. 290

Montford, Hattie (Wheeler) 294

Montfort, E. H. (Rutherford) 220

Montfort, J. E. 220

Montfort, Sallie E. (Neisler) 220

Montfort, W. T. 220

Montgomery, Charles H. 72

Montgomery, Edna (McCrary) 120

Montgomery, Jennie (Wall) 110

Montgomery, John I. 110

Montgomery, Samuel 97

Montgomery, Virginia (Chamberlain) 72

Mood, Augustus H. 289

Mood, Florence A. (Moorer) 289

Mood, Henry M. 55, 68, 136, 146

Mood, J. A. 96, 122, 243

Mood, Jno. A. 291

Mood, M. E. (Gregory) 136

Mood, Mary Catharine (Hoyt) 68

Mood, W. W. 187, 238

Mood, Wm. M. 136, 183,

Mood, Wm. W. 10,13, 17, 20, 64, 77, 82, 158, 163, 174, 243, 260, 272, 274, 275, 288

Moody, E. Florence (Ham) 273

Moody, Mollie M. (Browne) 164

Mooe, W. A. 175

Moomaugh, E. F. (Farrior) 32

Moomaugh, R. H. 32

Moon, Bell V. (Sherrill) 10

Moon, Crawford 22

Moon, Emily (Reynolds) 22

Moon, Mary E. (Smith) 45

Moon, Samuel S. A. 45

Moon, Selina A. (Culp) 15

Moor, H. J. 10

Moor, Henry B. 165

Moor, N. E. (Hutchens) 165

Moore, A. W. 83

Moore, Angie (Hurst) 264

Moore, Ann J. (Heartsfield) 155

Moore, Anna (Moore) 72

Moore, Anna M. (Brooks) 143

Moore, Annie (Scott) 121

Moore, Benning 186

Moore, Bertram 168

Moore, Carrie E. (Simmons) 261

Moore, Carrie M. (Tait) 182

Moore, Charles 153

Moore, Christiana (Brown) 145

Moore, Clara E. (Rumph) 186

Moore, Cornelia (Wind) 230

Moore, D. A. (Treadwell) 278

Moore, D. H. 139

Moore, Ellen (Shavers) 229

Moore, Emily J. (Fanning) 180

Moore, Emily Raifield (Armor) 153

Moore, Emma (Cozbey) 142

Moore, Emma G. (Aven) 196

Moore, Emma G. (Cook) 248

Moore, Eugene 142

Moore, Fannie (Williams) 263

Moore, Georgia E. (Ivy) 270

Moore, H. Berry (Wilson) 260

Moore, H. D. 2, 28, 49, 86

Moore, Hennie (Pritchard) 283

Moore, Henry D. 7, 9, 46, 182

Moore, Ira W. 155

Moore, Isham 174

Moore, J. B. 61

Moore, J. C. 261

Moore, J. J. 259

Moore, J. P. 168

Moore, Jennie E. (Reynolds) 87

Moore, Jennie R. (Rumph) 186

Moore, Joel 229

Moore, John M. 174

Moore, Josephine E. (Stokes) 248

Moore, L. M. 248

Moore, Lilla W. (Flynt) 175

Moore, Lucinda (Morrison) 40

Moore, Lucius A. 72

Moore, Lucy Ann (Ogletree) 190

Moore, M. J. (Smith) 28

Moore, M. Janie (Hill) 174

Moore, M. P. (King) 60

Moore, Martha E. (Cary) 190

Moore, Mary (Eley) 61

Moore, Mary H. (Sanders) 259

Moore, Mattie (Eley) 168

Moore, Missouri M. (Culver) 125

Moore, R. A. 34

Moore, R. T. 264

Moore, Richard H. 125

Moore, Robert H. 40

Moore, Rosalie A. (Sullivan) 34

Moore, S. Ollie (Wallis) 168

Moore, S. S. 106, 117, 125, 145, 183

Moore, Sallie (Sebastian) 158

Moore, Samanthia (Sewell) 257

Moore, Samuel L. 230

Moore, Sarah V. (Thornton) 108

Moore, Susan (Long) 62

Moore, T. W. 60, 99, 124, 253

Moore, Talula (Warner) 177

Moore, Thos. 257

Moore, W. A. 175

Moore, Wm. B. 62

Moorer, Ada (Appleby) 234

Moorer, Bell (Largley) 164

Moorer, Daniel F. 234

Moorer, Eliza (Murray) 68

Moorer, Ella J. (Moorer) 173

Moorer, Enora M. (Sloan) 98

Moorer, Florence A. (Mood) 289

Moorer, Frances 173

Moorer, Hansford 91

Moorer, Irene E. (Shuler) 191

Moorer, John E. 173

Moorer, Julia B. (Wannamaker) 193

Moorer, Leander S. 193

Moorer, Mary (Weathers) 91

Moorer, P. P. 68

Moorman, Bettie (Wardlaw) 209

Moorman, Marie Witherspoon (Wardlaw) 114

Moorman, Thomas S. 114

Mooty, A. P. 188

Moran, Lizzie B. (Scott) 92

More, Alice V. (Sims) 186

More, Maxey (Dukes) 264

More, Thomas 186

Morehead, Clarisa (Smith) 162

Morehouse, H. D. 148

Morehouse, N. D. 67, 73, 77, 80, 81, 121, 127, 147,

Nix, Leonora G. (Belcher) 183
Nix, Marietta (Taylor) 54
Nix, Tunny (Yarborough) 166
Nixon, Emma O. (Pinson) 121
Nixon, Mary E. (Willis) 207
Nixon, W. C. 121
Nobell, J. E. 178
Nobell, R. J. (Caldwell) 178
Noble, Alfred M. 280
Noble, Ellinor (Enzor) 280
Nobles, A. T. 203
Nobles, Zach (Owens) 203
Noblet, Charlotte V. (Yeagle) 73
Nolan, Alice H. (Robertson) 78
Nolan, D. 21, 52
Nolan, David 75, 142
Nolan, J. Emory 78
Nolan, John 29
Nolan, Mattie (Elliott) 29
Nolan, Mattie A (Evans) 63
Nolan, Q. R. 63
Noland, Annie M. (Lemon) 280
Noland, Thos. K. 280
Nolby, Daniel 127
Nolby, Delia (Crookshank) 127
Nolen, Anna M. (Roberts) 237
Norman, G. G. 86
Norman, Hattie J. (Jobson) 246
Norman, J. F. 6
Norman, J. W. 246
Norman, Lydia E. (Farris) 86
Norman, Mary E. (Brinkley) 86
Norman, Sallie L. (Jobson) 120
Norman, W. F. 86
Norman, Wm. T. 101
Norris, Fanny (Johnson) 257
Norris, George M. 207
Norris, Henrietta H. (Connor) 207
Norris, J. T. 44
Norris, John T. 105, 137, 183
Norris, Lucia O. (Livingston) 252
Norris, Narcissa (Owens) 109
Norris, Sallie A. (Bush) 144
Norris, Tallulah (Bird) 81
North, Sallie E. (Read) 195

Northcutt, Sarah E. (Jones) 86
Northington, Sandford M. 147
Northington, Sarah H. (Shackelford) 147
Norton, F. C. (Kendall) 171
Norton, M. D. 293
Norton, Mattie (Stewart) 210
Norton, Miles D. 290
Norton, W. F. 95
Norton, W. N. 171
Norton, W. R. 210
Norvill, A. J. (Spires) 222
Norvill, H. F. 222
Norwood, Anna (White) 193
Norwood, Anna M. (Ponder) 165
Norwood, Bunnie E. (Jackson) 27
Norwood, E. P. (Brewer) 132
Norwood, J. O. 193
Nottingham, A. M. (Zorn) 248
Nowell, Elizabeth S. (Arnold) 204
Noyes, Mary A. (Crabb) 177
Nugent, Hannah (Spann) 175
Nugent, John 175
Nun, E. R. (Daniel) 182
Nun, Elijah T. 182
Nun, J. 182
Nun, Sarah E. 182
Nunerly, R. D. 67
Nunerly, Susan (Scott) 67
Nunn, Anna (Perkins) 192
Nunnally, Mattie S. (England) 69
Nunnaly, Laura V. (Scott) 21
Nusum, Georgeanna A. (McGill) 285
Nutting, Cattie (Morris) 152
Nutting, James F. 152
O'Brien, Alice (Sims) 267
O'Cain, Jennie C. (Richards) 84
O'Cain, John 84
O'Caine, Callie P. P. (Hutchinson) 42
O'Caine, W. W. 42
O'Conner, Sarah J. (Meadows) 39
O'Connor, Mollie E. (Martin) 73
O'Driscoll, D. 50, 56, 59, 61, 128
O'Ferrell, Jas. 8

O'Ferrell, Martha F. (Mason) 8
O'Kelly, Dicy L. (Clotfelter) 233
O'Kelly, Erin (Clegg) 202
O'Neal, Alice (Bryan) 25
O'Neal, Bettie H. (Boykin) 83
O'Neal, C. B. 40
O'Neal, Dessie (Funderburke) 231
O'Neal, Georgia A. (Funderburke) 216
O'Neal, J. M. 221
O'Neal, Jas 231
O'Neal, Mary J. (Passmore) 40
O'Neal, R. (Carden) 221
O'Neale, J. T. 63
O'Neale, Sidney (Reid) 63
O'Sheals, Janie (Dunnaway) 288
O'Sheals, Wm. F. 288
Ocain, W. P. 171
Oder, M. (Merrit) 224
Odoin, John H. 167
Odoin, Sallie E. (Menifer) 167
Odom, Anna T. (Milhous) 289
Odom, B. B. 293
Odom, Charles M. 289
Odom, Cornelia A. (McCreary) 255
Odom, Dicey (Pitman) 39
Odom, G. I. 255
Odom, Ione (Whaley) 293
Odom, John 47
Odom, Julia D. (Brigham) 133
Odom, Levi 266
Odom, Martha M. (Williams) 47
Odom, Nannie (Black) 266
Odom, Rosa (Straman) 98
Odum, Ellen M. (Peeples) 291
Odum, P. L. 291
Oeland, Christian B. (Fickling) 265
Oeland, P. J. 265
Ogburn, S. (Stralnaker) 46
Oglesby, Eugenia H. (Cottingham) 230
Oglesby, Junius G. 230
Oglesby, Marian C. (Thomas) (Greer) 218
Oglesby, Mittie (Brown) 63
Oglesby, Silas 63
Ogletree, Catherine E. (Roberts) 158
Ogletree, Edmund H. 190

Pace, C. D. 166
Pace, Elkana 79
Pace, Ella V. (Yarbrough) 178
Pace, F. Alice (Laveigne) 228
Pace, Francis H. 149
Pace, Georgia A. (Walker) 79
Pace, J. A. 149
Pace, John C. 228
Pace, John W. 201
Pace, Julia A. (McLaren) 2
Pace, Mary E. (Hix) 264
Pace, Mary Havillah (Kimbrough) 62
Pace, Mary P. (Marshall) 194
Pace, Mary V. (Jones) 251
Pace, Noel W. 251
Pace, S. E. A. (Hardeman) 201
Pace, S. Loulie (Chambless) 166
Pace, Susie J. (McGee) 289
Pace, Thos. 194
Pace, Thos. M. 79
Pace, Virginia M. (Rune) 149
Pace, Warren A. 282
Pacetty, Alexander A. 62
Pacetty, Ella S. (Snow) 62
Packard, Lizzie (Adams) 215
Paden, R. S. 186, 190
Padget, Susan (Hollman) 173
Padgett, E. O. (Taylor) 154
Padgett, M. M. 154
Page, Clara B. (Roundtree) 233
Page, Cornelia W. (McDonald) 262
Page, Georgia (Windsor) 288
Page, Sarah R. 68
Page, William P. 288
Page, Z. T. 233
Paine, Fannie (Gambell) 50
Paine, James 50
Palmer, A. J. 186
Palmer, Annie E. (Harrison) 216
Palmer, C. A. (Rowland) (Hollinshed) 187
Palmer, Carrie (Smith) 221
Palmer, Cornelia A. (Fields) 177
Palmer, E. C. 187
Palmer, Edwin N. 2
Palmer, Ella E. (Salter) 286
Palmer, Ella E. (Bullard) 2
Palmer, Emma (Stone) 278

Palmer, Florence S. (Huggins) 197
Palmer, Howard E. W. 278
Palmer, J. A. 184
Palmer, James E. 221
Palmer, James H. 88, 194
Palmer, Joseph R. 197
Palmer, Julia E. (Jones) 233
Palmer, Laura A. (Brantley) 194
Palmer, M. B. (Milford) 217
Palmer, Mary (Burks) 182
Palmer, Mary E. (Palmer) 186
Palmer, Mary E. (Rheney) 207
Palmer, Mollie E. (Cox) 88
Palmer, William C. 207
Parade, Virginia (Young) 55
Pardue, Mahalia (Brown) 234
Parham, Caroline (Harris) 74
Parham, Ella J. (Evans) 112
Parham, Mary Anna (Cheeley) 200
Parham, Thomas M. 200
Parham, W. A. 112
Parish, Anna (Bazemore) 139
Parish, C. G. 216
Parish, H. O. 41
Parish, Henry 210
Parish, Joseph W. 135
Parish, Katie (Shaw) 135
Parish, Laura Eva (Fitchett) 216
Parish, Rebecca G. (Dorough) 41
Parish, Sarah W. (Green) 129
Park, Addie (Bigham) 197
Park, Ella H. (Holt) 200
Park, Howard Pope 268
Park, John W. 80
Park, Josie E. (Colton) 222
Park, L. M. 197
Park, Robert E. 200
Park, Sallie C. (Bull) 80
Park, Sannie J. (McDade) 268
Park, William 197, 198, 222
Parker, Edith R. (Ward) 218
Parker, Emma J. (Collins) 275
Parker, Emma J. (McCrone) 203
Parker, Esther (Gamage) 166
Parker, Geo. E. 218
Parker, Howell A. 291

Parker, John F. 45
Parker, John R. 2, 18, 20, 36, 37, 42, 58, 86, 101, 160, 211, 247, 279, 286, 293, 295
Parker, Joshua M. 135, 175
Parker, Julia (Claibern) 217
Parker, L. (Hardwick) 274
Parker, Laura V. Neal 135
Parker, M. Z. (Lloyd) 11
Parker, Mary G. (Verdier) 291
Parker, Mollie J. (Stuart) 129
Parker, S. D. 267, 278
Parker, Sallie A. (Low) 42
Parker, Sallie E. (McGee) 284
Parker, Sarah (Ruffin) 45
Parker, Sarah F. (Robinson) 11
Parker, William J. 203
Parker, William L. 11, 275
Parks, B. H. 259
Parks, Dudley 2
Parks, Eliza (Bryans) 157
Parks, Ella (Allen) 95
Parks, Emma (Bridges) 2
Parks, G. W. 21
Parks, H. H. 5, 8, 15, 19, 23, 25, 33, 51, 56, 70, 88, 90, 94, 105, 118, 177, 178, 200, 208, 211, 213, 245, 279, 295
Parks, H. M. (Blakey) 242
Parks, I. G. 203
Parks, Isaac H. 271
Parks, J. 82
Parks, J. G. 120
Parks, Jane C. (Quillian) 110
Parks, Jas. W. 101
Parks, Jennie C. (Simons) 208
Parks, Jimmie (Tarver) 271
Parks, Leroy 250
Parks, Lou D. (Neal) 82
Parks, Lou H. (Hunter) 82
Parks, M. F. (Albert) 21
Parks, Margaret (Gillespie) 259
Parks, Mary A. (Holleyman) 118
Parks, Mary O. (Smith) 169
Parks, T. 82
Parks, W. A. 27, 28, 36, 42, 45
Parks, W. G. 126
Parks, W. W. 242
Parks, William A. 65, 190
Parks, William H. 169
Parks, William P. 208
Parlor, Eugene M. 196
Parlor, Mary M. (Evans) 196

Parnel, Eliza H. (Brown) 73
Parnel, Willis J. 73
Parnells, H. M. 51
Parnells, Hattie C. (Solomons) (Johnson) 51
Parr, J. C. 92
Parr, Ophelia (Agniero) 92
Parrott, Fanny (Jones) 83
Parrott, James 157
Parrott, Judge 182
Parrott, Lizzie (DeWitt) 157
Parrott, Mary M. (Hollinshead) 182
Parrott, T. H. 83
Parsons, L. M. 249
Parsons, Vickie (Harlan) 249
Partridge, H. E. 161, 162, 183, 270
Partridge, H. M. 183
Partridge, Jesse 203
Partridge, M. A. E. J. (Russell) 203
Partridge, Sallie A. (Neilson) 161
Paschal, Mattie (Upshaw) 50
Paschal, Thos. S. 50
Pasco, F. 206
Pasco, Frederic 98
Pasco, Maria C. (Doggett) 98
Passmore, Julia (Green) 168
Passmore, Marie L. (Redding) 93
Passmore, Mary J. (O'Neal) 40
Pasteur, George 210
Pasteur, Jane (Forbes) 210
Patat, Anne E. (Royal) 15
Patat, F. 15
Patat, J. A. 15
Pate, J. F. 52
Pate, J. R. 246
Pate, John R. 244
Pate, Mary (Oliver) 115
Pate, Minnie E. (Brown) 207
Pate, R. O. 207
Pate, Rachel L. (Cobb) 52
Paten, Sallie (Copeland) 128
Paten, William 128
Patrick, A. W. 26
Patrick, Annie (Weaver) 119
Patrick, Cinthia (Proctor) 26
Patrick, E. D. 58
Patrick, E. Henrietta (England) 33
Patrick, Eliza J. (Walters) 197

Patrick, Frances (Nettles) 59
Patrick, J. W. 72
Patrick, James J. 150
Patrick, John 70
Patrick, Julia C. (Knight) 58
Patrick, L. E. (Turnison) 156
Patrick, M. J. (Anderson) (Wilkins) 72
Patrick, Matilda (Ackerman) 70
Patrick, Mollie E. (Hunter) 150
Patrick, Olivia (Bouzard) 167
Patrick, Perry 167
Patterson, A. E. 232
Patterson, Albert E. 12
Patterson, Camillus M. 84
Patterson, David W. 25
Patterson, Eliza (Freeman) 190
Patterson, Emma D. (Beall) 84
Patterson, Flora (Brown) 132
Patterson, Gertrude (Cook) 278
Patterson, H. L. 71
Patterson, Henrietta (Stilwell) 25
Patterson, J. C. 71
Patterson, J. N. 195
Patterson, Job C. 233
Patterson, Lavinia (Swift) 232
Patterson, Lizzie S. (Dalden) 12
Patterson, M. C. (Hebert) 9
Patterson, Mollie (Rodgers) 125
Patterson, N. A. (McNair) 49
Patterson, Ruth E. (Ellis) 71
Patterson, S. A. (Hoover) 71
Patterson, S. English (Tillinghast) 156
Patterson, S. M. R. (Stephens) 50
Patterson, Sarah C. (Stubbs) 233
Patterson, W. C. 125, 258, 260, 266
Patterson, W. H. 9
Patterson, William H. 132
Pattilla, May (Hargrove) 85
Pattilla, N. 85
Pattillo, 281
Pattillo, A. T. 195
Pattillo, C. L. 270, 293

Pattillo, Charles L. 106
Pattillo, Era (Woodward) 195
Pattillo, G. H. 18, 23, 25, 26, 51, 75, 82, 223
Pattillo, M. L. (Pharr) 270
Pattillo, Mary E. (Moss) 76
Pattillo, Mary F. (Guthrie) 48
Pattillo, Nancy E. (Aycock) 106
Pattillo, Sallie V. (Cole) 13
Pattillo, W. Frank 76
Pattillo, Wm. T. 13
Patton, E. A. (Nesbitt) 13
Patton, Lou S. (Johnson) 266
Patton, Martha J. (Shaw) 198
Paul, Eliza E. (Hamilton) 199
Paul, Mary E. (Jarvis) 255
Paul, R. J. (Burnett) 176
Paul, Susie V. (Cherry) 292
Paulling, Sallie (Laws) 64
Paxon, John C. 84
Paxon, Lanora (Niblack) 84
Paxton, David B. 111
Paxton, Florida V. (Mattox) 111
Payne, Cate (Garrison) 292
Payne, Fannie L. (Riviere) 86
Payne, J. B. 164, 188, 206, 252, 265, 293
Payne, J. T. 65, 68, 204
Payne, L. B. 182
Payne, Mary F. (Thomas) 273
Payne, Robert N. 88
Payne, Sade Q. (Davis) 18
Payne, Sallie E. (Payne) 88
Payne, Sue (Brown) 109
Payne, T. J. 273
Payne, W. D. 264
Paynes, Anna P. (Holmes) 253
Paynes, Edwin T. 253
Peacock, Delamar C. 291
Peacock, Delia P. (Crawford) 59
Peacock, E. M. (Barrow) 283
Peacock, Elbert 59
Peacock, Emma (Guttenberger) 5
Peacock, Eudora J. (Campbell) 82
Peacock, Ida (Lambert) 239
Peacock, J. R. 112
Peacock, Jesse 59
Peacock, Josephine (Foreman) 97

Peacock, Katie (Neely) 112
Peacock, Marietta R. (Anderson) 59
Peacock, Mary H. (Williams) 97
Peacock, Moselle (Roberts) 291
Peacock, Patience (Tanner) 213
Peacock, Perry 183
Peacock, Rebecca M. (Ivey) 92
Peacock, W. Dudley 97
Pearce, Benjamin N. 201
Pearce, Sallie S. D. (Tiller) 201
Pearre, Albert L. 180
Pearre, E. C. (Cody) 180
Pearre, E. E. (Williams) 194
Pearson, Alice A. (Freeman) 169
Pearson, Bettie E. (Ansley) 224
Pearson, Carrie (Gilbert) 25
Pearson, Carrie E. (Dennis) 109
Pearson, Carrie Lou (Booker) 286
Pearson, F. 37
Pearson, Fannie (Hill) 110
Pearson, Jos. G. 169
Pearson, Leonora D. (Dean) 165
Pearson, Lula (Cox) 199
Pearson, Mary (Mathews) 61
Pearson, Mary E. (Briscoe) 34
Pearson, Sallie (Blease) 37
Pearson, Seaborn T. 165
Pearson, Steven J. 61
Pearson, Wm. T. 34
Peavy, Hattie (Williams) 95
Peavy, Jno. W. 95
Pechner, Herman 209
Pechner, Mamie (Dickson) 209
Peck, Ella M. (Rackliff) 119
Peck, Orlando W. 119
Peddy, Elizabeth (Barnes) 33
Peddy, G. 92
Peddy, Sally (Twilley) 92
Peddy, T. J. 33
Peden, A. G. 242
Peed, M. E. (Avery) 281
Peed, Thos. U. 281
Peek, L. C. 65, 81, 125, 131
Peek, Susie M. (Scruggs) 116
Peel, Josie E. (Campbell) 287
Peeler, A. 152, 283

Peeler, Anderson 140
Peeler, E. A. (Souter) 219
Peeler, James P. 263
Peeler, Julia V. (Goodbread) 263
Peeler, Lillie E. (Brown) 140
Peeler, Wm. 219
Peeple, Eugenia E. (Craig) 70
Peeples, Ellen M. (Odum) 291
Peeples, Florence G. (Holland) 247
Peeples, Sarah M. (Logan) 237
Pegg, A. M. (Foran) 72
Pegg, James B. 72
Pegg, W. H. 132
Pegues, Hattie G. (Hodges) 230
Pegues, W. L. 17, 121, 230, 244, 276
Peirce, Geo. 251
Peirce, Margaret A. E. (Ackerman) 251
Peirson, Ellie C. (Johnston) 116
Pelham, Talulah (Hansel) 28
Pelham, Wm. 28
Pelot, Ella R. (Boring) 292
Pelot, Hannah N. Rawls 122
Pelot, Hattie C. (Hearn) 130
Pelot, Wm. J. 292
Pelote, M. C. (Vincent) 27
Pelote, W. H. 27
Pemberton, Helen M. (Boulden) 259
Pemberton, Martha L. (Peters) 65
Pemberton, Mary A. (Bates) 68
Pemberton, Sarah J. (Peters) 61
Pemberton, W. W. 68
Pendarvis, Annie (Rhodes) 218
Pendarvis, Hettie (Whetsel) 102
Pendarvis, Jacob D. C. 68
Pendarvis, Rachel L. (Weathers) 68
Pendington, Elizabeth L. (Stipe) 292
Pendleton, Bertha (Swift) 281
Pendleton, J. C. 281
Pendleton, Lizzie D. (Talmage) 82
Pendleton, Mattie A. (Nelson) 74

Pendleton, P. T. 74
Pendleton, Wm. M. 82
Pendry, George E. (Clarke) 200
Pendry, S. A. (Peterson) 5
Pendry, Samuel 5, 200
Peninger, Miria E. (Thompson) 32
Penington, Alice I. (Wilkerson) 248
Penington, Elizabeth (Beckum) 172
Penington, Thomas E. 248
Penn, Benjamin 272
Penn, John A. 217
Penn, M. A. (Morgan) 27
Penn, Martha E. R. (Sharp) 272
Penn, Mary T. (Grubbs) 217
Penney, Andrew J. 135
Penney, Haggie (Penney) 135
Penney, J. E. 135
Pennick, A. C. (Choate) 116
Pennick, M. R. (Ryle) 119
Pennington, Amma L. (Weaver) 279
Pennington, E. J. 159
Pennington, J. R. 218
Pennington, James L. 279
Pennington, Leila (Battles) 218
Pennington, Susannah E. (Stall) 159
Penny, J. 242
Penny, J. E. 175
Penny, J. _. 26
Penny, John 160, 169
Pentecost, Frank T. 296
Pentecost, Ophelia T. (Born) 296
Peoples, J. A. 184
Peoples, Mary A. (Mann) 184
Perdue, Ellen W. (Nelson) 246
Perdue, Fannie E. (Graves) 58
Perdue, Kittie (Nipper) 58
Perdue, Thos. B. 246
Perkerson, Lizzie F. (Butler) 85
Perkins, A. C. 36
Perkins, A. M. (Steed) 105
Perkins, Anna (Nunn) 192
Perkins, Augusta Paris (Lake) 238
Perkins, Belle P. (Chrietzberg) 61
Perkins, Caroline (Gibson) 134
Perkins, E. E. (Goff) 270

Perkins, Eliza J. (Heartley) 134
Perkins, Furney G. 134
Perkins, J. Albert 5
Perkins, John J. 192
Perkins, M. V. (Searcy) 45
Perkins, Mary (Ponder) 133
Perkins, Mary C. (Leseuer) 36
Perkins, Mary L. (Price) 134
Perkins, Mattie (Ponder) 232
Perkins, Mattie E. (Lundie) 5
Perkins, S. Cebie (Campbell) 222
Perkins, S. E. 238
Perkins, Samuel 153
Perkins, Sarah A. (Smith) 70
Pernell, J. E. (Milling) 140
Pernell, John E. 140
Pernell, Mary F. (Smith) 127
Pernell, Simpson 127
Perry, Anna (Estes) 275
Perry, Charlotte E. (Carter) 31
Perry, Eugenia (Tanner) 100
Perry, Georgia A. (Tucker) 7
Perry, Georgia C. (Willis) 18
Perry, H. H. 31
Perry, J. S. 115
Perry, James G. 275
Perry, James M. 86
Perry, Joseph T. 7
Perry, M. A. (Morris) 115
Perry, Mark A. 179
Perry, Martha J. (Rogers) 47
Perry, Mary E. (Price) 103
Perry, Mattie Y. (Price) 86
Perry, Mollie (Wright) 248
Perry, Nancy (McCants) 179
Perry, Sallie E. (Smith) 203
Perry, Sallie J. (Boon) 24
Perry, Stobo R. 18
Perry, William H. 100
Perryman, Algernon J. 134
Perryman, Hattie C. (Smith) 134
Persons, Anna W. (Dozier) 83
Persons, G. W. 27, 145, 171, 281
Persons, Mary (Barry) 60
Persons, R. T. 60
Pert, Nannie (Jester) 153
Peteet, M. A. 134

Peteet, Ola A. (Robertson) 134
Peters, A. S. 61
Peters, H. G. 97
Peters, John L. 65
Peters, Lou (Stoffragen) 97
Peters, Martha L. (Pemberton) 65
Peters, Sarah J. (Pemberton) 61
Peterson, J. A. 195
Peterson, Jacob 67
Peterson, Olivia (Lampkin) 67
Peterson, S. A. (Pendry) 5
Pettigrew, Mollie (Harkness) 193
Petty, Sallie A. (Zellars) 147
Peurifoy, Hettie (Maddux) 91
Peurifoy, J. W. 91
Peurifoy, Katie E. (Kelley) 233
Pfohl, M. A. M. (Fogle) 93
Pfohl, Wm. Lewis 93
Pharr, Emma (Willingham) 232
Pharr, J. P. 270
Pharr, M. J. 102
Pharr, M. L. (Pattillo) 270
Pharr, T. A. 3
Phelps, Ansel B. 96
Phelps, Eugenia 286
Phelps, Fannie V. (Wade) 110
Phelps, Nancy F. (Bowden) 99
Phelps, S. Emma (Leonard) 96
Phelps, Sallie (Cooper) 286
Phelps, William H. 99
Phelts, Emma C. (Daniels) 265
Phelts, Rufus J. 265
Phillips, A. E. 247
Phillips, Angie (Colville) 291
Phillips, Cornelia (Inabinet) 225
Phillips, Dorcas (Way) 120
Phillips, Duncan C. 86
Phillips, Elvira (Jeffcoat) 266
Phillips, Eugenia (Rawls) 247
Phillips, Fannie (Jeter) 34
Phillips, Florence (Summers) 225
Phillips, G. C. (Lamar) 59
Phillips, Hugh E. 233
Phillips, James 242

Phillips, Julia C. (Smith) 244
Phillips, Lydia Anna (Watts) 242
Phillips, Marcilla J. (Woolf) 233
Phillips, Mary Elizabeth (Miller) 2
Phillips, Mary J. (Taylor) 290
Phillips, Robert 120
Phillips, S. E. (Fretwell) 130
Phillips, Sallie A. E. (Bickley) 86
Phillips, T. H. 34
Phillips, T. J. 205, 215, 217, 263
Phillips, T. P. 290, 292
Phillips, Thomas S. 59
Phillips, W. F. 266
Phillips, W. M. 291
Phillips, Wm. 244
Philpot, Irvin H. 74
Philpot, Jane M. (Alexander) 74
Phin, A. C. 219
Phin, Adela B. (Baer) 219
Phipps, Annie (Griffith) 180
Phipps, Joseph P. 180
Picket, Louisa (Harvey) 40
Pickett, Emma F. (King) 82
Pickett, Onarine L. (Brown) 236
Picketts, Major 82
Pickran, Lizzie (Tresdway) 229
Pickrel, 292
Pierce, 105, 197, 265
Pierce, Anne T. (Harley) 71
Pierce, Annie Foster (Thornton) 89
Pierce, Carrie R. (Cotton) 197
Pierce, Cyntha (Vanlandingham) 20
Pierce, Emma (Williamson) 119
Pierce, F. M. (Kelley) 66
Pierce, George F. 68, 71, 119
Pierce, Harrie Hayes (Harley) 68
Pierce, J. L. 55, 85
Pierce, James 20
Pierce, Kate (Williams) 89
Pierce, Lizzie (McLeane) 198
Pierce, Lovick 32, 50, 71
Pierce, Luvicy (Quillian) 153
Pierce, Martha A. (Reid) 14
Pierce, Mary S. (Allfriend) 71

Pope, Mary F. (Logue) 190
Pope, Mattie (Wicker) 32
Pope, Mattie (Wylie) 162
Pope, Mittie (Bilbro) 53
Pope, S. L. (Potter) 85
Pope, T. A. 239
Poppel, E. A. (Seaver) 185
Poppel, P. J. 185
Poppell, Paul J. 102
Poppell, Susan A. (Houck) 102
Porcher, Julien H. 69
Porcher, M. Marion (Kirkland) 137
Porcher, Susan B. (Jones) 69
Porter, Amelia K. (Berry) 220
Porter, Benj. A. 9
Porter, Edwin T. 230
Porter, Fannie A. (Roden) 143
Porter, H. H. 72, 141, 145
Porter, J. A. 12, 258
Porter, J. N. (Shields) 182
Porter, John A. 133
Porter, Julia A. (Camp) 71
Porter, Mattie L. (McMillan) 12
Porter, Minnie H. (Robertson) 258
Porter, Mollie L. (Pitts) 67
Porter, O. S. 71
Porter, Orietta D. (Wilson) 230
Porter, Peter A. 220
Porter, Sarah Waring (Huggins) 133
Porter, Susan A. (Berry) 9
Post, S. G. (Arnold) 57
Post, W. A. 57
Postell, Jehu G. 13
Postell, Lizzie J. (Walton) 13
Poteet, Jane (Goforth) 88
Poteet, M. 49
Poteet, Mary (Smith) 49
Potter, A. C. 85
Potter, George A. 62
Potter, J. M. 154, 257, 262, 268, 287, 289
Potter, M. Della (Harmon) 198
Potter, S. L. (Pope) 85
Potter, Sophronia (Dixon) 62
Potter, W. H. 29, 42, 53, 174, 198, 236, 267
Potter, W. M. 234
Potts, James N. 227
Potts, M. A. (Freeman) 227
Potts, Margaret (Millirous) 73

Potts, Mary E. (Freeman) 22
Pou, Eliza M. (King) 129
Pound, Barbara 259
Pound, Belle (Goodwyn) 247
Pound, Louisa (Richter) 259
Pounds, Susan K. (Scott) 145
Pounds, William M. 145
Powel, Lucy (Hinnant) 1
Powell, B. Frank 187
Powell, C. A. (Prather) 187
Powell, Camilla W. (Simmons) 24
Powell, Carrie (Dudley) 223
Powell, Dollie (Simmons) 125
Powell, E. C. (Register) 241
Powell, Fannie (Davenport) 223
Powell, Frank R. 223
Powell, H. T. 241
Powell, John S. 125
Powell, LaFayette 24
Powell, M. L. (McWhorter) 38
Powell, Rhoda M. (Galloway) 296
Powell, S. E. (Johnston) 131
Powell, Sallie E. (Bell) 290
Powell, Sallie M. (Brown) 224
Powell, Sue (Brewster) 91
Powell, Tunis W. 223
Powell, W. F. 296
Powell, W. F. S. 91
Power, Mary S. (Lester) 151
Power, Wm. C. 35, 71, 106, 121, 140, 146, 149, 151, 196, 208, 217, 261, 263, 281
Powers, Annie Lollie (Throne) 195
Powers, Corinne (Smith) 205
Powers, E. W. (Cantrell) 143
Powers, Edward P. 38
Powers, Florence E. (Douglass) 38
Powers, G. T. 278
Powers, Homer O. 195
Powers, J. H. (Lumsden) 253
Powers, John H. 205
Powers, M. Louisa (Evans) (McEachin) 9
Powers, Mattie I. (Rogers) 278
Powers, Sarah E. (Rahn) 93
Powers, Virginia E. (Gugel) 144

Powers, W. C. 9
Powers, Z. H. 93
Powledge, C. B. (Barnes) 250
Powledge, J. M. 186
Powledge, Lizzie Means 108
Powledge, Mollie (Fuller) 186
Powledge, Philip 108
Prater, Bettie (Chambers) 245
Prater, Ida (McKay) 8
Prater, James B. 144
Prater, Jno. 8
Prater, Mary A. J. (Smith) 144
Prater, Sarah E. S. (Syfrett) 170
Prater, Wm. C. 170
Prather, C. A. (Powell) 187
Prather, Nannie (Crook) 203
Pratt, Mary I. (Barr) 239
Pratt, N. F. 239
Prescott, A. (Herrington) 23
Prescott, Kittie (Reeves) 23
Preskitt, Ausier 278
Preskitt, Lillie May (Syms) 278
Pressley, Sue (Smith) 193
Prevatt, B. C. 47
Prevatt, Celia (Sasser) 47
Prevatt, Elsie (Vinzant) 47
Price, 54
Price, Callie A. (Overby) 109
Price, Carrie A. (Rice) 55
Price, E. S. 55
Price, Eliza (Jordan) 152
Price, Emily (Duncan) 235
Price, George W. 103
Price, J. W. 12
Price, Jno. R. 63
Price, Joseph 86
Price, Laura R. (Turner) 63
Price, Leak C. (Bell) 92
Price, Lula (Hinton) 54
Price, Mary E. (Perry) 103
Price, Mary L. (Perkins) 134
Price, Mattie Y. (Perry) 86
Price, Robert A. 92
Price, S. B. 134
Price, Sallie (Lowe) 191
Price, Susan O. (Merk) 36
Price, T. N. 55
Price, W. H. 36
Price, Weldon W. 109
Price, Wm. P. 191
Pricket, Julia (Lee) 108
Prickett, Jos. P. 31
Prince, George E. 284
Prince, Mattie (Lander) 284

Prince, Mollie (Fouche) 191
Printup, Mary C. (Martin) 169
Pritchard, C. H. 41, 195
Pritchard, Hennie (Moore) 283
Pritchard, J. H. (Fox) 265
Pritchard, J. P. 195
Pritchard, L. Laval (Ewart) 195
Pritchard, L. N. 283
Pritchard, Wm. G. 64
Proctor, Anna H. (Forbes) 43
Proctor, Cinthia (Patrick) 26
Proctor, D. R. 246
Proctor, J. D. 90
Proctor, Jno. 84
Proctor, Jno. M. 43
Proctor, Julia I. (Mays) 90
Proctor, Lou B. (Cooper) 84
Proctor, Mary E. (Williams) 146, 149
Proctor, S. Gertrude (Mizell) 246
Propst, John W. 137
Propst, Sallie (Littlejohn) 137
Pruitt, M. E. (Lockhart) 69
Pruitt, M. Y. 69
Pruitt, Moses Y. 111
Pruitt, R. C. (Allen) 111
Pryor, Ceredia Auretta (Harris) 249
Puckett, Aaron M. 18
Puckett, Georgia Emma (Weatherbee) 189
Puckett, Lou 273
Puckett, M. 104, 225
Puckett, Mattie (Wharton) 273
Puckett, Olivia C. (Daniel) 18
Puckett, William Richard 189
Pue, Rebecca F. (Jordan) 65
Pue, Wesley A. 65
Puett, Laura E. (Cochran) 56
Pugeley, M. E. (Arnold) 66
Pugh, Eliza (Whiddon) 173
Pugh, Querny (McRay) 223
Pugh, Rebecca J. (Humphrey) 107
Pughesley, John 146
Pullen, Sallie W. (Webb) 214
Purdom, Mary E. (Causey) 238

Purrnal, Laurah A. (Binson) 128
Purrnal, N. B. 128
Purvis, J. B. 150
Purvis, S. C. S. (Wiggins) 283
Puryear, Emory S. 123
Puryear, Mary E. (Trible) 80
Puryear, Nannie (Davis) 252
Puryear, Ophelia F. (Cox) 123
Putman, J. G. 18
Putman, Margaret (Thurman) 18
Pye, B. 118
Pye, Henrietta M. (Sanders) 170
Pye, Javan 170
Pye, Mary R. (Talley) 118
Pyles, M. C. (Baker) 136
Pyles, Mary D. (Barnes) 192
Pyles, Samuel 192
Pyror, Emma (Griffeth) 113
Pyson, M. J. (Wood) 234
Quaige, Mattie J. (Sanderford) 9
Quarles, Sarah J. (Walker) 271
Quattlebaum, Ella (Whittle) 287
Quattlebaum, M. M. 287
Quillian, A. C. 110
Quillian, A. H. 220
Quillian, Amanda (Underwood) 95
Quillian, B. B. 3, 67, 78, 79, 85, 97, 11, 129, 136, 137, 141, 164, 189
Quillian, Clarissa M. (Dean) 54
Quillian, Cornelia M. A. (Stricklin) 51
Quillian, Ella (Smith) 162
Quillian, G. F. 162
Quillian, George 95
Quillian, George K. 185
Quillian, H. M. 285, 296
Quillian, Harwell P. 181
Quillian, India J. (Chapman) 185
Quillian, Isabella (Campbell) 220
Quillian, J. B. C. 51, 114, 164, 203
Quillian, James C. 153
Quillian, Jane C. (Parks) 110
Quillian, Jose T. 19
Quillian, Lizzie (Gaines) 85
Quillian, Lucy (Vail) 153

Quillian, Luvicy (Pierce) 153
Quillian, M. E. A. (Garriett) 203
Quillian, M. R. (Willson) 82
Quillian, Margaret E. (Smith) 19
Quillian, Mary E. (Oliver) 181
Quillian, Mattie J. (Finger) 217
Quillian, Robert A. 220
Quillian, Robert F. 185
Quillian, Sarah J. (Tye) 21
Quillian, W. A. 54
Quillian, W. F. 49, 54, 70, 83, 110, 127, 130, 132, 153, 153, 204, 217, 226, 234, 238, 265, 291
Quillian, William C. 21
Quillin, M. A. (Mitchell) 67
Quinker, Ella E. (Sanford) 169
Quinker, Jos. H. 169
Rackley, James F. 242
Rackley, Julia P. (Brickett) 242
Rackliff, Ella M. (Peck) 119
Radford, 126
Radford, J. O. A. 205
Ragan, L. E. (McKlewreath) 101
Ragan, M. A. 101
Ragan, Nancy (Manning) 246
Ragan, Sallie L. (Jones) 16
Ragan, Turissa R. (Sheridan 216
Ragan, Wm. B. 16
Ragans, J. E. 249
Ragans, N. A. E. (Roe) 249
Ragland, Augusta B. (Kimbrough) 43
Ragland, Fannie (Wales) 47
Ragland, John 47
Ragland, Mary J. (Boozer) 70
Ragland, W. P. 70
Ragland, William E. 43
Rahn, A. E. (Shearouse) 63
Rahn, Anna J. (Enicks) 252
Rahn, Edwin B. 122
Rahn, J. R. 63
Rahn, Maggie (Berry) 171
Rahn, Rebecca M. (Morgan) 124
Rahn, Sarah E. (Powers) 93
Rahn, Sarah J. (Berry) 122
Rahn, Thos. E. 124
Raiford, C. 92, 119, 273
Raiford, Capel 85
Raiford, Cyrus L. 199

Raiford, Emma L. (Marshall) 199
Railey, Georgean (Garvis) 163
Railey, Randal 163
Raines, Mary F. (Stanton) 204
Raines, Owen P. 204
Rainey, Carrie (Rea) 141
Rainey, J. H. 196
Rainey, Katie B. (Hall) 196
Rainey, Martha E. (Bradley) 102
Rainey, Nuton J. 141
Rains, C. P. (Sotory) 223
Rains, Lavonia (Leach) 149
Rainwater, Jessie F. (Saunders) 14
Rainwater, Marion G. 14
Rakestraw, George 69
Rakestraw, Louisa (Eason) 183
Rakestraw, Mary E. (Etheredge) 69
Raleigh, A. L. 249
Raleigh, Lizzie (Singer) 249
Rambo, John D. 277
Rambo, Mary E. (Caskill) 277
Ramply, Mattie E. (Dobbins) 112
Rampy, G. W. 68
Ramsau, James P. 281
Ramsau, Jennie C. (Kingsberry) 281
Ramsey, Ella (Ramsey) 141
Ramsey, F. J. (Ranson) 39
Ramsey, Fannie A. (Kelly) 287
Ramsey, J. W. 141
Ramsey, Nannie (Nichols) 179
Ramsey, Nora P. (Smith) 278
Ramsey, W. C. 39
Ranchfuss, Julia C. (Clarke) 272
Randall, Benjamin P. 52
Randall, E. (Blume) (Bryan) 26
Randall, Hettie (Snow) 52
Randall, J. B. 52
Randall, Lucy A. (Griffin) 52
Randall, P. N. 141
Randall, Sarah Ann (Massey) 56
Randall, Thomas 26
Randit, H. J. 6
Randle, L. L. (Herring) 31
Randle, Lackington C. 31
Randle, Mary E. (Bryan) 31
Raney, George P. 162

Raney, Mary Elizabeth (Lamar) 162
Range, C. P. (Bowden) 91
Rankin, Fanny Lou (Denton) 213
Rankin, Geo. C. 213
Ransdale, Julia (Reeves) 283
Ransom, Clara M. (Williams) 89
Ransom, O. W. 213, 263
Ransome, B. B. 153
Ransome, Mary E. (Huff) 71
Ransome, William 71
Ranson, F. J. (Ramsey) 39
Rantin, Abigail (Reid) 125
Rantin, John 125
Raoul, Alfred 32
Raoul, Ella J. (Neal) 32
Rast, Asenath R. (Pooser) 92
Rast, Emma (Rickenbaker) 259
Rast, F. Marion 259
Rast, J. 32, 68, 73
Rast, John A. 92
Rast, L. W. 126, 193, 224, 259
Rast, Lewis W. 295
Rauchfuss, Charles 272
Raulason, Frances D. (Dicks) 235
Rausson, Mary (Melton) 236
Raven, Rebecca (Foster) 84
Rawlins, Georgia (Rogers) 256
Rawlins, J. A. 256
Rawls, Daniel 60
Rawls, Eugenia (Phillips) 247
Rawls, Fannie (Stapler) 60
Rawls, H. 18
Rawls, Hannah N. Pelot 122
Rawls, Jane E. (Carter) 18
Rawls, Junius 60
Rawls, Samuel B. 122
Rawls, Statira A. (Watts) 60
Rawls, Thos. J. 247
Rawson, E. E. 14, 128
Rawson, Emma (Johnson) 128
Rawson, Florida I. (Fort) 76
Rawson, Mary P. (Ray) 14
Rawson, William A. 76, 267
Ray, A. G. (Harris) 248
Ray, Annie (Elliott) 203
Ray, D. J. 291
Ray, Ella (Hatchel) 240
Ray, Harriet L. (Armstrong) 43

Ray, John D. 14
Ray, M. A. S. 43
Ray, Mary C. (Sloan) 9
Ray, Mary P. (Rawson) 14
Ray, Mollie W. (Geise) 291
Ray, N. C. (Elliott) 239
Ray, S. N. 239
Ray, W. Jerome 248
Ray, Willie 203
Rayborn, Penellie (Kitchens) 77
Raybun, J. C. 150
Raybun, Susan A. (Louge) 150
Raysor, Alfred William 196
Raysor, Ella L. (Nally) 165
Raysor, Ida C. (Mabbit) 248
Raysor, John M. 125
Raysor, Mary (Barton) 107
Raysor, Mary Emma (Chiles) 125
Raysor, Petnah Adelia (Nalley) 196
Raysor, Thos. 107
Rea, Carrie (Rainey) 141
Rea, Fanny J. (Smith) (Stout) 141
Rea, Mattie (Maddox) 145
Rea, W. J. 152
Rea, W. T. 141, 145
Read, Emma (Yarborough) 70
Read, J. P. 70
Read, Jonathan H. 195
Read, Sallie B. (Owen) 83
Read, Sallie E. (North) 195
Read, Sallie G. (Carpenter) 280
Read, W. T. 38, 194
Reaney, Lucy E. (Mitchell) 166
Reaves, Joseph 142
Reaves, Lizzie (Hilliard) 142
Reaves, Thomas 128
Rece, H. 172
Rece, M. H. 173
Rector, Emma A. Lovejoy 103
Rector, Wm. L. 103
Redd, Geo. T. 185
Redd, Laura (Loper) 244
Redd, Lizzie (Harrington) 185
Redder, Anna M. (Taylor) 271
Redder, John 271
Reddick, A. M. (Burch) 270
Reddick, Georgia A. (Lowrey) 268
Redding, A. S. 114
Redding, Abner 216

Redding, Anna G. (Collier) 293

Redding, Chas. H. 187

Redding, Clara E. (Jackson) 187

Redding, Geo. A. 93

Redding, Ida Stripling 213

Redding, J. F. 148

Redding, J. T. 264

Redding, Kittie S. (Toole) 216

Redding, Lizzie (Worrel) 265

Redding, M. A. (Cowart) 121

Redding, Maggie F. (Ross) 264

Redding, Marie L. (Passmore) 93

Redding, R. J. 265

Redding, Sallie (Alvis) 235

Redding, Sally E. (White) 188

Redding, Susan Ridley (Duncan) 148

Redding, Thomas 213

Redding, Vista (Allen) 114

Redding, Wade H. 235

Redding, Wylie 188

Redfearn, Annie (Bates) 50

Redford, Sallie (Tindal) 26

Redwine, Elgivia E. (Campbell) 2

Redwine, Emma Florence (Hooker) 287

Redwine, W. M. 287

Reed, A. T. (Clyburn) 105

Reed, Drusilla (Rucker) 295

Reed, Eugenia J. (Bivins) 52

Reed, George M. 199

Reed, I. Alex. 200

Reed, Jacob V. 295

Reed, Leona (Robertson) 168

Reed, Mattie (Splawn) 28

Reed, Mollie A. (Dooly) 199

Reed, Mollie Fannie (Reese) 200

Reed, Samuel 30

Reed, Sarah C. (Simmons) 213

Reed, Sarah W. (Gramblin) 36

Reed, T. W. 168

Reed, Thos. W. 168

Reed, Titha A. (Splawn) 30

Reed, Wm. M. 28

Rees, A. G. (Booker) 220

Rees, E. B. 249

Rees, Katie E. (Dozier) 249

Rees, T. L. 220

Reese, 161

Reese, A. L. 281

Reese, Corall (Pitner) 247

Reese, J. L. (Walker) 281

Reese, Jere 118

Reese, Julia J. (Houser) 247

Reese, Mollie Fannie (Reed) 200

Reese, Oscar L. 200

Reese, Rowena (Walton) 161

Reese, Sarah E. (Young) 271

Reese, Wm. M. 247

Reeves, Annie A. (Herrington) 23

Reeves, Eliza (Bowen) 132

Reeves, Eliza F. (Cariker) 43

Reeves, Ellen (Stafford) 21

Reeves, Florence M. (Chance) 21

Reeves, Frances (Chance) 133

Reeves, Geo. W. 23

Reeves, John T. 21

Reeves, Julia (Ransdale) 283

Reeves, Kittie (Prescott) 23

Reeves, L. E. (Head) 2

Reeves, Maggie M. (Haton) 190

Reeves, Mark 130

Reeves, Mollie A. (Ward) 199

Reeves, Nancy A. (Oliver) 11

Reeves, Nancy E. (Haygood) 130

Reeves, Sallie E. (Floyd) 261

Reeves, Sherrod A. 283

Reeves, W. S. 199

Reeves, Wm. W. 2

Refo, C. L. 245

Refo, Maria L. (Williams) 245

Register, E. C. (Powell) 241

Register, Nannie E. (Smith) 254

Reid, 125

Reid, A. T. 151

Reid, Abigail (Rantin) 125

Reid, Agnes (Broddus) 58

Reid, Amanda M. (Gantt) 132

Reid, Augustus 63

Reid, Cornelia (Walsh) 47

Reid, Dinque (Whitaker) 211

Reid, E. E. 211

Reid, Florence A. (Adams) 114

Reid, G. T. 158

Reid, Jas. F. 105

Reid, L. G. 14

Reid, L. Josie (Stokes) 158

Reid, Martha A. (Pierce) 14

Reid, Mary B. (Adams) 60

Reid, Mary F. (Howard) 151

Reid, Mollie (Dennard) 151

Reid, Mollie (Simms) 211

Reid, R. H. 282

Reid, S. Kate (Davidson) 281

Reid, Samuel 47, 63

Reid, Sarah (Somelian) 270

Reid, Sidney (O'Neale) 63

Reid, W. L. J. 281

Reid, W. S. 60

Reid, W. T. 132

Reid, Wm. A. 58

Reidel, A. E. Seago 251

Reidel, Geo. 251

Remington, E. S. 24

Remington, Ellan Leigh (Leigh) 258

Remington, Jane L. (Livingston) 24

Renew, Aaron 291

Renew, Susan (Corley) 291

Renfro, Mattie L. (Solomon) 292

Renfro, V. C. (Gamlin) 4

Renfroe, Martha A. (Stubbs) 194

Renfroe, Martha L. (Weddon) 35

Renfroe, William H. 194

Renneker, E. J. Steinmyer 87

Renneker, F. W. 87

Renolds, Laura S. (Edding) 102

Rentfrow, Palestine (Jones) 142

Rents, E. J. 179, 220, 248, 294

Rentz, E. J. 82, 127, 188

Respress, Antoinett E. (Atwater) 106

Reudy, Joe (Johnson) 75

Revell, Katie (Jefferson) 198

Revell, W. B. 198

Reville, Alice (Langston) 157

Reville, Alpheus 157

Reynolds, A. (English) 120

Reynolds, A. 34

Reynolds, Adie (McClatchey) 34

Reynolds, Benj. A. 87

Rosser, Julia E. (Foster) 182
Rosser, L. D. F. 60
Rosser, Leonora (Freeman) 60
Rosser, Mattie M. (Means) 251
Rosser, R. P. 65
Rosser, Sryphosia M. (Johnson) 134
Rosser, W. E. (Lee) 66
Rosser, W. T. 251
Round, G. H. 56
Round, Geo. F. 9
Round, Julia (Hammond) 9
Roundtree, Anna J. (Webb) 123
Roundtree, Clara B. (Page) 233
Roundtree, James W. 123
Roundtree, Manson D. 110
Roundtree, Sallie (Harris) 110
Rountree, Daniel M. 276
Rountree, Mary E. (Collins) 276
Rowan, J. R. 155
Rowe, D. M. 166
Rowe, Lou (Hurt) 166
Rowe, Missouri A. (Glass) 188
Rowe, Sarah W. (Small) 174
Rowe, Wm. H. 174
Rowell, 210
Rowell, C. D. 215, 270
Rowell, M. E. 215
Rowell, Mary A. (Ledingham) 215
Rowland, A. W. 78, 192, 226
Rowland, Alice V. (Shy) 192
Rowland, Anna P. (Martin) 148
Rowland, C. A. (Hollinshed) (Palmer) 187
Rowland, Charlotte I. (Lockhart) 167
Rowland, Oscar P. 192
Rowland, Wm. C. 167
Royal, Anne E. (Patat) 15
Royal, C. S. (Waite) 85
Royal, Charlotte (McMurrian) 142
Royal, Chas. L. 142
Royal, Elizabeth (Harris) 30
Royal, John 30
Royal, Katie F. (Woodward) 88
Royal, Mary L. (Villard) 105

Royal, Susan M. (Wilson) 189
Royston, Andrew J. 24
Royston, Lucy A. (Thompson) 24
Rucker, Bettie (Fanning) 13
Rucker, Drusilla (Reed) 295
Rucker, J. L. 13
Rucker, Margaret (Stivender) 151
Rucker, Martha A. (Nelson) 91
Rucker, Richard 259
Rucker, Sallie (Knight) 259
Rude, Emma G. (Thompson) 171
Rudolph, A. 199
Rudolph, Amzi 23
Rudolph, Annie E. (Bessent) 276
Rudolph, B. E. (Latimer) 199
Rudolph, Fannie (Boyd) 23
Ruff, David E. 121
Ruff, Lucinda E. (Harris) 121
Ruff, Nannie (Lever) 6
Ruff, Samuel A. 120
Ruff, Sarah V. (Floyd) 85
Ruff, Sue (Lever) 1
Ruff, Susan F. (Martin) 120
Ruff, W. A. 1
Ruffin, H. J. 46
Ruffin, Sarah (Parker) 45
Ruffin, W. V. (Jinks) 46
Rump, Ida J. (Crawford) 285
Rump, Irving P. 285
Rumph, Clara E. (Moore) 186
Rumph, D. A. 53
Rumph, E. Emma (McGehee) 43
Rumph, Emma (Adams) 85
Rumph, I. N. (Houser) 16
Rumph, Jennie R. (Moore) 186
Rumph, Lewis A. 43, 186
Rumph, Sallie J. (Murray) 53
Rumph, Samuel H. 186
Rune, Virginia M. (Pace) 149
Rush, Annie E. (Jenkins) 23
Rush, C. O. 97
Rush, Edward B. 103
Rush, Ella T. (Bevens) 97
Rush, J. 2
Rush, J. W. 29
Rush, L. 23, 128
Rush, Mary (Martin) 89
Rush, Salena (Layton) 88

Rush, Sallie E. (Massengale) 128
Rushton, Susan E. (Hamilton) 272, 274
Rushton, William 272, 274
Russ, Laura (Hutto) 258
Russ, Lewis 258
Russel, A. M. C. 135
Russel, Annie E. (Mounger) 135
Russell, Aurelia (Nelson) 148
Russell, E. W. 203
Russell, Hattie (Brinson) 206
Russell, J. B. (Inman) 294
Russell, J. S. 86, 91, 270
Russell, Jacob W. 148
Russell, Lucy A. (Wolf) 86
Russell, M. A. E. J. (Partridge) 203
Russell, Mary C. (Wooten) 224
Russell, Mary Lou (Smith) 31
Russell, Mattie A. (Murphey) 91
Russell, R. B. 78
Russell, Susan C. (Cobb) 270
Russell, T. B. 17, 31, 45, 144, 168, 169, 189, 207, 208, 215, 219, 222, 272, 277, 281, 288, 294
Rutherford, Alfred 49
Rutherford, Arie H. (Hughey) 78
Rutherford, Carrie E. (Cowart) 290
Rutherford, E. B. (Ross) 1
Rutherford, E. H. (Montfort) 220
Rutherford, Elizabeth C. D. (Jenkins) 78
Rutherford, John 78
Rutherford, Sallie (Goode) 49
Rutland, Fannie (Van Landingham) 192
Rutledge, D. A. 34
Rutledge, Emma J. (Flowers) 34
Rutledge, Eugenia A. (Brown) 138
Rutledge, Lizzie (Jones) 225
Rutledge, P. R. 225
Rutledge, T. J. 12, 53, 55, 59, 61
Rutledge, William F. 138
Ryalls, Emaline (Watts) 148
Ryals, Caroline (Morrison) 254

Scarborough, Alfred 2
Scarborough, Emma T. (Lowe) 31
Scarborough, Jas. B. 57
Scarborough, Mary(Brinn) 2
Scarborough, P. W. (Cheak) 57
Schmitt, John 231
Schmitt, Sarah E. (Thompson) 231
Schnessler, Lewis S. 38
Schnessler, Sallie S. (Trammell) 38
Schofield, Martha E. (Booker) 14
Schoolfield, Mary S. (Jackson) 79
Schuessler, Ella Ida (Brown) 156
Schuessler, Zach 156
Score, Angus M. 48
Score, Sue A. (Stovall) 48
Scott, A. E. (Boswell) 48
Scott, Annie (Moore) 121
Scott, Augusta (Wilder) 105
Scott, B. S. 92
Scott, Benj. F. 21
Scott, Carrie S. (Gradick) 228
Scott, Emily (Roberson) 25
Scott, Frances (Tompkins) 71
Scott, H. Warren 270
Scott, Ida (Scott) 187
Scott, John A. 71
Scott, John E. 20
Scott, John O. 279
Scott, John R. 121
Scott, Julia (Kennedy) 20
Scott, Laura V. (Nunnaly) 21
Scott, Lizzie B. (Moran) 92
Scott, Louisa (Coyl) 9
Scott, Lula C. (Smith) 279
Scott, M. C. 228
Scott, Mary C. (Anderson) 76
Scott, Mary O. (Bonner) 118
Scott, Sallie L. (Stokes) 215
Scott, Sallie Lee (Hentz) 270
Scott, Sophia (Batts) 10
Scott, Susan (Nunerly) 67
Scott, Susan K. (Pounds) 145
Scott, Taylor 10
Scott, Temperance E. (Stewart) 8
Scott, Thomas G. 74
Scott, W. J. 102, 103
Scott, Walter 105, 234
Scott, William C. 187

Scott, William J. 76
Scott, Wilmer C. (Halzendorf) 234
Scovill, H. W. 288
Scovill, M. C. (Bateman) 288
Scoville, Edwin 66
Scoville, Susan E. (Hoyl) 66
Scroggins, M. E. (Jones) 10
Scruggs, Anna (Burkhalter) 83
Scruggs, Etta M. (Herrin) 281
Scruggs, Fannie C. (Gary) 240
Scruggs, J. L. 240
Scruggs, John T. 281
Scruggs, Joseph L. 123
Scruggs, Sarah J. (Scruggs) 123
Scruggs, Susie M. (Peek) 116
Scruggs, W. H. 116
Scudder, Jas. L. 205
Scudder, Mary Louie (Myrick) 205
Scurry, Sallie V. (Huff) 90
Seago, A. E. Reidel 251
Seago, Carrie E. W. (Glazier) 54
Seago, Florrie K. (Styles) 201
Seago, Georgie F. (Buzhardt) 201
Seago, J. M. 201
Seago, J. T. 59
Seago, Mattie L. (Brown) 59
Seago, Wm. 54
Seale, Anna (Larricott) 97
Seale, D. W. 97
Seale, R. A. 251, 265, 276
Seale, S. A. (Keener) 265
Sealey, J. J. 282
Sealey, Susan E. (Adams) 42
Sealey, W. A. 42
Seally, Joseph J. 253
Seals, A. 111
Seals, Fannie A. (Moss) 171
Seals, James M. 171
Seals, T. A. 55, 83, 86, 96, 105, 148, 166, 213, 241, 245, 280
Sealy, J. J. 31, 91
Sealy, Sarah Elizabeth (Williams) 201
Seaman, Sallie P. (Williams) 177
Searcy, Eugenia Pauline (Rogers) 48
Searcy, Henry 45
Searcy, John S. 208

Searcy, M. V. (Perkins) 45
Searcy, Sallie E. (Riley) 117
Searcy, William E. H. 48
Sears, Emilie C. (Stowe) 98
Sears, Joseph H. 98
Sears, M. A. (Hunt) 107
Sease, Minnie F. (Kistler) 216
Sease, W. G. 216
Seaver, E. A. (Poppel) 185
Seay, Benjamin 5
Seay, Frances M. (Baker) 80
Seay, Kitty (George) 5
Seay, William 80
Sebastian, L. H. 158
Sebastian, Sallie (Moore) 158
Seed, E. A. 38
Seely, J. J. 8
Sefers, Josephine (Finche) 7
Sefers, Michael 7
Sefstrum, Mollie (Lampkin) 73
Sefstrum, William 73
Segrest, A. Elizabeth (Foures) 248
Segrest, W. Laurance 248
Seibels, Lavinia Banks 176
Seibels, Thomas T. 176
Seibles, Maggie (Harmon) 168
Seixas, P. S. E. 96
Self, A. (Pitts) 63
Self, W. G. 63
Sellers, Henrietta M. (Jamison) 184
Sellers, John P. 184
Sellors, Fannie M. (Vinzant) 112
Senn, Ella Irine (Roach) 50
Senn, Hattie A. (Wolfe) 55
Senn, Rufus D. 50, 55
Sentell, Charlie 95
Sentell, J. E. 12, 53, 54, 60, 116, 150, 198, 200, 224, 277, 281, 292
Sentell, John 4
Sentell, John E. 4, 9, 16, 24, 35, 44
Senter, Lizzie C. (Dagnall) 98
Sessions, 246
Sessions, A. S. (Fentress) 71
Sessions, Anna R. (Brown) 201
Sessions, Esther A. (Nesmith) 121
Sessions, J. J. 71, 268
Sessions, Kareen Elizabeth (Wimberly) 268
Sessions, Lewe 65

Shields, Henry C. 239
Shields, J. N. (Porter) 182
Shields, Lucy (Word) 211
Shields, Mary Olena (Bond) 239
Shields, Mollie E. (Brooks) 163
Shields, Robert 145
Shields, Samuel S. 163
Shields, Samuel T. 211
Shields, Sophia M. (Sheilds) 145
Shine, Donie W. (Marr) 141
Shine, E. E. 47
Shine, J. B. 159
Shine, Millie E. (Vinson) 47
Shine, Mollie (Barker) 159
Shines, Henrietta J. (Griffith) 2
Shingler, Dora E. (Dantzler) 204
Shinholser, Audent V. (Wood) 105
Shinholser, Clifford N. (Haywood) 184
Shinholser, J. H. 105
Shinholser, John W. 108
Shinholser, Joseph H. 184
Shinholser, Martha A. (Heard) 108
Shipp, 262
Shipp, A. M. 155, 251
Shipp, Julius 59
Shipp, Lily (Webb) 251
Shipp, Mary W. (Sanders) 262
Shipp, Mollie (Hewell) 59
Shirah, Lou (Hays) 55
Shirley, Edna R. (Tucker) 258
Shirley, James 144
Shirley, Jonathan 258
Shirley, Nancy E. (Sauls) 144
Shiver, Amand (Murray) 267
Shiver, Carrie M. (Coleman) 105
Shiver, H. B. 105
Shockley, V. F. (Turk) 30
Shoemaker, John H. 295
Shoemaker, Willie A. (Land) 295
Shoer, Julia B. (Hall) 14
Shores, J. W. 22, 30, 32, 36, 38, 46, 53, 86
Shores, J. Wilson 44
Short, Sallie F. (Hampton) 171
Short, Walter J. 171
Shropshire, Fannie T. (Oliver) 91
Shrumpert, Francis M. 122

Shrumpert, Lillie E. (Merchant) 122
Shuford, J. L. 77, 80, 101, 154, 185, 270, 284
Shuford, Mary A. (Bell) 77
Shuler, Abram E. 98
Shuler, Ada (Wetherford) 76
Shuler, Henrietta (Kizer) 82
Shuler, Irene E. (Moorer) 191
Shuler, John 82
Shuler, Julia L. (Hutto) 146
Shuler, Julia W. (Edwards) 98
Shuler, Lovey C. (Edwards) 234
Shuler, M. E. (Avinger) 94
Shuler, Martha (Evans) 74
Shuler, Mary Ann (Dantzler) 72
Shuler, Mary Ann (McDaniel) 295
Shuler, P. 53
Shuler, Rosa (Kizer) 225
Shuler, Samuel R. 191
Shuler, Virginia G. (Murrer) 53
Shuler, Wm. M. 295
Shuler, Young G. 146
Shumate, B. D. 205
Shumate, Michael J. (Horn) 205
Shuptrine, Mary (Bradley) 47
Shuttles, Ella (Floyd) 77
Shuttles, John E. 77
Shy, Alice V. (Rowland) 192
Shy, M. T. (Hamilton) 80
Shy, S. H. 80
Sian, Agnes (Thompson) 92
Sibley, Elizabeth (Evans) 119
Sibley, James A. 119
Sibley, Mary J. (Mathews) 1
Sibley, W. T. 1
Siemons, Mary E. (Duren) 150
Sifley, J. F. 284
Sifley, J. L. 88, 107, 251, 267, 276
Sifly, J. F. 263
Sifly, J. L. 53, 100, 131, 149, 164, 230, 271
Silvey, Molly (Connally) 26
Simes, Mary N.(Beavers) 15
Simmons, Agnes J. (Shearouse) 124
Simmons, Andrew J. 124
Simmons, Camilla W. (Powell) 24

Simmons, Carrie E. (Moore) 261
Simmons, D. J. 26, 87, 102, 106, 107, 114, 115, 148, 149, 150, 158, 162, 166, 172, 183, 190, 197, 214, 218, 221, 233, 255, 256, 258, 263, 266, 268
Simmons, Dollie (Powell) 125
Simmons, Eddie (Connor) 34
Simmons, Ella (Babb) 115
Simmons, Emily (McCutchen) 274
Simmons, Henrietta (Berry) 177
Simmons, J. A. 179
Simmons, J. C. 125
Simmons, J. W. 48, 65, 73, 90, 101, 173, 193, 228, 235, 236
Simmons, James 288
Simmons, Jane (Flemming) 49
Simmons, John R. 49
Simmons, John W. 12
Simmons, Julia E. (Stubbs) 153
Simmons, Lavinia (Crawford) 179
Simmons, Lizzie (Willis) 134
Simmons, M. H. (McWhorter) 131
Simmons, Maddox M. 274
Simmons, Mary C. (Singer) 12
Simmons, Mary E. (Gower) 113
Simmons, Missouri (Johnson) 160
Simmons, O. C. 261
Simmons, Opelia P. (Lenning) 266
Simmons, Rowland 177
Simmons, S. Addie (Wilbanks) 174
Simmons, Sarah (Young) 292
Simmons, Sarah A. (Mote) 26
Simmons, Sarah C. (Reed) 213
Simmons, Sarah M. (Godfrey) 221
Simmons, Sarah Taylor 288
Simmons, Shelton 34
Simmons, T. J. 125, 151, 158, 162
Simmons, Thos. J. 73
Simmons, W. H. 266
Simmons, W. T. B. 213
Simmons, Wm. A. 131

Simms, A. B. 284
Simms, A. M. (Houston) 11
Simms, Ellen A. (Arnold) 79
Simms, Mollie (Reid) 211
Simms, Sarah S. T. (Jackson) 284
Simons, Fannie (Lott) 149
Simons, George W. 248
Simons, Havey 150
Simons, J. C. 12
Simons, Jennie C. (Parks) 208
Simons, Josiah 149
Simons, Susan F. (Langford) 248
Simonton, F. R. 133
Simonton, F. Rosalie (Jordan) 158
Simonton, J. Henry 158
Simonton, John A. 145
Simonton, John R. 161
Simonton, Leila G. (Harris) 145
Simonton, Mary A. (Smith) 5
Simonton, Sallie E. (Harris) 133
Simonton, Sallie V. (Cozart) 161
Simpon, M. J. (Graham) 93
Simpson, Fannie 239
Simpson, Harriet (Wages) 259
Simpson, J. N. 59
Simpson, Kittie E. (Mobley) 28
Simpson, Lucy A. (DuBose) 76
Simpson, M. A. (Martin) 27
Simpson, Mary M. (Williams) 75
Simpson, Mattie (Munro) 281
Simpson, R. F. 75
Simpson, Robert S. 281
Simpson, S. M. (Taylor) 59
Simpson, T. B. 27
Simpson, W. W. 76
Simpson, Wylie C. (Smith) 50
Sims, Alice (O'Brien) 267
Sims, Alice V. (More) 186
Sims, Amanda D. (Betts) 142
Sims, Amanda M. (Marshall) 75
Sims, Anna M. (Gocto) 44
Sims, E. C. (Nicholson) 66
Sims, Ellen E. (Cunningham) 162
Sims, Francis 267
Sims, Jennie (Fender) 169

Sims, Julia O. (Lucky) 183
Sims, Margaret (Tatum) 124
Sims, S. Y. 45
Sims, Sallie B. (Overby) 194
Sims, W. P. 66
Sims, W. W. 162
Sims, William 124
Sinclair, Davis S. 183
Sinclair, Emma C. (Bealer) 183
Sineth, Mahala B. (Wannamaker) 286
Sineth, Richard 286
Sinford, Amanda (Smith) 226
Singer, J. G. 12
Singer, Lizzie (Raleigh) 249
Singer, Mary C. (Simmons) 12
Singleton, Bettie H. (Bayne) 58
Singleton, Cordelia (Turk) 216
Singleton, J. J. 61, 114, 134, 135, 136, 142, 161, 177, 219, 242, 255, 257, 269
Sinius, G. W. 19
Sinius, Odie (Rylander) 19
Sinquefield, Louisa (Chapman) 114
Sinquefield, Lula E. (Burke) 293
Sistrunk, Amy C. (Hodges) 94
Sistrunk, Eva (Griffin) 282
Sistrunk, Newton 228
Sistrunk, S. H. J. 13, 23, 33, 64, 130, 159, 251
Sistrunk, Sarah W. (Chapman) 41
Sistrunk, T. W. 41
Sitton, E. Ann (King) 17
Sitton, Joseph E. 163
Sitton, Lizzie (Handrup) 163
Skeen, Mollie (Garrett) 293
Skelton, Francis M. (Sexon) 86
Skelton, V. H. 86
Skinner, Cornelia (Rockwell) 9
Skinner, Edgar 230
Skinner, Elizabeth (Dobson) 2
Skinner, Emily S. (Joiner) 87
Skinner, Francis (Lamberts) 21
Skinner, Mary Ann (Durant) 230
Skinner, Sarah S. (Taylor) 53

Skinner, W. S. 2
Skipper, Daniel 121
Skipper, J. L. 128
Skipper, Sally (Gittems) 121
Skrine, Vivianna B. (Boyer) 80
Slack, Matilda M. (Brown) 105
Slagle, J. M. 39
Slagle, Nancy E. (Collins) 39
Slappey, Jacob C. 64
Slappey, Lizzie (Lilly) 233
Slappey, Reuben H. 233
Slappey, Stella (Neal) 64
Slappy, Emma (Stewart) 217
Slappy, R. H. 217
Slapy, Anson 223
Slapy, Jennie (Stewart) 223
Slater, Emma S. (Hodges) 257
Slater, W. A. 106
Slaton, David L. 30
Slaton, Margaret J. (Higginbothan) 156
Slattery, Sarah C. (Kelly) 69
Slaughter, Cornelius 18
Slaughter, Emma (Watson) 150
Slaughter, Lizzie (Candler) 91
Slaughter, Mary E. (Hinton) 105
Slaughter, Mary F. (Dinkel) 231
Slaughter, Mary S. P. (Hightower) 18
Slaughter, Sallie C. (Cade) 49
Slaughter, Sallie E. (Faulkner) 233
Slayton, Colistia A. (Lynch) 95
Slayton, Wm. 156
Sledge, Ella L. (Pitman) 40
Sledge, J. W. 99
Sledge, James H. 248
Sledge, Mary E. (Hill) 99
Sledge, Mary Louise (Cox) 248
Sledge, N. H. 40
Sledge, Sallie O. (Green) 137
Sleigh, Carrie (Whitaker) 185
Sleigh, J. F. 140
Sleight, Caroline (Morgan) 146
Sleight, J. H. 146
Sloan, Emma J. (Blackburn) 49

Smith, Silo S. 70
Smith, Simeon G. 222
Smith, Sue (Pressley) 193
Smith, Sue E. (Garrett) 229
Smith, Susan A. (Andrew)
184
Smith, Susan A. 155
Smith, Susan J. (Middleton)
106
Smith, Susan R. (Crossby)
277
Smith, Susie (Ross) 116
Smith, Susie (Yates) 155
Smith, Susie Ellis 220
Smith, Susie M. (Berry) 50,
51
Smith, T. G. 40
Smith, Tabitha J. (Arwood)
161
Smith, Talula (Cooper) 14
Smith, Theo. E. 258
Smith, Theodosia J. (Hart)
103
Smith, Thomas 86
Smith, Thomas B. 283
Smith, Thomas D. 10
Smith, Thomas R. 223
Smith, Virginia S. (Brazier)
154
Smith, W. A. 285
Smith, W. F. 35, 49, 133,
268
Smith, W. P. 26, 212
Smith, W. T. 38
Smith, Walker 277
Smith, Wesley F. 1, 6, 10,
21, 27, 54, 70, 83, 86, 92,
123, 124, 135, 138, 153, 160,
165, 180, 185, 289
Smith, Wesley J. 82
Smith, Wesley P. 120
Smith, Whitefoord 229
Smith, Wiley 278
Smith, William 155, 166
Smith, William B. 194
Smith, William H. 250
Smith, William J. 173, 278
Smith, William J. J. 46
Smith, William M. 245
Smith, William T. B. (Wilson) 118
Smith, Williamson 270
Smith, Willie 288
Smith, Wilson 108
Smith, Wylie C. (Simpson)
50
Smoak, Perry 260
Smoak, Sallie (Means) 260
Smoke, Henrietta A. (Riley) 284
Smoke, Izorah E. (Westbury) 198

Smoke, Lucia (Saunders)
289
Smoot, Maggie (Trueluck)
276
Smoot, Thos. 276
Smyth, 50
Smyth, Ellison A. 50
Smyth, Julia (Gambell) 50
Snead, Catharine A. (Hightower) 43
Snead, F. T. 249
Snead, Fletcher T. 197
Snead, Garland 88
Snead, Hennie R. (McGolrick) 88
Snead, Lizzie W. (Wooten)
249
Snead, Mary L. (Wardlaw)
197
Sneed, Mary O. (Cottenham) 16
Sneed, Thomas 16
Snell, Ann R. (Whetsel) 195
Snell, Danie D. 234
Snell, David W. 228
Snell, Emma L. J. (Hutto)
234
Snell, Jubie C. (Oliver) 228
Snellings, G. T. 28
Snellings, S. E. (Kinckesw)
28
Snellings, Susan (Dadisman) 22
Snipes, MaryAnn (Willis) 9
Snipes, William Thomas 9
Snow, Ella S. (Pacetty) 62
Snow, Emma G. (Freeman)
213
Snow, Hettie (Randall) 52
Snow, Mary A. (Florence)
192
Solomon, John W. 219
Solomon, Lewis 103
Solomon, Mattie L. (Renfro) 292
Solomon, William C. 292
Solomons, Hattie C. (Parnells) (Johnson) 51
Solomons, Henry E. 51
Solomons, Lillie M. (Box)
233
Solomons, Samuel G. 233
Somelian, H. B. 270
Somelian, Sarah (Reid) 270
Sotory, Benjamin B. 223
Sotory, C. P. (Rains) 223
Souter, E. A. (Peeler) 219
Souter, E. D. 219
South, James A. 190
South, Mary E. (Coker) 190
Southerland, A. S. (Whitehead) 89
Southerland, J. G. 65

Southerland, M. S. (Whitehead) 65
Space, Charles A. 195
Space, Laura M. (Nelson)
195
Space, Mady M. (McIntosh)
249
Spain, Lucy B. (Brown) 252
Spalding, 281
Spalding, Bourke 188
Spalding, Ella P. (Barrow)
188
Spann, Hannah (Nugent)
175
Sparkman, Lizzie (Rigell)
290
Sparkman, Margaret L.
(Hundley) 125
Sparkman, Simeon L. 135
Sparks, J. G. 183
Sparks, James W. 276
Sparks, Jane E. (Beaton)
183
Sparks, Katie L. (Kilpatrick) 276
Sparrow, Martha C. (Pitts)
267
Spear, Dee (MacMillan)
180
Spear, Ellen C. (McCord)
117
Spear, Eustace W. 97
Spear, Henry H. 180
Spear, Laura (Blitch) 67
Spear, R. 67
Spearman, Cepkas R. 99
Spearman, J. L. (Geiger) 79
Spearman, M. W. 79
Spearman, Matilda R. (St.
John) 99
Spears, Conie (Thurman)
113
Spears, Frances C. (Dupree) 44
Spears, James 44
Spears, James A. 113
Spears, Mary P. (Moseley)
108
Speer, Alice (Roper) 263
Speer, Arthur 263
Speer, Fletcher B. 168
Speer, Geraldine Z. (Moreland) 54
Speer, H. W. 163
Speer, Harriet (McGaughey) 265
Speer, Henry S. 168
Speer, Jane T. (Carter) 55
Speer, John H. 265
Speer, Mary Hulit (Lewis)
109
Speer, Nancy (Bean) 168
Speer, W. H. 235, 261

Stokes, Mattie S. (Salley) 225

Stokes, Nancy A. (Mc-Swain) 78

Stokes, Olivia Ann (Malone) 34

Stokes, Peter 276

Stokes, S. Lilian (Lachicotte) 282

Stokes, Sallie L. (Scott) 215

Stokes, William A. 78

Stokes, Z. F. 215

Stoll, J. C. 65

Stoll, James C. 62, 69, 74, 75, 76, 89, 94, 116, 123, 132, 294

Stolvey, America (Marchman) 107

Stolvey, G. W. 107

Stone, Alice A. (Toney) 26

Stone, Anna R. (Lewis) 190

Stone, E. Jennie (Hutchinson) 93

Stone, Eliza H. (Whitfield) 63

Stone, Ellison D. 281

Stone, Emily (Eaddy) 130

Stone, Emma (Palmer) 278

Stone, Emma C. (Bradford) 281

Stone, Emma E. (Borrow) 2

Stone, G. W. W. 278

Stone, Geo. W. 145

Stone, Geo. W. W. 157

Stone, J. M. (Camp) 126

Stone, James H. 188

Stone, John H. 190

Stone, Julia (Word) 188

Stone, Lizzie E. (Hammett) 115

Stone, Maggie (Boyd) 51

Stone, Mary (McCain) 49

Stone, Nannie (Baker) 58

Stone, Rachel (Buchanan) 73

Stoner, Mary R. (Donalson) 191

Stoner, Peter T. 191

Story, Sallie (Howel) 84

Story, Thos. W. 84

Stoudemire, J. L. 68

Stout, Daniel 141

Stout, Fanny J. (Rea) (Smith) 141

Stovall, B. M. 83

Stovall, D. M. 123

Stovall, Eva E. (Marable) 24

Stovall, Lula (Osborn) 282

Stovall, M. O. (Few) 83

Stovall, Mark E. 24

Stovall, Matilda F. (Magruder) 93

Stovall, S. 93

Stovall, Sue A. (Score) 48

Stover, M. A. (Horton) 227

Stowe, Emilie C. (Sears) 98

Stoy, Ida E. (Cameron) 157

Stoy, Julien M. 157

Stralnaker, J. D. 46

Stralnaker, S. (Ogburn) 46

Straman, C. J. 98

Straman, Rosa (Odom) 98

Strange, Benj. 94

Strange, Bettie (Cassady) 94

Strange, E. A. (Mott) 256

Strange, Emma (Massey) 256

Strange, J. C. 256

Strange, Josie (Hames) 248

Stratford, Bettie (Farmer) 191

Stratford, Mattie E. (Godwin) 200

Stratford, Wm. E. 200

Strauss, Josephine 149

Street, Elizabeth B. (Heaton) 219

Street, Gertrude A. (Harrison) 85

Street, John J. 149

Street, Sallie E. (Berry) 210

Street, Sue (Evans) 116

Street, William F. 219

Streetman, (Johnson) 46

Streyer, Eliza S. (Gibson) 168

Streyer, William 168

Stribling, Anna (Mundy) 140

Stribling, Warren 140

Strickland, Albert 253

Strickland, Elisha W. 35

Strickland, Eunice (Baxter) 90

Strickland, Giles (Hague) 253

Strickland, James S. 259

Strickland, Jennie L. (Lee) 45

Strickland, Mary (Hopson) 38

Strickland, Mary E. (Strickland) 259

Strickland, Mattie A. (Bragdon) 35

Strickland, Willie E. 204

Stricklin, Cornelia M. A. (Quillian) 51

Stricklin, R. 51

Stringer, Mettie (Lykes) 178

Stringer, Sheldon 178

Stringfellow, L. G. 47

Stringfellow, Rebecca (Turner) 47

Stripling, Annie (Roberts) 258

Stripling, Ida Redding 213

Stripling, Mary C.(Emory) 1

Stripling, Robt. 1

Stripling, S. E. (Bains) 31

Strobhart, H. N. 200

Strobhart, Sarah Ellen (Miller) 200

Strong, Flewellin (Evans) 164

Strong, L. C. 164

Strong, R. A. (Vance) 155

Strother, Alphonso T. 56

Strother, Charles S. 99

Strother, Fannie (May) 215

Strother, G. E. (Hill) 100

Strother, Georgia (Holliday) 56

Strother, Lula (Lamar) 99

Stroud, D. A. 247

Stroud, Ella (Sanders) 82

Stroud, Lula V. (Blalock) 247

Stroud, M. D. 82

Stroud, M. Ella (Sanders) 83

Stroud, Mack D. 83

Stroud, Mary (Grove) 21

Stroud, S. B. (Smith) 165

Strozier, B. P. 277

Strozier, Fannie (Cowart) 147

Strozier, Leonora (Hailes) 277

Stuart, C. H. 142

Stuart, D. L. 23

Stuart, E. E. (Bostick) 142

Stuart, Eliza L. (Gibson) 23

Stuart, George D. 129

Stuart, Mollie J. (Parker) 129

Stubbs, Annie M. (Goodwin) 237

Stubbs, Charles B. 201

Stubbs, Charles F. 237

Stubbs, E. J. (Lester) 161

Stubbs, E. L. M. (Pool) 152

Stubbs, E. R. (Pitts) 283

Stubbs, F. M. (Stephens) 66

Stubbs, James W. 283

Stubbs, Julia E. (Simmons) 153

Stubbs, L. L. (Jenkins) 117

Stubbs, M. F. 66

Stubbs, Martha A. (Renfroe) 194

Stubbs, Mattie J. (Mithell) 201

Stubbs, Sarah C. (Patterson) 233

Stubbs, Walter P. 153

Stuckey, Antoinette (Dixon) 172
Stuckey, C. L. 217
Stuckey, Edmund 82
Stuckey, J. W. 138
Stuckey, Janie (Dixon) 217
Stuckey, Laney (Baskin) 82
Sturdivant, J. P. 267
Sturdivant, S. Fannie (Brooke) 267
Sturgis, Cynthia A. (Chreighton) 148
Sturgiss, T. W. 148
Styles, Florrie K. (Seago) 201
Suber, Mollie Z. (McRee) 98
Suber, Peter 140
Suber, Sarah (Seybt) 140
Subers, Amos A. 108
Subers, Wayne (Massey) 108
Suddath, E. A. (Winters) 132
Suddath, Z. T. 132
Suggs, M. A. (Cannon) 75
Sullings, Mary 193
Sullins, Mary Keitt (Bomar) 290
Sullivan, Annie E. (Anderson) 44
Sullivan, Chas. P. 172
Sullivan, Claudia (Hough) 273
Sullivan, Fannie M. (McDavid) 13
Sullivan, Fannie S. (Jobson) 240
Sullivan, G. W. 54
Sullivan, Hattie E. (Holland) 41
Sullivan, I. Mims 36
Sullivan, J. M. 13, 41
Sullivan, Janie K. 185
Sullivan, Jared D. 34
Sullivan, Jefferson 273
Sullivan, Jennie (Stokes) 36
Sullivan, Joshua D. 240
Sullivan, Kate (Willis) 172
Sullivan, Mary H. (Goodgion) 54
Sullivan, P. Alice (Greer) 172
Sullivan, Rosalie A. (Moore) 34
Sullivan, William G. 282
Sullivan, Winnnie (Lester) 282
Sumerall, L. (Allen) 192
Summerlin, E. C. 94
Summerlin, Ellen (Gnan) 94

Summerour, Mattie S. (Gregory) 268
Summers, Carrie (Ehney) 232
Summers, E. A. (Thompson) 286
Summers, Florella (Livingstone) 221
Summers, Florence (Phillips) 225
Summers, G. Asbury 232
Summers, J. W. 210
Summers, John A. 225, 286
Summerville, Mary (Martin) 102
Sumner, Geo. 125
Sumner, Mary (Cray) 125
Sutherlin, Charles A. 228
Sutherlin, Jane (Willis) 228
Sutley, Rebecca (Gray) 252
Sutley, Wm. D. 252
Sutton, Fannie A. (Owen) 260
Sutton, Mittie (Lyon) 146
Swain, Mary (Mayes) 111
Swan, Callie (Nichols) 216
Swann, Lizzie 163
Swann, Sallie (Smith) 91
Swann, Sallie C. (McLarin) 267
Swearengin, J. C. 208
Swearengin, Lucy (Brewer) 208
Swearingen, Dora C. (Chapman) 15
Swearingen, Jas. H. 199
Swearingen, M. J. C. (Lasseter) 199
Sweat, Georgiana (Brunner) 262
Sweatman, Mary (Grooms) 204
Sweatman, Robert 204
Sweeny, Anna (Morgan) 109
Sweeny, William E. 109
Sweet, Julia (Bunch) 120
Sweet, Middleton 120
Sweet, S. S. 48, 56, 57, 70, 105, 108, 109, 130, 131, 140, 141, 144, 150, 156, 168, 172, 184, 203, 216, 217, 220, 227, 253, 265
Swett, M. E. (Coward) 266
Swett, N. L. 266
Swift, Bertha (Pendleton) 281
Swift, John A. 111
Swift, Lavinia (Patterson) 232
Swift, Nettie (Johnson) 111
Swindall, M. E. (Cook) 155
Swindall, Thos. 155

Swindle, E. E. (Martin) 66
Swink, Jesse L. 241
Swink, Maggie A. (Bishop) 241
Swint, M. (Tidwell) 1
Switzer, Emma (Shell) 172
Switzer, J. R. 172
Swygert, Anna (Swygert) 260
Swygert, John H. 260
Swygert, John S. 239
Swygert, Mary E. (Wicker) 239
Swygert, Sanders 260
Syfrett, Sarah E. S. (Prater) 170
Sykes, Alice E. (Brockington) 244
Syms, Lillie May (Preskitt) 278
Tabor, M. A. (Cole) 123
Tabor, T. W. 123
Tackets, B. Gertrude (Freeman) 218
Tait, Carrie M. (Moore) 182
Tait, Felix 182
Talbot, Mary E. (Twitty) 128
Taliafero, Emma (Gilbert) 199
Taliafero, Samuel 199
Taliaferro, Annie W. (Freeman) 94
Taliaferro, Mildred A. (Freeman) 26
Talivar, Mary (Mazingo) 282
Talley, Alexander N. 225
Talley, Carrie (Harry) 125
Talley, D. Ann (Howell) 261
Talley, D. H. 118
Talley, Elizabeth Whitner (Jones) 225
Talley, J. W. 57, 116, 180, 261
Talley, Jas. W. 62
Talley, M. (Holtzendorf) 62
Talley, Mary R. (Pye) 118
Talley, Nathan 180
Talley, Rachel (Vanguson) 180
Talley, Sallie C. (Morse) 116
Talley, W. R. 41, 47
Talley, W. Rothchild 57
Talley, William R. 125
Talmadge, H. Z. (Key) 279
Talmadge, S. Emma (Tollison) 108
Talmadge, William J. 279

Talmage, Lizzie D. (Pendleton) 82
Tankersley, --llie Ann (Albea) 224
Tankersley, James M. 224
Tankersly, Ella J. (Tankersly) 278
Tankersly, George 278
Tanner, Eugenia (Perry) 100
Tanner, James G. 99
Tanner, John S. 213
Tanner, M. E. (McLendon) 275
Tanner, M. Lizzie (Tanner) 43
Tanner, Maggie E. (Blalock) 99
Tanner, Patience (Peacock) 213
Tanner, W. A. 43
Tanner, Wm. R. 43
Tant, Daniel 227
Tant, Winnie (Williams) 227
Tapp, H. H. (Burns) 98
Tappan, William L. 251
Tappan, Willie (Jernigan) 251
Tapper, J. T. 30
Tapper, Jane P. (Bowen) 30
Tapscott, Pocahontas (Hinson) 7
Tarbutton, Benjamin J. 151
Tarbutton, Mary H. (Bags) 151
Tarpley, A. F. (Vanlandingham) 85
Tarpley, Edward J. 65
Tarpley, Hellen A. (Brannan) 161
Tarpley, Mattie J. (Roberts) 65
Tarpley, T. M. 85
Tarply, Anna (Linder) 75
Tarply, Thos. M. 75
Tarrance, Charity A. (Martin) 243
Tarrance, George W. 243
Tarrant, R. B. 94, 98, 111, 138, 150, 221, 225, 232, 245, 289
Tart, J. H. 21
Tart, James H. 10, 26
Tarver, A. E. 271
Tarver, Belle C. (Murphy) 271
Tarver, C. A. (Malone) 274
Tarver, E. W. 257
Tarver, Jas. B. 174
Tarver, Jimmie (Parks) 271
Tarver, Laura G. (Cone) 257

Tarver, Sallie H. (Banks) 174
Tarver, Sallie K. (Banks) 193
Tat, M. M. 9
Tat, Sarah J. (Webster) 9
Tate, Cora E. (Thomas) 104
Tate, Martha A. (Wood) 189
Tate, Z. A. 104
Tates, Christiana (Webster) 188
Tates, George W. 188
Tatum, Fannie (Gammon) 245
Tatum, Jno. A. 151
Tatum, Lizzie (Baker) 151
Tatum, Margaret (Sims) 124
Tatum, Sarah E. (Hawkins) 179
Taylor, Alice L. (Wimberly) 95
Taylor, Anna (Wilkison) 127
Taylor, Anna M. (Redder) 271
Taylor, Charles E. 290
Taylor, Cinderella (Mann) 170
Taylor, E. O. (Padgett) 154
Taylor, E. Roberta (Watts) 210
Taylor, Elisabeth (Rogers) 50
Taylor, Elizabeth (Glenn) 72
Taylor, H. S. 87
Taylor, Harry 234
Taylor, Hugh G. 175
Taylor, J. T. 154
Taylor, James J. 54
Taylor, John E. 95
Taylor, John J. 177
Taylor, L. V. (Stevens) 236
Taylor, Lewis 170
Taylor, Louisa (Witt) 94
Taylor, Marietta (Nix) 54
Taylor, Mary (McClure) 87
Taylor, Mary J. (Phillips) 290
Taylor, Mary J. (Tomson) 234
Taylor, N. H. (McMullen) 178
Taylor, Nora M. (Miller) 188
Taylor, Ophelia A. (Kimbrough) 53
Taylor, R. N. 163
Taylor, Rebecca (Wooten) 150
Taylor, S. M. (Simpson) 59

Taylor, Sarah (Gainey) 20
Taylor, Sarah M. (Butts) 175
Taylor, Sarah S. (Skinner) 53
Taylor, Sarah Simmons 288
Taylor, Simmons 50
Taylor, Susan E. (Carmine) 230
Taylor, Susie H. (Lucas) 236
Taylor, T. J. 53
Taylor, Wm. C. 236
Taylor, Wm. R. 53
Taylor, Wm. T. 175
Teague, Stella C. (Fuller) 156
Teague, Thaddeus S. 156
Teasley, Emma (Brown) 294
Teasley, James A. 294
Teasley, Jennie (Brown) 294
Teasley, Mary M. (Crisler) 158
Teasley, Sallie E. (Brown) 23
Teasley, W. A. 158
Teasley, W. E. 79
Teat, J. R. 12
Tedards, Sallie A. (Claxton) 276
Telbests, 78
Temple, A. (Farmer) 72
Temple, Georgia H. (Hayns) 251
Temple, J. D. 72
Templeton, C. E. (Colbert) 219
Templeton, John C. 2
Templeton, Mary E. (McColough) 2
Tenison, Mary H. (Hays) 99
Tensley, Mary E. (Berry) 189
Tensley, N. A. 189
Terell, G. A. (Bonner) 65
Terell, J. A. 65
Terrell, Ida T. Spence 244
Terrell, Robert R. 244
Terrell, W. D. 117
Terry, 81
Terry, D. T. W. 285
Terry, Ellen (Thomason) 260
Terry, Fannie B. (Freeman) 107
Terry, J. P. 107
Terry, Josie B. (Hendrix) 196
Terry, S. J. (Thomason) 285
Terry, White 260
Thames, G. W. 111

410

411

Thompson, Mattie J. (Smith) 245
Thompson, Miria E. (Peninger) 32
Thompson, N. A. 238
Thompson, Nannie M. (Davis) 201
Thompson, Rebecca D. (Gentry) 112
Thompson, S. C. 171
Thompson, S. J. (Johnson) 48
Thompson, Sallie (Mathews) 164
Thompson, Sallie A. (Waters) 3
Thompson, Sarah E. (Schmitt) 231
Thompson, Susan J. (Longino) 261
Thompson, T. J. 60
Thompson, Thomassa (Galluchat) 287
Thompson, Thos. F. 177
Thompson, W. T. 55
Thompson, William 92
Thompson, William O. 32
Thomson, A. 251
Thomson, A. C. C. 101
Thomson, Ann E. (Leak) 125
Thomson, Annie E. (McLendon) 101
Thomson, Claudia (Whittle) 288
Thomson, E. J. (Wilson) 244
Thomson, Ellendor (Nicholson) 288
Thomson, Jas. C. 229
Thomson, Lizzie (Flowers) 229
Thomson, M. Eunice (Whitehead) 181
Thomson, M. S. 181
Thomson, Nena (Danner) 106
Thomson, Sam'l 260
Thomson, Wm. R. 125
Thomson, Wm. S. 106
Thornburgh, A. 208, 213
Thorne, Annie Lollie (Powers) 195
Thorne, Joseph 195
Thornton, Annie Foster (Pierce) 89
Thornton, E. R. 35
Thornton, Ellorah (Bryant) 87
Thornton, Ida (Felder) 281
Thornton, Joel F. 89
Thornton, Julia (Weeks) 58

Thornton, Nancy J. (Baxley) 35
Thornton, Nettie (Hearn) 108
Thornton, Novilla (Adams) 45
Thornton, R. A. 108
Thornton, S. W. 58
Thornton, Sallie E. (Branch) 230
Thornton, Sarah V. (Moore) 108
Thornton, Susan A. (Carroll) 241
Thornton, W. J. 281
Thornton, W. N. 108
Thornton, Wiley T. 45
Thorpe, Frances (Ferrell) 288
Thorpe, Horace 288
Thrasher, A. B. 45, 117
Thrasher, Barton E. 126
Thrasher, Celestia A. (Griffith) 24
Thrasher, Clara A. (Fulilove) 126
Thrasher, Fannie P. (Baxter) 126
Thrasher, J. S. 178
Thrasher, M. Callie (Collier) 178
Thrasher, Mattie A. (Bishop) 241
Thrasher, Sallie F. (Hattaway) 126
Threadgill, Mary E. (Motley) 31
Threadgill, Wm. 31
Thriff, M. (Wadsworth) 92
Thriff, S. 92
Thrower, O. A. 290, 291, 293
Thurman, Conie (Spears) 113
Thurman, Lucy (Tribble) 215
Thurman, Margaret (Putman) 18
Tibbs, Mary B. (Kenner) 79
Tibert, Mattie (Mayson) 49
Ticen, Mary S. R. (Dunevent) 99
Tidwell, James A. C. 2
Tidwell, L. B. (Coppage) 2
Tidwell, M. (Swint) 1
Tidwell, M. L. 1
Tidwell, Minnie G. (Murphy) 240
Tidwell, W. W. 62, 105
Tigner, A. W. 132
Tigner, Miriam (Boynton) 132
Tigner, U. G. 66

Tigner, Y. F. 114
Tignor, Eliza M. (Cottingham) 61, 62
Tignor, Eunice E. (Smith) 222
Tignor, I. C. (Kaigler) 182
Tignor, U. C. 182
Tignor, Wesley F. 61, 62
Tiley, Fannie (Barron) 203
Tiller, D. 198
Tiller, J. S. 255
Tiller, Joseph L. 201
Tiller, Mattie E. (Callaway) 255
Tiller, Sallie S. D. (Pearce) 201
Tilley, Fletcher 290
Tilley, Willie (Ford) 290
Tillinghast, S. English (Patterson) 156
Tillinghast, W. S. 156
Tillman, B. W. 28
Tillman, Belle (Blake) 138
Tillman, J. L. 258
Tillman, John 44
Tillman, M. Lawson (Wyche) 44
Tillman, Mary S. (Yoder) 258
Tillman, S. A. (Starke) 28
Tilly, Lou (Jones) 69
Tilly, Nannie (Smith) 207
Tilly, Roland C. 69
Timanus, Anna Gertrude (Tomkins) 158
Timanus, Henry 164
Timanus, Josephine (McDowell) 164
Timanus, T. 158
Timanus, T. P. (Bowden) 212
Timmons, B. E. L. 62, 83, 87, 95, 107, 200, 203, 207, 261, 286
Timmons, B. L. (Miller) 101
Timmons, D. F. C. 223, 255
Timmons, F. E. (Johnson) 216
Timmons, Jane (Robison) 101
Timmons, Lucy C. H. (Menifee) 200
Timmons, Mary E. (Booth) 82
Timmons, R. A. 143
Timmons, R. H. 54
Timmons, S. B. 216
Timmons, T. H. 147, 153, 156, 162, 167, 185, 194, 201, 213, 216, 221, 223, 224, 239, 245, 246, 250
Timmons, Thomas 101

412

Trible, Mary E. (Puryear) 80

Trible, Sarah A. E. (Edwards) 80

Trible, Thomas F. 80

Trice, B. A. 84

Trice, Donie E. (Cook) 84

Trimble, Carrie (Sawyer) 228

Trimble, Louis O. 228

Trimble, Mollie (Walker) 70

Trippe, Anna P. (Smith) 10

Trotter, Fanny (Fuller) 139

Trotter, Reuben 139

Trueluck, G. 276

Trueluck, Maggie (Smoot) 276

Trueluck, Mary A. (Lord) 47

Truesdel, Benjamin 235

Truesdel, Laura T. (Horton) 235

Truesdel, M. A. (Kelley) 261

Truett, E. W. (Bass) 6

Truett, S. C. 6

Truitt, Mary A. (Duke) 55

Truman, Martha (Hardy) 26

Trunnell, Lula J. (Lupo) 122

Truslow, John L. 129

Truslow, Julia B. (Howard) 129

Trussel, C. 198

Trussell, C. 222, 225

Trussell, F. Eugenia (Williams) 113

Trussell, H. C. 113

Trynum, S. T. (Ivy) 160

Trynum, W. L. 160

Tuck, Mattie (Macon) 202

Tuck, William R. 202

Tucker, C. W. 229

Tucker, Charles J. 152

Tucker, Edna R. (Shirley) 258

Tucker, Eliza C. (Adams) 155

Tucker, Emily (Kimrell) 115

Tucker, Emma R. (Wannamaker) 229

Tucker, Fannie (Tucker) 266

Tucker, G. C. (Beckwith) 45

Tucker, Georgia A. (Perry) 7

Tucker, J. L. 115

Tucker, J. R. 70

Tucker, Jesse 241

Tucker, M. V. (Williams) 71

Tucker, Margaret (Stokes) 288

Tucker, Milton 266

Tucker, Milton P. 45

Tucker, Pleasant A. 258

Tucker, S. N. 289

Tucker, Sallie J. (Merritt) 108

Tucker, Susie (Tounsley) 132

Tuggle, Louise M. (Cotter) 288

Tullis, A. F. 210

Tullis, Jennie (Ainsworth) 210

Tully, A. J. 175

Tully, L. S. (Coggins) 175

Tumlin, Frances Ophelia (Wilkes) 38

Tumlin, N. 38

Tunison, Mary S. (Hightower) 175

Turk, Cordelia (Singleton) 216

Turk, Dora V. (Evans) 114

Turk, James W. 216

Turk, John M. 30

Turk, Sarah L. (Traywick) 85

Turk, V. F. (Shockley) 30

Turman, Mary E. (Alston) 230

Turnell, Sudie A. (Mallory) 179

Turner, A. B. (Mason) 65

Turner, A. M. 290

Turner, Abthia L. (Hamby) 104

Turner, Achsah (Marsha) 38

Turner, Adam 288

Turner, Alice (Hudson) 139

Turner, C. F. 135

Turner, Catharine G. (Fryer) 39

Turner, Catharine M. C. (McLaughlin) 288

Turner, Charles H. 131

Turner, Eda E. (Webb) 209

Turner, Eliza (Smith) 135

Turner, Elizabeth (Hickmon) 168

Turner, Fannie (Orr) 143

Turner, Fannie J. (Smith) 290

Turner, Geo. W. 179

Turner, Georgia A. (Jones) 74

Turner, Harriet C. (Maxwell) 269

Turner, J. 53

Turner, J. A. 146

Turner, J. T. 76

Turner, J. W. 47, 56

Turner, James B. 161, 209

Turner, Jennie (Barrow) 118

Turner, Julia (Allgood) 179

Turner, Laura R. (Price) 63

Turner, Lena A. (Pope) 239

Turner, Levi A. 38

Turner, Lewis M. 139

Turner, Lizzie F. (Marone) 281

Turner, Ludie F. (Willingham) 193

Turner, Luther S. 188

Turner, Mary J. (Hewlett) 53

Turner, Mary J. (Hunnicutt) 56

Turner, Mattie C. (Marshall) 147

Turner, Mattie E. (Coker) 213

Turner, Molisia (Cook) 146

Turner, Raleigh 281

Turner, Rebecca (Stringfellow) 47

Turner, Riley O. 193

Turner, Robert A. 269

Turner, Sallie (Guest) 161

Turner, Sallie (Middlebrook) 170

Turner, Sue C. (Fletcher) 131

Turner, Susie B. (McKinley) 188

Turner, Susie W. (Thomas) 105

Turner, T. C. 65

Turner, Tommie L. (Glass) 38

Turner, W. K. 82, 86, 121

Turner, W. W. 213

Turner, Wm. G. 147

Turnison, G. H. 156

Turnison, L. E. (Patrick) 156

Turrentine, Jas. R. 19

Turrentine, Loula (Laidler) 283

Turrentine, M. C. 4

Turrentine, Nannie (Bazemore) 19

Turrentine, S. 195

Tutt, S. Leonard (Freeman) 123

Tutt, William D. 123

Tutwiler, M. Fletcher 132

Tutwiler, Nina E. (Johnson) 132

Twilley, Sally (Peddy) 92

Twitty, F. R. 128

Twitty, Henry D. 276

Twitty, Lizzie (Bailey) 276

Twitty, Lizzie (Crawford) 273

Walker, Loula (Moring) 91
Walker, Lucy J. (Lloyd) 120
Walker, M. D. (Webster) 27
Walker, Marcilla E. (Lively) 122
Walker, Margaret R. (Jones) 219
Walker, Martha (Billue) 39
Walker, Martha Frances (Wright) 140
Walker, Mary (Carlisle) 285
Walker, Mary A. (Neisler) 188
Walker, Mary E. (Boyd) 229
Walker, Mary Lou (Beason) 207
Walker, Mary Willie (Enlow) 205
Walker, Mattie S. (Pitts) 226
Walker, Mollie (Trimble) 70
Walker, Mollie E. (Ward) 6
Walker, R. M. 258
Walker, Robert 10
Walker, S. E. (Hudson) 206
Walker, Sallie H. (Beaty) 114
Walker, Sallie L. (Bramblett) 59
Walker, Sarah J. (Quarles) 271
Walker, Susan J. (Kellum) 113
Walker, T. J. 123
Walker, Thaddeus 205
Walker, Thomas D. 271
Walker, Thomas J. 113, 140
Walker, V. R. (Baxter) 193
Walker, Virginia (Kirkland) 226
Walker, W. F. 294
Walker, W. M. 177
Walker, W. W. 91, 93
Walker, Wal-- J. 239
Walker, Watson 70
Walker, Wm. G. 254
Walker, Wm. W. 219
Walker, Z. T. 168
Walkton, O. H. 13
Wall, 54
Wall, Adda (Smith) 91
Wall, Helon (Billingsley) 35
Wall, J. M. 35
Wall, J. S. 91
Wall, Jas. 230
Wall, Jennie (Montgomery) 110
Wall, M. E. (Cox) 10
Wall, Margaret J. (Thompson) 230

Wallace, Annie L. (English) 229
Wallace, Bland 15
Wallace, Elizabeth A. (Barrett) 103
Wallace, Gideon 220
Wallace, John 15
Wallace, Joseph P. 103
Wallace, M. C. 229
Wallace, M. J. (McSwain) 92
Wallace, Martha (Lasier) 15
Wallace, Mary M. (Mann) 102
Wallace, Nannie (DeVan) (Carter) 220
Waller, Mary E. (Dozier) 222
Waller, Sarah E. (Collins) 46
Wallis, H. B. 168
Wallis, S. Ollie (Moore) 168
Walsh, Admira R. (Riley) 185
Walsh, Anna (Inabinet) 83
Walsh, Cornelia (Reid) 47
Walsh, J. P. 185
Walsh, Josephine T. (McCollum) 18
Walsh, Tracy R. 18, 47
Walters, Eliza J. (Patrick) 197
Walters, J. W. 282
Walters, Lummie A. (Jossie) 167
Walters, Margaret Ann (Moye) 134
Walters, R. B. G. 17, 56, 134, 167
Walters, Sallie Ella (Littlejohn) 282
Walters, Stephen S. 197
Walthall, John W. 254
Walthall, Josephine (Brown) 254
Walton, Ceana J. (Hurdle) 35
Walton, H. M. (Willis) 27
Walton, Indiana G. (Joyner) 87
Walton, Isaiah 35
Walton, Jane (McLean) 6
Walton, L. D. 6
Walton, Lizzie J. (Postell) 13
Walton, Lou (Cates) 255
Walton, R. J. 27
Walton, Rowena (Reese) 161
Walton, Wm. D. 161
Waltz, Celestra R. (Crosby) 121

Wamack, Evaline (Pitts) 233
Wamack, James 233
Wannamaker, Annie R. (Watson) 52
Wannamaker, Corrie (Jones) 283
Wannamaker, Ella Lou (Banks) 274
Wannamaker, Emma R. (Tucker) 229
Wannamaker, G. W. 255
Wannamaker, J. C. J. 181
Wannamaker, J. S. 289
Wannamaker, Julia B. (Moorer) 193
Wannamaker, Lilly E. (Bates) 255
Wannamaker, Mahala B. (Sineth) 286
Wannamaker, Minerva A. (Robinson) 181
Wannamaker, Minnie B. (Bates) 141
Wannamaker, Pattie (Duncan) 289
Wannamaker, Rosa G. (Hudgins) 128
Wannamaker, T. E. 43, 52, 64, 128, 141, 217, 229
Wannamaker, W. W. 52, 141
Wannamaker, Whitfield W. 274
Ward, Adolphus 145
Ward, Alice (Gomiley) 249
Ward, Amanda (Massey) 28
Ward, B. F. 6
Ward, Bettie (Saybt) 294
Ward, Calvin J. 177
Ward, Camilla V. (McLendon) 17
Ward, Catherine (Sherman) 38
Ward, Chas. E. 286
Ward, Cornelia F. (Allen) 30
Ward, Cynthia C. (Crews) 124
Ward, Edith R. (Parker) 218
Ward, Ella (Dantzler) 177
Ward, Fanie (Ward) 55
Ward, H. C. 257
Ward, J. K. 55
Ward, J. M. 30
Ward, Jas 28
Ward, John C. 249
Ward, Josiah 124
Ward, Julia K. (Wilson) 286
Ward, L. A. (Thomas) 105
Ward, L. C. (Kesler) 259
Ward, Loutie (Dickson) 117

Ward, Low (Sanders) 145
Ward, Major 14
Ward, Mary S. (Johnson) 25
Ward, Mildred P. (Hardwich) 14
Ward, Missouri (Glass) 45
Ward, Mollie A. (Reeves) 199
Ward, Mollie E. (Walker) 6
Ward, Permelia O. (Ledbetter) 250
Ward, R. 105
Ward, Sallie J. (Jones) 166
Ward, Susie (Stancil) 233
Ward, T. A. 45
Ward, T. H. 117
Ward, William C. 250
Ward, Willie F. (Goldwin) 249
Wardlaw, A. Simmie (Coachman) 197
Wardlaw, Bettie (Moorman) 209
Wardlaw, Bettie (Moorman) 209
Wardlaw, E. S. (Drake) 112
Wardlaw, Georgia (Hickby) 140
Wardlaw, J. B. 10, 15, 20, 142, 153, 156, 163, 166, 197, 269
Wardlaw, J. Clarke 209
Wardlaw, J. P. 186, 187, 208, 245, 273, 280, 281, 291, 296
Wardlaw, Joseph L. 114
Wardlaw, Joseph P. 197
Wardlaw, Marie Witherspoon (Moorman) 114
Wardlaw, Mary L. (Snead) 197
Wardlaw, Susan J. (Connally) 20
Wardlaw, W. J. 12, 20, 26, 85, 213, 274
Wardlaw, W. L. 19
Ware, Annie W. (Chapple) 248
Ware, Fannie (Hammond) 165
Ware, J. L. 83
Ware, J. M. 100
Ware, M. A. (Cameron) 119
Ware, N. C. 281
Ware, Nannie (Green) 100
Ware, T. E. (Bussey) 83
Ware, Thomas L. 119
Warnell, J. S. 35
Warnell, Mary S. (Bradley) 35
Warner, Geo. H. 177

Warner, Talula (Moore) 177
Warnock, Margaret (Murphy) 287
Warnock, William 287
Warren, Josephene E. (Balkcom) 108
Warren, Lee America (Cain) 47
Warren, M. T. (Bryan) 135
Warren, Marshal 47
Warren, Rebecca (Lary) 142
Warrill, Cornelia E. (McBryde) 271
Warrill, L. W. 271
Warterson, F. M. (Morrow) 103
Warterson, W. L. 103
Warwick, Martha Jane (Edna) 206
Warwick, William 206
Washburn, H. 187
Washburn, Hattie F. (Wade) 187
Washington, George S. 188
Washington, Mancy S. (Myers) 188
Waterhouse, Edward W. 157
Waterhouse, Mattie Loula (Brinn) 157
Waterman, Anna E. (Brown) 111
Waterman, C. G. 101
Waterman, Charlotte (Hunter) 240
Waterman, Henrietta (Burleson) 8
Waterman, Jettie R. (Forbes) 101
Waterman, John T. 111
Waters, (Bars) 73
Waters, Amanda (Townsend) 263
Waters, Belle (Morris) 240
Waters, E. B. 41
Waters, John 263
Waters, John C. 117
Waters, Mattie Taylor (Riley) 117
Waters, Middleton 73
Waters, Nannie C. (Irby) 246
Waters, R. B. G. 75
Waters, Rebecca (Smith) 38
Waters, Roselle C. (Winbush) 6
Waters, Sallie A. (Thompson) 3
Waters, W. A. (Lawrence) 141
Waters, W. T. 141

Waters, William 3
Watkins, E. A. (Roberson) 182
Watkins, Georgia (Hammond) 286
Watkins, Gus. 286
Watkins, J. W. G. 247, 266
Watkins, Martha J. (Dudly) 55
Watkins, Mary A. (Smith) 108
Watkins, Talulah (Chapman) 247
Watkins, W. F. (Coffee) 101
Watkins, W. T. 101
Watkins, Wm. H. 182
Wats, M. C. (Spinks) 12
Watson, A. 52
Watson, A. Oline 29
Watson, Amanda C. (Hilton) 45
Watson, Annie R. (Wannamaker) 52
Watson, Bettie M. (Towns) 261
Watson, Catharine (Mullen) 212
Watson, Dollie A. E. (Mullins) 123
Watson, Emma (Slaughter) 150
Watson, Flora E. (Lane) 178
Watson, H. C. 16
Watson, Harriet 18
Watson, J. E. 9, 14, 25, 103, 104, 117, 148, 182, 260, 269
Watson, J. M. F. 261
Watson, James 18
Watson, James R. 178
Watson, John W. 123
Watson, Julia A. (Graham) 18
Watson, Kitty (Harmon) 218
Watson, L. L. (Langford) 16
Watson, L. L. 109
Watson, Lavinia (Catchings) 111
Watson, Lizzie (Burke) 225
Watson, Lizzie (Littlejohn) 288
Watson, Lizzie (McAlpin) 8
Watson, Mary A. (Jones) 109
Watson, Mary A. (Michael) 45
Watson, N. E. (Chiles) 292
Watson, Robert N. 218
Watson, S. Addie (Humbert) 29

Watson, S. E. (Greaves) 183
Watson, S. G. 150
Watson, Sallie L. (Boone) 267
Watson, W. C. 183
Watson, William A. 8
Watson, William B. 111
Watt, Cornelia F. (Walker) 83
Watt, Indiana (Lloyd) 128
Watt, Thomas J. 128
Watters, James M. 236
Watters, Sarah Cornelia (Wynne) 236
Wattles, Mattie J. (Averett) 136
Watts, Bettie (Adams) 288
Watts, E. Roberta (Taylor) 210
Watts, Emaline (Ryalls) 148
Watts, Fannie E. (Vanlandingham) 237
Watts, H. D. 19
Watts, Isaac 148
Watts, J. B. 210
Watts, Jennie Lela (Maddux) 29
Watts, Kanses E. 213
Watts, Lucia P. (Vinson) 139
Watts, Lydia Anna (Phillips) 242
Watts, M. L. (Smith) 119
Watts, Mary C. (Brooks) 237
Watts, Mary L. (Wilson) 55
Watts, Mittie (Beall) 188
Watts, Mollie J. (Hammond) 19
Watts, Statira A. (Rawls) 60
Watts, W. M. 52, 58 ,63, 66, 73, 90, 107, 126, 173, 179, 222, 224, 232, 237, 252, 268, 290, 292
Watts, Walter P. 188
Waugh, H. P. 52, 60
Way, (Glenn) 219
Way, Aaron 195
Way, Arcena R. (Cummings) 221
Way, Dorcas (Phillips) 120
Way, Emma C. (Kiser) 195
Way, J. A. 221
Way, James 89
Way, Mary (Curry) 79
Way, Missouri (Bull) 89
Way, R. E. 219
Way, William 79
Waymer, Mary J. (Brownlee) 235
Wealch, 224

Weatherbee, Georgia Emma (Puckett) 189
Weatherford, Anna (Vogt) 167
Weatherford, Middleton E. 167
Weatherley, Ida (Morrison) 290
Weatherley, Jno. 290
Weatherly, Bettie (Bernard) 15
Weathers, B. A. 201
Weathers, M. J. (Ferguson) 201
Weathers, Mary (Moorer) 91
Weathers, Rachel L. (Pendarvis) 68
Weathers, Sarah L. (Jackson) 73
Weathers, Susan (Murray) 82
Weaver, 208
Weaver, Amma L. (Pennington) 279
Weaver, Annie (Patrick) 119
Weaver, Bryant 4
Weaver, Claude (McCall) 45
Weaver, Cornelia (Jordan) 208
Weaver, Elizabeth (Colson) 4
Weaver, J. R. 53
Weaver, John L. 119
Weaver, S. R. 48, 80, 103, 107, 112, 113, 154, 218, 256
Weaver, Shelton R. 31
Weaver, Stella Florence (Biggs) 103
Webb, Anna J. (Roundtree) 123
Webb, Annie J. (Broddus) 113
Webb, Charls 78
Webb, Eda E. (Turner) 209
Webb, Giles T. 214
Webb, J. F. 113
Webb, J. M. 139, 251
Webb, J. T. 123, 197
Webb, Jennie (Bowdoin) 275
Webb, Lily (Shipp) 251
Webb, Maggie (Major) 88
Webb, Mary (Harrison) 56
Webb, Mary E. (Bobo) 186
Webb, Mary E. (Brown) 68
Webb, Matilda C. (Coker) 186
Webb, Mattie P. (Brown) 111
Webb, Myra F. (Benson) 78

Webb, Ruth (Owens) 206
Webb, Sallie W. (Pullen) 214
Webb, Sanders C. 186
Webb, Susie (McNeice) 139
Webb, W. G. 56
Weber, S. A. 71, 138, 191, 199, 204, 282, 283, 289
Weber, Samuel A. 166
Webster, A. T. (Haskins) 142
Webster, Christiana (Tates) 188
Webster, Cornelia B. (McFarland) 172
Webster, Joseph W. 113
Webster, M. D. (Walker) 27
Webster, Mary J. (Barrett) 113
Webster, S. J. 27
Webster, Sarah J. (Tat) 9
Webster, Willie F. (Mobley) 285
Weddon, J. E. 35
Weddon, Martha L. (Renfroe) 35
Weekes, W. J. 39
Weeks, Eugenie (Nash) 241
Weeks, Hattie A. (Carson) 120
Weeks, James W. 241
Weeks, Julia (Thornton) 58
Weeks, Laura J. (Elmore) 143
Weeks, Sarah (Blum) 33
Weeks, Thomas H. 143
Weeks, W. J. 58
Weems, D. J. 122, 155, 181, 189, 218
Weems, Emma M. (Richey) 94
Weems, Lula L. (Burch) 181
Weems, Mary E. (Ferguson) 33
Weems, N. E. (Smith) 119
Weisbroad, Hermon 110
Welborn, P. A. (Jordan) 154
Welch, J. N. 212
Welch, J. T. 257
Welch, Lizzie R. (Anderson) 212
Welchel, A. S. 91
Welchel, Julia A. (Neisler) 91
Welder, E. B. 165
Welder, Fannie (Harp) 165
Weldon, Mary Grant (English) 284
Wellborn, M. J. 70
Weller, R. H. 98
Wells, A. N. 27, 30

419

Whitaker, Dinque (Reid) 211

Whitaker, Dollie (Hardeman) 6

Whitaker, Elladecia (Florence) 150

Whitaker, Emma (Holtzclaw) 280

Whitaker, Hugh W. 185

Whitaker, James M. 211

Whitaker, Jno. B. 280

Whitaker, Jno. T. 139, 203, 237

Whitaker, Lula P. (Hicks) 211

Whitaker, Thos. H. 211

Whitaker, William 150

White, Althea (Wright) 296

White, Amanda (Collins) 287

White, Anna (Norwood) 193

White, Annie (McIntosh) 144

White, Aurora M. (Crutchfield) 181

White, C. H. 181

White, Carrie E. (Goolsby) 95

White, Cleora (Johnson) 191

White, Daniel 250

White, David 183

White, Dora C. (Hutchings) 46

White, E. B. (Byrom) 238

White, Emily F. (Burdan) 9

White, Emma C. (Cutter) 44

White, F. J. (Dale) 18

White, Fannie S. (Dana) 52

White, George C. 44

White, Grazilla M. (Mills) 69

White, Harriet (Rollins) 249

White, J. J. 46

White, James 235

White, James J. 191

White, James M. 287

White, Mary (Williams) 5

White, Melissa (Bowles) 250

White, Melissa N. (McMillan) 183

White, Mollie (Reynolds) 195

White, Moses M. 5

White, Rosa (Smith) 51

White, Russell C. 69

White, Sallie A. (Griffith) 6

White, Sallie A. (Knight) 14

White, Sallie K. (Wagner) 181

White, Sallie S. (Anderson) 70

White, Sally E. (Redding) 188

White, Sarah A. (Verstille) 198

White, Sumantha H. (Thomaston) 90

White, T. Ward 251

White, Telitha C. (Spradling) 195

White, Thos. A. 18

White, Virgil A. 6

White, Vollie (Johnson) 162

White, William M. 244

White, William R. 14

White, Willie (Sewell) 244

Whitehead, A. S. (Southerland) 89

Whitehead, G. W. M. 54

Whitehead, H. (Williams) 54

Whitehead, James E. 89

Whitehead, Jane (Bateman) 55

Whitehead, Lizzie (Graham) 184

Whitehead, M. E. 236

Whitehead, M. Eunice (Thomson) 181

Whitehead, M. S. (Southerland) 65

Whitehead, Mary (Sheppard) 54

Whitehead, Rebecca J. (Futch) 73

Whitehead, W. H. 181

Whitehurst, Ella L. (Leak) 220

Whiteley, Chas. H. 266

Whiteley, Mary Joe (Downer) 266

Whitely, Susie (Hill) 131

Whitfield, B. H. 63

Whitfield, Eliza H. (Stone) 63

Whitfield, Julia A. (Carpenter) 238

Whitfield, Maggie (Pledger) 79

Whitfield, W. F. 79

Whiting, W. M. 295

Whitlow, Sallie E. (Key) 58

Whitmore, Mary (Christopher) 223

Whitney, E. M. 260

Whitten, Mary A. (Chesnutt) 278

Whitten, O. J. (Lamb) 15

Whitten, Samuel F. 278

Whittimore, N. L. 100

Whittle, Claudia (Thomson) 288

Whittle, Ella (Quattlebaum) 287

Whittle, Henry 288

Whitworth, Mollie J. (Clack) 198

Whorton, Annie C. (Camp) 23

Wi---, F. H. (Brogdon) 196

Wickenberg, F. R. 120

Wickenberg, J. Anna (Dargan) 120

Wicker, Almira (Bird) 5

Wicker, Mary E. (Swygert) 239

Wicker, Mattie (Pope) 32

Wicker, R. 32

Wicker, Thos. O. 5

Wicker, W. H. 6

Wier, Mary E. (Bradberry) 279

Wiggin, Emma (Brown) 81

Wiggin, G. W. 81

Wiggins, A. E. (Kimbrough) 139

Wiggins, C. E. (Grey) 17

Wiggins, Emily S. (Leroy) 94

Wiggins, Geo. W. 283

Wiggins, Minny E. (Connor) 294

Wiggins, Olivia L. (McCoy) 159

Wiggins, R. L. 69, 139, 226, 233, 234, 260, 283

Wiggins, Robert L. 84, 118, 120, 130, 145, 190

Wiggins, S. C. S. (Purvis) 283

Wightman, Anna W. (Griffiths) 215

Wightman, Carrie Louisa Lawton 211

Wightman, J. T. 234

Wightman, John Wesley 215

Wightman, W. M. 68

Wightman, W. S. F. 211

Wigins, Robert L. 107

Wiker, Katie (Herrington) 181

Wilbanks, Milton A. 174

Wilbanks, S. Addie (Simmons) 174

Wilcox, J. N. 133

Wilcox, John H. 174

Wilcox, John N. 87, 143, 144

Wilcox, Mattie F. (Clark) 243

Wilcox, Mattie W. (Curry) 152

Wilcox, Sallie M. (Shell) 127

Wild, H. H. 42

Wilder, Aminda (Gasset) 145

Wilder, Augusta (Scott) 105

Wilder, Bettie (Keenan) 183

Wilder, F. N. 119

Wilder, Geo. 183

Wilder, Hattie E. (Davis) 74

Wilder, James 235

Wilder, Laura V. (Allen) 119

Wilder, M. C. (Bunkley) 235

Wiley, A. O. (Brandan) 90

Wiley, E. S. 90

Wiley, Florence (Rodgers) 295

Wilhelm, Ann Eliza (Gilmore) 89

Wilhelm, Frederick 89

Wilkerson, Alice I. (Penington) 248

Wilkerson, Lenora (Hopkins) 253

Wilkerson, Martha T. (Daniel) 5

Wilkes, Frances Ophelia (Tumlin) 38

Wilkes, Ida C. (Dozier) 162

Wilkie, H. Virginia (Hubert) 49

Wilkie, M. O. 49

Wilkie, Sallie (Goldsmith) 200

Wilkie, Theodore C. 200

Wilkins, Emily C. (Wheatley) 41

Wilkins, J. H. 41, 197, 250, 291

Wilkins, J. J. 41

Wilkins, M. J. (Patrick) (Anderson) 72

Wilkins, Martha W. (Cochran) 189

Wilkins, R. A. (Sheftell) 63

Wilkinson, 62

Wilkinson, E. V. (Williams) 1

Wilkinson, Lucia (Harben) 62

Wilkinson, M. C. 198

Wilkinson, M. F. (Werdon) 198

Wilkinson, Malodia M. (Baily) 137

Wilkinson, Mattie M. (Hill) 7

Wilkinson, R. W. 34

Wilkinson, T. F. 7

Wilkison, Anna (Taylor) 127

Wilkison, R. E. 127

Wilks, Martha (Cambbell) 210

Willard, J. J. 98

Willard, Jessie S. (Candler) 98

Willcox, Sudie E. (Williams) 175

Willer, DeWitt C. 171

Willer, Mary (Daniels) 171

Willett, B. B. 167

Willett, Ella I. (Armstrong) 42

Willett, Geo. M. 147

Willett, Mattie (Stanley) 167

Willett, Melina H. (Dawson) 147

Williams, A. (Ellerby) 140

Williams, A. H. (Allan) 101

Williams, A. M. 192, 221, 234, 238, 249, 252, 267, 273

Williams, A. P. 101

Williams, A. W. 67, 73, 181

Williams, Albert M. 290

Williams, Alice (Cashon) 186

Williams, Alice C. (Nance) 56

Williams, Allen D. (Smith) 141

Williams, Amicus W. 56

Williams, Anna (Sadler) 163

Williams, Annie M. O. (Smith) 237

Williams, Ardella A. J. (Allerson) 179

Williams, B. W. 156

Williams, Bascom 189

Williams, Benj. W. 163

Williams, C. D. 16

Williams, C. M. 186

Williams, Carrie (Morris) 46

Williams, Clara M. (Ransom) 89

Williams, Deacon 39

Williams, E. (Arrington) 19

Williams, E. E. (Pearre) 194

Williams, E. J. Ivey 219

Williams, E. M. (Martin) 24

Williams, E. V. (Wilkinson) 1

Williams, Ed G. 89

Williams, Edgar P. 73

Williams, Edwin P. 12

Williams, Eliza (Boyd) 106

Williams, Emily P. (Flournoy) 94

Williams, Emma S. (Ridgeway) 81

Williams, F. Eugenia (Trussell) 113

Williams, Fannie (Gresham) 16

Williams, Fannie (Moore) 263

Williams, Fannie H. (Miller) 57

Williams, Fannie P. (Hightower) 261

Williams, G. Q. 175

Williams, G. W. 4

Williams, George H. 263

Williams, H. (Whitehead) 54

Williams, H. H. 194

Williams, H. P. (Morgan) 189

Williams, Harriet M. (Hull) 16

Williams, Hattie (Peavy) 95

Williams, Hattie P. (Johnston) 242

Williams, Henry O. 45

Williams, Henry W. 89

Williams, Ida J. (Giles) 226

Williams, Imogene (McHan) 207

Williams, J. H. 278

Williams, J. L. 182, 231

Williams, J. P. 157

Williams, J. W. 3, 71

Williams, James W. 81

Williams, Jane M. (McKinnon) 106

Williams, Jennie (Bailey) 146

Williams, Jere S. 230, 231, 227

Williams, John A. 237

Williams, John M. 109

Williams, Kate (Pierce) 89

Williams, Kinchen H. 177

Williams, Laura H. (Smith) 163

Williams, Laura N. (Smith) 182

Williams, Leila E. (Muse) 109

Williams, Lewis James 54

Williams, Lilly H. (Andrews) 2

Williams, Lorena L. (Brown) 252

Williams, Lou (Askin) 47

Williams, M. (Freeman) 261

Williams, M. A. (Waldin) 143, 145

Williams, M. Q. (Jefferson) 267

Williams, M. V. (Tucker) 71

Williams, Mamie (Brabham) 253

Heritage Books by Brent H. Holcomb:

Bute County, North Carolina, Land Grant Plats and Land Entries

*CD: Early Records of Fishing Creek Presbyterian Church,
Chester County, South Carolina, 1799–1859*

CD: Kershaw County, South Carolina, Minutes of the County Court, 1791–1799

CD: Marriage and Death Notices from The Charleston *[S.C.] Observer, 1827–1845*

CD: South Carolina, Volume 1

*CD: Winton (Barnwell) County, South Carolina Minutes of
County Court and Will Book 1, 1785–1791*

Charleston District, South Carolina, Journal of the Court of Ordinary, 1812–1830
Caroline T. Moore, Edited by Brent H. Holcomb

*Chester County, South Carolina, Deed Abstracts,
Volume I: 1785–1799 [1768–1799] Deed Books A-F*

Deaths and Obituary Notices from the
Southern Christian Advocate, *1867–1878*

*Early Records of Fishing Creek Presbyterian Church, Chester County,
South Carolina, 1799–1859, with Appendices of the Visitation List of
Rev. John Simpson, 1774–1776 and the Cemetery Roster, 1762–1979*
Brent H. Holcomb and Elmer O. Parker

Kershaw County, South Carolina, Minutes of the County Court, 1791–1799

Laurens County, South Carolina, Minutes of the County Court, 1786–1789

*Lower Fairforest Baptist Church, Union County, South Carolina:
Minutes 1809–1875, Membership Lists through 1906*

*Marriage and Death Notices from Baptist Newspapers of South Carolina,
Volume 2: 1866–1887*

*Marriage and Death Notices from Columbia, South Carolina Newspapers,
1838–1860; Including Legal Notices from Burnt Counties*

Marriage and Death Notices from The Charleston Observer, *1827–1845*

Marriage Notices from the Southern Christian Advocate, *1867–1878*

Memorialized Records of Lexington District, South Carolina, 1814–1825

*Newberry County, South Carolina Deed Abstracts,
Volume I: Deed Books A-B, 1785–1794 [1751–1794]*

*Newberry County, South Carolina Deed Abstracts,
Volume II: Deed Books C, D-2, and D, 1794–1800 [1765–1800]*

*Parish Registers of Prince George Winyah Church,
Georgetown, South Carolina, 1815–1936*

*Petitions for Land from the South Carolina Council Journals
Volume V: 1757–1765*

*Record of Deaths in Columbia, South Carolina, and
Elsewhere as Recorded by John Glass, 1859–1877*

South Carolina Deed Abstracts, 1773–1778, Books F-4 through X-4

South Carolina Deed Abstracts, 1776–1783, Books Y-4 through H-5

South Carolina Deed Abstracts, 1783–1788, Books I-5 through Z-5

*The Bedenbaugh-Betenbaugh Family:
Descendants of Johann Michael Bidenbach from
Germany to South Carolina, 1752*

www.ingramcontent.com/pod-product-compliance
Lightning Source LLC
Chambersburg PA
CBHW060130280326
41932CB00012B/1474